HOW THE BIBLE IS WRITTEN

HOW THE BIBLE IS WRITTEN

GARY A. RENDSBURG

HENDRICKSON
PUBLISHERS

How the Bible Is Written

Hendrickson Publishers Marketing, LLC
P. O. Box 3473
Peabody, Massachusetts 01961-3473
www.hendrickson.com

ISBN 978-1-68307-197-6

Printed in the United States of America

First Printing — April 2019

The image used on the jacket of this book is a carpet page from the Damascus Keter (Burgos, Spain, 1260), now housed in the National Library of Israel, Ms. Heb. 24° 790, fol. 114r. Photograph by Zev Radovan and provided by www.BibleLandPictures.com / Alamy Stock Photo.

Library of Congress Cataloging-in-Publication Data

Names: Rendsburg, Gary, author.
Title: How the Bible is written / Gary A. Rendsburg.
Description: Peabody, Massachusetts : Hendrickson Publishers, [2019] | Includes bibliographical references.
Identifiers: LCCN 2018053612 | ISBN 9781683071976 (alk. paper)
Subjects: LCSH: Hebrew language--Grammar. | Bible.--Old Testament--Language, style. | Bible. Old Testament--Criticism, interpretation, etc. | Bible as literature.
Classification: LCC PJ4556 .R46 2019 | DDC 221.6/6--dc23
LC record available at https://lccn.loc.gov/2018053612

For Melissa

CONTENTS

ACKNOWLEDGMENTS

This book was written over the course of seven years (2010–2017), during which time I was privileged to be granted several sabbaticals by my home institution, Rutgers University. While I love to teach, and remain energized each time I enter the lecture hall or the seminar room even after almost forty years, a book of this magnitude requires time away from the classroom for extended periods. The singular location where the largest portion of this book was written was the Oxford Centre for Hebrew and Jewish Studies at Yarnton Manor (October 2010–February 2011 / June–December 2012 / June–July 2014). Those who have enjoyed the warm hospitality of the Centre and the unsurpassed allure of Yarnton Manor will understand my words here. To my mind, there is no better place in the world to conduct research in the field of Jewish studies, with easy access to the magical city of Oxford and all its treasures in one direction and to the English countryside and all its charm in the other. Alas, the Centre no longer is housed at Yarnton Manor, but I will recall my stays there with great fondness for years to come.

I also was able to spend extended periods at the University of Sydney (February–April 2011), the University of Cambridge (June–July 2015), Tyndale House (June–July 2015), and the University of California at Los Angeles (September–October 2015). I am grateful to my academic hosts at all these institutions, who afforded me library privileges, office space, accommodation, good cheer, and more.

My research has been generously funded by the Blanche and Irving Laurie Chair of Jewish History at Rutgers University. I am honored to be the inaugural holder of this chair (2004–present), and I remain grateful to the Laurie Foundation board members for their support, friendship, appreciation, and encouragement.

As I explain in the Introduction, sections of this book are based on my previously published work. Hence, I am grateful to the editors of the various journals and monographs who saw fit to publish my articles relevant to the general topic of "How the Bible Is Written." These essays, in turn, often were based on oral presentations of the material, delivered over the years at Johns Hopkins University, the University of Leiden, the University of Oxford, the University of Cambridge, Pennsylvania State University, Bar-Ilan University, and my own academic home, Rutgers University. These opportunities allowed for feedback from colleagues, always an important element in the advancement of research.

I am especially indebted to two special individuals whose diligent work made this a better book. The first is Charles Loder, who served as my research assistant for two years (2014–2016) and who has continued to assist me in manifold ways during the three years since. Charles tracked down references, read the entire manuscript in its pre-final version, read the proofs, and produced the indices and bibliography that accompany this volume. Every researcher should be as fortunate to have someone like Charles at his or her side, assisting the process at every stage.

The second is Jonathan Kline, senior editor at Hendrickson Publishers. As those who have worked with Jonathan know well, he is brilliant at shepherding a book from manuscript to finished product. He has both the technical know-how and the pleasant disposition to make the entire process a delight—all the more so in the present case, given the size of this book and the technical material (Hebrew, transliteration, etc.) inherent herein.

The pleasure of working with Charles and Jonathan was all the more gratifying because both of these young scholars were my students: Charles completed his M.A. degree with me at Rutgers University (2016), before assuming his current position as library coordinator at Southern Baptist Theological Seminary; while Jonathan completed his B.A. degree with me at Cornell University (2002) en route to his graduate training and professional career.

This book is dedicated to my wife Melissa: my love, my muse, my inspiration, my everything. Our journeys together, from Concord to Highclere; our readings together, from Blake to Thoreau; indeed our life together—all is embraced within the pages of this book. You bring my dreams to reality, and you make my reality a dream.

PERMISSIONS

Eight of the chapters appearing in the present volume are based on previously published articles. The author is grateful to the following publishers for permission to reuse this material herein:

Eisenbrauns (an imprint of Penn State University Press)—for permission to reuse the following articles, included herein as Chapters Five, Six, and Twelve, respectively:

"Alliteration in the Book of Genesis," in Elizabeth R. Hayes and Karolien Vermeulen, eds., *Doubling and Duplicating in the Book of Genesis: Literary and Stylistic Approaches to the Text* (Winona Lake, IN: Eisenbrauns, 2016), 79–95.

"Alliteration in the Exodus Narrative," in Chaim Cohen et al., eds., *Birkat Shalom: Studies in the Bible, Ancient Near Eastern Literature, and Postbiblical Judaism Presented to Shalom M. Paul on the Occasion of His Seventieth Birthday* (Winona Lake, IN: Eisenbrauns, 2008), 83–100.

"Repetition with Variation in Legal-Cultic Texts of the Torah," in Shamir Yona et al., eds., *Marbeh Ḥokmah: Studies in the Bible and the Ancient Near East in Loving Memory of Victor Avigdor Hurowitz* (Winona Lake, IN: Eisenbrauns, 2015), 435–63.

Journal of Hebrew Scriptures (http://www.jhsonline.org/) and Gorgias Press—for permission to reuse the following article, incorporated herein as Chapter Eight:

"Confused Language as a Deliberate Literary Device in Biblical Hebrew Narrative," *Journal of Hebrew Scriptures*, vol. 2, article

6 (1998–1999); available at http://www.jhsonline.org/Articles /article_12.pdf.

Reprinted in: Ehud Ben Zvi, ed., *Perspectives on Hebrew Scriptures I* (Perspectives on Hebrew Scriptures and Its Contexts 1; Piscataway, NJ: Gorgias, 2006), 197–213.

University Press of Maryland—for permission to reuse the following article, incorporated herein as Chapter Nine:

"Variation in Biblical Hebrew Prose and Poetry," in Maxine L. Grossman, ed., *Built by Wisdom, Established by Understanding: Essays on Biblical and Near Eastern Literature in Honor of Adele Berlin* (Bethesda: University Press of Maryland, 2013), 197–226.

Brill—for permission to reuse the following article, incorporated herein as Chapter Thirteen:

"Marking Closure," *Vetus Testamentum* 66 (2016): 280–303.

CDL Press for permission to reuse the following article, incorporated herein as Chapter Seventeen:

"Word Play in Biblical Hebrew: An Eclectic Collection," in Scott B. Noegel, ed., *Puns and Pundits: Word Play in the Bible and in Near Eastern Literature* (Bethesda, MD: CDL, 2000), 137–62.

SBL Press—for permission to reuse the following article, incorporated herein as Chapter Twenty-Four:

"Style-Switching in Biblical Hebrew," in Jeremy M. Hutton and Aaron D. Rubin, eds., *Epigraphy, Philology, and the Hebrew Bible: Methodological Perspectives on Philological and Comparative Study of the Hebrew Bible in Honor of Jo Ann Hackett* (SBL Ancient Near East Monographs 12; Atlanta: SBL Press, 2015), 65–85; available at http://www.sbl-site.org/assets/pdfs /pubs/9780884140801_OA.pdf via the SBL Press open access policy.

ABBREVIATIONS

General

ad loc.	to or at the place
B.C.E.	Before the Common Era
ca.	circa
C.E.	Common Era
cf.	confer, compare, see also
ch(s).	chapter(s)
col(s).	column(s)
def.	definition
e.g.	*exempli gratia*, for example
esp.	especially
fem.	feminine
frg.	fragment
i.e.	*id est*, that is
lit.	literally
masc.	masculine
Ms.	Manuscript
n.	note
no(s).	number(s)
pl.	plural
r.	reigned
sc.	*scilicet* (namely)
sg.	singular
s.v.	*sub verbo* (see under the word)
v(v).	verse(s)

viz.	*videlicet* (namely)
vol(s).	volume(s)
x	times

Dictionaries and Reference Works

BDB	Francis Brown, S. R. Driver, and Charles A. Briggs, *A Hebrew and English Lexicon of the Old Testament* (Oxford: Clarendon, 1906).
CAT	Manfried Dietrich, Oswald Loretz, and Joaquín Sanmartín, *The Cuneiform Alphabetic Texts from Ugarit, Ras Ibn Hani and Other Places*, 2nd ed. (Münster: Ugarit-Verlag, 1995).
DCH	David J. A. Clines, *Dictionary of Classical Hebrew*, 8 vols. (Sheffield: Sheffield Academic, 1993–2011).
HALOT	M. E. J. Richardson, ed., *The Hebrew and Aramaic Lexicon of the Old Testament*, 5 vols. (Leiden: Brill, 1994–2000).
KB	Ludwig Koehler and Walter Baumgartner, *Lexicon in Veteris Testamenti Libros*, 2 vols. (Leiden: Brill, 1985).
OED	*Oxford English Dictionary*, 2nd edition (Oxford: Clarendon, 1989), available online at http://www.oed.com/.

Bible Versions

BHS	*Biblia Hebraica Stuttgartensia*
JPS	*The Holy Scriptures: According to the Masoretic Text* (1916)
KJV	King James Version (1611)
LXX	Septuagint
NAB	New American Bible (1970)
NIV	New International Version (1984/2011)
NJB	New Jerusalem Bible (1985)
NJPS	*Tanakh: The Holy Scriptures: The New JPS Translation according to the Traditional Hebrew Text* (1985)
NRSV	New Revised Standard Version (1989)
REB	Revised English Bible (1989)
RSV	Revised Standard Version (1952)

LIST OF FIGURES

INTRODUCTION

Learned colleagues have written books entitled *Who Wrote the Bible?*, *How to Read the Bible*, *How the Bible Became a Book*, and *How the Bible Became Holy.*[1] The present volume poses a different question, *How the Bible Is Written.* My goal in this book is to reveal the manner in which language is used to produce exquisite literature, no less for the ancient Israelite literati who crafted the compositions that eventually were canonized as the Bible than for William Shakespeare or Jane Austen or J. R. R. Tolkien or any other writer whose literature we admire and continue to enjoy. Which is to say, in the most simple of terms: there are many books on what the Bible says; this is a book on how the Bible says it.

To be sure, a knowledge of Hebrew is helpful in fully understanding my analysis, but my goal has been to make the material accessible to non-specialists as well. The Bible continues to be widely read by millions of Jews and Christians who attend church and synagogue on a regular (or even less than regular) basis. Its contents are well known, but the manner in which those contents are crafted is not as well understood. My intended audience in this book, accordingly, is both scholars and educated lay people. My academic colleagues, who spend their lives poring over the biblical text, hopefully will find much of value from my own close readings contained herein. But the Jewish lay reader who follows the recitation of the Torah in the synagogue each Shabbat, the Christian lay reader who knows well the church

---

1. See, for example, Richard E. Friedman, *Who Wrote the Bible?* (Englewood Cliffs, NJ: Prentice-Hall, 1987); Marc Z. Brettler, *How to Read the Bible* (Philadelphia: Jewish Publication Society, 2005); Marc Z. Brettler, *How to Read the Jewish Bible* (New York: Oxford University Press, 2007); James Kugel, *How to Read the Bible: A Guide to Scripture, Then and Now* (New York: Free Press, 2007); William M. Schniedewind, *How the Bible Became a Book: The Textualization of Ancient Israel* (New York: Cambridge University Press, 2004); and Michael L. Satlow, *How the Bible Became Holy* (New Haven: Yale University Press, 2014).

lectionary, and indeed people of any faith or in fact of no faith who simply wish to know more about one of the world's great religious texts and its literary workings, also will benefit from reading these pages. To that end, each passage treated in this book is presented in the Hebrew original, in a relatively literal translation (see below), and, where appropriate, in a simplified transliteration (again, see below).

Many of us, the present author included, received an excellent education in English literature (or in some other literary corpus), as our teachers revealed to us the superb artistry introduced by the authors of the 'great books'. We reveled in the alliteration of *Beowulf*, the wordplay of Chaucer's *Canterbury Tales*, the unsurpassed poetry of Shakespeare's plays and sonnets, the wit and humor of Samuel Johnson, the subtlety of Jane Austen's prose, both the pure English and the Dorset dialect of William Barnes, the colloquialisms of Mark Twain, the obscurities of Lewis Carroll, the peculiarities precipitated by the stream-of-consciousness writing of James Joyce, the dialect representation inherent in William Faulkner, the philological wizardry of J. R. R. Tolkien, and much more. And of course all the crossovers between and among these writers and their techniques. Consider, for example, the alliteration in the following definition in Samuel Johnson's *A Dictionary of the English Language*, to wit, "*network*: Any thing reticulated or decussated, at equal distances, with interstices between the intersections"; or the alliterations present in the opening and closing words of Joyce's *Finnegans Wake*, namely, "from swerve of shore to bend of bay" and "by a commodius vicus of recirculation" (both in the opening sentence) and "a way a lone a last a loved a long the" (the ending).

We, that is to say, educated readers of English literature (including British, American, and other) are generally familiar with all of the above. The most widely read 'book' in the world, however, remains the Bible—and yet, when readers open its pages, most are totally ignorant of the manner in which its language is used to create its literature. Much of this ignorance, to be sure, is due to the linguistic divide: since the Bible is written in Hebrew, most contemporary readers access the ancient text via translation into their chosen vernacular.[2] Though one

---

2. When I refer to 'the Bible' in this work, I intend solely the Jewish canon, what some scholars call 'the Jewish Bible' or 'the Hebrew Bible' and what

must note that even readers with facility in Hebrew often miss some of the literary brilliance, until it is pointed out to them.

This lack of attention to the literary artistry of the Bible frequently is due to the goal and the expectation of the reader. For one typically approaches the biblical compositions for their moral teachings, theological insights, historical information, and the like, without considering the literary aspect of the material.

But there is so much that is missed in such a reading experience. The chief goal of the present volume, accordingly, is to bridge that divide, to bring interested readers—scholars and lay people alike—closer to the original text, with all of its literary artistry and linguistic virtuosity. For the person interested in the history of literature, the compositions of the ancient Israelite literati surely deserve greater attention. These writers are generally unknown to us by name,[3] but they clearly were as clever as Joyce, Johnson, and the author of *Jabberwocky*. In the pages that follow, I hope to make this point self-evident.

In order to allow both the scholar and the educated reader of the Bible in translation to follow my exposition, every verse is, as noted above, presented both in the Hebrew original and in English translation. At times the entire verse and always the key word, phrase, or clause discussed also appears in transliteration. A word about each of these three representations is in order, with the most detailed treatment coming first, the one about the Hebrew text itself.

The Hebrew original is presented in all its Masoretic garb, by which I mean the graphic representation of the oral reading tradition created by the savants of Tiberias in the ninth century C.E. Given my adherence to

---

Christians commonly call 'the Old Testament'. The vast majority of the canon is written in Hebrew, with only the following passages in Aramaic: Gen 31:47 (a two-word phrase), Jer 10:11 (a single verse), Daniel 2:4–7:28 (constituting the most substantial portion), and Ezra 4:8–6:18, 7:12–26 (quoting archival documents from the Persian government). This amounts to about ten chapters of text, compared to about 919 chapters in Hebrew.

3. The only authors whose names have been transmitted to us are the prophets Isaiah, Jeremiah, Ezekiel, and the twelve individuals responsible for the books known as the Minor Prophets (Hosea through Malachi). Though even here we do not know the name of one of the key writers, namely, the person responsible for the exquisite poetry and the monotheistic message of Isaiah 40–66; hence he is known in the scholarly literature simply as Second Isaiah.

the Masoretic Text (MT), I should outline here my understanding of its history and development. From the moment that a text was composed in ancient Israel, it was transmitted through a dual process: a written one and an oral one. The most telling passage in the Bible is Exod 17:14, where God instructs Moses as follows: כְּתֹב זֹאת זִכָּרוֹן בַּסֵּפֶר וְשִׂים בְּאָזְנֵי יְהוֹשֻׁעַ *kətob zoʾt zikkaron bas-sefer wə-śim bə-ʾozne yəhošuaʿ* 'write this (as) a memorial in the book, and put (it) in the ears of Joshua'.[4] This is the first time that the root כ-ת-ב *k-t-b* 'write' is used in the Bible: but writing the text is only one step in the process, for in addition Moses is to put the text in the ears of Joshua, representative of the next generation.

If we can extrapolate from this single key example, we can reconstruct the process of both the scribal transmission of the written text and the parallel oral transmission of the reading tradition.[5] Professional scribes were responsible for the former, as they copied and recopied the written text over the course of centuries and even millennia, while professional tradents were responsible for the latter, as they bequeathed the proper reading of the text from one generation to the next.[6] The two were equally necessary, for as readers of Hebrew know, the written text is but a consonantal skeleton, with no vowels, accents, punctuation, and so on indicated. The preservers of the oral reading tradition were responsible for those features, so that they knew, to use examples from the above passage: (a) to intone the first word (written simply כתב) as *kətob* 'write' (imperative form) and not as *katab* (masc. sg. past tense), *koteb* (masc. sg. active participle), or *katob* (infinitive absolute form); (b) to intone the fourth word (written simply בספר) as *bas-sefer* 'in the book' (with definite article) and not as *bə-seper* 'in a book' (without the article); and (c) to pause on the words בספר *bas-sefer* 'in the book'

4. My use of the word 'book' here is simply a convention. The actual text would have been inscribed on a scroll, not what we envision by the English word 'book', with a binding, writing on both sides of the page, and so on.

5. For the approach outlined here, I am indebted to the little-known but superb article by Saul Levin, "The 'Qeri' as the Primary Text of the Hebrew Bible," *General Linguistics* 35 (1997): 181–223.

6. The term 'tradent' refers to someone who passes on the tradition, in this case the oral reading tradition of the ancient Hebrew text. English has a well-known word, 'scribe', to refer to an invidividual who copies and transmits the written text, but no such word for one who learns and transmits the recitation of the text; hence I use the scholarly designation 'tradent' for such an individual.

(hence the comma in my translation) and יהושע *yᵊhošuaᶜ* 'Joshua' (which would be followed by a semicolon, were I to have continued with the rest of the verse in my translation). Multiply this passage by thousands of instances, and one can see just how remarkable the oral transmission of the text truly was. The term for this oral reading tradition in Jewish parlance is 'Masora', rendered best as 'tradition', but with specific reference to the process outlined here.

This is not to say that variant texts did not exist, for clearly they did;[7] but eventually a single text type emerged within the Jewish tradition, during the first millennium C.E.[8] Generally speaking, that text type, as scholars now recognize, was the most conservative of the variant texts in circulation. For almost always this proto-Masoretic text, as we may call it, reflects an older linguistic layer of Hebrew, a more conservative orthography (that is, spelling), and a more complex and sophisticated literary style.

Under the influence of both Islam and its devotion to the Qur'an, and the emerging Karaite movement within Judaism, during the ninth century C.E. the Jewish scribes and tradents in the city of Tiberias in northern Israel developed a system to graphically represent the oral reading tradition that had been passed down for anywhere between ca. 1000–2000 years (depending on the age of the specific biblical book). These scholars, whom we call the Masoretes, created two sets of signs consisting of a series of dots and dashes and similar markings, one to

---

7. The best evidence for variant Hebrew texts derives from the biblical manuscripts among the Dead Sea Scrolls found at Qumran, dating to the second and first centuries B.C.E. Further evidence is forthcoming from the Torah as transmitted by the Samaritans (= Samaritan Torah), since it departs from the Jewish Torah in hundreds of instances. In addition, the Septuagint (= LXX = the Greek translation produced by the Jews of Alexandria in the third and second centuries B.C.E.) often reflects a different Hebrew *Vorlage* than what would emerge as the Masoretic Text. I will refer to these other textual traditions on various occasions below, in my treatments of particular passages.

8. In fact, this single text type, with only the most minor of variants, seems to have emerged relatively early in the first millennium C.E., which is to say, by the second century C.E. Evidence for this is forthcoming from the biblical manuscripts uncovered in Naḥal Ḥever, Wadi Murabbaᶜat, and other nearby sites. See Emanuel Tov, *Textual Criticism of the Hebrew Bible*, 3rd ed. (Minneapolis: Fortress, 2012), 29.

indicate the vowels and the other to simultaneously indicate where a word is to be accented and how an entire phrase, clause, or verse is to be punctuated.[9] The result is the masterful Masoretic Text, a product unparalleled in the history of world literature, to the best of my knowledge. The result, accordingly, was the difference between the following two representations, once more using Exod 17:14 as our example:

(a) כתב זאת זכרון בספר ושים באזני יהושע

(b) כְּתֹב זֹאת זִכָּרוֹן בַּסֵּפֶר וְשִׂים בְּאָזְנֵי יְהוֹשֻׁעַ

The former constitutes the way the text appears with only its consonantal skeleton; the latter represents the text with all its Masoretic garb.[10]

One additional point is worth emphasizing here: the prominence given to the oral reading tradition within Judaism, even after it was graphically represented by the Masoretic enterprise, is indicated by the Hebrew term 'Miqra᾿', used for the Bible (as the canon, as a portion thereof, or even for a single passage). The etymological meaning of this word is 'that which is read', by which is meant 'that which is intoned or read aloud', hence more simply 'the Reading'. We English speakers are accustomed to the term 'Scripture', meaning, for the Bible, 'that which is written';[11] but in Jewish tradition, as indicated by the term 'Miqra᾿', the emphasis is on

---

9. As Jewish communities around the world developed traditions of chanting the text (especially the Torah), these markings also took on a third role, serving to note the specific cantillation.

10. As experts will realize, actually there were three different Masoretic systems created during this time period: the Tiberian one, the Palestinian one (also from the land of Israel), and the Babylonian one. Eventually the Tiberian one emerged as the standard within Jewish society. To further complicate matters, even within the Tiberian system there are some minor differences between the Ben Asher and Ben Naphtali schools, though the former eventually emerged as the standard. None of this finesse need concern us here, so that when I refer to 'the Masoretic Text', I refer to the text type developed by the Tiberian Masoretes, especially as embodied in the two great early codices of Aleppo (ca. 920 C.E.) and St. Petersburg (formerly Leningrad) (dated to precisely 1008–1009 C.E., based on the information provided in the colophon).

11. Or in German, *Die Schrift* (or with adjective, *Die heilige Schrift*), and similarly in other European languages (Dutch *de Heilige Schrift*, French *les Saintes Écritures* or *l'Écriture sainte*, etc.).

that which is read, not necessarily on that which is written.[12] The same holds for the Qur'an in Islam, the name of which is derived from the same Semitic root, hence 'the Reading' and not 'the Scripture'; and ditto for the name of the Karaite (more properly Qaraite) movement within Judaism, with its emphasis on Miqra', that is, 'the Reading', the Bible.[13]

As indicated above, each Hebrew word, passage, or verse quoted in this book is presented in English translation. My translation method follows that of such pioneering scholars as Everett Fox and Robert Alter,[14] with a style slightly more in line with the former than with the latter. That is to say, I aim for a more literal rendering, one that allows the reader of this book (whether he or she knows Hebrew or not) the opportunity to follow the flow, syntax, and cadence of the Hebrew original. At times, the English may sound stilted, but frequently this reflects the Hebrew. For example, in Gen 1:11, I render the Hebrew phrase תַּדְשֵׁא הָאָרֶץ דֶּשֶׁא *tadše' ha-'areṣ dɛšɛ'* 'let the earth vegetate vegetation' (see below, Chapter 1, p. 18), because the verb and the noun are built from the same root. The verb is atypical in Hebrew (it appears again only in Joel 2:22), though the noun is standard (occurring 14x altogether).[15] So the English sounds a bit odd because the Hebrew is a bit odd, and I want the reader to recognize this point. When I extend the English language

---

12. In fact, in those instances where the scribal tradition and the oral reading tradition diverged during the course of their parallel transmissions, Jewish practice is to follow the latter and not the former! This demonstrates that the oral tradents were seen as more reliable than the writerly scribes. The result is what is known as the Ketiv-Qeri system (that which is written vs. that which is read), as also indicated in the Masoretic Text. See further below, Chapter 2, p. 36, n. 2.

13. This emphasis on the Bible within Karaite Judaism stands in contrast to Rabbinic Judaism, with its focus on postbiblical texts, such as the Mishna and the two Talmudim.

14. Everett Fox, *The Five Books of Moses* (New York: Schocken, 1995); Everett Fox, *The Early Prophets* (New York: Schocken, 2014); Robert Alter, *The Five Books of Moses* (New York: Norton, 2004); Robert Alter, *The Book of Psalms* (New York: Norton, 2007); Robert Alter, *The Wisdom Books* (New York: Norton, 2010); and Robert Alter, *Ancient Israel* (New York: Norton, 2013).

15. This is true of postbiblical Hebrew as well, where the verb does not occur at all and the noun appears an additional 9x (5x in Qumran texts, 4x in Tannaitic texts [Mishna and Tosefta]).

in such fashion, almost always I include a justification, frequently one
that is in fact based on historical evidence from the language itself.[16]

I borrow from Fox the technique of using a hyphenated English
phrase to indicate that the Hebrew is actually a single word. Thus, for
example, I use 'dry-land' to render יַבָּשָׁה *yabbaša* and 'creeping-things'
to render רֶמֶשׂ *remeś*, just to cite two nouns from Genesis 1 (on which
see below, Chapter 1). Note that when I cite just a word or two (as here),
I typically delete the Masoretic accent marks, especially because said
markings may differ from one usage of the word to the next.

My transliteration scheme is a simplified one. Each of the consonants has a single representation, as shown on the following page.[17]
Over time, and as preserved within the Masoretic system, six of these
letters received a double pronunciation, but I have not introduced
such subtlety into my transliteration system. Thus, for example, בּ *bet*
is always transcribed as *b*, even when it might be pronounced as [v]
in certain environments according to the later Masora; פ *pe* is always
transcribed as *p*, even when it might be pronounced as [f] in certain
environments according to the later Masora; and so on. Since my work
is situated in ancient Israel, before this development occurred, I feel
justified in using the simplified system. Those who know Hebrew,
of course, are free to read the passages in whatever pronunciation
feels comfortable.

---

16. In this particular case, note the older (now largely obsolete) usage of
the verb 'vegetate', meaning 'grow, develop, produce vegetation'. Today, the
verb 'vegetate' has a different (indeed rather negative) connotation, which is
not intended here naturally. For details, see *OED*, s.v. 'vegetate' *v*. On the importance of the *Oxford English Dictionary* (*OED*), see below, pp. 10–11 and n. 18.

17. Note that each of these consonants bore a unique pronunciation during the biblical period of Iron Age Israel, and thus each of them is signified
differently. Later Jewish pronunciations, especially in the Ashkenazic world,
either altered or merged some of these pronunciations. My chart does not
include the five final letter forms ך, ם, ן, ף, and ץ (respectively, *k*, *m*, *n*, *p*, and
ṣ), which are simply graphic variants and have no effect on the matter.

There are some complications to the system outlined here, however.
First, as the chart indicates, the grapheme שׁ *šin/śin* represented two different
sounds that were kept distinct during the biblical period. Second, though not
reflected in the chart, the graphemes ח *ḥet* and ע *ʿayin* also represented two
distinct sounds, for which see Chapter 5, p. 81, n. 22.

Hebrew letter form	Hebrew letter name	Transliteration
א	ʾaleph	ʾ
ב	bet	b
ג	gimel	g
ד	dalet	d
ה	he	h
ו	waw	w
ז	zayin	z
ח	ḥet	ḥ
ט	ṭet	ṭ
י	yod	y
כ	kaf	k
ל	lamed	l
מ	mem	m
נ	nun	n
ס	samekh	s
ע	ʿayin	ʿ
פ	pe	p
צ	ṣade	ṣ
ק	qof	q
ר	reš	r
שׂ	śin	ś
שׁ	šin	š
ת	taw	t

My system of transcribing the vowels is even more simplified. I have not indicated length; thus, for example, *o* is used regardless of the precise realization of the vowel, in contrast to other, more detailed systems, which may distinguish ǒ, *o*, ō, and ô. None of this hyper-sophistication is necessary for our present purposes. I have, however, indicated *shewa* throughout with the siglum ə; and I also have taken advantage of two distinct letter forms, *e* and *ε*, in order to distinguish *ṣere* (̣) and *segol* (̣), respectively.

For the uninitiated reader, all of this may seem very arcane and difficult at times. In addition, there will be technical asides concerning phonology, cognates to Hebrew words in other Semitic languages, and more. But I would beg such a reader, especially one with an interest in text and in language, to persevere. For only through such perseverance will said reader come to marvel at all that the biblical text has to offer. The chapters ahead cover such topics as wordplay, alliteration, marking closure, form following content, repetition with variation, style-switching (or dialect representation), and the effect of placing the shorter word before the longer (along with departures from this norm)—all of which constitute the building blocks from which the biblical text is constructed. To truly know the Bible is to know this material. To put this another way, I would recommend that the reader of this work gain from it what he or she may gain, and disregard anything that he or she finds too technical.

As I stated at the outset, in writing this book I have sought to reach both an audience of scholars and an audience of interested and educated lay people. There are many asides to English literature, cinema, and more, which will serve as parallels to what I am describing within the biblical text. For example, in Chapter 24, which is devoted to 'style-switching', I use examples such as German 'mach schnell' in World War II movies (even when the Germans otherwise are speaking English) and the unsurpassed use of language by William Shakespeare in *Henry V* to represent the distinctive speeches of Captain Jamy the Scot, Captain Fluellen the Welshman, and Captain Macmorris the Irishman. As seen already above (p. 8, n. 16), the book is also replete with references to the English language, as recorded in the authoritative

Oxford English Dictionary (OED).[18] Hopefully, these analogues will assist the reader in understanding what transpires within the workings of the ancient Hebrew text as well.

The topics listed above, and the others that appear in the Table of Contents and in the chapters that follow, are meant to be seen as selective. In general, I have not reviewed literary devices already well surveyed in the scholarly literature. Most importantly, this book is devoted mainly to prose, with less interest in poetry. Hence, for example, there is no chapter devoted to parallelism, especially since Adele Berlin has treated this issue from a literary-linguistic perspective in her superb monograph *The Dynamics of Biblical Parallelism*.[19] What possibly could I add to her elegant statement? The term is mentioned occasionally in the work that follows, and I include a basic explanation of the phenomenon at Chapter 17, no. 2, but I have not included a sustained treatment of the subject.

If I have explored topics 'a', 'b', and 'c', but not topics 'd', 'e', and 'f', this is due largely to my own personal interests and previous publications. I have published on many of the matters discussed here, but my treatments are found in diverse articles and book chapters written over the course of several decades. The current project attempts to bring much of that information, along with new material, into a single book. One hopes, moreover, that the whole will be greater than the sum of its parts, so that the book is not seen merely as a volume of 'collected studies' (which it is not), but rather as a way of envisioning the multifaceted means by which the biblical authors created the texts that have come down to us from the distant past.

By and large my examples come from the most familiar of biblical texts, that is, the prose books of the Torah (Genesis and Exodus

18. My references to the *OED* are taken from the online edition, available at http://www.oed.com/, to which I have ready access via the Rutgers University Libraries. All citations were checked via online access as recently as September 2018. Those without full access to the online edition may find more or less the same information in the most recent print edition (or for that matter in earlier editions).

19. Adele Berlin, *The Dynamics of Biblical Parallelism* (Bloomington: University of Indiana Press, 1985; 2nd ed., Grand Rapids: Eerdmans, 2008).

especially) and other well-known prose narratives (the stories of Ruth, Samson, David, et al.). My emphasis, therefore, is on prose, especially narrative. At times I venture into the world of legal and cultic texts of the Torah, while at other times I address issues relevant to poetry (notwithstanding less focus on that genre, as indicated above). But even in such instances, I once again attempt to use more familiar passages. A glance at the Index of Biblical References at the end of the book illuminates this point well: lots of Genesis, lots of Exodus, some Leviticus, some Psalms, no Obadiah, no Malachi.[20]

At certain points in this book I use the expression 'biblical author' (or in the plural, 'biblical authors'). I am well aware that this term is anachronistic, because at the time of the floruit of these authors, the Bible did not exist—and in fact would not exist for centuries. I use the term, accordingly, as shorthand for the author of a passage, a chapter, a story, or even an entire composition that eventually would emerge as a book of the Bible, once the canonization process commenced, starting in ca. 450 B.C.E., with the elevation of the Torah to a new status (see Nehemiah 8 especially). In other words, 'biblical author' is a term of convenience: said individuals almost assuredly did not consider that they were writing anything akin to what would materialize as 'the Bible' centuries later. The more accurate term I use is 'ancient Israelite literati' (ah, the alliteration), but I felt the need to mix it up a bit and vary my language (ah, variation), hence the use of 'biblical authors' as a stand-in term in this book.

I close here with mention of two other terms of convenience. While we know precious little, if anything, about the people who wrote the biblical books,[21] almost undoubtedly these individuals were men.[22] For

---

20. True, Obadiah and Malachi appear in the Index of Biblical Passages (along with every other biblical book), but the verses registered there are not treated as primary illustrations herein. N.B. Chapter and verse numbers used herein follow the Hebrew tradition. The verse numbers used in English translations differ at times, for example, in Exodus 7–8, where Hebrew 7:26–29 = English 8:1–4, and Hebrew 8:1–28 = English 8:5–32.

21. Though see above, p. 3, n. 3, concerning the prophets.

22. Though I hasten to add that the first author known by name in the history of the world is a woman, namely, Enheduanna, high priestess of the moon-god Nanna in the city of Ur, ca. 2500 B.C.E. We possess several dozen

this reason, I will use masculine pronouns throughout to refer to the author of a text, the oral presenter of a text, the redactor of material, and so on. To balance this usage, I adopt the parallel convention of using feminine pronouns throughout to refer to the listener of the text, that is, an individual member of the audience gathered to hear the oral performance of the text.[23] These corresponding uses of 'he' and 'she' in this book absolve me of the need to say 'he or she' each time I refer to an author or a listener.

With all of the above as an introduction to the intent and purpose of this book, along with its procedures and conventions, I invite the reader to join me on the journey through the Bible's pages, with an eye to the nexus of language and literature, commencing with Genesis 1.

---

hymns written by her, the most extensive of which is 'The Exaltation of Inanna'. Other female authors may have existed, but Enheduanna seems to have been the exception more than the rule. Moreover, the fact that we know her name may be due to her exceptional quality as a women, in contrast to the presumed maleness of the vast majority of authors.

23. On the oral reading of ancient literature, the Bible included, see Chapter 1, pp. 25–29.

CHAPTER ONE

READING CREATION

To repeat the comment from the Introduction: there are lots of books on what the Bible says; this is a book about how the Bible says it. And there is no better place to begin our journey into how the Bible is written than at the beginning, with Genesis 1. The opening words of the canonical text present a grammatical conundrum: בְּרֵאשִׁית בָּרָא *bə-re'šit bara'*, lit., 'in-the-beginning-of he-created' > 'in the beginning of [God's] creating'. The first word includes the preposition -בְּ *bə-* 'in' plus a noun in the construct state, רֵאשִׁית *re'šit* 'beginning (of)', which according to standard Hebrew grammatical rules (in particular, one that every student of Hebrew learns early on) would demand another noun in the absolute state to follow.[1] Instead, however, the second word in the text is a suffix-conjugation verb in the past tense, בָּרָא *bara'* 'he created'. We have no immediate explanation for this grammatical oddity, other than to note that this two-word phrase sets the stage for the reader to pay heed. The text she is to hear is not a simple text, built on the grammatical rules found in a primer or even an intermediate-level textbook, but rather one in which challenging linguistic issues and literary formulations abound. Rashi, the great medieval Jewish commentator, pointed to the parallel construction in Hos 1:2, תְּחִלַּת דִּבֶּר *təḥillat dibbɛr* 'the-start-of he-spoke' > 'at the start of [Yнwн's]

---

1. Compare, for example, Jer 27:1 בְּרֵאשִׁית מַמְלֶכֶת יְהוֹיָקִם *bə-re'šit mamlɛkɛt yəhoyakim* 'in the beginning of the reign of Jehoiakim'; Jer 28:1 בְּרֵאשִׁית מַמְלֶכֶת צִדְקִיָּה *bə-re'šit mamlɛkɛt ṣidqiyya* 'in the beginning of the reign of Zedekiah'; etc. For more familiar phrases, consider בֵּית יִשְׂרָאֵל *bet yiśra'el* 'house of Israel', בְּנֵי יִשְׂרָאֵל *bane yiśra'el* 'children of Israel', אֶרֶץ כְּנַעַן *'ereṣ kəna'an* 'land of Canaan', Rabbinic and Modern Hebrew בֵּית כְּנֶסֶת *bet kənɛsɛt* 'synagogue' (lit., 'house of assembly'), Modern Hebrew בֵּית סֵפֶר *bet sefɛr* 'school' (lit., 'house of the book'), etc.

speaking [to Hosea]', which indeed represents an analogous syntagma,[2] though this does not resolve the problem—and thus the conundrum in Gen 1:1 remains nonetheless.

Naturally, when I refer to grammatical rules that one may find in a primer or even an intermediate-level textbook, I do not mean to imply that such volumes existed in ancient Israel. What I intend, rather, is to suggest that the antennae of an ancient reader of our text, a native speaker of ancient Hebrew, would have been raised upon encountering the expression בְּרֵאשִׁית בָּרָא *bə-reʾšit baraʾ*. What mean these words, she might have said to herself—and this at the very outset of a narrative, indeed at the very outset of a narrative that appears at the very outset of a book, which in turn one day would find its position at the very outset of a canonical text, the Torah. We will not resolve this grammatical structure here (other than to note that Hos 1:2 is not the only parallel; there are others in the Bible),[3] but I repeat the notion that a native speaker would have raised an eyebrow at this starting point in the narrative—and indeed one can only imagine how she would have interpreted the phrase.

As we proceed with Genesis 1, the reader notices the appearance of several refrains. For each act of creation (one per day on days one, two, four, and five; two per day on days three and six) the text begins with the phrase וַיֹּאמֶר אֱלֹהִים *wayyoʾmɛr ʾelohim* 'and God said'. Next, once the desired act is accomplished, the text informs us that God saw כִּי־טוֹב *ki tob* 'that it was good' (vv. 4, 10, 12, 18, 21, 25). And then finally, we read for each day of creation וַיְהִי־עֶרֶב וַיְהִי־בֹקֶר *wayhi ʿɛrɛb wayhi boqɛr* 'and it was evening and it was morning', plus the appropriately numbered day of creation (vv. 5, 8, 13, 19, 23, 31).

Except wait—the second of these refrains does not occur on day two! And so again the reader of this text must ponder a question, not a linguistic anomaly, but rather a literary curiosity. Why would the author of our text have omitted mention of the fact that God saw the creation of the רָקִיע *raqiaʿ* 'firmament' (named more simply שָׁמַיִם *šamayim* 'sky, heaven'; see v. 8) as good? The answer lies in the fact that the object

---

2. For another instance of the same syntagma, see below, Chapter 15, no. 10.

3. For example, Isa 29:1 קִרְיַת חָנָה דָוִד *qiryat ḥana dawid* 'the-city-of camped David' > 'the city (where) David camped', an epithet for Jerusalem.

of God's creative activity on day two was the water. A close reading of vv. 1–3 (especially v. 2) reveals that water was preexistent matter, in the form of the deep (Hebrew תְהוֹם *təhom*)—which is to say, water is never created in Genesis 1, but rather is the dominant presence on the earth, comprised of תֹהוּ וָבֹהוּ *tohu wa-bohu* 'wild and waste' (v. 2).[4] This water, in turn, represents the cosmic sea or abyss, which in other ancient Near Eastern cosmogonies (most famously, the Babylonian story *Enuma Elish*) is symbolized by an evil deity (for example, the goddess Tiamat in said story).[5] In short, water, in the form of the salt water that covers the surface of the earth, is seen as an evil force. After all, this salt water is of no use: one cannot drink it, one's animals will not drink it, and one cannot irrigate with it. In addition, the ocean is a potent force, which can wreck ships and destroy coastlines; most of us have witnessed the stormy sea and know its destructive power, and thus can understand why the ancients envisaged the watery mass in a negative light.

All of this is background for the omission of the second refrain noted above on day two. God creates the רָקִיעַ *raqiaʿ* 'firmament', which serves to separate the waters above and the waters below. And while there is nothing inherently negative about this created element, since the waters were acted upon, so to speak (and note the fivefold use of the word מַיִם *mayim* 'water' in the three verses that comprise the description of day two), the author intentionally omits the declaration וַיַּרְא אֱלֹהִים כִּי־טוֹב *wayyarʾ ʾɛlohim ki tob* 'and God saw that it was good' in his description of day two.

When we turn to day three, we are able to identify yet another element of our author's literary virtuosity, namely, his desire not to repeat phrases. A comparison of vv. 11–12 reveals an array of minor differences between the command (v. 11) and fulfillment (v. 12) regarding the creation of vegetation.[6]

---

4. I here borrow Everett Fox's rendering of the two-word Hebrew phrase.

5. Note that Babylonian *tiamat* is cognate to Hebrew תְהוֹם *təhom* 'deep, abyss', which, notwithstanding the lack of a feminine ending, is a feminine noun in Hebrew.

6. Here and elsewhere, when appropriate, I have formatted the Hebrew text in a way that allows the reader to compare more readily the corresponding phrase and expressions.

Genesis 1:11–12

11 וַיֹּאמֶר אֱלֹהִים

תַּדְשֵׁא הָאָרֶץ דֶּשֶׁא עֵשֶׂב מַזְרִיעַ זֶרַע עֵץ פְּרִי עֹשֶׂה פְּרִי לְמִינוֹ

אֲשֶׁר זַרְעוֹ־בוֹ עַל־הָאָרֶץ

וַיְהִי־כֵן:

12 וַתּוֹצֵא הָאָרֶץ דֶּשֶׁא עֵשֶׂב מַזְרִיעַ זֶרַע לְמִינֵהוּ וְעֵץ עֹשֶׂה־פְּרִי

אֲשֶׁר זַרְעוֹ־בוֹ לְמִינֵהוּ

וַיַּרְא אֱלֹהִים כִּי־טוֹב:

[11] And God said, "Let the earth vegetate vegetation, plants that seed seed, fruit trees that produce fruit (each) according to its kind with its seed in it, upon the earth"; and it was so.[7] [12] And the earth brought-forth vegetation, plants that seed seed (each) according to its kind, and trees that produce fruit with its seed in it (each) according to its kind; and God saw that it was good.

An uncreative author could simply have repeated the phraseology in v. 11 in his wording of v. 12, or perhaps he could have omitted the verse altogether, especially since the last two words of v. 11 already indicate וַיְהִי־כֵן *wayhi ken* 'and it was so'. But our ingenious writer desires to show off his talent, and this stage in the narrative appears to be an apt opportunity.

A comparison of vv. 11 and 12 reveals the following distinctions: (a) different verbs serving as the predicate of the subject הָאָרֶץ *ha-ʾareṣ* 'the earth'; (b) the wording עֵץ פְּרִי עֹשֶׂה *ʿeṣ pəri ʿośɛ pəri* 'fruit trees that produce fruit' in the former versus the shorter וְעֵץ עֹשֶׂה־פְּרִי *wə-ʿeṣ ʿośɛ pəri* 'and trees that produce fruit' in the latter, though this time preceded by conjunctive -וְ *wə-* 'and'; (c) the placement of the single occurrence of לְמִינוֹ *lə-mino* 'according to its kind' in v. 11 versus the placement of the first לְמִינֵהוּ *lə-minehu* 'according to its kind' in v. 12, not to mention the use of a second instance of לְמִינֵהוּ *lə-minehu* 'according to its kind' in v. 12; and (d) perhaps the most instantly recognizable difference, namely, the

---

7. On my use of the verb 'vegetate' in the translation, see above, Introduction, p. 8, n. 16.

variant forms לְמִינוֹ *lə-mino* and לְמִינֵהוּ *lə-minehu*, both meaning 'according to its kind' (the first is the standard form, the second is more archaic).[8]

But wait, there is more! When the vegetation is referenced again in v. 29, at the point where God grants the first human couple the plants of the earth to eat, we note still other variations.

Genesis 1:29

וַיֹּאמֶר אֱלֹהִים

הִנֵּה נָתַתִּי לָכֶם אֶת־כָּל־עֵשֶׂב | זֹרֵעַ זֶרַע אֲשֶׁר עַל־פְּנֵי כָל־הָאָרֶץ

וְאֶת־כָּל־הָעֵץ אֲשֶׁר־בּוֹ פְרִי־עֵץ זֹרֵעַ זָרַע

לָכֶם יִהְיֶה לְאָכְלָה:

And God said, "Behold, I give to you all the plants that seed seed that are on the face of all the earth, and all trees that have in it the fruit of the tree that seed seed; for you they will be food."

Here we note: (a) אֲשֶׁר־בּוֹ פְרִי־עֵץ *'ašer bo pəri 'eṣ* 'that have in it the fruit of the tree' instead of אֲשֶׁר זַרְעוֹ־בוֹ *'ašer zar'o bo* 'with its seed in it' of vv. 11–12; and (b) the twofold use of זֹרֵעַ זֶרַע *zorea' zera'* 'seed seed', using the Qal participle, in place of the earlier מַזְרִיעַ זֶרַע *mazria' zera'* 'seed seed' in vv. 11–12, using the Hiphʿil participle, with no apparent lexical distinction.[9]

---

8. This is an apposite place to mention Robert J. Ratner, "Morphological Variation in Biblical Hebrew Rhetoric," in Robert J. Ratner et al., eds., *Let Your Colleagues Praise You: Studies in Memory of Stanley Gevirtz*, Part II = *Maarav* 8 (1992): 143–59. Ratner's fine essay is devoted to smaller items revealing variation, whereas the present study focuses on larger matters of phraseology—though to be sure, some of the former serve the latter (e.g., the morphological variants just mentioned, to wit, לְמִינוֹ *lə-mino* and לְמִינֵהוּ *lə-minehu* in Gen 1:11–12). As such, one might say that the current study is Ratner writ large. Moreover, virtually everything that Ratner states in his essay, especially the concluding thoughts (157–59)—for example, the comment that "the authors considered them [sc. the variations in language] to be an enhancement of the reading and listening pleasure" (159)—applies to the current discussion as well.

9. Qal and Hiphʿil refer to two different forms that the Hebrew verb may take. The former is the basic form, while the latter bears a causative

Now, why would our author engage in such minor changes while composing the narrative? The answer, to my mind, is simply variation for the sake of variation. A mind game, as it were, is present. The author, through the text that he created and the performer who presents the text orally, entertains his reader, who consumes the text aurally, as she listens attentively to the oral performance (more on this aspect of ancient literature later). In short, there are no hidden meanings or esoteric significances to these minor changes. Rather, they are present in the text as part of the very fabric from which it is created.

Naturally, if our author is able to accomplish this variation in his description of the vegetation, we would expect him to do the same with his account of the creation of the animals. We are not disappointed. The same command-and-fulfillment approach is used in vv. 24–25, which read as follows:[10]

Genesis 1:24–25

²⁴ וַיֹּאמֶר אֱלֹהִים

תּוֹצֵא הָאָרֶץ נֶפֶשׁ חַיָּה לְמִינָהּ בְּהֵמָה וָרֶמֶשׂ וְחַיְתוֹ־אֶרֶץ לְמִינָהּ

וַיְהִי־כֵן:

²⁵ וַיַּעַשׂ אֱלֹהִים

אֶת־חַיַּת הָאָרֶץ לְמִינָהּ וְאֶת־הַבְּהֵמָה לְמִינָהּ וְאֵת כָּל־רֶמֶשׂ הָאֲדָמָה

לְמִינֵהוּ

וַיַּרְא אֱלֹהִים כִּי־טוֹב:

²⁴ And God said, "Let the earth bring-forth living beings
(each) according to its kind, beasts and creeping-things,
and animals of the earth (each) according to its kind"; and
it was so.

---

connotation. Thus, for example, if a verbal root means 'eat' in the Qal, it will mean 'cause to eat' > 'feed' in the Hiphʿil, and similarly with verbs meaning 'come' ~ 'cause to come' > 'bring'; 'go out' ~ 'cause to go out' > 'bring out'; etc. In the present instance, however, the Hiphʿil form in v. 29 connotes the same as the Qal verbs in vv. 11–12.

10. Once more I have presented the Hebrew text in a way that allows the reader to easily compare the key passages.

²⁵ And God made the animals of the earth (each) according
to its kind, and the beasts (each) according to its kind, and all
the creeping-things of the soil (each) according to its kind;
and God saw that it was good.

It is difficult for us to judge the various nuances in some of the terms
used in these verses (and thus another scholar's rendering may be
slightly different), but we can state the following, with an emphasis
on the different wordings. (a) The command line includes the general
term נֶפֶשׁ חַיָּה *nεpεš ḥayya* 'living beings', which is then subdivided into
three classes, in this order: בְּהֵמָה *bəhema* 'beasts', רֶמֶשׂ *rεmεś* 'creeping-
things', and חַיְתוֹ־אֶרֶץ *ḥayto ʾεrεṣ* 'animals of the earth'. In the fulfillment
line, the aforementioned general term is omitted, and we then read the
three subdivisions in different order: first חַיַּת הָאָרֶץ *ḥayyat ha-ʾareṣ* 'the
animals of the earth', then הַבְּהֵמָה *hab-bəhema* 'the beasts', and finally
כָּל־רֶמֶשׂ הָאֲדָמָה *kol rεmεś ha-ʾadama* 'all the creeping-things of the soil'.
(b) In v. 11, the three terms appear without the definite article; in v. 12,
they appear with the definite article. (c) In the first iteration, we have
only two instances of the phrase '(each) according to its kind', while
in the second iteration, we have three such expressions. (d) The author
uses the archaic phrase חַיְתוֹ־אֶרֶץ 'animals of the earth' in v. 24, which
is then replaced by the standard expression חַיַּת הָאָרֶץ 'the animals of
the earth' in v. 25. (e) The simple word רֶמֶשׂ *rεmεś* 'creeping-things' in
v. 24 is changed to the more complex phrase כָּל־רֶמֶשׂ הָאֲדָמָה *kol rεmεś
ha-ʾadama* 'all the creeping-things of the soil' in v. 25.

But wait, once again there is more! The animals are mentioned again
in v. 30, for they too are granted the vegetation for food. Here one reads:

Genesis 1:30

וּלְכָל־חַיַּת הָאָרֶץ וּלְכָל־עוֹף הַשָּׁמַיִם וּלְכֹל ׀ רוֹמֵשׂ עַל־הָאָרֶץ אֲשֶׁר־בּוֹ
נֶפֶשׁ חַיָּה אֶת־כָּל־יֶרֶק עֵשֶׂב לְאָכְלָה וַיְהִי־כֵן׃

"And to all the animals of the earth and to all the fowl of
heaven and to all that creeps on the earth, in which is a
living being, [I give] all the green plants for food"; and
it was so.

Which is to say: the one category has been changed to כָּל־חַיַּת הָאָרֶץ
kol ḥayyat ha-ʾareṣ 'all the animals of the earth', and the other has
been changed to כֹל רוֹמֵשׂ עַל־הָאָרֶץ *kol romeś ʿal ha-ʾareṣ* 'all that creeps
on the earth' (note the use of a verb now), while the third ('beasts')
is lacking altogether! And while we are contending with this verse,
let us also note that our author introduces a new word for vegetation,
namely, יֶרֶק *yεrεq* 'green', a lexeme hitherto not encountered—just to
keep the reader further on her toes.

In addition, since they too eat plants, the birds, which were created
on day five, are mentioned here as well—though yes, you guessed it,
with an expression not previously encountered. In the day five account,
the author placed into God's mouth the words עוֹף יְעוֹפֵף עַל־הָאָרֶץ *ʿop
yəʿopep ʿal ha-ʾareṣ* 'let fowl fly over the earth' (v. 20); and then upon
their creation he referred to them as כָּל־עוֹף כָּנָף לְמִינֵהוּ *kol ʿop kanap
lə-minehu* 'all winged fowl (each) according to its kind' (v. 21). The next
time we hear of them, in v. 30 (see above), yet a different wording is
used: כָּל־עוֹף הַשָּׁמַיִם *kol ʿop haš-šamayim* 'all the fowl of the heaven'.

The lesson derived from the detailed analysis presented in the foregoing paragraphs is as adumbrated above: our ancient author would go
to any length in order not to repeat himself. At every turn he introduced
variation into his text, sometimes of very minor significance, sometimes
of greater significance—but variation always. He clearly took pleasure
in demonstrating his virtuosity in this way. Though now we can expand
the discussion to include the consumer of this ancient text. After all, an
author's display of his agility with words is most likely intended not
just to please himself, but his audience as well. And if that is so, then
we also must conclude that the members of his audience were able
to both recognize the variations inherent in Genesis 1 and appreciate
the author's remarkable skill and accomplishment. More importantly,
let us recall that one listening to an ancient text processed the words
aurally only. We, as modern readers of the Bible, are able to check the
variations by comparing and contrasting parallel passages in writing, by checking each phrase against the other (as often as we would
like), or by working through the listings presented above. The ancient
reader, by contrast, was really an 'ancient listener', and she needed
to process all of the information noted above while listening to the
text. While listening to a presenter of Genesis 1 who had reached, say,

v. 30, a member of the audience could not go back to have a look at vv. 24–25 to recall how the creeping things were expressed. She simply would have known, I would aver, that the wording in all three cases was different. She would, moreover, have delighted in the pleasure.[11]

We turn now to another feature of Genesis 1, triggered by the wording in Gen 1:16, relevant to the creation of the luminaries on day four:

Genesis 1:16

וַיַּעַשׂ אֱלֹהִים אֶת־שְׁנֵי הַמְּאֹרֹת הַגְּדֹלִים

אֶת־הַמָּאוֹר הַגָּדֹל לְמֶמְשֶׁלֶת הַיּוֹם וְאֶת־הַמָּאוֹר הַקָּטֹן לְמֶמְשֶׁלֶת

הַלַּיְלָה וְאֵת הַכּוֹכָבִים:

And God made the two great lights; the greater light for the
rule of day, and the smaller light for the rule of night, and
the stars.

While seen most visibly in this verse, the point is true of the entirety of vv. 14–19, which concern day four: nowhere in these verses does the author use the common nouns שֶׁמֶשׁ *šεmεš* 'sun' and יָרֵחַ *yareaḥ* 'moon'. The reason is almost without a doubt due to a desire to avoid these words, because they evoke the names of pagan deities, worshipped in the local Canaanite culture as Shamash and Yarikh, the sun and moon deities, respectively, as known most importantly from the Ugaritic myths that feature both characters. That is to say, the author of Genesis 1 did not wish for an innocent reader to come away with the impression that the single God whom the people of Israel worshipped was responsible for the creation of pagan deities.

Once we have recognized the point here, in v. 16, we gain an understanding of the wording in vv. 9–10, which describe the first half of God's creative activity on day three:

---

11. Various animal terms also appear in vv. 26 and 28, and almost all of these occur with yet other variant phraseology. I refrain from presenting the details (lest I be accused of "overkill") and instead direct the reader to these passages to discover the alterations—and thereby the joy, hopefully—for herself.

Genesis 1:9–10

⁹ וַיֹּאמֶר אֱלֹהִים יִקָּווּ הַמַּיִם מִתַּחַת הַשָּׁמַיִם אֶל־מָקוֹם אֶחָד וְתֵרָאֶה
הַיַּבָּשָׁה וַיְהִי־כֵן:
¹⁰ וַיִּקְרָא אֱלֹהִים | לַיַּבָּשָׁה אֶרֶץ וּלְמִקְוֵה הַמַּיִם קָרָא יַמִּים וַיַּרְא
אֱלֹהִים כִּי־טוֹב:

⁹ And God said, "Let the water be gathered from below the heaven into one place, and let the dry-land be seen"; and it was so.
¹⁰ And God called the dry-land 'earth', and the collection of water he called 'seas'; and God saw that it was good.

The waters are to be collected 'into one place' (v. 9), and yet this collection of waters is called יַמִּים *yammim* 'seas' (v. 10), in the plural. All the other objects created receive names in the singular, including 'day' (v. 5), 'night' (v. 5), 'heaven' (v. 8),[12] and 'earth' (v. 10). The answer to this enigma once more has to do with ancient deities, for Yamm was another member of the ancient Canaanite pantheon, the powerful sea-god who serves as an adversary to Baʻal. The author of Genesis 1, accordingly, opted for the plural form יַמִּים *yammim* 'seas'. True, the phrase דְּגַת הַיָּם *dǝgat hay-yam* 'the fish of the sea' occurs in vv. 26, 28, with 'sea' in the singular. But note the presence of the definite article in this construction, which serves to distance our word from the name of the Canaanite sea-god, along with the fact that the ancient Hebrew brain may have processed the entire phrase[13] as a single "word."[14]

Variation also serves a very specific function in the Bible. Ancient Hebrew style often called for alternative language to mark closure, that is, to inform the reader that she has reached the end of a particu-

---

12. Admittedly, in this case the Hebrew noun is dual, or perhaps what we may call a pseudo-dual (since 'heaven' is not quite like 'hand', 'feet', 'eyes', etc., which are real dual nouns), which cannot appear in either the singular or the plural—but the point still stands.

13. What scholars call a 'construct phrase'; see above regarding Gen 1:1.

14. On the issue of identifying a single 'word', in particular in the mind of a traditional Serbo-Croatian *guslar*, see Raymond F. Person, "The Ancient Israelite Scribe as Performer," *Journal of Biblical Literature* 117 (1998): 601–9, esp. 603–4.

lar pericope. Such language is found in Genesis 1, particularly in the verses that complete day six of creation and thus conclude the entire narrative. Several examples are present. First, during the first five days of creation, the names of the days of the week are presented without the definite article, thus: יוֹם אֶחָד *yom ’εḥad* 'day one' (v. 5), יוֹם שֵׁנִי *yom šeni* 'a second day' (v. 8), יוֹם שְׁלִישִׁי *yom šəliši* 'a third day' (v. 13), יוֹם רְבִיעִי *yom rəbiʿi* 'a fourth day' (v. 19), and יוֹם חֲמִישִׁי *yom ḥamiši* 'a fifth day' (v. 23).[15] For the final day of creation, however, we read יוֹם הַשִּׁשִּׁי *yom haš-šišši* 'the sixth day' (v. 31), with the definite article.

Similarly, one of the other refrains noted above is changed. Instead of the usual כִּי־טוֹב *ki tob* 'that it was good' (vv. 4, 10, 12, 18, 21, 25), to conclude the account the author writes וְהִנֵּה־טוֹב מְאֹד *wə-hinne tob məʾod* 'and behold, very good' (v. 31) (or in more fluid English, 'and behold, it was very good') with two discernible differences: (a) The particle כִּי *ki* 'that' is changed to וְהִנֵּה *wə-hinne* 'and behold'; and (b) the word טוֹב *tob* 'good' receives the adverb מְאֹד *məʾod* 'very'.[16]

IMPORTANT DIGRESSION: By this point, you may be wondering whether it was indeed possible for the ancient reader of Genesis 1 to apprehend all of the literary devices inherent in the text, as delineated herein. My view on the matter is as follows, rehearsing some of the remarks above. If the author went to the trouble of interweaving all these items into his text, then one would imagine that yes, a considerable number of his audience members would have grasped and understood well all that he was attempting to accomplish.

Let us compare a modern movie director, for example. Does everyone who attends the cinema catch every nuance, especially during

---

15. Standard Hebrew usage calls for the cardinal number 'one' in this instance, as opposed to the ordinal number 'first' (for another instance, see Gen 2:11–14, where the rivers of Eden are enumerated). Accordingly, the ordinals commence only with 'second'. My glosses include the indefinite article 'a', which is necessary in English, though note that there is no such part of speech in Hebrew.

16. Ancient Jewish exegesis made much of the addition of מְאֹד *məʾod* 'very' in Gen 1:31, reading all sorts of meaning into the word. To my mind, however, we can explain the usage as simply another instance of variation, though with the specific function of marking closure.

the first viewing? No. But upon watching a film repeatedly, one sees things that one did not notice during a previous viewing. This is certainly my experience, and yes, there are films that I watch again and again. And this is my sense with the compositions that eventually found their way into the books of the Bible. These texts were the national literature of the people of ancient Israel, whose lives were not encumbered with all that we may have filling our "personal hard drives." In fact, research by anthropologists and folklore specialists into certain contemporary cultures still largely untouched by modernity reveals that consumers of texts can be very sophisticated in their understanding of literature.

One of the best examples of such individuals are the Somalis, among whom poetry continues to be appreciated as a traditional art form via oral performance. In fact, many Somalis, especially the poets and reciters (who may be one and the same at times), know their native poetic corpus intimately. B. W. Andrzejewski and I. M. Lewis wrote as follows:

> Unaided by writing they learn long poems by heart and some have repertoires which are too great to be exhausted even by several evenings of continuous recitation. Moreover, some of them are endowed with such powers of memory that they can learn a poem by heart after hearing it only once, which is quite astonishing, even allowing for the fact that poems are chanted very slowly, and important lines are sometimes repeated. The reciters are not only capable of acquiring a wide repertoire but can store it in their memories for many years, sometimes for their lifetime. We have met poets who at a ripe age could still remember many poems which they learnt in their early youth.[17]

Furthermore, it is not only the poets/reciters who have this ability: in public gatherings those listening to the poems often will correct the reciter if he makes a mistake. In the words of Andrzejewski and Lewis: "moreover, among the audience there are often people who already know by heart the particular poem, having learnt it from another

---

17. B. W. Andrzejewski and I. M. Lewis, *Somali Poetry: An Introduction* (Oxford: Clarendon, 1964), 45.

source. Heated disputes sometimes arise between a reciter and his audience concerning the purity of his version."[18]

If I may be permitted my little fantasy, I like to envision the people of ancient Israel similarly. Gathered around the campfire (in a pastoral setting) or at the piazza inside the city-gate complex (in an urban setting),[19] one can imagine groups enjoying the recital of texts, as part of their national heritage, indeed, as entertainment—with all religious overtones and implications set aside for the moment. And when a particular point was debated, as with the contemporary Somalis, one can imagine the discussion that ensued.

I proceed, accordingly, here and throughout this volume with the assumption that the people of ancient Israel had an uncanny appreciation for belles lettres. Certain small countries have made major contributions in certain fields (such as the Irish with poetry and the Dutch and Flemish with painting, and with a concomitant appreciation thereof by the populace at large). In like fashion, I see the people of ancient Israel totally immersed in their national literature.

And while I cannot cite an academic study on the matter, my travels and life experience have informed me that even ordinary readers in certain countries know their national poets well, can recite the poetry by heart, and are able to thoroughly understand and analyze both the style and the contents. Here I have in mind, for example, the Irish with W. B. Yeats, the Scots with Robert Burns, the Russians with Alexander Pushkin, the Iranians with Rumi and Ferdowsi, and no doubt many more examples, perhaps less known to me and the readers of this book.

One question for which we cannot supply a satisfactory answer is the following: Did the ancient Israelite reciters, performers, and presenters recite/perform/present the text from memory (see above, regarding the contemporary Somali reciters), or did they hold a written

---

18. Ibid., 46. Other well-known examples of such 'singers of tales' are the Serbo-Croatian *guslar* reciters, studied by Milman Parry and described by Albert B. Lord, *The Singer of Tales* (Harvard Studies in Comparative Literature 24; Cambridge: Harvard University Press, 1960); and the Uzbek *bakshy* reciters (among others), described by Nora K. Chadwick and Victor Zhirmunsky, *Oral Epics of Central Asia* (Cambridge: Cambridge University Press, 1969).

19. The former is suggested by Robert Alter, *The Art of Biblical Narrative*, 2nd ed. (New York: Basic Books, 2011), 114.

text in front of them, to serve as their guide? Possibly both options were available.[20] Based on the research of scholars who have investigated oral performance, clearly reciters could commit large chunks of text to memory, to be tapped when necessary. At the same time, though, we know that ancient Near Eastern literature was written down, on papyrus (in the case of Egypt and Canaan)[21] and on clay tablets (in the case of Ugarit, Mesopotamia, etc.). Generally speaking, I will assume the latter option, to wit, an ancient Israelite reciter holding the written text, which served as a mere skeleton (long before the development of the Masoretic apparatus [see above, pp. 3–7]), but which served him (and by extension his audience) during the oral performance. At times, as we shall see, the written version includes visual plays, which only the person holding the text would appreciate. I admit that this does not constitute foolproof evidence for the 'written text' hypothesis, but to my mind it certainly points in that direction.

Since I am assuming here an *oral* reading of the text, I should add a comment or two about this aspect of ancient literature. For moderns, reading is largely a silent affair, a task performed by the eyes before the text is decoded and processed by the brain. For the ancients, however, reading was an aural experience: one *heard* the text before it was processed by the brain.[22]

One proof for this point is the following oft-cited comment by Augustine (354–430 C.E.) regarding his senior colleague Ambrose, bishop of Milan (340–397 C.E.): "When he read, his eyes scanned the page and his heart sought out the meaning, but his voice was silent and his

---

20. There is, of course, the following key difference: the Somali, Serbo-Croatian, Uzbek, and other materials mentioned above are poems, whereas much of the biblical literature discussed herein is written in narrative prose (on which see below, Chapter 21). It may be easier to commit poetry to memory than prose, but I set that issue aside for the moment.

21. At a later time, starting in the Persian period, the Israelites began to write their literature on parchment scrolls. Such remains the practice among Jews to the present day, in particular for texts used for liturgical purposes (the Torah, Esther, etc.).

22. This activity persists in the manner in which young children listen to stories, read to them by parents, teachers, and others. Eventually, however, from kindergarten onward, they learn to read silently, and the experience of aurally processing books becomes less and less frequent.

tongue was still. Anyone could approach him freely and guests were not commonly announced, so that often, when we came to visit him, we found him reading like this in silence, for he never read aloud" (*Confessions*, Book 6, ch. 3).[23] From Augustine's observation, it is patently clear that Ambrose's ability to read silently was something at which to marvel, even as late as the fourth century c.e.; for the norm, as we have indicated, was to read a text aloud.

To return to the Hebrew realm, two observations may be raised to demonstrate the same point for ancient Israel. The first is the very simple observation that the Hebrew verb קרא *q-r-ʾ* means both 'call aloud' (its primary designation) and 'read' (its derived connotation). The second is the statement in Isa 29:18 ־וְשָׁמְעוּ בַיּוֹם־הַהוּא הַחֵרְשִׁים דִּבְרֵי סֵפֶר *wəšamʿu bay-yom ha-huʾ ha-ḥeršim dibre sepεr* 'and on that day the deaf shall hear the words of the book'. In the topsy-turvy world that the prophet describes (vv. 17–20), the Lebanon will become choice farmland, the blind will see, tyrants will cease, the poor will rejoice in Yahweh, and the deaf will gain the ability to hear.

In our contemporary society, where reading is mainly a visual activity, it is the blind who are handicapped and who require special assistance (through Braille mainly), while the deaf are able to read. In ancient Israel, by contrast, where reading was largely an aural activity, the blind could "read," by *listening* to an oral presentation, whereas the deaf could not.[24]

Back now to the first creation account: We conclude our detailed analysis of the Bible's first story with an eye to the three verses that describe day seven of creation, Gen 2:1–3. Two of the devices already expounded occur in these verses. First we note the variation present in the nonverbatim repetition of the key phrase:[25]

---

23. I quote the text from Alberto Manguel, *A History of Reading* (New York: Viking, 1996), 42—with much more valuable information on the topic to be found throughout Chapter 2, "The Silent Readers" (41–53).

24. With the increased use of audiobooks in our society, certainly among the blind, but even among sighted people, contemporary people are recapturing a bit of the ancient experience of oral/aural reading.

25. These words will be familiar to traditionally minded Jewish readers, since these verses are used to introduce the Kiddush (the sanctification of the

Genesis 2:2a

מְלַאכְתּוֹ אֲשֶׁר עָשָׂה

his work that he had made

Genesis 2:2b

מִכָּל־מְלַאכְתּוֹ אֲשֶׁר עָשָׂה:

from all his work that he had made

Genesis 2:3

מִכָּל־מְלַאכְתּוֹ אֲשֶׁר־בָּרָא אֱלֹהִים לַעֲשׂוֹת:

from all his work that God created in making

These three phrases summarize God's creative activity during the six days of creation. So as not to repeat the same words in v. 2, the author introduces the word כָּל *kol* 'all' in the latter part of the verse—though this simple adjustment only sets the stage for the splash of linguistic talent in what follows. For after rehearsing the phrase מִכָּל־מְלַאכְתּוֹ אֲשֶׁר *mik-kol məlaʾkto ʾašɛr* 'from all his work that', found in both v. 2b and v. 3, the author then (a) changes the verb from עָשָׂה *ʿaśa* 'he made' to בָּרָא *baraʾ* 'he created'; (b) introduces the explicit nominal subject אֱלֹהִים *ʾɛlohim* 'God'; and (c) ends the passage with the infinitive לַעֲשׂוֹת *laʿaśot* 'to make', thereby constructing a peculiar syntagma, one that rings a bit strange to the Hebrew ear. This last point speaks to one made earlier: the ancient author went to great lengths to vary his wording, even to the extent of fashioning a most unusual phraseology. For it is often via the abnormal that one's attention is captured, as exemplified by this instance.

Sabbath), recited each Friday night over wine. I invite said readers to ponder these words more carefully, taking note of the variation with repetition, which so characterizes biblical literature.

The second technique utilized in these verses is the absence of the word שַׁבָּת *šabbat* 'Sabbath'. One encounters the expressions בַּיּוֹם הַשְּׁבִיעִי *bay-yom haš-šəbiʿi* 'on the seventh day' (2x) and יוֹם הַשְּׁבִיעִי *yom haš-šəbiʿi* 'the seventh day' (1x), but the critical word 'Sabbath' is wanting. If this institution was so central to ancient Israelite culture and religion (as it clearly was, based on its mention in the Decalogue [Exodus 20 // Deuteronomy 5] and its position at the head of the calendar in texts such as Leviticus 23 and Numbers 28–29),[26] why is the word not used at the start of the Torah in Gen 2:1–3? The answer is the same one offered above for the non-mention of 'sun' and 'moon' and the use of plural 'seas' instead of singular 'sea', for Shabbat (or Shabbatay) is the classical Hebrew word for the planet Saturn, which naturally was worshipped as a god by the ancients.[27] As we saw earlier, the author of our text wished to avoid any mention of pagan deities—to the extent even of not incorporating the key word 'Sabbath' into his prose. The ancient reader, meanwhile, no doubt would have understood.

We have spent a good portion of our analysis describing intricate details about the language used to create Genesis 1:1–2:3. We now pull back the lens to reveal one more aspect of this well-known composition. As the chart below demonstrates, the first creation story contains a well-crafted literary structure:

Day 1:	Light	Day 4:	Lights
Day 2:	Sky (and Water)	Day 5:	Fish and Fowl
Day 3a:	Dry Land	Day 6a:	Land Animals
Day 3b:	Vegetation	Day 6b:	Humans

Day 7: Sabbath

---

26. The reader will be interested to learn that Sabbath is also mentioned in a Hebrew inscription discovered at Meṣad Ḥašavyahu in Israel. For more information, see Shmuel Ahituv, *Echoes from the Past: Hebrew and Cognate Inscriptions from the Biblical Period* (Jerusalem: Carta, 2008), 156–63, esp. 161.

27. We are most familiar with the Roman god by that name, but the worship of the planet Saturn in the form of a deity goes back to the ancient Near East as well.

The first set of three days is paralleled by the second set of three days. Above we gave a cogent explanation for the non-use of the words 'sun' and 'moon' in day four. In their place, the author refers to these items as שְׁנֵי הַמְּאֹרֹת הַגְּדֹלִים *šəne ham-mə'orot hag-gədolim* 'the two great lights', i.e., הַמָּאוֹר הַגָּדֹל לְמֶמְשֶׁלֶת הַיּוֹם *ham-ma'or hag-gadol lə-mɛmšɛlɛt hay-yom* 'the great light for the rule of day' and הַמָּאוֹר הַקָּטֹן לְמֶמְשֶׁלֶת הַלַּיְלָה *ham-ma'or haq-qaton lə-mɛmšɛlɛt hal-layla* 'the small light for the rule of night'. These circumlocutions not only avoid the need to use the basic words 'sun' and 'moon', but they also allow the reader to hear the basic word אוֹר *'or* 'light' over and again, thereby creating a lexical link back to day one. Indeed, the word אוֹר *'or* 'light' occurs 5x in Gen 1:3–5, just as the word מָאוֹר *ma'or* 'light' (in the sense of 'luminary') occurs 5x (in both singular and plural forms) in Gen 1:14–16.

On day two, water is the main object of God's creative act—though as we have noted, it was not actually created, but rather was bounded by the formation of the firmament, called 'sky, heaven', used to separate the waters into those above and those below. In the corresponding day five, accordingly, fish and fowl are created. As one would expect, the words מַיִם *mayim* 'water' and שָׁמַיִם *šamayim* 'sky, heaven' occur in both paragraphs.

Both day three and day six contain two stages to creation. On the former, the dry land and the vegetation are created; on the latter, the land animals and the humans, which live on the dry land and eat the vegetation, are created. The correspondence is self-evident, and as we saw above, the description of the vegetation reverberates in the descriptions of days three and six (with consummate variation, of course).

Finally, crowning the six days of creative activity is day seven, the Sabbath, which naturally lacks a corresponding day, for it has no equal.

The result is a blueprint for creation. One of the major points that the narrative as a whole wishes to impart is the manner in which God created an orderly world out of preexistent chaos. The latter is indicated most of all by the expression תֹהוּ וָבֹהוּ *tohu wa-bohu* 'wild and waste' (v. 2). As the action proceeds, God brings order into said world, indicated perhaps most of all by the fivefold use of the root ב-ד-ל *b-d-l* 'separate, divide' (vv. 4, 6, 7, 14, 18). Imagine the negative impression you would gain were you to enter my office and find a chaotic desktop, filled with 'wild and waste' comprised of indiscriminate piles of books, papers, and more. Imagine the very different impression you would gain were you to enter the next day and find that I had organized everything, dividing these books that belong here from those books that belong there, separating papers connected to my research from my students' papers relevant to my course instruction, and so on. So it is with Genesis 1. There is a blueprint to creation, which the literary structure signifies. Add to this design the refrains that repeat (even when one is omitted, for the reason stated above), and one senses even greater orderliness. The result is a brilliant example of "form follows content" (to use the literary term) or "form follows function" (to use the architectural term).[28] God created an orderly universe; the author of Genesis 1 fashioned an orderly narrative.

This opening chapter gives you a sense of our overall approach. The texts of the Hebrew Bible are about three thousand years old (on dating, see Chapter 21), and yet in no way should they be considered simple tales. At every turn they reveal a deep literary sophistication. Our ancient author, anonymous though he may be, was a master of language and a brilliant literary craftsman. His audience no doubt appreciated his every effort.

---

28. We will explore this literary device further in Chapter 27.

CHAPTER TWO

REPETITION WITH VARIATION: THE ANIMALS IN THE FLOOD STORY (GENESIS 6–9)

Our analysis of Genesis 1:1–2:3 in the previous chapter included several stellar examples of the technique of repetition with variation. As we saw in the descriptions of the plant kingdom and the animal kingdom, along with the wording of 'all his work' from which God rested on the seventh day, at every turn the author of the Bible's introductory narrative varies his language. As the reader already may suspect, this device is not limited to Genesis 1:1–2:3, but indeed permeates the biblical text throughout, both in prose and in poetry. In this and the following chapters, I will provide many additional examples of non-verbatim repetition in order to demonstrate the point. Indeed, as will become clear by the time we reach the end of Chapter 4 (with further excursions in Chapters 9, 12, and 15), this technique constitutes one of the most essential building blocks of biblical Hebrew literature, both prose and poetry.

We begin by focusing our attention on the various expressions used for the members of the animal kingdom, especially as those creatures are mentioned repeatedly in the flood story of Genesis 6–9, an account that follows the first creation story in relatively close proximity.

The relevant expressions are as follows:[1]

---

1. I have omitted from the long list of verses below Gen 7:2–3 and 8:20, in which a few of the terms appear, though these passages are more restricted in scope, contending with only the pure animals and birds intended for sacrificial purposes.

1. Genesis 6:7

וַיֹּ֣אמֶר יְהֹוָ֗ה אֶמְחֶ֨ה אֶת־הָאָדָ֤ם אֲשֶׁר־בָּרָ֙אתִי֙ מֵעַל֙ פְּנֵ֣י הָֽאֲדָמָ֔ה מֵֽאָדָם֙
עַד־בְּהֵמָ֔ה עַד־רֶ֖מֶשׂ וְעַד־ע֣וֹף הַשָּׁמָ֑יִם כִּ֥י נִחַ֖מְתִּי כִּ֥י עֲשִׂיתִֽם:

And Yhwh said, "I will wipe out the human whom I created from the face of the soil: from human until beast, until
creeping-thing, and until the fowl of heaven; for I regret that
I made them."

2. Genesis 6:20

מֵהָע֣וֹף לְמִינֵ֗הוּ וּמִן־הַבְּהֵמָה֙ לְמִינָ֔הּ מִכֹּ֛ל רֶ֥מֶשׂ הָֽאֲדָמָ֖ה לְמִינֵ֑הוּ שְׁנַ֧יִם
מִכֹּ֛ל יָבֹ֥אוּ אֵלֶ֖יךָ לְהַחֲיֽוֹת:

"From the fowl (each) according to its kind, and from
the beasts (each) according to its kind, (and) from all the
creeping-things of the soil (each) according to its kind—two
of each shall come unto you to remain alive."

3. Genesis 7:8

מִן־הַבְּהֵמָה֙ הַטְּהוֹרָ֔ה וּמִן־הַ֨בְּהֵמָ֔ה אֲשֶׁ֥ר אֵינֶ֖נָּה טְהֹרָ֑ה וּמִ֨ן־הָע֔וֹף וְכֹ֖ל
אֲשֶׁר־רֹמֵ֥שׂ עַל־הָֽאֲדָמָֽה:

From the pure beasts and from the beasts that are not pure,
and from the fowl, and (from) all that creeps on the soil.

4. Genesis 7:14

הֵ֜מָּה וְכָל־הַֽחַיָּ֣ה לְמִינָ֗הּ וְכָל־הַבְּהֵמָה֙ לְמִינָ֔הּ וְכָל־הָרֶ֛מֶשׂ הָרֹמֵ֥שׂ עַל־
הָאָ֖רֶץ לְמִינֵ֑הוּ וְכָל־הָע֣וֹף לְמִינֵ֔הוּ כֹּ֖ל צִפּ֥וֹר כָּל־כָּנָֽף:

They and every living-thing (each) according to its kind,
and all the beasts (each) according to its kind, and all the
creeping-things that creep on the earth (each) according to
its kind; and all the fowl (each) according to its kind, every
bird, every winged-thing.

5. Genesis 7:21

וַיִּגְוַ֞ע כָּל־בָּשָׂ֣ר ׀ הָרֹמֵ֣שׂ עַל־הָאָ֗רֶץ בָּע֤וֹף וּבַבְּהֵמָה֙ וּבַ֣חַיָּ֔ה וּבְכָל־הַשֶּׁ֖רֶץ הַשֹּׁרֵ֣ץ עַל־הָאָ֑רֶץ וְכֹ֖ל הָאָדָֽם:

And all flesh that creeps on the earth expired: among the
fowl, and among the beasts, and among the living-things,
and among all swarming-things that swarm upon the earth;
and all the humans.

6. Genesis 7:23

וַיִּ֜מַח אֶֽת־כָּל־הַיְק֣וּם ׀ אֲשֶׁ֣ר ׀ עַל־פְּנֵ֣י הָֽאֲדָמָ֗ה מֵאָדָ֤ם עַד־בְּהֵמָה֙ עַד־
רֶ֙מֶשׂ֙ וְעַד־ע֣וֹף הַשָּׁמַ֔יִם וַיִּמָּח֖וּ מִן־הָאָ֑רֶץ וַיִּשָּׁ֧אֶר אַךְ־נֹ֛חַ וַֽאֲשֶׁ֥ר אִתּ֖וֹ
בַּתֵּבָֽה:

And he erased all that exists on the face of the soil: from
human until beast, until creeping-thing, and until the fowl
of heaven—and they were erased from the earth; and there
remained only Noah and those with him in the ark.

7. Genesis 8:1

וַיִּזְכֹּ֤ר אֱלֹהִים֙ אֶת־נֹ֔חַ וְאֵ֣ת כָּל־הַֽחַיָּ֗ה וְאֶת־כָּל־הַבְּהֵמָ֔ה אֲשֶׁ֥ר אִתּ֖וֹ
בַּתֵּבָ֑ה וַיַּעֲבֵ֨ר אֱלֹהִ֥ים ר֙וּחַ֙ עַל־הָאָ֔רֶץ וַיָּשֹׁ֖כּוּ הַמָּֽיִם:

And God remembered Noah and all the living-things and all
the beasts that were with him in the ark; and God dispatched
a wind over the earth, and the waters receded.

8. Genesis 8:17

כָּל־הַחַיָּ֨ה אֲשֶֽׁר־אִתְּךָ֜ מִכָּל־בָּשָׂ֗ר בָּע֧וֹף וּבַבְּהֵמָ֛ה וּבְכָל־הָרֶ֛מֶשׂ הָרֹמֵ֥שׂ
עַל־הָאָ֖רֶץ [הוצא] הַיְצֵא* אִתָּ֑ךְ וְשָׁרְצ֣וּ בָאָ֔רֶץ וּפָר֥וּ וְרָב֖וּ עַל־הָאָֽרֶץ:[2]

---

2. Here and elsewhere my practice is to place the Ketiv (the written
form) in square brackets and to mark the Qeri (the orally recited form) with
an asterisk following the word. See further above, Introduction, p. 7, n. 12.
At other places in the manuscript, the reader will notice an asterisk before a

"All the living-things who are with you: from all flesh, of the fowl and of the beasts, and of all the creeping-things that creep on the earth—take out with you; and they shall swarm on the earth, and they shall be fruitful and shall multiply on the earth."

9. Genesis 8:19

כָּל־הַחַיָּה כָּל־הָרֶמֶשׂ וְכָל־הָעוֹף כֹּל רוֹמֵשׂ עַל־הָאָרֶץ לְמִשְׁפְּחֹתֵיהֶם יָצְאוּ מִן־הַתֵּבָה:

All the living-things, all the creeping-things and all the fowl, all that creeps on the earth, according to their families they exited from the ark.

10. Genesis 9:2

וּמוֹרַאֲכֶם וְחִתְּכֶם יִהְיֶה עַל כָּל־חַיַּת הָאָרֶץ וְעַל כָּל־עוֹף הַשָּׁמָיִם בְּכֹל֙ אֲשֶׁר תִּרְמֹשׂ הָאֲדָמָה וּבְכָל־דְּגֵי הַיָּם בְּיֶדְכֶם נִתָּנוּ:

"And fear of you and dread of you shall be over all the living-things of the earth, and over all the fowl of heaven; over all that the soil creeps,[3] and over all the fishes of the sea—into your hand they are given."

11. Genesis 9:3

כָּל־רֶמֶשׂ אֲשֶׁר הוּא־חַי לָכֶם יִהְיֶה לְאָכְלָה כְּיֶרֶק עֵשֶׂב נָתַתִּי לָכֶם אֶת־כֹּל:

"And all creeping-things that live, to you they shall be for food; as (with) green plants, I give to you all."

---

particular word or reading; in such instances this symbol marks a hypothetical reading or a potentially alternative reading, though one not actually attested.

3. For an explanation of this admittedly odd rendering, see below.

12. Genesis 9:10

וְאֵת כָּל־נֶפֶשׁ הַחַיָּה אֲשֶׁר אִתְּכֶם בָּעוֹף בַּבְּהֵמָה וּבְכָל־חַיַּת הָאָרֶץ
אִתְּכֶם מִכֹּל יֹצְאֵי הַתֵּבָה לְכֹל חַיַּת הָאָרֶץ׃

"And every living being who is with you, among the fowl,
among the beasts, and among all the living-things of the
earth with you, from among all who exit the ark, of all the
living-things of the earth."

Now, the presentation of these twelve verses clearly falls into the
category of 'data overload', and yet I include all of them here to demonstrate the point. The flood story provides occasion for repeated
mention of the constituent members of the animal kingdom, and the
author of Genesis 6–9 takes full advantage of this situation to vary his
language at every turn. I will forego identifying every single variation
in this litany of verses—for the point is rather self-evident—though a
few comments may be helpful to direct the reader's attention.

In Gen 6:7, the three main elements are ordered as בְּהֵמָה *bəhema*
'beasts', רֶמֶשׂ *rɛmeś* 'creeping-things', and עוֹף הַשָּׁמַיִם *'op haš-šamayim*
'fowl of the heaven'; while in Gen 6:20 the order is עוֹף *'op* 'fowl'
(without the word 'heaven'), בְּהֵמָה *bəhema* 'beasts', and רֶמֶשׂ הָאֲדָמָה
rɛmeś ha-'adama 'creeping-things of the soil' (using a more complete
expression). In Gen 7:8 the text presents yet a different order, with בְּהֵמָה
bəhema 'beasts' (divided into the pure and the impure), עוֹף *'op* 'fowl',
and then וְכֹל אֲשֶׁר־רֹמֵשׂ עַל־הָאֲדָמָה *wə-kol 'ašɛr romeś 'al ha-'adama* 'and
all that creeps on the soil', using a different wording than the first two
references to the 'creeping-things'.

The next mention of the animal kingdom appears in Gen 7:14, where
the order is once again 'beasts', 'creeping things', and 'fowl' (as it was
in the first instance in Gen 6:7), but the series now is introduced by the
catch-all term וְכָל־הַחַיָּה *wə-kol ha-ḥayya* 'and every living-thing'. In
addition, each item is qualified both by the word וְכָל־ *wə-kol* 'and all/
every' and by the term לְמִינָהּ / לְמִינֵהוּ *lə-minah / lə-minehu* '(each) according to its kind' (fem. and masc., respectively). Moreover, yet a new
expression is used for the 'creeping things', namely, וְכָל־הָרֶמֶשׂ הָרֹמֵשׂ
עַל־הָאָרֶץ *wə-kol ha-rɛmeś ha-romeś 'al ha-'areṣ* 'and all the creeping-
things that creep on the earth', hitherto not encountered (though see

Gen 1:26). Similarly, another new expression is attached to the end of the verse, with כֹּל צִפּוֹר כָּל־כָּנָף *kol ṣippor kol kanap* 'every bird, every winged-thing' now defining 'fowl'.

We next arrive at Gen 7:21, which presents yet further variation. In this verse, the key word רֹמֵשׂ *romeś* 'creeps' now appears near the head of the passage to modify 'all flesh'; the animals that follow are in the order 'fowl', 'beasts', and 'living-things'; and then an entirely new root, שׁ-ר-ץ *š-r-ṣ* 'swarm' (2x), is introduced at the end, in the phrase וּבְכָל־הַשֶּׁרֶץ הַשֹּׁרֵץ עַל־הָאָרֶץ *u-bə-kol haš-šɛrɛṣ haš-šoreṣ ʿal ha-ʾareṣ* 'and among all swarming-things that swarm upon the earth'.

After all of these variant wordings, our author plays with his readers (or at least that is how I would explain the verbatim repetition) by faithfully reproducing the initial expression from Gen 6:7 word-for-word in Gen 7:23: מֵאָדָם עַד־בְּהֵמָה עַד־רֶמֶשׂ וְעַד־עוֹף הַשָּׁמַיִם *me-ʾadam ʿad bəhema ʿad rɛmɛś wə-ʿad ʿop haš-šamayim* 'from human until beast, until creeping-thing, and until the fowl of heaven'. Though, to be sure, he returns to variant diction upon reaching Gen 8:1 and all successive iterations.

There is no need to continue this exercise for all of Genesis 8–9, for the point is clear. Instead, of the remaining locutions in the flood story, we may focus on what is certainly the most atypical: Gen 9:2, בְּכֹל אֲשֶׁר תִּרְמֹשׂ הָאֲדָמָה *bə-kol ʾašɛr tirmoś ha-ʾadama* 'and over all that the soil creeps'. Only here in the Bible (and in the exact replication of these words in Lev 20:25) is the verbal root ר-מ-שׂ *r-m-ś* 'creep' predicated of the earth,[4] and not of the creatures who actually creep, in which case a better rendering of the passage might be 'and over all (those creatures) with which the soil teems'. This last expression treated here demonstrates the extent to which the ancient writers would go in their efforts to vary language. As we saw in the previous chapter regarding Gen 2:3, מִכָּל־מְלַאכְתּוֹ אֲשֶׁר־בָּרָא אֱלֹהִים לַעֲשׂוֹת *mik-kol məlaʾkto ʾašɛr baraʾ ʾɛlohim laʿaśot* 'from all his work that God created in making', at times authors would create neologisms or invoke unusual usages to enhance their literary creation. To my mind, the aforecited passage from Gen 9:2 is another such example.

---

4. BDB, 942–43; and *DCH* 7:500.

One last point may be noted, however. The fish are not mentioned in the flood narrative, for naturally they were not affected by the great devastation. But they do appear in Gen 9:2, when the entire animal kingdom is described with all of its component parts: וּבְכָל־דְּגֵי הַיָּם *u-bə-kol dəge hay-yam* 'and over all the fishes of the sea'. I mention this particular phrase in order to highlight how here too the text uses variant language. For in the first mention of the fish, from day five of creation, the expression used was בִּדְגַת הַיָּם *bi-dgat hay-yam* 'over the fish of the sea' (Gen 1:26, 1:28). My focus is not so much on the use or non-use of the word כָּל *kol* 'all', but rather on the two different forms of the word for 'fish'. In Gen 1:26, 1:28, the text uses the feminine form of the noun as a collective (thus my rendering 'fish'), while in Gen 9:2, the text uses the masculine plural form of the noun (thus my rendering 'fishes').

At this point, the reader once again may wonder whether or not the ancient listener to this intoned prose was able to recall the various iterations of a phrase occurring at some distance (or, more properly, time interval) from one another. As I intimated in the first chapter, I believe the answer to this question is 'yes'. There is so much repetition with variation in the Bible—and we have only begun to scratch the surface here—that one is left to conclude that this practice represents an intentional literary device, employed by diverse authors, who indeed could expect their audiences to recall the previous locutions.

Another question also raises itself. Anyone familiar with the development of modern biblical scholarship during the nineteenth and twentieth centuries will know that most scholars divide the Torah into different sources.[5] Three of these reputed sources (Yahwist [J], Elohist [E], and Priestly [P]) are assumed to underlie the book of Genesis, two of which (J and P) are present in the first eleven chapters, that is, the creation and flood narratives, along with other material. The question thus needs to be asked whether perhaps the variant phrases are due to the presence of different authors employing different terminology. And yet this approach is not sustained by the evidence. To take the last illustration, for example, both Gen 1:26, 28 and Gen 9:2 are assigned to

---

5. For basic introduction, see Friedman, *Who Wrote the Bible?*; and Richard E. Friedman, *The Bible with Sources Revealed* (San Francisco: Harper, 2003).

the P source, and yet the passages use different forms of the word for 'fish'. Or to use an example presented at the start of this discussion, Gen 6:7 and 7:8 are both assigned to the J source, and yet they use different orders for the components of the animal kingdom (Gen 6:20, with yet another order, is allocated to P). Conversely, Gen 6:7 and 7:14 both use the order 'beasts', 'creeping things', and 'fowl' (see above), and yet the former is considered part of the J source, while the latter is reckoned as part of the P source. Now, as we shall see in a subsequent discussion (in Chapter 22), I reject the division of the narrative portions of the Torah into separate sources, so to some extent I find the matter at hand largely irrelevant. And yet I raise the topic here, since I assume that at least some if not many readers of this monograph are familiar with the Documentary Hypothesis (as the source theory is known) and will wonder if in some way this approach is not relevant to the identification of variant phraseology. As I hope to have demonstrated here, however, the sources play no role whatsoever. Instead (and here I anticipate my treatment in Chapter 22), we should view the narrative portions of the Torah as speaking with a single narrative voice, produced by an author (or authors) who delighted in dazzling his listeners with the literary technique studied here.

At this point, one may wish to know whether this device has a specific name within the scholarly jargon that typically dominates academic research (that is, beyond 'repetition with variation'). The answer is 'no', or at least not until recently. My colleague Scott Noegel deserves credit for coining the term *polyprosopon* (speaking of neologisms [see above, p. 39]), based on the Greek words for 'many' and 'face'.[6] Which is to say, the authors strived to present their language with 'many faces', never (or hardly ever) repeating the same expression in verbatim fashion.

---

6. See Scott B. Noegel and Gary A. Rendsburg, *Solomon's Vineyard: Literary and Linguistic Studies in the Song of Songs* (SBL Ancient Israel and Its Literature 1; Atlanta: Society of Biblical Literature, 2009), 108–9. Our co-authored volume does not make clear which of us coined this term, so here I happily note that full credit goes to Professor Noegel.

CHAPTER THREE

REPETITION WITH VARIATION: THE PLAGUES NARRATIVE (EXODUS 7–10)

The previous chapter focused on a particularly complex instance of polyprosopon, the manner in which the author of the flood narrative in Genesis 6–9 continually varies the phrases used to denote the constituent branches of the animal kingdom. A dozen verses formed the basis of our analysis, representing eleven different usages (only Gen 6:7 and Gen 7:23 repeat the same phrase word-for-word) for describing essentially the same thing: the various animals taken onto the ark by Noah. In the present chapter, we continue to explore this literary device by turning our attention to two interwoven expressions in the plagues narrative in Exodus 7–10: (a) the various warnings expressed by Moses to Pharaoh; and (b) the various phrases used to describe the hardening of Pharaoh's heart.[1]

1. Exodus 7–10 — the warnings to Pharaoh

Repeatedly in the book of Exodus, Moses appears before Pharaoh to warn him of a forthcoming plague. As scholars have noticed, these warnings appear before plagues 1, 4, and 7 in one formulation, and before plagues 2, 5, and 8 in another formulation. (No warning occurs before plagues 3, 6, and 9, while the warning for the tenth plague is worded in an altogether different fashion.)

---

1. For a parallel treatment, see Gary A. Rendsburg, "The Literary Unity of the Exodus Narrative," in James K. Hoffmeier, Alan Millard, and Gary A. Rendsburg, eds., *"Did I Not Bring Israel Out of Egypt?": Biblical, Archaeological, and Egyptological Perspectives on the Exodus Narratives* (Bulletin for Biblical Research Supplement 13; Winona Lake, IN: Eisenbrauns, 2016), 119–25.

The first set of verses, constituting what may be called 'the morning warning', are the following:

(1a) Exodus 7:15

לֵךְ אֶל־פַּרְעֹה בַּבֹּקֶר הִנֵּה יֹצֵא הַמַּיְמָה וְנִצַּבְתָּ לִקְרָאתוֹ עַל־שְׂפַת הַיְאֹר וְהַמַּטֶּה אֲשֶׁר־נֶהְפַּךְ לְנָחָשׁ תִּקַּח בְּיָדֶךָ:

"Go to Pharaoh in the morning—behold, he (will be) coming out to the water—and you shall position (yourself) to greet him at the edge of the Nile; and the staff that turned into a snake, you shall take in your hand."

(1b) Exodus 8:16

וַיֹּאמֶר יְהֹוָה אֶל־מֹשֶׁה הַשְׁכֵּם בַּבֹּקֶר וְהִתְיַצֵּב לִפְנֵי פַרְעֹה הִנֵּה יוֹצֵא הַמַּיְמָה וְאָמַרְתָּ אֵלָיו כֹּה אָמַר יְהֹוָה שַׁלַּח עַמִּי וְיַעַבְדֻנִי:

And Yʜᴡʜ said to Moses, "Arise-early in the morning and position yourself before Pharaoh—behold, he (will be) coming out to the water—and you shall say to him, 'Thus says Yʜᴡʜ: Send-forth my people, so that they may worship me'."

(1c) Exodus 9:13

וַיֹּאמֶר יְהֹוָה אֶל־מֹשֶׁה הַשְׁכֵּם בַּבֹּקֶר וְהִתְיַצֵּב לִפְנֵי פַרְעֹה וְאָמַרְתָּ אֵלָיו כֹּה־אָמַר יְהֹוָה אֱלֹהֵי הָעִבְרִים שַׁלַּח אֶת־עַמִּי וְיַעַבְדֻנִי:

And Yʜᴡʜ said to Moses, "Arise-early in the morning and position yourself before Pharaoh; and you shall say to him, 'Thus says Yʜᴡʜ the God of the Hebrews: Send-forth my people, so that they may worship me'."

I am not concerned with the lack of an introduction to (1a), for the phrase וַיֹּאמֶר יְהֹוָה אֶל־מֹשֶׁה "And Yʜᴡʜ said to Moses" occurs in the previous verse, serving to introduce the long direct speech that spans vv. 14–18 (including v. 15, cited above). Instead, the differences between and among the three verses lie elsewhere. First, in (1a) the author uses the Niphʿal form of the verb נ-צ-ב *n-ṣ-b* / י-צ-ב *y-ṣ-b* 'be positioned'

44   How the Bible Is Written

(and thus I have placed the word 'yourself' in parentheses); while in
(1b) and (1c) he employs the Hitpaʿel form of the same verb, meaning 'to
position oneself' (and thus I have not used parentheses with the word
'yourself'). Second, in (1a) God commands Moses לֵךְ אֶל־פַּרְעֹה בַּבֹּקֶר *lek
ʾel parʿo bab-boqɛr* 'go to Pharaoh in the morning'; while in (1b) and
(1c) the directive is worded הַשְׁכֵּם בַּבֹּקֶר *haškem bab-boqɛr* 'arise-early
in the morning'. Third, in (1a) the expression הִנֵּה יֹצֵא הַמַּיְמָה *hinne
yoṣeʾ ham-mayma* 'behold, he (will be) going out to the water' appears
relatively early in the verse; in (1b) these words are delayed until later
in the sentence; while in (1c) the phrase is omitted. In addition, the
language of the "Thus says Yʜwʜ" clause, along with the words actually spoken by God, are varied. (I will present these differences below,
once I have introduced the other relevant passages.)

The second set of verses, constituting what may be called 'the
general warning', are the following:

(1d) Exodus 7:26

וַיֹּאמֶר יְהוָה אֶל־מֹשֶׁה בֹּא אֶל־פַּרְעֹה וְאָמַרְתָּ אֵלָיו כֹּה אָמַר יְהוָה
שַׁלַּח אֶת־עַמִּי וְיַעַבְדֻנִי:

And Yʜwʜ said to Moses, "Come to Pharaoh, and you shall
say to him, 'Thus says Yʜwʜ: Send-forth my people, so that
they may worship me'."

(1e) Exodus 9:1

וַיֹּאמֶר יְהוָה אֶל־מֹשֶׁה בֹּא אֶל־פַּרְעֹה וְדִבַּרְתָּ אֵלָיו כֹּה־אָמַר יְהוָה
אֱלֹהֵי הָעִבְרִים שַׁלַּח אֶת־עַמִּי וְיַעַבְדֻנִי:

And Yʜwʜ said to Moses, "Come to Pharaoh, and you shall
speak to him, 'Thus says Yʜwʜ the God of the Hebrews:
Send-forth my people, so that they may worship me'."

(1f) Exodus 10:1

וַיֹּאמֶר יְהוָה אֶל־מֹשֶׁה בֹּא אֶל־פַּרְעֹה כִּי־אֲנִי הִכְבַּדְתִּי אֶת־לִבּוֹ וְאֶת־לֵב
עֲבָדָיו לְמַעַן שִׁתִי אֹתֹתַי אֵלֶּה בְּקִרְבּוֹ:

And Yhwh said to Moses, "Come to Pharaoh, for I have
made-heavy his heart, and the heart of his servants, in order
that I may place these my signs in their midst."

The three verses begin in identical manner, though naturally they
diverge after the first seven words. In (1d) the verb used is א-מ-ר *ʾ-m-r*
'say' (which also is used throughout the first set of warnings), while in
(1e) the verb used is ד-ב-ר *d-b-r* 'speak'.[2] The author introduces the most
significant change in (1f), with the statement כִּי־אֲנִי הִכְבַּדְתִּי אֶת־לִבּוֹ *ki
ʾani hikbadti ʾet libbo* 'for I have made-heavy his heart (etc.)' appearing
at the spot where one would expect to find a "Thus says Yhwh" clause.

With these six verses before us, we now can focus on the different
locutions utilized in the "Thus says Yhwh" clauses, regarding both
(a) the presence or absence of epithets associated with Yhwh, and
(b) the presence or absence of the grammatical particle אֶת *ʾet* (not to
be translated—see further below). I omit from our discussion the first
plague, since the wording there is altogether different. Thus we have
five different expressions to consider, presented here in canonical order,
with the last iteration appearing not in 10:1 (see above), but rather in
10:3 (see below):

(1d) Exodus 7:26

כֹּה אָמַר יְהוָֹה שַׁלַּח אֶת־עַמִּי וְיַעַבְדֻנִי׃

"Thus says Yhwh: Send-forth my people, so that they may
worship me."

---

2. As such, I consider the change from א-מ-ר *ʾ-m-r* 'say' (4x) to ד-ב-ר
d-b-r 'speak' in Exod 9:1 to be a prose analogue to the poetic device identified
by David Noel Freedman, "Deliberate Deviation from an Established Pattern
of Repetition in Hebrew Poetry as a Rhetorical Device," in *Proceedings of the
Ninth World Congress of Jewish Studies, Division A: The Period of the Bible*
(Jerusalem: World Congress of Jewish Studies, 1986), 45–52 [reprinted in
John R. Huddlestun, ed., *Divine Commitment and Human Obligation: Selected
Writings of David Noel Freedman* (Grand Rapids: Eerdmans, 1997), 2:205–12].
For the alliteration generated by the use of the verb ד-ב-ר *d-b-r* 'speak' in
this verse, see below, Chapter 6, no. 8.

(1b) Exodus 8:16

כֹּה אָמַר יְהוָה שַׁלַּח עַמִּי וְיַעַבְדֻנִי:

"Thus says Yhwh: Send-forth my people, so that they may worship me."

(1e) Exodus 9:1

כֹּה־אָמַר יְהוָה אֱלֹהֵי הָעִבְרִים שַׁלַּח אֶת־עַמִּי וְיַעַבְדֻנִי:

"Thus says Yhwh the God of the Hebrews: Send-forth my people, so that they may worship me."

(1c) Exodus 9:13

כֹּה־אָמַר יְהוָה אֱלֹהֵי הָעִבְרִים שַׁלַּח אֶת־עַמִּי וְיַעַבְדֻנִי:

"Thus says Yhwh the God of the Hebrews: Send-forth my people, so that they may worship me."

(1f) Exodus 10:3

כֹּה־אָמַר יְהוָה אֱלֹהֵי הָעִבְרִים עַד־מָתַי מֵאַנְתָּ לֵעָנֹת מִפָּנָי שַׁלַּח עַמִּי וְיַעַבְדֻנִי:

"Thus says Yhwh the God of the Hebrews: Until when will you refuse to humble yourself before me? Send-forth my people, so that they may worship me."

In the first two passages, the deity is simply Yhwh, while in the last three passages, the text uses the expression יְהוָה אֱלֹהֵי הָעִבְרִים *yhwh ʾɛlohe ha-ʿibrim* 'Yhwh the God of the Hebrews'. In three instances (7:26, 9:1, 9:13) the famous "Let my people go" expression (rendered here more literally as 'Send-forth my people') includes the particle אֶת *ʾɛt*, which typically is used before a definite direct object (as in עַמִּי *ʿammi* 'my people'); while in two cases (8:16, 10:3), this particle is lacking. And then most glaringly, version (1f) delays the speech from its expected place in 10:1 until 10:3, plus it inserts a new phrase, the query to Pharaoh עַד־מָתַי מֵאַנְתָּ לֵעָנֹת מִפָּנָי *ʿad matay meʾanta leʿanot mippanay* 'Until when will you refuse to humble yourself before me?'.

The result of these differences is that only two of the iterations (9:1, 9:13) include verbatim language. On the one hand, such an unusual situation may serve to deny my general approach, since one expects variation at every turn. On the other hand, we also need to contend with our author's playing with his readers from time to time (as we saw in Chapter 2, regarding Gen 6:7 and 7:23, which also display verbatim repetition) via the surprise maneuver of repeating himself word-for-word on this occasion.

2. Exodus 7–10 — the hardening of Pharaoh's heart

The succession of plagues provides the opportunity for the author of the Exodus narrative to invoke polyprosopon in another series of passages. I refer to the oft-repeated mention of the hardening of Pharaoh's heart. As scholars have noted, three different Hebrew verbal roots are used to denote this motif: ח-ז-ק *ḥ-z-q* 'strengthen' (9x), כ-ב-ד *k-b-d* 'make heavy' (6x), and ק-שׁ-ה *q-š-h* 'harden' (1x).[3] In many of these cases, we also read that Pharaoh did not agree to release the Israelites from their bondage.

The nine passages that use the first verb, ח-ז-ק *ḥ-z-q* 'strengthen', are as follows:

(2a) Exodus 4:21

וַאֲנִי אֲחַזֵּק אֶת־לִבּוֹ וְלֹא יְשַׁלַּח אֶת־הָעָם׃

"And I will strengthen his heart, and he will not send-forth the people."

(2b) Exodus 7:13

וַיֶּחֱזַק לֵב פַּרְעֹה וְלֹא שָׁמַע אֲלֵהֶם כַּאֲשֶׁר דִּבֶּר יְהוָה׃

And the heart of Pharaoh was strong, and he did not listen to them, as Yʜwʜ had spoken.

---

3. As per this section heading, most of these attestations occur in Exodus 7–10, though I also include in my counts the examples from Exod 4:21 (which introduces the theme) and Exod 11:10 (a culminating usage, in anticipation of the tenth plague).

(2c) Exodus 7:22

וַיֶּחֱזַק לֵב־פַּרְעֹה וְלֹא־שָׁמַע אֲלֵהֶם כַּאֲשֶׁר דִּבֶּר יְהוָה׃

And the heart of Pharaoh was strong, and he did not listen to them, as Yʜwʜ had spoken.

(2d) Exodus 8:15

וַיֶּחֱזַק לֵב־פַּרְעֹה וְלֹא־שָׁמַע אֲלֵהֶם כַּאֲשֶׁר דִּבֶּר יְהוָה׃

And the heart of Pharaoh was strong, and he did not listen to them, as Yʜwʜ had spoken.

(2e) Exodus 9:12

וַיְחַזֵּק יְהוָה אֶת־לֵב פַּרְעֹה וְלֹא שָׁמַע אֲלֵהֶם כַּאֲשֶׁר דִּבֶּר יְהוָה אֶל־מֹשֶׁה׃

And Yʜwʜ strengthened the heart of Pharaoh, and he did not listen to them, as Yʜwʜ had spoken to Moses.

(2f) Exodus 9:35

וַיֶּחֱזַק לֵב פַּרְעֹה וְלֹא שִׁלַּח אֶת־בְּנֵי יִשְׂרָאֵל כַּאֲשֶׁר דִּבֶּר יְהוָה בְּיַד־מֹשֶׁה׃

And the heart of Pharaoh was strong, and he did not send-forth the children of Israel, as Yʜwʜ had spoken via the hand of Moses.

(2g) Exodus 10:20

וַיְחַזֵּק יְהוָה אֶת־לֵב פַּרְעֹה וְלֹא שִׁלַּח אֶת־בְּנֵי יִשְׂרָאֵל׃

And Yʜwʜ strengthened the heart of Pharaoh, and he did not send-forth the children of Israel.

(2h) Exodus 10:27

וַיְחַזֵּק יְהוָה אֶת־לֵב פַּרְעֹה וְלֹא אָבָה לְשַׁלְּחָם׃

And Yʜwʜ strengthened the heart of Pharaoh, and he did not consent to send-forth them.

(2i) Exodus 11:10

וַיְחַזֵּק יְהוָהֿ אֶת־לֵב פַּרְעֹה וְלֹא־שִׁלַּח אֶת־בְּנֵי־יִשְׂרָאֵל מֵאַרְצֹו׃

And Yʜᴡʜ strengthened the heart of Pharaoh, and he did
not send-forth the children of Israel from his land.

As indicated above, Exod 4:21, placed in the mouth of God (note the
first-person speech), simply sets the stage for the motif that will
recur throughout the plagues account. Once more, the author plays
with his readers, by using verbatim language in (2b), (2c), and (2d).
Though one should note the slight change introduced in (2c) and (2d),
which connects both the second and third words, that is, לֵב־פַּרְעֹה *leb
parʿo* 'heart of Pharaoh', and the fourth and fifth words, that is, וְלֹא־
שָׁמַע *wə-loʾ šamaʿ* 'and he did not listen', with a *maqqef* (similar to a
hyphen)—a feature that is lacking in (2b). This represents the most
meager distinction that can be indicated in the Masoretic Text, and yet
I would aver that the use of *maqqef* creates a slightly different modu-
lation when the reader intones the text for his listeners. Nonetheless,
it must be admitted that since both (2c) and (2d) use the *maqqef* in
both combinations, these two iterations are truly verbatim; and in any
case they are only ever-so-slightly different from (2b). The effect of
the three verses as a whole (to which should be added 8:11 [see below,
(2k)] as a fourth instance), I would submit, is to indicate how Pharaoh
remained stubborn. He does not change, and the language does not
change—a stellar example of 'form follows content', a device to be
explored further in Chapter 27 (with this specific example registered
as Chapter 27, no. 3).

Had the author continued in such fashion, however, his text would
have run counter to the standard of repetition with variation. Accordingly, with the point of Pharaoh's stubbornness now made, he returns
to the norm by incorporating polyprosopon into the composition,
commencing with (2e). If we use the wording of (2b), (2c), and (2d) as
the base language, then we may note how in (2e) the verb shifts from
the Qal intransitive וַיֶּחֱזַק *wayyɛḥɛzaq* 'and [the heart of Pharaoh] was
strong' to the Piʿel transitive וַיְחַזֵּק *wayḥazzeq*, with Yʜᴡʜ as subject,
thus, 'and [Yʜᴡʜ] strengthened [the heart of Pharaoh]'. In addition,
the phrase at the end has been expanded to now read כַּאֲשֶׁר דִּבֶּר יְהוָה

אֶל־מֹשֶׁה *ka-ʾašɛr dibbɛr* YHWH *ʾɛl mošɛ* 'as YHWH had spoken to Moses', with the addition of the final two words.

(2f) returns to the use of the intransitive verb at the head of the passage, but now inserts a new clause, וְלֹא שִׁלַּח אֶת־בְּנֵי יִשְׂרָאֵל *wa-loʾ šillaḥ ʾɛt bəne yiśraʾel* 'and he did not send-forth the children of Israel'; plus the phrase at the end is changed to כַּאֲשֶׁר דִּבֶּר יְהוָה בְּיַד־מֹשֶׁה *ka-ʾašɛr dibbɛr* YHWH *bə-yad mošɛ* 'as YHWH had spoken via the hand of Moses' (with בְּיַד *bə-yad* 'via the hand' replacing the simpler אֶל *ʾɛl* 'to').

(2g) incorporates elements of the preceding two iterations, to create yet a different variant wording. It employs the opening of (2e), וַיְחַזֵּק יְהוָה אֶת־לֵב פַּרְעֹה *wayḥazzeq* YHWH *ʾɛt leb parʿo* 'and YHWH strengthened the heart of Pharaoh', followed by the expression, encountered for the first time in (2f), וְלֹא שִׁלַּח אֶת־בְּנֵי יִשְׂרָאֵל *wa-loʾ šillaḥ ʾɛt bəne yiśraʾel* 'and he did not send-forth the children of Israel'.

(2h) opens in the same manner as (2e) and (2g), but then utilizes an entirely new construction to complete the verse: וְלֹא אָבָה לְשַׁלְּחָם *wa-loʾ ʾaba ləšalləḥam* 'and he did not consent to send-forth them', with recourse to a relatively rare verbal root, א-ב-ה *ʾ-b-h* 'consent' (it appears only here in Exodus and only 2x in all of Genesis). This maneuver also allows the repeated verbal root שׁ-ל-ח *š-l-ḥ* 'send, send-forth' to now appear in the infinitive form לְשַׁלְּחָם *ləšalləḥam* 'to send-forth them', as opposed to the recurring (negated) past-tense form וְלֹא שִׁלַּח *wa-loʾ šillaḥ* 'and he did not send-forth'.

Finally, the audience is led to believe that (2i) is simply a repeat of (2g), for it proceeds word-for-word through the series of ten words—until the author discloses the difference by the addition of the final word מֵאַרְצוֹ *me-ʾarṣo* 'from his land'. The result of all these minor changes, as we have seen throughout our study, is a masterful use of language in which the ancient Israelites listening to the plagues narrative would have delighted.

There is much more, however. As noted above, the verbal root ח-ז-ק *ḥ-z-q* 'strengthen' is only the most common lexeme utilized to express the hardening of Pharaoh's heart. The text displays even greater variation when employing the verbal root כ-ב-ד *k-b-d* 'make heavy', as in the following passages:

(2j) *Exodus 7:14*

וַיֹּאמֶר יְהֹוָה אֶל־מֹשֶׁה כָּבֵד לֵב פַּרְעֹה מֵאֵן לְשַׁלַּח הָעָם:

And Yhwh said to Moses, "The heart of Pharaoh is heavy; he refuses to send-forth the people."

(2k) *Exodus 8:11*

וְהַכְבֵּד אֶת־לִבּוֹ וְלֹא שָׁמַע אֲלֵהֶם כַּאֲשֶׁר דִּבֶּר יְהֹוָה:

And he made-heavy his heart, and he did not listen to them, as Yhwh had spoken.

(2l) *Exodus 8:28*

וַיַּכְבֵּד פַּרְעֹה אֶת־לִבּוֹ גַּם בַּפַּעַם הַזֹּאת וְלֹא שִׁלַּח אֶת־הָעָם:

And Pharaoh made-heavy his heart also this time, and he did not send-forth the people.

(2m) *Exodus 9:7*

וַיִּכְבַּד לֵב פַּרְעֹה וְלֹא שִׁלַּח אֶת־הָעָם:

And the heart of Pharaoh was heavy, and he did not send-forth the people.

(2n) *Exodus 9:34*

וַיַּכְבֵּד לִבּוֹ הוּא וַעֲבָדָיו:

And he made-heavy his heart, he and his servants.

(2o) *Exodus 10:1*

כִּי־אֲנִי הִכְבַּדְתִּי אֶת־לִבּוֹ וְאֶת־לֵב עֲבָדָיו לְמַעַן שִׁתִי אֹתֹתַי אֵלֶּה בְּקִרְבּוֹ:

"For I have made-heavy his heart, and the heart of his servants, in order that I may place these my signs in their [lit., 'his'] midst."

The differences between and among these wordings may be summa-
rized as follows. First, in (2j) and (2m), the verbal stem is Qal, expressing
the intransitive 'is/was heavy', with the former using the stative form
of the suffix-conjugation, כָּבֵד *kabed*, and the latter using the standard
narrative tense *wayyiqtol* form, וַיִּכְבַּד *wayyikbad*. By contrast, the other
four passages use the Hiph'il stem, expressing the transitive 'made-
heavy (his heart)', though once more different specific verbal forms
are used. (2l) and (2n) employ the standard narrative tense *wayyiqtol*
form וַיַּכְבֵּד *wayyakbed*, while (2k) utilizes the infinitive absolute form
וְהַכְבֵּד *wə-hakbed*, lit., 'and to make-heavy', thereby invoking an unusual
syntagma for the sake of variation. Finally, in the last iteration, (2o), we
note that now God is the one responsible for Pharaoh's heavy heart:
כִּי־אֲנִי הִכְבַּדְתִּי *ki ʾani hikbadti* 'for I have made-heavy', with the Hebrew
grammatical construction placing special emphasis on the pronoun 'I'.

   In addition, we note a series of other phrases in these passages,
some of which were encountered in the aforecited verses from the
plagues narrative, in either the same or similar wording, including:
(2j) מֵאֵן לְשַׁלַּח הָעָם *me'en ləšallaḥ ha-ʿam* 'he refuses to send-forth the
people'; (2k) וְלֹא שָׁמַע אֲלֵהֶם כַּאֲשֶׁר דִּבֶּר יְהוָה *wə-lo' šamaʿ ʾalehɛm ka-ʾašer
dibbɛr* YHWH 'and he did not listen to them, as YHWH had spoken';
(2l) and (2m) וְלֹא שִׁלַּח אֶת־הָעָם *wə-lo' šillaḥ ʾet ha-ʿam* 'and he did not
send-forth the people'; and (2n) הוּא וַעֲבָדָיו *hu' wa-ʿabadaw* 'he and his
servants'. (2l), moreover, introduces a new clause: גַּם בַּפַּעַם הַזֹּאת *gam
bap-paʿam haz-zoʾt* 'also this time'. And naturally the wording of (2o)
is the most variant, stemming from the shift to YHWH's involvement
in Pharaoh's heavy heart, along with the first-person speech represented here.

   Lastly, to conclude this long section, I present here the one instance
of the verbal root ק-שׁ-ה *q-š-h* 'harden',[4] which naturally—given the
lexical choice—distinguishes this passage from the preceding fifteen:

---

   4. This is the appropriate place to note that throughout this book I refer to
verbs such as ק-שׁ-ה *q-š-h* 'harden', ר-א-ה *r-ʾ-h* 'see', כ-ב-ה *k-b-h* 'extinguish',
ח-נ-ה *ḥ-n-h* 'camp', י-ר-ה *y-r-h* 'instruct', etc., in the manner presented, as if
the third root letter were *he*. As Hebraists know well, the third root letter of
these so-called weak verbs is actually *yod*, and the grammar books typically
note this. See, for example, Paul Joüon and Takamitsu Muraoka, *A Grammar
of Biblical Hebrew* (Subsidia Biblica 14; Rome: Pontifical Biblical Institute, 1996),

(2p) Exodus 7:3

וַאֲנִי אַקְשֶׁה אֶת־לֵב פַּרְעֹה

"And I will harden the heart of Pharaoh."

Given the repetitive nature of the plagues, narrated in quick succession, one after the other, an uncreative author easily could have opted for the same wording, again and again. The result of our investigation in the two sections of this chapter, however, demonstrates the very opposite tack. At every turn (save for the unchanging language used to reflect Pharaoh's stubbornness, as noted above), the author of Exodus 7–10 utilizes variant language with the aim of dazzling his audience with this virtuosity.

203, §79a. But as the standard dictionaries of Biblical Hebrew continue to list this class of verbs with *he* as the third root letter, and since most who learn the language learn them in such fashion, I have followed that practice here.

CHAPTER FOUR

REPETITION WITH VARIATION: THE BALAAM NARRATIVE (NUMBERS 22–24)

The present chapter is indebted almost entirely to research conducted by my student Clinton Moyer, whose 2009 PhD dissertation at Cornell University (my former home institution) is a model of scholarship.[1] Moyer analyzed a host of literary and linguistic features in the Balaam narrative (Numbers 22–24), including the device of repetition with variation. His examination of these chapters revealed the following pertinent examples.

1. 'these three times'

(1a) Numbers 22:28

"(on) three occasions now"   זֶה שָׁלֹשׁ רְגָלִים

(1b) Numbers 22:32

"(on) three occasions now"   זֶה שָׁלוֹשׁ רְגָלִים

(1c) Numbers 22:33

"(on) three occasions now"   זֶה שָׁלֹשׁ רְגָלִים

(1d) Numbers 24:10

"three times now"   זֶה שָׁלֹשׁ פְּעָמִים

---

1. Clinton J. Moyer, "Literary and Linguistic Studies in *Sefer Bil'am* (Numbers 22–24)" (PhD dissertation, Cornell University, 2009).

The first three phrases appear toward the beginning of the narrative, within the episode concerning Balaam's ass. In fact, we first hear the phrase in the mouth of the jenny, who, immediately upon God's opening her mouth, asks her master why he has struck her '(on) three occasions now' (1a). The phrase then occurs twice in the mouth of the angel, who first asks Balaam why he has struck his donkey '(on) three occasions now' (1b) and then notes that '(on) three occasions now' (1c) the jenny attempted to turn aside when she saw the angel. (1d) occurs at some distance from the first three phrases; here the expression is placed in the mouth of the enraged Balak, who castigates Balaam for blessing (instead of cursing) Israel 'three times now'.

This example constitutes a rather simple illustration of polyprosopon, but there may be more to these passages than meets the eye. The word רְגָלִים *rəgalim* 'occasions' is a rare usage in the Bible; in fact, outside of the occurrences in Numbers 22, it is attested again only in Exod 23:14.[2] By contrast, the word פְּעָמִים *pəʿamim* 'times' is the standard usage in Biblical Hebrew, occurring 45x in the corpus.[3] Are we to understand that the donkey is capable of speaking a more elevated Hebrew, with a richer vocabulary, than that of the ordinary individual? And then naturally the angel of God continues to use the same phrase, given his prominent status. Balak, by contrast, is capable of employing only standard language, as indicated by his use of פְּעָמִים *pəʿamim* 'times'.[4] We have no sure way to answer this question, but the distinction between the two key words suggests the possibility. We also need to note, however, that the presence of the word רֶגֶל *regɛl* 'leg, foot' in Num 22:25 (with reference to Balaam's leg, which is pressed against the wall when the donkey turns aside so as not to encounter the angel in the way) most likely serves as the catalyst for the author's invoking רְגָלִים *rəgalim* 'occasions' in the three verses that follow closely (vv. 28, 32, 33).

---

2. On this passage, see further in Chapter 12, no. 1.

3. It is for this reason that I have rendered רְגָלִים *rəgalim* as 'occasions', while reserving 'times' for פְּעָמִים *pəʿamim*. This stratagem conforms with my desire to use common English words to render common Hebrew words and to select less common English words to render less common Hebrew usages.

4. Note, incidentally, that the Samaritan Torah harmonizes, using שלש רגלים *šlš rglym* '(on) three occasions' also here in Num 24:10.

2. God appears to Balaam and speaks (well, sort of)

(2a) Numbers 22:9

וַיָּבֹ֥א אֱלֹהִ֖ים אֶל־בִּלְעָ֑ם וַיֹּ֕אמֶר

And God came to Balaam, and he said,

(2b) Numbers 22:20

וַיָּבֹ֨א אֱלֹהִ֥ים ׀ אֶל־בִּלְעָם֮ לַ֒יְלָה֒ וַיֹּ֣אמֶר ל֗וֹ

And God came to Balaam at night, and he said to him,

(2c) Numbers 23:4

וַיִּקָּ֥ר אֱלֹהִ֖ים אֶל־בִּלְעָ֑ם וַיֹּ֣אמֶר אֵלָ֔יו

And God encountered Balaam, and he said to him,

(2d) Numbers 23:16

וַיִּקָּ֤ר יְהוָה֙ אֶל־בִּלְעָ֔ם וַיָּ֥שֶׂם דָּבָ֖ר בְּפִ֑יו וַיֹּ֥אמֶר

And Yhwh encountered Balaam, and he put (the) word in his mouth; and he said,

Four times in the Balaam narrative God appears to Balaam and then speaks to him. Or at least such is the surface reading of these four verses (thus my use of 'well, sort of' in the heading of this section), for as we shall see in a moment, the author introduces a surprise element in the third instance.

(2a) is a rather basic formulation, with other examples to be found in Gen 20:3 ('And God came to Abimelech') and Gen 31:24 ('And God came to Laban').[5] (2b) expands upon (2a) by explicitly using the word לַיְלָה *layla* 'at night' (this time frame is only implicit in the the first iteration, as a glance at Num 22:8 makes clear) and by including לוֹ *lo* 'to him'.

---

5. In both instances the phrase בַּחֲלֹום הַלַּיְלָה *ba-ḥalom hal-layla* 'in a dream of the night' follows.

(2c) introduces even greater variation by (i) employing the rarer verb וַיִּקָּר *wayyiqqar* 'and he encountered'[6] instead of the standard וַיָּבֹא *wayyabo'* 'and he came'; (ii) utilizing the longer prepositional phrase אֵלָיו *'elaw* 'to him'; and (iii) most importantly, springing the surprise element, namely, that in this case, it is not God speaking to Balaam, but rather Balaam speaking to God. This last point is not indicated in the quoted material above, though the reader quickly realizes such upon reading further in the verse, "The seven altars I have arranged, and I have sacrificed bull and ram on the altar," plainly the prophet's words to the deity, and not the other way around.

Finally, (2d) injects even more variation by (i) now using the divine name יְהוָה 'Yhwh' in place of the generic term אֱלֹהִים *'elohim* 'God'; and (ii) interposing the expression וַיֵּשֶׂם דָּבָר בְּפִיו *wayyaśem dabar bə-piw* 'and he put (the) word in his mouth' (see similar wordings in Num 22:38, 23:5, 23:12). This last expression may be used here to dispel any ambiguity; that is, it serves to state overtly that once again God speaks to Balaam—and not the other way around, as witnessed in (2c).

3. The angel stands in the way

(3a) Numbers 22:22–23

22 וַיִּחַר־אַף אֱלֹהִים כִּי־הוֹלֵךְ הוּא וַיִּתְיַצֵּב מַלְאַךְ יְהוָה בַּדֶּרֶךְ לְשָׂטָן לוֹ
וְהוּא רֹכֵב עַל־אֲתֹנוֹ וּשְׁנֵי נְעָרָיו עִמּוֹ:

23 וַתֵּרֶא הָאָתוֹן אֶת־מַלְאַךְ יְהוָה נִצָּב בַּדֶּרֶךְ וְחַרְבּוֹ שְׁלוּפָה בְּיָדוֹ וַתֵּט
הָאָתוֹן מִן־הַדֶּרֶךְ וַתֵּלֶךְ בַּשָּׂדֶה וַיַּךְ בִּלְעָם אֶת־הָאָתוֹן לְהַטֹּתָהּ הַדָּרֶךְ:

22 And God was angry, for he was going, and an angel of Yhwh positioned himself in the way, as an adversary to him; and he was riding on his jenny, and his two servants with him.

23 And the jenny saw the angel of Yhwh positioned in the way, with his sword drawn in his hand, and the jenny turned-aside from the way, and he went into the field; and Balaam struck the jenny, to turn her back to the way.

---

6. For similar usage, see Ruth 2:3, though the verb ק-ר-ה *q-r-h* occurs in the Qal pattern there, as opposed to the rarer Niphʿal pattern used in Num 23:4, 23:16.

(3b) Numbers 22:24–25

24 וַיַּעֲמֹד מַלְאַךְ יְהוָה בְּמִשְׁעוֹל הַכְּרָמִים גָּדֵר מִזֶּה וְגָדֵר מִזֶּה:

25 וַתֵּרֶא הָאָתוֹן אֶת־מַלְאַךְ יְהוָה וַתִּלָּחֵץ אֶל־הַקִּיר וַתִּלְחַץ אֶת־רֶגֶל
בִּלְעָם אֶל־הַקִּיר וַיֹּסֶף לְהַכֹּתָהּ:

24 And the angel of Yhwh stood in the path (among) the vineyards—a hedge on this side, and a hedge on that side.
25 And the jenny saw the angel of Yhwh, and she was pressured to the wall, and she pressed Balaam's leg into the wall; and he continued to strike her.

(3c) Numbers 22:26–27

26 וַיּוֹסֶף מַלְאַךְ־יְהוָה עֲבוֹר וַיַּעֲמֹד בְּמָקוֹם צָר אֲשֶׁר אֵין־דֶּרֶךְ לִנְטוֹת
יָמִין וּשְׂמֹאול:

27 וַתֵּרֶא הָאָתוֹן אֶת־מַלְאַךְ יְהוָה וַתִּרְבַּץ תַּחַת בִּלְעָם וַיִּחַר־אַף בִּלְעָם
וַיַּךְ אֶת־הָאָתוֹן בַּמַּקֵּל:

26 And the angel of Yhwh continued to pass; and he stood in a narrow place, where there was no way to turn aside, right or left.
27 And the jenny saw the angel of Yhwh, and she lay-recumbent under Balaam; and Balaam was angry, and he struck the jenny with the staff.

Three times in the narrative, the angel of Yhwh is positioned in the roadway; on each occasion, the donkey sees the angel (while Balaam obviously does not) and attempts to avoid him in some way; and the prophet's response in each case is to strike the donkey. The action is not strictly parallel in each of the three occurrences: for example, on the first occasion, the donkey is able to move aside into a field, so nothing major happens; on the second occasion, she has no room to move aside, and thus has no choice but to press Balaam's leg against the wall; and on the third occasion (presumably having learned her lesson and with no other option) she simply lies down, though naturally to no avail since once again her master beats her. In such cases, therefore, one can understand the use of different wordings to describe these different actions.

And yet, given the repeated scene, certain phrases do repeat, though naturally with variation. We may point to the following specific examples.

In (3a) we read rather simply וַיִּתְיַצֵּב מַלְאַ֤ךְ יְהוָה֙ בַּדֶּ֔רֶךְ *wayyityaṣṣeb malʾak* YHWH *bad-dεrεk* 'and an angel of Yʜwʜ positioned himself in the way'; in (3b) the wording is וַיַּעֲמֹד֙ מַלְאַ֣ךְ יְהוָ֔ה בְּמִשְׁע֖וֹל הַכְּרָמִ֑ים *wayyaʿamod malʾak* YHWH *bə-mišʿol hak-kəramim* 'and the angel of Yʜwʜ stood in the path (among) the vineyards', providing more specific details of the setting; while in (3c) the author states וַיּ֥וֹסֶף מַלְאַךְ־ יְהוָ֖ה עֲב֑וֹר וַיַּֽעֲמֹד֙ בְּמָק֣וֹם צָ֔ר *wayyosεp malʾak* YHWH *ʿabor wayyaʿamod bə-maqom ṣar* 'and the angel of Yʜwʜ continued to pass; and he stood in a narrow place', setting the stage for the donkey having no choice but to crouch at this point.

The donkey's perception of the angel is also stated differently. The most detail is provided in the first iteration: וַתֵּ֣רֶא הָאָת֡וֹן אֶת־מַלְאַךְ֩ יְהוָ֨ה נִצָּ֤ב בַּדֶּ֙רֶךְ֙ *wattεreʾ ha-ʾaton ʾεt malʾak* YHWH *niṣṣab bad-dεrεk* 'and the jenny saw the angel of Yʜwʜ positioned in the way' (with the added note 'with his sword drawn in his hand'); while in the second and third restatements, the simpler phrase is used: וַתֵּ֤רֶא הָֽאָתוֹן֙ אֶת־מַלְאַ֣ךְ יְהוָ֔ה *wattεreʾ ha-ʾaton ʾεt malʾak* YHWH 'and the jenny saw the angel of Yʜwʜ' (with no specific remark about the sword, though the reader may presume that it remains drawn on these occasions as well [see further below]).

The third series of varied wordings concerns Balaam's striking of the ass. In (3a) we read in basic language וַיַּ֥ךְ בִּלְעָ֖ם אֶת־הָאָתֽוֹן *wayyak bilʿam ʾεt ha-ʾaton* 'and Balaam struck the jenny'. In (3b) we read of the repeated action וַיֹּ֖סֶף לְהַכֹּתָֽהּ *wayyosεp ləhakkotah* 'and he continued to strike her'—with the use of the personal pronoun 'her', instead of the nominal formulation 'the jenny', to express the object. In (3c), meanwhile, a new element is introduced: וַיַּ֥ךְ אֶת־הָאָת֖וֹן בַּמַּקֵּֽל *wayyak ʾεt ha-ʾaton bam-maqqel* 'and he struck the jenny with the staff'. The object is once more expressed as a noun, 'the jenny', though most significantly the instrument, 'the staff', is incorporated into the expression. Lest the reader think that Balaam was using his hand to strike the donkey on the previous occasions (though such remains possible), we now learn that most likely (and most naturally, as anyone who has witnessed the world of donkeys to this day in the Middle East) he was using his staff all along.

4. Initial perception of the angel

(4a) Numbers 22:23

וַתֵּרֶא הָאָתוֹן אֶת־מַלְאַךְ יְהוָה נִצָּב בַּדֶּרֶךְ וְחַרְבּוֹ שְׁלוּפָה בְּיָדוֹ

And the jenny saw the angel of YHWH positioned in the way, with his sword drawn in his hand.

(4b) Numbers 22:31

וַיַּרְא אֶת־מַלְאַךְ יְהוָה נִצָּב בַּדֶּרֶךְ וְחַרְבּוֹ שְׁלֻפָה בְּיָדוֹ

And he saw the angel of YHWH positioned in the way, with his sword drawn in his hand.

Above we noted that the reader of this story may assume that the sword remained drawn in the angel's hand throughout, even if such was stated explictly only in the first instance (3a/4a) and not in (3b) and (3c). This assumption is confirmed once God opens Balaam's eyes (which occurs in [4b] immediately before the quoted text above), thus allowing the prophet now to perceive the angel in the way as well.

The passages quoted here permit the reader to experience the initial discernment of the presence of the angel both by the donkey (without difficulty) and now by Balaam (at long last). I am little concerned about the use of the expressed subject 'the jenny' in (4a) versus the lack thereof in (4b). An expressed subject would not be expected in the latter, given the fact that 'Balaam' is the word immediately prior to the quoted text above; which is to say, a simple 'and he saw' is perfectly normal here. The result, accordingly, is verbatim phraseology of what was seen: 'the angel of YHWH positioned in the way, with his sword drawn in his hand'. In this case, quite strikingly, polyprosopon is not invoked, though it is not difficult to ascertain why the author departs from the standard technique of varied language. For in this instance,

the verbatim repetition serves an excellent purpose: Balaam now sees
precisely what the donkey saw from the outset!

Though clearly the author or his later scribe could not resist the
opportunity to inject variant spelling into the only place where the text
would bear such, with שְׁלוּפָה *šəlupa* 'drawn', using *plene* spelling, in
(4a), and שְׁלֻפָה *šəlupa* 'drawn', using *defectiva* spelling, in (4b).[7]

5. The ritual sacrifices preceding the oracles

(5a) Numbers 22:41–23:2

[41] וַיְהִי בַבֹּקֶר וַיִּקַּח בָּלָק אֶת־בִּלְעָם וַיַּעֲלֵהוּ בָּמוֹת בָּעַל וַיַּרְא מִשָּׁם
קְצֵה הָעָם:

[1] וַיֹּאמֶר בִּלְעָם אֶל־בָּלָק בְּנֵה־לִי בָזֶה שִׁבְעָה מִזְבְּחֹת וְהָכֵן לִי בָּזֶה
שִׁבְעָה פָרִים וְשִׁבְעָה אֵילִים:

[2] וַיַּעַשׂ בָּלָק כַּאֲשֶׁר דִּבֶּר בִּלְעָם וַיַּעַל בָּלָק וּבִלְעָם פָּר וָאַיִל בַּמִּזְבֵּחַ:

[41] And it was in the morning, and Balak took Balaam, and he
brought him up (to) Bamoth-baal; and he saw from there the
entirety of the people.
[1] And Balaam said to Balak, "Build for me in this (place)
seven altars; and prepare for me in this (place) seven bulls
and seven rams."
[2] And Balak did as Balaam had spoken; and Balak and
Balaam offered bull and ram on the altar.

(5b) Numbers 23:14

וַיִּקָּחֵהוּ שְׂדֵה צֹפִים אֶל־רֹאשׁ הַפִּסְגָּה וַיִּבֶן שִׁבְעָה מִזְבְּחֹת וַיַּעַל פָּר
וָאַיִל בַּמִּזְבֵּחַ:

And he brought him to the field of the scouts, to the summit
of the Pisgah; and he built seven altars, and he sacrificed bull
and ram on the altar.

---

7. Again the Samaritan Torah harmonizes, using the longer spelling,
שלופה šLWPH, in both instances.

(5c) Numbers 23:28–30

28 וַיִּקַּח בָּלָק אֶת־בִּלְעָם רֹאשׁ הַפְּעוֹר הַנִּשְׁקָף עַל־פְּנֵי הַיְשִׁימֹן:

29 וַיֹּאמֶר בִּלְעָם אֶל־בָּלָק בְּנֵה־לִי בָזֶה שִׁבְעָה מִזְבְּחֹת וְהָכֵן לִי בָּזֶה
שִׁבְעָה פָרִים וְשִׁבְעָה אֵילִים:

30 וַיַּעַשׂ בָּלָק כַּאֲשֶׁר אָמַר בִּלְעָם וַיַּעַל פָּר וָאַיִל בַּמִּזְבֵּחַ:

28 And Balak took Balaam (to) the summit of Peor, which
looks-out over the face of the wasteland.
29 And Balaam said to Balak, "Build for me in this (place)
seven altars; and prepare for me in this (place) seven bulls
and seven rams."
30 And Balak did as Balaam had said; and he offered bull and
ram on the altar.

Each of Balaam's first three oracles is preceded by sacrifices, which
apparently are necessary before the divine word may be received. The
repeated scenes create yet another opportunity for the author of this
composition to display his talent for variant phraseology.

The first step in each scene is for Balak to take Balaam to the indicated place. (5a) reads וַיְהִי בַבֹּקֶר וַיִּקַּח בָּלָק אֶת־בִּלְעָם *wayhi bab-boqɛr
wayyiqaḥ balaq ʾɛt bilʿam* 'and it was in the morning, and Balak took
Balaam'—the only time that the time of day is indicated. (5b) utilizes
only one word, וַיִּקָּחֵהוּ *wayyiqaḥehu* 'and he brought him', with pronouns used for both subject and object (though who's who is clear).
And then (5c) rehearses the phrase used in the first iteration, וַיִּקַּח בָּלָק
אֶת־בִּלְעָם *wayyiqaḥ balaq ʾɛt bilʿam* 'and Balak took Balaam', though
(as noted above) without the mention of morning.

The second step in each scene is Balaam's instructions to Balak to
build for him seven altars on the spot and to prepare seven bulls and
seven rams. Strikingly, (5a) and (5c) use precisely the same language,
a point that stands in stark contrast to the total omission of any such
instructions in (5b)!

The third step is for Balak to carry out Balaam's instructions—even
when they are not explicitly stated, as in (5b). Thus, in (5a) we read:
וַיַּעַשׂ בָּלָק כַּאֲשֶׁר דִּבֶּר בִּלְעָם *wayyaʿaś balaq ka-ʾašɛr dibbɛr bilʿam* 'And
Balak did as Balaam had spoken', followed by וַיַּעַל בָּלָק וּבִלְעָם פָּר וָאַיִל
בַּמִּזְבֵּחַ *wayyaʿal balaq u-bilʿam par wa-ʾayil bam-mizbeaḥ* 'and Balak

and Balaam offered bull and ram on the altar'. The wording in (5c) reveals several slight changes. In the opening phrase, וַיַּעַשׂ בָּלָק כַּאֲשֶׁר אָמַר בִּלְעָם *wayyaʿaś balaq ka-ʾašɛr ʾamar bilʿam* 'and Balak did as Balaam had said', we note the shift from the verb ד-ב-ר *d-b-r* 'speak' to the verb א-מ-ר *ʾ-m-r* 'say'; while in the second phrase, וַיַּעַל פָּר וָאַיִל בַּמִּזְבֵּחַ *wayyaʿal par wa-ʾayil bam-mizbeaḥ* 'and he offered bull and ram on the altar', the unexpressed subject informs us that Balak alone performed the sacrifices. Since the second step was elided in (5b)— that is, there were no instructions conveyed by Balaam to Balak—for the third step, in (5b), a more overt description is necessary. We read, accordingly, וַיִּבֶן שִׁבְעָה מִזְבְּחֹת *wayyiben šibʿa mizbǝḥot* 'and he built seven altars', instead of 'and Balak did as Balaam had spoken/said'; after which the text states וַיַּעַל פָּר וָאַיִל בַּמִּזְבֵּחַ *wayyaʿal par wa-ʾayil bam-mizbeaḥ* 'and he sacrificed bull and ram on the altar', exactly as occurs in (5c)—though I present these two identical passages in reverse order here.

In general, as can be seen by even a quick glance at the verses presented above, the second incident is told in minimalist style, as indicated by the one-word phrase וַיִּקָּחֵהוּ *wayyiqaḥehu* 'and he brought him' and the lack of any instructions from Balaam to Balak. The entire scene, accordingly, is narrated in a single verse.

6. God encounters Balaam

(6a) Numbers 23:3–6

3 וַיֹּאמֶר בִּלְעָם לְבָלָק הִתְיַצֵּב עַל־עֹלָתֶךָ וְאֵלְכָה אוּלַי יִקָּרֵה יְהוָה
לִקְרָאתִי וּדְבַר מַה־יַּרְאֵנִי וְהִגַּדְתִּי לָךְ וַיֵּלֶךְ שֶׁפִי׃

4 וַיִּקָּר אֱלֹהִים אֶל־בִּלְעָם וַיֹּאמֶר אֵלָיו אֶת־שִׁבְעַת הַמִּזְבְּחֹת עָרַכְתִּי
וָאַעַל פָּר וָאַיִל בַּמִּזְבֵּחַ׃

5 וַיָּשֶׂם יְהוָה דָּבָר בְּפִי בִלְעָם וַיֹּאמֶר שׁוּב אֶל־בָּלָק וְכֹה תְדַבֵּר׃

6 וַיָּשָׁב אֵלָיו וְהִנֵּה נִצָּב עַל־עֹלָתוֹ הוּא וְכָל־שָׂרֵי מוֹאָב׃

3 And Balaam said to Balak, "Position yourself over your offering, and let me go, perhaps Yʜᴡʜ will encounter me, to greet me, and some word he will show me, and I will tell you," and he went (to the) heights.

⁴ And God encountered Balaam; and he said to him, "The
seven altars I have arranged, and I offered bull and ram on
the altar."
⁵ And Y<small>HWH</small> put the word in the mouth of Balaam; and he
said, "Return unto Balak, and thus you should speak."
⁶ And he returned unto him, and behold, he was positioned
over his offering, he and all the officers of Moab.

(6b) Numbers 23:15–17

15 וַיֹּאמֶר אֶל־בָּלָק הִתְיַצֵּב כֹּה עַל־עֹלָתֶךָ וְאָנֹכִי אִקָּרֶה כֹּה:

16 וַיִּקָּר יְהוָה אֶל־בִּלְעָם וַיָּשֶׂם דָּבָר בְּפִיו וַיֹּאמֶר שׁוּב אֶל־בָּלָק וְכֹה
תְדַבֵּר:

17 וַיָּבֹא אֵלָיו וְהִנּוֹ נִצָּב עַל־עֹלָתוֹ וְשָׂרֵי מוֹאָב אִתּוֹ וַיֹּאמֶר לוֹ בָלָק מַה־
דִּבֶּר יְהוָה:

¹⁵ And he said to Balak, "Position yourself here over your of-
fering; and I, I will be encountered here."
¹⁶ And Y<small>HWH</small> encountered Balaam, and he put (the) word in
his mouth; and he said, "Return unto Balak, and thus you
shall speak."
¹⁷ And he came to him, and behold him, positioned over his
offering, and the officers of Moab with him; and Balak said to
him, "What did Y<small>HWH</small> speak?"

The two scenes in this section, (6a) and (6b), follow immediately upon
the two scenes presented above, (5a) and (5b). Remarkably, while in the
previous section we also needed to treat a third incident (5c), no parallel third incident, a theoretical (6c), follows upon (5c)—already an
indication of major variation.

Our task, then, is to compare (6a) and (6b), in order to reveal the
more subtle distinctions in phraseology. The former begins with וַיֹּאמֶר
בִּלְעָם לְבָלָק *wayyoʾmɛr bilʿam lə-balaq* 'and Balaam said to Balak'; while
the latter commences with וַיֹּאמֶר אֶל־בָּלָק *wayyoʾmɛr ʾɛl balaq* 'and he
said to Balak', omitting the expressed nominal subject and employing
a different preposition.

In (6a), Balaam's words to Balak are as follows: הִתְיַצֵּב֙ עַל־עֹלָתֶ֔ךָ וְאֵלְכָ֗ה אוּלַ֞י יִקָּרֵ֤ה יְהוָה֙ לִקְרָאתִ֔י וּדְבַ֥ר מַה־יַּרְאֵ֖נִי וְהִגַּ֥דְתִּי לָֽךְ 'position yourself over your offering, and let me go, perhaps Yнwн will encounter me, to greet me, and some word he will show me, and I will tell you'. In (6b), Balaam states more tersely, הִתְיַצֵּ֥ב כֹּ֖ה עַל־עֹלָתֶ֑ךָ וְאָנֹכִ֖י אִקָּרֶ֥ה כֹּֽה 'position yourself here over your offering; and I, I will be encountered here'. In the former, the command is expressed as הִתְיַצֵּב֙ עַל־עֹלָתֶ֔ךָ *hityaṣṣeb ʿal ʿolateka* 'position yourself over your offering', while in the latter an additional element occurs: הִתְיַצֵּ֥ב כֹּ֖ה עַל־עֹלָתֶ֑ךָ *hityaṣṣeb ko ʿal ʿolateka* 'position yourself here over your offering'. In the first case, Balaam continues, וְאֵלְכָ֗ה אוּלַ֞י יִקָּרֵ֤ה יְהוָה֙ לִקְרָאתִ֔י *wə-ʾelka ʾulay yiqqare Yнwн liqraʾti* 'and let me go, perhaps Yнwн will encounter me, to greet me', to which he adds still another phrase (see above). In the second case, Balaam continues in shorter fashion: וְאָנֹכִ֖י אִקָּרֶ֥ה כֹּֽה *wə-ʾanoki ʾiqqare ko* 'and I, I will be encountered here', with no additional phrase. Moreover, (6a) ends with the action וַיֵּ֖לֶךְ שֶֽׁפִי *wayyelek šepi* 'and he went (to the) heights', for which no parallel exists in (6b).

(6a) continues: וַיִּקָּ֥ר אֱלֹהִ֖ים אֶל־בִּלְעָ֑ם *wayyiqqar ʾelohim ʾel bilʿam* 'and God encountered Balaam'; next comes Balaam's report to God about his activities (setting up the altars, etc.); and then the action resumes with וַיָּ֧שֶׂם יְהוָ֛ה דָּבָ֖ר בְּפִ֣י בִלְעָ֑ם *wayyaśem Yнwн dabar bə-pi bilʿam* 'and Yнwн put (the) word in the mouth of Balaam'. (6b), by contrast, reads as follows: וַיִּקָּ֤ר יְהוָה֙ אֶל־בִּלְעָ֔ם וַיָּ֥שֶׂם דָּבָ֖ר בְּפִ֑יו *wayyiqqar Yнwн ʾel bilʿam wayyaśem dabar bə-piw* 'and Yнwн encountered Balaam, and he placed the word in his mouth'. Here we note the use of 'Yнwн' instead of 'God'; the omission of any report by Balaam to God concerning his activities; and the use of בְּפִ֑יו *bə-piw* 'in his mouth' replacing the earlier בְּפִ֣י בִלְעָ֑ם *bə-pi bilʿam* 'in the mouth of Balaam'.

These parallel lines then converge with the verbatim phrase וַיֹּ֛אמֶר שׁ֥וּב אֶל־בָּלָ֖ק וְכֹ֥ה תְדַבֵּֽר *wayyoʾmer šub ʾel balaq wə-ko tədabber* 'and he said, "Return unto Balak, and thus you shall speak"'.

The scenes conclude with Balaam's returning to Balak to report God's words. (6a) uses the expression וַיָּ֣שָׁב אֵלָ֔יו *wayyašob ʾelaw* 'and he returned unto him'; while (6b) prefers a different verb, וַיָּבֹ֣א אֵלָ֔יו *wayyaboʾ ʾelaw* 'and he came to him'. The *hinne*-clause in the former reads וְהִנֵּ֥ה נִצָּ֖ב עַל־עֹלָתֽוֹ *wə-hinne niṣṣab ʿal ʿolato* 'and behold, he was positioned over his offering'; while in the latter the phrase reads וְהִנּוֹ נִצָּב עַל־עֹלָתוֹ *wə-hinno niṣṣab ʿal ʿolato* 'and behold him, positioned over his offering'. In both cases, Balak is accompanied by his officers, though the wording is different: (6a) הוּא וְכָל־שָׂרֵי מוֹאָב *huʾ wə-kol śare moʾab* 'he and all the officers of Moab', versus (6b) וְשָׂרֵי מוֹאָב אִתּוֹ *wə-śare moʾab ʾitto* 'and the officers of Moab with him'. At this point (6a) concludes, and the next verse (Num 23:7) begins promptly with Balaam's first oracle. Not so (6b), however, which adds וַיֹּאמֶר לוֹ בָּלָק מַה־דִּבֶּר יְהוָה *wayyoʾmer lo balaq ma dibbɛr yhwh* 'and Balak said to him, "What did Yнwн speak?" ', before moving to the next verse (Num 23:18), which begins Balaam's second oracle.

7. God's instructions to Balaam regarding the divine word

(7a) Numbers 22:20

וְאַךְ אֶת־הַדָּבָר אֲשֶׁר־אֲדַבֵּר אֵלֶיךָ אֹתוֹ תַעֲשֶׂה:

"And only the word that I shall speak to you, it shall you do."

(7b) Numbers 22:35

וְאֶפֶס אֶת־הַדָּבָר אֲשֶׁר־אֲדַבֵּר אֵלֶיךָ אֹתוֹ תְדַבֵּר

"And just the word that I shall speak to you, it shall you
speak."

On two occasions the divine entity informs Balaam what message he is to convey to Balak and his officers: in (7a) the speaker is God, while in (7b) the speaker is the angel of Yнwн. The differences between the two statements are patent: (i) the former uses אַךְ *ʾak* 'only', while the latter uses אֶפֶס *ʾɛpɛs* 'just' (selecting a different English word to mark the distinction); and (ii) the first iteration ends with תַעֲשֶׂה *taʿaśɛ* 'you shall do', while the second iteration ends with תְדַבֵּר *tədabber* 'you shall speak'.[8]

---

8. For the passages in both this section, no. 7, and the next section, no. 8, see also Clinton J. Moyer, "Who Is the Prophet, and Who the Ass? Role-Reversing Interludes and the Unity of the Balaam Narrative (Numbers 22–24),"

8. Balaam to Balak regarding the divine word

(8a) Numbers 22:38

הַדָּבָ֗ר אֲשֶׁ֨ר יָשִׂ֧ים אֱלֹהִ֛ים בְּפִ֖י אֹת֥וֹ אֲדַבֵּֽר׃

"The word that God puts in my mouth, it I shall speak."

(8b) Numbers 23:12

הֲלֹ֗א אֵת֩ אֲשֶׁ֨ר יָשִׂ֤ים יְהוָה֙ בְּפִ֔י אֹת֥וֹ אֶשְׁמֹ֖ר לְדַבֵּֽר׃

"In fact, that which Yhwh puts in my mouth, it I shall be-careful to speak."

(8c) Numbers 23:26

הֲלֹ֗א דִּבַּ֤רְתִּי אֵלֶ֨יךָ֙ לֵאמֹ֔ר כֹּ֛ל אֲשֶׁר־יְדַבֵּ֥ר יְהוָ֖ה אֹת֥וֹ אֶעֱשֶֽׂה׃

"In fact, I have spoken to you, saying: all that Yhwh speaks, it I shall do."

On three occasions, Balaam informs Balak how the divine communication operates, namely, that which Yhwh speaks, the prophet in turn will convey to the king. (8a) represents the basic statement, which is relatively short and simple. (8b) introduces several changes: (i) most patently, יְהוָה 'Yhwh' now appears instead of אֱלֹהִים *'ɛlohim* 'God'; (ii) the word הַדָּבָר *had-dabar* 'the word' has been replaced by the grammatical particle אֵת *'et*, so that the second version is translated 'that which Yhwh puts in my mouth'; (iii) the entire statement commences with הֲלֹא *halo'*, rendered here as 'in fact', bearing the force of 'behold'; and (iv) the statement now concludes with the more complex construction אֶשְׁמֹר לְדַבֵּר *'ɛšmor lədabber* 'I shall be-careful to speak' instead of the much simpler אֲדַבֵּר *'adabber* 'I shall speak'.

(8c) incorporates still further changes. First, it begins with the clause הֲלֹא דִּבַּרְתִּי אֵלֶיךָ לֵאמֹר *halo' dibbarti 'elɛka le'mor* 'in fact, I have spoken to you, saying' (though actually Balaam never said the exact

Journal for the Study of the Old Testament 37 (2012): 167–83, esp. the chart on 171.

words that follow). Second, the main clause is now כֹּל אֲשֶׁר־יְדַבֵּר יְהוָה אֹתוֹ אֶעֱשֶׂה *kol ʾašer yǝdabber* YHWH *ʾoto ʾɛʿɛśɛ* 'all that YHWH speaks, it I shall do', which (i) inserts כֹּל *kol* 'all'; (ii) uses the expression אֲשֶׁר־יְדַבֵּר יְהוָה *ʾašer yǝdabber* YHWH 'that which YHWH speaks' (instead of a phrase using 'puts in my mouth'); and (iii) changes the verbal root at the end from ד-ב-ר *d-b-r* 'speak' to ע-שֹ-ה *ʿ-ś-h* 'do'.

9. Balaam's inability to transgress the divine word

(9a) Numbers 22:18

אִם־יִתֶּן־לִי בָלָק מְלֹא בֵיתוֹ כֶּסֶף וְזָהָב לֹא אוּכַל לַעֲבֹר אֶת־פִּי יְהוָה
אֱלֹהָי לַעֲשׂוֹת קְטַנָּה אוֹ גְדוֹלָה:

"If Balak would give me the fullness of his house, silver and gold, I would not be able to transgress the mouth of YHWH my God, to do (either) little or big."

(9b) Numbers 24:13

אִם־יִתֶּן־לִי בָלָק מְלֹא בֵיתוֹ כֶּסֶף וְזָהָב לֹא אוּכַל לַעֲבֹר אֶת־פִּי יְהוָה
לַעֲשׂוֹת טוֹבָה אוֹ רָעָה מִלִּבִּי אֲשֶׁר־יְדַבֵּר יְהוָה אֹתוֹ אֲדַבֵּר:

"If Balak would give me the fullness of his house, silver and gold, I would not be able to transgress the mouth of YHWH to do (either) good or bad in my heart; that which YHWH speaks, it I shall speak."

(9a) occurs near the beginning of the Balaam narrative and comprises the message that the prophet conveys to Balak's emissaries. (9b) appears near the end of the narrative and represents words that Balaam speaks directly to Balak, in which he repeats his earlier conversation. In typical biblical style, when direct speech is quoted at a later instance (whether by someone else or by the original speaker), the citation of the former within the latter is not verbatim, but rather reflects the same kind of variation that we have been surveying in this and the previous chapters. In fact, this specific literary technique has been treated in detail by George Savran in his monograph *Telling and Retelling*,[9] and I will devote a chapter to the subject as well (see below, Chapter 26). But since the example before us occurs among so many other examples of polyprosopon within Numbers 22–24, I have elected to include these verses in the present chapter.

The two tellings begin with the same fourteen words, until (9b) departs from (9a) by deleting אֱלֹהָי *ʾɛlohay* 'my God', apparently deeming the divine name יְהוָה 'Yнwн' to be sufficient. The second alternation occurs immediately following, with (9a) employing לַעֲשׂוֹת קְטַנָּה אוֹ גְדוֹלָה *laʿaśot qətanna ʾo gədola* 'to do (either) little or big' (that is to say, not even the slightest deviation from the divine word would be permissible), whereas (9b) uses לַעֲשׂוֹת טוֹבָה אוֹ רָעָה מִלִּבִּי *laʿaśot ṭoba ʾo raʿa mil-libbi* 'to do (either) good or bad in my heart'. The second iteration selects a different merism (with the same overall connotation) and then adds the word מִלִּבִּי *mil-libbi* 'in my heart' (lit., 'from my heart') for good measure.

Finally, Balaam adjoins an additional line, one that resonates with lines surveyed in the previous section, though the closest match is Num 23:26. We may, accordingly, contrast these two passages:

(8c) Numbers 23:26

כֹּל אֲשֶׁר־יְדַבֵּר יְהוָה אֹתוֹ אֶעֱשֶׂה

"all that Yнwн speaks, it I shall do."

(9b) Numbers 24:13

אֲשֶׁר־יְדַבֵּר יְהוָה אֹתוֹ אֲדַבֵּר

"that which Yнwн speaks, it I shall speak."

The latter passage deletes כֹּל *kol* 'all' and changes the final verbal root from ע-שׂ-ה *ʿ-ś-h* 'do' to ד-ב-ר *d-b-r* 'speak'. This latter alternation represents a reversal of the shift witnessed above regarding (8c) when compared to (8a) and (8b), though one very much in line with (7a) and (7b).

---

9. George W. Savran, *Telling and Retelling: Quotation in Biblical Narrative* (Bloomington: Indiana University Press, 1988). The present example is discussed on p. 33.

Yes, this is all very complicated and very difficult for even the most attentive reader/listener to follow. And yet such are the workings of the biblical text, fashioned by the master craftsmen literati of ancient Israel.

10. Balak's words to Balaam

(10a) Numbers 23:11

וַיֹּאמֶר בָּלָק אֶל־בִּלְעָם מֶה עָשִׂיתָ לִי לָקֹב אֹיְבַי לְקַחְתִּיךָ וְהִנֵּה בֵּרַכְתָּ בָרֵךְ׃

And Balak said to Balaam, "What you have done to me? To curse my enemies I took you, and behold, you have indeed blessed."

(10b) Numbers 24:10

וַיֹּאמֶר בָּלָק אֶל־בִּלְעָם לָקֹב אֹיְבַי קְרָאתִיךָ וְהִנֵּה בֵּרַכְתָּ בָרֵךְ זֶה שָׁלֹשׁ פְּעָמִים׃

And Balak said to Balaam, "To curse my enemies I called you, and behold, you have indeed blessed them now three times."

Twice Balak castigates Balaam for not having cursed Israel but rather having blessed them. As a comparison of (10a) and (10b) makes clear (a third passage, Num 23:25, is totally different), the king's language varies in several ways, though for our present purposes we may focus solely on the alternation between לָקֹב אֹיְבַי לְקַחְתִּיךָ *laqob ʾoybay ləqaḥtika* 'to curse my enemies I took you' in the former and לָקֹב אֹיְבַי קְרָאתִיךָ *laqob ʾoybay qəraʾtika* 'to curse my enemies I called you' in the latter, a classic instance of polyprosopon.

11. A single example from the oracles

(11a) Numbers 24:4

נְאֻם שֹׁמֵעַ אִמְרֵי־אֵל אֲשֶׁר מַחֲזֵה שַׁדַּי יֶחֱזֶה נֹפֵל וּגְלוּי עֵינָיִם׃

Oracle of one-who-hears the words of El, who views the vision of Shaddai, fallen, but with eyes uncovered.

(11b) Numbers 24:16

נְאֻם שֹׁמֵעַ אִמְרֵי־אֵל וְיֹדֵעַ דַּעַת עֶלְיוֹן מַחֲזֵה שַׁדַּי יֶחֱזֶה נֹפֵל וּגְלוּי
עֵינָיִם:

Oracle of one-who-hears the words of El, and one-who-knows the knowledge of Elyon, (who) views the vision of Shaddai, fallen, but with eyes uncovered.

This chapter, like most of the ones in this book, is devoted to literary matters emanating from our analysis of the prose portions of the Bible. It should be noted, however, that repetition with variation occurs also in the poetic portions of the Bible, with the current pair of passages a prime example thereof.[10] (11a) and (11b) commence with the same four-word phrase and end with the same pair of three-word expressions—but in between the language is varied. The former uses the relative marker אֲשֶׁר *ʼašer* 'who, that, which', which is quite rare in poetry, to introduce the second epithet 'who views the vision of Shaddai'; while the latter (i) deletes this grammatical particle and (ii) incorporates another epithet, 'and one-who-knows the knowledge of Elyon'.[11]

---

10. We will return to this topic in Chapter 15.
11. On other aspects of these two verses, see below, Chapter 24, p. 513.

CHAPTER FIVE

AN INTRODUCTION TO ALLITERATION, AND ALLITERATION IN THE BOOK OF GENESIS

The previous chapters have examined a key facet of biblical prose composition, repetition with variation. As we have seen in so many instances—in the Flood Story, in the Plagues Account, and in the Balaam Narrative (and as we shall see in future chapters in so many other places in the Bible)—the authors of the Bible opted to vary their text whenever and wherever possible. This chapter introduces the second key building block of biblical prose, namely, alliteration.[1]

The very word 'alliteration' typically conjures up notions of poetry, and as we shall see in a moment, alliteration is a feature of biblical poetry as well. Less widely recognized, however, is the manner in which alliteration functions within biblical prose—and it is this subject, after some introductory thoughts and explanations, that will dominate both this chapter and the following one.

Before proceeding further, however, we need to define the term 'alliteration' for our present purposes and explain how it functions within ancient Hebrew literature. The dictionary definition of 'alliteration' refers to the initial consonants of words. Thus, for example, the *Oxford English Dictionary*: "The commencing of two or more words in close connection, with the same letter, or rather the same sound."[2] Or the Wikipedia entry: "the repeated sound of the first consonant in a series

---

1. For an earlier version of this chapter, see Gary A. Rendsburg, "Alliteration in the Book of Genesis," in Elizabeth R. Hayes and Karolien Vermeulen, eds., *Doubling and Duplicating in the Book of Genesis: Literary and Stylistic Approaches to the Text* (Winona Lake, IN: Eisenbrauns, 2016), 79–95.

2. *OED*, s.v. 'alliteration'.

of multiple words, or the repetition of the same sounds or of the same kinds of sounds at the beginning of words or in stressed syllables of a phrase."[3] And this is precisely how alliteration operates in Old English poetry (e.g., *Beowulf, The Battle of Maldon*, etc.) and in other Old Germanic verse (e.g., the Old High German *Das Hildebrandslied*, the Old Norse [Icelandic] *Eddas*, etc.). Of the literally thousands of examples of alliterative verse that could be presented here, we need only consider several phrases from the opening lines of the Prologue to *Beowulf*:

Gardena in gear-dagum 'Spear-Danes in olden days' (line 1)

monegum mægþum 'from many tribes' (line 5)

egsode eorlas 'aweing the earls' (line 6)

weox under wolcnum 'he waxed under welkin'[4] (line 8)

In fact, alliteration is so pervasive in these early medieval poems that it is no exaggeration to state that the device is a *requirement* of the writing style. Obligatory alliteration lessened as the centuries passed, but one still finds the technique amply peppering the great works of early modern English literature, most prominently, perhaps, in the works of the greatest of the bards, William Shakespeare. One need only consider a phrase such as 'we band of brothers' (*Henry V*, Act IV, Scene 3), spoken by the title character in the famous St. Crispin's Day speech; or the expression 'the vapor of our valor' (*Henry V*, Act IV, Scene 2), used by the Constable of France, commanding the French troops at the Battle of Agincourt. In the latter phrase, 'vapor' is substituted for the more common 'breath', in order to produce the sought-after alliteration. Note how the latter word is more commonly used by Shakespeare, including, not surprisingly, for purposes of alliteration in phrases such as "The King shall drink to Hamlet's better breath" (*Hamlet*, Act V, Scene 2), spoken by Claudius, and "Ah balmy breath" (*Othello*, Act V, Scene 2), uttered by Othello to Desdemona.

And of course one can identify further instances of alliteration employed by Shakespeare, including examples of soundplay spread across an entire line. I limit myself here to two specimens, especially

---

3. http://en.wikipedia.org/wiki/Alliteration.

4. 'Welkin' is an old English word for 'clouds' (compare German *Wolken*).

since they allow the reader/hearer to perceive the use of rare words *alliterationis causa* (to use the Latin phrase, meaning 'for the sake of alliteration').[5] My first example is from the mouth of King Lear: "Here I disclaim all my paternal care, / Propinquity and property of blood" (*King Lear*, Act I, Scene 1). This line represents the only use of 'propinquity' in all of Shakespeare, so one may conclude (correctly) that the word was a relatively rare lexeme in the early seventeenth century—with the playwright's employment of this vocable between 'paternal' and 'property' providing the appropriate focus.

Our second example is from the mouth of John of Gaunt, with particular attention to the second half of the line: "Though Richard my life's counsel would not hear, / My death's sad tale may yet undeaf his ear" (*Richard II*, Act II, Scene 1). This is the first recorded instance of 'undeaf' in the English language, and it would not be too much of a leap to claim that Shakespeare invented the word for the present line. After all, the bard could have written, "My death's sad tale may yet open his ear," but he selected 'undeaf', rather than 'open', in order to create the aural effect of dental consonants across this line: **d**eath – sa**d** – **t**ale – ye**t** – un**d**eaf. Moreover, the words 'death' and 'deaf' (the main part of 'undeaf') share the same vowel and end in like-sounding consonants: the voiceless dental fricative /th/ (IPA [θ]) and the voiceless labiodental fricative /f/, respectively. The proximate nature of the two sounds is reflected by the fact that in some dialects of English (including Cockney) the voiceless /th/ sound shifts to /f/, in what linguists call th-fronting.[6] All of this, accordingly, explains the playwright's choice of 'undeaf', instead of the more banal and prosaic 'open'.[7]

Poets since Shakespeare have employed the device as well, though I limit myself here to two additional examples. First, note the couplet

---

5. One scholar in the field of biblical studies who commonly uses the term is Baruch Margalit; see his two studies: "Alliteration in Ugaritic Poetry: Its Role in Composition and Analysis," *Ugarit-Forschungen* 11 (1979), 537–57; and "Alliteration in Ugaritic Poetry: Its Role in Composition and Analysis (Part II)," *Journal of Northwest Semitic Languages* 8 (1980): 57–80.

6. For more on this phenomenon, see https://en.wikipedia.org/wiki/Th-fronting. The same shift occurs in some spoken Arabic dialects.

7. For further discussion, see David Crystal, *The Story of English in 100 Words* (New York: St. Martin's Press, 2011), 113–15.

employed by William Blake in "The Tyger," included in his illustrated collection *Songs of Innocence* (1789): "What immortal hand or eye / Could frame thy fearful symmetry?" (in the first stanza) ~ " What immortal hand or eye / Dare frame thy fearful symmetry?" (in the sixth and final stanza). In the words of Alfred Kazin: "The poem is hammered together with alliterative strokes. *Frame* is there . . . because he wants *fearful* as well."[8]

Second, note the final stanza of Robert Louis Stevenson's "Sing Me a Song of a Lad that is Gone," which employs the phrase "billow and breeze" to evoke the experience of sailing from the Scottish mainland to Skye—not "wind and squall" or "gust and wind" or any other possible combination, but rather the alliterative "billow and breeze."[9]

And not just poets, but also prose writers adept at the English language have employed alliteration to enhance their literary creations. Consider, for example, Henry David Thoreau's use, in his classic work *Walden*, of such phrases as "rippled but not ruffled," "guided and guarded," "as a dervis in the desert," and "the *shore* is *shorn.*"[10] For a sustained alliteration, we may observe the following:

---

8. Alfred Kazin, *The Portable Blake* (New York: Viking, 1968), 43.

9. We also should note here the recurring phrase "over the sea to Skye," which concludes the first, third, and fifth stanzas. Not Mull or Iona or Jura or any other of the Hebrides, but "over the sea to Skye," since this toponym creates the alliteration. Though I hasten to add that the expression is widely known in Scottish legend and writing, based on the actual sailing of Charles Edward Stuart (Bonne Prince Charlie) to Skye after his defeat at Culloden to mark the end of the Jacobite Rebellion in 1746—so that "over the sea to Skye" is the fitting phrase. I further note here that Stevenson's father was a lighthouse inspector, and that the future poet would accompany his father on these maritime journeys, so that the imagery of "billow and breeze" and "over the sea to Skye" was based on firsthand experience. This is the kind of thing we know about more modern writers, but which reminds us how little we know of the ancient authors whose compositions are no doubt similarly based on their life experiences. For at least one passage in the Bible that evokes its author's life experiences, see the beginning of Amos's words in Amos 1:2, with its shepherd imagery, made especially vivid by the statements in Amos 1:1 and 7:14–15.

10. The phrases may be found, respectively, on pp. 174, 176, 181, and 229 in the Penguin Classics edition: Henry David Thoreau, *Walden and Civil Disobedience*, with an Introduction by Michael Meyer (New York: Penguin,

I am no more lonely than the loon in the pond that laughs so loud, or than Walden Pond itself. What company has that lonely lake, I pray? And yet it has not the blue devils, but the blue angels in it. . . . God is alone,—but the devil, he is far from being alone; he sees a great deal of company; he is legion. I am no more lonely than a single mullein or dandelion in a pasture, or a bean leaf, or sorrel, or a horse-fly, or a humble-bee.[11]

The series of /l/ sounds, I submit, builds off the key words 'alone' and 'lonely' in this chapter entitled "Solitude." Furthermore, they evoke the sound of the lapping of the water at Walden Pond's edge, which the current writer himself has observed and enjoyed.

So Shakespeare, so Blake, so Stevenson, so Thoreau, so many great writers—and as we shall see below, so also the ancient Israelite literati.

To be sure, alliteration is not as prominent in biblical literature, neither in poetry nor in prose; for if it were, I would be absolved of needing to treat the subject here in the present manner, since scholars long ago would have written treatises thereupon. And yet the ancient Hebrew wordsmiths made effective use of the technique, spicing their compositions with alliteration when so desired in an effort to further enhance the reading (again, better: listening) pleasure.

Yes, the listening pleasure, for clearly the effects of alliteration are better sensed and better appreciated when hearing the string of the same or similar consonants in quick succession. One stellar example

---

1983). The italics in the fourth example are original. Incidentally, almost un-doubtedly Thoreau learned the expression "as a dervis in the desert" through the Alcotts (on their relationship see further below, Chapter 21, pp. 460–62). Note the treatment of the subject in W. A. Alcott, "On Reading, and Reading Books," in *The Common School Journal*, edited by Horace Mann, vol. 3, no. 2 (Jan. 15, 1841), 17–20, esp. 17–18. Note that William Alcott was the second cousin of Bronson Alcott, Thoreau's neighbor in Concord, Massachusetts; and that Horace Mann was the brother-in-law of Nathaniel Hawthorne, another of Thoreau's neighbor in the same town.

11. See 182 in the aforecited edition. Note that some of these words em-ployed by Thoreau are exceedingly rare; for example, 'mullein' and 'dandelion' appear only here in *Walden*, and 'sorrel' appears only one other time. As we will see below, both in this chapter and in subsequent chapters devoted to alliteration, the Hebrew authors also invoked rare words to foster soundplay.

from American history demonstrates the point nicely. Perhaps the most famous speech in the annals of American oratory is Abraham Lincoln's "Gettysburg Address," which begins, "Fourscore and seven years ago our fathers brought forth on this continent a new nation, conceived in liberty, and dedicated to the proposition that all men are created equal."[12] Here one notes the use of 'fourscore', 'fathers', and 'forth' in the opening phrase, followed by the two words 'continent' and 'conceived', which begin with the same syllable. American school-children, who typically are asked to memorize this line at some point in their primary school education, never stop to ask, "Why 'fourscore and seven years ago'? Why not the simpler 'eighty-seven years ago'?", which would not require the listener to engage in arithmetic calculations at the outset of the speech. One can similarly imagine other word choices, such as 'created' for 'brought forth'. If these substitutions were made, the passage would read, "Eighty-seven years ago our fathers created," a phrase devoid of the alliterative chord struck by Lincoln in the words that continue to resonate in the ears of Americans young and old a century and a half after they were uttered. The brilliance of Lincoln's address, I submit, lies not only in its stirring content, but in the manner of elocution that captures the audience from the start. I, for one, can picture myself standing on that cold November afternoon in 1863, absorbing the president's words, marveling at his oratorial skills.

And so it is (or was), if I may be permitted a leap further back into literary history, with the ancient Israelite consumers of (what would become) biblical literature, with its sounds and resonances echoing in the ears of the listeners.[13] But back to our definition of alliteration.

As indicated above, most consider alliteration to refer to the repetition of sounds at the *beginning* of a *series* of words. As we shall see below, though, the Hebrew writers enjoyed greater freedom and

---

12. All five manuscripts of the "Gettysburg Address" commence with this same line, with only punctuation differences between and among them. For convenient access to the documents, go to http://en.wikisource.org/wiki/Gettysburg_Address.

13. Equally so in other ancient literary corpora, including Latin, for which see the superb treatment by Frederick Ahl, *Metaformations: Soundplay and Wordplay in Ovid and Other Classical Poets* (Ithaca: Cornell University Press, 1985).

flexibility in creating the acoustic effect. First, given the root structure of Hebrew (and Semitic languages generally), the repeated sounds are not found at the beginning of words necessarily, but rather, they (a) may appear anywhere within a given word or words,[14] and (b) may be accompanied by other like-sounding consonants. Secondly, the alliteration was heard not necessarily within consecutive words, but also within words further apart, sometimes in close proximity, sometimes at a farther distance. As such, given all the possible permutations and combinations, alliteration in ancient Hebrew texts occurs with two or three identical consonants, two or three similar consonants, or any combination thereof; with the evocative sounds presented either in the same order or in scrambled fashion; with the sound effect placed in either the same verse or in adjacent verses; with the options either of highlighting just two crucial words in the text or of creating a veritable cluster of alliterative words; and so on.

The above description of alliteration in biblical Hebrew literature is best demonstrated by a typical example. Of the literally hundreds of passages that could be selected, I present the following stich from Ps 55:9:

Psalm 55:9

מֵרוּחַ סֹעָה מִסָּעַר׃

me-ruaḥ soʿa mis-saʿar

From the wind, sweeping from the storm.

The panoply of permutations and combinations noted in the previous paragraph may be illustrated by these three words. Identical sounds are naturally easy to identify. The *mem* and *reš* that occur in מֵרוּחַ *me-ruaḥ* and מִסָּעַר *mis-saʿar* represent, of course, the same sounds. The *samekh* and *ʿayin* that occur in סֹעָה *soʿa* and מִסָּעַר *mis-saʿar* are again the same sounds. Like-sounding consonants aid the alliteration in the follow-

---

14. As such, some may prefer to use the more general term 'consonance' for this device, of which 'alliteration' (with initial consonance) is a specific type thereof. But since the term 'alliteration' is so much better known, and since specifically 'initial consonance' is actually quite rare in Hebrew and thus not germane to our subject, I have elected to use 'alliteration' as the favored term here.

ing ways: The *ḥet* in רוּחַ *ruaḥ* and the *ʿayin* in the two words סֹעָה *soʿa* and סַעַר *saʿar* also alliterate, because both /ḥ/ and /ʿ/ are pharyngeal fricatives (see further below). Moreover, when we realize that סֹעָה *soʿa* 'sweeping' in Ps 55:9 is a *hapax legomenon*,[15] we understand the conscious lexical choice made by the ancient Israelite poet. Indeed, as we shall see time and again, rare words, including *hapax legomena*, were specifically chosen by the writers to create or enhance soundplay. And finally, in this particular case, we may note that the two *samekh*s within the three-word string create an onomatopoetic effect, as the reader hears the sound of the wind whistling in these words.[16] In short, I hope to have shown, through this single illustration, exactly how much thought goes into the creation of a single passage—indeed, in this case, a three-word poetic stich.[17] Multiply this example by hundreds, and one gains a greater appreciation of how the Bible is written, with conscious word choices made at every turn.[18]

The fact that writers could employ not only identical sounds but also similar sounds to produce alliteration means that, as the above example illustrates, some basic knowledge of phonology is required in order to follow the data that I will present in support of each example.[19]

---

15. That is, a word that occurs only once in the entire biblical corpus.

16. For a parallel to this effect in an Egyptian text, note Pyramid Text, Utterance 253, §275: *šw sšw sw šw sšw sw* "O Shu, lift him up! O Shu, lift him up!" with its invocation of Shu, the god of air. See Carleton T. Hodge, "Ritual and Writing: An Inquiry into the Origin of the Egyptian Script," in M. Dale Kinkade, Kenneth L. Hale, and Oswald Werner, eds., *Linguistics and Anthropology: In Honor of C. F. Voegelin* (Lisse: Peter de Ridder Press, 1975), 343 [reprinted in Scott B. Noegel and Alan S. Kaye, eds., *Afroasiatic Linguistics, Semitics, and Egyptology: Selected Writings of Carleton T. Hodge* (Bethesda, MD: CDL, 2004), 215]. The standard English translation is Raymond O. Faulkner, *The Ancient Egyptian Pyramid Texts* (Oxford: Clarendon, 1969), 63.

17. We will revisit this passage below, in Chapter 16, no. 15, within the context of alliteration in biblical poetry.

18. For some of the early pioneering work on the topic, see Ignaz Gábor, *Der hebräische Urrhythmus* (Beihefte zur Zeitschrift für die Alttestamentliche Wissenschaft 25; Giessen: Töpelmann, 1929), along with the important review essay of this book by Oliver S. Rankin, "Alliteration in Hebrew Poetry," *Journal of Theological Studies* 31 (1930): 285–91.

19. For a general introduction to the subject, see Gary A. Rendsburg, "Ancient Hebrew Phonology," in Alan S. Kaye, ed., *The Phonologies of Asia and*

Linguists classify the consonantal sounds that the mouth produces based on (a) place of articulation, and (b) manner of articulation. Thus, for example, /b/ and /p/ are both bilabial plosives (that is, sounds produced by the lips, with the airflow from the mouth temporarily stopped and then released), but the former is voiced (that is, the vocal cords vibrate), while the latter is voiceless (that is, the vocal cords do not vibrate). The consonant /m/ is another bilabial (that is, sound produced by the lips), though in this case the airflow is via the nose, so that we call this a nasal consonant. The consonant /n/, meanwhile, is a dental nasal, which means that, once more, the airflow is via the nose, but the sound is produced by positioning the tongue against the upper teeth. In Hebrew, as in almost all languages in the world, the nasal consonants /m/ and /n/ are voiced; that is, once more, the vocal cords vibrate during the production of these sounds. And so it goes with the classification of the other consonants.

The upshot of all this detailed analysis for our present purposes is this: labial consonants, be they /b/, /p/, or /m/, may alliterate with each other based on the use of the lips to produce these sounds, while the consonants /m/ and /n/ may alliterate with each other based on their shared nasal quality. But neither /b/ and /p/ will alliterate with /n/, since these sounds do not share sufficient acoustic qualities.[20]

The interested reader can explore these issues elsewhere, so for the nonce—with apologies for introducing some phonological terms here without defining them—let me simply note that in addition to the above consonant sets, the following alignments also serve alliteration. All voiced and voiceless counterparts alliterate with one another (thus, not only /b/ *bet* and /p/ *pe*, but also /z/ *zayin* and /s/ *samekh*, as well as /d/ *dalet* and /t/ *taw*). Sometimes the nasals (/m/ *mem* and /n/ *nun*) and the liquids (the rolled /r/ *reš* and the lateral /l/ *lamed*)—together these groups are known as sonorants—will alliterate with each other, including sounds across these groups (e.g., *nun*

Africa (Winona Lake, IN: Eisenbrauns, 1997), 65–83; and Gary A. Rendsburg, "Phonology: Biblical Hebrew," in Geoffrey Khan, ed., *Encyclopedia of Hebrew Language and Linguistics* (Leiden: Brill, 2013), 3:100–109.

20. True, both /b/ and /n/ are voiced consonants, but this single feature is insufficient to produce the required sound effect.

and *lamed*).[21] The three dentals, /d/ *dalet*, /t/ *taw*, and /ṭ/ *ṭet*, share the same point of articulation; and the same holds for the three velars, /g/ *gimel*, /k/ *kaf*, and /q/ *qof*. (The last member of these trios, incidentally, represents a so-called emphatic consonant, with the air originating deeper in the throat than with its standard counterpart.) There are, moreover, the various so-called guttural consonants, which include the pharyngeals, /ḥ/ *ḥet* and /ʿ/ *ʿayin*,[22] and the laryngeals, /h/ *he* and /ʾ/ *ʾaleph*. Certain consonants can be employed in a variety of ways. For example, the lateral /ś/ *śin* is most like the lateral /l/ *lamed*, but it also can be used in alliterative chains with the sibilants, /s/ *samekh*, /z/ *zayin*, /ṣ/ *ṣade*, and /š/ *šin*. (The third of these, incidentally, is once more a so-called emphatic consonant.)

The above represents a long and detailed digression into the arcane arena of phonology, and yet, as we shall see, a knowledge of how sounds are produced in the mouth is essential to an understanding and appreciation of alliteration in biblical literature. Above we presented but a single example, from Psalm 55. Let us proceed, then, to instances in the more familiar texts of the Bible, starting with the narrative portions of the Torah, with examples from Genesis presented in this chapter and examples from Exodus in the next.

---

21. In fact, these phonemes are so alike that /l/ and /n/ sometimes interchange in cognates within Semitic. See Edward Lipiński, *Semitic Languages: Outline of a Comparative Grammar* (Leuven: Peeters, 1997), 134–35.

22. To further complicate matters (see already in the Introduction, p. 8, n. 17), note that the graphemes ח *ḥet* and ע *ʿayin* each represent two separate phonemes—one pharyngeal fricative each and one velar fricative each: /ḥ/ and /ḫ/ for the former, /ʿ/ and /ġ/ for the latter. These sounds were kept distinct in ancient Hebrew, until ca. 250 B.C.E. (as determined through transcriptions of Hebrew proper names in the Septuagint), though the twenty-two-letter alphabet did not possess separate symbols to distinguish the two. (Compare, for example, the two different articulations of the *th* combination in English, the voiceless interdental fricative /θ/, as in 'thing', 'think', etc., and the voiced interdental fricative /ð/, as in 'the', 'that', 'those', etc.) In the treatments below, I typically will provide further specificity, in order to determine which of the phonemes is represented by either ח or ע (that is, /ḥ/ or /ḫ/ for the former, /ʿ/ or /ġ/ for the latter), in order to give the reader a sense of our knowledge about such matters. In general, though, for our present purposes this issue matters very little or not at all. Which is to say, regardless of whether the relevant sounds were velar fricatives or pharyngeal fricatives, the alliteration would have been perceived.

1. Genesis 2:25–3:1

‫²⁵ וַיִּהְיוּ שְׁנֵיהֶם עֲרוּמִּים הָאָדָם וְאִשְׁתּוֹ וְלֹא יִתְבֹּשָׁשׁוּ׃‬

‫¹ וְהַנָּחָשׁ הָיָה עָרוּם מִכֹּל חַיַּת הַשָּׂדֶה אֲשֶׁר עָשָׂה יְהוָה אֱלֹהִים . . .‬

²⁵ And the two of them were naked—the human and his
wife—but they were not embarrassed.
¹ And the snake was (more) cunning than all the animals of
the field that Yʜwʜ God had made . . .

We begin with one of the best-known—albeit one of the most simple
and most glaring, and thus to my mind less sophisticated (as we shall
see)—examples of alliteration. The last verse of chapter 2 of Genesis
portrays the first human couple as עֲרוּמִּים *'arummim* 'naked', while the
first verse of chapter 3 describes the snake as עָרוּם *'arum* 'cunning'.
The sound correspondences here are plain and obvious.

2. Genesis 6:14

‫עֲשֵׂה לְךָ תֵּבַת עֲצֵי־גֹפֶר קִנִּים תַּעֲשֶׂה אֶת־הַתֵּבָה וְכָפַרְתָּ אֹתָהּ מִבַּיִת‬
‫וּמִחוּץ בַּכֹּפֶר׃‬

Make for yourself an ark of gopher-wood; (from) reeds²³ you
shall make the ark; and you shall cover it inside and outside
with pitch-cover.

---

23. While my standard practice is not to emend the Masoretic Text, in this
case, given the prevailing evidence, one is led to repoint קִנִּים *qinnim* 'nests' to
קָנִים *qanim* 'reeds'. Prime evidence is forthcoming from the parallel flood narrative present in Gilgamesh Epic, Tablet XI, in which Utnapishtim constructs
his boat from wood, *reeds*, and pitch; this is also a native Middle Eastern custom down to the present day. For the former, see Cyrus H. Gordon and Gary
A. Rendsburg, *The Bible and the Ancient Near East* (New York: Norton, 1997), 48
and n. 34. For the latter, see Edward Ullendorff, "The Construction of Noah's
Ark," *Vetus Testamentum* 4 (1954): 95–96 [reprinted in Edward Ullendorff, *Is
Biblical Hebrew a Language?* (Wiesbaden: Harrassowitz, 1977), 48–49]. For the
most thorough treatment, see John Day, *From Creation to Babel: Studies in
Genesis 1–11* (Library of Hebrew Bible / Old Testament Studies 592; London:
Bloomsbury Academic, 2013), 113–22 [= Chapter 7, entitled "Rooms or Reeds
in Noah's Ark (Genesis 6.14)?"].

This verse returns us to the Flood Narrative, which we studied earlier in conjunction with the device of repetition with variation. Two unique usages are present in this verse. The first is the noun גֹּפֶר *gopɛr*, which occurs only here in the Bible: the word refers to a type of wood, typically translated as 'gopher-wood' since scholars are unsure of which specific tree is involved, though almost undoubtedly it is to be identified as cypress. This identification is based on (a) the similarity between the Hebrew form גֹּפֶר *gopɛr* and the Greek word κυπάρισσος *kyparissos*, whence Latin *cupressus* and eventually English *cypress*; and (b) the fact that cypress wood was used in ancient shipbuilding,[24] since long planks could be made from the tall tree and its wood is relatively impervious to rot from moisture. But Hebrew has a word for 'cypress', namely, בְּרוֹשׁ *bəroš*, which appears 20x elsewhere in the Bible—which raises the question: Why did the author of Genesis 6 use an atypical word and not the usual word in v. 14?

The answer is forthcoming from a look at the second unique locution in the verse, וְכָפַרְתָּ . . . בַּכֹּפֶר *wəkaparta . . . bak-kopɛr* 'and you shall cover . . . with pitch-cover'. The verbal root כ-פ-ר *k-p-r* is common in the Bible in other patterns, especially in the Piʿel, with the connotation 'atone'.[25] But only here in the Bible does the verb occur in the Qal, with the meaning 'cover'. The noun כֹּפֶר *kopɛr* 'pitch' (rendered above as 'pitch-cover' to show the connection between the verb and the noun) constitutes a *hapax legomenon*—though notably it is cognate with the Akkadian word *kupru* 'pitch', which occurs in the Babylonian flood story preserved in Gilgamesh Epic, Tablet XI, line 55. This unique Hebrew lexeme is used in our verse instead of other potential options, such as חֵמָר *ḥemar* 'loam' and זֶפֶת *zɛpɛt* 'bitumen' (see Exod 2:3, Isa 34:9).[26]

Clearly, the author of our text reached deep into the Hebrew lexicon to purposefully select these words, one with the consonants ג-פ-ר *g-p-r* and two with the consonants כ-פ-ר *k-p-r*, to alliterate with each

---

24. See Lionel Casson, *Ships and Seamanship in the Ancient World* (Princeton: Princeton University Press, 1971), 196, 212–13.

25. See, for example, יוֹם הַכִּפֻּרִים *yom hak-kippurim* (Lev 23:27) > the more familiar Yom Kippur 'Day of Atonement'.

26. The different English glosses 'pitch', 'loam', and 'bitumen' are used simply to distinguish the different words, without necessarily aligning one specific Hebrew noun with one specific English gloss.

other. To return to the subject of phonology, note that the only distinction between the two is the voiced velar stop /g/ in the former and the
voiceless velar stop /k/ in the latter.

3. Genesis 21:4, 7–8

וַיָּ֤מָל אַבְרָהָם֙ אֶת־יִצְחָ֣ק בְּנ֔וֹ בֶּן־שְׁמֹנַ֖ת יָמִ֑ים כַּאֲשֶׁ֛ר צִוָּ֥ה אֹת֖וֹ ⁴
אֱלֹהִֽים׃

וַתֹּ֗אמֶר מִ֤י מִלֵּל֙ לְאַבְרָהָ֔ם הֵינִ֥יקָה בָנִ֖ים שָׂרָ֑ה כִּֽי־יָלַ֥דְתִּי בֵ֖ן לִזְקֻנָֽיו׃ ⁷
וַיִּגְדַּ֥ל הַיֶּ֖לֶד וַיִּגָּמַ֑ל וַיַּ֤עַשׂ אַבְרָהָם֙ מִשְׁתֶּ֣ה גָד֔וֹל בְּי֖וֹם הִגָּמֵ֥ל אֶת־יִצְחָֽק׃ ⁸

⁴ And Abraham circumcised Isaac his son at eight days old,
as God had commanded him.

----

⁷ And she said, "Who would declare to Abraham (that) Sarah
would nurse sons, that I would bear a son in his old-age."
⁸ And the child grew, and he was weaned; and Abraham
made a big party on the day of the weaning of Isaac.

The attentive reader of or listener to this text will realize that the
verb מִלֵּל *millel* 'declare' in v. 7 is a rare verb, one totally unexpected
in the mouth of Sarah within the larger narrative. Apart from Gen
21:7, the verb is limited to poetry in the Bible, with the only other attestations being found in Ps 106:2[27] and Job 8:2, 33:3[28]—and here one
should note that poetry, not only in ancient Hebrew,[29] but in many

---

27. The knowledgeable reader may know the passage מִ֤י יְמַלֵּל֙ גְּבוּר֣וֹת יְהוָ֔ה
mi yəmallel gəburot YHWH 'who can utter the heroic-acts of YHWH', since it has
become a byword in Jewish tradition (connected especially with a Hanukkah
song); but in biblical times, as demonstrated, the verb was nevertheless rarely
used in everyday discourse.

28. The root מ-ל-ל *m-l-l* also produces two other (unrelated) verbs in
ancient Hebrew, one with the meaning 'rub, scrape' (Prov 6:13) and one with
the meaning 'languish, wither, fade' (Psalms 2x, Job 4x). Note that these verbs
are also limited to the domain of poetry.

29. The standard work remains G. R. Driver, "Hebrew Poetic Diction,"
in *Congress Volume: Copenhagen 1953* (Supplements to Vetus Testamentum 1;
Leiden: Brill, 1953), 26–39.

world literatures (such as ancient Greek and ancient Latin), possesses a richer vocabulary (both words and phrases), employed by the poets to express their passions and emotions.[30] Given the scant distribution of the verb מִלֵּל *millel* 'declare' in the Bible,[31] we are led to ask: why, then, did the writer of Genesis 21 place the word in Sarah's mouth in v. 7? Why did he not, for example, use one of any number of verbs for speech that are much more common in the Bible, especially in prose texts, such as אָמַר *'amar* 'say', דִּבֶּר *dibber* 'speak', הִגִּיד *higgid* 'tell', etc.? The answer lies in the author's desire to produce alliteration. I refer here not only to the string of /m/ and /l/ sounds produced in the expression -מִי מִלֵּל לְ *mi millel lə-* 'who would declare to' (which is, after all, a rather simplistic example of alliteration, given the ordinariness of both the interrogative pronoun מִי *mi* 'who' and the preposition -לְ *lə-* 'to'), but more importantly to the presence of two other verbs in this pericope with the same two sounds, to wit, וַיָּמָל *wayyamol* 'and he circumcised' in v. 4 and וַיִּגָּמַל *wayyiggamal* 'and he was weaned' / הִגָּמֵל *higgamel* 'weaning' in v. 8.

While this book is focused on the use of Hebrew in ancient times, the key word מִלֵּל *millel* 'declare' offers an opportunity to enter the world of medieval Jewish exegesis. Rashi (1040–1105 C.E.), the most popular of all medieval Jewish commentators, has an interesting comment on מִלֵּל *millel*. He notes, quite cleverly, that the *gematria* of *mem-lamed-lamed* equals 100,[32] the age of Abraham at the birth of Isaac (see Gen 21:5). Obviously, this is *not* the reason why the author of Genesis 21 selected this verb in our story (especially since the *gematria* device is a postbiblical development). But as so often happens when reading

---

30. Such was the case in English too, until the Romantics (led by William Wordsworth) and even more so the Modernists challenged the notion of a special poetic diction, so that the lexis of prose and poetry has merged to a great extent.

31. Even the noun מִלָּה *milla* 'word', which is derived from this verb (and which continues in use to the present day in Modern Hebrew), while more common in the Bible, is also limited to poetry: 2 Sam 23:2, Pss 19:5, 139:4, Prov 23:9, and 34x in the book of Job. Indeed, this distribution suggests that the noun was an Israelian Hebrew trait (for more on this subject, see Chapter 23). Note that both the verb and the noun belong more properly to the Aramaic lexicon.

32. The letter *mem* = 40, and the letter *lamed* = 30 (x2 = 60, in this particular case), thus yielding 100.

the medieval exegetes, the benefit gained is not the answer that a particular commentator provides, but rather the question that under-lies his remark. In this case, Rashi's sensitivity to the text was such that he understood that מִלֵּל *millel* represented a most unusual usage, necessitating comment. Had the author of Genesis 21 used any of the aforementioned options, each a much more common verb in Biblical Hebrew prose, one can be certain that Rashi would not have taken the time to comment.

4. Genesis 21:14–16

¹⁴ וַיַּשְׁכֵּ֨ם אַבְרָהָ֜ם ׀ בַּבֹּ֗קֶר וַיִּֽקַּֽח־לֶ֜חֶם וְחֵ֣מַת מַ֩יִם֩ וַיִּתֵּ֨ן אֶל־הָגָ֜ר שָׂ֣ם
עַל־שִׁכְמָ֤הּ וְאֶת־הַיֶּ֙לֶד֙ וַֽיְשַׁלְּחֶ֔הָ וַתֵּ֣לֶךְ וַתֵּ֔תַע בְּמִדְבַּ֖ר בְּאֵ֥ר שָֽׁבַע׃

¹⁵ וַיִּכְל֥וּ הַמַּ֖יִם מִן־הַחֵ֑מֶת וַתַּשְׁלֵ֣ךְ אֶת־הַיֶּ֔לֶד תַּ֖חַת אַחַ֥ד הַשִּׂיחִֽם׃

¹⁶ וַתֵּלֶךְ֩ וַתֵּ֨שֶׁב לָ֜הּ מִנֶּ֗גֶד הַרְחֵק֙ כִּמְטַחֲוֵ֣י קֶ֔שֶׁת כִּ֣י אָֽמְרָ֔ה אַל־אֶרְאֶ֖ה
בְּמ֣וֹת הַיָּ֑לֶד וַתֵּ֧שֶׁב מִנֶּ֛גֶד וַתִּשָּׂ֥א אֶת־קֹלָ֖הּ וַתֵּֽבְךְּ׃

¹⁴ And Abraham arose-early in the morning, and he took bread and a bottle-skin of water, and he gave (them) to Hagar, put (them) on her shoulder—and the child—and he sent her forth; and she went, and she wandered in the wil-derness of Beersheba.
¹⁵ And the water from the bottle-skin was finished; and she cast the child under one of the bushes.
¹⁶ And she went and she sat herself opposite (him), at a dis-tance of a bowshot, for she said, "Let me not see the death of the child"; and she sat opposite, and she lifted her voice, and she cried.

This passage includes two unique usages: (a) the pure *hapax legomenon* מְטַחֲוֵי *maṭaḥawe*, within the expression כִּמְטַחֲוֵי קֶשֶׁת *ki-mṭaḥawe qešet*, lit., 'like the shooters of a bow' > 'bowshot'; and (b) the quasi-*hapax* חֵמֶת *ḥemɛt* (construct form חֵמַת *ḥemat*) 'bottle-skin'. The former is a pure *hapax* because the noun and indeed the root (presumably ט-ח-ו *ṭ-ḥ-w* 'shoot') occurs only here in the Bible. The latter is classified as a quasi-*hapax* because the noun appears twice in our passage, and then again a few lines further down in v. 19—though nowhere else in the Bible.

Most important for our present concern is the manner in which the two forms incorporate the same sounds (or very similar ones in the case of /t/ and /ṭ/). The words were intentionally chosen *alliterationis causa*.

Moreover, additional words aid in the aural effect: (a) תַּחַת *taḥat* 'under' and אַחַד *'aḥad* 'one' both have /ḥ/ + /dental/; and (b) לֶחֶם *leḥem* 'bread' and שִׂיחִם *śiḥim* 'bushes' both have /ḥ/ + /m/. The first three of these words are common, but the fourth is another rare word: שִׂיחַ *śiaḥ* 'bush' occurs elsewhere in the Bible only in Gen 2:5 and Job 30:4, 30:7.

This might be the best place to introduce the effect of including a *hapax legomenon* in the text from the perspective of the reader—by which I intend both the one orally intoning the text and the audience listening thereto. No doubt these rare words, such as מִטַּחֲוֵי *məṭaḥawe* 'bowshot', slow down the entire process. One could imagine the oral presenter slowing his voice at this point, in order to allow the listeners to focus on the word for a moment. One might even question whether everyone in attendance would know these rare words. The philosopher Giorgio Agamben has called our attention to a passage in Augustine's *De Trinitate* in which the church father mentions his own experience upon encountering a *vocabulum emortuum* 'dead word', specifically, the noun *temetum*, instead of the typical word *vinum* 'wine'.[33] The experience with this rare or even unknown word places the reader "in the no-man's-land between sound and significance." And while we cannot be absolutely certain that the same would have occurred when an ancient Israelite listener heard the word מִטַּחֲוֵי *məṭaḥawe* 'bowshot', or any of the other *hapax legomena* treated herein, I for one like to imagine the Augustinian struggle in such cases a millennium earlier in a Hebrew literary context. Embedded in such usages is the author's message to his readership: slow down, hear the word, process its sounds, and understand why it is used specifically here.

---

33. Giorgio Agamben, "Pascoli and the Thought of the Voice" (originally published in Italian in 1982), in *The End of the Poem*, trans. Daniel Heller-Roazen (Stanford: Stanford University Press, 1999), 63–64. I am indebted to Rebecca Sacks for a very helpful discussion on the matter and for bringing this reference to my attention.

5. Genesis 24:18–22

¹⁸ וַתֹּאמֶר שְׁתֵה אֲדֹנִי וַתְּמַהֵר וַתֹּרֶד כַּדָּהּ עַל־יָדָהּ וַתַּשְׁקֵהוּ:

¹⁹ וַתְּכַל לְהַשְׁקֹתוֹ וַתֹּאמֶר גַּם לִגְמַלֶּיךָ אֶשְׁאָב עַד אִם־כִּלּוּ לִשְׁתֹּת:

²⁰ וַתְּמַהֵר וַתְּעַר כַּדָּהּ אֶל־הַשֹּׁקֶת וַתָּרָץ עוֹד אֶל־הַבְּאֵר לִשְׁאֹב וַתִּשְׁאַב
לְכָל־גְּמַלָּיו:

²¹ וְהָאִישׁ מִשְׁתָּאֵה לָהּ מַחֲרִישׁ לָדַעַת הַהִצְלִיחַ יְהוָה דַּרְכּוֹ אִם־לֹא:

²² וַיְהִי כַּאֲשֶׁר כִּלּוּ הַגְּמַלִּים לִשְׁתּוֹת וַיִּקַּח הָאִישׁ נֶזֶם זָהָב בֶּקַע מִשְׁקָלוֹ
וּשְׁנֵי צְמִידִים עַל־יָדֶיהָ עֲשָׂרָה זָהָב מִשְׁקָלָם:

¹⁸ And she said, "Drink, my lord"; and she hurried, and she lowered her jug from her hand, and she gave-drink to him. ¹⁹ And she finished to give-drink to him; and she said, "Also for your camels I will draw, until they have finished to drink." ²⁰ And she hurried, and she emptied her jug into the trough, and she ran again to the well to draw; and she drew for all his camels. ²¹ And the man is gazing at her, being-silent, to know whether or not Yʜwʜ had made his way successful. ²² And it was, after the camels had finished to drink, and the man took a golden nose-ring, a *bεqaʿ* its weight; and two bracelets on her hand, ten (shekels) of gold their weight.

This passage provides a paradigmatic example of the employment of a *hapax legomenon* in order to produce alliteration. The unique word is מִשְׁתָּאֵה *mišta'e* 'is gazing' in v. 21, a Hitpaʿel masc. sg. participle from the root שׁ-א-ה *š-ʾ-h* 'gaze, watch'. Two common roots appear in the surrounding verses in forms that alliterate with מִשְׁתָּאֵה: (a) שׁ-ת-ה *š-t-h* 'drink', occurring in vv. 18, 19, and 22 (plus four other times in the chapter); and (b) שׁ-א-ב *š-ʾ-b* 'draw (water)', occurring in vv. 19 and 20 (plus five other times in the chapter). Note especially the form וַתִּשְׁאַב *wattišʾab* 'she drew' in v. 20, which alliterates most closely with מִשְׁתָּאֵה *mišta'e* 'is gazing' in v. 21, with only three words intervening. These two words have the most pronounced aural effect, due to the presence of the third-person fem. sg. preformative *t-* in the former and the characteristic infixed *-t-* of the Hitpaʿel form in the latter, with the alliteration completed by the corresponding labial consonants /b/ and /m/ in these two words.[34]

6. Genesis 25:23–24

23 וַיֹּ֨אמֶר יְהֹוָ֜ה לָ֗הּ שְׁנֵ֤י [גֹיִים] גוֹיִם֙* בְּבִטְנֵ֔ךְ וּשְׁנֵ֣י לְאֻמִּ֔ים מִמֵּעַ֖יִךְ
יִפָּרֵ֑דוּ וּלְאֹם֙ מִלְאֹ֣ם יֶֽאֱמָ֔ץ וְרַ֖ב יַעֲבֹ֥ד צָעִֽיר:
24 וַיִּמְלְא֥וּ יָמֶ֖יהָ לָלֶ֑דֶת וְהִנֵּ֥ה תוֹמִ֖ם בְּבִטְנָֽהּ:

23 And YHWH said to her, "Two nations are in your womb, and two peoples from your innards shall divide; and (one) people will be stronger than the (other) people, and the greater shall serve the younger."
24 And her days of bearing were fulfilled; and behold, twins in her womb.[35]

The experienced reader of Biblical Hebrew immediately will recognize that לְאֹם *lə'om* 'people', used here 3x, is an unusual lexeme to encounter in a narrative prose text. Indeed, the word occurs 31x in the Bible, 27 of which are in poetry (Isaiah 11x, Jeremiah 1x, Habakkuk 1x, Psalms 10x, Proverbs 4x). Of the remaining four instances, three occur in Gen 25:23, with the one remaining attestation in Gen 27:29, which clearly evokes the verse interpreted here. The expected word in Hebrew prose is the exceedingly common עַם *'am* 'people'.

This survey of the noun לְאֹם *lə'om* 'people' leads one to inquire: why, then, does the author of Genesis 25 utilize the word 3x in v. 23? Now, it is true that the divine word (as we have here, an oracle from Yahweh to Rebekah)—even when embedded into narrative prose—often includes elevated (indeed, poetic) language. So that fact partially answers our question, but I believe that there is more at work here. A more complete answer is forthcoming from a look at the first word in v. 24: וַיִּמְלְאוּ *wayyimlə'u* 'and were fulfilled', in the expression 'and her

---

34. For another reason for the conscious employment of מִשְׁתָּאֵה *mišta'e* 'is gazing' in Gen 24:21, see below, Chapter 24, pp. 503–5, in particular p. 505, item (6). For still more relevant information to this scene, see below, Chapter 26, p. 533, n. 8.

35. On this expression and its variant mate in Gen 38:27, see Chapter 9, no. 3.

days of bearing were fulfilled'. The root of this common verb, מ-ל-א *m-l-ʾ* 'fill', constitutes an anagram of the noun לְאֹם *lə'om* 'people', with the alliteration heard clearly.

7. Genesis 48:19

וַיְמָאֵן אָבִיו וַיֹּאמֶר יָדַעְתִּי בְנִי יָדַעְתִּי גַּם־הוּא יִהְיֶה־לְּעָם וְגַם־הוּא יִגְדָּל וְאוּלָם אָחִיו הַקָּטֹן יִגְדַּל מִמֶּנּוּ וְזַרְעוֹ יִהְיֶה מְלֹא־הַגּוֹיִם:

And his father declined, and he said, "I know, my son, I know—he also will become a people, and he also will grow; however, his younger brother shall grow greater than he, and his seed will be the fullness of nations."

My general approach in this monograph is to proceed via the order of the passages within a particular biblical book or series of books. In the present instance, however, I have elected to treat Gen 48:19 out of order, because it involves once more the root מ-ל-א *m-l-ʾ* 'fill'. Jacob's words to Joseph concerning Ephraim, the younger who will supersede his older brother Manasseh, are on par with similar expressions found in similar situations in the book of Genesis (see especially Gen 17:18–21 regarding Isaac and Ishmael, and Gen 25:23–24 regarding Jacob and Esau [treated above]). Yet the verse concludes with a most enigmatic locution: מְלֹא־הַגּוֹיִם *məlo' hag-goyim* 'the fullness of nations'. This two-word phrase is encountered only here in the Bible,[36] and while the sense is clear (especially in light of the parallel texts just cited), the expression is puzzling nonetheless.

By now the reader should have discerned my approach, which I would summarize as follows: "Hark! An unusual word (or phrase)! Look for alliteration nearby!" Once more, our search yields the successful result, for in this verse we are able to identify the relatively rare term וְאוּלָם *wə-'ulam* 'however', which appears only 4x in the Torah (and in one of these places, Num 14:21, one notes alliteration with the root מ-ל-א *m-l-ʾ* 'fill' as well; see below, Chapter 10, no. 2).

---

36. The closest parallel is Isa 31:4 מְלֹא רֹעִים *məlo' ro'im*, lit., 'fullness of shepherds', meaning (most likely) 'a large band of shepherds' (or something on that order).

Our verse also includes another alliterative word, namely, וַיְמָאֵן *wayma'en* 'and he declined'. This is a standard verb in Biblical Hebrew, so there is nothing unusual about its presence at the head of the verse—and yet it too serves to enhance the auditory effect. Of the consonants that do not match perfectly between and among the three terms, note that the *nun* of the root מ-א-ן *m-ʾ-n* 'refuse, decline' and the *lamed* of the other two words studied herein fall under the general category of sonorants (comprised of liquids and nasals).

There is another reason for the use of מְלֹא־הַגּוֹיִם *məlo' hag-goyim* 'the fullness of nations' in Gen 48:19. As intimated above, there is a relationship between the scene in which this verse occurs and the earlier scene in which Rebekah receives the divine word. As we saw in our treatment of Gen 25:23–24, the noun גוֹיִם *goyim* 'nations' and the verbal root מ-ל-א *m-l-'* 'fill' appear there, with the latter alliterating with the noun לְאֹם *lə'om* 'people'. I would suggest that the author of Gen 48:19 intentionally alludes to the earlier scene by utilizing similar language. In fact, מְלֹא *məlo'* and לְאֹם *lə'om* evoke one another through assonance—a literary device that utilizes vowel patterns, in much the same way that alliteration operates with consonants. The technical name for this literary device is allusion or intertextuality, a topic surveyed by Benjamin Sommer and other scholars in recent years.[37]

In short, there are several motivations that led to the presence of the unusual expression מְלֹא־הַגּוֹיִם *məlo' hag-goyim* 'the fullness of nations' in Gen 48:19.[38] Not only does the first part of the phrase alliterate with other words in the verse, the entire phrase brings the listener back to the parallel scene in Gen 25:23–24.

37. The most significant monograph is Benjamin D. Sommer, *A Prophet Reads Scripture: Allusion in Isaiah 40–66* (Contraversions: Jews and Other Differences; Stanford: Stanford University Press, 1998). For a survey of research, see Geoffrey D. Miller, "Intertextuality in Old Testament Research," *Currents in Biblical Research* 9 (2010): 283–309.

38. Incidentally, as another key to the unusual nature of this two-word phrase, note that Targum Onqelos departs from its usual word-for-word rendering with either שלטין בעממיא 'rulers over peoples' (thus Ms. British Library Or. 2363) or מלכין דשליטין בעממיא 'kings who rule over peoples' (as well as similar wordings in early printed editions). See Alexander Sperber, *The Bible in Aramaic* (Leiden: Brill, 2004; reprint of the original 1959–1968 four-volume set), 84.

8. Genesis 27:12

אוּלַי יְמֻשֵּׁנִי אָבִי וְהָיִיתִי בְעֵינָיו כִּמְתַעְתֵּעַ וְהֵבֵאתִי עָלַי קְלָלָה וְלֹא
בְרָכָה:

"Perhaps my father will feel me, and I will be in his eyes as a
mocker; and I will bring upon myself a curse, and not a blessing."

Cf. the use of מַטְעַמִּים 'dainties, delicacies' 6x in the same
account (vv. 4, 7, 9, 14, 17, 31).

Two rare words are collocated in these verses. The noun מְתַעְתֵּעַ
mətaʿteaʿ 'mocker' (actually the masc. sg. participle of the verb ת-ע-ע
t-ʿ-ʿ 'mock' in the Pilpel pattern) occurs only here and in 2 Chr 36:16,
while the related noun תַּעְתֻּעִים *taʿtuʿim* 'mockery' appears only in Jer
10:15 and 51:18. The noun מַטְעַמִּים *maṭʿammim* 'dainties, delicacies'
occurs 6x in Genesis 27, as indicated in the parentheses above, and
again only in Prov 23:3 and 23:6 (albeit in slightly different form, with
the וֹת- nominal pl. ending). In light of the approach taken thus far, I
would submit that the author of Genesis 27 selected these two words
intentionally, in order to enhance the oral-aural process through their
similar sounds: /m/, /ʿ/, and voiceless dental (either /t/ or /ṭ/).

　While we have not attempted to capture the alliterations in the
verses surveyed thus far in our English renderings, in this case we take
the opportunity to do so. Instead of the more standard 'mocker', one
could imagine an English translation using either 'derider' or 'disdainer'
for מְתַעְתֵּעַ *mətaʿteaʿ*, paired with either 'dainties' or 'delicacies' for
מַטְעַמִּים *maṭʿammim*.[39]

9. Genesis 32:30, 33

[30] . . . וַיִּשְׁאַל יַעֲקֹב וַיֹּאמֶר הַגִּידָה־נָּא שְׁמֶךָ

[33] עַל־כֵּן לֹא־יֹאכְלוּ בְנֵי־יִשְׂרָאֵל אֶת־גִּיד הַנָּשֶׁה אֲשֶׁר עַל־כַּף הַיָּרֵךְ עַד
הַיּוֹם הַזֶּה כִּי נָגַע בְּכַף־יֶרֶךְ יַעֲקֹב בְּגִיד הַנָּשֶׁה:

39. On attempts to capture alliteration within translation, see Jonathan Roper, "Alliteration Lost, Kept and Gained: Translation as Indicator of
Language-Specific Prosaics," in Anneli Baran, Liisi Laineste, and Piret Voolaid,
eds., *Scala Naturae: Festschrift in Honour of Arvo Krikmann for His 75th Birthday*
(Tartu: ELM Scholarly Press, 2014), 419–34.

[30] And Jacob asked, and he said, "Tell, please, your name," . . .
[33] Therefore the children of Israel do not eat the *membrum virile* which is on the palm of the thigh unto this day; for he struck Jacob in the palm of the thigh, at the *membrum virile.*

The scene is the enigmatic encounter between Jacob and 'the man' (v. 25) at the Jabbok River. Jacob asks this figure, הַגִּידָה־נָּא שְׁמֶךָ *haggida na' šəmɛka* 'tell, please, your name'. Jacob's interlocutor responds that he is unable to reveal his name, thereby disclosing to both Jacob and the reader that he is not simply a 'man', but rather an angelic figure or divine being of some sort. This was, however, implied already in the previous verse (v. 29), where this figure informs Jacob that his name is herewith changed to 'Israel', because 'you have striven with divine-beings (Hebrew *'ɛlohim*, lit., 'gods') and with men'.

That point aside, the reader is treated to a remarkable alliteration in the last verse of the account.[40] Twice we hear the words גִּיד הַנָּשֶׁה *gid han-našɛ*, a unique phrase whose precise meaning has been debated for centuries. Of the various suggestions, the one which rises to the top, in my opinion, is the proposal of Stanley Gevirtz to understand the term as 'the male sinew', that is, the *membrum virile*, or penis.[41] Actually, this too is only a side point for our present concern, because regardless of the meaning of the term, the soundplay echoes loudly and clearly.

The syllable *gid* is the most manifest linkage between the two phrases *haggida na' šəmɛka* 'tell, please, your name' and גִּיד הַנָּשֶׁה *gid han-našɛ* 'the male sinew / *membrum virile*'; though one also hears the consonants /n/ and /š/ in both phrases. Regarding the sound /š/, which immediately follows הַגִּידָה־נָּא *haggida na'* 'tell, please', the following point should be noted. In the seven other cases of הַגִּידָה־נָּא *haggida na'* 'tell, please' in the Bible, the expression is followed by the self-reflective prepositional phrase לִי *li* 'to me' or לָנוּ *lanu* 'to us' (Gen 37:16, Judg 16:6, 16:10, 1 Sam 9:18, 10:15, Jer 38:25, Jonah 1:8). That particle is missing, however, in Gen 32:30, for had it been present the

---

40. I owe this example to David Stein (Culver City, CA), with gratitude.

41. Stanley Gevirtz, "Of Patriarchs and Puns: Joseph at the Fountain, Jacob at the Ford," *Hebrew Union College Annual* 46 (1975): 52–53. To be sure, later Jewish tradition understood the term as 'sciatic nerve', but that is a much later tradition, with no inherent underpinning in the text of Genesis itself.

/l/ sound would have interrupted the string of consonants necessary
to anticipate the twice-heard unique phrase גִּיד הַנָּשֶׁה *gid han-naše* 'the
male sinew / *membrum virile*'.[42]

Gevirtz goes even further, with another brilliant observation. Also
heard within the phrase גִּיד הַנָּשֶׁה *gid han-naše* 'the male sinew / *membrum
virile*' are the two tribal names גָּד *gad* 'Gad' and מְנַשֶּׁה *mənašše* 'Manasseh',
a point that comes into clearer focus when one realizes that the Jabbok
River serves as the boundary between the two tribal territories![43]

10. Genesis 38:21–23

²¹ וַיִּשְׁאַל אֶת־אַנְשֵׁי מְקֹמָהּ לֵאמֹר אַיֵּה הַקְּדֵשָׁה הִוא בָעֵינַיִם עַל־
הַדָּרֶךְ וַיֹּאמְרוּ לֹא־הָיְתָה בָזֶה קְדֵשָׁה:

²² וַיָּשָׁב אֶל־יְהוּדָה וַיֹּאמֶר לֹא מְצָאתִיהָ וְגַם אַנְשֵׁי הַמָּקוֹם אָמְרוּ לֹא־
הָיְתָה בָזֶה קְדֵשָׁה:

²³ וַיֹּאמֶר יְהוּדָה תִּקַּח־לָהּ פֶּן נִהְיֶה לָבוּז הִנֵּה שָׁלַחְתִּי הַגְּדִי הַזֶּה וְאַתָּה
לֹא מְצָאתָהּ:

²¹ And he asked the men of her place, saying, "Where is the
qedesha who (was) in Enayim on the roadway?" And they
said, "There has not been a *qedesha* in this [sc. 'here']."
²² And he returned to Judah, and he said, "I did not find her,
and even the men of the place said, 'There has not been a
qedesha in this [sc. 'here'].'"
²³ And Judah said, "Let her take (it) for herself, lest we become a ridicule; behold, I sent her this kid, but you could not
find her."

---

42. The glaring absence of the prepositional phrase לִי *li* 'to me' in Gen
32:30 is reflected in the fact that almost all English translations include 'me' in
their rendering (for it is so expected in this idiom), even though it is not present in our verse. For example, RSV: "Tell me, I pray, your name"; NJPS: "Pray
tell me your name"; NIV: "Please tell me your name"; Everett Fox: "Pray tell
me your name"; etc. Robert Alter appears to be the only one who (correctly)
omits the word, "Tell your name, pray."

43. Gevirtz, "Of Patriarchs and Puns," 53. This point could be made in
Chapter 18, "Wordplay on Names," but since I treat the verse in this chapter,
the observation is pertinent here.

Quite strikingly in this passage, the exact words that Judah's friend Hirah heard from the townspeople of Enayim (in v. 21) are used in his report to Judah (in v. 22): לֹא־הָיְתָה בָזֶה קְדֵשָׁה *loʾ hayta ba-zε qədeša* 'there has not been a *qedesha* in this [sc. 'here']'. As we have seen in the earlier chapters in this book, verbatim repetition is extremely rare in the Bible. This is also true when direct speech is reported at a later time, as we have here in Gen 38:21–22.[44]

Another rarity occurs in these verses, the root ב-ו-ז *b-w-z* 'scorn, ridicule', in the form לָבוּז *la-buz* '(become) a ridicule'. This is the only appearance of this verbal root in the entire biblical narrative prose corpus. The lexeme is relatively common in poetic texts (e.g., Psalms 4x, Proverbs 10x, Job 3x, etc.), but, as noted, only in Gen 38:23 does the word occur within prose.

The sounds of the words בָזֶה *ba-ze* 'in this' and לָבוּז *la-buz* '(become) a ridicule' evoke one another, with the soundplay operating with the *bet-zayin* combination. To enhance the alliteration, the author has Hirah repeat the same words that he heard from the townsfolk.

11. Genesis 38:22–23, 25

²² וַיָּשָׁב אֶל־יְהוּדָה וַיֹּאמֶר לֹא מְצָאתִיהָ וְגַם אַנְשֵׁי הַמָּקוֹם אָמְרוּ לֹא־הָיְתָה בָזֶה קְדֵשָׁה:

²³ וַיֹּאמֶר יְהוּדָה תִּקַּח־לָהּ פֶּן נִהְיֶה לָבוּז הִנֵּה שָׁלַחְתִּי הַגְּדִי הַזֶּה וְאַתָּה לֹא מְצָאתָהּ:

----

²⁵ הִוא מוּצֵאת וְהִיא שָׁלְחָה אֶל־חָמִיהָ לֵאמֹר לְאִישׁ אֲשֶׁר־אֵלֶּה לּוֹ אָנֹכִי הָרָה וַתֹּאמֶר הַכֶּר־נָא לְמִי הַחֹתֶמֶת וְהַפְּתִילִים וְהַמַּטֶּה הָאֵלֶּה:

²² And he returned to Judah, and he said, "I did not find her, and even the men of the place said, 'There has not been a *qedesha* in this [sc. 'here']'."

---

44. In fact, there are only ten such instances of verbatim repetition of the original speech within the narrative corpus stretching from Genesis through Kings (five in Genesis–Exodus; five in Samuel–Kings); see Savran, *Telling and Retelling*, 29. We will return to this topic below, in Chapter 26.

²³ And Judah said, "Let her take (it) for herself, lest we become a ridicule; behold, I sent her this kid, but you could not find her."

----

²⁵ She is brought-out—and she had sent to her father-in-law saying, "By the man to whom these (belong) I am pregnant"; and she said, "Recognize, please, to whom (belong) these: the seale [*sic*],⁴⁵ and the cords, and the staff."

The odd usage here is the Hophʿal fem. sg. passive participle form מוּצֵאת *muṣeʾt* '(she) is brought-out'.⁴⁶ The reader of biblical prose would expect to find here a suffix-conjugation form indicating the past tense. The author used the unexpected form, however, because the participle allows the *mem* to be prefixed to the root י-צ-א *y-ṣ-ʾ* 'go out' (Hiphʿil 'bring out', with the passive expressed by the Hophʿal), thereby creating the string of consonants *mem-ṣade-ʾaleph-taw*. This unusual form is employed *alliterationis causa*, to invoke the sounds of the earlier words מְצָאתִיהָ *maṣaʾtiha* 'I did (not) find her' (v. 22) and מְצָאתָהּ *maṣaʾtah* 'you did (not) find her' (v. 23), both of which contain the same *mem-ṣade-ʾaleph-taw* series.

12. Genesis 2:15–16, 18

¹⁵ וַיִּקַּח יְהוָה אֱלֹהִים אֶת־הָאָדָם וַיַּנִּחֵהוּ בְגַן־עֵדֶן לְעָבְדָהּ וּלְשָׁמְרָהּ:
¹⁶ וַיְצַו יְהוָה אֱלֹהִים עַל־הָאָדָם לֵאמֹר מִכֹּל עֵץ־הַגָּן אָכֹל תֹּאכֵל:

----

¹⁸ וַיֹּאמֶר יְהוָה אֱלֹהִים לֹא־טוֹב הֱיוֹת הָאָדָם לְבַדּוֹ אֶעֱשֶׂה־לּוֹ עֵזֶר כְּנֶגְדּוֹ:

¹⁵ And Yʜᴡʜ Elohim took the man, and he placed him in the garden of Eden, to till it and to guard it.
¹⁶ And Yʜᴡʜ Elohim commanded the man, saying, "From every tree of the garden you indeed may eat."

----

45. On my use of the spelling 'seale', see my second treatment of this verse, at Chapter 28, no. 2.
46. The oddity has been noticed by many scholars, e.g., Alter, *Art of Biblical Narrative*, 9: "a rare present passive participle."

[18] And Yʜwʜ Elohim said, "It is not good for the man to be alone, I will make for him a lady as his opposite."

Once more I have elected to treat a passage out of canonical order. I do so given the very thorny issues involved with the phrase עֵזֶר כְּנֶגְדּוֹ ʿezer kə-negdo. Had we proceeded in canonical order, these words would have come at the beginning of our explorations (since they appear in the second creation account). I felt it more prudent, however, to set the stage with examples such as Gen 6:14, 21:4, 21:7–8, etc., given the simpler wording in these verses. Only now at chapter's end, with the device of alliteration exemplifed and our method of interpretation elucidated, may we proceed to this illustration.

The expression עֵזֶר כְּנֶגְדּוֹ ʿezer kə-negdo (it occurs not only in v. 18, reproduced above, but in v. 20 as well) has bedeviled scholars for centuries. The rendering of the King James Version (1611), 'an help meet for him', became ensconced in the English language,[47] eventually yielding 'help-meet' (with hyphen, used by John Dryden, for example) and then either 'helpmeet' (without hyphen, common from the nineteenth century onward) or 'helpmate' (used by Daniel Defoe, for example).[48] The first element, 'help', is a suitable rendering of the Hebrew noun עֵזֶר ʿezer, which appears about a dozen times elsewhere in the Bible (e.g., Deut 33:7); while the second element, 'meet', meaning 'equal' (though it would have been archaic even in 1611), is an attempt to render the Hebrew prepositional phrase כְּנֶגְדּוֹ kə-negdo. In truth, though, this compound preposition (formed by -כְּ kə- + נֶגֶד neged) appears only in Gen 2:18 and 2:20, so we cannot be so certain about its meaning, especially since the simple preposition נֶגֶד neged nowhere else has the meaning 'equal', but rather typically means 'opposite, in front of' in a spatial sense.

The problem, then, is this: Does 'help meet' suitably capture the essence of this phrase? Have we, and readers for centuries before us,

---

47. The KJV translators seem to have originated the phrase, since their predecessors John Wycliffe (1382) and William Tyndale (1530) used different renderings, 'an help lijk to hym silf' and 'an helper to beare him company', respectively. Note that the former used the Vulgate as his source text, while the latter translated directly from the Hebrew original.

48. *OED*, s.v. 'helpmeet'.

been misled not only by the King James Version (and almost all English translations influenced thereby since 1611), but also by the presence of עֵזֶר ʿezɛr 'help' (along with the verbal root ע-ז-ר ʿ-z-r 'help') in the Hebrew lexicon? My even raising the question naturally directs our answer: yes, we have been misled—for there is nothing further in the text that suggests that the woman is to be a helper to the man. This point, of course, could become the subject of a long sermon on egalitarianism, women's rights, the role of women in religious life, and more—though notwithstanding my personal interest in these matters, for the nonce I prefer to remain with the subject at hand, the intersection of language and literature in the Bible.

Happily, a relatively recent suggestion points the way and to my mind provides the solution to the phrase עֵזֶר כְּנֶגְדּוֹ ʿezɛr kə-nɛgdo. The remarkable Zeʾev Ben-Ḥayyim (1907–2013), master Hebraist of the Hebrew University, who continued to produce scholarship well into his nineties, suggested in 1998 that the word עֵזֶר ʿezɛr indeed does not mean 'help', but rather is cognate with Arabic عذراء ʿaḏrā 'virgin, young woman' (the phonetics match perfectly, since Arabic /ḏ/ corresponds to Hebrew /z/).[49] Which is to say, ancient Hebrew had a word עֵזֶר ʿezɛr that meant 'woman' (in some fashion)—a meaning that fits the context of Gen 2:18 (and 2:20). If I have translated the word as 'lady' above, I do so only to evoke a different and rarer usage, in keeping with the exceptional nature of עֵזֶר ʿezɛr.[50] This word, accordingly, is a homonym

---

49. Zeʾev Ben-Ḥayyim, "ʾezɛr kə-nɛgdo: haṣṣaʿa," *Leshonenu* 61 (1998 / 5758): 45–50. Note that the Arabic word is used by Christian Arabs to refer to the Virgin Mary.

50. I thus reserve 'woman' for אִשָּׁה ʾišša, 'female' for נְקֵבָה naqeba, etc. Note, incidentally, that while the modern meaning of English 'lady' sounds very aristocratic, the etymology of the word bespeaks rather lowly origins. The source of 'lady' is actually rather convoluted, as it derives from a reconstructed Old English form *hlaf + dige*, that is, 'loaf' + 'kneader', that is, 'one who kneads dough into a loaf', very much woman's work in the premodern period. See further *OED*, s.v. 'lady' *n.*; and Crystal, *The Story of English in 100 Words*, 12. On women in the ancient world as grinders of grain into flour, molders of bread loaves, and bakers, see Carol L. Meyers, "Having Their Space and Eating There Too: Bread Production and Female Power in Ancient Israelite Households," *Nashim: A Journal of Jewish Women's Studies* 5 (2002): 14–44.

of עֵזֶר *'ezɛr* 'help', but the two are to be sharply distinguished, especially here in Genesis 2.

We thus are led to ask: Why did the author choose this phrase, עֵזֶר כְּנֶגְדּוֹ *'ezɛr kǝ-nɛgdo* 'a lady as his opposite'? By this point, the reader will not be surprised to learn that the answer lies in noticing the sounds at play. Two phrases heard earlier, בְגַן־עֵדֶן *bǝ-gan 'edɛn* 'in the garden of Eden' (v. 15) and עֵץ־הַגָּן *'eṣ hag-gan* 'the trees of the garden' (v. 16), incorporate the same or similar consonants as the expression עֵזֶר כְּנֶגְדּוֹ *'ezɛr kǝ-nɛgdo* 'a lady as his opposite' (v. 18). Note that /ʿ/, /n/, and /g/ appear in all three combinations; /d/ appears in two of them; the /ṣ/ in the second one evokes the /z/ of the third one; the /r/ of the last one shares the sonorant qualities of the /n/ in the other two; and the /k/ in the third one is the voiceless velar stop corresponding to the voiced velar stop /g/ that appears in all three. The result is an interweaving of sounds in the three expressions—an effect produced by our author's reaching deep into the Hebrew lexicon to pluck the word עֵזֶר *'ezɛr* 'lady', which then works in tandem with the unique compound preposition כְּנֶגֶד *kǝ-nɛged* 'as opposite' (or whatever its precise nuance may be).

Throughout this book, I have attempted to remain objective, without reading into the text anything not intrinsic thereto. In this case, I wish to depart from that norm and offer an aspirational understanding of the phrase. One would hope that my literal rendering 'a lady as his opposite' does not capture the true sense of the Hebrew phrase. Indeed, in light of the prominent and at times heroic roles assigned to women in biblical literature,[51] I would propose an understanding of עֵזֶר כְּנֶגְדּוֹ *'ezɛr kǝ-nɛgdo* (without pushing the Hebrew too far, in my estimation) as 'a woman as equal partner'.

Final note to this chapter: there is another superb illustration of alliteration in Genesis, though I will wait to present the relevant passages until later in this book—for reasons that will become apparent at such time.[52]

---

51. Gary A. Rendsburg, "Unlikely Heroes: Women as Israel," *Bible Review* 19.1 (Feb. 2003): 16–23, 52–53.

52. See below, Chapter 22, no. 2.

CHAPTER SIX

ALLITERATION IN THE EXODUS NARRATIVE

We continue our examination of alliteration in biblical prose in this chapter, with examples from the book of Exodus.[1]

1. Exodus 1:21

וַיְהִי כִּי־יָרְאוּ הַמְיַלְּדֹת אֶת־הָאֱלֹהִים וַיַּעַשׂ לָהֶם בָּתִּים:

And it was, because the midwives feared God, he made for them houses.

Previous scholars have noted that the word בַּת *bat* 'daughter' serves as a *Leitwort* (that is, 'leading word', a word that is woven into several interconnected episodes) in the first two chapters of Exodus (see 1:16, 1:22, 2:1, 2:5, etc.).[2] To further enhance the texture of this pericope, the author introduces the word בָּתִּים *battim*, lit., 'houses', in 1:21. When one realizes further that the idiom עָשָׂה בָּתִּים *ʿaśa battim*, lit., 'to make houses', is used here in a technical legal sense, with the meaning 'to found a family',[3] we gain an added appreciation of the author's tack in making use of the full range of connotations of words in his lexis.

---

1. For an earlier treatment, see Gary A. Rendsburg, "Alliteration in the Exodus Narrative," in Chaim Cohen et al., eds., *Birkat Shalom: Studies in the Bible, Ancient Near Eastern Literature, and Postbiblical Judaism Presented to Shalom M. Paul on the Occasion of His Seventieth Birthday* (Winona Lake, IN: Eisenbrauns, 2008), 83–100.

2. See, e.g., Umberto Cassuto, *A Commentary on the Book of Exodus*, trans. Israel Abrahams (Jerusalem: Magnes, 1967), 17; and Fox, *Five Books of Moses*, 260. For more on the *Leitwort* device, see below, Chapter 29, p. 578.

3. Shalom M. Paul, "Exodus 1:21: 'To Found a Family': A Biblical and Akkadian Idiom," in Robert J. Ratner et al., eds., *Let Your Colleagues Praise You: Studies in Memory of Stanley Gevirtz*, Part II = *Maarav* 8 (1992): 139–42.

2. Exodus 2:3

וְלֹא־יָכְלָה עוֹד הַצְּפִינוֹ וַתִּקַּח־לוֹ תֵּבַת גֹּמֶא וַתַּחְמְרָה בַחֵמָר וּבַזָּפֶת
וַתָּשֶׂם בָּהּ אֶת־הַיֶּלֶד וַתָּשֶׂם בַּסּוּף עַל־שְׂפַת הַיְאֹר:

And she could no longer hide him, and she took for him a
basket of papyrus, and she loamed it with loam and with
pitch; and she placed the child in it, and she placed (it)
amongst the reeds on the edge of the Nile.

In line with the above, we also may note the introduction of the word
תֵּבַת *tebat* 'basket of' in 2:3, in close proximity to the *Leitwort* בַּת *bat*
'daughter'. Clearly the former is a rare word in Hebrew, used in specific contexts only, namely, here in Exod 2:3 (and in v. 5 in the absolute
form) and in Genesis 6–9 (26x). As previous scholars have noted (see
n. 4 below), the author of Exodus 1–2 evokes the language of the early
chapters of Genesis (see, for example, the shared vocabulary of Exod
1:7 and Gen 1:28; and the expression כִּי־טוֹב *ki tob* 'that it/he was good'
in Exod 2:2 and Gen 1:4, etc.), with the theological message that the
two greatest events in the history of the world were the creation of the
world and the creation of the people of Israel (note the phrase עַם בְּנֵי
יִשְׂרָאֵל *'am bəne yiśra'el* 'the people of the children of Israel' used for
the first time in Exod 1:9). Accordingly, the use of תֵּבָה *teba* 'basket' in
the Exodus narrative can be explained along the same lines.[4]

At the same time, however, we may note the sound effect that
emerges from the presence of this word in our narrative, surrounded as
it is by repeated use of the word בַּת *bat* 'daughter'. In fact, the construct
form תֵּבַת *tebat* 'basket of' produces the exact same syllable as בַּת *bat*
'daughter'. But regardless of the construct form תֵּבַת *tebat* 'basket of',
the absolute form תֵּבָה *teba* itself alliterates with בַּת *bat* 'daughter', with
the two consonants of the two words in anagrammatic order. Naturally,
these two consonants, /b/ and /t/, are among the most common in the

---

4. See Isaac Kikawada, "Literary Convention of the Primeval History,"
Annual of the Japanese Biblical Institute 1 (1975): 3–22; James S. Ackerman,
"The Literary Context of the Moses Birth Story (Exodus 1–2)," in Kenneth
R. R. Gros Louis, James S. Ackerman, and Thayer S. Warshaw, eds., *Literary
Interpretations of Biblical Narratives* (Nashville: Abingdon, 1974), 74–119; and
Fox, *Five Books of Moses*, 256, 263.

language—and among the most common in many languages—but given the rarity of both the word תֵּבָה *teba* 'basket' and the technical use of the term בָּתִּים *battim*, I would claim that these lexemes were intentionally selected by the author to elicit the maximal sound effect possible.

3. Exodus 2:2–3

2 וַתַּהַר הָאִשָּׁה וַתֵּלֶד בֵּן וַתֵּרֶא אֹתוֹ כִּי־טוֹב הוּא וַתִּצְפְּנֵהוּ שְׁלֹשָׁה יְרָחִים:

3 וְלֹא־יָכְלָה עוֹד הַצְּפִינוֹ וַתִּקַּח־לוֹ תֵּבַת גֹּמֶא וַתַּחְמְרָה בַחֵמָר וּבַזָּפֶת וַתָּשֶׂם בָּהּ אֶת־הַיֶּלֶד וַתָּשֶׂם בַּסּוּף עַל־שְׂפַת הַיְאֹר:

2 And the woman became-pregnant, and she bore a son; and she saw that he was good, and she hid him three months.
3 And she could no longer hide him, and she took for him a basket of papyrus, and she loamed it with loam and with pitch; and she placed the child in it, and she placed (it) amongst the reeds on the edge of the Nile.

The Hebrew lexicon includes two words for 'month': the more common חֹדֶשׁ *hodeš* (attested 281x in the Bible) and the far less common יֶרַח *yeraḥ* (attested only 12x in the corpus). While all languages contain synonyms, in this particular case we are able to determine that these two lexemes were used in different regional dialects of ancient Hebrew. The former was the term employed in Judahite Hebrew, that is, the dialect of Judah, including Jerusalem, whence most of the biblical books emanate; while the latter was characteristic of Israelian Hebrew, that is, the dialect of northern Israel, where a minority of the biblical material was composed (to be explored in greater detail in Chapter 23). This conclusion is based on (a) the distribution of the word יֶרַח *yeraḥ* in the Bible (in such northern texts as Deut 33:14, 2 Kgs 15:13, etc.), and (b) the presence of cognates in dialects and languages spoken to the north of Israel (Ugaritic *yrḫ*, Phoenician ירח, Aramaic ירח).[5] The Moses birth story, however, is a narrative otherwise devoid of Israelian Hebrew fea-

---

5. Gary A. Rendsburg, *Israelian Hebrew in the Book of Kings* (Occasional Publications of the Department of Near Eastern Studies and the Program of Jewish Studies, Cornell University, 5; Bethesda, MD: CDL, 2002), 127–28; and

tures, so one cannot claim that these verses stem from northern Israel. Instead, the expression שְׁלֹשָׁה יְרָחִים *šəloša yəraḥim* 'three months' at the end of v. 2 must be explained differently.

In the following v. 3 we read וַתַּחְמְרָה בַחֵמָר *wattaḥməra ba-ḥemar* 'and she loamed it with loam'. Note how the three consonants of this root, ח-מ-ר *ḥ-m-r*, which appears here both as a verb and a noun, are the same three consonants present in the plural form יְרָחִים *yəraḥim* 'months'.[6]

Furthermore, while the word חֹמֶר *ḥomɛr* 'clay, mortar' in Exod 1:14 occurs at quite a distance from the like-sounding words in 2:2–3, its presence in the narrative also should be noted. All of this, then, explains the author's choice of the word יְרָחִים *yəraḥim* 'months' in 2:2. The use of the standard word חֳדָשִׁים *ḥodašim* 'months' would not have produced the same literary result. Our Judahite author, accordingly, took advantage of the presence of יְרָחִים *yəraḥim* 'months' as a northern regional dialect feature. Under normal circumstances he would not have used this word, but he could not resist its inclusion here *alliterationis causa*. His (presumably Judahite) listeners, meanwhile, would have raised an eyebrow upon hearing the word, a gesture soon to be followed by an appreciative smile upon hearing the alliterative phrase וַתַּחְמְרָה בַחֵמָר *wattaḥməra ba-ḥemar* 'and she loamed it with loam' in the next verse.

For a parallel to the employment of a dialectal word or form with an eye to enhancing its literary role, we note the use of 'wood', associated with British English,[7] instead of 'woods', by two American writers to generate more precise rhyme in their compositions. First, observe how Robert Frost uses 'wood' in the opening stanza of "The Road Not Taken" (1916), so that it could rhyme perfectly with 'stood' and 'could':

Gary A. Rendsburg, "A Comprehensive Guide to Israelian Hebrew: Grammar and Lexicon," *Orient* 38 (2003): 26.

6. Actually, this statement is not totally accurate, because the *ḥet*s in these two lexemes represent different consonants: cognate data inform us that the root חֵמָר *ḥemar* 'loam' contains the pharyngeal fricative /ḥ/, while יְרַח *yɛraḥ* 'month' contains the velar fricative /ḫ/ (thus more properly one would transcribe the sounds as *yɛraḫ*). But this minor difference in the articulation of these two phonemes does not lessen the aural impact created by the juxtaposition of these words, especially in light of the exact match between the other two consonants, /m/ *mem* and /r/ *resh*.

7. See *OED*, s.v. 'wood' *n.*[1].

Two roads diverged in a yellow wood,
And sorry I could not travel both
And be one traveler, long I stood
And looked down one as far as I could
To where it bent in the undergrowth;

The unexpected use of 'wood' in this well-known poem comes into greater focus when one encounters Frost's fivefold use of 'woods' in his second famous poem, "Stopping by Woods on a Snowy Evening" (1922), including in the title and in the opening line, "Whose woods these are I think I know."

Similarly, consider Stephen Sondheim's single use of the word 'wood', in place of the expected and ubiquitous 'woods', in the lyrics to his song "No One Is Alone" (sung by Cinderella) from "Into the Woods" (1986–1987), as follows:

Sometimes people leave you.
Halfway through the wood.
Others may deceive you.
You decide what's good.

Once again we notice how here British English 'wood' replaces American English 'woods' in order to elicit a more precise rhyme with the following word 'good'.

4. Exodus 2:2–3

This same pair of verses includes another set of alliterative words. The verbal root צ-פ-ן ṣ-p-n 'hide' occurs twice, in both vv. 2 and 3: וַתִּצְפְּנֵהוּ wattiṣpǝnehu 'and she hid him' and הַצְּפִינוֹ haṣṣǝpino 'hide him'. Its presence elicits the use of three words with the combination sibilant + /p/ pe: זֶפֶת zɛpɛt 'pitch', a rare word, attested only 3x in the Bible; סוּף sup 'reeds', another rare word, attested only 4x (not including instances of יַם סוּף yam sup 'Sea of Reeds'); and שְׂפַת śǝpat 'edge of (the Nile)' = 'riverbank', a common usage. While none of these words is as unexpected as the presence of יְרָחִים yǝrahim 'months' in the preceding example, the overall effect produces a first-rate alliterative chain.

5. Exodus 5:9

תִּכְבַּ֧ד הָעֲבֹדָ֛ה עַל־הָאֲנָשִׁ֖ים וְיַעֲשׂוּ־בָ֑הּ וְאַל־יִשְׁע֖וּ בְּדִבְרֵי־שָֽׁקֶר׃

Let the work be hard on the men, so that they may labor at
it; and let them not pay-heed to lying words.

The root שׁ-ע-ה *š-ʿ-h* 'pay heed, have regard' occurs in the narrative
corpus of Genesis through Kings only here and in Gen 4:4–5 in the Cain
and Abel story (2x).[8] The lexical choice made by our author is clearly
for the sake of alliteration: the verb יִשְׁעוּ *yišʿu* 'let them (not) pay-heed'
evokes the sounds of the preceding verb וְיַעֲשׂוּ *wǝ-yaʿaśu* 'so that they
may labor', from the common root ע-שׂ-ה *ʿ-ś-h* 'do, work, make'.[9]

6. Exodus 5:11, 14

‏¹¹ אַתֶּ֗ם לְכ֨וּ קְח֤וּ לָכֶם֙ תֶּ֔בֶן . . .
¹⁴ מַדּ֗וּעַ לֹ֨א כִלִּיתֶ֧ם חָקְכֶ֛ם לִלְבֹּ֖ן

¹¹ You, go, take for yourselves straw . . .
¹⁴ Why did you not complete your quota of making-bricks?

The latter of these verses utilizes the word חֹק *ḥoq* 'quota' in a most
unusual way (its usual meaning is 'law, decree, regulation').[10] And
while there is nothing unusual about the verb כִלִּיתֶם *killitɛm* 'complete'
(from the verbal root כ-ל-ה *k-l-h*) in this context, by collocating these
two words the author creates an echo of a short phrase that appears
three verses earlier: לְכוּ קְחוּ *lǝku qǝḥu* 'go, take' (v. 11). Furthermore,
although there is not an exact correspondence of the speakers issuing
these commands in the name of the Pharaoh—5:11 is spoken by נֹגְשֵׂי
הָעָם וְשֹׁטְרָיו *nogśe haʿam wǝšoṭraw* 'the taskmasters of the people and
their officers' (v. 10), while 5:14 is spoken by שֹׁטְרֵי בְּנֵי יִשְׂרָאֵל *šoṭre bǝne
yiśraʾel* 'the officers of the Israelites'—note that these are the only two

---

8. The root occurs 12x in poetic texts; it is especially common in Isaiah,
wherein are found seven attestations.

9. Thus already Cassuto, *Commentary on the Book of Exodus*, 68.

10. Thus BDB, 349. Similar meanings are attested in passages such as Gen
47:22 (2x) and Prov 31:15.

instances in the narrative where the שֹׁטְרִים 'officers' address the people directly. Accordingly, near the beginning of their words one finds the consonantal string /l/–/k/–/q/–/ḥ/ (with the letters *lamed-kaf* in one word and then *qof-ḥet* in the other), and then near the end of their words one hears the string /k/–/l/–/ḥ/–/q/ (with the letters *kaf-lamed* in one word, and then *ḥet-qof* in the other), all in the same voice.

7. Exodus 8:10

וַיִּצְבְּרוּ אֹתָם חֳמָרִם חֳמָרִם וַתִּבְאַשׁ הָאָרֶץ׃

And they piled them up, heaps (upon) heaps, and the land stunk.

צְפַרְדְּעִים: 10x in Exod 7:27–8:9 ~ צְפַרְדֵּעַ: once in Exod 8:2

The verbal root צ-ב-ר *ṣ-b-r* 'pile up', present in the form וַיִּצְבְּרוּ *wayyiṣbərū* 'they piled up' in Exod 8:10, is a relatively rare lexeme in the Bible. It appears only 6x in the corpus (plus once more in a noun form). Its presence in our text, within the description of the second plague, follows immediately upon the elevenfold mention of frogs: צְפַרְדְּעִים *ṣəpardəʿim* 'frogs' (10x) ~ צְפַרְדֵּעַ *ṣəpardeaʿ* 'frog' (1x).[11] The first and third consonants of these words and the root צ-ב-ר *ṣ-b-r* 'pile up' are identical, while the corresponding second letters represent the voiced and voiceless labials /p/ and /b/, respectively.

8. Exodus 9:1

וַיֹּאמֶר יְהוָה אֶל־מֹשֶׁה בֹּא אֶל־פַּרְעֹה וְדִבַּרְתָּ אֵלָיו כֹּה־אָמַר יְהוָה
אֱלֹהֵי הָעִבְרִים שַׁלַּח אֶת־עַמִּי וְיַעַבְדֻנִי׃

And Yнwн said to Moses, "Go unto Pharaoh, and you shall speak to him: 'Thus says Yнwн the God of the Hebrews: Send-forth my people, so that they may worship me'."

As we saw in Chapter 3, no. 1, in five places in the plagues narrative, God instructs Moses to warn Pharaoh of the impending disaster. In four of

---

11. See already, in very general terms, Richard E. Friedman, *A Commentary on the Torah* (San Francisco: Harper, 2001), 195.

these cases, God uses the word וְאָמַרְתָּ wə'amartá 'and you shall say' (7:16
[first plague], 7:26 [second plague], 8:16 [fourth plague], and 9:13 [seventh
plague]).[12] In one passage, at 9:1, in anticipation of the fifth plague, we
encounter the divergent form וְדִבַּרְתָּ wədibbartá 'and you shall speak'.[13]

The author has altered the verb of speech at this specific point in
order to produce alliteration with the name of the fifth plague, that is,
דֶּבֶר deber 'pestilence'. This noun form appears for the first time in v. 3
and then again in v. 15.

Furthermore, the noun דָּבָר dabar 'thing, matter' occurs 3x in this
pericope, in vv. 4, 5, and 6. This lexeme is exceedingly common in the
Bible, and it therefore may not be used here intentionally. One should
note, however, that this is the only place in the long account of the ten
plagues where the word דָּבָר dabar appears.

In sum, three separate lexemes from the root ד-ב-ר d-b-r (by this
statement I do not mean to imply that the noun דֶּבֶר deber 'pestilence'
derives from the same etymological root as the other two items) are
placed in close proximity to produce a fine example of alliteration.

9. Exodus 9:3

הִנֵּה יַד־יְהוָה הוֹיָה בְּמִקְנְךָ אֲשֶׁר בַּשָּׂדֶה בַּסּוּסִים בַּחֲמֹרִים בַּגְּמַלִּים
בַּבָּקָר וּבַצֹּאן דֶּבֶר כָּבֵד מְאֹד:

Behold, the hand of YHWH is upon your livestock that are in
the field—upon the horses, upon the donkeys, upon the camels,
upon the herd, and upon the flock—a very heavy pestilence.

In Exod 9:3 we encounter the only example of the participle of the verb
ה-י-ה h-y-h 'be' in the Bible.[14] G. S. Ogden noted a discernible pattern
in the use of the participle within the plagues narrative:

---

12. See also Exod 4:22 in the portion of the narrative leading up to the
plagues account.

13. We may note that in general וְדִבַּרְתָּ wədibbartá 'and you shall speak'
is rare, especially in contrast to the more common וְאָמַרְתָּ wə'amartá 'and you
shall say'. In the Torah, for example, the former occurs only 3x (Exod 4:15,
9:1, Deut 6:7), while the latter occurs 40x.

14. That is, strictly speaking. Participles of the byform ה-ו-ה h-w-h 'be'
occur in Qoh 2:22 and Neh 6:6.

On five occasions Moses and Aaron are depicted as presenting themselves before the Pharaoh in order to petition for approval of an Israelite pilgrimage into the desert. On each of these occasions their words involve statements as to what Yahweh would do should the Pharaoh fail to comply with their request. In each of the five statements the pattern of speech is almost identical.[15]

Ogden presented the following chart:[16]

Exod 7:17	בַּמַּטֶּה אֲשֶׁר־בְּיָדִי 'with the staff that is in my hand'	מַכֶּה '(will) strike'	אָנֹכִי 'I'	הִנֵּה 'behold'
Exod 7:27	אֶת־כָּל־גְּבוּלְךָ 'all your borders'	נֹגֵף '(will) plague'	אָנֹכִי 'I'	הִנֵּה 'behold'
Exod 9:3	בְּמִקְנְךָ 'upon your livestock'	הוֹיָה '(will) be'	יַד־יְהוָֹה 'the hand of Yʜᴡʜ'	הִנֵּה 'behold'
Exod 9:14	אֶת־כָּל־מַגֵּפֹתַי 'all my plagues'	שֹׁלֵחַ 'am sending'	אֲנִי 'I'	
Exod 10:4	מָחָר אַרְבֶּה 'tomorrow locusts'	מֵבִיא '(will) bring'		הִנְנִי 'behold I'

It is clear that each of the statements requires a participle, and that each, save one, is expressed in the first-person singular with reference to God. The exception is the passage in Exod 9:3, where the subject is 'the hand of Yʜᴡʜ'. Ogden's contribution was to note why a participle form is required in this verse, thereby eliciting the unique feminine singular active participle of ה-י-ה *h-y-h* 'be'. What he did not note is

---

15. G. S. Ogden, "Notes on the Use of הויה in Exodus ix 3," *Vetus Testamentum* 17 (1967): 483–84, in particular 484.

16. I have corrected the errors that Ogden included in his transcription of Exod 7:17 (on p. 484), plus I have added the vowels and the *ṭaʿamim*.

that the combination of the exceptional form הֹוֶיה *hoya* 'is' and the divine name יהוה *YHWH* creates an exquisite alliteration, thus providing us with another case of a rare or unique word or form invoked for the purposes of alliterative exigency.[17]

10. Exodus 9:8–10

⁸ וַיֹּאמֶר יְהוָה אֶל־מֹשֶׁה וְאֶל־אַהֲרֹן קְחוּ לָכֶם מְלֹא חָפְנֵיכֶם פִּיחַ כִּבְשָׁן
וּזְרָקוֹ מֹשֶׁה הַשָּׁמַיְמָה לְעֵינֵי פַרְעֹה:

⁹ וְהָיָה לְאָבָק עַל כָּל־אֶרֶץ מִצְרָיִם וְהָיָה עַל־הָאָדָם וְעַל־הַבְּהֵמָה
לִשְׁחִין פֹּרֵחַ אֲבַעְבֻּעֹת בְּכָל־אֶרֶץ מִצְרָיִם:

¹⁰ וַיִּקְחוּ אֶת־פִּיחַ הַכִּבְשָׁן וַיַּעַמְדוּ לִפְנֵי פַרְעֹה וַיִּזְרֹק אֹתוֹ מֹשֶׁה
הַשָּׁמַיְמָה וַיְהִי שְׁחִין אֲבַעְבֻּעֹת פֹּרֵחַ בָּאָדָם וּבַבְּהֵמָה:

⁸ And Yhwh said to Moses and to Aaron, "Take for yourselves a fill of your fists (of) soot of the furnace, and Moses should throw it heavenward in the eyes of Pharaoh.
⁹ And it will become dust-powder on all the land of Egypt, and it will be upon human and upon beast, as boils sprouting eruptions, in all the land of Egypt.
¹⁰ And they took the soot of the furnace, and they stood before Pharaoh, and Moses threw it heavenward; and it became boils, eruptions, sprouting on human and on beast.

The word פִּיחַ *piaḥ* 'soot' occurs only here in the Bible, in vv. 8 and 10, within the description of the sixth plague. It has been specifically chosen by the author to alliterate with words in close proximity, namely, חָפְנֵיכֶם *ḥopnekεm* 'your fists' in v. 8 and פֹּרֵחַ *poreaḥ* 'sprouting' in vv. 9–10 (2x).[18]

---

17. Note further that graphically the two forms are anagrams of each other.

18. Due to lack of cognates, we are unable to determine the exact phonetic value of the *ḥet* in פִּיחַ *piaḥ*. For the other two words involved in this series, as in example no. 3 above, we are dealing with different *ḥets*. Cognates for the noun חֹפֶן *ḥopεn* 'fist' (e.g., Akkadian *upnu*, Arabic *ḥafna*) point to the presence of the pharyngeal fricative /ḥ/, while cognates for the verb פ-ר-ח *p-r-ḥ* 'sprout, blossom' (e.g., Arabic *faraḥa*) point to the presence of the velar fricative /ḫ/. Nonetheless, as noted in no. 3 above, this issue has only a minor effect on the overall impact of the alliteration created by the collocation of these three lexemes.

11. Exodus 9:23–24

וַיֵּ֣ט מֹשֶׁ֣ה אֶת־מַטֵּהוּ֮ עַל־הַשָּׁמַיִם֒ וַֽיהוָ֗ה נָתַ֤ן קֹלֹת֙ וּבָרָ֔ד וַתִּֽהֲלַךְ־אֵ֖שׁ ²³
אָ֑רְצָה וַיַּמְטֵ֧ר יְהוָ֛ה בָּרָ֖ד עַל־אֶ֥רֶץ מִצְרָֽיִם׃
וַיְהִ֣י בָרָ֔ד וְאֵ֕שׁ מִתְלַקַּ֖חַת בְּת֣וֹךְ הַבָּרָ֑ד כָּבֵ֣ד מְאֹ֗ד אֲשֶׁ֤ר לֹֽא־הָיָ֤ה ²⁴
כָמֹ֙הוּ֙ בְּכָל־אֶ֣רֶץ מִצְרַ֔יִם מֵאָ֖ז הָיְתָ֥ה לְגֽוֹי׃

²³ And Moses inclined his staff toward the heaven, and YHWH
gave-forth thunders and hail, and fire proceeded earthward;
and YHWH rained hail upon the land of Egypt.
²⁴ And there was hail and fire taking-hold-of-itself in the
midst of the hail—very heavy, the likes of which were not in
all the land of Egypt, since it became a nation.

The rare word מִתְלַקַּ֖חַת *mitlaqqaḥat*, lit., 'taking-hold-of-itself' (with
its exact connotation unclear) occurs in v. 24, as one of only two attestations of the Hitpaʿel of the root ל-ק-ח *l-q-ḥ* 'take'.[19] The only
other instance is Ezek 1:4, where the same expression וְאֵ֕שׁ מִתְלַקַּ֖חַת
wə-ʾeš mitlaqqaḥat 'and fire taking-hold-of-itself' occurs—no doubt
modeled after our Exodus passage. By now, the reader will grasp our
approach: upon encountering a rare word or form in the Bible, look in
the surrounding verses for other lexemes (especially other rare ones)
that evoke the same sounds. Once more our search yields positive
results, for the preceding verse contains two lexemes that alliterate
with מִתְלַקַּ֖חַת *mitlaqqaḥat* 'taking-hold-of-itself'.

The first is קֹלֹת *qolot*, lit., 'voices' (= 'thunder'), which includes three
of the identical sounds occurring in מִתְלַקַּ֖חַת *mitlaqqaḥat*, in scrambled
fashion. The second is the rare verbal form וַתִּֽהֲלַךְ *wattihalak* 'and (fire)
proceeded'. This verb derives from the exceedingly common root ה-ל-ך
h-l-k 'go', though the form in Exod 9:23 reflects the atypical preserva-
tion of the first root letter *he* (there are only 11 such cases in the Bible,
compared to 630 instances without the *he* in prefix-conjugation forms).
This peculiarity enhances the aural effect, with the sounds /t/–/h/–/l/–/k/
of וַתִּֽהֲלַךְ *wattihalak* corresponding closely to the string of sounds
/t/–/ḥ/–/l/–/q/ of מִתְלַקַּ֖חַת *mitlaqqaḥat*, again in scrambled fashion.

---

19. For discussion on the meaning of the term, see William H. C. Propp,
Exodus 1–18 (Anchor Bible 2; New York: Doubleday, 1999), 334.

12. Exodus 9:30

וְאַתָּה וַעֲבָדֶיךָ יָדַעְתִּי כִּי טֶרֶם תִּירְאוּן מִפְּנֵי יְהוָה אֱלֹהִים׃

"And as for you and your servants, I know that you do not
yet fear Yʜwʜ Elohim."

מַמְטִיר '(behold I) am raining' (v. 18)

וַיַּמְטֵר 'and (God) rained' (v. 23)

מָטָר 'rain' (2x: vv. 33, 34)

Within the description of the seventh plague, the text includes a statement of a sort not previously encountered. I refer to the following:
יָדַעְתִּי כִּי טֶרֶם תִּירְאוּן מִפְּנֵי יְהוָה אֱלֹהִים 'I know that you do not yet fear
Yʜwʜ Elohim' (v. 30).[20] This statement allows for the use of the adverb
טֶרֶם *ṭerem* 'yet' amidst the fourfold use of the root מ-ט-ר *m-ṭ-r* 'rain',
twice as a verb (vv. 18 and 23) and twice as a noun (vv. 33 and 34), all
of which are presented above. The alliteration created by these anagrammatic lexemes is obvious.

13. Exodus 10:26, 28

²⁶ וְגַם־מִקְנֵנוּ יֵלֵךְ עִמָּנוּ לֹא תִשָּׁאֵר פַּרְסָה כִּי מִמֶּנּוּ נִקַּח לַעֲבֹד אֶת־
יְהוָה אֱלֹהֵינוּ וַאֲנַחְנוּ לֹא־נֵדַע מַה־נַּעֲבֹד אֶת־יְהוָה עַד־בֹּאֵנוּ שָׁמָּה׃

----

²⁸ וַיֹּאמֶר־לוֹ פַרְעֹה לֵךְ מֵעָלָי הִשָּׁמֶר לְךָ אַל־תֹּסֶף רְאוֹת פָּנַי כִּי בְּיוֹם
רְאֹתְךָ פָנַי תָּמוּת׃

²⁶ "And also our livestock must go with us, (not even) a hoof
shall remain, for from-among them we must take, to worship
Yʜwʜ our God; and we do not know (with) which to worship Yʜwʜ until we come there."

----

²⁸ And Pharaoh said to him, "Go from me, guard yourself not
to see my face again, for on the day of your seeing my face,
you shall die."

----

20. The inclusion of this statement in the narrative is another indication
of the special character of the seventh plague; see Scott B. Noegel, "The Significance of the Seventh Plague," *Biblica* 76 (1995): 532–39.

The word פַּרְסָה *parsa* 'hoof' occurs in v. 26. This is the only place in the Torah, outside of Leviticus 11 and Deuteronomy 14 (where the dietary laws are presented), where this noun occurs. Moreover, this is the only place in the entire Bible where it is used synecdochically: פַּרְסָה *parsa* here does not mean 'hoof' per se, but rather stands for 'domesticated animal' in general.

The listener to the text may raise an eyebrow upon encountering this term in v. 26, but her question is soon answered upon reaching v. 28. Here we read the expression אַל־תֹּסֶף רְאוֹת פָּנָי *'ɛl tosɛp rə'ot panay* '(you are) not to see my face again' in the mouth of the Pharaoh. Note the string of consonants that bridges the middle two words of this phrase: /s/ *samekh* – /p/ *pe* – /r/ *reš*, precisely the same three consonants that appear in the word פַּרְסָה *parsa* 'hoof'. Given the unique usage of this word in v. 26, as described above, especially the metonymy present, there can be little doubt that the author employed the word *allitera-tionis causa*.

14. Exodus 11:1–2

וַיֹּאמֶר יְהוָה אֶל־מֹשֶׁה עוֹד נֶגַע אֶחָד אָבִיא עַל־פַּרְעֹה וְעַל־מִצְרַיִם 1
אַחֲרֵי־כֵן יְשַׁלַּח אֶתְכֶם מִזֶּה כְּשַׁלְּחוֹ כָּלָה גָּרֵשׁ יְגָרֵשׁ אֶתְכֶם מִזֶּה:
דַּבֶּר־נָא בְּאָזְנֵי הָעָם וְיִשְׁאֲלוּ אִישׁ | מֵאֵת רֵעֵהוּ וְאִשָּׁה מֵאֵת רְעוּתָהּ 2
כְּלֵי־כֶסֶף וּכְלֵי זָהָב:

[1] And YHWH said to Moses, "One more plague I will bring upon Pharaoh and upon Egypt. Afterward he will send-forth you from this (place)—as a sending-forth, completely—indeed he will expel you from this (place).
[2] Speak now in the ears of the people, so that each-man shall ask from his neighbor, and each woman from her neighbor, (for) objects of silver and objects of gold."

The word כָּלָה *kala* 'completely' (which normally functions as a noun meaning 'completion, complete destruction, annihilation, etc.') is used in 11:1 adverbially, one of only two such occurrences in the Bible (the other is in Gen 18:21).[21] The usage is considered odd enough by scholars

---

21. See BDB, 478.

that the text is often viewed as suspect, with various textual emendations proposed.[22]

But this atypical usage may be explained by the desire to produce alliteration. In the next verse we read that the Israelites are to ask their Egyptian neighbors for כְּלֵי־כֶסֶף וּכְלֵי זָהָב *kəle kɛsɛp u-kle zahab* 'objects of silver and objects of gold' (v. 2). The twofold use of כְּלֵי *kəle* 'objects of' rehearses the sounds of כָּלָה *kala* 'completely' in the previous verse.

15. Exodus 13:17

וַיְהִי בְּשַׁלַּח פַּרְעֹה אֶת־הָעָם וְלֹא־נָחָם אֱלֹהִים דֶּרֶךְ אֶרֶץ פְּלִשְׁתִּים כִּי
קָרוֹב הוּא כִּי | אָמַר אֱלֹהִים פֶּן־יִנָּחֵם הָעָם בִּרְאֹתָם מִלְחָמָה וְשָׁבוּ
מִצְרָיְמָה:

And it was, when Pharaoh sent-forth the people, and God
did not lead them (via) the way of the land of the Philistines,
though it was closer; for God said, "Lest the people regret,
upon their seeing war, and return to Egypt."

This passage has been noted by previous scholars.[23] Two relatively common roots are used here, but this does not lessen the overall effect. The first relevant word is נָחָם *naham* '(God did not) lead them', from the root נ־ח־ה *n-ḥ-h* 'lead'; while the second one is יִנָּחֵם *yinnaḥem* '(lest the people) regret', from the root נ־ח־ם *n-ḥ-m* 'regret, change one's mind'. The resemblance of sound is made even more complete by the addition of the third masc. pl. pronominal suffix -*am* on the former, creating the form נָחָם *naham* 'lead them', with the same three consonants as the root of the verb נ־ח־ם *n-ḥ-m* 'regret, change one's mind'.[24]

---

22. See, e.g., KB, 438, and *HALOT*, 477. This holds for both passages, ours and the one in Gen 18:21. The emendations proposed, however, typically deal with the vowels only, in which case the alliteration still would be present. For a brief survey of proposed emendations, see Propp, *Exodus 1–18*, 342.

23. E.g., Cassuto, *Commentary on the Book of Exodus*, 156, and Fox, *Five Books of Moses*, 327.

24. In this case, moreover, the phonetic likeness is exact, since the *ḥet* in each case represents /ḥ/—cf. Arabic *naḥa* 'go, walk, wend one's way'; and the Ugaritic personal names *mnḥm* and *ynḥm*, both widely attested.

In addition, note the presence of the noun מִלְחָמָה *milḥama* 'war' in the verse, which enhances the alliteration.[25] The *lamed* in this word corresponds to the *nun* in the two verbal roots: as noted earlier, liquids and nasals share similar phonetic characteristics.

16. Exodus 16:29–35

הַשַּׁבָּת	*haš-šabbat* 'the Sabbath' (v. 29)
וַיִּשְׁבְּתוּ	*wayyišbətu* 'they rested' (v. 30)
דְּבָשׁ	*dəbaš* 'honey' (v. 31)
מִשְׁמֶרֶת	*mišmɛrɛt* 'preserve' (3x: vv. 32–34)
צִנְצֶנֶת	*ṣinṣɛnɛt* 'jar' (v. 33)
אֶרֶץ נוֹשָׁבֶת	*ʾɛreṣ nošabɛt* 'inhabitable land' (v. 35)

In this instance I do not produce a verse or several verses, but rather simply list the alliterative words that cluster in Exod 16:29–35—with at least one word in each verse. The trigger for this discussion is the unique expression in v. 35: אֶרֶץ נוֹשָׁבֶת *ʾɛreṣ nošabɛt* 'inhabitable land'. While the closest alliterative words come at some distance, five and six verses earlier, I nevertheless believe that the presence of הַשַּׁבָּת *haš-šabbat* 'the Sabbath' in v. 29 and וַיִּשְׁבְּתוּ *wayyišbətu* 'and they rested' in v. 30 explains the author's employment of the above phrase in v. 35. Note, moreover, that given the choice of the morphological variants נוֹשָׁבֶת *nošabɛt* and נוֹשָׁבָה *nošaba*, both of which mean 'inhabitable' (for the latter see Jer 6:8, in a similar expression), the author chose the former because of the presence of the /t/ *taw*, thus completing the alliteration with the root שׁ-ב-ת *š-b-t* 'rest' (verb), 'Sabbath' (noun), appearing in vv. 29–30.

Bridging the long range of these like-sounding words are several other words with less-than-perfect alliteration that nonetheless serve to augment the auditory effect. I refer here to the following items: the common noun דְּבָשׁ *dəbaš* 'honey' in v. 31; the noun מִשְׁמֶרֶת *mišmɛrɛt*

---

25. Once more the *ḥet* here represents the phoneme /ḫ/—cf. Ugaritic *mlḫmt*, Arabic *malḫama*, etc.

'preserve' (in this context) in vv. 32–34 (3x, once in each verse); and the *hapax legomenon* צִנְצֶנֶת *ṣinṣenet* 'jar' in v. 33. Note the following sound links. דְבָשׁ *dəbaš* is comprised of two of the same consonants as the root שׁ-ב-ת *š-b-t* and the form נוֹשֶׁבֶת *nošabet*, while the third one, the /d/ *dalet*, is the voiced counterpart of the voiceless dental /t/ *taw*. מִשְׁמֶרֶת *mišmeret* has the /š/ *šin* and the /t/ *taw* of our original two words, while the third key consonant is the twice-heard /m/ *mem*, a labial with phonetic similarities to /b/ *bet*. And finally, צִנְצֶנֶת *ṣinṣenet* has /n/ *nun* and /t/ *taw*, as in נוֹשֶׁבֶת *nošabet*, along with the emphatic sibilant /ṣ/ *ṣade*, which has at least some minimal correspondence to /š/ *šin*. The overall result is a string of words, two of them unusual (נוֹשֶׁבֶת *nošabet* and צִנְצֶנֶת *ṣinṣenet*), with alliteration throughout.

Finally, we may note the presence of assonance in three of the words discussed here, specifically those that occur at the end of this section, in vv. 32–35: מִשְׁמֶרֶת *mišmeret* (2x), מִשְׁמָרֶת *mišmaret* (1x), צִנְצֶנֶת *ṣinṣenet*, and נוֹשֶׁבֶת *nošabet*. Three of the five occurrences are in the standard form, while two of them appear in pause, though during the Iron Age the ending on all of these words would have been exactly the same, most likely closest to the pausal forms, viz., -*aCt* (without anaptyxis) or -*aCet* (with anaptyxis).[26]

17. Exodus 19:20–24

20 וַיֵּרֶד יְהוָה עַל־הַר סִינַי אֶל־רֹאשׁ הָהָר וַיִּקְרָא יְהוָה לְמֹשֶׁה אֶל־רֹאשׁ
הָהָר וַיַּעַל מֹשֶׁה:

21 וַיֹּאמֶר יְהוָה אֶל־מֹשֶׁה רֵד הָעֵד בָּעָם פֶּן־יֶהֶרְסוּ אֶל־יְהוָה לִרְאוֹת
וְנָפַל מִמֶּנּוּ רָב:

22 וְגַם הַכֹּהֲנִים הַנִּגָּשִׁים אֶל־יְהוָה יִתְקַדָּשׁוּ פֶּן־יִפְרֹץ בָּהֶם יְהוָה:

23 וַיֹּאמֶר מֹשֶׁה אֶל־יְהוָה לֹא־יוּכַל הָעָם לַעֲלֹת אֶל־הַר סִינָי כִּי־אַתָּה
הַעֵדֹתָה בָּנוּ לֵאמֹר הַגְבֵּל אֶת־הָהָר וְקִדַּשְׁתּוֹ:

24 וַיֹּאמֶר אֵלָיו יְהוָה לֶךְ־רֵד וְעָלִיתָ אַתָּה וְאַהֲרֹן עִמָּךְ וְהַכֹּהֲנִים וְהָעָם
אַל־יֶהֶרְסוּ לַעֲלֹת אֶל־יְהוָה פֶּן־יִפְרָץ־בָּם:

---

26. In these transcriptions, C = consonant, that is, the consonant immediately preceding the final /t/ *taw*. The term anaptyxis refers to the helping vowel /ε/ inserted between the /C/ and the /t/.

²⁰ And YHWH went-down upon Mount Sinai to the summit
of the mountain; and YHWH called to Moses to the summit of
the mountain, and Moses went-up.
²¹ And YHWH said to Moses, "Go-down, exhort the people,
lest they penetrate unto YHWH, to see, and many among
them shall fall.
²² And also the priests who approach unto YHWH shall sanc-
tify themselves, lest YHWH break-forth upon them."
²³ And Moses said to YHWH, "The people are not able to
go-up onto Mount Sinai, because you exhorted us, saying,
'Set-bounds (around) the mountain and sanctify it'."
²⁴ And YHWH said to him, "Go, go-down, and you shall
go-up, and Aaron with you; and the priests and the people,
let them not penetrate to go-up unto YHWH, lest he break-
forth upon them."

In v. 21 the following expression occurs: פֶּן־יֶהֶרְסוּ אֶל־יְהוָה לִרְאוֹת *pɛn
yɛhɛrsu ʾɛl* YHWH *lirʾot* 'lest they penetrate unto YHWH, to see'. A similar
expression occurs in v. 24: אַל־יֶהֶרְסוּ לַעֲלֹת אֶל־יְהוָה *ʾal yɛhɛrsu laʿalot
ʾɛl* YHWH 'let them not penetrate to go-up unto YHWH'. Normally the
root ה-ר-ס *h-r-s* means 'destroy', though that connotation would be
a bit too strong for these passages. Accordingly, translators and in-
terpreters prefer a slightly milder nuance, such as 'penetrate, break
through'.²⁷ This meaning is further suggested by the twice-stated threat
that should the people penetrate, then God will break forth at them,
in a form of tit-for-tat: פֶּן־יִפְרֹץ בָּהֶם יְהוָה *pɛn yiproṣ bahɛm* YHWH 'lest
YHWH break-forth upon them' (v. 22); פֶּן־יִפְרָץ־בָּם *pɛn yiproṣ bam* 'lest
he break-forth upon them' (v. 24).

Given the uniqueness of this usage of the root ה-ר-ס *h-r-s*, in line
with our approach in this book we are entitled to ask: Why did the
author select this verb in this context? The answer to this question
is readily forthcoming from the presence of the key toponym הַר סִינַי
har sinay 'Mount Sinai', occurring in vv. 20 and 23 (as well as in vv. 11

---

27. 'Break through' is used by RSV; NJPS; and Fox, *Five Books of Moses*,
367, 369. I have elected to use 'penetrate', to distinguish the usage more clearly
from the root פ-ר-ץ *p-r-ṣ* 'break-forth'.

and 18 earlier). Note how the root ה-ר-ס *h-r-s* appears in the toponym, bridging the two-word construct phrase.

While we are focused on these verses, we also take the opportunity to note in passing the variations that occur, most visibly with the two expressions פֶּן־יֶהֶרְסוּ *pɛn yɛhɛrsu* 'lest they penetrate' (v. 21) and אַל־יֶהֶרְסוּ *'al yɛhɛrsu* 'let them not penetrate' (v. 24), though with other phrases as well. A more detailed discussion may be found in Chapter 9, no. 7, within the treatment of repetition with variation in prose narratives.

18. Exodus 32:12–17

בְּרָעָה	*bə-ra'a*	'with evil' (v. 12)
הָרָעָה	*ha-ra'a*	'the evil' (v. 12)
אַרְבֶּה	*'arbɛ*	'I will multiply' (v. 13)
זַרְעֲכֶם	*zar'akɛm*	'your seed' (v. 13)
הָרָעָה	*ha-ra'a*	'the evil' (v. 14)
עֶבְרֵיהֶם	*'ɛbrehɛm*	'their (two) sides' (v. 15)
בְּרֵעֹה	*bə-re'o*	'in its [sc. the people's] shouting' (v. 17)

These verses contain a cluster of words with the same or similar sounds, as listed above. The consonantal trio /b/ *bet* – /r/ *reš* – /ʿ/ *ʿayin* forms the basis for the alliteration, as seen in the first, sixth, and seventh of these words. Three others (the second, fourth, and fifth) include the /r/ *reš* and /ʿ/ *ʿayin* elements; while the remaining one (the third) includes the /r/ *reš* and /b/ *bet* sounds.

Included in this string of lexemes are two unusual items. First, the word עֶבְרֵיהֶם *'ɛbrehɛm* 'their (two) sides' (v. 15), with reference to the two sides of the two tablets of the Decalogue, presents a usage that occurs only here in the Bible[28] (and indeed this is the only passage in the Bible that comments on this feature of the tablets).[29] Second, the noun רֵעַ 'shouting' (v. 17), within the form בְּרֵעֹה *bə-re'o* 'in its [i.e., the people's]

---

28. Note BDB, 719: "even מִשְּׁנֵי עֶבְרֵיהֶם Ex 32¹⁵ (E) *on their two sides* (i.e. of tablets)," with the word "even" highlighting the unusual nature of this usage.

29. As noted by R. Alan Cole, *Exodus* (London: Tyndale House, 1973), 218.

shouting', appears in only two other places in the Bible (Mic 4:9, Job 36:33), though admittedly the verbal root ר-ו-ע *r-w-ᶜ* 'roar, shout' occurs more commonly.[30]

One also may note the orthography of this last item, with the archaic spelling ה- for the third masc. sg. pronominal suffix (normally one expects ו-), thus permitting ברעה 'with evil' (v. 12) and ברעה 'in its shouting' (v. 17) to look exactly alike.[31]

19. Exodus 32:22–27

בְרָע	*bə-raᶜ*	'in evil' (v. 22)
הִתְפָּרְקוּ	*hitparaqu*	'break off' (v. 24)
פָּרֻעַ	*paruaᶜ*	'wild' (v. 25)
פְרָעֹה	*pəraᶜo*	'let them (lit., him) be wild' (v. 25)
שַׁעַר	*šaᶜar*	'gate' (3x: vv. 26–27)
חַרְבּוֹ	*ḥarbo*	'his sword' (v. 27)
עִבְרוּ	*ᶜibru*	'pass' (v. 27)
רֵעֵהוּ	*reᶜehu*	'his friend' (v. 27)
קְרֹבוֹ	*qərobo*	'his kinsman' (v. 27)

A second, related cluster of words, listed above, appears later in the same chapter.[32] As in the previous example, we may begin with /b/

---

30. Unfortunately, we are unable to determine the exact phoneme that lies behind the grapheme ᶜ*ayin* in the roots ר-ע-ע *r-ᶜ-ᶜ* 'be evil' and ר-ו-ע *r-w-ᶜ* 'roar, shout', for lack of cognates in Arabic and Ugaritic (some have been proposed [see the lexica], but they are not convincing). The first root letter of ע-ב-ר *ᶜ-b-r* 'pass, cross' (as in עָבְרֵיהֶם *ᶜɛbrehɛm* 'their sides') is the pharyngeal fricative /ᶜ/ (cf. Ugaritic ᶜ*rb*), but this piece of information serves us little without the additional information. Regardless, all these words would have alliterated with one another.

31. As noted already by Cassuto, *Commentary on the Book of Exodus*, 418. I intentionally omit the vowel signs and accent marks here, in order to have the two words appear as they would in a pre-Masoretic manuscript (or, for that matter, in a Torah scroll unto the present day).

32. As noted already by Cassuto, *Commentary on the Book of Exodus*, 421.

bet – /r/ *reš* – /ʿ/ *ʿayin* as the consonantal basis for this alliteration, thus: בְּרָע *bə-raʿ* 'in evil' (v. 22) and עָבְרוּ *ʿibru* 'pass' (v. 27). The slight change from voiced /b/ to voiceless /p/ allows the twofold use of the root פ-ר-ע *p-r-ʿ* 'be wild' (third and fourth items above) to alliterate. A similar slight change from one pharyngeal fricative to another (/ʿ/ to /ḥ/) permits חַרְבּוֹ *ḥarbo* 'his sword' (v. 27) to serve.[33] The /r/ *reš* – /ʿ/ *ʿayin* combination is present in the words שַׁעַר *šaʿar* 'gate' (3x: vv. 26–27) and רֵעֵהוּ *reʿehu* 'his friend' (v. 27). Building from the root פ-ר-ע *p-r-ʿ* 'be wild' is the root פ-ר-ק *p-r-q* in the form הִתְפָּרְקוּ *hitparaqu* 'break off' (v. 24). And finally, the shift back from voiceless /p/ in this root to voiced /b/ produces the form קְרֹבוֹ *qərobo* 'his kinsman' (v. 27).[34]

As in the previous example, so here we may point to some atypical usages. First, the expression בְּשַׁעַר הַמַּחֲנֶה 'at the gate of the camp' in v. 26 (see also v. 27) is most striking, for naturally a camp does not have a proper gate. The only parallel is 2 Chr 31:2, where בְּשַׁעֲרֵי מַחֲנוֹת יְהוָה 'at the gates of the camps of Yhwh' is used metaphorically, since the setting is the Temple, a structure with actual gates.

Second, we may note the unique string אִישׁ־אֶת־אָחִיו וְאִישׁ אֶת־רֵעֵהוּ וְאִישׁ אֶת־קְרֹבוֹ *ʾiš ʾet ʾaḥiw wə-ʾiš ʾet reʿehu wə-ʾiš ʾet qərobo* 'each-man his brother, and each-man his friend, and each-man his kinsman' in v. 27. Obviously, only one of these three expressions is needed. Indeed, in only two other passages in the Bible do we find two of the phrases side by side: Jer 23:35 אִישׁ עַל־רֵעֵהוּ וְאִישׁ אֶל־אָחִיו *ʾiš ʿal reʿehu wə-ʾiš ʾel ʾaḥiw* 'each-man to his friend, and each-man to his brother', and Jer 31:34 אִישׁ אֶת־רֵעֵהוּ וְאִישׁ אֶת־אָחִיו *ʾiš ʾet reʿehu wə-ʾiš ʾet ʾaḥiw* 'each-man his friend, and each-man his brother'.[35] Thus, this is the only case in the Bible of the

---

33. Cf. Ugaritic *ḥrb*.

34. Once more we have only partial evidence concerning the phonemes that lie behind the grapheme *ʿayin* in these words. The Ugaritic cognates *ʿrb* and *ṯǵr* reveal a pharyngeal fricative in ע-ב-ר *ʿ-b-r* 'pass' and a velar fricative in שַׁעַר *šaʿar* 'gate'. We do not possess reliable evidence for the roots ר-ע-ע *ʿ-ʿ-r* 'be evil' and פ-ר-ע *p-r-ʿ* 'be wild' (though again the lexica suggest some [to my mind, unconvincing] possibilities). Once more, however, regardless of the precise pronunciation of all these words, their sounds were sufficiently proximate to produce the alliterative effect.

35. On the interchange of the prepositions אל *ʾel* and על *ʿal* in the former passage, which is relatively common in the book of Jeremiah, see the discussion in Rendsburg, *Israelian Hebrew in the Book of Kings*, 32–36.

threefold chain. In addition, this is the only attestation of the expression אִישׁ אֶת־קְרֹבוֹ ʾiš ʾet qərobo 'each-man his kinsman' in the canon.

These two usages, I submit, were introduced into the text by our author in order to enhance the oral-aural effect of the interlocking series of consonantal sounds that infuse the entire chapter.

20. Exodus 36:6

וַיְצַו מֹשֶׁה וַיַּעֲבִירוּ קוֹל בַּמַּחֲנֶה לֵאמֹר אִישׁ וְאִשָּׁה אַל־יַעֲשׂוּ־עוֹד
מְלָאכָה לִתְרוּמַת הַקֹּדֶשׁ וַיִּכָּלֵא הָעָם מֵהָבִיא:

And Moses commanded, and they passed the voice through
the camp, saying, "Neither man nor woman should do any
more labor for the benefaction of the Holy-Place"; and the
people were restrained from bringing.

My final example occurs in a brief narrative embedded within the Tabernacle account. The expression וַיִּכָּלֵא הָעָם מֵהָבִיא wayyikkaleʾ haʿam me-habiʾ 'and the people were restrained from bringing' occurs within the greatest concentration of the use of the word מְלָאכָה məlaʾka 'work, labor' in the Bible (13x within the fourteen verses of the pericope of Exodus 35:30–36:8, three of which surround the above expression in exceedingly close proximity). At first glance, there is nothing exceptional about either of these words; and thus, on the one hand, we may simply observe that the roots כ-ל-א k-l-ʾ 'restrain' and ל-א-ך l-ʾ-k 'be on a mission' (from which מְלָאכָה məlaʾka 'work, labor' is derived) are anagrams of each other, and leave it at that.

On the other hand, two additional points may be raised. First, the author of Exod 36:6 could have selected another verbal root with the same or similar meaning, for example, ח-שׂ-ך ḥ-ś-k 'withhold' (see 2 Sam 18:16) or ע-צ-ר ʿ-ṣ-r 'stop, constrain' (see Judg 13:15, 1 Sam 21:8). It also may be significant that this is one of only three cases of the root כ-ל-א k-l-ʾ 'restrain' in the Niphʿal, and that the other two refer to the restraining of water (Gen 8:2, Ezek 31:15). This is, therefore, the only instance of כ-ל-א k-l-ʾ 'restrain' in the Niphʿal where people are restrained.[36] Second, in at least the first occurrence of מְלָאכָה məlaʾka

---

36. Though admittedly examples in the Qal can be cited, e.g., Gen 23:6 (with the byform כ-ל-ה k-l-h).

in v. 7, and possibly in the instance in v. 6 as well, the meaning of this common word has been extended from its usual sense of 'work, labor, handiwork, craftsmanship' to the unusual sense of 'stuff, wares, items'.[37] After all, if the people are to stop bringing (see the last word of v. 6), the word cannot carry the connotation 'work, labor, etc.', but rather must refer to specific items (I, for one, enjoy the translation 'stuff' used by KJV and RSV). All of which is to say, by selecting the root כ-ל-א *k-l-ʾ* 'restrain' and by extending the meaning of מְלָאכָה *mala'ka* 'work, labor', the author of this passage made specific lexical choices, thereby pushing the limits of his language *alliterationis causa*.

---

37. Biblical commentators who have noted the usage include Cassuto, *Commentary on the Book of Exodus*, 461, and Alter, *Five Books of Moses*, 519. For several other examples in Biblical Hebrew, see KB, 527, and *HALOT*, 586.

CHAPTER SEVEN

MICAH 1: THE CASE FOR ALLITERATION

By this point, the reader of this book rightly may ask: Did listeners to the text in ancient Israel really grasp all this? Did authors really have alliteration in mind when they composed their texts? Are these sound connections real? Or are we simply reading too much into these passages?

After two chapters on alliteration (one on Genesis, one on Exodus), the reader will gather that I would answer the first three questions in the affirmative and only the last one in the negative. Fortunately, the Bible includes a passage that allows us to judge the matter on internal grounds. I refer to Mic 1:10–15, in which the prophet plays upon eleven place names (my own alliteration here intentional?)—evoking the sounds of the toponyms with his lexical choices at every turn. Sometimes the aural nexus is close, sometimes it is less proximate—but in all cases the alliteration is present.

10 בְּגַת אַל־תַּגִּידוּ בָּכוֹ אַל־תִּבְכּוּ בְּבֵית לְעַפְרָה עָפָר [התפלשתי]
הִתְפַּלָּשִׁי*׃

11 עִבְרִי לָכֶם יוֹשֶׁבֶת שָׁפִיר עֶרְיָה־בֹשֶׁת
לֹא יָצְאָה יוֹשֶׁבֶת צַאֲנָן מִסְפַּד בֵּית הָאֵצֶל יִקַּח מִכֶּם עֶמְדָּתוֹ׃

12 כִּי־חָלָה לְטוֹב יוֹשֶׁבֶת מָרוֹת כִּי־יָרַד רָע מֵאֵת יְהֹוָה לְשַׁעַר יְרוּשָׁלָ͏ִם׃

13 רְתֹם הַמֶּרְכָּבָה לָרֶכֶשׁ יוֹשֶׁבֶת לָכִישׁ
רֵאשִׁית חַטָּאת הִיא לְבַת־צִיּוֹן כִּי־בָךְ נִמְצְאוּ פִּשְׁעֵי יִשְׂרָאֵל׃

14 לָכֵן תִּתְּנִי שִׁלּוּחִים עַל מוֹרֶשֶׁת גַּת בָּתֵּי אַכְזִיב לְאַכְזָב לְמַלְכֵי
יִשְׂרָאֵל׃

15 עֹד הַיֹּרֵשׁ אָבִי לָךְ יוֹשֶׁבֶת מָרֵשָׁה עַד־עֲדֻלָּם יָבוֹא כְּבוֹד יִשְׂרָאֵל׃

v. 10a (Gath):

בְּגַת / תַּגִּידוּ   *bə-gat / taggidu*

v. 10b (Beth-leaphrah):

בְּבֵית לְעַפְרָה / עָפָר   *bə-bet lə-ʿapra / ʿapar*

v. 11a (Shaphir):

שָׁפִיר / בֹשֶׁת   *šapir / bošɛt*

v. 11b (Zaanan, Beth-ezel):

צַאֲנָן / הָאֵצֶל / לֹא יָצְאָה   *ṣaʾanan / ha-ʾeṣɛl / loʾ yaṣʾa*

v. 12a (Maroth):

מָרוֹת / לְטוֹב / רְתֹם [v. 13a]   *marot / lə-ṭob / rətom* [v. 13a]

v. 13a (Lachish):

לָכִישׁ / לָרֶכֶשׁ   *lakiš / la-rɛkɛš*

v. 14a (Moresheth-gath):

מוֹרֶשֶׁת גַּת / שִׁלּוּחִים   *morɛšɛt gat / šilluḥim*

v. 14b (Achzib):

אַכְזִיב / לְאַכְזָב   *ʾakzib / lə-ʾakzab*

v. 15a (Mareshah):

מָרֵשָׁה / הַיֹּרֵשׁ   *mareša / hay-yoreš*

v. 15b (Adullam):

עֲדֻלָּם / עַד   *ʿadullam / ʿad*

(There appear to be no alliterations for Jerusalem/Zion in vv. 12b, 13b. While this could be a coincidence, more likely the prophet did not feel the need to produce soundplay, given the city's fundamental role in the culture of ancient Judah.)

> [10] Tell it not in Gath, weep not at all; in Beth-leaphrah roll yourselves in the dust.
> [11] Pass on your way, inhabitants of Shaphir, (in) naked-ness (and) shame; the inhabitants of Zaanan do not come forth; the wailing of Beth-ezel shall take away from you its standing-place.
> [12] For the inhabitants of Maroth wait anxiously for good, because evil has come down from Y HWH to the gate of Jerusalem.
> [13] Harness the chariot to the steeds, inhabitants of Lachish; she is the beginning of sin to the daughter of Zion, for in you were found the transgressions of Israel.
> [14] Therefore you shall give parting-gifts to Moresheth-gath; the houses of Achzib shall be a deceitful-thing to the kings of Israel.
> [15] I will again bring the dispossessor upon you, inhabitants of Mareshah; unto Adullam shall come the glory of Israel.

(1) v. 10a:

$$בְּגַת אַל־תַּגִּידוּ \quad \textit{bə-gat 'al taggidu}$$
tell it not in Gath

The consonants of the city name גַּת *gat* 'Gath' are echoed in the following verb תַּגִּידוּ *taggidu* 'tell', with /g/ repeated and with /t/ and /d/, the voiceless and voiced dental plosives, corresponding.

(2) v. 10b:

$$בְּבֵית לְעַפְרָה עָפָר \quad \textit{bə-bet lə-ʿapra ʿapar}$$
in Beth-leaphrah . . . dust

The city name בֵּית לְעַפְרָה *bet lə-ʿapra* 'Beth-leaphrah' occurs only here in the Bible. Regardless of its actual connotation, the author of Micah 1 relates the toponym to the word עָפָר *ʿapar* 'dust', with the same three consonants.

(3) v. 11a:

שָׁפִיר . . . בֹּשֶׁת   *šapir . . . bošɛt*
Shapir . . . shame

Compared to the first two examples, in this instance the correspondence of sounds is more discreet—and yet the author apparently considered the match to suffice for his purposes. The city name שָׁפִיר *šapir* 'Shapir' and the following noun בֹּשֶׁת *bošɛt* 'shame' share only one consonant, namely, /š/, though we also observe the tally between the voiceless labial plosive /p/ and its voiced counterpart /b/. Note that the respective third consonants, /r/ and /t/, do not correspond, and yet in the ears of an ancient Israelite the alliteration was present nonetheless.

(4) v. 11b:

לֹא יָצְאָה / צַאֲנָן / בֵּית הָאֵצֶל   *loʾ yaṣʾa / ṣaʾanan / bet ha-ʾeṣɛl*
do not come forth / Zaanan /
Beth-ezel

Two toponyms occur here, צַאֲנָן *ṣaʾanan* 'Zaanan' and בֵּית הָאֵצֶל *bet ha-ʾeṣɛl* 'Beth-ezel' (neither of them known from elsewhere). The two forms share /ʾ/ and /ṣ/, plus we note the soundplay created by the two liquids /n/ (in the former) and /l/ (in the latter). The prophet anticipates these consonants by beginning the clause with לֹא יָצְאָה *loʾ yaṣʾa* 'do not come forth', with /l/, /ṣ/, and /ʾ/ present.

(5) v. 12a:

לְטוֹב . . . מָרוֹת   *lə-ṭob . . . marot*
for good . . . Maroth

Once more we encounter a toponym, מָרוֹת *marot* 'Maroth', known only from Micah 1. Its corresponding term לְטוֹב *lə-ṭob* 'for good' shares not a single exact consonant, and yet the match works well. Note the aural association afforded by /m/ and /b/ (labials), /r/ and /l/ (liquids), and /t/ and /ṭ/ (dentals). Assonance also plays a role in this case, with the long /o:/ vowel assisting. In this case, moreover, the author carried the alliteration (and the assonance) into the next verse, which begins with רְתֹם *rətom* 'harness' (v. 13a), comprised of /r/, /t/, long /o:/, and /m/.

(6) v. 13a:

לָרֶכֶשׁ . . . לָכִישׁ   *la-rɛkɛš . . . lakiš*
                             to the steeds . . . Lachish

לָכִישׁ *lakiš* 'Lachish' was the second-largest city in Judah; the sounds
of its name are adumbrated by the rare word רֶכֶשׁ *rɛkɛš* 'steeds' (a
collective noun that occurs elsewhere only in 1 Kgs 5:8 and Esth 8:10,
8:14), to which has been prefixed the preposition plus definite article
combination -לְ *la-* 'to the'. The aural effect is obvious.

(7) v. 14a:

שִׁלּוּחִים . . . מוֹרֶשֶׁת   *šilluḥim . . . morɛšɛt*
                               parting-gifts . . . Moresheth

Again the alliteration is not overt, though closer inspection reveals at
least a minor aural nexus. The sounds of the name of Micah's home-
town (see Mic 1:1), מוֹרֶשֶׁת *morɛšɛt* 'Moresheth', are anticipated by the
rare noun שִׁלּוּחִים *šilluḥim* 'parting-gifts' (elsewhere only in 1 Kgs 9:16,
with the connotation 'dowry'). Both forms have /m/ and /š/, with the
liquids /r/ and /l/ providing support.

(8) v. 14b:

אַכְזִיב לְאַכְזָב   *ʾakzib lə-ʾakzab*
                      Achzib shall be a
                      deceitful-thing

The connection is so obvious here, no further comment is necessary.

(9) v. 15a:

הַיֹּרֵשׁ . . . מָרֵשָׁה   *hay-yoreš . . . mareša*
                             the dispossessor . . . Mareshah

Two of the consonantal sounds of the city name מָרֵשָׁה *mareša*
'Mareshah' occur earlier in the verse in the noun הַיֹּרֵשׁ *hay-yoreš* 'the
dispossessor'. Once more we note that the respective third consonants,
/m/ and /y/ in this case, lack phonetic similarity, and yet in the ears of
an ancient Israelite the alliteration was operative nevertheless.

(10) v. 15b:

עַד־עֲדֻלָּם   *ʿad ʿadullam*
unto Adullam

Only two of the four consonants in the place name עֲדֻלָּם *ʿadullam* 'Adullam' are anticipated in the preposition עַד *ʿad* 'unto, until', though even this rather minor effort suffices to achieve the desired auditory effect.

As stated at the outset of this chapter, the ten alliterative wordplays produced by the prophet Micah provide sufficient evidence to enable us, as modern readers, to apprehend how the ancient Israelite listener processed the aural effect inherent in the orally performed literature.

CHAPTER EIGHT

CONFUSED LANGUAGE

We will return later to the two key building blocks of biblical literature canvassed up to this point—namely, (a) repetition with variation and (b) alliteration—but at this juncture I wish to shift gears to introduce another device employed by the ancient Israelite literati. I refer to the use of confused language as a deliberate literary device, invoked by the authors to portray confusion, excitement, or bewilderment.[1]

Before turning to the Bible, however, we direct our attention to a paradigm example of confused language that appears in the ancient Egyptian tale known as The Shipwrecked Sailor. This composition imposes few difficulties on its readers: Our only extant manuscript is in excellent condition, hardly a sign is in doubt, and the reading is smooth.[2] The main exception to the smooth reading is lines 36–37 (repeated in lines 105–106): *in ḫt ḥwi n-i s(y)*, lit., 'by wood, struck, to me, it'. This line occurs in the Sailor's description of his adventures, first to his Commanding Officer (lines 36–37) and then to the Snake (lines 105–106), with specific reference to the shipwreck itself.

---

1. This chapter is based on two earlier articles: Gary A. Rendsburg, "Confused Language as a Deliberate Literary Device in Biblical Hebrew Narrative," *Journal of Hebrew Scriptures*, vol. 2, article 6 (1998–1999), on the Web at http://www.arts.ualberta.ca/JHS/ [reprinted in: Ehud Ben Zvi, ed., *Perspectives on Hebrew Scriptures I* (Perspectives on Hebrew Scriptures and Its Contexts 1; Piscataway, NJ: Gorgias, 2006), 197–213]; and Gary A. Rendsburg, "Lašon Mebulbelet ke-Takhsis Sifruti ba-Sippur ha-Miqra'i," in Shmuel Vargon et al., eds., *Menaḥot, Yedidut, ve-Hoqra le-Moshe Garsiel* (Ramat-Gan: Bar-Ilan University Press, 2009) = *'Iyyune Miqra' u-Paršanut* 9 (5769), 27–43.

2. The standard edition is A. M. Blackman, *Middle-Egyptian Stories* (Bibliotheca Aegyptiaca 2; Brussels: Édition de la Fondation Égyptologique Reine Élisabeth, 1932), 41–48.

The syntax is so confusing that scholar after scholar has deemed the phrase too difficult to render with any certainty.[3] Here is a sampling: Adolf Erman: 'It was a piece of wood that . . . it to me', with a footnote "The whole account of the storm is unintelligible to us."[4] William Kelly Simpson: 'There was a plank which struck it (the wave) for me', with a footnote "This passage difficult in the original."[5] Miriam Lichtheim: 'The mast—it (the wave) struck (it)', with a long footnote justifying her rendering and an honest statement that "this admittedly imperfect solution is presented largely in order to emphasize that the passage remains problematic."[6] Richard B. Parkinson: 'Only the mast broke it for me', with a footnote "An obscure phrase: *it* is probably the wave, so that the sense is that the mast sheltered the sailor from the storm."[7] Note further the difficulty and uncertainty reflected in the Hebrew translation of Yehoshua M. Grintz, with two different renderings: עץ (?) נאחזתי for lines 36–37 and נאחזתי בו . . . -עץ for lines 105–106, even though the Egyptian original is the same in both places.[8]

But the difficulty and unintelligibility of this passage are precisely the point.[9] I propose that we view these words from the mouth of the Sailor as a clever literary device in which confused syntax is utilized to portray the confusion that characterized the moment. A ship is in danger at sea, the wind is howling, and an eight-foot wave (see line 36 [= 105]) strikes the ship (by this statement I do not mean to imply

---

3. For detailed discussion, see Hans Goedicke, *Die Geschichte des Schiff-brüchigen* (Wiesbaden: Harrassowitz, 1974), 21–22.

4. Adolf Erman, *The Ancient Egyptians: A Sourcebook of Their Writings*, trans. A. M. Blackman (New York: Harper & Row, 1966; German original 1923, first English edition 1927), 30 and n. 5.

5. William Kelly Simpson, *The Literature of Ancient Egypt* (New Haven: Yale University Press, 1972), 52 and n. 6.

6. Miriam Lichtheim, *Ancient Egyptian Literature* (Berkeley: University of California Press, 1973), 1:212 (translation) and 215 n. 1 (comment).

7. Richard B. Parkinson, *The Tale of Sinuhe and Other Ancient Egyptian Poems 1940–1640 BC* (Oxford: Clarendon, 1997), 93 and 98 n. 6.

8. Yehoshua M. Grintz, *Mivḥar ha-Sifrut ha-Miṣrit ha-ʿAtiqa* (Tel Aviv: Devir, 1958), 5, 7.

9. For further discussion and for other stylistic devices in this text, see Gary A. Rendsburg, "Literary Devices in the Story of the Shipwrecked Sailor," *Journal of the American Oriental Society* 120 (2000): 13–23.

that I accept Lichtheim's rendering, others are equally possible). In the
very next sentence we read that 'the ship stood a death' (lines 37–38
[= 106]). What occurred between the great wave and the ship sinking
is one minute of mass confusion for the Sailor. The language bears this
out with its confused and irregular syntax.[10]

With this example in mind,[11] we now may turn to the Bible and see
the same technique in use in a variety of contexts. I begin with two
passages that have been discussed previously in the literature; the re-

---

10. This approach serves as a counter to the view of John Baines, "Interpreting the Story of the Shipwrecked Sailor," *Journal of Egyptian Archaeology*
76 (1990), 58 and n. 15: "The story's status as written literature, as against a
papyrus that records an oral composition, is demonstrated by textual cor-
ruptions that must have a written origin," with the footnote adding: "The
best example is the phrase *jn-ḥt ḥḥ n.j-s(w)* (36–7, 105–6), which occurs twice
but is not meaningful as it stands." I agree with Baines's conclusion that the
narrative is written literature (though I doubt very much whether an ancient
Egyptian or anyone in the ancient Near East would have understood the
modern scholarly distinction between written composition and oral composition), but I disagree with his presumption of scribal error in lines 36–37 (=
105–106) as evidence thereof.

11. For a second illustration from an ancient Near Eastern literary text, in
the Apology of Esarhaddon, see Hayim Tadmor, "Autobiographical Apology
in the Royal Assyrian Literature," in Hayim Tadmor and Moshe Weinfeld, eds.,
*History, Historiography and Interpretation: Studies in Biblical and Cuneiform
Literatures* (Jerusalem: Magnes, 1983), 40. In addition, see Nick C. Veldhuis,
"The Fly, the Worm, and the Chain: Old Babylonian Chain Incantations," *Orientalia Lovaniensia Periodica* 24 (1993): 41–64. Veldhuis dealt with a specific
literary genre, namely, incantation texts, but his statement about grammar is
applicable to all literature: "The rules of grammar are not laws of nature—the
existence of which, after all, is generally doubted. Ungrammaticality, or deviant
grammar, is often a mark in that it draws our attention to something special,
as readers of modern poetry well know. Therefore the object of our interest
must be the deviation as well as the rule" (p. 46). My kind thanks to Scott
Noegel for this reference. As the late Victor Avigdor Hurowitz reminded me
(oral communication), one interpretation of the confused language in lines
2–3 of the Meṣad Ḥashavyahu inscription entails understanding these words
as representing the emotional status of the petitioner. Thus already Joseph
Naveh in the *editio princeps*: "A Hebrew Letter from the Seventh Century
B.C.," *Israel Exploration Journal* 10 (1960): 131–32. Note that Naveh cited Gen
37:30, one of the biblical texts that we will consider below, as a parallel. For
general treatment of this inscription, see Ahituv, *Echoes from the Past*, 156–63.

mainder (presented in the order of their appearance in the canon) have occasioned comment by scholars, but typically the approach has been to assume that the text is in error and in need of correction. In some cases, the confused language appears in the speech of the characters (see nos. 1, 2, 3, 5, 10), while in other cases the muddled words occur within the third-person narration (see nos. 4, 6, 7, 8, 9). In all these instances, I propose that we view the confused language as a deliberate literary device invoked to portray confusion, excitement, or bewilderment. In the main, our focus is on narrative prose texts, though I also conclude the discussion with one illustration from poetry (no. 11), in which the difficult syntax reflects the message conveyed.

1. 1 Samuel 9:12–13 — the maidens answer Saul

In 1 Sam 9:10–11, Saul and his attendant, on the outskirts of Samuel's city, encounter a group of young maidens who have exited the city to draw water. They ask a simple, three-word question: הֲיֵשׁ בָּזֶה הָרֹאֶה *ha-yeš ba-ze ha-ro'ɛ* 'is the seer here?'—to which the girls respond with the rambling two verses as follows (vv. 12–13):

וַתַּעֲנֶינָה אוֹתָם וַתֹּאמַרְנָה יֵּשׁ הִנֵּה לְפָנֶיךָ מַהֵר | עַתָּה כִּי הַיּוֹם בָּא ^{12}
לָעִיר כִּי זֶבַח הַיּוֹם לָעָם בַּבָּמָה:

כְּבֹאֲכֶם הָעִיר כֵּן תִּמְצְאוּן אֹתוֹ בְּטֶרֶם יַעֲלֶה הַבָּמָתָה לֶאֱכֹל כִּי ^{13}
לֹא־יֹאכַל הָעָם עַד־בֹּאוֹ כִּי־הוּא יְבָרֵךְ הַזֶּבַח אַחֲרֵי־כֵן יֹאכְלוּ הַקְּרֻאִים
וְעַתָּה עֲלוּ כִּי־אֹתוֹ כְהַיּוֹם תִּמְצְאוּן אֹתוֹ:

I offer here an attempt at a translation:

> ^{12} And they answered them, and they said, "Yes, here before you; hurry now, because today he is coming to the city, because the sacrifice is today for the people at the high-place. ^{13} When you come to the city, thus you will find him, before he goes up to the high-place to eat, because the people cannot eat until he comes, because he must bless the sacrifice, afterward the invited-ones can eat; so now go up, because him, this very day you will find him."

Avi Hurvitz described the Hebrew of this passage in this way:

> Now if we judge the quality of the style employed in the pas-
> sage solely according to strict formal linguistic standards of
> grammar and syntax, we would undoubtedly conclude that
> this is deficient Hebrew. However, if we consider the peculiar
> circumstances of the episode, it becomes clear that the con-
> fused speech created here by the biblical writer is an attempt
> to reproduce the effect of the girls all talking at once in their
> excitement at meeting Saul. The confused style is thus a deliber-
> ate device intended to reflect the heroines' mood and feelings.[12]

Although Hurvitz developed the notion further, he was indebted to
a simple remark by Martin Buber, who referred to these verses as
"Mädchenschwatz."[13] In sum, in their excitement over seeing the tall,
handsome Saul, the girls prattle all at once, creating a cacophony of
voices represented by the language of the text.

2. Ruth 2:7 — the foreman answers Boaz

Ruth 2:7 is one of the famous cruces of the Bible. The foreman
reports to Boaz as follows: וַתָּבוֹא וַתַּעֲמוֹד מֵאָז הַבֹּקֶר וְעַד־עַתָּה זֶה שִׁבְתָּהּ
הַבַּיִת מְעָט: 'and she came, and she stood since the morning until now,
this, her sitting (in) the house, a little'. The last four Hebrew words
(which I have rendered here literally, as 'this, her sitting (in) the house,
a little') have engendered considerable discussion in the secondary

---

12. Avi Hurvitz, "Ruth 2:7—'A Midrashic Gloss'?" *Zeitschrift für die Alttestamentliche Wissenschaft* 95 (1983): 122.

13. Martin Buber, "Die Erzählung von Sauls Königswahl," *Vetus Testamentum* 6 (1956): 126. It appears that Jan P. Fokkelman, *Narrative Art and Poetry
in the Books of Samuel*, vol. 4, *Vow and Desire* (Assen: Van Gorcum, 1993), 387,
had Buber's specific comment in mind when he wrote, after attempting to
show some order to the chaos of these lines, that "these observations yield
enough material to prevent our labelling the contribution of the women 'chat-
ter'." Fokkelman did not cite Buber on this particular passage, but he cited
Buber's lengthy treatment of the Saul narrative in several other places (e.g.,
p. 383 n. 31).

literature.[14] Of the proposed solutions, the one that rises above the others, especially because it entails no emendation of the traditional text,[15] is once more that of Hurvitz. Indeed, it was his reading of Ruth 2:7 that led him to the aforecited discussion of 1 Sam 9:12–13. Once more I quote Hurvitz at length:

> We suggest, then, that a similar approach be adopted in the case of Ruth 2:7. Namely, here the overseer speaks in an apologetic and confused manner because he is not sure whether the 'boss' will approve of the fact that the overseer has given Ruth his permission to stay (שבתה—from ישב) *inside* the house reserved specifically for Boaz's workers. . . . [T]he overseer is emphasizing the fact that this (זה) Ruth's stay in 'the house' was very brief and that the whole day 'from early morning until now' (מאז הבוקר ועד עתה) she has remained [working] (ותעמד) *outside* in the field. If this interpretation is accepted, then the peculiar wording of Ruth 2:7 makes perfect sense in its context and need not be attributed to hypothetical scribal errors which occurred in the course of transmission. The awkward formulation of the overseer's words, then, should not be considered a textual corruption created by a *later copyist*, but, rather, an artistic device deliberately employed for dramatic purposes by the *original author* of Ruth.[16]

---

14. See Michael S. Moore, "Two Textual Anomalies in Ruth," *Catholic Biblical Quarterly* 59 (1997): 238–43, for a survey of opinions.

15. By traditional text, I mean the Masoretic Text with all its parts. Thus, e.g., Daniel Lys, "Résidence ou repos? Notule sur Ruth ii 7," *Vetus Testamentum* 21 (1971): 497–501, proposed a reading that ignored the accent marks; and D. R. G. Beattie, "A Midrashic Gloss in Ruth 2:7," *Zeitschrift für die Alttestamentliche Wissenschaft* 89 (1977): 122–24, proposed an interpretation based on a repointing of the vowels. Of course, other scholars have suggested more radical alterations, i.e., emendation of the consonantal text.

16. Hurvitz, "Ruth 2:7—'A Midrashic Gloss'?" 122–23. The last line, with the italicized words (in the original) for emphasis, speaks directly to the suggestion of Beattie, "A Midrashic Gloss in Ruth 2:7," that the phrase is a later addition to the original story.

3. Genesis 19:12 — who is in Lot's house?

The scene is well known: Two visitors (called אֲנָשִׁים *'anašim* 'men') are in Lot's house, and a rabble of townsmen outside the house requests that Lot surrender his guests so that they may have sexual relations with them. Lot refuses and instead offers his two virgin daughters, but the townsmen only press further, almost to the point of breaking the door (Gen 19:4–9). At this point, the visitors rescue Lot from the crowd and strike the townsmen with sudden blindness (סַנְוֵרִים *sanwerim*) (vv. 10–11). The text continues (v. 12):

וַיֹּאמְרוּ הָאֲנָשִׁים אֶל־לוֹט עֹד מִי־לְךָ פֹה חָתָן וּבָנֶיךָ וּבְנֹתֶיךָ וְכֹל אֲשֶׁר־
לְךָ בָּעִיר הוֹצֵא מִן־הַמָּקוֹם:

And the men said to Lot, "Who else is here with you? A son-in-law and your sons and your daughters, and all who are yours in the city—take-out from (this) place."

In the haste of the moment, the men/angels ask Lot who else is in the house. Their mention of 'your sons and your daughters' is perfectly understandable. Oddly, however, the men lead with חָתָן *hatan* 'son-in-law', when obviously 'sons and daughters' would be more expected and would rank more importantly. Moreover, the men do not say 'your son-in-law' but simply 'son-in-law' (or 'a son-in-law'; recall that Hebrew lacks an indefinite article).[17] While we do not know to what extent the visitors have canvassed Lot's family to know exactly who lives with him, or who among his relatives may reside elsewhere in the city, we may presume that at this point they know only of his two unmarried (indeed, virgin) daughters, whom Lot had offered to

---

17. The usage is so odd that some scholars simply omit the word in their translations! This includes, most uncharacteristically, Alter, *Five Books of Moses*, 93. For detailed discussion, see David Marcus, "How Many Daughters Did Lot Have?" in Shamir Yona, ed., *Or le-Mayer: Studies in Bible, Semitic Languages, Rabbinic Literature, and Ancient Civilizations Presented to Mayer Gruber on the Occasion of His Sixty-Fifth Birthday* (Beersheva: Ben-Gurion University of the Negev Press, 2010), 109*–20*. For other scholars who omit 'son-in-law' in Gen 19:12, along with the versional evidence, see 115* nn. 35–37.

the mob (v. 8)—assuming that the visitors were in earshot of this declaration. All of this, naturally, leads us to raise an eyebrow, when the men/angels lead with the word חָתָן *ḥatan* 'son-in-law'. The explanation for this word placed into the mouth of the speaker(s) is evident: too much action is happening all at once to allow the visitors (even angelic ones) to compose a coherent sentence/question. The words roll off the tongue, even if they lack perfect sense.

Interestingly, in response to the visitors informing Lot that Yʜᴡʜ has sent them to destroy the city (v. 13), the first people whom Lot addresses are indeed his sons-in-law (v. 14), though his appeal to them meets with scorn. So there is a balance between the words spoken by the men/angels in v. 12 and Lot's action in v. 14. Though clearly this does not explain the presence of חָתָן *ḥatan* 'son-in-law' at the head of the clause in v. 12. To further complicate matters, the men/angels use חָתָן *ḥatan* 'son-in-law' (in the singular) in v. 12, though we learn in v. 14 that Lot has plural sons-in-law: וַיְדַבֵּר | אֶל־חֲתָנָיו | לֹקְחֵי בְנֹתָיו *waydabber 'el ḥatanaw loqḥe bənotaw* 'and Lot spoke to his sons-in-law, the ones-married (to) his daughters'.

We may contrast the hurried speech of the men/angels in v. 12 with what transpires the next morning (v. 15). While time still is of the essence, the guests show greater composure, perhaps with newfound knowledge of who is in Lot's household and who is important to him. The text now reads: קוּם קַח אֶת־אִשְׁתְּךָ וְאֶת־שְׁתֵּי בְנֹתֶיךָ הַנִּמְצָאֹת 'arise, take your wife and your two daughters who are present'. The command is grammatical and straightforward, and the ordering of the family members demonstrates forethought, with Lot's wife (whom we learn about now for the first time) mentioned first, and his two remaining daughters (presumably the unmarried ones, with the assumption that the married ones followed the lead of their mocking husbands) mentioned as well.

As we as speakers of our own native languages know well, not every sentence that we utter is produced with grammatical clarity. When haste is of the essence, our words are just as likely to be disorderly and ungrammatical—exactly as the author of Genesis 19 has done in representing the speech of Lot's guests in v. 12.

4. Genesis 37:28 — Joseph pulled from the pit

In the ongoing debate as to how to make sense of the three different ethnic groups that appear in Genesis 37 within the context of the
transporting of Joseph to Egypt,[18] the most crucial verse is v. 28:

וַיַּעַבְרוּ אֲנָשִׁים מִדְיָנִים סֹחֲרִים וַיִּמְשְׁכוּ וַיַּעֲלוּ אֶת־יוֹסֵף מִן־הַבּוֹר
וַיִּמְכְּרוּ אֶת־יוֹסֵף לַיִּשְׁמְעֵאלִים בְּעֶשְׂרִים כָּסֶף וַיָּבִיאוּ אֶת־יוֹסֵף
מִצְרָיְמָה׃

> And Midianite merchant men passed, and they pulled and
> they raised Joseph from the pit, and they sold Joseph to
> the Ishmaelites for twenty silver; and they brought Joseph
> to Egypt.

In a future chapter (see below, Chapter 22), we will consider the Documentary Hypothesis, which views the narrative portions of the Torah
as a patchwork of earlier sources. This approach 'solves' the difficulty
inherent in v. 28 by assigning different portions of the verse to separate sources, generally attributing the middle section, וַיִּמְכְּרוּ אֶת־יוֹסֵף
לַיִּשְׁמְעֵאלִים בְּעֶשְׂרִים כָּסֶף *wayyimkəru ʾet yosep lay-yišməʿeʾlim bə-ʿɛśrim
kasɛp* 'and they sold Joseph to the Ishmaelites for twenty silver', to the
J-source and the remainder to the E-source. We will proceed on different grounds, following the lead of those scholars who have read the
story as an integrated literary unit. The most sophisticated reading of
the story, in my opinion, is that of Edward Greenstein, whom I quote
here at length:

> A close reading of this verse reveals that it is ambiguous. Two
> readings converge on one clause. . . . The clause in question is
> *wayyimkᵉru ʾet yoseph layyishmᵉʿelim*—"they-sold Joseph to-
> the-Ishmaelites." According to the syntax of the verse, the verb
> *wayyimkᵉru*, "they sold," follows as the fourth in a sequence of
> verbs of which "Midianite trading men" is the explicit subject.

---

18. Most scholars contend with only two different ethnic groups, the
Midianites and the Ishmaelites, but Gen 37:36 introduces a third group, the
Medanites. That the Midianites and the Medanites are distinct entities ac-
cording to the biblical tradition may be seen in Gen 25:2.

Therefore, the syntactic reading is: the Midianites sold Joseph
to the Ishmaelites. However, the attentive reader is aware of
another reading, which I call the "allusive" reading. The phrase
wayyimkᵉru ʾet yoseph layyishmᵉʿelim, "they-sold Joseph to-the-
Ishmaelites," only alludes to the words of Joseph to his brothers:
lᵉkhu wᵉnimkᵉrennu layyishmᵉʿelim—"Come, let-us-sell-him to-
the-Ishmaelites" (verse 27). With this association in mind, the
reader can disregard the syntactic sequence and understand the
subject of *wayyimkᵉru*, "they-sold," in verse 28 to be Joseph's
brothers. . . . In a faithful reading, the reader must be sensitive
to both messages, leaving them both open. . . . In any event, the
clause "they-sold Joseph to-the-Ishmaelites" is equivocal in its
context, that is, at that point in the narrative's self-disclosure
to us. The equivocation in this clause is merely a microcosm for
the equivocal effect created for the surrounding narrative of the
sale of Joseph as a whole by the twofold sequence of action.[19]

Though I would go further in presenting the ambiguities inherent
in this verse (see below), I am in essential agreement with Greenstein.
I also am willing to accept Greenstein's conclusion: "In the end, the
reader cannot be certain of what human events actually took Joseph
down to Egypt. . . . By blurring the human factors leading to the enslavement of Joseph, the narrative sharpens our image of the divine
factor in bringing it about."[20]

In the specific case of the confusion present in Gen 37:28, I believe
that an additional factor is at play, namely, that the language reflects
Joseph's point of view. As the literary study of biblical narrative has
demonstrated, the text often shifts, ever so subtly, from the narrator's
objective, third-person point of view to the point of view of one of
the story's characters, and then back again.[21] Such is the case in our

---

19. Edward L. Greenstein, "An Equivocal Reading of the Sale of Joseph,"
in Kenneth R. R. Gros Louis, ed., *Literary Interpretations of Biblical Narratives,*
Volume II (Nashville: Abingdon, 1982), 119–21.

20. Ibid., 122–23.

21. See, for example, Adele Berlin, *Poetics and Interpretation of Biblical
Narrative* (Sheffield: Almond Press, 1983; repr., Winona Lake, IN: Eisenbrauns,
1994), 59–73.

passage. Joseph is at the bottom of a pit, unable to see what transpires above, and catching only a few sounds and voices here and there. He cannot put all the clues together, and thus for Joseph the events transpiring above are unclear. Things happen so quickly, without his full knowledge, and without his ability to process them fully, that for Joseph the quick moment of being yanked from the pit is one big blur. The text bears this out with its ambiguous language.

In fact, as I intimated above, Greenstein understated the ambiguities of this verse. Not only is it not clear who sold Joseph to the Ishmaelites, it is equally unclear who pulled Joseph from the pit. The Midianites might be the subject of וַיִּמְשְׁכוּ וַיַּעֲלוּ אֶת־יוֹסֵף מִן־הַבּוֹר *wayyimšəku wayyaʿalu ʾet yosep min hab-bor* 'and they pulled and they raised Joseph from the pit', but the brothers also might be the subject. True, the Masora connects this clause more closely to the previous one (with 'Midianite merchant men' as the explicit subject) than to the following one, but any number of readings is possible. The Midianites could have pulled Joseph out and then sold him to the Ishmaelites; the Midianites could have pulled Joseph out and the brothers could have sold him to the Ishmaelites; or the brothers could have pulled Joseph out and sold him to the Ishmaelites. Then, whoever winds up with Joseph, in whichever of these scenarios, brings Joseph to Egypt, as per the last clause of v. 28.

It is important to note that יוֹסֵף *yosep* 'Joseph' appears 3x in this verse, each time as the object of the verb, and that never does the text replace the name with a pronominal form (with either אֹתוֹ *ʾoto* 'him' or as a suffixed pronoun attached directly to the verb). The threefold mention of Joseph's name has two functions. First, it marks each clause as an independent one, thereby allowing the possibility of a different subject for each clause. For example, if the reading were וַיִּמְכְּרוּ אֹתוֹ לַיִּשְׁמְעֵאלִים **wayyimkəru ʾoto lay-yišməʿeʾlim* *'and they sold him to the Ishmaelites', then we would be forced to assume, with no evidence to the contrary, that whoever pulled Joseph out of the pit also sold him to the Ishmaelites. Secondly, the mention of 'Joseph' by name three times brings him into the reader's mind more forcefully than pronominal references would, thereby directing the reader to see Joseph's point of view in this verse. In sum, the ambiguity in Gen 37:28 reflects Joseph's confusion in processing the events as they occurred.

5. Genesis 37:30 — Reuben to his brothers (or is it to himself?)

Upon discovering that Joseph is missing from the pit, Reuben returns to his brothers and says הַיֶּ֣לֶד אֵינֶ֔נּוּ וַאֲנִ֖י אָ֥נָה אֲנִי־בָֽא 'the child is not, and I, to where shall I come?' (Gen 37:30). I emphasize the final word in the phrase, בָא, and my English rendering thereof, 'come'. Not a single modern translation (in any language) that I have checked renders the word in this fashion, but that of course is the plain meaning of the verbal root ב-ו-א *b-w-ʾ* 'come'. The reason why translators do not render בָא as 'come' in this instance, but instead are compelled to use 'go' (thus, e.g., RSV and Everett Fox[22]) or a word such as 'turn' (thus, e.g., NAB, NRSV, and Robert Alter[23]), is clear. In Leo Depuydt's words, "In questions asking for the destination to which a person is moving, the verb 'to go' is compulsory, because using 'to come' equals assuming that the destination is already known, namely [to] the speaker (or hearer). So, we do not say 'Where are you coming?', but rather: 'Where are you going?'"[24] Depuydt further noted, correctly and not surprisingly, that "this is the only case where אנה goes together with בוא, against 11 examples with הלך."[25] Accordingly, we have here another case of confused—or in this case, impossible—syntax.[26]

---

22. Fox, *Five Books of Moses*, 179.

23. Alter, *Five Books of Moses*, 212.

24. Leo Depuydt, "On the Notion of Movement in Egypto-Coptic and Biblical Hebrew," in Sarah Israelit-Groll, ed., *Pharaonic Egypt: The Bible and Christianity* (Jerusalem: Magnes, 1985), 37. The bracketed word "to" at the end of the first sentence in this quotation is missing in the original; I have added it because I think it is necessary to bring out Depuydt's intended meaning (unless I have misunderstood him in some way).

25. Ibid., 37.

26. I fully recognize that words for 'come' and 'go' do not equate in all cases in all languages. There may be instances of הלך where 'come' is the desired English equivalent, and there may be instances of בוא where 'go' is the desired English equivalent (see also the use of both words collocated in וּלְכוּ־בֹ֔אוּ *u-lku boʾu* 'and go, come' in Gen 45:17). But Depuydt is correct in this case, since with the interrogative particle אָ֫נָה *ʾana* 'to where', the only "correct" option is ה-ל-ך *h-l-k* 'go', while the use of ב-ו-א *b-w-ʾ* 'come' creates confused syntax.

The use of this syntax in Gen 37:30 is once more a case of form following content.[27] Reuben, in a fretful state and with no knowledge of what has become of Joseph, can barely speak. His twofold use of the word אֲנִי 'ani 'I' is one indication of this. Though an even more glaring indication is the phrase אָנָה אֲנִי־בָא 'ana 'ani ba' 'to where shall I come', the product of a confused mind.

The surface meaning of the text is that Reuben is speaking to his brothers. But in a penetrating study of this passage, Maren Niehoff made a strong case for reading these words as Reuben speaking to himself.[28] The presence of confused syntax in Reuben's words could support Niehoff's proposal—Reuben's mind, filled with pain and "inner conflict,"[29] has not quite sorted out the individual words.

6. Joshua 2:4 — Rahab hides the men

In Josh 2:3, the messengers of the king of Jericho arrive at Rahab's door and order her to produce the men who have come to her house. Verse 4 then reads as follows:

וַתִּקַּח הָאִשָּׁה אֶת־שְׁנֵי הָאֲנָשִׁים וַתִּצְפְּנוֹ וַתֹּאמֶר | כֵּן בָּאוּ אֵלַי
הָאֲנָשִׁים וְלֹא יָדַעְתִּי מֵאַיִן הֵמָּה:

And the woman took the two men, and she hid him; and she said, "Yes, the men came to me, and I do not know where they are from."

First we must marvel at the action of Rahab, the heroine of the story—an action that is in fact impossible in reality, but this is literature, not reality. I refer to the fact that with the king's men—we know that there is more than one representative of the king present, because she addresses them with plural verb forms in v. 5—standing at her

---

27. In theory, all the examples presented in this chapter could qualify as instances of "form follows content." We will explore this technique further in Chapter 27, in which nos. 1 and 7 of the current chapter will be rehearsed again.

28. Maren Niehoff, "Do Biblical Characters Talk to Themselves? Narrative Modes of Representing Inner Speech in Early Biblical Fiction," *Journal of Biblical Literature* 111 (1992): 577–95, esp. 587–88.

29. Ibid., 588.

door, Rahab is able to accomplish the ultimate in multitasking. She is at once able to hide the men at this moment *and* speak to the king's messengers. In reality this cannot be done, but I repeat, we are reading literature here, and the author clearly wishes to portray Rahab as the greatest of heroines, even able to accomplish the impossible—but then again everyone knows that women, more so than men, are the ultimate multitaskers.

English translations of this passage attempt to smooth out the difficulty by rendering the words וַתִּקַּח הָאִשָּׁה אֶת־שְׁנֵי הָאֲנָשִׁים וַתִּצְפְּנוֹ *wattiqqaḥ ha-'iššā 'et šəne ha-'anašim wattiṣpəno* in the pluperfect, e.g., NAB: 'The woman had taken the two men and hidden them'; NJPS: 'The woman, however, had taken the two men and hidden them'; RSV: 'But the woman had taken the two men and hidden them'. The use of the verbal form 'had taken' implies that Rahab had taken and hidden the men *before* the king's men arrived at her door. The Hebrew of Josh 2:4, however, suggests no such reading, for it uses the basic narrative tense, the *wayyiqtol* form וַתִּקַּח *wattiqqaḥ* 'and she took'.[30] Had the author wished to state that Rahab hid the men earlier, he would have used the anterior construction וְהָאִשָּׁה לָקְחָה* *wə-ha-'iššā laqḥa* *'and the woman had taken'.[31] Indeed, the author did use this construction at the beginning of v. 6, וְהִיא הֶעֱלָתַם הַגָּגָה *wə-hi' heʿɛlatam hag-gaga* 'and she had brought them up to the roof', where it is most appropriate, as the story now resumes with new action.[32]

But this piece of literary brilliance in v. 4—all to indicate, once more, the ultimate ability and heroism of Rahab—is not the main issue on which I wish to focus in this section. Instead, I wish to call attention to just one word occurring at the end of the half-verse just discussed. We expect to encounter the word וַתִּצְפְּנֵם* *wattiṣpənem* *'and

---

30. I am happy to note, however, that not all English translations diverge from the Hebrew syntax. Already KJV got it right: 'And the woman took the two men, and hid them'; and NRSV returns to such a rendering: 'But the woman took the two men and hid them'.

31. On this syntagma, see Ziony Zevit, *The Anterior Construction in Classical Hebrew* (Society of Biblical Literature Monograph Series 50; Atlanta: Society of Biblical Literature, 1998).

32. This verse is listed by Zevit (ibid., 27), though it is not one of the passages that receives detailed treatment in his monograph.

she hid them' at this point, for after all there were two Israelite spies
in her house. And indeed that is how *all* English translations render
the verse; see the five quoted above as a representative sampling. But
the Hebrew is very clear: וַתִּצְפְּנוֹ *wattiṣpəno* 'and she hid him'.[33] It is
not just English translations that attempt to smooth out the difficulty;
almost all commentators feel compelled to emend the word either to
וַתִּצְפְּנֵם* (with final *mem* for *waw*) *wattiṣpənem* *'and she hid them', or
to וַתִּצְפֹּן* *wattiṣpon* (assuming dittography of *waw*, since the next word
begins with the same letter) *'and she hid', with the implicit though
unexpressed object 'them'.[34]

But let us accept the reading וַתִּצְפְּנוֹ *wattiṣpəno* 'and she hid him'
and attempt to explain it along the lines laid out in this chapter. I
would argue that the author used the third masc. sg. pronominal suffix intentionally, to indicate that Rahab—who in reality had no time
to hide either man—astonishingly managed to hide at least one of the
men, with the other spy presumably tagging along or finding his own
quick hiding spot (one can imagine how this would be depicted in a
film version, even with a comedic aspect to it).[35] This is a very hurried
moment for Rahab, there is hardly time to think, and no time to act;
and she does the best she can at this critical juncture in order to hide
even one man. The text should stand as it is, with the third masc. sg.
pronominal suffix, as an indication of the animation and excitement
present in her house at this crucial moment.

Another indication of something amiss in the text is the specific
form of וַתִּצְפְּנוֹ *wattiṣpəno* 'and she hid him'. Standard Biblical Hebrew
would call for וַתִּצְפְּנֵהוּ *wattiṣpənehu* 'and she hid him', exactly as occurs

---

33. Happily, Tikva Frymer-Kensky, *Reading the Women of the Bible* (New
York: Schocken, 2002), 34, translated the text similarly.

34. Not surprisingly, earlier Jewish commentators dealt with the text as
best they could, including the imaginative midrash recorded in Tanhuma,
Shelah 1, that the two spies were Caleb and Phineas, but that Phineas could
not be seen, like an angel. This midrash was cited by Radaq, who also provided
more sober, grammatical explanations (as did Rashi et al.).

35. On comic aspects to the story of Rahab, see Yair Zakovitch, "Humor
and Theology or the Successful Failure of Israelite Intelligence: A Literary-
Folkloric Approach to Joshua 2," in Susan Niditch, ed., *Text and Tradition: The
Hebrew Bible and Folklore* (Atlanta: Society of Biblical Literature, 1990), 75–98.

in Exod 2:2.[36] Indeed, there are 287 cases of הוּ‎ - *-ehu* 'him' suffixed to *wayyiqtol* forms in the Bible (that is, third masc. sg., third fem. sg., second masc. sg., first common sg., and first common pl. forms, viz., those that end in a consonant), in contrast to only three or four examples with suffixed וֹ‎ *-o* 'him' (our passage, along with 1 Sam 21:14 and 2 Sam 14:6; and see also 1 Sam 18:1 Ketiv).[37] I would suggest that the atypical form וַתִּצְפְּנוֹ *wattiṣpəno* 'and she hid him' in Josh 2:4 is invoked by the author to add yet another element of confused language to the story. The moment of Rahab's hiding the men is so rushed that not even the correct grammatical form can be used; instead, the author introduces this atypical form to enhance the storytelling.

In short, both the use of the third masc. sg. pronominal suffix and the form that it takes here (specifically, וֹ‎ *-o* 'him') indicate the excitement present in Rahab's house at this point in the narrative. By no means should the text be emended.

7. Judges 18:14–20 — the disturbance at Micah's house

Judges 18 relates the story of the migration of the tribe of Dan from its original homeland in the southern coastal plain to the town of Laish/Dan in northern Israel. En route, while passing through the territory of Ephraim, the five men who had reconnoitered the land inform their fellow tribesmen that in the house of a certain Micah there is present אֵפוֹד וּתְרָפִים וּפֶסֶל וּמַסֵּכָה *'epod u-trapim u-pesɛl u-masseka* 'an ephod and teraphim, and an idol and a molten-image' (Judg 18:14). The five men then add the words וְעַתָּה דְּעוּ מַה־תַּעֲשׂוּ *wə-ʿatta dəʿu ma taʿaśu* 'and now, know what you are to do', no doubt coded language for 'let's take action'.[38] With six hundred armed Danites surrounding

---

36. For more on the relationship between Josh 2:4 and Exod 2:2, see Frymer-Kensky, *Reading the Women of the Bible*, 36. On the larger picture concerning interconnections between Joshua and Exodus, see Elie Assis, "Ha-Mivneh ha-Sifruti šel Sippur Kibbuš ha-ʾAreṣ be-Sefer Yehošuaʿ (Peraqim 1–11) u-Mašmaʿuto" (PhD dissertation, Bar-Ilan University, 1999), for example, the summary chart on p. 30.

37. Data courtesy of A. Dean Forbes (personal communication).

38. In the words of George Foot Moore, *A Critical and Exegetical Commentary on Judges* (International Critical Commentary; Edinburgh: T&T Clark, 1895), 395: "No more than the hint was needed."

the house, the five men enter the house and take אֶת־הַפֶּ֙סֶל֙ וְאֶת־הָאֵפ֔וֹד
וְאֶת־הַתְּרָפִ֖ים וְאֶת־הַמַּסֵּכָ֑ה ʾet hap-pɛsɛl wə-ʾɛt ha-ʾepod wə-ʾɛt hat-tərapim
wə-ʾɛt ham-masseka 'the idol and the ephod, and the teraphim and the
molten-image' (v. 17). Immediately the reader notices that the order of
the four items has changed. The normal pairings of 'ephod and teraphim' and 'idol and molten-image', which appear in v. 14, and which
occur as early as Judg 17:3–5, in the introduction to this story,[39] now
are changed to the unnatural pairings 'idol and ephod' and 'teraphim
and molten-image'. The effect is to give a sense of ransacking.[40]

But there is more. In the second telling of what occurred—a telling that most likely gives us the perspective of the priest in Micah's
house—the narrator refers to the items as אֶת־פֶּ֣סֶל הָאֵפוֹד֮ וְאֶת־הַתְּרָפִים֒
וְאֶת־הַמַּסֵּכָה ʾet pesɛl ha-ʾepod wə-ʾɛt hat-tərapim wə-ʾɛt ham-masseka
'the idol of the ephod, and the teraphim and the molten-image' (v. 18).
Now the confusion is even greater, since there can be no such combination as 'an idol of the ephod'. The looting is intensified, or at least the
priest perceives the scene as even more chaotic than it actually was.
Finally, when the priest decides to join the Danites, we read that he
took אֶת־הָאֵפ֤וֹד וְאֶת־הַתְּרָפִים֙ וְאֶת־הַפֶּ֔סֶל ʾet ha-ʾepod wə-ʾɛt hat-tərapim
wə-ʾɛt hap-pasɛl 'the ephod, and the teraphim and the idol' (v. 20), omitting one of the four items. The effect is to convey the haste with which
the priest departed, leaving behind הַמַּסֵּכָה ham-masseka 'the molten-
image'. Furthermore, as the priest grabs the things, note that now the
ephod is by itself, no longer paired in the impossible construction פֶּסֶל
הָאֵפוֹד pesɛl ha-ʾepod 'the idol of the ephod' as earlier, but that there still
is a bit of a mix-up since the traditional pair 'ephod and teraphim' is
still not quite together—the Masoretic accents separate the two items
and place the teraphim with the idol. The cumulative effect of the four
phrases—beginning with the normal pairings in v. 14, then creating
abnormal pairings in v. 17, then positing an impossible construction in
v. 18, and finally omitting one item in v. 20—is to portray the confusion
that reigned in Micah's house.

---

39. For an additional example of 'ephod and teraphim', see Hos 3:4; for
additional examples of 'idol and molten-image', see Deut 27:15, Nah 1:14.

40. Though he did not go far enough in recognizing the true import of the
change in wording, see the suggestion of David Noel Freedman *apud* Robert
G. Boling, *Judges* (Anchor Bible 6A; Garden City, NY: Doubleday, 1975), 264.

It is apposite to observe how the standard translations—both ancient and modern—smooth over the difficulties in this text. For example, the Septuagint omits the listing in v. 17; reads 'the graven-image and the ephod and the teraphim and the molten-image' in v. 18 (with no recognition of the construct phrase פֶּסֶל הָאֵפוֹד *pɛsɛl ha-ʾepod* 'the idol of the ephod'); and then recreates the original string 'the ephod and the teraphim and the graven-image and the molten-image' in v. 20, thereby putting everything back in order and including הַמַּסֵּכָה *ham-masseka* 'the molten-image', which is lacking in the Masoretic Text.[41] The interested reader can check the various English versions and see what modern translators have done. The most egregious change is represented in both NJPS and REB at v. 18, with an implied Hebrew text אֶת־הַפֶּסֶל ** ʾɛt hap-pɛsɛl wə-ʾɛt ham-masseka wə-ʾɛt ha-ʾepod wə-ʾɛt hat-tərapim* *'the idol and the molten-image and the ephod and the teraphim', thereby presenting the four items in their normal pairing (though, to their credit, both translations included a footnote presenting the literal rendering of the Hebrew text).

While we are studying this pericope, I also take the opportunity to comment on another stylistic device utilized by the author, especially since it too has not been properly understood by commentators. In v. 17 the actions of the five men are described as follows: בָּאוּ שָׁמָּה לָקְחוּ *baʾu šamma laqḥu* 'they came there, they took' (followed by the listing of the four items taken, as noted above). Several scholars have disapproved of this phrase, given (a) the uncharacterisic absence of a conjunction between the two verbal phrases, and (b) the use of simple past tense verbs instead of typical *wayyiqtol* forms. George Foot Moore noted that "the asyndeton is without parallel in simple narrative,"[42] while Arnold Ehrlich used the rather strong term "unhebräisch."[43] But certainly this view is a misunderstanding of what the author is attempting to convey here. The lack of the conjunction is an indication of the suddenness by which the men swooped into the house and took the desired items.

---

41. Based on the Septuagint, many modern scholars emend the Masoretic Text to include מַסֵּכָה *masseka* 'molten-image' in v. 20; thus, e.g., Boling, *Judges*, 264.

42. Moore, *Judges*, 397.

43. Arnold B. Ehrlich, *Randglossen zur Hebräischen Bibel* (Leipzig: Hinrichs, 1910), 3:146.

The text is not "un-Hebraic" here, but rather, once more, form follows content. Just as confused syntax is utilized to indicate the confusion of the moment, so is speeded syntax (if I may use that term) used to indicate the speed with which an event occurs. A parallel usage is found in Song 5:6, where the wording וְדוֹדִי חָמַק עָבָר wə-dodi ḥamaq ʿabar 'but my beloved turned, passed [i.e., was gone]' indicates the instantaneous disappearance of the male lover from the female lover's fantasy.[44]

To return to the main point: the narrative in Judges 18 employs confused language to portray the ransacking of Micah's house. This reading stands in contrast to that of a distinguished previous commentator: "The account of the way in which they got possession of the images is badly confused by interpolations and glosses, and baffles emendation or analysis."[45] Confused, yes; but that is the very point.

8. 1 Samuel 14:21 — confusion in the Philistine camp

First Samuel 14:20–21 describes an Israelite encounter with the Philistines. In the latter half of v. 20 we learn that the confusion among the latter was so great that the Philistines actually attacked each other. The narrator adds curtly: מְהוּמָה גְדוֹלָה מְאֹד məhuma gədola məʾod 'a very great confusion'. The next verse, v. 21, is another example of confused syntax:

וְהָעִבְרִים הָיוּ לַפְּלִשְׁתִּים כְּאֶתְמוֹל שִׁלְשׁוֹם אֲשֶׁר עָלוּ עִמָּם בַּמַּחֲנֶה
סָבִיב וְגַם־הֵמָּה לִהְיוֹת עִם־יִשְׂרָאֵל אֲשֶׁר עִם־שָׁאוּל וְיוֹנָתָן:

And the Hebrews, they had been to the Philistines as before, who had gone up with them into the camp all around;
and even they, to be with Israel, who were with Saul and
Jonathan.

I have translated the passage as it reads, without any attempt at smoothing over the difficulties. The latter, of course, is what typically occurs in English translations, e.g., NRSV: 'Now the Hebrews who previously had been with the Philistines and had gone up with them

---

44. See further below, in Chapter 27, p. 545.
45. Moore, *Judges*, 394.

into the camp turned and joined the Israelites who were with Saul and
Jonathan'.[46] Now something like this is presumably what happened in
the battle, but the biblical writer did not describe it in such smooth
terms. Instead, to evoke the tumult in the Philistine camp, he produced
language that by its very confusion describes the battlefield.

The difficulties in this verse are several. I present here a sampling
of what some commentators have noted. First, as many scholars have
noted, it would be helpful to have a relative pronoun, presumably אֲשֶׁר
'ašer 'who, that, which' after וְהָעִבְרִים wə-ha-ʿibrim 'and the Hebrews',
thus enabling a reading such as 'and the Hebrews who were with the
Philistines'.[47] Secondly, the word עִמָּם ʿimmam 'with them' is a bit
odd, since by stating that the Hebrews had gone up with them, i.e.,
the Philistines, the text implies that Philistines had gone up into their
own camp. Note that the Septuagint omits any equivalent to 'with
them'.[48] Third, in the words of Jan Fokkelman, "The verse founders on
the atnāḥ in the MT and requires correction."[49] His proposal, like that
of many, is to move the *'atnah* (that is, the accent/punctuation mark)
back one word, and to emend slightly, producing a text that would look
like בַּמַּחֲנֶה סָבְבוּ גַּם־הֵמָּה * *bam-maḥanɛ sabəbu gam hemma* (with the
'atnah on בַּמַּחֲנֶה* to mark the disjuncture, as indicated) *ʿ. . . into the

---

46. The translation in NJPS, 'And the Hebrews who had previously sided
with the Philistines, who had come up with them in the army [from] round
about—they too joined with the Israelites who were with Saul and Jonathan',
with a footnote marking the entire sentence save the last six words with the
comment "meaning of Heb. uncertain," is a bit better at preserving some of
the difficulty of this verse.

47. Thus, e.g., S. R. Driver, *Notes on the Hebrew Text of the Books of Samuel*
(Oxford: Clarendon, 1890), 84–85; Henry Preserved Smith, *A Critical and
Exegetical Commentary on the Books of Samuel* (International Critical Commentary; Edinburgh: T&T Clark, 1899), 113; and Ehrlich, *Randglossen zur
Hebräischen Bibel* 3:213. Jan P. Fokkelman, *Narrative Art and Poetry in the
Books of Samuel*, vol. 2, *The Crossing Fates* (Assen: Van Gorcum, 1986), 61–62,
n. 53, proposed adding -ה *h-* (the definite article), a less radical emendation,
instead of אֲשֶׁר *'ašer* 'who, that, which' (the relative pronoun). But he qualified his remark on p. 721.

48. See P. Kyle McCarter, *I Samuel* (Anchor Bible 8; Garden City, NY:
Doubleday, 1980), 237.

49. Fokkelman, *The Crossing Fates*, 61 n. 53.

camp; they too turned . . .'.[50] Fourth, though I have found no scholar who has stated the point explicitly, the infinitive construct לִהְיוֹת *lihyot* 'to be' has no verb to support it, though of course by emending the text to read סָבְבוּ* **sababu* *'turned' this difficulty is alleviated.

But the free hand of the emender is the wrong approach here. The verse is intentionally confused: it depicts the confusion that reigned in the Philistine camp. Any attempt either to emend the Hebrew original or to smooth over its difficulties in a modern translation misses the point entirely.

9. 1 Samuel 17:38 — Saul dresses David with his armor

Our next example is 1 Sam 17:38:

וַיַּלְבֵּשׁ שָׁאוּל אֶת־דָּוִד מַדָּיו וְנָתַן קוֹבַע נְחֹשֶׁת עַל־רֹאשׁוֹ וַיַּלְבֵּשׁ אֹתוֹ
שִׁרְיוֹן׃

This passage is uniformly rendered as a series of consecutive acts, as in NJPS: 'Saul clothed David in his own garment; he placed a bronze helmet on his head and clothed him in a breastplate'.[51] But if we take a closer look at the verbs in this passage, we note that only the first and the third are in the *wayyiqtol* form and that the second of them is in the *wa-qatal* form. A typical approach is to declare that "*wntn* is syntactically impossible" and to emend the verse.[52] More sober is the approach of two recent studies from the field of discourse analysis, one by Robert Longacre and one by C. H. J. van der Merwe, both of whom isolated this passage as among the most difficult nuts to crack in the biblical narrative corpus.[53] While neither was able to supply an

---

50. Thus McCarter, *I Samuel*, 234, 237, with an eye to the Septuagint. See also Driver, *Notes on the Hebrew Text*, 84; Smith, *Samuel*, 113; Ehrlich, *Randglossen zur Hebräischen Bibel* 3:213; *BHS*, ad loc. This emendation underlies those translations that include the word 'turned' in their rendition, e.g., the aforecited NRSV, as well as RSV and NAB. Probably REB 'changed sides' and NJB 'defected' have a similar basis.

51. Reading the last part of the verse with the footnote; the main text reads 'and fastened a breastplate on him'.

52. McCarter, *I Samuel*, 288.

53. Robert E. Longacre, "*Weqatal* Forms in Biblical Hebrew Prose: A Discourse-modular Approach," in Robert D. Bergen, ed., *Biblical Hebrew and*

answer to the problem of why וְנָתַן *wə-natan* (instead of the expected וַיִּתֵּן *wayyitten* 'and he gave/placed') is used here (and their respect for the text precluded emendation as a solution), it was their discussion of this passage that motivated me to hunt for a solution.

In keeping with the approach taken above, I propose to explain the linguistic peculiarity of 1 Sam 17:38 as follows. Given the three items mentioned in this verse, the expected order of dressing would be מַדִּים *maddim* 'body-suit', then שִׁרְיוֹן *širyon* 'breastplate', and finally קוֹבַע *qobaʿ* 'helmet'.[54] In the entire history of human armor, the last item to be donned is always the helmet. The most explicit evidence is provided by the fifteenth-century Hastings manuscript, a document that includes a tract entitled "How a man schall be armyd at his ese when he schal fighte on foote" (folios 122v–123v).[55] In great detail the author of this text describes the manner of dressing, with the 'basinet', or helmet, affixed last.[56] In addition, there are numerous references to

---

Discourse Linguistics (Dallas: Summer Institute of Linguistics, 1994), 75; and C. H. J. van der Merwe, "Discourse Linguistics and Biblical Hebrew Grammar," in Bergen, *Biblical Hebrew and Discourse Linguistics*, 28.

54. I admit to some difficulty here in rendering the terms מַדִּים *maddim* and שִׁרְיוֹן *širyon*. The former is a generic word for 'garment', and the latter is typically translated 'body armor' or 'coat of mail'. In the present instance, it appears that מַדִּים *maddim* must be a body-suit with some protective function and that שִׁרְיוֹן *širyon* would then be the breastplate. Note that Mark J. Fretz, "Weapons and Implements of Warfare," in David Noel Freedman, ed., *The Anchor Bible Dictionary* (New York: Doubleday, 1992), 6:894, allowed for מַד *mad* = 'armor' and שִׁרְיוֹן *širyon* = 'breastplate'. In any case, the precise designations of these terms in the present context is not the main concern here, since however one understands them, it is clear that the helmet should be donned last.

55. The manuscript is held by the Pierpont Morgan Library (New York), with the official title "Ordonances of Chivalry" (accession number MS M.775). For the first relevant page of this manuscript, go to: http://corsair.morganlibrary.org/icaimages/7/m775.122v.jpg.

56. For detailed treatment of the text, see (Viscount) H. A. Dillon, "On a MS. Collection of Ordinances of Chivalry of the Fifteenth Century, Belonging to Lord Hastings," *Archaeologia, or Miscellaneous Tracts Relating to Antiquity Published by the Society of Antiquaries of London* 57 (1900): 29–70, esp. 43–46. A briefer discussion may be found in Charles Ffoulkes, *The Armourer and His Craft from the XIth to the XVIth Century* (Boston: Small, Maynard, 1912), 107–8. On the term 'basinet', see George Cameron Stone, *A Glossary of the Construction, Decoration and Use of Arms and Armor* (New York: Jack Brussel, 1961), 102–5.

the donning of armor in medieval literary compositions (*La Chanson de Roland* and many other works), and they consistently refer to the helmet as the last item to be affixed.[57]

Perhaps more germane than these medieval references are the following passages from the *Iliad*, a text roughly contemporary with the authorship of 1 Samuel 17.[58] In four places (3:330–338 [Alexandros/ Paris]; 11:17–43 [Agamemnon]; 16:131–139 [Patroclus]; 19:369–383 [Achilles]), Homer portrays the hero preparing for battle by donning the armor. In each case the order is greaves, corselet, shield, helmet. A fifth hero does likewise, as we can see from 3:339, following immediately upon Alexandros's suiting: 'In the same way warlike Menelaos put on his armour'.[59] Finally, note that when Moses dresses Aaron with the priestly vestments in Lev 8:6–9, the last item donned is the headdress.

One of the overall goals of the author of 1 Samuel, as many scholars have noted,[60] is to show the inadequacy of Saul. The present passage

---

57. For numerous examples from medieval literature, see François Buttin, *Du costume militaire au moyen âge et pendant la renaissance* (Memorias de la Real Academia de Buenas Letras de Barcelona 12; Barcelona: Real Academia de Buenas Letras, 1971), 15–16, 20, 154–59. In addition, the final placement of the helmet can be inferred from numerous medieval artworks depicting the wearing of armor; for general orientation, see Ffoulkes, *The Armourer and His Craft*. I take this opportunity to thank Pierre Terjanian, formerly Andrew W. Mellon Curatorial Fellow in European Arms and Armor at the Philadelphia Museum of Art, for his assistance in this matter and for these references to medieval literature and art.

Even Mark Twain got it right in his very detailed description of donning armor, ending with the helmet: "your iron rat-trap onto your head, with a rag of steel web hitched onto it to hang over the back of your neck—and there you are, snug as a candle in a candlemould." See Mark Twain, *A Connecticut Yankee in King Arthur's Court* (New York: Oxford University Press, 1996 [orig. 1889]), 134–35 (in Chapter XI, entitled "The Yankee in Search of Adventures").

58. For detailed discussion of the *Iliad* references, see John Pairman Brown, *Israel and Hellas* (Beihefte zur Zeitschrift für die Alttestamentliche Wissenschaft 231; Berlin: de Gruyter, 1995), 163–70.

59. Translation of Richard Lattimore, *The Iliad of Homer* (Chicago: University of Chicago Press, 1951), 109.

60. See, for example, David M. Gunn, *The Fate of King Saul* (Journal for the Study of the Old Testament Supplement Series 14; Sheffield: JSOT Press, 1980), and Moshe Garsiel, *The First Book of Samuel: A Literary Study of Comparative Structures, Analogies and Parallels* (Ramat-Gan: Revivim, 1983), as

should be understood as part of the portrayal. Saul's bafflement at the presence of the shepherd boy David on the battlefield and his volunteering to fight Goliath has caused the king to become so flustered that he is unable even to dress another man properly.

The language of 1 Sam 17:38 parallels the scene, both through the order of the objects mentioned (with helmet not last) and by use of the *wə-qatal* form וְנָתַן *wə-natan* 'and he placed' (clearly, the verb is not a perfect or a pluperfect here). I propose an English rendering of 1 Sam 17:38 such as: 'Saul clothed David in his body-suit, then he even placed a bronze helmet on his head, and he clothed him with a breastplate', with the highlighting of the *wə-qatal* verb indicated by the expression 'then he even placed'; or more radically, 'Saul clothed David in his body-suit, then placed he a bronze helmet on his head, and he clothed him with a breastplate', with the inverted word order 'then placed he' replicating the most unusual presence of the Hebrew *wə-qatal* form.[61]

10. 1 Kings 3:26 — the mother of the living child cries out

The scene is well known: the two women stand before Solomon, who must use his wisdom to decide the case of the one living baby. The king's solution is to divide the child in half, giving one half to one woman and the other half to the second woman. Upon hearing the king's proposal, the mother of the baby cries out:

תְּנוּ־לָהּ אֶת־הַיָּלוּד הַחַי וְהָמֵת אַל־תְּמִיתֻהוּ

tənu lah ʾɛt hay-yalud ha-ḥay wə-hamet ʾal təmituhu

"Give her the living newborn, and do not put him to death!"

---

well as the succinct remarks by Joel Rosenberg, "1 and 2 Samuel," in Robert Alter and Frank Kermode, eds., *The Literary Guide to the Bible* (Cambridge: Harvard University Press [Belknap], 1987), 127–28.

61. For an earlier treatment, with special attention to the translation issue, see Gary A. Rendsburg, "The Literary Approach to the Bible and Finding a Good Translation," in Frederick W. Knobloch, ed., *Biblical Translation in Context* (Bethesda: University Press of Maryland, 2002), 179–94, in particular 187–90.

As Yoo-Ki Kim has observed, 1 Kgs 3:26 represents the only instance in the entire Bible in which an infinitive absolute is negated by אַל *'al*.[62] The standard usage, of course, is negation by לֹא *lo'*, e.g., Num 23:25 (2x) גַּם־קֹב לֹא תִקֳּבֶנּוּ גַּם־בָּרֵךְ לֹא תְבָרֲכֶנּוּ *gam qob lo' tiqqobɛnnu gam barek lo' təbarakɛnnu* 'indeed curse, do not curse him, indeed bless, do not bless him'. Naturally, one can appreciate the wording in 1 Kgs 3:26, as the mother of the living child invokes the particle אַל *'al*.[63] At this crucial point in the narrative, one imagines her struggling to utter any set of words, regardless of grammatical correctness, given her passion and the excitement of the moment.

Indeed, her words come into greater focus when we hear Solomon speak in the next verse. Notwithstanding his intense interest in the judicial matter before him, the king-magistrate is able to speak dispassionately, thus employing proper grammar with the negative particle לֹא *lo'*: 1 Kgs 3:27 תְּנוּ־לָהּ אֶת־הַיָּלוּד הַחַי וְהָמֵת לֹא תְמִיתֻהוּ *tənu lah 'et hay-yalud ha-ḥay wə-hamet lo' təmituhu* 'Give her the living newborn, and you shall not put him to death'.

These two verses, accordingly, constitute yet another example of repetition with variation—with the simple switch from אַל *'al* in v. 26 to לֹא *lo'* in v. 27 (see below, Chapter 9, no. 19). More germane to the present discussion, however, we have identified in v. 26 another instance of confused language, in this case placed in the mouth of one of the characters—not just any character, of course, but the mother of the baby about to be severed into two, whose ability to produce grammatically correct language clearly must have been compromised in the emotional strain of the moment.

11. Deuteronomy 32:5 — a crooked and twisted generation

There are, of course, dozens if not hundreds of exceedingly difficult poetic stichs in the Bible. One would not wish to claim that all of

---

62. Yoo-Ki Kim, *The Function of the Tautological Infinitive in Classical Biblical Hebrew* (Harvard Semitic Studies 60; Winona Lake, IN: Eisenbrauns, 2009), 51.

63. Typically, the negator אַל *'al* is used before prefix-conjugation verbs to issue a one-time negative command; see Joüon and Muraoka, *Grammar of Biblical Hebrew*, 377, §114i.

these can be explained as deliberate attempts by the poets to present confused language to indicate a sense of confusion. But in light of the prose examples presented above, I wish to suggest—even if through one example only—that such be considered by scholars when studying difficult poetic passages.

The example I have chosen is among the most abstruse in the Bible. Deuteronomy 32:5 reads as follows (presented here so as to display the parallelism):[64]

שִׁחֵת לֹו לֹא בָּנָיו מוּמָם
דּוֹר עִקֵּשׁ וּפְתַלְתֹּל:

The second stich is straightforward; it means 'a crooked and twisted generation'. The first stich, on the other hand, has caused endless difficulties for commentators. One need only cite Jeffrey H. Tigay, who wrote the following concerning these five words: "Their syntactic connection is unclear, as can be seen from a literal translation: 'He has dealt corruptly with Him not His children their blemish'."[65] I particularly like the way that Tigay avoids using punctuation marks, especially because the *ṭəʿamim* present a reading that otherwise does not suggest itself, viz., separating לֹא *loʾ* 'not' from בָּנָיו *banaw* 'his sons'.[66] As Tigay further notes, the individual words in the first half of the verse—שִׁחֵת *šiḥet* 'dealt corruptly', לֹא בָּנָיו *loʾ banaw* 'not his sons' (assuming that they are to be read as one phrase), and מוּם *mum* 'blemish'—all suit the context, each in its own way referring to the manner in which Israel has apostatized. The problem is, as indicated, how to put this string of words together to create a smooth reading.

But that is exactly the point, I would suggest. The poet has utilized awkward syntax—awkward even within the parameters of poetry, which allows for looser word order, etc.—to reflect the clear message presented in the second half of the verse and indeed in the poem in

---

64. On poetic parallelism, see my basic treatment below, Chapter 17, no. 2.

65. Jeffrey H. Tigay, *Deuteronomy* (JPS Torah Commentary; Philadelphia: Jewish Publication Society, 1996), 301; citing A. D. H. Mayes, *Deuteronomy* (Grand Rapids: Eerdmans, 1981), 383.

66. On this issue, see most importantly Simcha Kogut, *Ha-Miqraʾ ben Ṭeʿamim le-Paršanut* (Jerusalem: Bialik, 1996), 144–45, 212–14, 240–41, with a rich survey of readings of this verse culled from traditional Jewish sources.

general. Israel is a crooked and twisted people, they do not follow the correct path, they are replete with blemishes, and they no longer deserve the label of God's children. To drive home the point, the poet creates a hemistich in v. 5a that itself is twisted and confused.

The translation of the NJPS is worth citing in this regard:

Children unworthy of Him—
That crooked, perverse generation—
Their baseness has played Him false.

Note how the first stich of this translation renders לֹא בָנָיו *lo' banaw* 'children unworthy of him'; the second stich renders דּוֹר עִקֵּשׁ וּפְתַלְתֹּל *dor 'iqqeš u-ptaltol* 'that crooked, perverse generation'; and the third stich renders שִׁחֵת לוֹ ... מוּמָם *šiḥet lo ... mumam* 'their baseness has played Him false', though naturally these words are separated in the actual Hebrew text, with לֹא בָנָיו *lo' banaw* 'children unworthy of him' interposed. While the NJPS takes more liberties in the translation than most English versions, and it represents only one possible solution to a difficult verse, this rendering nevertheless serves our purpose well: for it indicates how the Hebrew might be read, by scrambling the individual words to create a smooth reading. This is fine, of course, for an English translation, as long as one realizes that the Hebrew text is intentionally confused, as a prime example of form following content.

CHAPTER NINE

REPETITION WITH VARIATION: PROSE NARRATIVES

We return now to our treatment of repetition with variation, garnered from a variety of prose texts.[1]

1. Genesis 4:26; 10:21

Gen 4:26

וּלְשֵׁת גַּם־הוּא יֻלַּד־בֵּן

and to Seth, also he, was born a son

Gen 10:21

וּלְשֵׁם יֻלַּד גַּם־הוּא

and to Shem was born, also he

As several scholars have noted, two sections within the Primeval History (that is, Genesis 1–11) deal with the development of human-kind: Gen 4:17–26 and Gen 10:1–32.[2] The two sections share a series of theme-words and expressions that serve to seal the literary bond.

---

1. For an earlier treatment of some of these passages, see Gary A. Rendsburg, "Variation in Biblical Hebrew Prose and Poetry," in Maxine Grossman, ed., *Built by Wisdom, Established by Understanding: Essays in Honor of Adele Berlin* (Bethesda: University Press of Maryland, 2013), 197–226.

2. Jack M. Sasson, "The 'Tower of Babel' as a Clue to the Redactional Structuring of the Primeval History (Genesis 1:1–11:9)," in Gary A. Rendsburg et al., eds., *The Bible World: Essays in Honor of Cyrus H. Gordon* (New York: Ktav, 1980), 211–19 [reprinted in Richard S. Hess and David T. Tsumura, eds., *I Studied Inscriptions from Before the Flood: Ancient Near Eastern, Literary, and Linguistic Approaches to Genesis 1–11* (Winona Lake, IN: Eisenbrauns, 1994),

Prime among them are the two passages presented here, announcing offspring born to the sons of the leading protagonists of the Primeval History: Seth son of Adam and Shem son of Noah. Not one to repeat the phrases in verbatim fashion (save for the change in the character's name), the author of this material varied his wording in several ways. Most prominently, in 4:26 the key phrase גַּם־הוּא *gam hu'* 'also he' appears before the passive verb יֻלַּד *yullad* 'was born', while in 10:21 these two elements appear in reverse order. In addition, the first iteration includes the noun בֵּן *ben* 'son', which is lacking in the second instance—though, to be sure, there is a substantive reason for this variation, since in Seth's case the focus will be on his single son Enosh, while in Shem's case the focus will be on his multiple offspring.

2. Genesis 19:33, 35

Gen 19:33

וַתַּשְׁקֶיןָ אֶת־אֲבִיהֶן יַיִן בַּלַּיְלָה הוּא וַתָּבֹא הַבְּכִירָה וַתִּשְׁכַּב אֶת־
אָבִיהָ וְלֹא־יָדַע בְּשִׁכְבָהּ וּבְקוּמָהּ׃

And they plied their father with wine that night, and the elder came and she lay with her father, though he did not know her lying down and her rising up.

Gen 19:35

וַתַּשְׁקֶיןָ גַּם בַּלַּיְלָה הַהוּא אֶת־אֲבִיהֶן יַיִן וַתָּקָם הַצְּעִירָה וַתִּשְׁכַּב
עִמּוֹ וְלֹא־יָדַע בְּשִׁכְבָהּ וּבְקֻמָהּ׃

And they plied even that night their father with wine, and the younger arose and she lay with him, though he did not know her lying down and her rising up.

These two verses describe the events surrounding the acts of intercourse between Lot and his two daughters. While they begin with the same word, וַתַּשְׁקֶיןָ *wattašqɛna* 'and they plied', the sentences quickly depart from one another: (a) v. 33 follows immediately with אֶת־אֲבִיהֶן *'ɛt abihɛn* 'their father', while v. 35 places this expression slightly later;

448–57]; and Gary A. Rendsburg, *The Redaction of Genesis* (Winona Lake, IN: Eisenbrauns, 1986; repr., with a new foreword, 2014), 15–18.

(b) the former uses the more archaic בַּלַּיְלָה הוּא *bal-layla hu²* 'on that night' (note the lack of the definite article on the demonstrative pronoun), while the latter uses the more standard בַּלַּיְלָה הַהוּא *bal-layla ha-hu²* 'on that night' (with the definite article on the demonstrative pronoun);[3] (c) v. 33 uses the verb ב-ו-א *b-w-²* 'come', whereas v. 35 uses the verb ק-ו-ם *q-w-m* 'arise'; and (d) in the first instance we read וַתִּשְׁכַּב אֶת־אָבִיהָ *wattiškab ²et ²abiha* 'and she lay with her father', with the object expressed as a noun, while in the second case we read וַתִּשְׁכַּב עִמּוֹ *wattiškab ʿimmo* 'and she lay with him', with the object expressed as a pronoun—and note, moreover, the use of different synonymous prepositions (both אֶת *²et* and עִם *ʿim* mean 'with') in these phrases.

This last difference, moreover, offers a subtle adumbration of the names of the two respective sons (see vv. 37–38), with the former phrase anticipating מוֹאָב *mo²ab* 'Moab', the name of the first daughter's son (note the common element אָב *²ab* 'father'), and with the latter phrase anticipating בֶּן־עַמִּי *ben ʿammi*, lit., 'son of my people', the second daughter's son and the ancestor of עַמּוֹן *ʿammon* 'Ammon' (note the common element created by the *ʿayin-mem* combination).[4]

In sum, far from a simple 'here we go again', the author introduces variation at every possible turn in v. 35. In fact, in light of these changes, I would further submit that the *defectiva* spelling וּבְקֻמָה [wBQMH] *u-bqumah* 'and her rising up' in v. 35 (the only case in the Bible of *defectiva* spelling with the infinitive construct of ק-ו-ם *q-w-m* 'arise'—see the Masoretic note) represents another slight alteration, in contrast to the expected *plene* spelling וּבְקוּמָה [wBQWMH] *u-bqumah* 'and her rising up', which is found in v. 33.[5] Obviously, this orthographic matter would be sensed only by the reader holding the written text and not by the listener enjoying the recitation—and yet I would appeal to variation for the sake of variation here as well,[6] especially when one

---

3. Incidentally, the Samaritan Torah reads בלילה ההוא BLYLH HHW² in both instances, a clear effort at harmonization. See also below, n. 5.

4. I am indebted to Roni Shweka (Hebrew University) for this very insightful observation.

5. Not surprisingly, once more the Samaritan Torah harmonizes the spelling, with ובקומה WBQWMH in both instances.

6. I thus accept the approach of Alfred Rahlfs and James Barr concerning the variant spellings in the Bible. See Alfred Rahlfs, "Zur Setzung der Lesemütter

realizes that the final clause of both iterations is otherwise identical.[7] Indeed, this most likely explains the supralineal dot over the *waw* in וּבְקוּמָה in v. 33, alerting the scribe to pay heed, to write the form in v. 33 with *waw* and then the form in v. 35 without.[8]

3. Genesis 25:24; 38:27

Gen 25:24

וַיִּמְלְאוּ יָמֶיהָ לָלֶדֶת וְהִנֵּה תוֹמִם בְּבִטְנָהּ׃

And her days to give birth were fulfilled, and behold, twins in her womb.

Gen 38:27

וַיְהִי בְּעֵת לִדְתָּהּ וְהִנֵּה תְאוֹמִים בְּבִטְנָהּ׃

And it was, at the time of her giving birth, and behold, twins in her womb.

The word for 'twins' in Hebrew is clearly one of the most unstable vocables in the language.[9] Apart from the two passages cited above, this lexeme occurs again in the Bible only in Song 4:5 and 7:4.[10] In passages that are otherwise identical (at least as far as the key six-word string is

---

im Alten Testament," in *Nachrichten von der Königlichen Gesellschaft der Wissenschaften zu Göttingen: Philologisch-historische Klasse* (Berlin: Weidmannsche Buchhandlung, 1916), 315–47; and James Barr, *The Variable Spellings of the Hebrew Bible* (Oxford: Oxford University Press, 1989), esp. 186–95.

7. For two more similar cases, see below, Chapter 9, no. 23.

8. On dotted letters in the Torah, see James S. Diamond, *Scribal Secrets: Extraordinary Texts in the Torah and Their Implications*, ed. Robert Goldenberg and Gary A. Rendsburg (Eugene, OR: Pickwick, 2019), 29–74, with Gen 19:33 treated on pp. 44–49.

9. For some factors which may have led to this instability, see Saul Levin, *Semitic and Indo-European: The Principal Etymologies* (Amsterdam: John Benjamins, 1995), 44–51; and Saul Levin, *Semitic and Indo-European II: Comparative Morphology, Syntax and Phonetics* (Amsterdam: John Benjamins, 2002), 532–33.

10. The root also occurs in the parallel passages Exod 26:24 and 36:29, though it functions there more as a verb (in the participial form, to be specific). On all these passages, see Karolien Vermeulen, "Two of a Kind: Twin Language in the Hebrew Bible," *Journal for the Study of the Old Testament* 37 (2012): 135–50.

concerned), the Masoretic Text presents only the most minor deviation for 'twins' (both in construct): תְּאוֹמֵי *təʾome* in 4:5, תְּאָמֵי *taʾome* in 7:4 (for many other instances of this phenomenon in Song of Songs, see further below, Chapter 15).

This information serves as background for the two similar lines from Genesis, which record the two occasions of the birthing of twins mentioned in the Bible. The wordings are parallel, save for the use of different forms of the key noun: תוֹמִם *tomim* in 25:24 (regarding Rebekah) and תְאוֹמִים *təʾomim* in 38:27 (regarding Tamar). Are we to imagine an ancient Israelite audience entertained by a single continuous reading of the book of Genesis (or perhaps just the ancestor narratives) that would recognize the different forms of the key word used at a distance of 13 chapters from one another? In light of what we have presented thus far, I would answer that question in the affirmative. Note further that the earlier form תוֹמִם *tomim* is presumably the less standard one (with ʾ*aleph* elided), with the more proper form תְאוֹמִים *təʾomim* (with ʾ*aleph* in place) reserved for the second encounter.

4. Genesis 34:5, 13

Gen 34:5

וַיַּעֲקֹב שָׁמַע כִּי טִמֵּא אֶת־דִּינָה בִתּוֹ

And Jacob heard that he had defiled Dinah his daughter.

Gen 34:13

וַיַּעֲנוּ בְנֵי־יַעֲקֹב אֶת־שְׁכֶם וְאֶת־חֲמוֹר אָבִיו בְּמִרְמָה וַיְדַבֵּרוּ אֲשֶׁר
טִמֵּא אֵת דִּינָה אֲחֹתָם:

And the sons of Jacob answered Shechem and Hamor
his father, with deceit, and they spoke; because he had
defiled Dinah their sister.

The latter verse includes one of but a handful of instances in Biblical Hebrew where the particle אֲשֶׁר ʾ*ašer* retains not its usual usage as the relative marker 'that, which, who', but rather functions akin to the conjunction כִּי *ki* 'for, because' used to introduce a causal clause.[11]

---

11. Robert D. Holmstedt, "The Story of Ancient Hebrew ʾ*ašer*," *Ancient Near Eastern Studies* 43 (2006): 7–26, esp. 21.

The author has invoked this atypical usage to avoid repeating the same string of words that occurs in v. 5. In the former verse, the word כִּי *ki* appears with its other usage, akin to English 'that' introducing a subordinate clause. Which is to say, one would expect v. 13 to read כִּי טִמֵּא אֶת דִּינָה **ki timme' 'et dina* *'because he had defiled Dinah'; but since v. 5 used these words (albeit with the slightly different meaning 'that he had defiled Dinah'), the author of Genesis 34 elected to vary his language by introducing אֲשֶׁר *'ašer* in v. 13, even if this maneuver entailed pushing the language to the edge of its grammaticality.

5. Genesis 35:26; 36:5

Gen 35:26

אֵלֶּה בְּנֵי יַעֲקֹב אֲשֶׁר יֻלַּד־לוֹ בְּפַדַּן אֲרָם:

These are the sons of Jacob, who was born to him in
Paddan Aram.

Gen 36:5

אֵלֶּה בְּנֵי עֵשָׂו אֲשֶׁר יֻלְּדוּ־לוֹ בְּאֶרֶץ כְּנָעַן:

These are the sons of Esau, who were born to him in
the land of Canaan.

The first verse (actually half-verse: Gen 35:26b) follows upon the listing of Jacob's sons (including Benjamin [see v. 24], even though he was born in Canaan and not in Aram). The passage presents a linguistic peculiarity, to wit, the use of the singular יֻלַּד *yullad* 'was born', even though the subject 'the sons of Jacob' is patently plural. The grammar is 'corrected', as it were, in the second go-round, in the summary statement concerning Esau's sons (again, a half-verse: Gen 36:5b)—note the plural verb יֻלְּדוּ *yulladu* 'were born'. The alert reader's antennae go up upon hearing Gen 35:26, but her attention is rewarded eight verses later upon reaching Gen 36:5. If I may be permitted such fancy, one may imagine the smile on her face upon perceiving the second iteration: good for you, dear author, you corrected your 'mistake' from eight verses earlier.[12]

---

12. As we have seen in other cases, the Samaritan tradition already 'corrected' the error, by changing the singular form ילד YLD in Gen 35:26 to the plural form ילדו YLDW.

6. Exodus 14:22, 29

Exod 14:22

וַיָּבֹאוּ בְנֵי־יִשְׂרָאֵל בְּתוֹךְ הַיָּם בַּיַּבָּשָׁה וְהַמַּיִם לָהֶם חֹמָה מִימִינָם
וּמִשְּׂמֹאלָם:

And the children of Israel came in the midst of the sea,
on the dry-land, and the waters were to them (as) a wall,
on their right and on their left.

Exod 14:29

וּבְנֵי יִשְׂרָאֵל הָלְכוּ בַיַּבָּשָׁה בְּתוֹךְ הַיָּם וְהַמַּיִם לָהֶם חֹמָה מִימִינָם
וּמִשְּׂמֹאלָם:

And the children of Israel had gone on the dry-land, in
the midst of the sea, and the waters were to them (as) a
wall, on their right and on their left.

In the dramatic narrative describing the Israelites' crossing of the
Sea of Reeds, twice we read that the people traversed the dry land in
the midst of the sea. The first passage above presents the action as
it first occurs; while the second one recounts the action in contrast
to the Egyptians' drowning in the sea upon the return of the waters.
These different settings demand different syntax (verb-subject in the
first, subject-verb in the second) and different verbal roots (ב-ו-א
b-w-ʾ 'come' in the first, ה-ל-ך *h-l-k* 'go' in the second), which by
themselves create the variation—but then the author goes further by
reversing the order of the two key phrases: בְּתוֹךְ הַיָּם בַּיַּבָּשָׁה *bə-tok*
hay-yam bay-yabbaša 'in the midst of the sea, on the dry-land' in
v. 22; בַּיַּבָּשָׁה בְּתוֹךְ הַיָּם *bay-yabbaša bə-tok hay-yam* 'on the dry-
land, in the midst of the sea' in v. 29. Contrary to typical biblical
style, the second half of each of these passages is identical: וְהַמַּיִם
לָהֶם חֹמָה מִימִינָם וּמִשְּׂמֹאלָם *wə-ham-mayim laḥεm ḥoma mi-minam*
u-miś-śəmoʾlam 'and the waters were to them (as) a wall, on their
right and on their left'. This verbatim repetition may have served
as a factor in the development of the Jewish tradition (observed in
many synagogues) of the congregation joining the Torah reader in
the chanting of this recurring line.

7. Exodus 19:21–22, 24

Exod 19:21–22

²¹ פֶּן־יֶהֶרְסוּ אֶל־יְהוָה֙ לִרְאוֹת֙ . . . ²² פֶּן־יִפְרֹץ בָּהֶם יְהוָה׃

²¹ "Lest they penetrate unto Yʜᴡʜ to see . . . ²² lest Yʜᴡʜ break-forth upon them."

Exod 19:24

אַל־יֶהֶרְסוּ לַעֲלֹת אֶל־יְהוָה פֶּן־יִפְרָץ־בָּם׃

"Let them not penetrate to go-up unto Yʜᴡʜ, lest he break-forth upon them."

Twice in the Mount Sinai scene, God tells Moses to warn the people not to come forward, with use of the verb ה-ר-ס *h-r-s*, normally meaning 'destroy', though here 'penetrate, break through'. The reader will recall that this unusual lexical choice appears *alliterationis causa*; see Chapter 6, no. 17. We now focus on the variations that occur within the repeated passages: (a) In the most obvious variation, פֶּן־יֶהֶרְסוּ *pɛn yɛhɛrsu* 'lest they penetrate' (v. 21) and אַל־יֶהֶרְסוּ *ʾal yɛhɛrsu* 'do not let them penetrate' (v. 24), different particles appear before the verb. (b) The former is followed by אֶל־יְהוָה לִרְאוֹת *ʾɛl yhwh lirʾot* 'unto Yʜᴡʜ to see', with the prepositional phrase אֶל־יְהוָה *ʾɛl yhwh* 'unto Yʜᴡʜ' preceding the infinitive of the root ר-א-ה *r-ʾ-h* 'see'; while the latter is followed by לַעֲלֹת אֶל־יְהוָה *laʿalot ʾɛl yhwh* 'to go-up unto Yʜᴡʜ', with the infinitive of the root ע-ל-ה *ʿ-l-h* 'go-up' preceding the prepositional phrase אֶל־יְהוָה *ʾɛl yhwh* 'unto Yʜᴡʜ'. (c) In the first iteration, the second part of the extended sentence reads פֶּן־יִפְרֹץ בָּהֶם יְהוָה *pɛn yipros bahɛm yhwh* 'lest Yʜᴡʜ break-forth upon them', with the subject expressly stated; while in the second iteration the matching clause reads פֶּן־יִפְרָץ־בָּם *pɛn yipros bam* 'lest he break-forth upon them', with the subject signified by an embedded pronoun indicator. (d) Finally, these last two phrases witness two different options for 'upon them', בָּהֶם *bahɛm* and בָּם *bam*. In short, as is to be expected given the survey of material in this monograph, at every turn our author introduced variation into his narrative.

8. Exodus 24:3, 7

Exod 24:3

כָּל־הַדְּבָרִים אֲשֶׁר־דִּבֶּר יְהוָה נַעֲשֶׂה:

"All the words that Yʜwʜ has spoken, we will do."

Exod 24:7

כֹּל אֲשֶׁר־דִּבֶּר יְהוָה נַעֲשֶׂה וְנִשְׁמָע:

"All that Yʜwʜ has spoken, we will do and we will obey."

Twice during the Sinai narrative in Exodus 24, the people proclaim their willingness to obey all that Yʜwʜ has spoken. The proclamation is different, however, in the two places, (a) with the first one using the word הַדְּבָרִים *had-dəbarim* 'the words', which is lacking in the second; and (b) with the second one appending the word וְנִשְׁמָע *wə-nišmaʿ* 'and we will obey', which is lacking in the first. The result is not only variant expressions, but more-or-less balanced ones in length.[13]

9. Exodus 24:10–11

Exod 24:10

וַיִּרְאוּ אֵת אֱלֹהֵי יִשְׂרָאֵל

And they saw the God of Israel.

Exod 24:11

וַיֶּחֱזוּ אֶת־הָאֱלֹהִים

And they beheld God.

Twice during the same narrative, the text informs us that the people saw God—a striking statement given the presence of other passages in the Bible that mention the danger inherent in such an action (Gen 32:31, Exod 19:21, 33:20, Judg 13:22, etc.). More to the point of the present enterprise, we note the variation in the two verses: (a) The first

---

13. For more on Exod 24:7, see below, Chapter 20, p. 430.

iteration uses the standard verb וַיִּרְאוּ *wayyir'u* 'and they saw', while
the restatement employs the atypical verb וַיֶּחֱזוּ *wayyeḥezu* 'and they
behold'; and (b) the first iteration uses the atypical אֱלֹהֵי יִשְׂרָאֵל *'elohe
yiśra'el* 'God of Israel', while the second mention employs the standard
term הָאֱלֹהִים *ha-'elohim* 'God' (lit., 'the God').

The uncommon nature of the two atypical usages is determined
from the following facts. The verb ח-ז-ה *ḥ-z-h* 'behold' is used in biblical
prose elsewhere only in Exod 18:21.[14] Its presence in Exod 24:11 would
have been seen by the attentive ancient reader as quite arresting, to
be explained, according to the present approach, as an attempt to introduce variation.[15] At the same time, though, the atypical verb ח-ז-ה
ḥ-z-h 'behold' is employed here to serve the 'form following content'
technique, as a parallel to the arresting action of beholding God.

The divine epithet אֱלֹהֵי יִשְׂרָאֵל *'elohe yiśra'el* 'God of Israel' is
common when preceded by יְהוָה 'Yhwh' (99x in the Bible) or by יהוה
צְבָאוֹת *yhwh ṣəba'ot* 'Yhwh of Hosts' (37x in the Bible, especially in
Jeremiah), but it is relatively rare when standing on its own, especially
in prose. In the grand narrative of Genesis–Kings, the only other passages where the term stands on its own are Num 16:9 and 1 Kgs 8:26.[16]

---

14. On the atypical language in Exodus 18, see Edward L. Greenstein, "Jethro's Wit: An Interpretation of Wordplay in Exodus 18," in Stephen L. Cook
and S. C. Winter, eds., *On the Way to Nineveh: Studies in Honor of George M.
Landes* (Atlanta: Scholars Press, 1999), 155–71; and Mordechay Mishor, "On
the Language and Text of Exodus 18," in Steven E. Fassberg and Avi Hurvitz,
eds., *Biblical Hebrew in Its Northwest Semitic Environment: Typological and
Historical Perspectives* (Jerusalem: Magnes; Winona Lake, IN: Eisenbrauns,
2006), 225–29. The only other attestations of the verb ח-ז-ה *ḥ-z-h* 'behold' in
the Torah, which are found in Num 24:4, 24:16, appear in the poetic oracles of
Balaam (on which see Chapter 24). In the rest of the Bible, the verbal root is
limited to poetry (Psalms, Job) and prophetic books (frequently with reference
to prophetic vision). For the reader not conversant with Hebrew, note that
the verb ח-ז-ה *ḥ-z-h* 'behold' is not related to the particle *hinne* 'behold', the
subject of Chapter 19, even though I have used the same English translation
(in the former case, as a verb; in the latter case, as an interjection).

15. See Bernard P. Robinson, "The Theophany and Meal of Exodus 24,"
Scandinavian Journal of the Old Testament 25 (2011): 167: "the shift of verb is
simply a matter of elegant variation."

16. In Gen 33:20, the phrase stands in apposition to אֵל *'el* 'El'. In 1 Sam
5:7–6:3 (7x), the term appears as part of the expression אֲרוֹן אֱלֹהֵי יִשְׂרָאֵל *'aron*

10. Exodus 34:30, 35

Exod 34:30

וַיַּרְא אַהֲרֹן וְכָל־בְּנֵי יִשְׂרָאֵל אֶת־מֹשֶׁה וְהִנֵּה קָרַן עוֹר פָּנָיו

And Aaron and all the children of Israel saw Moses, and
behold, the skin of his face was horned.

Exod 34:35

וְרָאוּ בְנֵי־יִשְׂרָאֵל אֶת־פְּנֵי מֹשֶׁה כִּי קָרַן עוֹר פְּנֵי מֹשֶׁה

And the children of Israel would see the face of Moses,
that the skin of the face of Moses was horned.

Clearly there is a distinction between these two verses, with the first
one describing Aaron's and the Israelites' *first* perception of Moses
with his face horned,[17] while the second describes the *ongoing* realization of said physical observation.[18] Nonetheless, we note the following
changes in wording.

(a) In v. 30 the object of the verb ר-א-ה *r-ʾ-h* 'see' is simply אֶת־מֹשֶׁה
ʾet moše 'Moses', while in v. 35 the object is אֶת־פְּנֵי מֹשֶׁה *ʾet pǝne moše*
'the face of Moses'. The reason is clear: in v. 30 Aaron and the people
see Moses from afar as a whole person (indeed for the first time as he
descends Mount Sinai), and only upon his approaching closer do the
viewers perceive his extraordinary face (such is the effect, I submit);
while in v. 35 they cannot help but look at Moses's face, each time they

---

ʾelohe yiśraʾel 'the Ark of the God of Israel', providing the Philistine perspective (six of the seven occurrences are within direct speech uttered by the
Philistines). The attestation in 2 Sam 23:3 is within a poem embedded into
the narrative prose.

17. Yes, 'horned' and not 'radiant', on which see further Gary A. Rendsburg, "Moses as Equal to Pharaoh," in Gary M. Beckman and Theodore J. Lewis,
eds., *Text, Artifact, and Image: Revealing Ancient Israelite Religion* (Brown
Judaic Studies 346; Providence: Brown Judaic Studies, 2006), 201–19, in particular 216–18.

18. See recently Tamar Zewi, "On רָאָה כִּי and רָאָה וְהִנֵּה in Biblical Hebrew,"
in Gregor Geiger, ed., *En pāsē grammatikē kai sophiā: Saggi di linguistica
ebraica in onore di Alviero Niccacci, ofm* (Jerusalem: Franciscan Printing Press
/ Edizioni Terra Sancta, 2011), 405–14, esp. 413.

encounter him. Which is to say, the variation here is not simply for stylistic effect, but rather incorporates a true distinction.

(b) In line with this is the shift from וְהִנֵּה *wə-hinne* 'and behold' in v. 30 to כִּי *ki* 'that' in v. 35. The former particle reflects the first-time perception by Aaron and the people (as noted above); as we will explicate further in Chapter 19, this use of וְהִנֵּה *wə-hinne* 'and behold' allows the reader to see the event through the eyes of these characters. Said particle would be out of place in v. 35, since the people already know what to expect each time they see Moses, and thus the relative marker כִּי *ki* 'that' is used.

(c) The third variation, however, is for stylistic effect alone. Note the difference between קָרַן עוֹר פָּנָיו *qaran ʿor panaw* 'the skin of his face was horned' in v. 30 and קָרַן עוֹר פְּנֵי מֹשֶׁה *qaran ʿor pəne mošɛ* 'the skin of the face of Moses was horned' in v. 35, with the name 'Moses' repeated in this verse, even though the form פָּנָיו *panaw* 'his face' (as in v. 30) would have sufficed here again.

11. Judges 16 (first set of verses)

Judg 16:7

וְחָלִיתִי וְהָיִיתִי כְּאַחַד הָאָדָם׃

"and I will be weak and I will be as any man"

Judg 16:11

וְחָלִיתִי וְהָיִיתִי כְּאַחַד הָאָדָם׃

"and I will be weak and I will be as any man"

(round three: lacking)

Judg 16:17

וְחָלִיתִי וְהָיִיתִי כְּכָל־הָאָדָם׃

"and I will be weak and I will be as every man"

Four times in Judges 16, Delilah attempts to extract the secret of Samson's strength from her suitor, and four times the hero responds with information (false or real). In the first two instances (vv. 7 and 11), Samson declaims the same phrase: וְחָלִיתִי וְהָיִיתִי כְּאַחַד הָאָדָם *wəḥaliti wəhayiti kə-ʾaḥad ha-ʾadam* 'and I will be weak and I will be as any man'. No such statement occurs during the third scene (one would expect it at the end of v. 13). In the fourth scene, Samson's words are varied: וְחָלִיתִי וְהָיִיתִי כְּכָל־הָאָדָם *wəḥaliti wəhayiti kə-kol ha-ʾadam* 'and I will be weak and I will be as every man'.

12. Judges 16 (second set of verses)

Judg 16:9

וְהָאֹרֵב יֹשֵׁב לָהּ בַּחֶדֶר וַתֹּאמֶר אֵלָיו פְּלִשְׁתִּים עָלֶיךָ שִׁמְשׁוֹן

And the ambush was waiting for her in the room, and she said to him, "The Philistines are upon you, Samson."

Judg 16:12

וַתֹּאמֶר אֵלָיו פְּלִשְׁתִּים עָלֶיךָ שִׁמְשׁוֹן וְהָאֹרֵב יֹשֵׁב בֶּחָדֶר

And she said to him, "The Philistines are upon you, Samson," and the ambush was waiting in the room.

Judg 16:14

וַתֹּאמֶר אֵלָיו פְּלִשְׁתִּים עָלֶיךָ שִׁמְשׁוֹן

And she said to him, "The Philistines are upon you, Samson."

Judg 16:20

וַתֹּאמֶר פְּלִשְׁתִּים עָלֶיךָ שִׁמְשׁוֹן

And she said, "The Philistines are upon you, Samson."

The four enticements in Judges 16 provide additional opportunities for the author to vary his text, as exemplified by the verses above. In the first two scenes, the verses are matched closely, though the order of the two main clauses is reversed: v. 9 mentions the ambush first and then proceeds to Delilah's warning; while in v. 12 Delilah's warning appears first and is followed by mention of the presence of the ambush. A more minor variation is present as well, with v. 9 including the word לָהּ *lah* 'for her' and with v. 12 removing this word. In the third and fourth instances, the author omits any mention of the ambush. To vary these two statements, the author continues with וַתֹּאמֶר אֵלָיו *watto'mɛr 'elaw* 'and she said to him' to introduce Delilah's cautioning in v. 14, but he then deletes the latter term in v. 20, with a simple וַתֹּאמֶר *watto'mɛr* 'and she said' sufficing.[19]

13. 1 Samuel 3:5–6, 8–9

1 Sam 3:5

> וַיָּרָץ אֶל־עֵלִי וַיֹּאמֶר הִנְנִי כִּי־קָרָאתָ לִּי וַיֹּאמֶר לֹא־קָרָאתִי שׁוּב
> שְׁכָב וַיֵּלֶךְ וַיִּשְׁכָּב:

And he ran to Eli, and he said, "Here I am, for you called me"; and he said, "I did not call, return, lie down," and he went, and he lay down.

1 Sam 3:6

> וַיֹּסֶף שְׁמוּאֵל וַיֵּלֶךְ אֶל־עֵלִי וַיֹּאמֶר הִנְנִי כִּי קָרָאתָ לִי וַיֹּאמֶר לֹא־
> קָרָאתִי בְנִי שׁוּב שְׁכָב:

And Samuel arose, and he went to Eli, and he said, "Here I am, for you called me"; and he said, "I did not call, my son, return, lie down."

1 Sam 3:8–9

> ⁸ וַיָּקָם וַיֵּלֶךְ אֶל־עֵלִי וַיֹּאמֶר הִנְנִי כִּי קָרָאתָ לִי . . .
> ⁹ וַיֹּאמֶר עֵלִי לִשְׁמוּאֵל לֵךְ שְׁכָב . . .
> וַיֵּלֶךְ שְׁמוּאֵל וַיִּשְׁכַּב בִּמְקוֹמוֹ:

⁸ And he arose, and he went to Eli, and he said, "Here I am, for you called me"; . . .
⁹ and Eli said to Samuel, "Go, lie down . . ." And Samuel went, and he lay down in his place.

---

19. We will return to this point below, Chapter 13, no. 18.

The scene is the young Samuel living with Eli in the sanctuary of Yahweh. Three times God calls to Samuel, though the lad does not understand the source of the call, since he assumes that Eli has called him. Three times Samuel tells Eli הִנְנִי כִּי קָרָאתָ לִי *hinəni ki qara'ta li* 'Here I am, for you called me'; and three times Eli replies that he has not. During the third incident, Eli realizes (not reproduced above) that in fact God has called Samuel. The repeated scene allows the author to introduce variation, with such alternations set against the verbatim words uttered by Samuel each time. In a literary style where variation is the norm, in this case the reader is asked to focus on the lack of variation in the young Samuel's speech, a device, I would propose, that mirrors the lad's innocence and unawareness.

The repetitions in the prose are as follows. (1) Samuel's approach to Eli is worded as (a) וַיָּרָץ אֶל־עֵלִי *wayyaroṣ 'el 'eli* 'and he ran to Eli'; (b) וַיָּקָם שְׁמוּאֵל וַיֵּלֶךְ אֶל־עֵלִי *wayyaqom šəmu'el wayyelek 'el 'eli* 'and Samuel arose, and he went to Eli'; and (c) וַיָּקָם וַיֵּלֶךְ אֶל־עֵלִי *wayyaqom wayyelek 'el 'eli* 'and he arose, and he went to Eli'. Note the verb ר-ו-ץ *r-w-ṣ* 'run' in the first occasion versus the two-verb idiom ק-ו-ם *q-w-m* 'arise' + ה-ל-ךְ *h-l-k* 'go' in the second and third occasions, along with the expressed subject שְׁמוּאֵל *šəmu'el* 'Samuel' in the second occasion versus the use of (embedded) pronouns in the first and third.

(2) Eli's command to return to sleep is expressed differently in the three events: (a) לֹא־קָרָאתִי שׁוּב שְׁכָב *lo' qara'ti šub šəkab* 'I did not call, return, lie down'; (b) לֹא־קָרָאתִי בְנִי שׁוּב שְׁכָב *lo' qara'ti bəni šub šəkab* 'I did not call, my son, return, lie down', which introduces the word בְנִי *bəni* 'my son'; and (c) לֵךְ שְׁכָב *lek šəkab* 'go, lie down', without an assertion that Eli had not called Samuel, though at this point Eli continues with further instructions, should Samuel hear the voice again.

(3) Finally, there is Samuel's return to sleep: (a) וַיֵּלֶךְ וַיִּשְׁכָּב *wayyelek wayyiškab* 'and he went, and he lay down'; (b) the lack of any such statement in the second occurrence; and (c) וַיֵּלֶךְ שְׁמוּאֵל וַיִּשְׁכַּב בִּמְקוֹמוֹ *wayyelek šəmu'el wayyiškab bi-mqomo* 'and Samuel went, and he lay down in his place', with both the explicit subject and a prepositional phrase providing additional specific information.

14. 1 Samuel 17:55–56

1 Sam 17:55

בֶּן־מִי־זֶה הַנַּעַר

"the son of whom is this young-man?"

1 Sam 17:56

בֶּן־מִי־זֶה הָעֶלֶם

"the son of whom is this lad?"

These two phrases, both in the mouth of Saul, occur within the narrative of the encounter between David and Goliath. When Saul observes the young man entering the fray with the aim of slaying the Philistine giant, he asks his general Abner, בֶּן־מִי־זֶה הַנַּעַר *ben mi zɛ han-naʿar* 'the son of whom is this young-man?' When Abner replies that he does not know, Saul instructs him to inquire as to the person's identify, though he now uses the phrase בֶּן־מִי־זֶה הָעֶלֶם *ben mi zɛ ha-ʿalɛm* 'the son of whom is this lad?' For the sake of variation, the word used to denote the unknown individual is changed from the standard word נַעַר *naʿar* 'young-man' to the rare noun עֶלֶם *ʿɛlɛm* (pausal *ʿalɛm*) 'lad'.[20]

15. 1 Samuel 25:22, 34

1 Sam 25:22

אִם־אַשְׁאִיר מִכָּל־אֲשֶׁר־לוֹ עַד־הַבֹּקֶר מַשְׁתִּין בְּקִיר׃

"if I leave from all that is his by the morning a pisser on the wall."

1 Sam 25:34

כִּי אִם־נוֹתַר לְנָבָל עַד־אוֹר הַבֹּקֶר מַשְׁתִּין בְּקִיר׃

"there would not have remained to Nabal by the light of morning a pisser on the wall."

---

20. Hence my preference for 'young-man' (more standard in English) for the former, and 'lad' (less standard, except in certain regions of Great Britain) for the latter.

In v. 22 David vows to destroy all the males in Nabal's entourage with the words reproduced above. Due to Abigail's intervention, such does not occur, an action that then leads David to declaim the words presented in v. 34. The most obvious change in phraseology is from עַד־הַבֹּקֶר *ʿad hab-boqɛr* 'by the morning' (v. 22) to עַד־אוֹר הַבֹּקֶר *ʿad ʾor hab-boqɛr* 'by the light of morning' (v. 34). One also observes the change in verbal root and voice, from אַשְׁאִיר *ʾašʾir* 'I leave' (v. 22), an active Hiphʿil form of the root שׁ-א-ר *š-ʾ-r* 'leave', to נוֹתַר *notar* 'have remained' (v. 34), a passive Niphʿal form of the root י-ת-ר *y-t-r* 'remain'.[21]

16. 1 Samuel 27:3; 30:5

1 Sam 27:3

אֲחִינֹעַם הַיִּזְרְעֵאלִית וַאֲבִיגַיִל אֵשֶׁת־נָבָל הַכַּרְמְלִית:

Ahinoam the Jezreelite (fem.) and
Abigail the wife of Nabal the Carmelite (fem.)

1 Sam 30:5

אֲחִינֹעַם הַיִּזְרְעֵלִית וַאֲבִיגַיִל אֵשֶׁת נָבָל הַכַּרְמְלִי:

Ahinoam the Jezreelite (fem.) and
Abigail the wife of Nabal the Carmelite (masc.)

Twice during the narrative of David's rise to kingship we encounter a reference to his two wives, Ahinoam and Abigail (one need not ask what happened to Michal in these passages). Note the variation with reference to the latter: in 27:3, Abigail is the Carmelite (fem.); while in 30:5, her late husband Nabal is the Carmelite (masc.).[22] Presumably, the attentive listener would grasp the difference in wording, even at a distance of three chapters. We further note another scribal

---

21. On other delightful literary aspects in these verses, see Peter Leithart, "Nabal and His Wine," *Journal of Biblical Literature* 120 (2001): 525–27. On alliteration in this chapter, see below, Chapter 10, no. 16.

22. Note that the *təʿamim* (along with the *maqqef*) work in conjunction with this distinction. There is certainly no reason for textual emendation here, as suggested by many scholars; see further McCarter, *I Samuel*, 412.

variation, for the reader/performer to feast his eyes upon: in the first
passage, the epithet of Ahinoam is written correctly, with (quiescent)
’aleph; while in the second passage the ’aleph is missing from the
orthography.

17. 2 Samuel 11:9, 13

2 Sam 11:9

. . . אֶת כָּל־עַבְדֵי אֲדֹנָיו וְלֹא יָרַד אֶל־בֵּיתוֹ:

. . . with all the servants of his lord; and he did not go-
down to his house.

2 Sam 11:13

. . . עִם־עַבְדֵי אֲדֹנָיו וְאֶל־בֵּיתוֹ לֹא יָרָד:

. . . with the servants of his lord, and to his house he did
not go-down.

These two verses bring us to the story of David and Bathsheba, to my
mind the absolute pinnacle of biblical prose storytelling.[23] Hence it is
good to be able to include two examples from 2 Samuel 11, both this
one and the next one. The verses above describe Uriah's remaining
with the king's servants in the palace, as opposed to his going home
to sleep with his wife, which of course was David's intention in bringing him back to Jerusalem from the battlefront. Three main differences
occur: (a) in v. 9 the preposition 'with' is expressed by אֶת ’et, while
in v. 13 the alternative form עִם ‘im is used; (b) the first iteration uses
the expression כָּל־עַבְדֵי אֲדֹנָיו kol ‘abde ’adonaw 'all the servants of his
lord', while the second iteration uses simply עַבְדֵי אֲדֹנָיו ‘abde ’adonaw
'the servants of his lord'; and (c) the word order of the last phrase is
reversed, so that for the first night the narrator states וְלֹא יָרַד אֶל־בֵּיתוֹ
wə-lo’ yarad ’ɛl beto 'and he did not go-down to his house', while for

---

23. See the masterful analysis by Meir Sternberg, *The Poetics of Biblical
Narrative: Ideological Literature and the Drama of Reading* (Bloomington:
Indiana University Press, 1985), 190–222.

the second night he relates וְאֶל־בֵּיתֹו לֹא יָרָד *wə-ʾel beto loʾ yarad* 'and to his house he did not go-down'. This last alteration may constitute more than stylistic effect, since the syntax could evoke something like 'and to his house he *still* did not go-down', that is, not even after an evening of feasting and drinking with David (see the first part of v. 13)—but it remains a case of repetition with variation regardless.

18. 2 Samuel 11:20–21

2 Sam 11:20

מַדּוּעַ נִגַּשְׁתֶּם אֶל־הָעִיר לְהִלָּחֵם

"Why did you approach to the city to fight?"

2 Sam 11:21

לָמָּה נִגַּשְׁתֶּם אֶל־הַחֹומָה

"Why did you approach to the city-wall?"

These two passages occur slightly later in the David and Bathsheba story. The context is Joab's speech to the messenger, who is to report to David what has transpired in the siege of Rabbah—the battle that includes the orchestrated murder of Uriah. Joab anticipates that David will speak the words cited above, with the passage in v. 20 at the start of said 'quotation' and the passage in v. 21 at the end of it. Literary style demands repetition with variation, so that the words are not repeated verbatim. In the first instance, Joab anticipates that David will use the word מַדּוּעַ *maddua*ʿ 'why', while in the second instance, Joab envisions David employing the alternative word לָמָּה *lamma* 'why'.[24] In v. 20, moreover, the phrase is אֶל־הָעִיר לְהִלָּחֵם *ʾel ha-ʿir ləhillaḥem* 'to the city to fight', using one noun followed by the infinitival verb; while in v. 21, the phrase is the simpler אֶל־הַחֹומָה *ʾel ha-ḥoma* 'to the city-wall', using a different noun without a verb following.

---

24. If I wanted to extend the English language to capture the difference between the two interrogatives, I might use the phrase 'what for' in the second instance, which captures the etymological basis of לָמָּה *lamma* 'why'.

19. 1 Kings 3:26–27

1 Kgs 3:26

תְּנוּ־לָהֹ אֶת־הַיָּלוּד הַחַי וְהָמֵת אַל־תְּמִיתֻהוּ

"Give her the living newborn, and do not put him to death!"

1 Kgs 3:27

תְּנוּ־לָהֹ אֶת־הַיָּלוּד הַחַי וְהָמֵת לֹא תְמִיתֻהוּ

"Give her the living newborn, and you shall not put him to death."

These two verses were analyzed in the previous chapter, which was devoted to confused language in the Bible. As I observed there, v. 26 represents the only instance in the entire Bible in which an infinitive absolute is negated by אַל *'al*.[25] The standard usage, of course, is negation by לֹא *lo'*, as in v. 27. To repeat what was stated earlier: Naturally, one can appreciate the wording in v. 26, for at this crucial juncture in the narrative, one imagines the mother of the living child struggling to utter any set of words, regardless of grammatical correctness, given her passion and the excitement of the moment. Solomon, by contrast, notwithstanding his intense interest in the matter, is able to speak dispassionately, thus employing proper grammar with the negative particle לֹא *lo'*.

To the earlier discussion I now add the following: In light of my analysis, this example does not constitute a case of variation simply for the sake of variation, but rather once again demonstrates the extent to which ancient Hebrew authors would vary their language, even to the point of fashioning a unique or highly abnormal (shall we say, ungrammatical) syntagma. Finally, note that while the first five words of the parallel phrases are identical, the author utilizes these verbatim sentences most artfully: with the former (in the mouth of the mother of the living child) pointing to Woman A of the story, and with the latter (in the mouth of Solomon) pointing to Woman B in the story.[26]

---

25. See Kim, *The Function of the Tautological Infinitive in Classical Biblical Hebrew*, 51.

26. For the designations "Woman A" and "Woman B," along with my literary analysis of 1 Kings 3:16–28, see Gary A. Rendsburg, "The Guilty Party in

20. 1 Kings 11:31, 35

1 Kgs 11:31

הִנְנִי קֹרֵעַ אֶת־הַמַּמְלָכָה מִיַּד שְׁלֹמֹה וְנָתַתִּי לְךָ אֵת עֲשָׂרָה
הַשְּׁבָטִים:

Behold, I am tearing the kingdom from the hand of Solomon, and I will give to you the ten tribes.

1 Kgs 11:35

וְלָקַחְתִּי הַמְּלוּכָה מִיַּד בְּנוֹ וּנְתַתִּיהָ לְךָ אֵת עֲשֶׂרֶת הַשְּׁבָטִים:

And I will take the kingship from the hand of his son,
and I will give it to you, the ten tribes.

In these two verses the prophet Ahijah states and restates God's intention to wrest the ten tribes from the Davidic dynasty and to present
them to Jeroboam. Variable phraseology is used throughout: (a) v. 31
begins with a הִנֵּה *hinne* 'behold' clause, while v. 35 commences with a
wǝqatal form; (b) v. 31 uses the verb ק-ר-ע *q-r-ʿ* 'tear', while v. 35 uses
ל-ק-ח *l-q-ḥ* 'take'; (c) the former verse uses the noun הַמַּמְלָכָה *ham-
mamlaka* 'the kingdom', with אֶת *ʾet* before it, whereas the latter uses
the noun הַמְּלוּכָה *ham-mǝluka* 'the kingship', without the *nota accusativi*; (d) in the first iteration the kingdom will be torn מִיַּד שְׁלֹמֹה *miy-yad
šǝlomo* 'from the hand of Solomon', while in the second instance the
kingship will be taken מִיַּד בְּנוֹ *miy-yad bǝno* 'from the hand of his [sc.
Solomon's] son'; (e) v. 31 reads וְנָתַתִּי לְךָ *wǝnatatti lǝka* 'and I will give
to you', while v. 35 states וּנְתַתִּיהָ לְךָ *unǝtattiha lǝka* 'and I will give it
to you'; and finally (f) we note the variation between עֲשָׂרָה *ʿaśara* 'ten'
(in the absolute form) and עֲשֶׂרֶת *ʿaśeret* 'ten' (in the construct form).

This last fluctuation, not surprisingly, occurs elsewhere in the Bible,
as authors took advantage of the different manners of expressing nu-
merals. Here I simply present several examples: Lev 27:5 וְלַנְּקֵבָה עֲשֶׂרֶת
וְלַנְּקֵבָה עֲשָׂרָה שְׁקָלִים *wǝ-lan-nǝqeba ʿaśeret šǝqalim* ~ Lev 27:7 שְׁקָלִים

1 Kings iii 16–28," *Vetus Testamentum* 48 (1998): 534–41; and Gary A. Rendsburg,
"The Literary Approach to the Bible and Finding a Good Translation," 179–94,
esp. 190–93, and with my English translation of the entire episode on p. 194.

wə-lan-nəqeba ʿaśara šəqalim, both 'and for a female, ten shekels'; Judg 11:38 שְׁנֵי חֳדָשִׁים *šəne ḥodašim* ~ Judg 11:37, 11:39 שְׁנַיִם חֳדָשִׁים *šənayim ḥodašim*, both 'two months'; and Dan 10:2 שְׁלֹשָׁה שָׁבֻעִים יָמִים *šəloša šabuʿim yamim* ~ Dan 10:3 שְׁלֹשֶׁת שָׁבֻעִים יָמִים *šəlošɛt šabuʿim yamim*, both 'three weeks' time' (even if the latter may suggest definiteness in this context, viz., 'the three weeks' time').

21. 1 Kings 19

(21a) 1 Kgs 19:5

וַיֹּאמֶר לוֹ קוּם אֱכֹל:

And he said to him, "Arise, eat."

1 Kgs 19:7

וַיֹּאמֶר קוּם אֱכֹל

And he said, "Arise, eat."

(21b) 1 Kgs 19:6

וַיֹּאכַל וַיֵּשְׁתְּ

And he ate and he drank.

1 Kgs 19:8

וַיָּקָם וַיֹּאכַל וַיִּשְׁתֶּה

And he arose, and he ate and he drunk.

(21c) 1 Kgs 19:9

וְהִנֵּה דְבַר־יְהוָה אֵלָיו וַיֹּאמֶר לוֹ מַה־לְּךָ פֹה אֵלִיָּהוּ:

And behold, the word of Yʜᴡʜ unto him, and he said to him, "Why are you here, Elijah?"

1 Kgs 19:13

וְהִנֵּה אֵלָיו קוֹל וַיֹּאמֶר מַה־לְּךָ פֹה אֵלִיָּהוּ:

And behold, unto him a voice, and he said, "Why are you here, Elijah?"

Within the narrative of 1 Kings 19, scenes repeat (made most explicit by the use of the word שֵׁנִית *šenit* 'a second time' in v. 7), a situation that allows the author to enliven his prose with skillfully fashioned alternative phraseology.[27] In (21a) the author first uses וַיֹּאמֶר לוֹ *wayyo'mɛr lo* 'and he said to him', followed by the simpler וַיֹּאמֶר *wayyo'mɛr* 'and he said';[28] plus he introduces variable spelling with both אֱכוֹל and אֱכֹל, the

---

27. The word שֵׁנִית *šenit* 'second time' serves as an indicator of "build-up and climax" in ancient Hebrew prose texts; cf. Cyrus H. Gordon, "Build-up and Climax," in Yitzhak Avishur and Joshua Blau, eds., *Studies in the Bible and Ancient Near East Presented to Samuel E. Loewenstamm* (Jerusalem: E. Rubinstein, 1978), 29–34 (in the non-Hebrew volume); and Esther H. Roshwalb, "Build-up and Climax in Jeremiah's Visions and Laments," in Meir Lubetski, Claire Gottlieb, and Sharon Keller, eds., *Boundaries of the Ancient Near Eastern World: A Tribute to Cyrus H. Gordon* (Journal for the Study of the Old Testament Supplement Series 273; Sheffield: Sheffield Academic Press, 1998), 111–35. As another instance of repetition with variation in a text surveyed by the latter author, note Jer 1:11 מָה־אַתָּה רֹאֶה יִרְמְיָהוּ *ma 'atta ro'ɛ yirməyahu* 'what do you see, Jeremiah?' and Jer 1:13 מָה אַתָּה רֹאֶה *ma 'atta ro'ɛ* 'what do you see?', to be discussed below in Chapter 15, no. 7.

28. On such formulae, see Robert E. Longacre, *Joseph: A Story of Divine Providence* (Winona Lake, IN: Eisenbrauns, 1989), 158–84 (the chapter entitled "Variations in Formulas of Quotation"). Longacre's method revealed different shades of meaning in the various formulae that he studied, a point I would accept for examples such as Gen 44:15 וַיֹּאמֶר לָהֶם יוֹסֵף *wayyo'mɛr lahɛm yosep* 'and Joseph said to them' versus Gen 45:3 וַיֹּאמֶר יוֹסֵף אֶל־אֶחָיו *wayyo'mɛr yosep 'ɛl 'ɛhaw* 'and Joseph said to his brothers'. But I doubt that such an approach could explain the difference noted here for 1 Kgs 19:5, 19:7, where variation simply for the sake of variation is at play. I also would resist the criticism of Samuel E. Meier, *Speaking of Speaking: Marking Direct Discourse in the Hebrew Bible* (Supplements to Vetus Testamentum 46; Leiden: Brill, 1992), 16–17, who noted that the "nominal and pronominal constituents that accompany the verb are among the most unstable elements in the textual tradition" (p. 16). My approach, like that of Longacre, is to take the Masoretic Text seriously on such matters. After all, regardless of how one judges the Masoretic Text, it remains a significant textual witness (or perhaps reflects a group of relatively uniform textual witnesses) to the ancient Hebrew compositions included in the canon. Notwithstanding our contrary opinions reflected in the above remarks, I am grateful to Samuel Meier (Ohio State University) for directing me both to Longacre's book (cited here) and to Revell's book (cited below, p. 180, n. 35).

two forms of *’ɛkol* 'eat'. Regarding (21b), God had commanded Elijah קוּם אֱכֹל *qum ’ɛkol* 'arise, eat' in v. 5, though the narrative describes the prophet's response as וַיֹּאכַל וַיֵּשְׁתְּ *wayyo’kal wayyešt* 'he ate and he drank' in v. 6. In the second instance, the command is the same (v. 7), but the narrative then states וַיָּקָם וַיֹּאכַל וַיִּשְׁתֶּה *wayyaqom wayyo’kal wayyištɛ* 'and he arose, and he ate and he drunk' (v. 8), including both an appropriate response to the 'arise' command and a nonstandard *wayyiqtol* form, וַיִּשְׁתֶּה *wayyištɛ*.[29] The latter point is crucial here: the author is willing to go to any extreme to vary his language, even to the point of employing a nonstandard usage. I have attempted to reflect this variation in my translation via the use of 'drunk', the sub-standard past tense of 'drink' in English.[30]

In (21c) God's question to Elijah מַה־לְּךָ פֹה אֵלִיָּהוּ *ma ləka po ’eliyyahu* 'why are you here, Elijah?' is repeated verbatim. Accordingly, to ensure variation the author introduces the question through different means: (i) through different וְהִנֵּה *wə-hinne* 'and behold' clauses; and (ii) with the alternation of וַיֹּאמֶר לוֹ *wayyo’mɛr lo* 'and he said to him' and וַיֹּאמֶר *wayyo’mɛr* 'and he said', as we saw above in (21a) as well. Conversely, Elijah's long (twenty-four-word!) answer in v. 10 to God's question appears verbatim in v. 14 (letter for letter, vowel for vowel, *ṭaʿam* for *ṭaʿam*). Presumably, the fact that God's question was repeated word for word paves the way for his prophet's response to be stated verbatim. In addition, given all the other variable phraseology inherent in this text (and throughout the Bible), the lack of such variation in Elijah's retort may provide the reader/listener with some insight into the prophet's character, as one who does not stray, unlike those Israelites whom he describes with the statement כִּי־עָזְבוּ בְרִיתְךָ *ki ʿazbu bəritka* 'for they have forsaken your covenant'.[31]

---

29. On such forms, see Joüon and Muraoka, *Grammar of Biblical Hebrew*, 208, §79m. Note their comment, "The long forms are particularly frequent in the books of Kings."

30. See the discussion in the *American Heritage Dictionary* at http://dictionary.reference.com/browse/drink, s.v. 'Usage Note'.

31. See further below, Chapter 27, no. 6.

22. Jonah 1:2; 3:2

Jonah 1:2

קוּם לֵךְ אֶל־נִינְוֵה הָעִיר הַגְּדוֹלָה וּקְרָא עָלֶיהָ כִּי־עָלְתָה רָעָתָם
לְפָנָי:

"Arise, go to Nineveh the great city, and call upon it, for their evil has arisen before me."

Jonah 3:2

קוּם לֵךְ אֶל־נִינְוֵה הָעִיר הַגְּדוֹלָה וּקְרָא אֵלֶיהָ אֶת־הַקְּרִיאָה אֲשֶׁר
אָנֹכִי דֹּבֵר אֵלֶיךָ:

"Arise, go to Nineveh the great city, and call unto it this call, which I speak to you."

Much has been written about the alternation between וּקְרָא עָלֶיהָ *u-qra' 'alɛha* 'and call upon it', as part of God's original command to Jonah, and וּקְרָא אֵלֶיהָ *u-qra' 'elɛha* 'and call unto it', as part of God's repetition of the command. On the one hand, Athalya Brenner claimed that this alternation originates "from a desire to vary the language of the opening of ch. 3, which is almost word-for-word the language of the opening of ch. 1" (hence her view is in line with the present study);[32] while on the other hand, Jack Sasson contended that the change in preposition reflects a different semantic nuance.[33] George Landes, meanwhile, considered both positions, calling the usage in 3:2 "simply a stylistic variant" of the usage in 1:2, while at the same time noting that possibly "the author intended a somewhat stronger expression with על in 1:2 than with אל in 3:2, because of the different content that follows each of the constructions."[34] While I tend to agree with Brenner (and

---

32. Athalya Brenner, "Lešono šel Sefer Yona ke-Maddad li-Qviʿat Zeman Ḥibburo," *Bet Miqra'* 39 (1978–1979 / 5739): 396–405, in particular p. 400. The Hebrew original is: ודאי ברצון לגוון את נוסחת הפתיחה של פרק ג׳ שהיא זהה כמעט מילולית לנוסחת הפתיחה בפרק א׳.

33. Jack M. Sasson, "On Jonah's Two Missions," *Henoch* 6 (1984), 23–30; and Jack M. Sasson, *Jonah* (Anchor Bible 24B; New York: Doubleday, 1990), 72–75.

34. George M. Landes, "Linguistic Criteria and the Date of the Book of Jonah," in *Eretz-Israel* 16 (Harry Orlinsky Volume; Jerusalem: ha-Ḥevra le-Ḥaqirat Ereṣ-Yisra'el ve-ʿAtiqoteha, 1982): 158*.

Landes's first suggestion), the question need not be decided here—for even if Sasson (and Landes's second suggestion) are correct, from a purely stylistic viewpoint polyprosopon is operative in these two comparable verses.[35] Which is to say, while some readers may have intuited a semantic difference between 1:2 and 3:2, all discerning readers would have grasped the slight change from וְקָרָא עָלֶיהָ *u-qraʾ ʿalɛha* 'and call upon it' in the former to וְקָרָא אֵלֶיהָ *u-qraʾ ʾelɛha* 'and call unto it' in the latter—in addition to the larger shifts in wording toward the end of the two verses.

23. Job 1–2

(23a) Job 1:1

תָּם וְיָשָׁר וִירֵא אֱלֹהִים וְסָר מֵרָע׃

perfect and just, and fearing God, and turning from evil.

Job 1:8

תָּם וְיָשָׁר יְרֵא אֱלֹהִים וְסָר מֵרָע׃

perfect and just, fearing God, and turning from evil.

Job 2:3

תָּם וְיָשָׁר יְרֵא אֱלֹהִים וְסָר מֵרָע

perfect and just, fearing God, and turning from evil.

(23b) Job 1:12

וַיֵּצֵא הַשָּׂטָן מֵעִם פְּנֵי יְהוָה׃

And the Satan went out from before God.

Job 2:7

וַיֵּצֵא הַשָּׂטָן מֵאֵת פְּנֵי יְהוָה

And the Satan went out from before God.

---

35. Other scholars also have found meaning in the varied language of biblical prose. See, most prominently perhaps, E. J. Revell, *The Designation of the Individual: Expressive Usage in Biblical Narrative* (Kampen: Kok Pharos, 1996). See also above, p. 177, n. 28.

(23c) Job 1:16

עוֹד | זֶה מְדַבֵּר וְזֶה בָּא וַיֹּאמַר֫

This one still was speaking, and this one came and said.

Job 1:17

עוֹד | זֶה מְדַבֵּר וְזֶה בָּא וַיֹּאמַר֫

This one still was speaking, and this one came and said.

Job 1:18

עַד זֶה מְדַבֵּר וְזֶה בָּא וַיֹּאמַר

This one yet was speaking, and this one came
and said.

(23d) Job 1:6

וַיְהִי הַיּוֹם וַיָּבֹאוּ בְּנֵי הָאֱלֹהִים לְהִתְיַצֵּב עַל־יְהוָה וַיָּבוֹא גַם־הַשָּׂטָן
בְּתוֹכָם:

And it was on the day, and the *bǝne ʾɛlohim* came to
present themselves before Yhwh, and also the Satan
came in their midst.

Job 2:1

וַיְהִי הַיּוֹם וַיָּבֹאוּ בְּנֵי הָאֱלֹהִים לְהִתְיַצֵּב עַל־יְהוָה וַיָּבוֹא גַם־הַשָּׂטָן
בְּתֹכָם לְהִתְיַצֵּב עַל־יְהוָה:

And it was on the day, and the *bǝne ʾɛlohim* came to
present themselves before Yhwh, and also the Satan
came in their midst, to present himself before Yhwh.

(23e) Job 1:7

וַיֹּאמֶר יְהוָה אֶל־הַשָּׂטָן מֵאַיִן תָּבֹא וַיַּעַן הַשָּׂטָן אֶת־יְהוָה וַיֹּאמַר
מִשּׁוּט בָּאָרֶץ וּמֵהִתְהַלֵּךְ בָּהּ:

And Yhwh said to the Satan, "From where have you
come?" And the Satan answered Yhwh, and he said,
"From traversing the earth and going to-and-fro on it."

Job 2:2

וַיֹּ֤אמֶר יְהוָה֙ אֶל־הַשָּׂטָ֔ן אֵ֥י מִזֶּ֖ה תָּבֹ֑א וַיַּ֨עַן הַשָּׂטָ֤ן אֶת־יְהוָה֙ וַיֹּאמַ֔ר
מִשֻּׁ֣ט בָּאָ֔רֶץ וּמֵֽהִתְהַלֵּ֖ךְ בָּֽהּ׃

And YHWH said to the Satan, "Whence have you
come?" And the Satan answered YHWH, and he said,
"From traversing the earth and going to-and-fro on it."

(23f) Job 1:11

וְאוּלָם֙ שְֽׁלַֽח־נָ֣א יָֽדְךָ֔ וְגַ֖ע בְּכָל־אֲשֶׁר־ל֑וֹ אִם־לֹ֥א עַל־פָּנֶ֖יךָ יְבָרֲכֶֽךָּ׃

"However, send forth your hand, and harm all that is
his—[and see] if he will not 'bless' you upon your face."

Job 2:5

אוּלָם֙ שְֽׁלַֽח־נָ֣א יָֽדְךָ֔ וְגַ֥ע אֶל־עַצְמ֖וֹ וְאֶל־בְּשָׂר֑וֹ אִם־לֹ֥א אֶל־פָּנֶ֖יךָ
יְבָרֲכֶֽךָּ׃

"However, send forth your hand, and harm his bone
and his flesh—[and see] if he will not 'bless' you
unto your face."

As with 1 Kings 19, so with Job 1–2: repeated scenes provide the author
ample opportunity to display his linguistic virtuosity for the benefit of
his readers/listeners. In (23a), it is simply the presence or absence of
the conjunction -וְ wə- 'and': the author includes the conjunction in the
narratorial voice (1:1), then deletes it when God addresses the Satan (1:8,
2:3). In (23b), we note the change from מֵעִם me'im to מֵאֵת me'et, both
meaning 'from' (and thus I have rendered the two passages the same).
In (23c), the first two iterations use the standard Hebrew adverb עוֹד
'od 'still'; while in the third passage the author elects to employ עַד 'ad
'yet' (in order to distinguish the two usages in my renderings, I opt for
'yet' here). In Standard Biblical Hebrew, עַד 'ad is a preposition meaning 'until'; in Late Biblical Hebrew, this particle takes on the adverbial
usage 'still, yet, while'.[36] The author of Job 1–2 took full advantage of
this fact in his selection of עַד 'ad 'yet' in 1:18.

---

36. For initial treatment, see Avi Hurvitz, "The Date of the Prose-Tale
of Job Linguistically Reconsidered," *Harvard Theological Review* 67 (1974):

The two passages in (23d) begin in like fashion (in fact, the first eight words match each other letter for letter, vowel for vowel, *ṭaʿam* for *ṭaʿam*) and continue as such—until the author plays with the reader's/listener's expectations with the surprise inclusion of a second לְהִתְיַצֵּב עַל־יְהוָה *ləhityaṣṣeb ʿal* Yhwh 'to present himself before Yhwh' at the end of 2:1. Here we also note another scribal/visual distinction, between the *plene* writing בְּתוֹכָם [BTWKM] *bə-tokam* 'in their midst' in 1:6 and the *defectiva* orthography בְּתֹכָם [BTKM] *bə-tokam* 'in their midst' in 2:1 (the latter noted by the Masoretes as a unique form in the Bible). In (23e) we observe the change from the more common (17x in the Bible) interrogative מֵאַיִן *me-ʾayin* 'from where' in 1:7 to the less common (7x in the Bible) interrogative אֵי מִזֶּה *ʾe miz-ze* 'whence' in 2:2 (again using different English terms available to reflect the two different Hebrew terms). And once more we recognize different orthography in these two verses, with the standard מִשּׁוּט [MŠWṬ] *miš-šuṭ* 'from traversing' in 1:7 and the unusual מִשֻּׁט [MŠṬ] *miš-šuṭ* 'from traversing' in 2:2 (again, see the Masoretic note).[37] Finally, in (23f) a series of small changes is present: (i) again, the use or non-use of the conjunction -וְ *wə-* (not reflected in the translation, though) at the start; (ii) the use of either -בְּ *bə-* or אֶל *ʾel* following the verb נ-ג-ע *n-g-ʿ* 'touch, harm';[38] and (iii) the use of either עַל *ʿal* 'upon' or אֶל *ʾel* 'unto' in the last phrase.

The result of all these slight changes is obvious. With the scenes repeating throughout Job 1–2 (the *bəne ʾelohim* presenting themselves

---

17–34, in particular 26–28, where Hurvitz discusses the specific combination of עַד *ʿad* + participle. For further discussion, see Gary A. Rendsburg, "Late Biblical Hebrew in the Book of Haggai," in Rebecca Hasselbach and Naʿama Pat-El, eds., *Language and Nature: Papers Presented to John Huehnergard on the Occasion of His 60th Birthday* (Studies in Ancient Oriental Civilization 67; Chicago: The Oriental Institute of the University of Chicago, 2012), 331. For adverbial עַד *ʿad* 'still, while, yet' as an Israelian Hebrew feature, see Rendsburg, *Israelian Hebrew in the Book of Kings*, 116–17. For a challenge to the Hurvitz position concerning the prose narrative of Job, see Ian Young, "Is the Prose Tale of Job in Late Biblical Hebrew?" *Vetus Testamentum* 59 (2009): 606–29, with particular attention to עַד *ʿad* on pp. 615–17 (though I side with Hurvitz against Young on this issue).

37. This parallels the difference noted above (Chapter 9, no. 2) for the infinitive construct forms in Gen 19:33, 35.

38. For examples of both usages in the Bible, see *DCH* 5:608–9.

before God twice; God's two conversations with the Satan; messengers arriving in quick succession to relay devastating news to Job; etc.), a less creative writer simply may have repeated the same words verbatim. Ancient Hebrew literary style, however, called for a much more imaginative use of language—one that no doubt the consumers of these texts appreciated with pleasure.

CHAPTER TEN

ALLITERATION IN PROSE NARRATIVES

I have devoted two chapters of this monograph to alliteration in the books of Genesis and Exodus (see above, Chapters 5 and 6). In this chapter, we return to the subject of alliteration in biblical narrative prose, with a sampling of two dozen passages taken from the larger compositions Numbers, Joshua, Judges, Samuel, and Kings, as well as the smaller prose texts Ruth, Jonah, and Job 1–2.

1. Numbers 11:1–2

וַיְהִי הָעָם כְּמִתְאֹנְנִים רַע בְּאָזְנֵי יְהוָה וַיִּשְׁמַע יְהוָה וַיִּחַר אַפּוֹ וַתִּבְעַר־ ¹
בָּם אֵשׁ יְהוָה וַתֹּאכַל בִּקְצֵה הַמַּחֲנֶה:
וַיִּצְעַק הָעָם אֶל־מֹשֶׁה וַיִּתְפַּלֵּל מֹשֶׁה אֶל־יְהוָה וַתִּשְׁקַע הָאֵשׁ: ²

¹ And the people were complaining, evil in the ears of Yʜwʜ; and Yʜwʜ heard, and he angered, and a fire of Yʜwʜ burned among them, and it consumed the edge of the camp.
² And the people cried-out to Moses; and Moses prayed to Yʜwʜ, and the fire abated.

Numbers 11 presents the first sustained narrative since the arrival at Sinai in Exodus 19. Which is to say, from Exodus 20 to the end of that book, then the entirety of Leviticus, and then the first ten chapters of Numbers, the Israelites have been encamped at Sinai, with the Torah focused on the subjects of law and cult, especially within the priestly tradition. Finally, the Israelites are on the march again (see Num 10:12), so that prose storytelling resumes at this point. It does not take long for the narrative voice of the Torah to introduce alliteration into the composition.

The phrase that attracts our attention is at the end of v. 2: וַתִּשְׁקַע הָאֵשׁ wattišqaʿ ha-ʾeš 'and the fire abated'. The verbal root שׁ-ק-ע š-q-ʿ

'abate' occurs only five other times in the Bible, all in poetry and prophecy, typically with reference to the abatement of water, in particular the waters of the Nile River (Ezek 32:14, Amos 8:8, 9:5).

The normal verb used for putting out a fire is כ-ב-ה *k-b-h* 'extinguish', as can be seen in Lev 6:5, 6:6, Isa 66:24, Jer 4:4, 17:27, 21:12, Ezek 21:3, Amos 5:6, Prov 26:20 (9x altogether). The usage in Num 11:2, accordingly, is atypical on several grounds: (a) it is the only attestation of the root שׁ-ק-ע *š-q-ʿ* 'abate' in the narrative prose corpus; and (b) it is the only instance where the verb is collocated with אֵשׁ *ʾeš* 'fire', in place of the regular verb כ-ב-ה *k-b-h* 'extinguish'.

The reason for this peculiar word choice is obvious. Two other main verbs in these verses are וַיִּשְׁמַע *wayyišmaʿ* 'and (Yhwh) heard' (v. 1) and וַיִּצְעַק *wayyiṣʿaq* 'and (the people) cried-out'. The former shares *šin* and *ʿayin* with the key word וַתִּשְׁקַע *wattišqaʿ*, while the latter shares *ʿayin* and *qof*.

2. Numbers 14:21

וְאוּלָם חַי־אָנִי וְיִמָּלֵא כְבוֹד־יְהוָה אֶת־כָּל־הָאָרֶץ׃

"However, as I live, and as the glory of Yhwh fills all the earth."

In Chapter 5, no. 7, we observed the alliteration between the emphatic word וְאוּלָם *wə-ʾulam* 'however' and the root מ-ל-א *m-l-ʾ* 'fill' in Gen 48:19. The same soundplay appears here in Num 14:21, with the two forms וְאוּלָם *wə-ʾulam* 'however' and וְיִמָּלֵא *wə-yimmaleʾ* 'fill' containing the same four consonants (I include in this count the initial /w/ sound in each form). There is more, however (no pun intended), for as we shall see below, other biblical authors produced alliteration between וְאוּלָם *wə-ʾulam* 'however' and another Hebrew phrase.

3. Numbers 21:9

וַיַּעַשׂ מֹשֶׁה נְחַשׁ נְחֹשֶׁת וַיְשִׂמֵהוּ עַל־הַנֵּס וְהָיָה אִם־נָשַׁךְ הַנָּחָשׁ אֶת־
אִישׁ וְהִבִּיט אֶל־נְחַשׁ הַנְּחֹשֶׁת וָחָי׃

wayyaʿaś mošɛ nəḥaš nəḥošɛt wa-yśimehu ʿal han-nes
wəhaya ʾim našak han-naḥaš ʾɛt ʾiš wəhibbiṭ ʾɛl nəḥaš
han-nəḥošɛt wahay

And Moses made a snake of copper, and he placed it on the standard; and it would be, when the snake [that is, a real snake] would bite a person, he would look at the snake of copper, and he would live.

Faced with yet one more instance of the Israelites' murmuring (see v. 5), God sends poisonous snakes to bite the people, with the result that many die (v. 6). The people admit their sin, and Moses intercedes before God (v. 7). God instructs Moses to make a copper serpent and to place it on a standard (v. 8), and the result is the verse quoted above. The most fascinating aspect of the cited passage is the repetition of sibilants, as follows: /ś/–/š/–/š/–/š/–/ś/–/s/–/š/–/š/–/š/–/š/–/š/. Not only is this an instance of alliteration, but more significantly the chain of sibilants reproduces in human language the hissing sounds of snakes.[1]

4. Numbers 25:8

וַיָּבֹא אַחַר אִישׁ־יִשְׂרָאֵל אֶל־הַקֻּבָּה וַיִּדְקֹר אֶת־שְׁנֵיהֶם אֵת אִישׁ
יִשְׂרָאֵל וְאֶת־הָאִשָּׁה אֶל־קֳבָתָהּ וַתֵּעָצַר הַמַּגֵּפָה מֵעַל בְּנֵי יִשְׂרָאֵל:

And he [i.e., Pinḥas] came after the Israelite man unto the
tent-chamber, and he pierced the two of them, the Israelite
man, and the woman in her abdomen; and the plague upon
the children of Israel stopped.

The author of Numbers 25 seizes the opportunity to collocate two unusual words in v. 8: הַקֻּבָּה *haq-qubba* 'the tent-chamber' and קֳבָתָהּ *qobatah* 'her abdomen'. The former is a *hapax legomenon* (the normal word, of course, is אֹהֶל *’ohɛl* 'tent', though possibly if not probably הַקֻּבָּה *haq-qubba* refers to the innermost part of a tent, hence my gloss 'the tent-chamber'); while the latter appears only here and in Deut 18:3, in a slightly different form, הַקֵּבָה *haq-qeba*, with reference to the stomach of an animal as among those portions of the sacrifice due to the priest.[2]

---

1. Victor A. Hurowitz, "Healing and Hissing Snakes: Listening to Numbers 21:4–9," *Scriptura* 87 (2004): 278–87.

2. To capture the alliteration in an English rendering, the translator might consider using the words 'billet' and 'belly', respectively—even though I have opted for more standard terms here, 'tent-chamber' and 'abdomen'.

Assisting the aural effect here is the word הַמַּגֵּפָה *ham-maggepa* 'the plague', whose voiced velar /g/ sound corresponds to the voiceless emphatic velar /q/ of the other two words, and whose labials /m/ and /p/ echo the sound of the labial /b/ of the other two words.

5. Joshua 5:10–12

10 וַיַּחֲנוּ בְנֵי־יִשְׂרָאֵל בַּגִּלְגָּל וַיַּעֲשׂוּ אֶת־הַפֶּסַח בְּאַרְבָּעָה עָשָׂר יוֹם לַחֹדֶשׁ בָּעֶרֶב בְּעַרְבוֹת יְרִיחוֹ:

11 וַיֹּאכְלוּ מֵעֲבוּר הָאָרֶץ מִמָּחֳרַת הַפֶּסַח מַצּוֹת וְקָלוּי בְּעֶצֶם הַיּוֹם הַזֶּה:

12 וַיִּשְׁבֹּת הַמָּן מִמָּחֳרָת בְּאָכְלָם מֵעֲבוּר הָאָרֶץ וְלֹא־הָיָה עוֹד לִבְנֵי יִשְׂרָאֵל מָן וַיֹּאכְלוּ מִתְּבוּאַת אֶרֶץ כְּנַעַן בַּשָּׁנָה הַהִיא:

10 And the children of Israel encamped at Gilgal; and they made the Pesaḥ on the fourteenth day of the month, in the evening, on the plains of Jericho.
11 And they ate of the harvest of the land, from the morrow of the Pesaḥ, *matzot* and roasted-grain, on that very day.
12 And the manna ceased on the morrow, upon their eating of the harvest of the land, and there no longer was manna for the children of Israel; and they ate of the produce of the land of Canaan during that year.

It will come as no surprise to learn that an agrarian society such as Israel possessed numerous words to express 'harvest, produce, ingathering, etc.' The commonest of these words in the Bible are קָצִיר *qaṣir* (54x) and תְּבוּאָה *təbu'a* (43x, including once here in v. 12); other terms are more specific ones, such as בָּצִיר *baṣir* (6x, used especially for fruit [grapes, olives, etc.]), אֹסֶף *'osep* (3x, including once with reference to locusts), and אָסִיף *'asip* (2x, both with reference to Sukkot).[3]

---

3. The Gezer Calendar, line 1, also attests to the word אסף 'harvest', presumably vocalized as either *'osep* or *'asip*, both just cited—though more likely the latter, which fits the *qatīl* pattern of season times; cf. קָצִיר *qaṣir* and בָּצִיר *baṣir*, both mentioned above, as well as אָבִיב *'abib* 'spring', זָמִיר *zamir* 'pruning', etc. See further below, Chapter 17, pp. 361–62, n. 6.

With all of these (near or virtual) synonyms available, the author of Joshua 5 instead elected to use עֲבוּר *ʿabur* 'harvest' (vv. 11–12), the only two attestations of this usage in the Bible. The effect of this lexical choice is rather obvious, since this word is surrounded by אַרְבָּעָה *ʾarbaʿa* 'four', עֶרֶב *ʿɛrɛb* 'evening', עַרְבוֹת *ʿarbot* 'plains of'—all in v. 10, and all of which share the same three consonants as our key word. Adding support to the auditory pleasure is the twofold use of מִמָּחֳרַת *mim-maḥorat* 'on/from the morrow' (vv. 10–11), with shared /r/, corresponding labials /b/ and /m/, and corresponding gutturals /ʿ/ and /ḥ/.

6. Judges 3:17–18, 20, 24

¹⁷ וַיַּקְרֵב֙ אֶת־הַמִּנְחָ֔ה לְעֶגְל֖וֹן מֶ֣לֶךְ מוֹאָ֑ב וְעֶגְל֕וֹן אִ֥ישׁ בָּרִ֖יא מְאֹֽד׃

¹⁸ וַֽיְהִי֙ כַּאֲשֶׁ֣ר כִּלָּ֔ה לְהַקְרִ֖יב אֶת־הַמִּנְחָ֑ה וַיְשַׁלַּח֙ אֶת־הָעָ֔ם נֹשְׂאֵ֖י הַמִּנְחָֽה׃

----

²⁰ וְאֵה֣וּד ׀ בָּ֣א אֵלָ֗יו וְהֽוּא־יֹ֠שֵׁב בַּעֲלִיַּ֨ת הַמְּקֵרָ֤ה אֲשֶׁר־לוֹ֙ לְבַדּ֔וֹ וַיֹּ֣אמֶר אֵה֔וּד דְּבַר־אֱלֹהִ֥ים לִ֖י אֵלֶ֑יךָ וַיָּ֖קָם מֵעַ֥ל הַכִּסֵּֽא׃

----

²⁴ וְה֣וּא יָצָא֮ וַעֲבָדָ֣יו בָּאוּ֒ וַיִּרְא֗וּ וְהִנֵּ֛ה דַּלְת֥וֹת הָעֲלִיָּ֖ה נְעֻל֑וֹת וַיֹּ֣אמְר֔וּ אַ֣ךְ מֵסִ֥יךְ ה֛וּא אֶת־רַגְלָ֖יו בַּחֲדַ֥ר הַמְּקֵרָֽה׃

¹⁷ And he brought-close the tribute to Eglon, king of Moab; and Eglon (was) a very hefty man.
¹⁸ And it was, when he finished to bring-close the tribute, and he sent-forth the people, the tribute bearers.

----

²⁰ And Ehud had come unto him, as he was sitting in the upper-room of the cool-place, which was his, alone, and Ehud said, "I have a word of God for you"; and he arose from the chair.

----

²⁴ And he had gone out, and his servants had come, and they saw—and behold, the doors of the upper-room are locked; and they said, "indeed, he is covering his legs in the chamber of the cool-place."

I have intentionally translated the Hiphʿil verb הִקְרִיב *hiqrib* as 'bring-close', in order to bring out the etymological sense of the word, from the root ק-ר-ב *q-r-b* 'be near, be close'. By so doing, I also am able to distinguish this verb from its synonym, the Hiphʿil verb הֵבִיא *hebi'* 'bring', from the root ב-ו-א *b-w-'* 'come'. I do so because both verbs are used with the object מִנְחָה *minḥa* 'gift, offering, tribute', though typically with an important distinction.

When מִנְחָה *minḥa* is used in reference to a sacrifice for God, in the majority of cases, especially within the cultic material in the Torah, the verb is הִקְרִיב *hiqrib* 'bring-close' > 'offer, sacrifice'; thus, for example, Lev 2:1, 2:4, 2:8, 2:11, 2:14, 6:7, 6:14, 7:9, 9:17, 23:16, Num 5:25, 28:26. True, the verb הֵבִיא *hebi'* 'bring' > 'offer, sacrifice' also may be used, but such instances appear only occasionally: thus, in a narrative context in Gen 4:3, 4:4, and in the prophetic texts in Isa 1:13, Jer 17:26, 41:5, Mal 1:13.

By contrast, the latter usage dominates when מִנְחָה *minḥa* refers to 'tribute' conveyed by one person to another or by one nation to another; thus, Gen 43:26, 1 Sam 10:27, 1 Kgs 10:25, 2 Chr 9:24, 17:11. The exception is Judg 3:17–18, in which occur the two verbs וַיַּקְרֵב *way-yaqreb* 'and he brought-close' and לְהַקְרִיב *ləhaqrib* 'to bring close', with reference to the tribute that Ehud brings on behalf of the Israelites to Eglon, king of Moab.

Now, there may be an allusion to sacrificial terminology here, because, as many scholars have noted, the name of the soon-to-be-killed king, עֶגְלוֹן *ʿɛglon* 'Eglon', derives from the word עֵגֶל *ʿɛgɛl* 'calf, young bull', not to mention the author's use of בָּרִיא *bari'* 'fat, hefty' to describe him (v. 17), a term typically associated with animals (e.g., 6x in Genesis 41, with reference to the good cows in Pharaoh's dream, plus Ezek 34:20, Zech 11:16), including those used for sacrifice (1 Kgs 5:3, Ezek 34:3). All of which is to say, the author's choice of הִקְרִיב *hiqrib* 'bring-close' for the tribute offering to Eglon may hint at the monarch's eventual demise.

Whether this be the case or not, it is certain that one factor contributing to the author's twofold use of הִקְרִיב *hiqrib* 'bring-close' in Judg 3:17–18 is the alliteration produced via its proximity to הַמְּקֵרָה *ham-məqera* 'the cool-place' (vv. 20, 24). This term is used only here in the Bible, so we cannot be sure of its precise meaning, though clearly it refers to a private room with a lock (see vv. 23–25)—and indeed most scholars, myself included, assume that מְקֵרָה *məqera* 'cool-place' refers to the privy or toilet room.

In short, the narrative adopts a formula known from sacrificial language—that is, הִקְרִיב *hiqrib* 'bring-close' + מִנְחָה *minḥa* 'offering'—for use in the context of tribute (where the expected verb would have been הֵבִיא *hebi'* 'bring'), in order to have the sounds of הִקְרִיב *hiqrib* 'bring-close' echo with הַמְּקֵרָה *ham-məqera* 'the cool-place'. The words share the consonants /q/ and /r/, with the third (near) match generated by the labials /b/ and /m/.

7. Judges 3:22–23

וַיָּבֹא גַם־הַנִּצָּב אַחַר הַלַּהַב וַיִּסְגֹּר הַחֵלֶב בְּעַד הַלַּהַב כִּי לֹא שָׁלַף ²²
הַחֶרֶב מִבִּטְנוֹ וַיֵּצֵא הַפַּרְשְׁדֹנָה:
וַיֵּצֵא אֵהוּד הַמִּסְדְּרוֹנָה וַיִּסְגֹּר דַּלְתוֹת הָעֲלִיָּה בַּעֲדוֹ וְנָעָל: ²³

²² And also the hilt entered after the blade, and the fat closed
around the blade, because he did not withdraw the sword
from his stomach; and the feces went-out.
²³ And Ehud went-out via the side-porch, and he closed the
doors of the upper-chamber behind him, and he locked.

We remain with the same story. In a brilliant display of depth of lexicon, the author of the Ehud pericope places two *hapax legomena* within a cluster of four words, bridging vv. 22 and 23: הַפַּרְשְׁדֹנָה *hap-paršədona* 'the feces'[4] and הַמִּסְדְּרוֹנָה *ham-misdərona* 'via the side-porch' (or some such architectural term). The match of consonants is quite remarkable: both contain /r/ and /d/, in addition to sharing the suffix -*on* (in fact, in these two forms, more specifically -*ona*; see anon); while the two sets of sibilants /š/ and /s/ and labials /p/ and /m/ correspond.

The adverbial locative-directional -*a* suffix on the latter term, הַמִּסְדְּרוֹנָה *ham-misdərona*, makes grammatical sense, 'and Ehud went-out *via* the side-porch'. The presence of this morpheme on the former noun, הַפַּרְשְׁדֹנָה *hap-paršədona*, is at first glance problematic, since it serves as the subject of the sentence. Undoubtedly the author reinforced

---

4. On this word and its definition, see Michael L. Barré, "The Meaning of PRŠDN in Judges iii 22," *Vetus Testamentum* 41 (1991): 1–11.

the linkage between the two words by adapting the pattern הַמִּסְדְּרוֹנָה
ham-misdərona 'via the side-porch' to הַפַּרְשְׁדֹנָה *hap-paršədona* 'the
feces', notwithstanding the grammatical difficulty created thereby.[5]

Finally, we note what the scribal tradition accomplished with these
two words. In an attempt to vary the spelling of the two matched words,
convention necessitated that one noun (in this case, the former) be
written *plene* (that is, with *waw* to mark the long /o:/ vowel), while the
other noun (in this case, the latter) be written *defectiva* (note the lack
of *waw*). Remarkably, this point was not lost on the Masoretes, who
felt the need to comment on the two words, indicating the different
spelling usages.[6]

8. Judges 7:3–4

³ וְעַתָּה קְרָ֣א נָ֗א בְּאָזְנֵ֤י הָעָם֙ לֵאמֹ֔ר מִי־יָרֵ֣א וְחָרֵ֔ד יָשֹׁ֥ב וְיִצְפֹּ֖ר מֵהַ֣ר
הַגִּלְעָ֑ד וַיָּ֣שָׁב מִן־הָעָ֗ם עֶשְׂרִ֤ים וּשְׁנַ֙יִם֙ אֶ֔לֶף וַעֲשֶׂ֥רֶת אֲלָפִ֖ים נִשְׁאָֽרוּ׃
⁴ וַיֹּ֙אמֶר יְהֹוָ֜ה אֶל־גִּדְע֗וֹן עוֹד֮ הָעָ֣ם רָב֒ הוֹרֵ֤ד אוֹתָם֙ אֶל־הַמַּ֔יִם וְאֶצְרְפֶ֥נּוּ
לְךָ֖ שָׁ֑ם . . .

³ "And now, call, please, in the ears of the people, saying,
'Whoever is fearful and trembling, he should return and he
should leap from Mount Gilead'"; and twenty-two thousand from among the people returned, and ten thousand
remained.
⁴ And Yнwн said to Gideon, "Still the people are too many,
take them down to the water, so that I may refine them for
you there . . ."

No one quite knows what the *hapax legomenon* וְיִצְפֹּ֖ר *wə-yiṣpor*, from
the root צ-פ-ר *ṣ-p-r*, connotes in Judg 7:3, though for our present purposes it matters not. My use of 'leap' above is a serviceable gloss, for
the context calls for a verb of motion, something to be paired with

---

5. We will return to this story on two further occasions, at Chapter 13,
no. 17, and Chapter 19, no. 10.

6. I owe this observation concerning both the different orthographies
and the Masoretic recognition thereof to my very able student Baek Hee Kim
(Brite Divinity School).

'return', as one descends from a mountain.[7] As is clear by now, upon encountering a rare or unique word in the Bible, the reader should look at the surrounding words, among which she most likely will find a like-sounding word. In this instance, said inspection results once more in success, for in the next verse one comes across the key verb וְאֶצְרְפֶנּוּ *wə-'eṣrəpennu* 'so that I may refine them' (lit., 'him', since the antecedent הָעָם *ha-'am* 'the people' is masc. sg.), from the root צ-ר-ף *ṣ-r-p* 'refine'. The two verbal roots, of course, are anagrams of each other.

9. Judges 11:35

וַיְהִי כִרְאוֹתוֹ אוֹתָהּ וַיִּקְרַע אֶת־בְּגָדָיו וַיֹּאמֶר אֲהָהּ בִּתִּי הַכְרֵעַ
הִכְרַעְתִּנִי וְאַתְּ הָיִיתְ בְּעֹכְרָי וְאָנֹכִי פָּצִיתִי־פִי אֶל־יְהוָה וְלֹא אוּכַל
לָשׁוּב:

And it was, when he saw her, and he tore his clothes, and
he said, "Ah, my daughter, you indeed have brought me low,
and you, you have become my trouble; and I, I opened my
mouth unto Yhwh, and I cannot take (it) back."

Four alliterative words from three separate roots appear in close proximity to each other in this verse: וַיִּקְרַע *wayyiqra'* 'and he tore'; הַכְרֵעַ הִכְרַעְתִּנִי *hakrea' hikra'tini* 'you indeed have brought me low'; and בְּעֹכְרָי *bə-'okray* 'my trouble'. The three roots are ק-ר-ע *q-r-'* 'tear'; כ-ר-ע *k-r-'* 'kneel (Qal), bring low (Hiph'il)'; and ע-כ-ר *'-k-r* 'trouble'. In addition, one notes the presence of כִרְאוֹתוֹ *kir'oto* 'when he saw', from the root ר-א-ה *r-'-h* 'see', in which one observes the consonantal string כ /k/ – ר /r/ – א /'/, which aligns with the aforementioned words. In fact, one might have expected our author to begin this verse with a simple וַיַּרְא *wayyar'* 'and he saw', one of the commonest forms in the Bible, though this form would not have provided additional sound effect. By selecting the expression וַיְהִי כִרְאוֹתוֹ *wayhi kir'oto* 'and it was, when he saw', the author enhances the alliteration by including this fifth word.[8]

---

7. As such, I interpret the verb as a denominative from צָפִיר *ṣəpir* 'goat', an animal well known for its ability to leap up and down the mountain sides. Though I admit that other explanations are equally possible.

8. On the wordplay involving the root פ-צ-ה *p-ṣ-h* 'open' in this verse, see below, Chapter 18, no. 7.

10. Judges 14:18

וַיֹּאמְרוּ לוֹ אַנְשֵׁי הָעִיר בַּיּוֹם הַשְּׁבִיעִי בְּטֶרֶם יָבֹא הַחַרְסָה מַה־מָּתוֹק
מִדְּבַשׁ וּמֶה עַז מֵאֲרִי וַיֹּאמֶר לָהֶם לוּלֵא חֲרַשְׁתֶּם בְּעֶגְלָתִי לֹא מְצָאתֶם
חִידָתִי׃

And the men of the city said to them on the seventh day,
before the solar set, "What is sweeter than honey, and what
is stronger than a lion?"; and he said to them, "Had you not
plowed with my heifer, you would not have found-out my
riddle."

The above verse comes near the end of the second narrative within
the Samson cycle. The author passed on the opportunity to play on the
name of the hero, for he elected not to use שֶׁמֶשׁ *šɛmɛš* 'sun' in conjunction with שִׁמְשׁוֹן *šimšon* 'Samson',[9] but instead invoked the rare word
הַחַרְסָה *ha-ḥarsa* 'the solar',[10] which appears again only in Job 9:7. The
listener to this text may express bafflement upon hearing this word, but
the puzzle is short-lived, for she soon encounters the key verb חֲרַשְׁתֶּם
ḥaraštɛm 'you plowed', which provides the alliterative link. The three
consonants of the earlier noun are /ḥ-r-s/, which are echoed in the
following verbal root /ḥ-r-š/.

I should mention that the expression לוּלֵא חֲרַשְׁתֶּם בְּעֶגְלָתִי *lule*ˀ
ḥaraštɛm bə-ˁɛglati 'had you not plowed with my heifer' constitutes a
delightful idiom in Hebrew, equal to English 'had you not fooled around
with my girl'. The word 'plow' bears sexual meaning in other world
languages (including English),[11] while words for young female animals

---

9. For the technique of plays on proper names, see below, Chapter 18.

10. In keeping with my practice of rendering common Hebrew words with
common English words and rare Hebrew words with rare English words, I
have elected to use 'solar' for חַרְסָה *ḥarsa* here. The noun 'sol' would be more
appropriate, but I fear that this word (Latin, Spanish, Portuguese; cf. Italian
sole, French *soleil*) would be too foreign to resonate as English, whereas the
adjective 'solar' is standard in English.

11. See, for example, the following lines by William Shakespeare: "And
if shee were a thornyer peece of ground then shee is, shee shall be plowed"
(*Pericles*, Act IV, Scene 6); and "She made great Cæsar lay his sword to bed,

often are applied to young women (cf., e.g., English 'filly'[12] and to a lesser extent also 'heifer'[13]). And of course, it was the employment of this idiom here that allowed for the alliteration to take place.

In short, Judg 14:18, with its manifold use of language (alliteration, expressive idiom, etc.), is among the most enjoyable passages in the Bible, the product of a gifted wordsmith.

11. 1 Samuel 1:5–6

וּלְחַנָּ֕ה יִתֵּ֥ן מָנָ֖ה אַחַ֣ת אַפָּ֑יִם כִּ֤י אֶת־חַנָּה֙ אָהֵ֔ב וַיהוָ֖ה סָגַ֥ר רַחְמָֽהּ׃ [5]

וְכִעֲסַ֤תָּה צָֽרָתָהּ֙ גַּם־כַּ֔עַס בַּעֲב֖וּר הַרְּעִמָ֑הּ כִּֽי־סָגַ֥ר יְהוָ֖ה בְּעַ֥ד רַחְמָֽהּ׃ [6]

[5] And to Hannah he would give one portion, twofold, because Hannah he loved, and (because) Yʜᴡʜ had closed-up her womb.

[6] And her rival would anger her—indeed, anger—in order to vex her, for Yʜᴡʜ had closed-up around her womb.

The rare word within these two verses that attracts our attention is הַרְּעִמָהּ *harrə'imah* 'vex her'. The lexeme is so rare (it clearly does not mean 'thunder' here, which is what the root ר-ע-ם *r-'-m* denotes elsewhere in the Bible) that many commentators have labeled it "dubious" and the text "corrupt."[14] Our approach, of course, is to treat the Masoretic Text with respect, without recourse to the facile tack of textual emendation, especially since the root occurs again in Ezek 27:35 and then commonly in Mishnaic Hebrew (admittedly in the Hitpaʿel usually; see also the noun תַּרְעֹמֶת *tar'omɛt* 'vexation, irritation, torment' [18x in the Tannaitic corpus]).[15]

He ploughed her, and she cropt" (*Antony and Cleopatra*, Act II, Scene 2)—both cited from the *OED*, s.v. 'plough, plow' *v.*, def. 3.

12. *OED*, s.v. 'filly', def. 2.

13. *OED*, s.v. 'heifer', def. c-d.

14. See, e.g., BDB, 947 (using the abbreviation 'dub.'); and Smith, *Critical and Exegetical Commentary on the Books of Samuel*, 8 ("the word is probably corrupt here").

15. For further discussion, see Gary A. Rendsburg, "Some False Leads in the Identification of Late Biblical Hebrew Texts: The Cases of Genesis 24 and 1 Samuel 2:27–36," *Journal of Biblical Literature* 121 (2002): 40.

The presence of הַרְּעִמָהּ *harrə‘imah* 'vex her' in our passage is due to the twofold presence of the like-sounding word רַחְמָהּ *raḥmah* 'her womb' (vv. 5–6). The /r/ and /m/ sounds in the two lexemes match perfectly (see also the use of /h/ in each form), while the /ḥ/ in the noun 'womb' and the /ʿ/ in the verb 'vex' are both guttural consonants.

Bolstering the soundplay in this passage is the use of בַּעֲבוּר 'in order to, on account of'; note the /ʿ/ and /r/ in this word, with the repeated labial consonant /b/ echoing the /m/ in the two key words.

12. 1 Samuel 6:12

וַיִּשַּׁ֣רְנָה הַפָּר֣וֹת בַּדֶּ֗רֶךְ עַל־דֶּ֙רֶךְ֙ בֵּ֣ית שֶׁ֔מֶשׁ בִּמְסִלָּ֣ה אַחַ֗ת הָלְכ֤וּ הָלֹךְ֙
וְגָע֔וֹ וְלֹא־סָ֥רוּ יָמִ֖ין וּשְׂמֹ֑אול וְסַרְנֵ֣י פְלִשְׁתִּים֙ הֹלְכִ֣ים אַחֲרֵיהֶ֔ם עַד־גְּב֖וּל
בֵּ֥ית שָֽׁמֶשׁ׃

And the cows went-straight on the way, upon the way (to)
Beth-shemesh, on one highway they walked, walking and
lowing, and they did not turn right or left; and the potentates
of the Philistines were walking after them, until the border
of Beth-shemesh.

The first word in this verse constitutes an irregular form of the third fem. pl. prefix-conjugation (in this case, within a *wayyiqtol* form).[16] The paradigm form would be וַתִּשַּׁרְנָה* *wattiššarna *'went-straight', with *t*- prefix (not *y*- prefix) and -*na* suffix. The atypical form וַיִּשַּׁרְנָה *wayyiššarna* 'went-straight' alerts the reader to the presence of alliterative words in this verse: סַרְנֵי *sarne* 'potentates of' and סָרוּ *saru* 'they (did) not turn', with מְסִלָּה *məsilla* 'highway' providing support.[17] In actuality, even the expected form וַתִּשַּׁרְנָה* *wattiššarna *'went-straight' would produce the same alliteration, since the key sounds remain: sibilant + /r/ + /n/, corresponding to the same string in סַרְנֵי *sarne* (with

---

16. For the other instances of this form, see Gen 30:38 and Dan 8:22, with discussion in E. Y. Kutscher, *A History of the Hebrew Language* (Leiden: Brill; Jerusalem: Magnes, 1982), 41.

17. For earlier discussion, see Fokkelman, *Narrative Art and Poetry in the Books of Samuel*, vol. 4, *Vow and Desire*, 282.

סָרוּ *saru* including sibilant + /r/, and with מְסִלָּה *məsilla* including sibilant + /l/ + /m/, in scrambled fashion). On the other hand, the final /e/ vowel in סָרְנֵי *sarne* (written with *yod*, though it marks only a vowel and does not bear consonantal force /y/) shares phonetic similarities to the consonantal /y/ at the beginning of וַיִּשָּׁרְנָה *wayyiššarna* (scholars call this a homorganic vowel/consonant pair).

13. 1 Samuel 15:9

וַיַּחְמֹל שָׁאוּל וְהָעָם עַל־אֲגָג וְעַל־מֵיטַב הַצֹּאן וְהַבָּקָר וְהַמִּשְׁנִים וְעַל־
הַכָּרִים וְעַל־כָּל־הַטּוֹב וְלֹא אָבוּ הַחֲרִימָם וְכָל־הַמְּלָאכָה נְמִבְזָה וְנָמֵס
אֹתָהּ הֶחֱרִימוּ׃

And Saul and the people had pity on Agag, and on the best
of the flocks and the herds, and (on) the second-borns and on
the young-rams, and on all the good, and they did not accede
to proscribe them; but all the despised and worthless craftwork, those they proscribed.

The root ח-מ-ל *ḥ-m-l* 'have pity' occurs 3x in 1 Samuel 15, while the root ח-ר-ם *ḥ-r-m* 'proscribe' appears 8x in the same chapter. This frequency allows the two verbs to intersect throughout the narrative, with each appearing once in vv. 3 and 15, though with the present v. 9 allowing the greatest coincidence, given the twofold use of the latter root. Thus, we read here וַיַּחְמֹל *wayyaḥmol* 'had pity', הַחֲרִימָם *haḥarimam* 'to proscribe them', and הֶחֱרִימוּ *heḥerimu* 'they proscribed'.

There is another soundplay at work, one that is especially evident as the reader's ears focus on the abnormal form נְמִבְזָה *nəmibza* 'despised'. The word is a Niphʿal fem. sg. participle of the root ב-ז-ה *b-z-h* 'despise', but there is a striking peculiarity present. This word represents the only Niphʿal participle in the Bible that includes both prefixed *n-* (as usual) *and* prefixed *m-* (which occurs in all the other derived conjugations, but not in the Niphʿal).[18] The combination is used here due to alliteration.

---

18. Historical grammars of the Hebrew language state, correctly in my opinion, that the original Niphʿal participle bore a *mem* prefix, like all the other derived conjugations (Piʿel, Hiphʿil, Hitpaʿel, etc.). Only at a later stage

Note that the next word is נָמֵס *names* 'worthless' (though this form also has its own oddity, since it is masculine, even though the noun הַמְּלָאכָה *ham-məlaʾka* 'the craftwork' is feminine), which begins with the same /n/ + /m/ combination, followed by a sibilant /s/, the voiceless counterpart to the voiced /z/ in נִמְבְזָה *nəmibza* 'despised'. Once the soundplay between these two words is recognized, we also gain an understanding for the inclusion of the word הַמִּשְׁנִים *ham-mišnim* 'the second-borns' (the reader will agree, I trust, that its insertion in the list of bovine and caprid terms at least raises an eyebrow); observe how this word also has /m/ + /n/ + sibilant (in this case /š/).

14. 1 Samuel 15:33, 35

³³ וַיֹּאמֶר שְׁמוּאֵל כַּאֲשֶׁר שִׁכְּלָה נָשִׁים חַרְבֶּךָ כֵּן־תִּשְׁכַּל מִנָּשִׁים אִמֶּךָ
וַיְשַׁסֵּף שְׁמוּאֵל אֶת־אֲגַג לִפְנֵי יְהוָה בַּגִּלְגָּל:

----

³⁵ וְלֹא־יָסַף שְׁמוּאֵל לִרְאוֹת אֶת־שָׁאוּל עַד־יוֹם מוֹתוֹ כִּי־הִתְאַבֵּל
שְׁמוּאֵל אֶל־שָׁאוּל וַיהוָה נִחָם כִּי־הִמְלִיךְ אֶת־שָׁאוּל עַל־יִשְׂרָאֵל:

³³ And Samuel said, "As your sword has made women bereaved, so shall your mother be bereaved among women";
and Samuel hacked Agag before Yʜwʜ in Gilgal.

----

³⁵ And Samuel did not continue to see Saul, until the day
of his death, though Samuel grieved over Saul; and Yʜwʜ
repented that he had made Saul king over Israel.

Hark! Another *hapax legomenon* in the Bible! The verb וַיְשַׁסֵּף *wayšassep* 'hacked' constitutes the only attestation of the root שׁ־ס־ף *š-s-p* in the entire canon. The ancient reader would be struck by the rarity of this verb,[19] though the purpose for its employment would not become ap-

---

was the *nun* prefix introduced (imported from the suffix-conjugation), presumably due to the similarity of the /m/ and /n/ consonants. The example
in 1 Sam 15:9, accordingly, both retains the original /m/ and presents the
innovative /n/.

19. Naturally, any single *hapax legomenon* in the Bible could appear
but once in the corpus simply by sheer coincidence. But as Frederick E.

parent until she heard the phrase וְלֹא־יָסַף שְׁמוּאֵל *wǝ-lo' yasap šǝmu'el* 'and Samuel did not continue' at the beginning of v. 35, with the anagrammatic consonantal string ס /s/ – פ /p/ – שׁ /š/ bridging the two key words.

15. 1 Samuel 19:20

וַיִּשְׁלַח שָׁאוּל מַלְאָכִים לָקַחַת אֶת־דָּוִד וַיַּרְא אֶת־לַהֲקַת הַנְּבִיאִים
נִבְּאִים וּשְׁמוּאֵל עֹמֵד נִצָּב עֲלֵיהֶם וַתְּהִי עַל־מַלְאֲכֵי שָׁאוּל רוּחַ אֱלֹהִים
וַיִּתְנַבְּאוּ גַּם־הֵמָּה:

And Saul sent messengers to take David, and he saw a cadre of prophets prophesying, and Samuel was standing positioned over them; and over the messengers of Saul was the spirit of God, and they too prophesied.

Yet again! Another *hapax legomenon* in the Bible! And of course by now the reader is well attuned to what to expect. The unique noun לַהֲקַת *lahaqat* 'cadre of' was selected by our ancient wordsmith *alliterationis causa*, since it occurs in close proximity to לָקַחַת *laqaḥat* 'to take', with מַלְאָכִים *mal'akim* 'messengers' and מַלְאֲכֵי *mal'ake* 'messengers of' augmenting the auditory effect. Each of these words has /l/ + velar consonant (either /q/ or /k/) + consonant produced even deeper in the throat (either /h/, /ḥ/, or /'/); the first two key words, moreover, share the final /t/ sound. One also observes the left-movement[20] of the phrase עַל־מַלְאֲכֵי שָׁאוּל *'al mal'ake ša'ul* 'over the messengers of Saul', that is, this prepositional phrase is placed before the subject (resulting in atypical word order, as reflected in my English rendering above); I would propose that the author contrived this maneuver in order to place the last alliterative member closer to the other three in the verse.

Greenspahn, *Hapax Legomena in Biblical Hebrew* (Society of Biblical Literature Dissertation Series 74; Chico, CA: Scholars Press, 1984), 31–46, demonstrated, unique words in the Bible typically constitute rare words within the ancient Hebrew lexis.

20. The relevant linguistic term, even if 'right-movement' would be more appropriate for Hebrew.

16. 1 Samuel 25

1 Sam 25:22

עַד־הַבֹּקֶר מַשְׁתִּין בְּקִיר

"until the morning, a pisser on the wall"

1 Sam 25:34

עַד־אוֹר הַבֹּקֶר מַשְׁתִּין בְּקִיר

"until the light of morning, a pisser on the wall"

1 Sam 25:36

עַד־אוֹר הַבֹּקֶר

until the light of morning

1 Sam 25:37

וַיְהִי בַבֹּקֶר

and it was in the morning

1 Sam 25:37

וַיָּמָת לִבּוֹ בְּקִרְבּוֹ

and his heart died in his midst

The phrase 'the heart in one's midst' (v. 37) constitutes an expression of poets and prophets, as suggested by the attestation of this idiom in Jer 23:9, 31:33, Pss 36:2, 39:4, 55:5, 109:22, and Lam 1:20. Accordingly, the ancient person listening to the story of Abigail and Nabal in 1 Samuel 25 would be struck by the presence of the words לִבּוֹ בְּקִרְבּוֹ *libbo bə-qirbo* 'his heart in his midst' within a prose narrative. At the same time, however, she would appreciate the aural effect, since the key words in the various phrases listed above not only alliterate with each other, but they also anticipate the unusual placement of 'the heart in one's midst' within the narrative storytelling in v. 37. Note בֹּקֶר *boqer* 'morning' (4x) and בְּקִיר *bə-qir* 'on the wall' (2x) as preludes to בְּקִרְבּוֹ *bə-qirbo* 'in his midst' (v. 37).[21]

---

21. The slight change between עַד־הַבֹּקֶר *'ad hab-boqer* 'until the morning' (v. 22) and עַד־אוֹר הַבֹּקֶר *'ad 'or hab-boqer* 'until the light of morning' (vv. 34,

17. 2 Samuel 13:8–9 (in conjunction with 13:6–7, 17–18)

⁸ וַתֵּלֶךְ תָּמָר בֵּית אַמְנוֹן אָחִיהָ וְהוּא שֹׁכֵב וַתִּקַּח אֶת־הַבָּצֵק [ותלוש]
וַתָּלָשׁ* וַתְּלַבֵּב לְעֵינָיו וַתְּבַשֵּׁל אֶת־הַלְּבִבוֹת:

⁹ וַתִּקַּח אֶת־הַמַּשְׂרֵת וַתִּצֹק לְפָנָיו וַיְמָאֵן לֶאֱכוֹל וַיֹּאמֶר אַמְנוֹן הוֹצִיאוּ
כָל־אִישׁ מֵעָלַי וַיֵּצְאוּ כָל־אִישׁ מֵעָלָיו:

⁸ And Tamar went to the house of Amnon her brother,
and he was lying-down; and she took the dough, and she
kneaded, and she formed (it) before him / was alluring to his
eyes, and she baked the heart-cakes.

⁹ And she took the pan, and she poured (it) out before him,
and he refused to eat; and Amnon said, "Take-out every man
from upon me," and every man went-out from upon him.

2 Sam 13:6

וַתְּלַבֵּב לְעֵינַי שְׁתֵּי לְבִבוֹת וְאֶבְרֶה מִיָּדָהּ:

"and let her form (it) before me (and let her be alluring
to my eyes) two heart-cakes, so that I may meal from her
hand"²²

---

36) was studied above in Chapter 9, no. 15. For the alliteration studied here,
see Fokkelman, *The Crossing Fates*, 495; and Moshe Garsiel, "The Story of
David, Nabal and Abigail (1 Samuel 25): A Literary Study of Wordplay on
Names, Analogies and Socially Structured Opposites," in Daniel Bodi, ed.,
Abigail, Wife of David, and Other Ancient Oriental Women (Sheffield: Sheffield
Phoenix Press, 2013), 66–78, esp. 75. On other literary aspects in these verses,
see Leithart, "Nabal and His Wine."

22. While I have not always justified the unusual translations I have used
in this book, in the present instance I feel the need to do so. The Hebrew
verb used here is ב-ר-ה *b-r-h*, used only 6x in the Bible, as opposed to the
common verb א-כ-ל *ʾ-k-l* 'eat', used 819x in the corpus. The former verb is
used especially within the context of eating bread (see 2 Sam 3:35, 12:17) or
other foodstuffs made from grain (as here in 2 Samuel 13), so I have selected
a rare and to some extent obsolete English verb, 'meal', for which see *OED*,
s.v. 'meal', *v.²*. Note that the etymology of this English verb and its attendant
noun relates to 'grind' and 'grain', respectively. To this day in British English
and elsewhere, 'whole-meal bread' is the term used for what Americans call
'whole-grain bread'. See also German *mahlen* 'grind' and *Mehl* 'flour'.

2 Sam 13:7

וַעֲשִׂי־לֹו הַבִּרְיָה:

"and make for him the meal"[23]

2 Sam 13:17

וַיִּקְרָא אֶת־נַעֲרֹו מְשָׁרְתֹו

and he called to his lad, who serves him

2 Sam 13:18

וַיֹּצֵא אוֹתָהּ מְשָׁרְתֹו הַחוּץ

and the one who serves him took her outside

2 Sam 13:18

כִּי כֵן תִּלְבַּשְׁןָ בְנוֹת־הַמֶּלֶךְ

for thus the daughters of the king would dress

The account of Tamar preparing cakes for Amnon in vv. 8–9 is filled with detail, as each step from dough to finished product (six altogether) is described with its own verbal clause. A countertext, for example, might simply have said וַתַּעַשׂ לֹו לְבִבוֹת *watta'aś lo ləbibot *'and she made for him heart-cakes' and then continued with the mention of Amnon's refusal to eat the delicacies. The author clearly wishes for the reader to focus on Tamar's actions, with the goal of indicating the loving manner in which Amnon's half-sister prepares the cakes for her ailing (albeit feigning) half-brother. In the course of doing so, moreover, he provides plenty of fodder for alliteration within the narrative.

Perhaps most striking in detail are the phrases וַתִּקַּח אֶת־הַמַּשְׂרֵת וַתִּצֹק לְפָנָיו *wattiqqaḥ 'et ham-maśret wattiṣoq ləpanaw* 'and she took the pan, and she poured (it) out before him' (v. 9). The second verb, וַתִּצֹק *wattiṣoq* 'and she poured-out', includes an immediate auditory echo of the noun בָּצֵק *baṣeq* 'dough' in the previous verse (v. 8), with both words sharing the /ṣ/–/q/ combination. The key word in the other phrase, מַשְׂרֵת *maśret* 'pan', is yet another *hapax legomenon* in

---

23. See the previous note. I use the noun 'meal' here not as the main nourishment taken twice or thrice daily, but rather as a foodstuff made of grain, such as Tamar's heart-cakes.

the Bible, employed here in anticipation of its alliterative mate מְשָׁרְתוֹ *məšarto* 'the one who serves him' (vv. 17–18), the individual who will usher Tamar away from Amnon when the latter seeks for her to be banished from his sight.[24]

More typical in a food-preparation scene are the two verbs וַתָּלָשׁ *wattaloš* 'and she kneaded' and וַתְּבַשֵּׁל *wattəbaššel* 'and she cooked' (v. 8), whose roots share the sounds /l/ and /š/; and then these two words (especially the second one) receive a long-distance echo with תִּלְבַּשְׁן *tilbašna* 'would dress' (v. 18), in a clause that once more provides (what might be considered) a superfluous detail.[25]

Our attention is further drawn to the clause וַתְּלַבֵּב לְעֵינָיו *wattəlabbeb lə-ʿenaw* 'she formed (it) before him / was alluring to his eyes'. My use of the slash here attempts to replicate the polysemy inherent in these words. More on that anon, though first let us consider the additional aural effect of these words, in particular the verb וַתְּלַבֵּב *wattəlabbeb* 'and she formed', continuing the use of וּתְלַבֵּב *u-tlabbeb* 'and let her form' placed in Amnon's mouth in v. 6, with reference to the forming of the dough into the heart-shaped baked goods (note the common noun לֵב *leb* 'heart'). These are the only two instances of this root (with this meaning) in the Bible; the rarity directs us to seek alliteration, which we find upon encountering the /l/ and /b/ sounds in both this root ל-ב-ב *l-b-b* and in the nearby word וַתְּבַשֵּׁל *wattəbaššel* 'and she cooked', from the root ב-שׁ-ל *b-š-l* 'cook' (see the previous paragraph). Further soundplay is at hand once we recognize the presence of another rare root, namely, ב-ר-ה *b-r-h* 'meal' (discussed above, nn. 22–23), present both in the verb וְאֶבְרֶה *wə-ʾebrɛ* 'so that I may meal' (v. 6) and the noun

---

24. The oddity of מַשְׂרֵת *maśret* 'pan' and its resemblance to its alliterative mate is so felt by some critics that they simply emend וַתִּקַּח אֶת־הַמַּשְׂרֵת *wattiqqaḥ ʾet ham-maśret* 'and she took the pan' to *וַתִּקְרָא (אֶת־) הַמְשָׁרֵת* (אֶת-) הַמְשָׁרֵת **wattiqraʾ (ʾɛt) ham-məšaret* *'and she called the one who serves', thereby both eliminating a unique word from the Bible and displaying lack of recognition of the literary artistry (see the entry in BDB, 602).

25. Obviously, no detail is extraneous in biblical narrative, and in this case the phrase כְּתֹנֶת פַּסִּים *kətonɛt passim* 'ornamented tunic' (vv. 18–19) serves as an intertextual link to Genesis 37. While I do not treat this specific example in Chapter 21 below, the reader will find a number of interconnections between the Genesis and Samuel narratives discussed in that chapter.

הַבִּרְיָה *hab-birya* 'the meal' (v. 7).[26] Based on the two other occurrences in the Bible (2 Sam 3:35, 12:17), we may conclude that this root bears specialized lexical force, with reference to eating a bread or cake product, something baked from dough. Its employment here allows the /b/ and /r/ of this root to alliterate with the /l/ and /b/ of the aforecited root, with the same labial consonant and with corresponding liquids.

There is more, however. We will devote a chapter in this book to wordplay in the Bible (see below, Chapter 17), though since we have encountered this verse in this chapter, we take a moment to divert from the subject of alliteration to the presence of wordplay in the clause וַתְּלַבֵּב לְעֵינָיו *wattəlabbeb lə-ʿenaw*. As we have seen, these words can mean 'and she formed (it, sc. the dough) before him'. Though in the one other place where the root ל-ב-ב *l-b-b* occurs in the Bible, namely Song 4:9 (2x)—where again it is collocated with the word for 'eyes' (not to mention 'sister')—the verb means 'entice, be alluring':

Song 4:9

לִבַּבְתִּנִי אֲחֹתִי כַלָּה לִבַּבְתִּינִי [באחד] בְּאַחַת* מֵעֵינַיִךְ

"you allure me, my sister, bride; you allure me with one
of your eyes"

With knowledge of this verse before us, especially given the context of the Amnon and Tamar story, the perceptive reader will grasp the author's clever use of wordplay in 2 Sam 13:8.

In sum, these verses include several layers of alliteration, crowned by the delightful wordplay.

18. 1 Kings 20:23

וְעַבְדֵי מֶלֶךְ־אֲרָם אָמְרוּ אֵלָיו אֱלֹהֵי הָרִים אֱלֹהֵיהֶם עַל־כֵּן חָזְקוּ
מִמֶּנּוּ וְאוּלָם נִלָּחֵם אִתָּם בַּמִּישׁוֹר אִם־לֹא נֶחֱזַק מֵהֶם:

And the servants of the king of Aram said to him, "Their god
is a god of the mountains, therefore they are stronger than
we are; however, let us fight them in the plain, and then we
will be stronger than they."

---

26. See in v. 10 for the two words again, along with v. 5 for another instance of the verb.

Several times in this monograph we have encountered alliteration involving the word וְאוּלָם *wə-ʾulam* 'however' (see above, Chapter 5, no. 7, and earlier here within Chapter 10, no. 2). The biblical authors seem always ready to pounce upon this word, which occurs 23x in the Bible and which elicits a disproportionate number of soundplays. The current verse has engendered much discussion regarding the manner in which a neighboring people, in this case the Arameans, understood the God of Israel as a mountain deity. Attention to not only what the verse says, but how it says it, alerts us to the interplay between וְאוּלָם *wə-ʾulam* 'however' and אִם־לֹא *ʾim loʾ*, a composite particle with the force of 'but rather' (rendered here as 'and then').

Two other instances of the same alliteration occur in the prose narrative at the beginning of Job:

Job 1:11

וְאוּלָם שְׁלַח־נָא יָדְךָ וְגַע בְּכָל־אֲשֶׁר־לוֹ אִם־לֹא עַל־פָּנֶיךָ יְבָרֲכֶךָּ:

"However, send forth your hand and harm all that is his—[and see] if he will not 'bless' you upon your face."

Job 2:5

אוּלָם שְׁלַח־נָא יָדְךָ וְגַע אֶל־עַצְמוֹ וְאֶל־בְּשָׂרוֹ אִם־לֹא אֶל־פָּנֶיךָ יְבָרֲכֶךָּ:

"However, send forth your hand and harm his bone and his flesh—[and see] if he will not 'bless' you unto your face."

We have studied these two verses above in Chapter 9, no. 23, as an example of repetition with variation within Biblical Hebrew prose. In this chapter, our attention is drawn to the same alliteration as occurs in 1 Kgs 20:23, with the words וְאוּלָם *wə-ʾulam* 'however' and אִם־לֹא *ʾim loʾ*, the composite particle with negative force, rendered here as 'if . . . not'.

19. 2 Kings 6:8–9

8 וּמֶלֶךְ אֲרָם הָיָה נִלְחָם בְּיִשְׂרָאֵל וַיִּוָּעַץ אֶל־עֲבָדָיו לֵאמֹר אֶל־מְקוֹם
פְּלֹנִי אַלְמֹנִי תַּחֲנֹתִי:
9 וַיִּשְׁלַח אִישׁ הָאֱלֹהִים אֶל־מֶלֶךְ יִשְׂרָאֵל לֵאמֹר הִשָּׁמֶר מֵעֲבֹר הַמָּקוֹם
הַזֶּה כִּי־שָׁם אֲרָם נְחִתִּים:

[8] And the king of Aram was fighting against Israel, and he took-counsel of his servants, saying, "Unto such-and-such place is my camp."
[9] And the man of God sent to the king of Israel, saying, "Beware not to pass this place, for there the Arameans are descending."

These two verses include two unique usages, the noun-form תַּחֲנֹתִי *taḥanoti* 'my camp' at the end of v. 8, and the verb נְחִתִּים *naḥitim* 'are descending' at the end of v. 9. The former is used instead of the more common noun מַחֲנֶה *maḥane* 'camp' (215x in the Bible), while the latter is used instead of the exceedingly common verb י-ר-ד *y-r-d* 'go down' (309x in the Qal pattern in the Bible). The lexical choices are made for several reasons. In a story set in northern Israel, involving the neighboring Arameans, one can expect dialectal features not known from Standard Biblical Hebrew, that is, Judahite Hebrew. First, while we can say nothing more about the ת- prefix (instead of מ-) on the word for 'camp',[27] for which there are no parallels within Northwest Semitic, we can observe how the fem. sg. nominal ending -*ot* is a grammatical trait of Israelian Hebrew, that is, the dialect of the north (again, see ahead, Chapter 23). Secondly, the usage at the end of v. 9 represents the only instance of the verbal root נ-ח-ת *n-ḥ-t* 'descend' in the biblical narrative corpus, though this is a common verb in Aramaic.[28] One will assume that at least some people in northern Israel, especially those living along the border with Aram, used this root either alongside of or in place of the more common root י-ר-ד *y-r-d*

---

27. Said prefixes convert the verbal root ח-נ-ה *ḥ-n-h* 'camp' into a noun.

28. Elsewhere in the Bible the root נ-ח-ת *n-ḥ-t* 'descend' is limited to poetic texts (Job 17:16, etc.). Note that the Targumim regularly use נ-ח-ת *n-ḥ-t* 'descend' to render the Hebrew verb י-ר-ד *y-r-d* 'go down'.

'go down'.[29] Thirdly, and most significantly for our present purposes, these two dialect words alliterate with one another, sharing the /t/, /ḥ/,[30] and /n/ sounds.[31]

20. Ruth 2:10

וַתִּפֹּל֙ עַל־פָּנֶ֔יהָ וַתִּשְׁתַּ֖חוּ אָ֑רְצָה וַתֹּ֣אמֶר אֵלָ֔יו מַדּ֗וּעַ מָצָ֤אתִי חֵן֙ בְּעֵינֶ֔יךָ
לְהַכִּירֵ֖נִי וְאָנֹכִ֥י נָכְרִיָּֽה׃

And she fell on her face, and she prostrated earthward; and she said to him, "Why have I found favor in your eyes, that you take-notice of me, and I am but a stranger?"

Scholars have long recognized the alliteration present in the final three words of this verse:[32] לְהַכִּירֵ֖נִי וְאָנֹכִ֥י נָכְרִיָּֽה *ləhakkireni wə-'anoki nokriyya* 'that you take-notice of me, and I am but a stranger'. The root of the verb is נ־כ־ר *n-k-r*, though as often occurs with I-*nun* verbs (that is, verbs with נ /n/ as the initial consonant), the vowelless *nun* is assimilated to the next consonant, so that the Hiphʿil infinitive form appears as לְהַכִּיר *ləhakkir* 'to take-note'. By adding the first common sg. pronominal suffix נִי ־ *-eni* 'of me', the author restores the third consonant of the root, albeit within a different morpheme. This maneuver anticipates

---

29. In addition, note the Aramaic-style passive form, though with an active sense. See further Joshua Blau, "Benoni Paʿul be-Horaʾa ʾAqṭivit," *Leshonenu* 18 (1951 / 5713): 67–81; and Rendsburg, *Israelian Hebrew in the Book of Kings*, 103.

30. As for the nature of the *ḥet* in the two key words, we can propose /ḥ/ for the root נ־ח־ת *n-ḥ-t* 'descend', based on a likely Ugaritic cognate; but we can say nothing about the root ח־נ־ה *ḥ-n-h* 'camp' due to lack of cognate Semitic evidence.

31. This approach answers to the approach of those scholars who would facilely emend both words. See, e.g., the comments in BDB, 334, 639, respectively: "but form very strange. Rd. prob. תֵּחָבְאוּ *ye shall hide yourselves*, so 𝔊 Th Klo"; and "but rd. prob. with Th Klo Benz after G נֶחְבִּים *hidden*."

32. See, for example, Edward F. Campbell, *Ruth* (Anchor Bible 7; Garden City, NY: Doubleday, 1975), 98, who calls "this unit a pure delight"; and Jack M. Sasson, *Ruth: A New Translation, with a Philological Commentary and a Formalist-Folkloristic Interpretation*, 2nd ed. (Sheffield: JSOT Press, 1989), 51, who remarks that the phrase contains both metaphonic and parasonantic wordplay.

the same root, with all three consonants present, in the nominal form נָכְרִיָּה *nokriyya* 'stranger' (fem. sg.). Inserted between these two words is the pronoun אָנֹכִי *'anoki* 'I', which shares the /n/ and /k/ sounds.[33] There is more, however: for no one, it appears, has noticed that the preceding word עֵינֶיךָ *'enɛka* 'your eyes' also includes the /n/ and /k/ sounds. The result is a four-word string placed in the mouth of Ruth with supreme auditory effect.

21. Ruth 2:14, 16

14 וַיֹּאמֶר לָהּ בֹּעַז לְעֵת הָאֹכֶל גֹּשִׁי הֲלֹם וְאָכַלְתְּ מִן־הַלֶּחֶם וְטָבַלְתְּ
פִּתֵּךְ בַּחֹמֶץ וַתֵּשֶׁב מִצַּד הַקּוֹצְרִים וַיִּצְבָּט־לָהּ קָלִי וַתֹּאכַל וַתִּשְׂבַּע
וַתֹּתַר:

----

16 וְגַם שֹׁל־תָּשֹׁלּוּ לָהּ מִן־הַצְּבָתִים וַעֲזַבְתֶּם וְלִקְּטָה וְלֹא תִגְעֲרוּ־בָהּ:

14 And Boaz said to her, at the time of the food, "Approach hither, and you shall eat of the bread, and you shall dip your morsel in the vinegar"; and she sat aside the reapers, and he grasped for her (some) roasted-grain, and she ate, and she was satiated, and she had-leftover.

----

16 "And also pull-out for her from the bundles, and you shall leave, so that she may glean, and you shall not rebuke her."

These verses present two *hapax legomena*, which, as we have come to expect during our study, are employed for literary effect, in this case, alliteration. The first is the verb וַיִּצְבָּט *wayyiṣboṭ* 'and he grasped' (v. 14), while the second is the noun הַצְּבָתִים *haṣṣəbatim* 'the bundles' (v. 16). The verbal root צ-ב-ט *ṣ-b-ṭ* 'grasp' and the nominal base צ-ב-ת

---

33. The pronoun אָנֹכִי *'anoki* 'I' is the expected lexical choice here (as opposed to אֲנִי *'ani* 'I'), since Ruth refers to herself in a debased fashion ("and I am but a stranger?"). See E. J. Revell, "The Two Forms of First Person Singular Pronoun in Biblical Hebrew: Redundancy or Expressive Contrast?" *Journal of Semitic Studies* 40 (1995): 204–5.

ṣ-b-t 'bundle' (the reconstructed singular form would be either צֶבֶת*
or צְבֶת*) share two consonants and then the like-sounding dental
consonants /ṭ/ and /t/, respectively. Even with v. 15 intervening, the
ancient listener would have recognized the use of two rare lexemes to
achieve the resonance.

22. Ruth 2:17, 19

¹⁷ וַתְּלַקֵּט בַּשָּׂדֶה עַד־הָעָרֶב וַתַּחְבֹּט אֵת אֲשֶׁר־לִקֵּטָה וַיְהִי כְּאֵיפָה
שְׂעֹרִים:

----

¹⁹ וַתֹּאמֶר לָהּ חֲמוֹתָהּ אֵיפֹה לִקַּטְתְּ הַיּוֹם וְאָנָה עָשִׂית יְהִי מַכִּירֵךְ
בָּרוּךְ

¹⁷ And she gleaned in the field until the evening; and she
beat-out that which she had gleaned, and it was about an
ephah of barley.

----

¹⁹ And her mother-in-law said to her, "Where did you glean
today, and to-where did you do—may he who takes-notice of
you be blessed."

The two key words are אֵיפָה *'epa* 'ephah' (a measurement of grain, akin
to our 'peck' or 'bushel') (v. 17) and אֵיפֹה *'epo* 'where' (v. 19). Both are
typical usages, plus they are separated by an intervening verse, and yet
the listening audience would recognize the soundplay nonetheless.³⁴ In
addition, we note that the two words are written exactly alike—both
would appear as איפה in the ancient scroll text (or as אפה before the
introduction of medial *matres lectionis*)—so that the one who held the
written document would enjoy a visual effect as well.

---

34. See the earlier comment by Campbell, *Ruth*, 105: "As for the word
'ēpōh, is the story-teller indulging his fancy for assonance? The sound is very
much like the word *'ēpāh* he used in verse 17!"

23. Ruth 3:7–8

7 וַיֹּ֨אכַל בֹּ֤עַז וַיֵּשְׁתְּ֙ וַיִּיטַ֣ב לִבּ֔וֹ וַיָּבֹ֕א לִשְׁכַּ֖ב בִּקְצֵ֣ה הָעֲרֵמָ֑ה וַתָּבֹ֣א בַלָּ֔ט וַתְּגַ֥ל מַרְגְּלֹתָ֖יו וַתִּשְׁכָּֽב:

8 וַיְהִי֙ בַּחֲצִ֣י הַלַּ֔יְלָה וַיֶּחֱרַ֥ד הָאִ֖ישׁ וַיִּלָּפֵ֑ת וְהִנֵּ֣ה אִשָּׁ֔ה שֹׁכֶ֖בֶת מַרְגְּלֹתָֽיו:

7 And Boaz ate, and he drank, and his heart was good, and
he came to lie at the edge of the heap; and she came secretly,
and she uncovered his legs, and she lay-down.
8 And it was, in the middle of the night, and the man trembled,
and he groped; and behold, a woman lying (at) his legs.

Our attention is drawn to the expression וַיִּיטַ֣ב לִבּ֔וֹ *wayyiṭab libbo* 'and
his heart was good', which provides a pleasant portrayal of Boaz's
condition upon his eating and drinking in celebration of the bountiful
harvest. The three consonants that bridge this phrase are rehearsed
in the word בַלָּ֔ט *ballaṭ* 'secretly' later in the verse. Which is to say,
the sounds -ל ב-ט- -*ṭ-b l*- in the former reoccur a few words later in
scrambled fashion as ט-ל-ב *b-l-ṭ*.

The soundplay gains further support from the rare verb וַיִּלָּפֵ֑ת
wayyillapet 'and he groped' (elsewhere only Judg 16:29)[35] in the next
verse, from the root ל-פ-ת *l-p-t* (with the voiceless labial /p/ corresponding to the voiced labial /b/ of the former two words; and with
the standard dental /t/ corresponding to the emphatic dental /ṭ/ of the
former two words).

The alliteration is further augmented via the use of the rare word
מַרְגְּלֹתָיו *margəlotaw* 'his legs' (in both vv. 7–8; see also vv. 4 and 14;
elsewhere only Dan 10:6). This form includes labial (/m/) + /l/ + dental
(/t/), exactly as occurs in the other three words studied here. Had the
standard form, רַגְלָיו *raglaw* 'his feet', been used, no such effect would
have been attained.[36]

---

35. The root also appears in Job 6:18, though with a different connotation.
36. For additional examples of soundplay in the book of Ruth, see Nachman Levine, "Ten Hungers/Six Barleys: Structure and Redemption in the Targum to Ruth," *Journal for the Study of Judaism* 30 (1999): 312–24, with attention
to מַרְגְּלֹתָיו *margəlotaw* 'his legs' in a different alliterative setting on p. 321.

24. Jonah 4:6

וַיְמַן יְהוָה־אֱלֹהִים קִיקָיוֹן וַיַּעַל ׀ מֵעַל לְיוֹנָה לִהְיוֹת צֵל עַל־רֹאשׁוֹ
לְהַצִּיל לוֹ מֵרָעָתוֹ וַיִּשְׂמַח יוֹנָה עַל־הַקִּיקָיוֹן שִׂמְחָה גְדוֹלָה:

And YHWH God prepared a gourd-plant, and it went-up over
Jonah, to be a shade over his head, to save him from his discomfort; and Jonah was happy over the gourd-plant, a great
happiness.

This verse includes the two words צֵל *ṣel* 'shade' and לְהַצִּיל *ləhaṣṣil* 'to
save' in close proximity.[37] The soundplay is self-evident. The purpose
of the phrase לְהַצִּיל לוֹ מֵרָעָתוֹ *ləhaṣṣil lo me-ra'ato* 'to save him from his
discomfort' (the last word is literally 'his evil') is not readily apparent,
especially since Jonah already was sitting in the shade provided by his
booth, as described in the previous verse. In addition, Biblical Hebrew
includes two options for 'save' in such contexts, with the object רָעָה
ra'a 'evil': the root נ־צ־ל *n-ṣ-l* (elsewhere only Ps 34:20) and the root
י־שׁ־ע *y-š-'* (1 Sam 10:19, Jer 2:27–28, 11:12). In light of the presence of *ṣel*
'shade' in the verse, the selection of the former verbal root (once the
three-word phrase was deemed advisable) was no doubt a conscious
decision.

25. Jonah 4:7

וַיְמַן הָאֱלֹהִים תּוֹלַעַת בַּעֲלוֹת הַשַּׁחַר לַמָּחֳרָת וַתַּךְ אֶת־הַקִּיקָיוֹן וַיִּיבָשׁ:

And God prepared a worm, at the coming-up of dawn on the
morrow; and it struck the gourd-plant, and it withered.

Our final example comes from the following verse in the book of Jonah.[38]
The alliterative words are common—תּוֹלַעַת *tola'at* 'worm' and עֲלוֹת
'alot 'coming-up' (within the phrase בַּעֲלוֹת הַשַּׁחַר *ba-'alot haš-šaḥar*

---

37. See already Nahum M. Waldman, "Some Aspects of Biblical Punning,"
Shofar 14 (1996): 42; and Sasson, *Jonah*, 291, who noted that the somewhat
unusual syntax is employed "so that the ear can hear repetitions of the consonants *ṣl* (*ṣēl . . . lehaṣṣîl*)."

38. Again, see already Waldman, "Some Aspects of Biblical Punning," 42;
and Sasson, *Jonah*, 301.

'at the coming-up of dawn')—and yet, given that they have the same consonants, /l/–/ʿ/–/t/, their juxtaposition is conspicuous.[39]

The twenty-five examples of alliteration in biblical narrative prose (beyond the books of Genesis and Exodus) presented in this chapter only touch the surface. The reader is invited to discover on her own the many more illustrations of this literary device lurking in the biblical text.

---

39. In fact, as Jonathan Kline observed to me, the string of consonants in the two words תולעת בעלות TWLʿT BʿLWT forms a near-palindrome. Furthermore, the vowel patterns of the two words (moving from long /oː/ at the start through a series of /a/ vowels and ending with long /oː/) enhance the near-palindromic effect.

CHAPTER ELEVEN

ALLITERATION IN THE LEGAL-CULTIC MATERIAL

It is hard to imagine a less obvious place to encounter literary devices in the Bible than the legal-cultic material that dominates much of the Torah (the latter half of Exodus, all of Leviticus, much of Numbers, the majority of Deuteronomy). After all, with no offense intended to the juridical mind at work, legal writing is not known for its literary flair. And yet even in this genre within the Bible one finds the authors employing the techniques surveyed in this monograph. This chapter presents examples of alliteration in the legal-cultic sections of the Torah, while the next chapter focuses on repetition with variation. Which is to say, unlike in the previous two chapters, in which we presented polyprosopon first and alliteration second, we now vary our own ordering of the material to first treat alliteration and only afterward to discuss variation with repetition in the same sections of Scripture.

1. Exodus 29:1

וְזֶה הַדָּבָר אֲשֶׁר־תַּעֲשֶׂה לָהֶם לְקַדֵּשׁ אֹתָם לְכַהֵן לִי לְקַח פַּר אֶחָד בֶּן־
בָּקָר וְאֵילִם שְׁנַיִם תְּמִימִם:

And this is the thing that you should do to them, to make-
holy them, to serve-as-priests to me: take one bull, a member
of the herd, and two unblemished rams.

Upon hearing this verse, the listener is immediately struck by the atypi-cal masculine singular imperative לְקַח *ləqaḥ* 'take', instead of the usual form קַח *qaḥ* 'take'. The former (as well as its feminine counterpart), with retention of the initial root letter *lamed*, occurs elsewhere in the Bible in 1 Kgs 17:11, Ezek 37:16, and Prov 20:16—a distribution that suggests that this grammatical form is a characteristic of Israelian Hebrew.[1] Note that in 1 Kgs 17:11, Elijah addresses the woman of Zarepath; in Ezek 37:16 the form is used in connection with the former northern kingdom of Israel (treated elsewhere in this book, Chapter 15, no. 22); and Prov 20:16 appears in a book replete with Israelian Hebrew features.[2]

Now there clearly is no concentration of Israelian Hebrew features in the priestly material that dominates the end of the book of Exodus. But authors of biblical texts would go to great lengths to introduce alliteration into their compositions, as this case well illustrates. The author of Exod 29:1 opted to use the Israelian Hebrew form לְקַח ləqaḥ 'take' because the inclusion of the lamed creates a threefold string of alliterative words: לְקַדֵּשׁ ləqaddeš 'to make-holy', לְכַהֵן ləkahen 'to serve-as-priests', and לְקַח ləqaḥ 'take', all in very close proximity, with /l/ lamed followed by either /k/ kaf or /q/ qof in all three instances.

2. Leviticus 10:10–11

10 וּלֲהַבְדִּיל בֵּין הַקֹּדֶשׁ וּבֵין הַחֹל וּבֵין הַטָּמֵא וּבֵין הַטָּהוֹר:

11 וּלְהוֹרֹת אֶת־בְּנֵי יִשְׂרָאֵל אֵת כָּל־הַחֻקִּים אֲשֶׁר דִּבֶּר יְהוָה אֲלֵיהֶם בְּיַד־מֹשֶׁה:

10 And to separate between the holy and the profane, and between the impure and the pure, 11 and to instruct the children of Israel all the laws that Yhwh has spoken to them through the hand of Moses.

The long description of the investiture of the priests (Leviticus 8–10) ends with a summary statement of their duties. Notwithstanding the overriding presence of the word תּוֹרָה tora 'Torah, law, instruction' throughout the legal-cultic portions of the Pentateuch, the verbal root י-ר-ה y-r-h 'instruct', on which the key noun is based, is strikingly rare

1. See Rendsburg, *Israelian Hebrew in the Book of Kings*, 46–47.
2. See Yiyi Chen, "Israelian Hebrew in the Book of Proverbs" (PhD dissertation, Cornell University, 2000); and Gary A. Rendsburg, "Literary and Linguistic Matters in the Book of Proverbs," in John Jarick, ed., *Perspectives on Israelite Wisdom: Proceedings of the Oxford Old Testament Seminar* (The Library of Hebrew Bible / Old Testament Studies 618; London: Bloomsbury T&T Clark, 2016), 112, 136–41.

within the same material. Thus, for example, the noun תּוֹרָה *tora* 'Torah,
law, instruction' occurs 16x in Leviticus, while the verb י-ר-ה *y-r-h* 'instruct' appears only twice, in both cases as the infinitive לְהוֹרֹת *ləhorot*
'to instruct' (Lev 10:11, 14:57). The placement of this infinitive form,
in both cases, is due to alliterative concerns. In the verses presented
above, one notes the juxtaposition of הַטָּהוֹר *haṭ-ṭahor* 'the pure' (end
of v. 10) and וּלְהוֹרֹת *u-ləhorot* 'and to instruct', with the shared /h/ and
/r/ sounds and the corresponding dental consonants /ṭ/ ~ /t/. On the
second instance of the infinitive form, see below, no. 4.

3. Leviticus 13:38–39

וְאִישׁ אוֹ־אִשָּׁה כִּי־יִהְיֶה בְעוֹר־בְּשָׂרָם בֶּהָרֹת בֶּהָרֹת לְבָנֹת: ³⁸
וְרָאָה הַכֹּהֵן וְהִנֵּה בְעוֹר־בְּשָׂרָם בֶּהָרֹת כֵּהוֹת לְבָנֹת בֹּהַק הוּא פָּרַח ³⁹
בָּעוֹר טָהוֹר הוּא:

³⁸ When a man or a woman has on the skin of their flesh
spots, white spots, ³⁹ the priest shall see, and behold, on the
skin of their flesh dull white spots; it is a tetter, blossoming
on the skin, he is pure.

Within the legal-cultic material in the Torah, probably no section is
less literary than the two chapters (Leviticus 13–14) concerning the
eruptions that may affect humans, household items, and houses, the
so-called 'leprosy' of the Bible, which extends to mean a variety of
skin diseases, mold, and mildew. Nonetheless—or perhaps because the
material is so long and detailed—here and there the author of these
sections peppered his writing with alliterative words.

The passage above (set off as its own sub-paragraph in the manuscript tradition) concerns a special sub-category of בֶּהֶרֶת *baheret*, a skin
disease characterized by spots of some sort, presented in the preceding
section, especially vv. 19–28 (see also v. 4). In vv. 38–39, the plural form
בֶּהָרֹת *beharot* 'spots' is used (3x), though these marks are described as
either בֶּהָרֹת לְבָנֹת *beharot ləbanot* 'white spots' (v. 38) or בֶּהָרֹת כֵּהוֹת
לְבָנֹת *beharot kehot ləbanot* 'dull white spots' (v. 39). Most importantly,
these spots are described as בֹּהַק *bohaq* 'tetter', that is, a less-serious
issue (pimples or blisters, for example) that does not render the afflicted
individual impure. The last cited word is a *hapax legomenon*, and while

we cannot know its meaning with any certainty ('tetter' is simply a convenient gloss), we are justified in presuming that its presence in the verse is due to the desire to generate alliteration. The sounds of the key word בֶּהָרֹת *bɛharot* 'spots', that is, /b/–/h/–/r/, are echoed in the unique word בֹּהַק *bohaq* 'tetter', with /b/–/h/–/q/. The first two consonants are a perfect match, while the third corresponding sounds, /r/ and /q/, are both pronounced deep in the throat. Further alliteration is achieved with the introduction of the word כֵּהוֹת *kehot* 'dull' in v. 39 (note its absence in v. 38), whose /k/–/h/ combination alliterates with the /h/–/q/ combination in the *hapax* בֹּהַק *bohaq* 'tetter'.

4. Leviticus 14:54–57

⁵⁴ זֹאת הַתּוֹרָה לְכָל־נֶגַע הַצָּרַעַת וְלַנָּתֶק:

⁵⁵ וּלְצָרַעַת הַבֶּגֶד וְלַבָּיִת:

⁵⁶ וְלַשְׂאֵת וְלַסַּפַּחַת וְלַבֶּהָרֶת:

⁵⁷ לְהוֹרֹת בְּיוֹם הַטָּמֵא וּבְיוֹם הַטָּהֹר זֹאת תּוֹרַת הַצָּרַעַת:

⁵⁴ This is the law concerning every affliction of eruptions and of scalls, ⁵⁵ and of eruptions of the clothing and of the house, ⁵⁶ and of swellings and of rashes and of spots; ⁵⁷ to instruct on the day of the impure and on the day of the pure; this is the law of eruptions.

These verses constitute the summary statement at the end of the two very long aforementioned chapters, though quite incongruously the order of the individual afflictions departs from the order of their detailed descriptions within Leviticus 13–14. For example, eruptions on clothing are discussed in Lev 13:47–59, and eruptions on the walls and accoutrements of the house are discussed in Lev 14:34–53, with בֶּהָרֶת *bahɛret* 'spots' explained earlier in Lev 13:19–28 (see also v. 2). In the summary statement, however, בֶּהָרֶת *bahɛret* 'spots' is the last of the items listed. The reason for this realignment is readily forthcoming upon recognizing the following word, לְהוֹרֹת *ləhorot* 'to instruct' (v. 57), the second attestation of this form in Leviticus (see above, no. 2), whose consonants echo those of וְלַבֶּהָרֶת *wə-lab-bɛharɛt* 'and of spots' (v. 56), with /l/–/h/–/r/–/t/ in the same order in both forms (though with /b/ included in the latter word, naturally).

5. Leviticus 14:41, 43

וְאֶת־הַבַּיִת יַקְצִעַ מִבַּיִת סָבִיב וְשָׁפְכוּ אֶת־הֶעָפָר אֲשֶׁר הִקְצוּ אֶל־ ⁴¹
מִחוּץ לָעִיר אֶל־מָקוֹם טָמֵא:

וְאִם־יָשׁוּב הַנֶּגַע וּפָרַח בַּבַּיִת אַחַר חִלֵּץ אֶת־הָאֲבָנִים וְאַחֲרֵי הִקְצוֹת ⁴³
אֶת־הַבַּיִת וְאַחֲרֵי הִטּוֹחַ:

⁴¹ And the house he shall scrape, inside-the-house all-around;
and they shall cast the (plaster-)dust that they scoured to
outside the city, to an impure place.

----

⁴³ And if the disease returns and blossoms in the house, after
he has removed the stones, and after the scouring of the
house, and after the plastering, . . .

The verb יַקְצִעַ *yaqṣia‘* 'he shall scrape' in v. 41 is a unique usage in the
Bible. Nouns from the root ק-צ-ע *q-ṣ-‘* occur in the Bible (with such
meanings as 'cassia', 'corner', and 'scraping tool'), but only here do we
encounter a verbal form. The verbs הִקְצוּ *hiqṣu* 'they scoured' (v. 41)
and הִקְצוֹת *hiqṣot* 'the scouring' (v. 43) are the only attestations of the
Hiph‘il pattern of the root ק-צ-ה *q-ṣ-h* in the Bible (elsewhere the root
appears in the Qal and Pi‘el patterns with the meaning 'cut off'). The
collocation of these two exceptional usages within the same context
results from the author's desire to introduce alliteration at this stage
in the composition.³

A second, independent auditory effect is attained by the introduction of the verb חִלֵּץ *ḥilleṣ* 'he removed' (v. 43), another unique usage
within the biblical corpus. Elsewhere the Pi‘el of the root ח-ל-ץ *ḥ-l-ṣ*
bears the connotation 'save, deliver'; only here does it refer to the
removal of stones (though to be fair, one should note that the Qal
means 'remove [shoes]'). This unfamiliar usage calls our attention to
this idiom, with the realization that the verb alliterates with אֶל־מִחוּץ
לָעִיר *'el mi-ḥuṣ la-‘ir* 'to outside the city' (v. 41). The main component

---

3. Note that my use of 'scrape' and 'scour' for the two verbs attempts
to capture the alliteration in the Hebrew original in my English rendering.

of this phrase is the adverbial לְ־חוּץ *ḥuṣ lə*- 'outside', with the same three consonants /ḥ/–/ṣ/–/l/ as in the key verb, in scrambled order.[4]

6. Leviticus 26

קֶרִי	*qɛri* 'opposite, contrary' (7x: vv. 21, 23, 24, 27, 28, 40, 41)
לָרִיק	*la-riq* 'in vain' (2x: vv. 16, 20)
וַהֲרִיקֹתִי	*wahariqoti* 'empty, unsheathe' (v. 33)

The noun קֶרִי *qɛri* 'opposite, contrary' occurs only here in the Bible, 7x in Leviticus 26 (spread through vv. 21–41), with reference to Israel's (potentially) contrary ways, in violation of the covenant. Just prior to this span of attestations the reader hears the word לָרִיק *la-riq* 'in vain' (v. 20, though see also v. 16), the less common formulation of this idea (elsewhere only Isa 49:4, 65:23, Job 39:16), in contrast to the synonymous construction לַשָּׁוְא *laš-šaw>* 'in vain' (11x, including twice each within the third commandment [Exod 20:7, Deut 5:11]). And within the span of seven uses of the key noun one perceives the same sounds in the verb וַהֲרִיקֹתִי *wahariqoti* 'empty, unsheathe' (v. 33), with reference to the sword that God will bring upon the Israelites for their untoward behavior. Accordingly, one hears the /q/–/r/ combination 10x in this penultimate chapter of the book of Leviticus.

7. Leviticus 26:34

אָז תִּרְצֶה הָאָרֶץ אֶת־שַׁבְּתֹתֶיהָ כֹּל יְמֵי הָשַּׁמָּה וְאַתֶּם בְּאֶרֶץ אֹיְבֵיכֶם
אָז תִּשְׁבַּת הָאָרֶץ וְהִרְצָת אֶת־שַׁבְּתֹתֶיהָ:

And then the land shall compensate for its sabbaticals, all the days of the destruction, while you are in the land of your enemies; then the land will rest, and it will cause-recompense for its sabbaticals.

---

4. The *ḥet* in the verb ח-ל-ץ *ḥ-l-ṣ* most likely represents /ḥ/, based on proposed Arabic and Ethiopic cognates; but we are unable to determine which consonant underlies the *ḥet* in the form חוּץ *ḥuṣ* 'outside'.

The renderings of the verbal root ר-צ-ה *r-ṣ-h* 'compensate' (Qal), 'cause-recompense' (Hiphʻil) in this passage are a best guess, since the typical meaning of this verb, 'be pleased, be favorable', does not fit in this verse. The employment of this root here, whatever its exact connotation, is explained by the overriding presence of the common noun אֶרֶץ *ʼereṣ* 'land'; this lexeme occurs 13x in this section (Lev 26:32–45),[5] with three of the attestations in our passage, v. 34. The /r/ and /ṣ/ combination, accordingly, is perceived 5x in the verse.

The second instance of the root ר-צ-ה *r-ṣ-h*, in the form וְהִרְצָת *wəhirṣat* 'and it will cause-recompense', is doubly odd. First, this represents the only time that this verb occurs in the Hiphʻil in the Bible, hence my peculiar rendering with 'cause' to indicate the causative force of this verbal pattern. Secondly, this third fem. sg. form ends in *-at*, instead of the usual and expected ending *-a*. The result is an even closer link between the two specific forms of the verbs, with the consonants /t/–/r/–/ṣ/ in both. In addition, one notes that the two verbs are anagrams of each other in terms of their consonants—תרצה and הרצת—thereby affording a visual delight for the oral presenter of the composition.

8. Leviticus 26:37, 39

³⁷ וְכָשְׁלוּ אִישׁ־בְּאָחִיו כְּמִפְּנֵי־חֶרֶב וְרֹדֵף אָיִן וְלֹא־תִהְיֶה לָכֶם תְּקוּמָה לִפְנֵי אֹיְבֵיכֶם:

----

³⁹ וְהַנִּשְׁאָרִים בָּכֶם יִמַּקּוּ בַּעֲוֺנָם בְּאַרְצֹת אֹיְבֵיכֶם וְאַף בַּעֲוֺנֹת אֲבֹתָם אִתָּם יִמָּקּוּ:

³⁷ And they shall stumble, each over the other, ahead of the sword—with none pursuing; and you shall not have power-to-stand before your enemies.

----

³⁹ And those who remain among you shall pine away on account of their sin, in the lands of your enemies; and even on account of the sins of their fathers, with them they shall pine away.

---

5. If my calculations are correct, this is the greatest concentration of attestations of אֶרֶץ *ʼereṣ* 'land' within a fourteen-verse span anywhere in the Bible.

As we have seen throughout our study, rare words frequently are invoked *alliterationis causa*. In these verses we encounter two rarities:
(a) תְּקוּמָה *təquma* 'power-to-stand' (v. 37), the only attestation of this
noun in the Bible, though it is based on the common root ק-ו-ם *q-w-m*
'arise, stand up'; and (b) the verb יִמָּקּוּ *yimmaqqu* 'shall pine away' (2x)
(v. 39), the only instance of the root מ-ק-ק *m-q-q* 'diminish, pine away,
waste way' in a prose text (of any genre: narrative, legal-cultic, etc.).[6]
The shared consonants /q/ and /m/ resonate.

9. Numbers 4:19–20

¹⁹ וְזֹאת | עֲשׂוּ לָהֶם וְחָיוּ וְלֹא יָמֻתוּ בְּגִשְׁתָּם אֶת־קֹדֶשׁ הַקֳּדָשִׁים אַהֲרֹן
וּבָנָיו יָבֹאוּ וְשָׂמוּ אוֹתָם אִישׁ אִישׁ עַל־עֲבֹדָתוֹ וְאֶל־מַשָּׂאוֹ:
²⁰ וְלֹא־יָבֹאוּ לִרְאוֹת כְּבַלַּע אֶת־הַקֹּדֶשׁ וָמֵתוּ:

¹⁹ And this you shall do to them, so that they shall live and
shall not die when they approach the Holy of Holies; Aaron
and his sons shall come, and they shall assign them, each
man, over his work and to his porterage.
²⁰ And they shall not come to see, even for a moment, the
Holy-Place, (lest) they die.

The unusual usage here is the expression כְּבַלַּע *kə-balla*ʿ, lit., 'as (one)
swallows', which by extension is understood to be a temporal adverb. The Septuagint rendered the phrase ἐξάπινα 'suddenly'; though
more recent commentators have suggested 'the time it takes for one
to swallow', hence 'for a moment'.[7] The question arises, why would
the author have introduced this term here? The answer is forthcoming
from the sounds heard at the end of the previous verse, in the phrase
עַל־עֲבֹדָתוֹ *ʿal ʿabodato* 'over his work', with the *lamed-ʿayin-bet* string
bridging the two words, thereby setting the stage for the anagrammatic
bet-lamed-ʿayin root in כְּבַלַּע *kə-balla*ʿ 'as (one) swallows'. Indeed, the

---

6. The other eight occurrences of the verb appear in Psalms and in prophetic texts.

7. For the parallel usage, see Job 7:19. As an analogy, though using a different body part and action, compare English 'in the blink of an eye', German
Augenblick, Hebrew כהרף עין *kə-hεrεf ʿayin*.

key noun עֲבֹדָה *ʿaboda* 'work, task' occurs 20x in Numbers 4, in a variety of grammatical forms, with reference to the various chores and duties to be carried out by the different Levitical subdivisions—though only here in v. 19 (and in its echo at chapter's end in v. 49) does the phrase עַל־עֲבֹדָתוֹ *ʿal ʿabodato* 'over his work' occur, thereby producing the full alliteration with the following כְּבַלַּע *kə-ballaʿ* 'as (one) swallows'.

10. Numbers 17:20, 23

²⁰ וְהָיָה הָאִישׁ אֲשֶׁר אֶבְחַר־בּוֹ מַטֵּהוּ יִפְרָח וַהֲשִׁכֹּתִי מֵעָלַי אֶת־תְּלֻנּוֹת
בְּנֵי יִשְׂרָאֵל אֲשֶׁר הֵם מַלִּינִם עֲלֵיכֶם:

----

²³ וַיְהִי מִמָּחֳרָת וַיָּבֹא מֹשֶׁה אֶל־אֹהֶל הָעֵדוּת וְהִנֵּה פָּרַח מַטֵּה־אַהֲרֹן
לְבֵית לֵוִי וַיֹּצֵא פֶרַח וַיָּצֵץ צִיץ וַיִּגְמֹל שְׁקֵדִים:

²⁰ And it will be, the man whom I will choose, his rod will blossom; and I will cause-to-diminish from upon me the complaints of the children of Israel, which they complain unto you.

----

²³ And it was on the morrow, and Moses came to the Tent of the Testimony, and behold, the rod of Aaron of the house of Levi blossomed; and it brought-forth a blossom, and it flowered a flower, and it produced almonds.

The reader's attention is immediately drawn to וַהֲשִׁכֹּתִי *wahašikkoti* 'and I will cause-to-diminish' (v. 20), the only Hiphʿil attestation in the Bible of what is already a rare root, שׁ-כ-ך *š-k-k* 'abate, lessen, diminish' (elsewhere only 3x: Gen 8:1, Esth 2:1, 7:10).[8] The puzzle in the reader's mind—why would the author use this unusual word here?—remains for a few verses, until the climactic word שְׁקֵדִים *šəqedim* 'almonds' (v. 23). The corresponding sounds are (in the same order within both forms): /š/–/š/, /k/ ~ /q/ (both velars), and /t/ ~ /d/ (both dentals). The linkage between the two words, admittedly at a slight distance from each other, is strengthened by the presence of the root פ-ר-ח *p-r-ḥ* 'blossom' in both verses (1x in v. 20; 2x in v. 23, once as verb, once as noun).

---

8. See also Jer 5:26, though the usage there is unclear.

11. Numbers 18

חֵלֶף   *ḥelεp* 'exchange' (vv. 21, 31)

חֵלֶב   *ḥelεb* 'fat, suet' (vv. 12 [2x], 17, 29, 30, 32)—but also 'best-portion'

חֵלֶק   *ḥelεq* 'portion' (v. 20 [2x])

לְחָק עוֹלָם   *lə-ḥoq ʿolam* 'as a law forever' (vv. 8, 11, 19)

חֵרֶם   *ḥerεm* 'proscribed-item' (v. 14)

רֶחֶם   *rεḥεm* 'womb' (v. 15)

The unusual usage in this list of items from Numbers 18 is חֵלֶף *ḥelεp* 'exchange' (vv. 21, 31), appearing only here in the Bible. The two at-testations are surrounded by four occurrences of the word חֵלֶב *ḥelεb* 'fat, suet' (vv. 17, 29, 30, 32; see also v. 12 [2x]); only in Leviticus 3–4, 7–8, with their major focus on the sacrifices, does one find such a concentration of usages of this word. As is plainly visible, both words begin with /ḥ/–/l/, with the former containing the voiceless labial plosive /p/ and the latter its voiced counterpart /b/. Yet another word beginning with /ḥ/–/l/ appears in close proximity, namely, חֵלֶק *ḥelεq* 'portion' (v. 20 [2x]). In addition, all three words share the same vowel pattern, hence, assonance is at work as well. The last of these words, namely, חֵלֶק *ḥelεq* 'portion', in turn alliterates with לְחָק *lə-ḥoq* 'as a law', in the phrase לְחָק עוֹלָם *lə-ḥoq ʿolam* 'as a law forever' (vv. 8, 11, 19). This expression occurs elsewhere in Exod 29:28, Lev 7:34, 10:15; its threefold presence in Numbers 18, accordingly, is rather striking. The result is a cluster of words whose aural resemblance is heard in the latter half of this chapter.

But the author of this portion of the book of Numbers treats his readers/listeners to even more, by also introducing the alliterative pair חֵרֶם *ḥerεm* 'proscribed-item' (v. 14) and רֶחֶם *rεḥεm* 'womb' (v. 15), which not only share the same sounds, but also to a great extent echo the sounds of the first set of words discussed in the previous paragraph.[9]

---

9. Comparative Semitic evidence informs us that the *ḥet* in four of the six words represents the pharyngeal fricative /ḥ/, while in the other two the velar

12. Deuteronomy 16:19–17:1

¹⁹ לֹא־תַטֶּה מִשְׁפָּט לֹא תַכִּיר פָּנִים וְלֹא־תִקַּח שֹׁחַד כִּי הַשֹּׁחַד יְעַוֵּר
עֵינֵי חֲכָמִים וִיסַלֵּף דִּבְרֵי צַדִּיקִם:

----

²¹ לֹא־תִטַּע לְךָ אֲשֵׁרָה כָּל־עֵץ אֵצֶל מִזְבַּח יְהוָה אֱלֹהֶיךָ אֲשֶׁר
תַּעֲשֶׂה־לָּךְ:

²² וְלֹא־תָקִים לְךָ מַצֵּבָה אֲשֶׁר שָׂנֵא יְהוָה אֱלֹהֶיךָ:

¹ לֹא־תִזְבַּח לַיהוָה אֱלֹהֶיךָ שׁוֹר וָשֶׂה אֲשֶׁר יִהְיֶה בוֹ מוּם כֹּל דָּבָר רָע
כִּי תוֹעֲבַת יְהוָה אֱלֹהֶיךָ הוּא:

¹⁹ You shall not pervert the law, you shall not take-notice of
a face, and you shall not take a bribe, for a bribe blinds the
eyes of the wise and subverts the words of the righteous.

----

²¹ You shall not plant for yourself an *asherah*, any tree, near
the altar of Yhwh your God, which you shall make for
yourself.
²² And you shall not erect for yourself a pillar, which Yhwh
your God hates.
¹ You shall not sacrifice to Yhwh your God a bull or a sheep
that has a blemish, anything wrong; for it is an abomination
to Yhwh your God.

Deuteronomy 16:18–20 introduces a long section of legal material concerning the jurisprudential procedures of ancient Israel. These verses
begin with the command to appoint judges and officials (v. 18), who
should not pervert the law and take bribes (v. 19, see above), but who
rather should pursue justice (v. 20). The discussion continues in Deut
17:2, with more details, including, for example, the need for multiple
witnesses in order to carry out the death penalty (v. 6).

Oddly, the presentation of this topic is interrupted by Deut 16:21–
17:1, three verses that have nothing to do with legal practices at all, but

---

fricative /ḥ/ is present. Regardless, the consonantal sounds are sufficiently
approximate to produce the necessary aural ring.

which rather relate to cultic and ritual practices.[10] If anything, these verses belong more properly to Deut 12:2–6, where such is the topic at hand, and where, in fact, the same key vocables are used: אֲשֵׁרָה ’ašera 'asherah' (12:3, 16:21); מַצֵּבָה maṣṣeba 'pillar' (12:3, 16:22); and the root ז-ב-ח z-b-ḥ, both as verb, i.e., 'sacrifice', and within nouns meaning 'altar' and 'sacrifice' (12:3, 12:6, 16:21, 17:1).

The question arises, then: Why are 16:21–17:1 inserted at this stage within the Deuteronomic presentation of Israelite law and cult?[11] The answer lies in the alliterative hook provided by the three (negated) verbs in 16:19, each of which is then echoed by the (negated) verb at the start of the next three verses. Thus:

> לֹא־תַטֶּה   lo' taṭṭε 'you shall not pervert' (v. 19)
>
> לֹא תַכִּיר   lo' takkir 'you shall not take-notice' (v. 19)[12]
>
> וְלֹא־תִקַּח   wə-lo' tiqqaḥ 'and you shall not take' (v. 19)
>
> ----------
>
> לֹא־תִטַּע   lo' tiṭṭaʿ 'you shall not plant' (v. 21)
>
> וְלֹא־תָקִים   wə-lo' taqim 'and you shall not erect' (v. 22)
>
> לֹא־תִזְבַּח   lo' tizbaḥ 'you shall not sacrifice' (17:1)

In truth, the aural linkages here are not as alliterative as other examples analyzed in this study, but the sounds evoke one another nonetheless, especially when assonance (that is, like-sounding vowel patterns) are brought into the picture. The first pair shares the key /t/ consonant; the second pair shares a velar consonant (either /k/ or /q/) plus the

---

10. Note how these verses are set off by the Masoretic *setuma* sub-paragraph breaks.

11. For previous attempts to deal with the question, see Alexander Rofé, "Sidduram šel ha-ḥuqqim be-Sefer Devarim," in Shemuʼel Reʼem, Haim Beinart, and Samuel E. Loewenstamm, eds., *Studies in the Bible: M. D. Cassuto Centennial Volume* (Jerusalem: Magnes, 1987), 217–35; and Stephen A. Kaufman, "The Structure of the Deuteronomic Law," *Maarav* 1 (1978–1979): 105–58.

12. The full phrase "you shall not take-notice of a face" (see the rendering above) instructs a judge not to show partiality.

long /i:/ vowel; and the third pair shares the final /ḥ/ plus the /i/–/a/ vowel pattern.[13] This example illustrates the extent to which the ancient Israelite literati would go to achieve literary effect—even to the point of interrupting a weighty discussion on one topic with an equally serious discussion on another.

13. Deuteronomy 24:7–8

7 כִּי־יִמָּצֵא אִישׁ גֹּנֵב נֶפֶשׁ מֵאֶחָיו מִבְּנֵי יִשְׂרָאֵל וְהִתְעַמֶּר־בּוֹ וּמְכָרוֹ וּמֵת

הַגַּנָּב הַהוּא וּבִעַרְתָּ הָרָע מִקִּרְבֶּךָ:

8 הִשָּׁמֶר בְּנֶגַע־הַצָּרַעַת לִשְׁמֹר מְאֹד וְלַעֲשׂוֹת כְּכֹל אֲשֶׁר־יוֹרוּ אֶתְכֶם

הַכֹּהֲנִים הַלְוִיִּם כַּאֲשֶׁר צִוִּיתִם תִּשְׁמְרוּ לַעֲשׂוֹת:

7 If a man is found stealing a person from his brothers, from the children of Israel, and he deals-harshly with him or he sells him, that thief shall die—and you shall extirpate evil from your midst.
8 Be on guard concerning the affliction of 'leprosy', very on guard and to do, according to all that the priests, the Levites, instruct you, that which I commanded them, you shall be on guard to do.

As discussed above (Chapter 11, no. 3 especially, but also nos. 4–5), the general category of skin diseases and related issues dominates two long chapters in the book of Leviticus; as witness thereto, the word נֶגַע *nega*ʿ 'affliction' appears 61x in chs. 13–14. By contrast, the subject arises only once in the book of Deuteronomy, here in 24:8,[14] a verse that includes the sole attestation of נֶגַע *nega*ʿ 'affliction' in this long book.[15] Once more (as with no. 12 above), the systematic, logical

---

13. True, these vowels are from the Masoretic tradition, though presumably even in Iron Age Israel there would have been a similar vowel pattern.

14. This contrast highlights one of the major ideological concerns distinguishing the Priestly Code (P), embodied most of all by Leviticus, from the Deuteronomic Code (D).

15. The word נֶגַע *nega*ʿ appears three other times in Deuteronomy (17:8 [2x], 21:5), but in these passages the noun bears the unrelated meaning 'legal case'.

presentation of legal material in Deuteronomy is set aside to allow
for the incorporation of alliteration. The key root גּ-נ-ב *g-n-b* appears
twice in v. 7, in the participial form גֹּנֵב *goneb* 'stealing' and as the noun
גַּנָּב *gannab* 'thief'. The sounds of this root serve as the catalyst for the
presence of בְּנֶגַע *bə-nεgaʿ* 'concerning the affliction of', with the three
initial consonants /b/–/n/–/g/ echoing the /g/–/n/–/b/ of the aforecited
vocables in v. 7, once more in anagrammatic fashion.[16]

As long as v. 7 is before us, we also may draw attention to וְהִתְעַ־
מֶּר *wəhitʿammεr* 'and he deals-harshly', one of only two instances of
this usage, the Hitpaʿel (or any verbal pattern) of the root ע-מ-ר *ʿ-m-r*
'deal harshly', in the Bible. Following this verb is the alliterative word
וּמְכָרוֹ *umkaro* 'or he sells him', with the subsequent concluding phrase
וּבִעַרְתָּ הָרָע מִקִּרְבֶּךָ *ubiʿarta ha-raʿ miq-qirbεka* 'and you shall extirpate
evil from your midst'. These words (וּמְכָרוֹ *umkaro*, וּבִעַרְתָּ *ubiʿarta*,
הָרָע *ha-raʿ*, and מִקִּרְבֶּךָ *miq-qirbεka*) share the following consonants,
respectively, with the aforecited rare word (וְהִתְעַמֶּר *wəhitʿammεr*):
/m/–/r/, /ʿ/–/r/, /r/–/ʿ/, /m/–/r/. Note, moreover, that while the refrain
וּבִעַרְתָּ הָרָע מִקִּרְבֶּךָ *ubiʿarta ha-raʿ miq-qirbεka* 'and you shall extirpate
evil from your midst' (with variants) is common in Deuteronomy, this
is the only instance thereof in ch. 24 (indeed in all of chs. 23–25, the
final portion of the legal material). Its placement in 24:7, accordingly,
is well considered.

Finally, while we are dealing with the Hitpaʿel of the root ע-מ-ר
ʿ-m-r 'deal harshly', we should mention the second attestation, which
is found in Deut 21:14: לֹא־תִתְעַמֵּר בָּהּ *loʾ hitʿammer bah* 'do not deal-
harshly with her'. While the cluster of aforecited alliterative mates is
not present in this verse, we may nonetheless observe the twofold use
of the verbal root מ-כ-ר *m-k-r* 'sell' in the same verse: וּמָכֹר לֹא־תִמְכְּרֶנָּה
u-makor loʾ timkərεnna 'and sell, do not sell her', with the longer form
sharing /t/–/m/–/r/ with תִתְעַמֵּר *hitʿammer*.

---

16. Again one observes how the Masora sets off the brief discussion of
'leprosy' (vv. 8–9, with the second verse referring to the story of Miriam in
Numbers 12), though it also must be admitted that virtually every new legal
topic in Deuteronomy is so delineated. For this example of alliteration within
a legal text, I am indebted to my student, the late Colin Smith.

14. Deuteronomy 26:13–14

Deut 26:13

בִּעַרְתִּי הַקֹּדֶשׁ מִן־הַבַּיִת

"I have eliminated the holy from the house"

Deut 26:13

לֹא־עָבַרְתִּי מִמִּצְוֹתֶיךָ

"I have not transgressed any of your commandments"

Deut 26:14

וְלֹא־בִעַרְתִּי מִמֶּנּוּ בְּטָמֵא

"I have not eliminated any of it while impure"

Our attention is drawn to the verb ב-ע-ר *b-ʿ-r*, rendered 'eliminate' here. Almost always in the Bible, the verb means simply 'burn' (e.g., Exod 3:2–3, 22:5, 35:3, etc.) or 'remove', with the object of said verb something evil or sinful. In the latter category, one may point to the oft-repeated command in Deuteronomy to remove evil from the community (Deut 13:6, 17:7, 17:12, 19:19, 21:21, 22:21, 22:22, 22:24, 24:7—on these passages, see Chapter 12, no. 20) and to a host of other biblical passages with specific objects (2 Sam 4:11, the assassins of Ish-bosheth; 1 Kgs 14:10, the house of Jeroboam, dung; 1 Kgs 22:47, *qədešim*; 2 Kgs 23:24, ghosts, wizards, teraphim, idols, abominations; 2 Chr 19:3, *ʾašerot*; etc.). It is thus rather striking to find the verb ב-ע-ר *b-ʿ-r* used in the declaration to be spoken by the Israelite farmer upon his presentation of the tithe to the priest at the sanctum, with his claims that (a) he has not retained any of the tithe for himself, but rather has granted it all to the Levite and others deserving (v. 13); and (b) he has not defiled the tithe by handling it while in a state of ritual impurity (v. 14). Jeffrey Tigay commented, "The verb is normally used for purging sin from society. Here it seems to indicate total removal: the farmer has not held back even the slightest amount."[17] All true, though still one

---

17. Tigay, *Deuteronomy*, 243.

must ask why the author of Deuteronomy selected the verb ב-ע-ר *b-ʿ-r* 'eliminate' in this context. The solution is forthcoming from another observation by Tigay, for he pointed to the manner in which the phrase לֹא־עָבַרְתִּי *loʾ ʿabarti* 'I have not transgressed' echoes בִּעַרְתִּי *biʿarti* 'I have eliminated'.[18] Deuteronomy 26:13–14 constitutes an oral declaration (by the farmer, anticipated to occur in the future, upon Israel's entry into the land of Canaan) within an oral discourse (by Moses on the plains of Moab to the people of Israel); it is this doubly oral-aural setting that generates the alliteration here, produced by extending the semantic range of ב-ע-ר *b-ʿ-r*.[19]

18. Ibid.

19. Note that the *ʿayin* in both verbs represents the pharyngeal fricative /ʿ/, as determined by Ugaritic cognates.

CHAPTER TWELVE

REPETITION WITH VARIATION: LEGAL AND CULTIC TEXTS

As with alliteration, so too with repetition with variation: the authors of the legal-cultic material in the Torah delighted in introducing this second literary device into their compositions.[1]

1. Exodus 23:14, 17; 34:23–24 — appearing before God three times each year

(a) 23:14

שָׁלֹשׁ רְגָלִים תָּחֹג לִי בַּשָּׁנָה׃

šaloš rəgalim taḥog li baš-šana

"(On) three occasions you shall celebrate me during the year."

(b) 23:17

שָׁלֹשׁ פְּעָמִים בַּשָּׁנָה יֵרָאֶה כָּל־זְכוּרְךָ אֶל־פְּנֵי הָאָדֹן | יְהוָה׃

šaloš pəʿamim baš-šana yeraʾɛ kol zəkurka ʾɛl pəne ha-ʾadon YHWH

"Three times during the year, every male of yours shall be seen before the face of the Lord Yʜᴡʜ."

---

1. See my earlier study, Gary A. Rendsburg, "Repetition with Variation in Legal-Cultic Texts of the Torah," in Shamir Yona et al., eds., *Marbeh Ḥokmah: Studies in the Bible and the Ancient Near East in Loving Memory of Victor Avigdor Hurowitz* (Winona Lake, IN: Eisenbrauns, 2015), 435–63.

(c) 34:23

שָׁלֹשׁ פְּעָמִים בַּשָּׁנָה יֵרָאֶה כָּל־זְכוּרְךָ אֶת־פְּנֵי הָאָדֹן | יְהוָה אֱלֹהֵי
יִשְׂרָאֵל:

*šaloš pǝ'amim baš-šana yera'ɛ kol zǝkurka 'ɛt pǝne
ha-'adon* YHWH *'ɛlohe yiśra'el*

"Three times during the year, every male of yours shall
be seen before the face of the Lord YHWH, the God of
Israel."

(d) 34:24

בַּעֲלֹתְךָ לֵרָאוֹת אֶת־פְּנֵי יְהוָה אֱלֹהֶיךָ שָׁלֹשׁ פְּעָמִים בַּשָּׁנָה:

ba-'alotka lera'ot 'ɛt pǝne YHWH *'ɛlohɛka šaloš pǝ'amim
baš-šana*

"when you go-up to be seen before the face of YHWH
your God three times during the year."

The book of Exodus presents the four passages above as an instruction
to the people of Israel to appear before God three times during the
calendar year. The first of these is the simplest and most direct wording, though it also includes the unusual usage שָׁלֹשׁ רְגָלִים *šaloš rǝgalim*
'three occasions' (attested elsewhere only in Num 22:28, 22:32–33, on
which see above, Chapter 4, no. 1). The other three iterations use the
more standard expression שָׁלֹשׁ פְּעָמִים *šaloš pǝ'amim* 'three times'. In
addition, in (a) the word בַּשָּׁנָה *baš-šana* 'during the year' is disjoined
from 'three occasions', while in the other three formulations this word
follows immediately after 'three times'.

The key verb is different also, for in (a) we read תָּחֹג *taḥog* 'you
shall celebrate' (in the second person), while the other three expressions employ the Niph'al of the verb ר-א-ה *r-'-h* 'see', hence 'be seen,
appear', with (b) and (c) using the prefix-conjugation form יֵרָאֶה *yera'ɛ*
'shall be seen' (in the third person), and with (d) using the infinitive
form לֵרָאוֹת *lera'ot* 'to be seen'.

Different prepositions also serve to differentiate the wordings:
(a) uses simple -לְ *lǝ-* 'to'; (b) uses אֶל־פְּנֵי *'ɛl pǝne* 'before the face of'
(thus literally, the force may be simply 'before'); and (c) and (d) use

אֶת־פְּנֵי *'et pəne* 'before the face of' (thus literally once more, though again the force may be simply 'before'). The object of the preposition is different as well: (a) reads לִי *li* 'to me' (in the first person); (b) uses הָאָדֹן יְהוָה *ha-'adon* YHWH 'the Lord YHWH'; (c) expands to הָאָדֹן יְהוָה אֱלֹהֵי יִשְׂרָאֵל *ha-'adon* YHWH *'ɛlohe yiśra'el* 'the Lord YHWH, God of Israel'; and (d) reads יְהוָה אֱלֹהֶיךָ YHWH *'ɛlohɛka* 'YHWH your God'.

The exact relationship between chs. 23 and 34 has been debated by scholars. Regardless of how that issue is resolved, in its final form the book of Exodus ensures variation, via the means presented above, in the repeated command to appear before God three times each year.

2. Exodus 23:18; 34:25

(a) 23:18

לֹא־תִזְבַּח עַל־חָמֵץ דַּם־זִבְחִי וְלֹא־יָלִין חֵלֶב־חַגִּי עַד־בֹּקֶר:

lo' tizbaḥ 'al ḥameṣ dam zibḥi wə-lo' yalin ḥelɛb ḥaggi 'ad boqɛr

"You shall not sacrifice the blood of my sacrifice upon anything-leavened; and you shall not let-remain the suet of my festival-offering until morning."

(b) 34:25

לֹא־תִשְׁחַט עַל־חָמֵץ דַּם־זִבְחִי וְלֹא־יָלִין לַבֹּקֶר זֶבַח חַג הַפֶּסַח:

lo' tišḥaṭ 'al ḥameṣ dam zibḥi wə-lo' yalin lab-boqɛr zɛbaḥ ḥag hap-pasaḥ

"You shall not slaughter the blood of my sacrifice upon anything-leavened; and you shall not let-remain till the morning the sacrifice of the festival of Pesaḥ."

The passages presented in (1b) and (1d) in the previous example are followed by the verses listed here. Each of them deals with the Passover sacrifice, and with similar yet divergent wording. The former begins with לֹא־תִזְבַּח *lo' tizbaḥ* 'you shall not sacrifice', while the latter commences with לֹא־תִשְׁחַט *lo' tišḥaṭ* 'you shall not slaughter'. The conclusion of (a) is: חֵלֶב־חַגִּי עַד־בֹּקֶר *ḥelɛb ḥaggi ʿad boqer* 'the suet of my festival-offering until morning'; while the parallel expression in (b) is: לַבֹּקֶר זֶבַח חַג הַפָּסַח *lab-boqɛr zɛbaḥ ḥag hap-pasaḥ* 'till the morning the sacrifice of the festival of Pesaḥ'. Note the different prepositions affixed to בֹּקֶר *boqɛr* 'morning' (עַד *ʿad* 'until' versus לְ־ *lə-* 'till'), plus the different placements of the phrase 'until/till morning' (at the end of the verse versus a bit earlier in the verse). Finally, 23:18 uses the term חֵלֶב־חַגִּי *ḥelɛb ḥaggi* 'the suet of my festival-offering', with no specific reference to Passover, though such clearly is implied by the prohibition of leaven in the first half of the verse; while 34:25 is more explicit, with the expression זֶבַח חַג הַפָּסַח *zɛbaḥ ḥag hap-pasaḥ* 'the sacrifice of the festival of Pesaḥ'.

To repeat what we noted in the previous section, regardless of the ultimate relationship between chs. 23 and 34, the final text of Exodus has ensured variation in these parallel verses via the changes just analyzed. Though we also must admit that the following verses, 23:19 and 34:26, read verbatim: רֵאשִׁית בִּכּוּרֵי אַדְמָתְךָ תָּבִיא בֵּית יְהוָה אֱלֹהֶיךָ לֹא־תְבַשֵּׁל גְּדִי בַּחֲלֵב אִמּוֹ *reʾšit bikkure ʾadmatka tabiʾ bet* YHWH *ʾelohɛka loʾ təbaššel gədi ba-ḥaleb ʾimmo* 'the prime first-fruits of your land you shall bring to the house of Yʜwʜ your God; you shall not boil a kid in its mother's milk'.

3. Exodus 25–27 — the blueprint of the Tabernacle

25:9 (general)

כְּכֹל אֲשֶׁר אֲנִי מַרְאֶה אוֹתְךָ אֵת תַּבְנִית הַמִּשְׁכָּן וְאֵת תַּבְנִית כָּל־כֵּלָיו וְכֵן תַּעֲשׂוּ:

"According to all that I show you, the design of the Tabernacle and the design of all its vessels; and thus you shall do."

25:40 (Menorah)

וּרְאֵה וַעֲשֵׂה בְּתַבְנִיתָם אֲשֶׁר־אַתָּה מָרְאֶה בָּהָר:

"And see and do; according to their design, which you are shown on the mountain."

26:30 (Tabernacle)

וַהֲקֵמֹתָ אֶת־הַמִּשְׁכָּן כְּמִשְׁפָּטוֹ אֲשֶׁר הָרְאֵיתָ בָּהָר׃

"And you shall erect the Tabernacle, according to its
plan, which you have been shown on the mountain."

27:8 (Altar)

נְבוּב לֻחֹת תַּעֲשֶׂה אֹתוֹ כַּאֲשֶׁר הֶרְאָה אֹתְךָ בָּהָר כֵּן יַעֲשׂוּ׃

"Hollow planks you should make it; according to what he
showed you on the mountain, thus they shall do."

Four times in Exodus 25–27, God directs Moses to construct the Tabernacle and its accoutrements according to the blueprint that he has
devised. I reproduce each verse *in toto* here, though our attention is
drawn to the variation present in the dependent clauses. The first
statement is clear and succinct, in anticipation of the forthcoming detailed instructions: כְּכֹל אֲשֶׁר אֲנִי מַרְאֶה אוֹתְךָ *kə-kol ʾašer ʾani marʾɛ ʾotka*
'according to all that I show you' (25:9). The next statement serves to
seal the Menorah section: אֲשֶׁר־אַתָּה מָרְאֶה בָּהָר *ʾašer ʾatta morʾɛ ba-har*
'which you are shown on the mountain' (25:40)—the form מָרְאֶה *morʾɛ*
'are shown' is the only Hophʿal participle of the verb ר-א-ה *r-ʾ-h* 'see'
in the Bible. The next iteration seals the Tabernacle section (that is,
the details concerning the tent itself, which is constructed of beams,
curtains, etc.): אֲשֶׁר הָרְאֵיתָ בָּהָר *ʾašer horʾeta ba-har* 'which you have
been shown on the mountain' (26:30)—with change from the Hophʿal
participle in the previous passage to the Hophʿal suffix-conjugation
form הָרְאֵיתָ *horʾeta* 'you have been shown', one of only three such cases
in the Bible (see also Lev 13:49, Deut 4:35). The fourth and final version
appears at the end of the Altar segment: כַּאֲשֶׁר הֶרְאָה אֹתְךָ בָּהָר *ka-ʾašer
hɛrʾa ʾotka ba-har* 'according to what he showed you on the mountain'
(27:8); notwithstanding the fact that God remains the speaker here, the
text uses a third-person verbal form (one would expect a first-person
form, as in 25:9), thereby raising the reader's eyebrow in the process.
After the common and expected wording in the first passage, the text
applies the technique of defamiliarization in the next three passages—
each with its own peculiarity, inviting the reader to ponder the unusual
and unexpected language.

4. Leviticus — 'and you shall say'

(a) 1:2, 23:2, 23:10, 25:2, 27:2

דַּבֵּר אֶל־בְּנֵי יִשְׂרָאֵל וְאָמַרְתָּ אֲלֵהֶם

"Speak to the children of Israel, and you shall say
to them"

18:2

דַּבֵּר אֶל־בְּנֵי יִשְׂרָאֵל וְאָמַרְתָּ אֲלֵהֶם

"Speak to the children of Israel, and you shall say
to them"

19:2

דַּבֵּר אֶל־כָּל־עֲדַת בְּנֵי־יִשְׂרָאֵל וְאָמַרְתָּ אֲלֵהֶם

"Speak to all the congregation of the children of
Israel, and you shall say to them"

Numerous times in the book of Leviticus, God instructs Moses to speak
to the children of Israel generally or to Aaron and the priests specifically. We begin this section with a look at the former formulations.
The priestly author sets the tone in 1:2 with the standard rendition
דַּבֵּר אֶל־בְּנֵי יִשְׂרָאֵל וְאָמַרְתָּ אֲלֵהֶם 'speak to the children of Israel, and you
shall say to them', which appears four other times with the exact set
of accent marks and one additional time (18:2) with a different array.
To mix things up a bit, the text adds an additional phrase in 19:2: דַּבֵּר
אֶל־כָּל־עֲדַת בְּנֵי־יִשְׂרָאֵל וְאָמַרְתָּ אֲלֵהֶם 'speak to all the congregation of
the children of Israel, and you shall say to them' (note the insertion of
כָּל־עֲדַת *kol 'adat* 'all the congregation of').

(b) 21:1

אֱמֹר אֶל־הַכֹּהֲנִים בְּנֵי אַהֲרֹן וְאָמַרְתָּ אֲלֵהֶם

"Say to the priests, the sons of Aaron, and you shall
say to them"

22:2–3

. . . אֱמֹר אֲלֵהֶם דַּבֵּר אֶל־אַהֲרֹן וְאֶל־בָּנָיו

"Speak to Aaron and to his sons . . . say to them"

In these two passages, God instructs Moses to speak to the priests. Apparently to mark this distinction (that is, only the priests are to be addressed, and not the Israelites generally), the language is modified greatly. For example, both of these passages use the imperative form אֱמֹר *ʾɛmor* 'say', the only two such instances in all of Leviticus. When the two texts are compared to each other, further distinctions are forthcoming: e.g., 21:1 אֶל־הַכֹּהֲנִים בְּנֵי אַהֲרֹן *ʾɛl hak-kohanim bəne ʾaharon* 'to the priests, the sons of Aaron', versus 22:2 אֶל־אַהֲרֹן וְאֶל־בָּנָיו *ʾɛl ʾaharon wə-ʾɛl banaw* 'to Aaron and to his sons'.

For the sake of completeness, I also note here two passages (verbatim in this case) in which the priests *and* the Israelites are specifically mentioned as the addressees:

(c) 17:2

דַּבֵּר אֶל־אַהֲרֹן וְאֶל־בָּנָיו וְאֶל כָּל־בְּנֵי יִשְׂרָאֵל וְאָמַרְתָּ אֲלֵיהֶם

"Speak to Aaron and to his sons and to all the children of Israel, and you shall say to them"

22:18

דַּבֵּר אֶל־אַהֲרֹן וְאֶל־בָּנָיו וְאֶל כָּל־בְּנֵי יִשְׂרָאֵל וְאָמַרְתָּ אֲלֵהֶם

"Speak to Aaron and to his sons and to all the children of Israel, and you shall say to them"

So, if the two passages are verbatim (even to the point of the accent marks), why do I reproduce them individually? In order to highlight the orthographic variation generated by the scribe, with *plene* אֲלֵיהֶם *ʾalehɛm* 'to them' in 17:2 and *defectiva* אֲלֵהֶם *ʾalehɛm* 'to them' in 22:18.

Finally, even greater linguistic variation is introduced in two other places:

(d) 17:8

וַאֲלֵהֶם תֹּאמַר

"and to them you shall say"

20:2

וְאֶל־בְּנֵי יִשְׂרָאֵל תֹּאמַר

"and to the children of Israel you shall say"

In these two passages, (i) the indirect object is placed first, with the prefix-conjugation verb תֹּאמַר *to'mar* 'you shall say' following; and (ii) the author uses וַאֲלֵהֶם *wa-'alehɛm* 'to them' (with pronoun) in one instance (presumably the priests and the Israelites mentioned in 17:2 [see above] constitute the antecedent of 'them' here), with the more patently stated וְאֶל־בְּנֵי יִשְׂרָאֵל *wə-'ɛl bəne yiśra'el* in the second iteration.

5. Leviticus 1:7–8

Lev 1:7

בְּנֵי אַהֲרֹן הַכֹּהֵן

the sons of Aaron the priest

Lev 1:8

בְּנֵי אַהֲרֹן הַכֹּהֲנִים

the sons of Aaron, the priests

The phrase בְּנֵי אַהֲרֹן הַכֹּהֲנִים *bəne 'aharon hak-kohanim* 'the sons of Aaron, the priests' occurs 5x in Leviticus 1–3 (1:5, 1:8, 1:11, 2:2, 3:2). Just to mix it up a bit, the author of this material uses the expression בְּנֵי אַהֲרֹן הַכֹּהֵן *bəne 'aharon hak-kohen* 'the sons of Aaron the priest' in 1:7, the only attestation of this wording in the Bible. The pattern, then, is: standard phrase first; the unusual (indeed, unique) phrase second; followed by a return to the standard phrase for the remainder.[2]

---

2. The Samaritan Torah reads plural הכהנים HKHNYM also in 1:7, and the Septuagint οἱ ἱερεῖς 'the priests' implies a similar reading. But these efforts are a clear sign of harmonization, reflecting an unawareness of the device studied here (see also above, Chapter 4, p. 55, n. 4, p. 61, n. 7, and Chapter 9, p. 157, nn. 3, 5, p. 160, n. 12). For various attempts to explain the wording of the Masoretic Text, see Jacob Milgrom, *Leviticus 1–16* (Anchor Bible 3; New York: Doubleday, 1991), 157, though to my mind the far simpler explanation is variation for the sake of variation.

6. Leviticus 11:13–19 — forbidden birds

¹³ וְאֶת־אֵ֙לֶּה֙ תְּשַׁקְּצ֣וּ מִן־הָע֔וֹף לֹ֥א יֵאָכְל֖וּ שֶׁ֣קֶץ הֵ֑ם
אֶת־הַנֶּ֙שֶׁר֙ וְאֶת־הַפֶּ֔רֶס וְאֵ֖ת הָעָזְנִיָּֽה׃
¹⁴ וְאֶת־הַדָּאָ֖ה וְאֶת־הָאַיָּ֥ה לְמִינָֽהּ׃
¹⁵ אֵ֥ת כָּל־עֹרֵ֖ב לְמִינֽוֹ׃
¹⁶ וְאֵת֙ בַּ֣ת הַֽיַּעֲנָ֔ה וְאֶת־הַתַּחְמָ֖ס וְאֶת־הַשָּׁ֑חַף וְאֶת־הַנֵּ֖ץ לְמִינֵֽהוּ׃
¹⁷ וְאֶת־הַכּ֥וֹס וְאֶת־הַשָּׁלָ֖ךְ וְאֶת־הַיַּנְשֽׁוּף׃
¹⁸ וְאֶת־הַתִּנְשֶׁ֥מֶת וְאֶת־הַקָּאָ֖ת וְאֶת־הָרָחָֽם׃
¹⁹ וְאֵת֙ הַחֲסִידָ֔ה הָאֲנָפָ֖ה לְמִינָ֑הּ וְאֶת־הַדּוּכִיפַ֖ת וְאֶת־הָעֲטַלֵּֽף׃

Because the identification of so many of the individual birds listed in Lev 11:13–19 is so uncertain, I refrain from producing a translation here (with apologies to the reader unable to access the Hebrew in this passage). Regardless of the specific meanings, one observes how this pericope is structured, with an eye toward variation in the grouping of the birds in each verse. We will consider vv. 17–18 to constitute the standard wording, with three species listed, each introduced by וְאֶת־ *wə-'ɛt* + definite article. Verse 13b represents only the slightest variation, with no -וְ *wə-* 'and' (as such would not be expected at the beginning of a list), and with וְאֵת *wə-'et* as a self-standing word (note the lack of *maqqef*) before the third bird. Verse 14 has only two birds and adds לְמִינָהּ *la-minah* 'according to its kind' to the second. Verse 15 reads אֵת כָּל־עֹרֵב לְמִינוֹ *'et kol 'oreb la-mino* 'every raven, according to its kind', with no -וְ *wə-* 'and' at the beginning, the addition of the word כָּל *kol* 'every', and the use of לְמִינוֹ *la-mino* 'according to its kind' (in the masculine, unlike the previous occurrence, which is in the feminine; obviously, the change in gender is mandated by the antecedent, but the variation is noteworthy nonetheless). Verse 16 lists four separate species and then adds לְמִינֵהוּ *la-minehu* 'according to its kind' to the last item, using a different (more archaic) form than in the previous verse. Finally, v. 19 lists four birds, but for the second species the *nota accusativi* (direct object indicator) is lacking, plus said item bears the word לְמִינָהּ *la-minah* 'according to its kind'.

A less creative writer, I submit, would have listed the twenty birds in a more orderly fashion, for example, by using five verses each with four species, or some such arrangement. The author of Leviticus 11, by contrast, displays his virtuosity with the text above.

7. Deuteronomy 14:12–18 — forbidden birds

וְזֶ֕ה אֲשֶׁ֥ר לֹֽא־תֹאכְל֖וּ מֵהֶ֑ם הַנֶּ֥שֶׁר וְהַפֶּ֖רֶס וְהָעָזְנִיָּֽה׃ 12

וְהָרָאָה֙ וְאֶת־הָ֣אַיָּ֔ה וְהַדַּיָּ֖ה לְמִינָֽהּ׃ 13

וְאֵ֥ת כָּל־עֹרֵ֖ב לְמִינֽוֹ׃ 14

וְאֵת֙ בַּ֣ת הַיַּֽעֲנָ֔ה וְאֶת־הַתַּחְמָ֖ס וְאֶת־הַשָּׁ֑חַף וְאֶת־הַנֵּ֖ץ לְמִינֵֽהוּ׃ 15

אֶת־הַכּ֥וֹס וְאֶת־הַיַּנְשׁ֖וּף וְהַתִּנְשָֽׁמֶת׃ 16

וְהַקָּאָ֥ת וְאֶת־הָֽרָחָ֖מָה וְאֶת־הַשָּׁלָֽךְ׃ 17

וְהַחֲסִידָ֣ה וְהָאֲנָפָ֗ה לְמִינָ֛הּ וְהַדּוּכִיפַ֖ת וְהָעֲטַלֵּֽף׃ 18

Due to the similarity and interdependence between Leviticus 11 and Deuteronomy 14, we depart from a book-by-book, chapter-by-chapter presentation of the data, and instead move directly to the second, parallel text. Unlike Leviticus 11, where a standard formulation was discernible, no two verses in Deuteronomy 14 contain the same pattern. We begin, accordingly, with the first set of birds, in v. 12, with three species listed and no use of the *nota accusativi*. In v. 13, once more three birds are registered, though in this case the second is introduced by וְאֶת *wa-ʾet* and the third bears the word לְמִינָהּ *lə-minah* 'according to its kind' (in the feminine, due to gender considerations). Verse 14 reads וְאֵת כָּל־עֹרֵב לְמִינוֹ *wa-ʾet kol ʿoreb lə-mino* 'and every raven, according to its kind', which (like its parallel in Lev 11:15 concerning this bird) adds both כָּל *kol* 'every' and לְמִינוֹ *lə-mino* 'according to its kind' (in the masculine, again due to gender considerations). Verse 15 (the verbatim equivalent of Lev 11:16) registers four separate species, with לְמִינֵהוּ *lə-minehu* 'according to its kind' affixed to the last item, using a different (more archaic) form than in the previous verse. Both vv. 16 and 17 record three birds, though in each case one of the three lacks the preceding וְאֶת *wa-ʾet*; not wishing to repeat the same pattern, the author deletes this particle on the third item in v. 16 and on the first item in v. 17. Finally, v. 18 lists four species, with none of them preceded by אֶת־ wə-ʾɛt, and with the second one followed by the term לְמִינָהּ lə-minah 'according to its kind'.

Once more, one may assume that a less imaginative author would have produced a more systematic list for the twenty-one birds in Deut 14:12–18.

When we compare the two lists of Leviticus 11 and Deuteronomy 14 to each other, we note that (with one exception) either authorial action or scribal tradition ensured that not only within each listing of the birds the verses should diverge, but that also from one text to the other variation should be present. Thus, for example, at first glance Lev 11:15 and Deut 14:14 appear to contain the same wording, until one realizes that the Deuteronomic version deviates by affixing the conjunction -וְ wə- 'and' at the head of the verse. A more complicated illustration of fluctuation between the two compositions arises from an inspection of Lev 11:17–18 and Deut 14:16–17. These verses include the same six species, though (a) they appear in scrambled order, with ABC/DEF in the former and ACD/EFB in the latter; (b) Lev 11:17 uses masculine רָחָם raham, while Deut 14:17 uses feminine רְחָמָה rahama, presumably referring to the same species, typically identified with the Egyptian vulture (cf. Arabic raham); and (c) Lev 11:17–18 uses the *nota accusativi* 6x (once before each bird), while Deut 14:16–17 deletes this particle once in each verse. On the other hand, one must admit that Lev 11:16 and Deut 14:15 are identical (word-for-word, accent-for-accent)—ah, just to keep the reader honest (I would propose), by varying the variation, with the retention of one verbatim parallel.

8. Leviticus 18 — laws of incest (round one)

עֶרְוַת אָבִיךָ וְעֶרְוַת אִמְּךָ לֹא תְגַלֵּה אִמְּךָ הִוא לֹא תְגַלֶּה עֶרְוָתָהּ: ⁷

עֶרְוַת אֵשֶׁת־אָבִיךָ לֹא תְגַלֵּה עֶרְוַת אָבִיךָ הִוא: ⁸

עֶרְוַת אֲחוֹתְךָ בַת־אָבִיךָ אוֹ בַת־אִמֶּךָ מוֹלֶדֶת בַּיִת אוֹ מוֹלֶדֶת חוּץ לֹא ⁹
תְגַלֶּה עֶרְוָתָן:

עֶרְוַת בַּת־בִּנְךָ אוֹ בַת־בִּתְּךָ לֹא תְגַלֵּה עֶרְוָתָן כִּי עֶרְוָתְךָ הֵנָּה: ¹⁰

עֶרְוַת בַּת־אֵשֶׁת אָבִיךָ מוֹלֶדֶת אָבִיךָ אֲחוֹתְךָ הִוא לֹא תְגַלֵּה עֶרְוָתָהּ: ¹¹

עֶרְוַת אֲחוֹת־אָבִיךָ לֹא תְגַלֵּה שְׁאֵר אָבִיךָ הִוא: ¹²

עֶרְוַת אֲחוֹת־אִמְּךָ לֹא תְגַלֵּה כִּי־שְׁאֵר אִמְּךָ הִוא: ¹³

עֶרְוַת אֲחִי־אָבִיךָ לֹא תְגַלֵּה אֶל־אִשְׁתּוֹ לֹא תִקְרָב דֹּדָתְךָ הִוא: ¹⁴

עֶרְוַת כַּלָּתְךָ לֹא תְגַלֵּה אֵשֶׁת בִּנְךָ הִוא לֹא תְגַלֵּה עֶרְוָתָהּ: ¹⁵

עֶרְוַת אֵשֶׁת־אָחִיךָ לֹא תְגַלֵּה עֶרְוַת אָחִיךָ הִוא: ¹⁶

עֶרְוַת אִשָּׁה וּבִתָּהּ לֹא תְגַלֵּה אֶת־בַּת־בְּנָהּ וְאֶת־בַּת־בִּתָּהּ לֹא תִקַּח ¹⁷

לְגַלּוֹת עֶרְוָתָהּ שַׁאֲרָה הֵנָּה זִמָּה הִוא:

⁷ "The nakedness of your father and the nakedness of your
mother you shall not uncover; she is your mother, you shall
not uncover her nakedness.

⁸ The nakedness of the wife of your father you shall not uncover; she is the nakedness of your father.

⁹ The nakedness of your sister, the daughter of your father or
the daughter of your mother, whether born in the house or
born outside; you shall not uncover their nakedness.

¹⁰ The nakedness of the daughter of your son or the daughter
of your daughter, you shall not uncover their nakedness; for
they are your nakedness.

¹¹ The nakedness of the daughter of the wife of your father,
born of your father, she is your sister; you shall not uncover
her nakedness.

¹² The nakedness of the sister of your father you shall not
uncover; she is the carnality of your father.

¹³ The nakedness of the sister of your mother you shall not
uncover, for she is the carnality of your mother.

¹⁴ The nakedness of the brother of your father you shall
not uncover; unto his wife you shall not come-near, she is
your aunt.

¹⁵ The nakedness of your daughter-in-law you shall not uncover; she is the wife of your son, you shall not uncover her
nakedness.

¹⁶ The nakedness of the wife of your brother you shall not
uncover; she is the nakedness of your brother.

¹⁷ The nakedness of a woman and her daughter you shall
not uncover; the daughter of her son or the daughter of her
daughter you shall not take to uncover her nakedness, they
are carnality, it is vile."

We return to the book of Leviticus, with an inspection of the laws of incest in 18:7–17. The reader will observe that no two wordings of the eleven verses are alike. The closest are vv. 12 and 13, parallel prohibitions of intercourse with your aunt, either the sister of your father or the sister of your mother—with the variation generated by inclusion of the word כִּי *ki* 'for' in the latter statement. Verses 7 and 15 comprise another pair of proximate wordings, with each one using the expression לֹא תְגַלֵּה *loʾ təgalle* (pausal) / לֹא תְגַלֶּה *loʾ təgallɛ* (standard) twice; the passages depart, however, via the inclusion of עֶרְוַת *ʿɛrwat* 'the nakedness of' 2x in the former (one for 'father', one for 'mother') versus only one instance of this word in the latter (for 'daughter-in-law'). We can expand this point by observing that the vital word עֶרְוַת *ʿɛrwat* 'the nakedness of' (including instances with pronominal suffixes) appears only once in vv. 12, 13, and 14, twice in vv. 8, 9, 11, 15, 16, and 17, and thrice in vv. 7 and 10, with no pattern present—that is, the number of times this noun appears is not connected to how many individual relatives are mentioned in each verse. One further observes that vv. 7, 9, 11, and 15 conclude with the expression 'you shall not uncover her/their nakedness'; whereas vv. 8, 10, 12, 13, 14, 16, and 17 end with a pronoun serving as the copula (the verb 'to be') in a nominal phrase. In these latter expressions, the commonest key noun is עֶרְוַת *ʿɛrwat* 'the naked-ness of' (vv. 8, 10, 16), with the following deviations: (a) vv. 12–13 use the word שְׁאֵר *šəʾer* 'carnality'; (b) no equivalent term is used in v. 14 (the verse ends simply with דֹּדָתְךָ הִוא *dodatka hiʾ* 'she is your aunt'); and (c) v. 17 reads שַׁאֲרָה הֵנָּה זִמָּה הִוא *šaʾara henna zimma hiʾ* 'they are carnality, it is vile', with two verbless clauses to seal the verse and thus the entire litany of prohibitions. Here there is also the additional change from masculine שְׁאֵר *šəʾer* 'carnality' (vv. 12–13, plus fourteen additional attestations in the Bible) to feminine שַׁאֲרָה *šaʾara* 'carnality', a form that appears only here in the canon, no doubt introduced into the text by our witty wordsmith *variationis causa*.

All of this, once more, to create a composition characterized by the ebbs and flows of the written word, in order to allow for maximum enjoyment at the oral/aural level.

9. Leviticus 20 — laws of incest (round two)

וְאִ֗ישׁ אֲשֶׁ֤ר יִנְאַף֙ אֶת־אֵ֣שֶׁת אִ֔ישׁ אֲשֶׁ֥ר יִנְאַ֖ף אֶת־אֵ֣שֶׁת רֵעֵ֑הוּ מֽוֹת־ ¹⁰
יוּמַ֥ת הַנֹּאֵ֖ף וְהַנֹּאָֽפֶת׃

וְאִ֗ישׁ אֲשֶׁ֤ר יִשְׁכַּב֙ אֶת־אֵ֣שֶׁת אָבִ֔יו עֶרְוַ֥ת אָבִ֖יו גִּלָּ֑ה מֽוֹת־יוּמְת֥וּ ¹¹
שְׁנֵיהֶ֖ם דְּמֵיהֶ֥ם בָּֽם׃

וְאִ֗ישׁ אֲשֶׁ֤ר יִשְׁכַּב֙ אֶת־כַּלָּת֔וֹ מ֥וֹת יוּמְת֖וּ שְׁנֵיהֶ֑ם תֶּ֥בֶל עָשׂ֖וּ ¹²
דְּמֵיהֶ֥ם בָּֽם׃

וְאִ֗ישׁ אֲשֶׁ֤ר יִשְׁכַּב֙ אֶת־זָכָר֙ מִשְׁכְּבֵ֣י אִשָּׁ֔ה תּוֹעֵבָ֥ה עָשׂ֖וּ שְׁנֵיהֶ֑ם מ֥וֹת ¹³
יוּמָ֖תוּ דְּמֵיהֶ֥ם בָּֽם׃

וְאִ֗ישׁ אֲשֶׁ֤ר יִקַּח֙ אֶת־אִשָּׁ֣ה וְאֶת־אִמָּ֔הּ זִמָּ֖ה הִ֑וא בָּאֵ֞שׁ יִשְׂרְפ֤וּ אֹתוֹ֙ ¹⁴
וְאֶתְהֶ֔ן וְלֹא־תִהְיֶ֥ה זִמָּ֖ה בְּתוֹכְכֶֽם׃

וְאִ֗ישׁ אֲשֶׁ֨ר יִתֵּ֧ן שְׁכָבְתּ֛וֹ בִּבְהֵמָ֖ה מ֣וֹת יוּמָ֑ת וְאֶת־הַבְּהֵמָ֖ה תַּהֲרֹֽגוּ׃ ¹⁵

וְאִשָּׁ֗ה אֲשֶׁ֨ר תִּקְרַ֤ב אֶל־כָּל־בְּהֵמָה֙ לְרִבְעָ֣ה אֹתָ֔הּ וְהָרַגְתָּ֥ אֶת־הָאִשָּׁ֖ה ¹⁶
וְאֶת־הַבְּהֵמָ֑ה מ֥וֹת יוּמָ֖תוּ דְּמֵיהֶ֥ם בָּֽם׃

וְאִ֣ישׁ אֲשֶׁר־יִקַּ֣ח אֶת־אֲחֹת֡וֹ בַּת־אָבִ֣יו א֣וֹ בַת־אִ֠מּוֹ וְרָאָ֨ה אֶת־עֶרְוָתָ֜הּ ¹⁷
וְהִֽיא־תִרְאֶ֤ה אֶת־עֶרְוָתוֹ֙ חֶ֣סֶד ה֔וּא וְנִ֨כְרְת֔וּ לְעֵינֵ֖י בְּנֵ֣י עַמָּ֑ם עֶרְוַ֧ת אֲחֹת֛וֹ
גִּלָּ֖ה עֲוֺנ֥וֹ יִשָּֽׂא׃

וְ֠אִישׁ אֲשֶׁר־יִשְׁכַּ֨ב אֶת־אִשָּׁ֜ה דָּוָ֗ה וְגִלָּ֤ה אֶת־עֶרְוָתָהּ֙ אֶת־מְקֹרָ֣הּ ¹⁸
הֶֽעֱרָ֔ה וְהִ֕וא גִּלְּתָ֖ה אֶת־מְק֣וֹר דָּמֶ֑יהָ וְנִכְרְת֥וּ שְׁנֵיהֶ֖ם מִקֶּ֥רֶב עַמָּֽם׃

וְעֶרְוַ֨ת אֲח֧וֹת אִמְּךָ֛ וַאֲח֥וֹת אָבִ֖יךָ לֹ֣א תְגַלֵּ֑ה כִּ֧י אֶת־שְׁאֵר֛וֹ הֶעֱרָ֖ה ¹⁹
עֲוֺנָ֥ם יִשָּֽׂאוּ׃

וְאִ֗ישׁ אֲשֶׁ֤ר יִשְׁכַּב֙ אֶת־דֹּ֣דָת֔וֹ עֶרְוַ֥ת דֹּד֖וֹ גִּלָּ֑ה חֶטְאָ֥ם יִשָּׂ֖אוּ עֲרִירִ֥ים ²⁰
יָמֻֽתוּ׃

וְאִ֗ישׁ אֲשֶׁ֥ר יִקַּ֛ח אֶת־אֵ֥שֶׁת אָחִ֖יו נִדָּ֣ה הִ֑וא עֶרְוַ֥ת אָחִ֖יו גִּלָּ֑ה עֲרִירִ֥ים ²¹
יִהְיֽוּ׃

¹⁰ "And a man who adulters with the wife of a man, who adulters with the wife of his fellow;³ indeed the adulterer shall die, and the adultress.

---

3. The phrasing of the Hebrew original is a bit odd, with essentially the same information conveyed in both the independent clause that begins the

[11] And a man who lies with the wife of his father, the nakedness of his father he has uncovered; indeed the two of them shall die, their blood is upon them.

[12] And a man who lies with his daughter-in-law, indeed the two of them shall die; an outrage they did, their blood is upon them.

[13] And a man who lies with a male (like) the bedding of a woman, an abomination they did, the two of them; indeed they shall die, their blood is upon them.

[14] And a man who takes a woman and her mother, it is vile; in the fire they shall burn him and them, and there shall not be vileness in your midst.

[15] And a man who gives his lying to an animal, indeed he shall die; and the animal you shall kill.

[16] And a woman who comes-near to any animal, to copulate with it, and you shall kill the woman and the animal; indeed they shall die, their blood is upon them.

[17] And a man who takes his sister, the daughter of his father or the daughter of his mother, and he sees her nakedness, and she sees his nakedness, it is immorality, and they shall be cut-off in the eyes of their fellow people; the nakedness of his sister he has uncovered, his sin he shall bear.

[18] And a man who lies with an infirm woman,[4] and he uncovers her nakedness, her fountain he has laid-bare, and she has uncovered the fountain of her blood; and the two of them shall be cut-off from the midst of their people.

---

verse and the dependent clause introduced by אֲשֶׁר *ʾašer* 'who', which follows. In my opinion, the double wording is to emphasize the seriousness of the sin of adultery.

As for my use of the verb 'adulter', I here follow the lead of Fox, *Five Books of Moses*, 372 (with note to Exod 20:13); see also p. 607 for the present verse. For the pedigree of the verb in English, see *OED*, s.v. 'adulter' *v.*; and the earlier entry in Samuel Johnson, *A Dictionary of the English Language* (London: W. Strahan, 1755), 89, "To commit adultery with another: a word not classical" (available online at http://johnsonsdictionaryonline.com/).

4. I have retained the translation 'infirm' for the Hebrew verbal root ד-ו-ה *d-w-h*, for such is its usual connotation, even though in this passage the reference is to a menstruating woman.

¹⁹ And the nakedness of the sister of your mother and the sister of your father you shall not uncover; for his carnality she has laid-bare, their sin they shall bear.
²⁰ And a man who lies with his aunt, the nakedness of his uncle he has uncovered; their transgression they shall bear, childless they shall die.
²¹ And a man who takes the wife of his brother, it is indecency; the nakedness of his brother he has uncovered, childless they shall be."

A second set of incest laws appears in Leviticus 20, this time with twelve individual statements (vv. 10–21). Not surprisingly, once more, not a single wording repeats in this pericope. Ten of the verses begin with וְאִישׁ אֲשֶׁר *wə-ʾiš ʾašɛr* 'and a man who', so that this is clearly a standard formula; variation is present in v. 16, which begins with וְאִשָּׁה אֲשֶׁר *wə-ʾišša ʾašɛr* 'and a woman who', and more significantly in v. 19, which fronts the object וְעֶרְוַת *wə-ʿɛrwat* 'and the nakedness of'. If we return to the ten verses with the standard formula, we note the variation generated first by the following verb (1x יִנְאַף *yinʾap* 'adulters' [v. 10],[5] 5x יִשְׁכַּב *yiškab* 'lies' [vv. 11, 12, 13, 18, 20], 3x יִקַּח *yiqqaḥ* 'takes' [vv. 14, 17, 21], and 1x יִתֵּן *yitten* 'gives' [v. 15]) and then through a variety of other mechanisms as each passage continues.

Among these other alternative phrases, we find the following series: מֹות־יוּמְתוּ שְׁנֵיהֶם דְּמֵיהֶם בָּם *mot yumtu šənehɛm dəmehɛm bam* 'indeed the two of them shall die, their blood is upon them' (v. 11); מֹות יוּמְתוּ שְׁנֵיהֶם תֶּבֶל עָשׂוּ דְּמֵיהֶם בָּם *mot yumtu šənehɛm, tɛbɛl ʿaśu dəmehɛm bam* 'indeed the two of them shall die; an outrage they did, their blood is upon them' (v. 12); תּוֹעֵבָה עָשׂוּ שְׁנֵיהֶם מֹות יוּמָתוּ דְּמֵיהֶם בָּם *toʿeba ʿaśu sənehɛm, mot yumatu dəmehɛm bam* 'an abomination they did, the two of them; indeed they shall die, their blood is upon them' (v. 13); and מֹות יוּמָתוּ דְּמֵיהֶם בָּם *mot yumatu dəmehɛm bam* 'indeed they shall die, their blood is upon them' (v. 16; note the absence of שְׁנֵיהֶם *sənehɛm* 'the two of them').

---

5. Actually, the form יִנְאַף *yinʾap* 'adulters' occurs twice in Lev 20:10, on which see above, n. 3.

Other comparable yet different phrasings in this pericope include the following:

(a) different terms for the objectionable act (including two just mentioned):

- תֶּבֶל *tɛbɛl* 'outrage' (v. 12)

- תּוֹעֵבָה *toʿeba* 'abomination' (v. 13)

- זִמָּה *zimma* 'vile' (v. 14)

- חֶסֶד *ḥɛsɛd* 'immorality' (v. 17), a most unusual usage, since normally the term means just the opposite

- נִדָּה *nidda* 'indecency' (v. 21), also atypical, since normally the word is used in connection with a menstruating woman, though that is not the case here

(b) the three comparable phrases:

- עֲוֹנוֹ יִשָּׂא *ʿawono yiśśaʾ* 'his sin he shall bear' (v. 17)

- עֲוֹנָם יִשָּׂאוּ *ʿawonam yiśśaʾu* 'their sin they shall bear' (v. 19)

- חֶטְאָם יִשָּׂאוּ *ḥɛṭʾam yiśśaʾu* 'their transgression they shall bear' (v. 20)

(c) the two parallel expressions:

- עֲרִירִים יָמֻתוּ *ʿaririm yamutu* 'childless they shall die' (v. 20)

- עֲרִירִים יִהְיוּ *ʿaririm yihyu* 'childless they shall be' (v. 21)

and (d) the two parallel clauses:

- וְנִכְרְתוּ לְעֵינֵי בְּנֵי עַמָּם *wənikrətu la-ʿene bəne ʿammam* 'and they shall be cut-off in the eyes of their fellow people' (lit., 'the children of their people') (v. 17)

- וְנִכְרְתוּ שְׁנֵיהֶם מִקֶּרֶב עַמָּם *wənikrətu šənehɛm miq-qɛrɛb ʿammam* 'and the two of them shall be cut-off from the midst of their people' (v. 18).

All of this, as we have seen on so many occasions, to guarantee that no single wording repeats anywhere within the same section.

10. Leviticus 23

Lev 23:3 (Shabbat)

שַׁבָּ֤ת הִוא֙ לַֽיהוָ֔ה בְּכֹ֖ל מוֹשְׁבֹֽתֵיכֶֽם׃

It is a Sabbath unto Yʜwʜ, in all your dwellings.

Lev 23:14 (Pesaḥ)

חֻקַּ֤ת עוֹלָם֙ לְדֹרֹ֣תֵיכֶ֔ם בְּכֹ֖ל מֹשְׁבֹֽתֵיכֶֽם׃

an eternal statute for your generations, in all your
dwellings.

Lev 23:21 (Shavuʿot)

חֻקַּ֤ת עוֹלָ֣ם בְּכָל־מוֹשְׁבֹֽתֵיכֶ֖ם לְדֹרֹֽתֵיכֶֽם׃

an eternal statute in all your dwellings, for your
generations.

[Lev 23:24–25 (Month 7, Day 1) — no statement]

Lev 23:31 (Yom Kippur)

חֻקַּ֤ת עוֹלָם֙ לְדֹרֹ֣תֵיכֶ֔ם בְּכֹ֖ל מֹשְׁבֹֽתֵיכֶֽם׃

an eternal statute for your generations, in all your
dwellings.

Lev 23:41 (Sukkot)

חֻקַּ֤ת עוֹלָם֙ לְדֹרֹֽתֵיכֶ֔ם

an eternal statute for your generations.

Leviticus 23 presents the ancient Israelite calendar, with the various
(non-verbatim) phrases presented above. The standard expression (in-
sofar as it occurs twice) appears in vv. 14 and 31, concerning Pesaḥ
and Yom Kippur, respectively (see also Lev 3:17, Num 35:29). In v. 21,
regarding Shavuʿot, the text reverses the two key phrases, with לְדֹרֹֽתֵיכֶֽם
lə-dorotekεm 'for your generations' occuring after בְּכָל־מוֹשְׁבֹֽתֵיכֶ֖ם bə-kol
mošbotekεm 'in all your dwellings' (plus note the maqqef in the latter

phrase). In v. 41, concerning Sukkot, the phrase בְּכָל מוֹשְׁבֹתֵיכֶם *bə-kol mošbotekεm* 'in all your dwellings' is omitted altogether, presumably because the threefold use of the verbal root י-שׁ-ב *y-š-b* 'sit, dwell' in the following two verses (vv. 42–43; 2x Qal, 1x Hiphʿil) renders the term unnecessary in the author's mind. Perhaps to balance this deletion toward the end of the chapter, the author omits the other term, לְדֹרֹתֵיכֶם *lə-dorotεkεm* 'for your generations', in the description of Shabbat at the beginning of the chapter. We further may note that the connection between Shabbat and 'the generations' is built into the system, as indicated by the twofold use of the term in Exod 31:13, 16. If we may evoke Abraham Joshua Heschel here,[6] Sukkot is the most "place"-defined holiday and therefore does not require 'in all your dwellings', whereas Shabbat is the most "time"-defined holiday and therefore does not require 'for your generations', at least as conceived and formulated by the author of Leviticus 23. Finally, the greatest divergence occurs in vv. 24–25, pertaining to the festival that occurs on month 7, day 1 (to emerge eventually as Rosh ha-Shana). Since Leviticus 23 provides only the most minimal information concerning this holiday, quite appropriately the non-verbatim refrain is omitted altogether in these two verses.

11. Numbers 1 — the census

Num 1:20

וַיִּהְיוּ בְנֵי־רְאוּבֵן בְּכֹר יִשְׂרָאֵל תּוֹלְדֹתָם לְמִשְׁפְּחֹתָם לְבֵית אֲבֹתָם
בְּמִסְפַּר שֵׁמוֹת לְגֻלְגְּלֹתָם כָּל־זָכָר מִבֶּן עֶשְׂרִים שָׁנָה וָמַעְלָה כֹּל
יֹצֵא צָבָא:

And the children of Reuben the firstborn of Israel were, their generations according to their families, of their ancestral house, by the number of names per capita, every male from age twenty years upward, all who go-out (in the) army.

---

6. Abraham Joshua Heschel, *The Sabbath* (New York: Farrar, Straus & Young, 1951).

Num 1:22

לִבְנֵי שִׁמְעוֹן תּוֹלְדֹתָם לְמִשְׁפְּחֹתָם לְבֵית אֲבֹתָם פְּקֻדָיו בְּמִסְפַּר
שֵׁמוֹת לְגֻלְגְּלֹתָם כָּל־זָכָר מִבֶּן עֶשְׂרִים שָׁנָה וָמַעְלָה כֹּל יֹצֵא צָבָא:

To the children of Simeon, their generations according
to their families, of their ancestral house, its accounting,
by the number of names per capita, every male from age
twenty years upward, all who go-out (in the) army.

Num 1:24 (etc.)

לִבְנֵי גָד תּוֹלְדֹתָם לְמִשְׁפְּחֹתָם לְבֵית אֲבֹתָם בְּמִסְפַּר שֵׁמוֹת מִבֶּן
עֶשְׂרִים שָׁנָה וָמַעְלָה כֹּל יֹצֵא צָבָא:

To the children of Gad, their generations according to
their families, of their ancestral house, by the number of
names, from age twenty years upward, all who go-out (in
the) army.

The formula in v. 24, introducing the census figure for the tribe of Gad,
is repeated without change (save for the tribal name) for tribes three
(Gad) through eleven (Asher). For the first two tribes, however, the
reader encounters different wordings. In v. 20, Reuben is introduced as
the בְּכֹר יִשְׂרָאֵל bəkor yiśra'el 'firstborn of Israel', and a verbal form of the
root ה-י-ה h-y-h 'be' is used. In v. 22, the Simeon passage includes the
word פְּקֻדָיו pəqudaw 'its accounting'. For both of the first two tribes,
we find the phrase לְגֻלְגְּלֹתָם כָּל־זָכָר lə-gulgəlotam kol zakar 'per capita,
every male'.[7] For the last tribe, introduced as בְּנֵי נַפְתָּלִי bəne naptali
(without the preposition -לְ lə- 'of, to'), see below, Chapter 13, no. 14.
Even in as mundane a text as a census, there is an effort to introduce
variation into the repetitive language.

_____

7. I take advantage of the Latin phrase *per capita*, lit., 'by heads', to render
Hebrew לְגֻלְגְּלֹתָם lə-gulgəlotam, lit., 'by their heads' (more literally, 'skulls'),
with a rarer noun in place of the basic lexeme רֹאשׁ ro'š 'head'.

12. Numbers 2 — the tribal encampment around the Tabernacle (flags)

וְהַחֹנִים֙ קֵ֣דְמָה מִזְרָ֔חָה דֶּ֛גֶל מַחֲנֵ֥ה יְהוּדָ֖ה לְצִבְאֹתָ֑ם ³

דֶּ֚גֶל מַחֲנֵ֣ה רְאוּבֵ֔ן תֵּימָ֖נָה לְצִבְאֹתָ֑ם ¹⁰

דֶּ֚גֶל מַחֲנֵ֣ה אֶפְרַ֔יִם לְצִבְאֹתָ֖ם יָ֑מָּה ¹⁸

דֶּ֚גֶל מַחֲנֵ֥ה דָ֖ן צָפֹ֑נָה לְצִבְאֹתָ֑ם ²⁵

³ And those encamped orient-ward, eastward, the flag of the camp of Judah according to their armies;

----

¹⁰ The flag of the camp of Reuben, southward, according to their armies;

----

¹⁸ The flag of the camp of Ephraim, according to their armies, sea-ward;

----

²⁵ The flag of the camp of Dan, northward, according to their armies;

According to Numbers 2, the Israelite encampment was divided into four parts, each one positioned on a different flank of the Tabernacle, with a flag or banner to mark the division. The second and fourth units are described in verbatim terms (save for the necessary differences of lead tribe and cardinal direction) and thus may be considered the standard wording: 'The flag of the camp of X-tribe, Y-direction, according to their armies'. The third unit is described with variant word order, with the phrase 'according to their armies' and the Y-direction switching slots. The first unit has the most variation, with (a) the word וְהַחֹנִים *wə-ha-ḥonim* 'and those encamped'; (b) two synonyms for the same direction, קֵ֣דְמָה מִזְרָ֔חָה *qedma mizraḥa* 'orient-ward, eastward'; and (c) with the direction preceding the mention of the flag.

13. Numbers 3 — the number of Levites (numbers)

²² פְּקֻדֵיהֶם בְּמִסְפַּר כָּל־זָכָר מִבֶּן־חֹדֶשׁ וָמָעְלָה פְּקֻדֵיהֶם שִׁבְעַת
אֲלָפִים וַחֲמֵשׁ מֵאוֹת:

----

²⁸ בְּמִסְפַּר כָּל־זָכָר מִבֶּן־חֹדֶשׁ וָמָעְלָה שְׁמֹנַת אֲלָפִים וְשֵׁשׁ מֵאוֹת
שֹׁמְרֵי מִשְׁמֶרֶת הַקֹּדֶשׁ:

----

³⁴ וּפְקֻדֵיהֶם בְּמִסְפַּר כָּל־זָכָר מִבֶּן־חֹדֶשׁ וָמָעְלָה שֵׁשֶׁת אֲלָפִים
וּמָאתָיִם:

²² Their accounting, by the number of all males, from one-month (old) and upward; their accounting, seven thousand and five hundred.

----

²⁸ By the number of all males, from one-month (old) and upward, eight thousand and six hundred, duty-guards of the duty of the Holy-Place.

----

³⁴ And their accounting, by the number of all males, from one-month (old) and upward, six thousand and two hundred.

The Levites are divided into three groups: Gershon-ites, Kohath-ites, and Merari-ites—with the census providing the number for each division. In the style to which we have become well accustomed, the data are not presented in a dull manner; instead, the author jumbles the material to allow for the reader's admiration of his literary flair. With the first group, the word פְּקֻדֵיהֶם *pəqudehɛm* 'their accounting' is used twice (v. 22); for the second group this key word is omitted (v. 28); and for the third group the conjunction *waw* is included to provide the form וּפְקֻדֵיהֶם *u-pqudehɛm* 'and their accounting'. In addition, the second group gains a special epithet: שֹׁמְרֵי מִשְׁמֶרֶת הַקֹּדֶשׁ *šomre mišmɛrɛt haq-qodɛš* 'duty-guards of the duty of the Holy-Place'.

14. Numbers 3 — the number of Levites (encamped + tribal leader)

²³ מִשְׁפְּחֹת הַגֵּרְשֻׁנִּי אַחֲרֵי הַמִּשְׁכָּן יַחֲנוּ יָמָּה:

²⁴ וּנְשִׂיא בֵית־אָב לַגֵּרְשֻׁנִּי אֶלְיָסָף בֶּן־לָאֵל:

----

²⁹ מִשְׁפְּחֹת בְּנֵי־קְהָת יַחֲנוּ עַל יֶרֶךְ הַמִּשְׁכָּן תֵּימָנָה:

³⁰ וּנְשִׂיא בֵית־אָב לְמִשְׁפְּחֹת הַקְּהָתִי אֱלִיצָפָן בֶּן־עֻזִּיאֵל:

----

³⁵ וּנְשִׂיא בֵית־אָב לְמִשְׁפְּחֹת מְרָרִי צוּרִיאֵל בֶּן־אֲבִיחָיִל עַל יֶרֶךְ הַמִּשְׁכָּן יַחֲנוּ צָפֹנָה:

²³ The families of the Gershon-ite; behind the Tabernacle, they encamped sea-ward.
²⁴ And the leader of the ancestral house of the Gershon-ite: Elyasap son of Lael.

----

²⁹ The families of the children of Kohath encamped; on the flank of the Tabernacle southward.
³⁰ And the leader of the ancestral house of the families of the Kohath-ite: Elizapan son of Uzziel.

----

³⁵ And the leader of the ancestral house of the families of Merari-ite: Zuriel son of Abihayil; on the flank of the Tabernacle, they encamped, northward.

In these comparable verses, further details are provided for the three Levite groups: (a) their position vis-à-vis the Tabernacle; and (b) the names of their division leaders. The most glaring difference is the use of two verses to present this information for the Gershon-ite and Kohath-ite groups (vv. 23–24 and 29–30, respectively), with only a single (albeit longer) verse used for the Merari-ite group (v. 35). And within this major variation, one notes the order of cardinal direction + name of leader for the first two groups, versus the order of name of leader + cardinal direction for the third group.

More minor divergences also are present. First, in the clause that
provides details about the encampment, we note the differences between and among: (a) מִשְׁפְּחֹת הַגֵּרְשֻׁנִּי *mišpǝḥot hag-geršunni* 'the families of the Gershon-ite' (v. 23), with definite article + gentilic form of the
group name, i.e., 'the Gershon-ite'; (b) מִשְׁפְּחֹת בְּנֵי־קְהָת *mišpǝḥot bene
qǝhat* 'the families of the children of Kohath' (v. 29), with the word בְּנֵי
bǝne 'children of' used; and (c) no such corresponding phrase for the
encamping of the Merari-ite group (v. 35).

Secondly, concerning where each group encamped, we note
the differences between and among: (a) אַחֲרֵי הַמִּשְׁכָּן יַחֲנוּ יָמָּה *'aḥare
ham-miškan yaḥanu yamma* 'behind the Tabernacle, they encamped sea-
ward' (v. 23); (b) יַחֲנוּ עַל יֶרֶךְ הַמִּשְׁכָּן תֵּימָנָה *yaḥanu ʿal yɛrɛk ham-miškan
temana* 'they encamped; on the flank of the Tabernacle southward'
(v. 29); and (c) עַל יֶרֶךְ הַמִּשְׁכָּן יַחֲנוּ צָפֹנָה *ʿal yɛrɛk ham-miškan yaḥanu
ṣapona* 'on the flank of the Tabernacle, they encamped, northward'
(v. 35). Each of these has a slightly different wording, with the most
striking feature being the attachment of יַחֲנוּ *yaḥanu* 'they encamped'
to the first clause of v. 29 (note the presence of the major disjuncture
marked by the *'atnaḥ*).

Third, for the name of the group leader, we note: (a) וּנְשִׂיא בֵית־אָב
לַגֵּרְשֻׁנִּי *u-nśiʾ bet ʾab lag-geršunni* 'and the leader of the ancestral house
of the Gershon-ite' (v. 24); (b) וּנְשִׂיא בֵית־אָב לְמִשְׁפְּחֹת הַקְּהָתִי *u-nśiʾ bet
ʾab lǝ-mišpǝḥot haq-qǝhati* 'and the leader of the ancestral house of the
families of the Kohath-ite' (v. 30); and וּנְשִׂיא בֵית־אָב לְמִשְׁפְּחֹת מְרָרִי *u-nśiʾ
bet ʾab lǝ-mišpǝḥot ha-mǝrari* 'and the leader of the ancestral house of the
families of Merari-ite' (v. 35). All three begin the same, with the phrase
וּנְשִׂיא בֵית־אָב *u-nśiʾ bet ʾab* 'and the leader of the ancestral house'—though
for the first simply the gentilic term is used, לַגֵּרְשֻׁנִּי *lag-geršunni* 'of the
Gershon-ite' (v. 24), while for the second and third the term לְמִשְׁפְּחֹת
lǝ-mišpǝḥot 'of the families of' is inserted (vv. 30, 35). Given this parallel
structure of the second and the third, a further distinction is introduced
by including the definite article with הַקְּהָתִי *haq-qǝhati* 'the Kohath-ite'
and by omitting this morpheme with מְרָרִי *mǝrari* 'Merari-ite'.

The result of these variant wordings is a panoply of differentia-
tions at which the reader/listener may marvel. Far from producing
banal repetition of the formulas to impart the data for the three Levite
subgroups, the author deliberately introduces variation at every level.

15. Numbers 7 — the tribal gifts to the Tabernacle

Num 7:12–13

¹² וַיְהִ֗י הַמַּקְרִ֥יב בַּיּ֛וֹם הָרִאשׁ֖וֹן אֶת־קָרְבָּנ֑וֹ נַחְשׁ֥וֹן בֶּן־עַמִּינָדָ֖ב

לְמַטֵּ֥ה יְהוּדָֽה: ¹³ וְקׇרְבָּנ֞וֹ קַֽעֲרַת־כֶּ֣סֶף אַחַ֗ת . . .

¹² And he was the offerer on the first day, his offering, Nahshon son of Amminadab of the tribe of Judah. ¹³ And his offering, one silver bowl . . .

Num 7:18–19

¹⁸ בַּיּוֹם֙ הַשֵּׁנִ֔י הִקְרִ֖יב נְתַנְאֵ֣ל בֶּן־צוּעָ֑ר נְשִׂ֖יא יִשָּׂשכָֽר: ¹⁹ הִקְרִ֨ב

אֶת־קׇרְבָּנ֜וֹ קַעֲרַת־כֶּ֣סֶף אַחַ֗ת . . .

¹⁸ And on the second day offered Nethanel son of Zuar, leader of Issachar. ¹⁹ He offered his offering, one silver bowl . . .

Num 7:24–25

²⁴ בַּיּוֹם֙ הַשְּׁלִישִׁ֔י נָשִׂ֖יא לִבְנֵ֣י זְבוּלֻ֑ן אֱלִיאָ֖ב בֶּן־חֵלֹֽן: ²⁵ קׇרְבָּנ֞וֹ

קַעֲרַת־כֶּ֣סֶף אַחַ֗ת . . .

²⁴ On the third day the leader of the children of Zebulun, Eliab son of Helon. ²⁵ His offering, one silver bowl . . .

Numbers 7 is the longest chapter in the Torah, made so by the verbatim repetition of each tribe's identical gift to the Tabernacle: silver bowl, silver basin (each filled with fine flour mixed with oil), gold spoon (bearing incense), one bull, one ram, one yearling sheep, one hairy-goat, two more bulls, five more rams, and five more yearling sheep (see vv. 13–17, 19–23, 25–29, etc., through vv. 79–83). In this case, one imagines that the author wished to show the equality of each tribe, and thus not a single word of the detailed listing is altered from tribe to tribe.

As a parallel to the verbatim repetition used during this presentation ceremony, I offer the verbatim repetition of the following words declaimed by the president of Rutgers University upon the presentation of each year's graduates by the respective deans of the several dozen units that comprise my academic institution: "Upon recommendation of the Faculty of [the named School] for the aforementioned degrees, and by virtue of the authority vested in me by the Boards of Governors and Trustees of Rutgers, The State University of New Jersey, I confer upon each of you and the candidates you represent, the degrees indicated with all the rights, responsibilities, privileges, and immunities appertaining thereunto, here and elsewhere." Over and over again the audience listens to this phrase, word-for-word, in this time-honored ceremony for Arts and Sciences, Business, Education, Engineering, Environmental and Biological Sciences, Medicine, Nursing, Social Work, etc., etc. In similar fashion, one imagines each tribe of ancient Israel listening to the recitation of the same words in Numbers 7, in whatever manner we may envision a public reading of the chapter.

In typical biblical style, however, the author allowed himself some variation at the beginning of this long pericope, not with the items contributed (as per the preceding paragraph), but rather with the introductory phrases. The standard phrase is the one listed as Num 7:24–25, with said wording repeated verbatim (save for the names of the tribe and its leader) for tribes three (Zebulun) through twelve (Naphtali).

For the first tribe, v. 12 presents the following modifications: (a) the introductory phrase וַיְהִי הַמַּקְרִיב *wayhi ham-maqrib* 'and he was the offerer'; (b) the additional phrase אֶת־קָרְבָּנוֹ *'et qorbano* 'his offering'; and (c) the tag לְמַטֵּה יְהוּדָה *lə-maṭṭe yəhuda* 'of the tribe of Judah' (without the word נָשִׂיא *nasi'* 'leader'). In addition, a slight change occurs at the beginning of v. 13, with (d) the addition of the conjunction -וְ *wə-* 'and' before קָרְבָּנוֹ *qorbano* 'his offering'.

For the second tribe, v. 18 reveals the following alterations: (a) the use of the verb הִקְרִיב *hiqrib* 'offered'; and (b) the epithet נְשִׂיא יִשָּׂשכָר *nəsi' yissakar* 'leader of Issachar' after the name of the tribal leader. A major variation is then introduced at the beginning of v. 19, with (c) the verbal clause הִקְרִב אֶת־קָרְבָּנוֹ *hiqrib 'et qorbano* 'he offered his offering'. And since the same verb is reiterated in close proximity, scribal variation is instituted via *plene* הִקְרִיב *hiqrib* (v. 18) versus *defectiva* הִקְרִב *hiqrib* (v. 19).

The pattern of Numbers 7 follows closely the pattern of Numbers 1, studied above. Variation is presented with the wording for the first two tribes, and then from the third tribe onward the author settles into a fixed wording. The two chapters depart only in the lack of variation for the final tribe, which is present in Numbers 1 (noted briefly above, no. 11, and studied more thoroughly below, Chapter 13, no. 14), though not in Numbers 7.

16. Numbers 28–29 — the goat-offering on festival days

Num 28:15 (Rosh Hodesh)

וּשְׂעִיר עִזִּים אֶחָד לְחַטָּאת לַיהוָה

*u-śʿir ʿizzim ʾɛḥad lə-ḥaṭṭaʾt la-*YHWH

and one hairy-one of the goats as a *ḥaṭṭaʾt* unto YHWH

Num 28:22 (Pesaḥ)

וּשְׂעִיר חַטָּאת אֶחָד לְכַפֵּר עֲלֵיכֶם

u-śʿir ḥaṭṭaʾt ʾɛḥad ləkapper ʿalekɛm

and one hairy-one *ḥaṭṭaʾt* to expiate for you

Num 28:30 (Shavuʿot)

שְׂעִיר עִזִּים אֶחָד לְכַפֵּר עֲלֵיכֶם

śəʿir ʿizzim ʾɛḥad ləkapper ʿalekɛm

one hairy-one of the goats to expiate for you

Num 29:5 [Rosh ha-Shana]

וּשְׂעִיר־עִזִּים אֶחָד חַטָּאת לְכַפֵּר עֲלֵיכֶם

u-śʿir ʿizzim ʾɛḥad ḥaṭṭaʾt ləkapper ʿalekɛm

and one hairy-one of the goats *ḥaṭṭaʾt* to expiate for you

Num 29:11 (Yom Kippur)

שְׂעִיר־עִזִּים אֶחָד חַטָּאת

śəʿir ʿizzim ʾɛḥad ḥaṭṭaʾt

one hairy-one of the goats *ḥaṭṭaʾt*

Numbers 28–29 outlines the individual sacrifices for each of the festival days, as envisioned by the Priestly source. Far from providing a repetitive litany of this offering and that sacrifice, the author of this pericope introduces variation whenever possible. The different word-ings in the individual paragraphs are too complicated to outline here, and thus we limit ourselves to the variation inherent in one specific formula, viz., the one concerning the goat-offering.

In four instances the animal is referred to as שְׂעִיר עִזִּים śəʿir ʿizzim 'hairy-one of the goats', while in 28:22 the term appears as שְׂעִיר חַטָּאת śəʿir ḥaṭṭaʾt 'hairy-one ḥaṭṭaʾt'. In three cases, the phrase begins with the conjunction -וּ u- 'and', while in 28:30 and 29:11 the conjunction is omitted. The word חַטָּאת ḥaṭṭaʾt (traditionally rendered 'sin-offering', though recent research reveals that 'purification-offering' is more appropriate)[8] appears in four places, though again not in 28:30. The phrase לְכַפֵּר עֲלֵיכֶם ləkapper ʿalekɛm 'to expiate for you' occurs 3x, but it does not appear in 28:15 and 29:11. The divine name יְהוָה 'YHWH' ap-pears in the first formulation, though not in the others.[9] These minor modifications guarantee that none of the five sentences is repeated verbatim.

17. Numbers 29 — the sacrifices for the individual days of Sukkot

Num 29:16 (Day 1)

וּשְׂעִיר־עִזִּים אֶחָד חַטָּאת מִלְּבַד עֹלַת הַתָּמִיד מִנְחָתָהּ וְנִסְכָּהּ:

u-śʿir ʿizzim ʾɛḥad ḥaṭṭaʾt mil-ləbad ʿolat hat-tamid minḥatah wə-niskah

and one hairy-one of the goats ḥaṭṭaʾt, in addition to the daily offering, its grain-offering and its libation-offering.

---

8. See ahead in Chapter 20, p. 428, n. 10.

9. As one might expect, given their sensitivity to the text, the classi-cal rabbis at times derived teachings, including theological insights, from the variant phrases and expressions. For this example, see Bavli Ḥullin 60b, Bereshit Rabba 6:3.

Num 29:19 (Day 2)

וּשְׂעִיר־עִזִּים אֶחָד חַטָּאת מִלְּבַד עֹלַת הַתָּמִיד וּמִנְחָתָהּ וְנִסְכֵּיהֶם׃

u-śʿir ʿizzim ʾɛhad hattaʾt mil-ləbad ʿolat hat-tamid u-minhatah wə-niskehɛm

and one hairy-one of the goats *hattat*, in addition to the daily offering, and its grain-offering and their libation-offerings.

Num 29:22 (Day 3)

וּשְׂעִיר חַטָּאת אֶחָד מִלְּבַד עֹלַת הַתָּמִיד וּמִנְחָתָהּ וְנִסְכָּהּ׃

u-śʿir hattaʾt ʾɛhad mil-ləbad ʿolat hat-tamid u-minhatah wə-niskah

and one hairy-one *hattaʾt*, in addition to the daily offering, and its grain-offering and its libation-offering.

Num 29:25 (Day 4)

וּשְׂעִיר־עִזִּים אֶחָד חַטָּאת מִלְּבַד עֹלַת הַתָּמִיד מִנְחָתָהּ וְנִסְכָּהּ׃

u-śʿir ʿizzim ʾɛhad hattaʾt mil-ləbad ʿolat hat-tamid minhatah wə-niskah

and one hairy-one of the goats *hattaʾt*, in addition to the daily offering, its grain-offering and its libation-offering.

Num 29:28 (Day 5)

וּשְׂעִיר חַטָּאת אֶחָד מִלְּבַד עֹלַת הַתָּמִיד וּמִנְחָתָהּ וְנִסְכָּהּ׃

u-śʿir hattaʾt ʾɛhad mil-ləbad ʿolat hat-tamid u-minhatah wə-niskah

and one hairy-one *hattaʾt*, in addition to the daily offering, and its grain-offering and its libation-offering.

Num 29:31 (Day 6)

וּשְׂעִיר חַטָּאת אֶחָד מִלְּבַד עֹלַת הַתָּמִיד מִנְחָתָהּ וּנְסָכֶיהָ׃

u-śʿir hattaʾt ʾɛhad mil-ləbad ʿolat hat-tamid minhatah u-nəsakɛha

and one hairy-one *hattaʾt*, in addition to the daily offering, its grain-offering and its libation-offerings.

Num 29:34 (Day 7)

וּשְׂעִיר חַטָּאת אֶחָד מִלְּבַד עֹלַת הַתָּמִיד מִנְחָתָהּ וְנִסְכָּהּ:

u-śʿir ḥaṭṭaʾt ʾɛḥad mil-ləbad ʿolat hat-tamid minḥatah
wə-niskah

and one hairy-one *ḥaṭṭaʾt*, in addition to the daily offering, its grain-offering and its libation-offering.

Num 29:38 (Day 8)

וּשְׂעִיר חַטָּאת אֶחָד מִלְּבַד עֹלַת הַתָּמִיד וּמִנְחָתָהּ וְנִסְכָּהּ:

u-śʿir ḥaṭṭaʾt ʾɛḥad mil-ləbad ʿolat hat-tamid u-minḥatah
wə-niskah

and one hairy-one *ḥaṭṭaʾt*, in addition to the daily offering, and its grain-offering and its libation-offering.

The enumeration of the sacrifices on the festival days (see above,
no. 16) concludes with the offerings ordained for the individual days
of Sukkot, with the technique of repetition with variation continuing
apace. In the present instance, we expand our analysis to include the
wording not only for the goat-offering, but for the daily offering (*tamid*)
and its accompanying grain- and libation-offerings (*minḥa* and *nɛsɛk*,
respectively) as well.

To begin, in three cases the animal is called שְׂעִיר־עִזִּים *śəʿir ʿizzim*
'hairy-one of the goats', with the word חַטָּאת *ḥaṭṭaʾt* following, while
in five cases the term used is שְׂעִיר חַטָּאת *śəʿir ḥaṭṭaʾt* 'hairy-one *ḥaṭṭaʾt*'.
The expression מִלְּבַד עֹלַת הַתָּמִיד *mil-ləbad ʿolat hat-tamid* 'in addition to
the daily offering' remains constant throughout all eight days, but the
final formula in each of the verses allows for variation once more. Four
days present מִנְחָתָהּ *minḥatah* 'its grain-offering', while four days present וּמִנְחָתָהּ *u-minḥatah* 'and its grain-offering'. The libation-offering
is termed וְנִסְכָּהּ *wə-niskah* 'and its libation-offering' (in the singular)
6x, though quite oddly once we read וְנִסְכֵּיהֶם *wə-niskehɛm* 'and their
libation-offerings' (Day 2) and once we read וּנְסָכֶיהָ *u-nsakɛha* 'and its
libation-offerings' (Day 6).

As a consequence of all these alterations, five different formulations are present: one set of passages appears verbatim for Days 1 and 4; another set of passages appears verbatim for Days 3, 5, and 8; while the other days (2, 6, and 7) attest to unique wordings.

When we expand these passages to include the full wording for each day of Sukkot,[10] we find still other minor variations. Thus, for example, v. 24 (Day 4) commences with מִנְחָתָם *minḥatam* 'their grain-offering', while the parallel verses for all other days begin with וּמִנְחָתָם *u-minḥatam* 'and their grain-offering' (that is, with the conjunction); and v. 33 (Day 7) ends with כְּמִשְׁפָּטָם *kə-mišpaṭam* 'according to their regulation', while the parallel verses for all other days use כַּמִּשְׁפָּט *kam-mišpaṭ* 'according to the regulation'.[11] On the orthography front, we also note the unique spelling וְנִסְכֵּהֶם *wə-niskehɛm* 'and their libation-offerings' in v. 33 (Day 7).[12]

A less creative author would have repeated the same language again and again for the seven (or eight) days of Sukkot. Instead, however, the reader is invited to pay attention to these very minor differences, all in the interest of keeping the mind alert in the continual play of author → text → reader/performer → listener/audience.

---

10. I exclude from the discussion Day 1, since an altogether different phrasing is used there to introduce the entire week-long holiday.

11. Once more we may point to a rabbinic teaching derived from the variant wordings. Judah ben Betera in Sifre be-Midbar 150 used the "extra *mem*" of וְנִסְכֵּיהֶם *wə-niskehɛm* 'and their libation-offerings' in v. 19 (Day 2), the "extra *yod*" of וּנְסָכֶיהָ *u-nsakɛha* 'and its libation-offerings' in v. 31 (Day 6), and the "extra *mem*" of כְּמִשְׁפָּטָם *kə-mišpaṭam* 'according to their regulation' in v. 33 (Day 7) to spell the word מַיִם *mayim* 'water', as "proof" for the Pentatuechal origin of the Simḥat Bet haš-Šoʼeba ("the Celebration of the Drawing of Water") ceremony that occurred during the festival of Sukkot—for in truth this ritual is nowhere mentioned in the Bible.

12. Though the word also could be taken as singular 'their libation-offering', given the spelling without *yod*, in which case a real difference (not one of spelling only) is present.

18. Deuteronomy 6:6–9; 11:18–20

Deut 6:6–9

⁶ וְהָי֞וּ הַדְּבָרִ֣ים הָאֵ֗לֶּה אֲשֶׁ֨ר אָנֹכִ֧י מְצַוְּךָ֛ הַיּ֖וֹם עַל־לְבָבֶֽךָ׃

⁷ וְשִׁנַּנְתָּ֣ם לְבָנֶ֔יךָ וְדִבַּרְתָּ֖ בָּ֑ם בְּשִׁבְתְּךָ֤ בְּבֵיתֶ֙ךָ֙ וּבְלֶכְתְּךָ֣ בַדֶּ֔רֶךְ
וּֽבְשָׁכְבְּךָ֖ וּבְקוּמֶֽךָ׃

⁸ וּקְשַׁרְתָּ֥ם לְא֖וֹת עַל־יָדֶ֑ךָ וְהָי֥וּ לְטֹטָפֹ֖ת בֵּ֥ין עֵינֶֽיךָ׃

⁹ וּכְתַבְתָּ֛ם עַל־מְזוּזֹ֥ת בֵּיתֶ֖ךָ וּבִשְׁעָרֶֽיךָ׃

⁶ And these words that I command you (sg.) today shall
be upon your (sg.) heart.
⁷ And you (sg.) shall inculcate them to your (sg.) children,
and you (sg.) shall speak of them; when you (sg.) sit in
your (sg.) house, and when you (sg.) walk on the way,
and when you (sg.) lie-down, and when you (sg.) rise-up.
⁸ And you (sg.) shall bind them as a sign upon your (sg.)
hand, and they shall be for frontlets between your (sg.) eyes.
⁹ And you (sg.) shall write them upon the doorposts of
your (sg.) house and upon your (sg.) gates.

Deut 11:18–20

¹⁸ וְשַׂמְתֶּם֙ אֶת־דְּבָרַ֣י אֵ֔לֶּה עַל־לְבַבְכֶ֖ם וְעַל־נַפְשְׁכֶ֑ם
וּקְשַׁרְתֶּ֨ם אֹתָ֤ם לְאוֹת֙ עַל־יֶדְכֶ֔ם וְהָי֥וּ לְטוֹטָפֹ֖ת בֵּ֥ין עֵינֵיכֶֽם׃

¹⁹ וְלִמַּדְתֶּ֥ם אֹתָ֛ם אֶת־בְּנֵיכֶ֖ם לְדַבֵּ֣ר בָּ֑ם בְּשִׁבְתְּךָ֤ בְּבֵיתֶ֙ךָ֙ וּבְלֶכְתְּךָ֣
בַדֶּ֔רֶךְ וּֽבְשָׁכְבְּךָ֖ וּבְקוּמֶֽךָ׃

²⁰ וּכְתַבְתָּ֛ם עַל־מְזוּזֹ֥ות בֵּיתֶ֖ךָ וּבִשְׁעָרֶֽיךָ׃

¹⁸ And you (pl.) shall place these my words upon your
(pl.) heart and upon your (pl.) life-essence; and you (pl.)
shall bind them as a sign upon your (pl.) hand, and they
shall be for frontlets between your (pl.) eyes.
¹⁹ And you (pl.) shall teach them to your (pl.) children, to
speak of them; when you (sg.) sit in your (sg.) house, and
when you (sg.) walk on the way, and when you (sg.) lie-
down, and when you (sg.) rise-up.
²⁰ And you (sg.) shall write them upon the doorposts of
your (sg.) house and upon your (sg.) gates.

These two paragraphs from the book of Deuteronomy contain the same instructions,[13] though with many changes, both major and minor.[14] Let us begin by noting the different orders of the key four elements. In Deut 6:6–9, the order is (using key phrases to identify the four elements):

(a) 'upon your heart'

(b) 'to your children', with the four different modes following

(c) 'upon your hand' and 'between your eyes'

(d) 'upon the doorposts of your house and upon your gates'.

In the rehearsal of this material in Deut 11:18–20, the order is (using the prime indicator to show the matches):

(a′) 'upon your heart'

(c′) 'upon your hand' and 'between your eyes'

(b′) 'to your children', with the four different modes following

(d′) 'upon the doorposts of your house and upon your gates'.

Which is to say, the central two elements have been reversed.

The second major change relates to the second-person pronouns used in the two pericopes. In ch. 6, the second-person singular forms are used consistently, while in ch. 11, the text commences with second-person plural forms and then shifts to second-person singular forms. This shift between singular addressee and plural addressee occurs throughout the book of Deuteronomy, so one is not surprised to find this technique here. Nonetheless, it is employed here specifically to introduce difference between these two interrelated sections.

---

13. One will admit that the book of Deuteronomy is much less legal-cultic than the three central books of the Torah (Exodus–Leviticus–Numbers), with a rhetorical flair and hortatory style all its own. This and the following examples, accordingly, are not strictly legal-cultic (except for no. 19), but I have elected to include them in this chapter nonetheless. For when all is said and done, the large central portion of Deuteronomy is a collection of laws.

14. Note that while these two pericopes are five chapters away from each other in the canonical book of Deuteronomy, Jewish readers in particular may be sensitive to these differences, since the two sets of verses are read in quick succession within the first and second paragraphs of the Shema prayer, the centerpiece of the Jewish liturgy, recited twice daily (morning and evening).

And then there is a host of smaller, especially lexical and morphological substitutions, to wit: (a) הַדְּבָרִים הָאֵלֶּה *had-dəbarim ha-ʾellɛ*
'these words' in 6:6, versus דְּבָרַי אֵלֶּה *dəbaray ʾellɛ* 'these my words'
in 11:18; (b) the addition of נֶפֶשׁ *nɛpɛš* 'life-essence' in 11:18, absent in
6:6; (c) וְשִׁנַּנְתָּם *wəšinnantam* 'and you (sg.) shall inculcate them' in 6:7,
versus וְלִמַּדְתֶּם אֹתָם *wəlimmadtɛm ʾotam* 'and you (pl.) shall teach them'
in 11:19; and (d) וְדִבַּרְתָּ בָּם *wədibbarta bam* 'and you (sg.) shall speak
of them' in 6:7, vs. לְדַבֵּר בָּם *lədabber bam* 'to speak of them' in 11:19.

Though, just to keep the reader on her toes, two entire phrases
are repeated verbatim: (a) בְּשִׁבְתְּךָ בְּבֵיתֶךָ וּבְלֶכְתְּךָ בַדֶּרֶךְ וּבְשָׁכְבְּךָ וּבְקוּמֶךָ
bə-šibtəka bə-betɛka u-b-lɛktəka bad-dɛrɛk u-b-šokbəka u-b-qumɛka
'when you (sg.) sit in your (sg.) house, and when you (sg.) walk on the
way, and when you (sg.) lie-down, and when you (sg.) rise-up' in 6:7
and 11:19; and (b) וּכְתַבְתָּם עַל־מְזוּזֹת בֵּיתֶךָ וּבִשְׁעָרֶיךָ *u-ktabtam ʿal məzuzot
betɛka u-bi-šʿarɛka* 'and you (sg.) shall write them upon the doorposts of
your (sg.) house and upon your (sg.) gates' in 6:9 and 11:20. In fact, note
that these verbatim phrases use the second-person singular pronoun
throughout, even in the second iteration, for otherwise they would not
be word-for-word repetitions. Though naturally the writer could not
resist the opportunity to introduce one spelling change, as a little game
between him and the reciter of these passages; hence מְזוּזֹת *məzuzot*
'doorposts' in 6:9 (with but one *waw*), but מְזוּזוֹת *məzuzot* 'doorposts'
in 11:20 (with second *waw*).

19. Deuteronomy 17:6; 19:15

(a) Deut 17:6

עַל־פִּי | שְׁנַיִם עֵדִים אוֹ שְׁלֹשָׁה עֵדִים יוּמַת הַמֵּת

(only) on the testimony of two witnesses or three witnesses may a person be put-to-death

(b) Deut 19:15

עַל־פִּי | שְׁנֵי עֵדִים אוֹ עַל־פִּי שְׁלֹשָׁה־עֵדִים יָקוּם דָּבָר׃

(only) on the testimony of two witnesses or on the testimony of three witnesses may (the) matter stand

Twice the book of Deuteronomy turns its attention to the question of how many witnesses are required in order to convict the accused in a legal proceeding.[15] The two laws agree in requiring two or three witnesses (that is, a minimum of two, though more are permitted), though we note the variant wording present in the text. In 17:6 the term עַל פִּי *'al pi* 'on the testimony of' (lit., 'on the mouth of') appears but once, governing both the following 'two witnesses' and 'three witnesses'; while in 19:15 the term עַל־פִּי *'al pi* 'on the testimony of' occurs twice, before both 'two witnesses' and 'three witnesses'. Moreover, in the first iteration the absolute form of the numeral is used: שְׁנַיִם עֵדִים *šǝnayim 'edim* 'two witnesses'; whereas in the echo two chapters later the construct form of the numeral is used: שְׁנֵי עֵדִים *šǝne 'edim* 'two witnesses'.[16] Finally, the slightest variation is present in the Masoretic Text, with the former passage invoking שְׁלֹשָׁה עֵדִים *šǝloša 'edim* 'three witnesses' as two separate words, and the second passage conjoining שְׁלֹשָׁה־עֵדִים *šǝloša 'edim* 'three witnesses' as a single entity via the *maqqef.*

20. Deuteronomic Code — 'and you shall extirpate evil' (and similar expressions)

(a) Deut 13:6, 17:7, 19:19, 21:21, 22:21, 22:24, 24:7

וּבִעַרְתָּ הָרָע מִקִּרְבֶּךָ:

ubi'arta ha-ra' miq-qirbɛka

and you shall extirpate evil from your midst[17]

---

15. In the first instance the death penalty is explicit, and this may be implied in the second instance as well; see n. 18 below.

16. This is another instance where the Samaritan Torah harmonizes, reading both passages as עַל פִּי שְׁנֵי עֵדִים אוֹ עַל פִּי שְׁלֹשָׁה עֵדִים 'L PY ŠNY 'DYM 'W 'L PY ŠLŠH 'DYM, thereby accommodating Masoretic 17:6 to Masoretic 19:15. On the Septuagint here, see Carmel McCarthy, *Deuteronomy* (Biblica Hebraica Quinta 5; Stuttgart: Deutsche Bibelgeschellschaft, 2007), 53, 103*. Note the *paseq/pǝsiq* (vertical line) mark in these two passages, which may be present to signal the variation; see further Frank Zimmerman, *Before the Masora* (Lanham, MD: University Press of America, 2001), 114.

17. To be technical, note that one of the accent marks is different in Deut 21:21, due to the placement of the expression in the verse.

(b) Deut 17:12, 22:22

וּבִעַרְתָּ הָרָע מִיִּשְׂרָאֵל:

ubiʿarta ha-raʿ miy-yiśraʾel

and you shall extirpate evil from Israel

These two variant phrases punctuate the laws of Deuteronomy, especially those where the death penalty is involved.[18] Version (a) is clearly the dominant one, though in two cases the author of Deuteronomy changes the final word from מִקִּרְבֶּךָ *miq-qirbeka* 'from your midst' to מִיִּשְׂרָאֵל *miy-yiśraʾel* 'from Israel' to produce version (b). Why does this change occur specifically at 17:12 and 22:22? For the latter, I would suggest that alliteration with a key word in the next verse served as the catalyst; one observes the use of מְאֹרָשָׂה *məʾoraśa* 'betrothed' five words after מִיִּשְׂרָאֵל *miy-yiśraʾel* 'from Israel', with the letters of the root א-ר-שׂ *ʾ-r-ś* 'betrothe' of the former appearing in reverse order within the ethnonym יִשְׂרָאֵל *yiśraʾel* 'Israel'. This might suggest that alliteration also is at play in 17:12, even if the soundplay between יִשְׂרָאֵל *yiśraʾel* 'Israel' and the key word לְשָׁרֶת *ləšaret* 'to serve' (earlier in the verse) is less immediate.

(c) Deut 19:13

וּבִעַרְתָּ דַם־הַנָּקִי מִיִּשְׂרָאֵל

u-biʿarta dam han-naqi miy-yiśraʾel

and you shall extirpate the blood of the innocent from Israel

(d) Deut 21:9

וְאַתָּה תְּבַעֵר הַדָּם הַנָּקִי מִקִּרְבֶּךָ

wə-ʾatta təbaʿer had-dam han-naqi miq-qirbeka

and you, you shall extirpate the innocent blood from your midst

The key verb ב-ע-ר *b-ʿ-r* 'purge, extirpate' from (a) and (b) above also appears in (c) and (d). In these passages, the focus is specifically on

---

18. Tigay, *Deuteronomy*, 131. The one apparent exception is Deut 19:19, though in the light of Deut 17:6, the law of false witnesses also may result in capital punishment. See above, n. 15.

the extirpation of innocent blood. Once more the author introduces variation: (c) uses (i) the *wəqatal* form of the verb, וּבִעַרְתָּ *ubiʿarta* 'and you shall extirpate', (ii) the expression דַּם־הַנָּקִי *dam han-naqi* 'the blood of the innocent', and (iii) מִיִּשְׂרָאֵל *miy-yiśraʾel* 'from Israel'; whereas (d) uses (i) the prefix-conjugation verb with the independent pronoun for emphasis, thus וְאַתָּה תְּבַעֵר *wa-ʾatta təbaʿer* 'and you, you shall extirpate', (ii) the expression הַדָּם הַנָּקִי *had-dam han-naqi* 'the innocent blood', and (iii) מִקִּרְבֶּךָ *miq-qirbɛka* 'from your midst'.

(e) Deut 13:12

וְכָל־יִשְׂרָאֵל יִשְׁמְעוּ וְיִרָאוּן וְלֹא־יוֹסִפוּ לַעֲשׂוֹת כַּדָּבָר הָרָע הַזֶּה בְּקִרְבֶּךָ:

wə-kol yiśraʾel yišməʿu wə-yiraʾun wə-loʾ yosipu laʿaśot kad-dabar ha-raʿ haz-zɛ bə-qirbɛka

And all Israel shall hear and shall fear, and they shall not continue to do according to this evil thing in your midst.

(f) Deut 19:20

וְהַנִּשְׁאָרִים יִשְׁמְעוּ וְיִרָאוּ וְלֹא־יֹסִפוּ לַעֲשׂוֹת עוֹד כַּדָּבָר הָרָע הַזֶּה בְּקִרְבֶּךָ:

wə-han-nišʾarim yišməʿu wə-yiraʾu wə-loʾ yosipu laʿaśot ʿod kad-dabar ha-raʿ haz-zɛ bə-qirbɛka

And those who remain shall hear and shall fear, and they shall not continue to do again according to this evil thing in your midst.

These two verses exhort the Israelites in similar fashion to the afore-cited passages, though without recourse to the verbal root ב־ע־ר *b-ʿ-r* 'purge, extirpate'. Instead, a different phraseology is employed, though a comparison of the two verses reveals, as we have come to expect, non-verbatim repetition. We note the following differences: (i) וְכָל־יִשְׂרָאֵל *wə-kol yiśraʾel* 'and all Israel' versus וְהַנִּשְׁאָרִים *wə-han-nišʾarim* 'and those who remain' (i.e., 'everyone else'); (ii) the archaic form וְיִרָאוּן *wə-yiraʾun* 'and they shall fear', with paragogic *nun*, versus the standard form וְיִרָאוּ *wə-yiraʾu* 'and they shall fear'; and (iii) the introduction of

עוֹד *'od* 'again' in (f) versus its absence in (e). An orthographic difference bolsters the alterations, with *plene* יוֹסִפוּ *yosipu* 'continue' in 13:12 versus *defectiva* יֹסִפוּ *yosipu* 'continue' in 19:20. One notes that these two verses appear six chapters apart, and yet one assumes that the listener to the text would apprehend the differences in wording, even at such a distance.

(g) Deut 17:13

וְכָל־הָעָם יִשְׁמְעוּ וְיִרָאוּ

> *wə-kol ha-ʿam yišməʿu wə-yiraʾu*
>
> and all the people shall hear and shall fear

(h) Deut 21:21

וְכָל־יִשְׂרָאֵל יִשְׁמְעוּ וְיִרָאוּ

> *wə-kol yiśraʾel yišməʿu wə-yiraʾu*
>
> and all Israel shall hear and shall fear

Shorter versions of (e) and (f) above appear in these two passages, though again the reader notices the variation. The former uses וְכָל־הָעָם *wə-kol ha-ʿam* 'and all the people', while the latter uses וְכָל־יִשְׂרָאֵל *wə-kol yiśraʾel* 'and all Israel'.

The book of Deuteronomy is distinguished (from Leviticus, for example) by its constant exhortations to the people of Israel to observe the law and to remove evil from their midst. The message remains essentially the same, though the wording is varied in order to provide the composition with appropriate literary flavor.

21. Deuteronomy 27:12–13

Deut 27:12

אֵלֶּה יַעַמְדוּ לְבָרֵךְ אֶת־הָעָם עַל־הַר גְּרִזִים בְּעָבְרְכֶם אֶת־הַיַּרְדֵּן
שִׁמְעוֹן וְלֵוִי וִיהוּדָה וְיִשָּׂשכָר וְיוֹסֵף וּבִנְיָמִן:

These shall stand to bless the people upon Mount Gerizim, when you cross-over the Jordan: Simeon, and Levi and Judah; and Issachar, and Joseph and Benjamin.

Deut 27:13

וְאֵלֶּה יַעַמְדוּ עַל־הַקְּלָלָה בְּהַר עֵיבָל רְאוּבֵן גָּד וְאָשֵׁר וּזְבוּלֻן דָּן
וְנַפְתָּלִי:

And these shall stand over the curse on Mount Ebal: Reuben, Gad and Asher; and Zebulun, Dan and Naphtali.

In these verses, Moses commands the people concerning the ceremonial proclamation of the blessings and the curses, which will occur once the Israelites cross the Jordan and arrive in Canaan proper, with specific attention to the arrangement of the twelve tribes, six on each mountain. While an uncreative author might have used the same phraseology in each verse, our author, with ever an eye to literary artistry, introduces variation in several key places.

(1) The action of the first group is worded אֵלֶּה יַעַמְדוּ לְבָרֵךְ אֶת־הָעָם *'elle ya'amdu ləbarek 'et ha-'am* 'these shall stand to bless the people', while the action of the second group is worded וְאֵלֶּה יַעַמְדוּ עַל־הַקְּלָלָה *wə-'elle ya'amdu 'al haq-qəlala* 'and these shall stand over the curse'. I am not concerned with the absence of the conjunction -וְ *wə-* 'and' in the first passage and its presence in the second, for such would be expected in almost any linguistic context. Instead, one notices the use of the infinitive verb לְבָרֵךְ *ləbarek* 'to bless' followed by the explicit direct object אֶת־הָעָם *'et ha-'am* 'the people' in v. 12, in contrast to the phrase עַל־הַקְּלָלָה *'al haq-qəlala* 'over the curse' in v. 13.

(2) In the first instance, the text reads עַל־הַר גְּרִזִים *'al har gərizim* 'upon Mount Gerizim'; while in the second instance the text uses a different preposition, in בְּהַר עֵיבָל *bə-har 'ebal* 'on Mount Ebal'. The Bible seems to use both prepositions with more or less equal frequency following the verb ע-מ-ד *'-m-d* 'stand', with reference to standing on a mountain: for עַל *'al* 'upon', see Ezek 11:23, Zech 14:4 (and when רֹאשׁ *ro'š* 'head, summit' is used, see also 1 Sam 26:13, 2 Kgs 1:9); for -בְּ *bə-* 'on' (lit., 'in'), see Deut 10:10, 1 Kgs 19:11 (and with רֹאשׁ *ro'š* 'head, summit', see also Judg 9:7). Which is to say, not only were both options available to the author of Deut 27:12–13, but not surprisingly, both were utilized, in order to vary the language.[19]

---

19. I do not treat here the presence of בְּעָבְרְכֶם אֶת־הַיַּרְדֵּן *bə-'obrəkɛm 'et hay-yarden* 'when you cross-over the Jordan' in v. 12, versus its absence in

(3) The first six tribes are presented as שִׁמְעוֹן וְלֵוִי וִיהוּדָה וְיִשָּׂשכָר
וְיוֹסֵף וּבִנְיָמִן *šimʿon wə-lewi wi-huda wə-yiśśakar wə-yosep u-binyamin*
'Simeon, and Levi and Judah; and Issachar, and Joseph and Benjamin',
with conjunction -וְ *wə-* 'and' appended to each name (save the first,
obviously); whereas the second six tribes are presented as רְאוּבֵן גָּד וְאָשֵׁר
וּזְבוּלֻן דָּן וְנַפְתָּלִי *rə'uben gad wə-'ašer u-zbulun dan wə-naptali* 'Reuben,
Gad and Asher; and Zebulun, Dan and Naphtali', with the conjunction
-וְ *wə-* 'and' omitted before the second and fifth tribal names. The ar-
rangements, accordingly, may be charted as follows (with [---] indicating the lack of the conjunction):

- first six tribes: A, and B and C; and D, and E and F

- second six tribes: A, [---] B and C; and D, [---] E and F

As we noted at the beginning of Chapter 11, one can hardly imagine
texts with as little literary character as the legal-cultic sections of the
Torah (though that characterization may reflect our modern bias), and
yet even here one notices the author's attempt to vary his language in
order to engage his readers/listeners.

---

v. 13, since it would be very unidiomatic to include such an expression a
second time.

CHAPTER THIRTEEN

MARKING CLOSURE

The Israeli scholar Aharon Mirsky wrote the seminal article on this subject, entitled "Stylistic Device for Conclusion in Hebrew" (1977).[1] With a fine eye to the manner in which literature operates, Mirsky noticed that in a series of corresponding passages (typically four or more), the syntax or wording of the last one in the sequence will be altered. This device alerts the reader that she has reached the end of the thought-unit. We begin with a paradigm example identified by Mirsky, Ps 115:5–7, a text that is familiar to Jews in particular because it is intoned several dozen times per year as part of the liturgical recitation of Hallel (Psalms 113–118) on the festivals and new moon. I then will present a sampling of additional passages recognized by Mirsky, before proceeding to further illustrations of the phenomenon detected by Meir Par'an, by Amos Frisch, and by the present writer.[2] Finally, we will continue the discussion in the next chapter of this book, where we expand the notion of marking closure from individual passages to larger swaths of material.

1. Psalm 115:5–7

פֶּה־לָהֶם וְלֹא יְדַבֵּרוּ עֵינַיִם לָהֶם וְלֹא יִרְאוּ׃ [5]

אָזְנַיִם לָהֶם וְלֹא יִשְׁמָעוּ אַף לָהֶם וְלֹא יְרִיחוּן׃ [6]

יְדֵיהֶם ׀ וְלֹא יְמִישׁוּן רַגְלֵיהֶם וְלֹא יְהַלֵּכוּ לֹא־יֶהְגּוּ בִּגְרוֹנָם׃ [7]

[5] A mouth they have, but they do not speak;
Eyes they have, but they do not see.

---

1. Aharon Mirsky, "Stylistic Device for Conclusion in Hebrew," *Semitics* 5 (1977): 5–23.

2. For my earlier treatment, see Gary A. Rendsburg, "Marking Closure," *Vetus Testamentum* 66 (2016): 280–303.

⁶ Ears they have, but they do not hear;
A nose they have, but they do not smell.
⁷ Their hands, but they do not feel,
Their legs, but they do not walk-about;
They do not utter in their throat.

In this passage, the psalmist mocks the idols of the foreign nations (see vv. 2–4) by enumerating seven body parts that they (seemingly) possess but which are unable to perform the applicable actions. For the first six body parts (mouth, eyes, ears, nose, hands, legs), the body part is listed first, with the verbal statement following: e.g., 'eyes they have, but they do not see' (v. 5b). In he seventh and final passage, however, the order is reversed, so that one reads 'they do not utter in their throat', with the verbal clause preceding the body part.

2. Genesis 23

Gen 23:4	וְאֶקְבְּרָה מֵתִי	'so that I may bury my dead'
Gen 23:6a	קְבֹר אֶת־מֵתֶךָ	'bury your dead'
Gen 23:6b	מִקְּבֹר מֵתֶךָ	'from burying your dead'
Gen 23:8	לִקְבֹּר אֶת־מֵתִי	'to bury my dead'
Gen 23:11	קְבֹר מֵתֶךָ	'bury your dead'
Gen 23:13	וְאֶקְבְּרָה אֶת־מֵתִי	'so that I may bury my dead'
Gen 23:15	וְאֶת־מֵתְךָ קְבֹר	'and your dead, bury'

Genesis 23:3–16 constitutes the contracted negotiations between Abraham and the Hittites of Hebron (or from v. 10 onward one particular such person, Ephron) to purchase a burial place for his deceased wife Sarah. For simplicity's sake, I have truncated the seven expressions above, but the main point is discernible nonetheless.[3] In the first six cases, regardless of who is speaking and what the tone or tenor may be, the verb ק-ב-ר *q-b-r* 'bury' appears before the object מֵת *met* 'dead, deceased'. In

---

3. Mirsky, "Stylistic Device for Conclusion in Hebrew," 21, attributed this example to the insightful Mordechai Breuer, though note that I have expanded the discussion from the three phrases treated by Mirsky and Breuer (vv. 6b, 11, 15) to the seven iterations listed here.

the last instance, however, one notes the change in word order in Ephron's final words: וְאֶת־מֵתְךָ קְבֹר *wə-ʾet metka qabor* 'and your dead, bury'
(v. 15), with the object preceding the verb in the imperative form. While
this modification by itself should signal the end of the negotiations, just
in case the reader missed the point, the next verse confirms the point
rather prosaically: וַיִּשְׁמַע אַבְרָהָם אֶל־עֶפְרוֹן וַיִּשְׁקֹל אַבְרָהָם לְעֶפְרֹן אֶת־הַכֶּסֶף
'and Abraham heeded Ephron, and Abraham weighed for Ephron the
silver' (v. 16). In Mirsky's words, "change in the order of words indicates
the end of the dialogue, and also the end of the incident."[4]

In previous chapters, we have focused on variation for the sake of
variation as a major literary device within biblical literature. These passages from Genesis 23 afford us further illustrations of the technique.
Note, for example: (a) וְאֶקְבְּרָה מֵתִי *wə-ʾeqbəra meti* (v. 4) versus וְאֶקְבְּרָה
אֶת־מֵתִי *wə-ʾeqbəra ʾet meti* (v. 13), both spoken by Abraham and both
meaning 'so that I may bury my dead'; and (b) קְבֹר אֶת־מֵתֶךָ *qabor ʾet
metɛka* (v. 6a) versus קְבֹר מֵתֶךָ *qabor metɛka* (v. 11), the first spoken by
the Hittites at large, the second spoken by Ephron, and both meaning
'bury your dead'. In both pairs of verses, in one case the particle אֵת *ʾet*
(the marker of the definite direct object) is present, while in the other it
is lacking. Though just to keep the reader on her toes, in the clauses of
illustration (a), it is the former that lacks אֵת *ʾet* and the latter that includes
it; while in the clauses of illustration (b) the opposite obtains, with the
former containing אֵת *ʾet* and the latter lacking the form. Our author
misses no chance to use language to advance his goal of literary artistry.

3. Isaiah 13:20–21

20 לֹא־תֵשֵׁב לָנֶצַח

וְלֹא תִשְׁכֹּן עַד־דּוֹר וָדֹר

וְלֹא־יַהֵל שָׁם עֲרָבִי

וְרֹעִים לֹא־יַרְבִּצוּ שָׁם:

21 וְרָבְצוּ־שָׁם צִיִּים

וּמָלְאוּ בָתֵּיהֶם אֹחִים

וְשָׁכְנוּ שָׁם בְּנוֹת יַעֲנָה

וּשְׂעִירִים יְרַקְּדוּ־שָׁם:

---

4. Ibid., 22.

[20] It shall not be inhabited for eternity,

And it shall not be dwelt-in for generation after generation;

And no Arab shall pitch-tent there,

And the shepherds will not make-lie-down [their flocks] there.

[21] Rather, hyenas shall lie-down there,

And owls shall fill their homes;

And ostriches shall dwell there,

And hairy-satyrs will dance there.

These verses describe the prophet Isaiah's vision for future Babylon, a city to be destroyed and never inhabited again. The first verse deals with the humans who will no longer settle the area (with each stich including the negative particle לֹא *loʾ* 'not'), while the second verse delineates the various wild creatures that will settle there.[5] Each verse has four stichs, the first three of which present one word order (verb-subject), with the fourth stich proffering a variant syntax (subject-verb). The variable word order of Hebrew poetry cannot be captured in English (in which subject must nearly always precede verb in declarative sentences), and thus I have elected to use 'shall' in the first three stichs of each verse, but 'will' in the fourth. This technique, one hopes, allows the English-speaking reader to ascertain the manner in which the fourth stich in each verse is marked with difference and hence closure.

4. Jeremiah 10:12

עֹשֶׂה אֶרֶץ בְּכֹחוֹ

מֵכִין תֵּבֵל בְּחָכְמָתוֹ

וּבִתְבוּנָתוֹ נָטָה שָׁמָיִם׃

He makes the earth with his strength,

He prepares the world with his wisdom,

And with his astuteness he stretched-out the heavens.

---

5. One also observes the build-up in v. 20: the first two stichs refer to permanent settlement, using the verbal roots י-שׁ-ב *y-š-b* 'sit, inhabit' and שׁ-כ-ן *š-k-n* 'dwell in'; while the second two stichs state that not even non-permanent settlers, imagined as tent-dwelling Arab shepherds with their flocks, will inhabit the former city. My rendering of צִיִּים *ṣiyyim* in v. 21 as 'hyenas' is purely conventional; the dictionaries typically provide the gloss 'wild creatures of the desert'.

As this passage illustrates, even three lines provide an opportunity for the skilled author to employ the device under consideration here. In the first two stichs, the word order is: (a) participle form of the verb (with God as the unstated subject); (b) the object acted upon; and (c) the instrument employed by God. The third stich marks closure by introducing several changes, most prominently the word order, which now is: (a) the instrument employed by God; (b) the verb; and (c) the object acted upon. But finer modifications also are introduced, including (i) the use of the conjunction -ו *u-* 'and' at the head of the line, and (ii) the use of the past-tense verb נָטָה *naṭa* 'stretched-out' instead of the participle, used twice earlier.

5. Ezekiel 21:12

וְנָמֵס כָּל־לֵב֙
וְרָפ֣וּ כָל־יָדַ֔יִם
וְכִהֲתָ֥ה כָל־ר֖וּחַ
וְכָל־בִּרְכַּ֛יִם תֵּלַ֥כְנָה מָּ֑יִם

And every heart shall melt,
And all hands shall weaken,
And every spirit shall be frail,
And all knees will run water.

This passage foretells what will happen to the people upon their witnessing the wrath personified by God's drawn sword (see v. 10). In the first three stichs, Ezekiel employs the typical verb-subject word order, utilizing the *wəqatal* form of the verb (pointing to the future) followed by the relevant body part. In the fourth stich, the prophet transposes the two main grammatical components, recasting them with atypical subject-verb word order, hence by necessity utilizing the *yiqtol* verb form: וְכָל־בִּרְכַּ֛יִם תֵּלַ֥כְנָה מָּ֑יִם *wə-kol birkayim telakna mayim* 'and all knees will run water'. Once more (as in no. 3 above), I have taken advantage of the nearly synonymous English modal forms 'shall' (3x) and 'will' (1x) in order to capture the alteration in the original Hebrew in English translation. As to the sense of the Hebrew expression in the last stich, apparently 'knees will run water' is a euphemism for 'urinate from fear', either with the image of urine dripping onto the knees or with 'knees' serving for 'penis'.[6]

6. Qohelet 12:3–7

³ בַּיּוֹם

שֶׁיָּזֻעוּ שֹׁמְרֵי הַבַּיִת

וְהִתְעַוְּתוּ אַנְשֵׁי הֶחָיִל

וּבָטְלוּ הַטֹּחֲנוֹת כִּי מִעֵטוּ

וְחָשְׁכוּ הָרֹאוֹת בָּאֲרֻבּוֹת:

⁴ וְסֻגְּרוּ דְלָתַיִם בַּשּׁוּק . . .

⁵ . . . וְיָנֵאץ הַשָּׁקֵד

וְיִסְתַּבֵּל הֶחָגָב

וְתָפֵר הָאֲבִיּוֹנָה . . .

⁶ עַד אֲשֶׁר

לֹא־יֵרָתֵק חֶבֶל הַכֶּסֶף

וְתָרֻץ גֻּלַּת הַזָּהָב

וְתִשָּׁבֶר כַּד עַל־הַמַּבּוּעַ

וְנָרֹץ הַגַּלְגַּל אֶל־הַבּוֹר:

⁷ וְיָשֹׁב הֶעָפָר עַל־הָאָרֶץ כְּשֶׁהָיָה

וְהָרוּחַ תָּשׁוּב אֶל־הָאֱלֹהִים אֲשֶׁר נְתָנָהּ:

³ On the day[7]
That the guardians of the house [sc. the arms] tremble,
And the men of strength [sc. the legs] are bent;

---

6. Moshe Greenberg, *Ezekiel 1–20* (Anchor Bible 22; Garden City, NY: Doubleday, 1983), 152; and Moshe Greenberg, *Ezekiel 21–37* (Anchor Bible 22A; New York: Doubleday, 1997), 422.

7. Along with many scholars, I understand the individual items listed here to represent parts of the human body (as indicated by bracketed inserts introduced by sc.), even if one cannot be certain about each one. For discussion, see Choon-Leong Seow, *Ecclesiastes* (Anchor Bible 18C; New York: Doubleday, 1997), 354–67 (comments interspersed). Though even if one wishes to accept the surface meanings of the terms, the literary device under examination here remains nonetheless.

And the grinders [sc. the teeth] cease, for they are few,
And the seers [sc. the eyes] are darkened behind windows.
[4] And the double-doors [sc. the ears] are closed in the street . . .
[5] . . . And the almond [sc. the white hair] blossoms,
And the locust [sc. the penis] droops,
And the caperberry [sc. the desire] is split open . . .
[6] Until
The cord of silver [sc. the spine] is not bound,
And the bowl of gold [sc. the skull] is shattered;
And the pitcher over the wellspring [sc. the penis and
        testicles] is broken,
And the wheel at the cistern [sc. bodily vigor] is shattered.
[7] And the dust returns to the earth as it was;
And the spirit returns to God who gave it.

These lines from the last chapter of Qohelet afford us an additional example of syntactic change to mark closure. Distributed over these five verses are thirteen stichs portraying the end of life. Twelve stichs use metaphors for body parts (even if we are uncertain of the symbolism in each case) no longer functioning properly, while the thirteenth one employs the simple prose word עָפָר *'apar* 'dust'. Throughout, the word order is the usual arrangement of verb-subject. In the last phrase (v. 7b), the word order is reversed, with the subject now preceding the verb: וְהָרוּחַ תָּשׁוּב *wə-ha-ruaḥ tašub* 'and the spirit returns'. The reader recognizes that she has reached the end, just as the entire pericope announces the end of an individual human's life.

Notwithstanding the seminal nature of Mirsky's article, in my perusal of dozens, nay, hundreds, of commentaries on biblical books, monographs devoted to particular selections of biblical literature, standard reference works, and so on, only a handful of scholars (to my knowledge) have taken notice of "Stylistic Device for Conclusion in Hebrew." These include Wilfred Watson, who provides a brief discussion on the endings of poems in his valuable handbook, though without offering further examples,[8] and Meir Par'an and Amos Frisch, both of

---

8. Wilfred G. E. Watson, *Classical Hebrew Poetry: A Guide to Its Techniques* (London: T&T Clark, 2005), 62–65.

whom identified additional instances of the phenomenon.[9] We continue
our treatment of this literary device with two passages ascertained by
Parʾan, the first of which simply sets the stage for the second, which
is more central to his project concerning stylistic devices within the
priestly material in the Torah.

7. Psalm 74:13–17

13 אַתָּה פוֹרַרְתָּ בְעָזְּךָ יָם
שִׁבַּרְתָּ רָאשֵׁי תַנִּינִים עַל־הַמָּיִם:
14 אַתָּה רִצַּצְתָּ רָאשֵׁי לִוְיָתָן
תִּתְּנֶנּוּ מַאֲכָל לְעָם לְצִיִּים:
15 אַתָּה בָקַעְתָּ מַעְיָן וָנָחַל
אַתָּה הוֹבַשְׁתָּ נַהֲרוֹת אֵיתָן:
16 לְךָ יוֹם אַף־לְךָ לָיְלָה
אַתָּה הֲכִינוֹתָ מָאוֹר וָשָׁמֶשׁ:
17 אַתָּה הִצַּבְתָּ כָּל־גְּבוּלוֹת אָרֶץ
קַיִץ וָחֹרֶף אַתָּה יְצַרְתָּם:

13 You crushed with your strength Yam,
You shattered the heads of the Tanninim over the waters.
14 You smashed the heads of Leviathan,
You give him (as) food to the people of the deserts.
15 You split spring and wadi,
You dried-up the everflowing streams.
16 To you is day, yea, to you is night,
You set luminary and sun.
17 You established all the boundaries of the earth,
Summer and winter, you created them.

In these poetic lines, the psalmist ascribes to God ten different acts of
creation (not necessarily derivative of Genesis 1, but rather exploits

---

9. Meir Parʾan, *Darkhe ha-Signon ha-Kohani ba-Torah* (Jerusalem: Magnes,
1989), 183–204; and Amos Frisch, "Hedim be-Sifre Neviʾim le-ʾIssure ʿHoq ha-
Melekʾ še-be-Sefer Devarim," in Shmuel Vargon et al., eds., *Menaḥot Yedidut
ve-Hoqra le-Menaḥem Kohen* (Ramat-Gan: Bar-Ilan University Press, 2005)
= *ʿIyyune Miqraʾ u-Paršanut* 7 (5765), 263–81, esp. 272, 276–77.

more typically associated with the mythologies of the ancient world, such as the defeat of Yam/Tannin/Leviathan, ascribed to Baʿal in Ugaritic myth). The first nine stichs begin with 'you', with the object following. The pronoun 'you' may appear as an independent form, אַתָּה ʾatta 'you', as it does 6x; it may be built into a suffix-conjugation verb, as happens once, in שִׁבַּרְתָּ šibbarta 'you shattered' (v. 13); it may be built into a prefix-conjugation verb, as also occurs once, תִּתְּנֶנּוּ tittənɛnnu 'you give him' (v. 14); or it may appear as a pronominal suffix attached to a preposition, as occurs with לְךָ ləka 'to you' (v. 16), though this is still the headword in the poetic line.[10] This pattern is altered in the tenth and last line of this section of Psalm 74; in the colon קַיִץ וָחֹרֶף אַתָּה יְצַרְתָּם qayiṣ wa-ḥorɛp ʾatta yəṣartam 'summer and winter, you created them', the two-noun object appears first, with the 'you' expression following.

8. Leviticus 1:4–9

⁴ וְסָמַךְ יָדוֹ עַל רֹאשׁ הָעֹלָה

וְנִרְצָה לוֹ לְכַפֵּר עָלָיו:

⁵ וְשָׁחַט אֶת־בֶּן הַבָּקָר לִפְנֵי יְהוָה

וְהִקְרִיבוּ בְּנֵי אַהֲרֹן הַכֹּהֲנִים אֶת־הַדָּם

וְזָרְקוּ אֶת־הַדָּם עַל־הַמִּזְבֵּחַ סָבִיב אֲשֶׁר־פֶּתַח אֹהֶל מוֹעֵד:

⁶ וְהִפְשִׁיט אֶת־הָעֹלָה

וְנִתַּח אֹתָהּ לִנְתָחֶיהָ:

⁷ וְנָתְנוּ בְּנֵי אַהֲרֹן הַכֹּהֵן אֵשׁ עַל־הַמִּזְבֵּחַ

וְעָרְכוּ עֵצִים עַל־הָאֵשׁ:

⁸ וְעָרְכוּ בְּנֵי אַהֲרֹן הַכֹּהֲנִים אֵת הַנְּתָחִים אֶת־הָרֹאשׁ וְאֶת־הַפָּדֶר

עַל־הָעֵצִים אֲשֶׁר עַל־הָאֵשׁ אֲשֶׁר עַל־הַמִּזְבֵּחַ:

⁹ וְקִרְבּוֹ וּכְרָעָיו יִרְחַץ בַּמָּיִם

וְהִקְטִיר הַכֹּהֵן אֶת־הַכֹּל הַמִּזְבֵּחָה עֹלָה אִשֵּׁה רֵיחַ־נִיחוֹחַ לַיהוָה:

---

10. In this particular case, the words that follow—namely, יוֹם *yom* 'day', and then later in the verse לַיְלָה *layla* 'night'—are technically the grammatical subjects of verbless clauses, and hence not strictly objects. But the point remains nonetheless, since the reader realizes of course that the line refers to God's creation of day and night (in this case, yes, something noted in the canonical creation account in Genesis 1).

⁴ And he shall lay his hand on the head of the burnt-offering,
And it shall be acceptable unto him, to expiate for him.
⁵ And he shall slaughter the herd-member before Yнwн,
And the sons of Aaron the priests shall bring-forth the blood,
And they shall dash the blood on the altar all-around,
    which is at the opening of the Tent of Meeting.
⁶ And he shall flay the burnt-offering,
And he shall section it into sections.
⁷ And the sons of Aaron the priest shall place fire upon the altar,
And they shall arrange wood upon the fire.
⁸ And the sons of Aaron the priests shall arrange the
    sections, the head, and the suet upon the wood that is
    upon the fire that is upon the altar.
⁹ And its entrails and its legs he shall wash in water;
And the priest shall burn-as-smoke the whole on the altar
    (as) a burnt-offering, a sacrificial-gift of pleasing odor
    unto Yнwн.

The book of Leviticus commences with a detailed presentation of the individual sacrifices, including a step-by-step description of the specific priestly actions. In Lev 1:4–8 nine separate activities are mentioned, conducted either by Aaron alone (4x, with appropriate verb in the singular) or by his sons as a collective unit (5x, with appropriate verb in the plural). In each case, the verb is clause-initial, with the object following. For the tenth and final stage in the ritual, the text presents a different ordering: וְקִרְבּוֹ וּכְרָעָיו יִרְחַץ בַּמָּיִם *wə-qirbo u-kraʿaw yirḥaṣ bam-mayim* 'and its entrails and its legs he shall wash in water' (v. 9a)—with object first and verb following, as reflected in my English rendering. The reader thereby realizes that this action represents the final stage in the ritual ceremony. The following half-verse (v. 9b), 'And the priest shall burn-as-smoke the whole on the altar (as) a burnt-offering, a sacrificial-gift of pleasing odor unto Yнwн', returns to the usual word order; however, this passage does not represent a specific action, but rather serves as a summary statement for the sacrificial ritual as a whole.

We next present several fine illustrations of the marking-closure device detected by Frisch.

9. Deuteronomy 17:16–17

16 רַקֹ לֹא־יַרְבֶּה־לּוֹ סוּסִים . . .

17 וְלֹא יַרְבֶּה־לּוֹ נָשִׁים . . .

וְכֶסֶף וְזָהָב לֹא יַרְבֶּה־לּוֹ מְאֹד:

[16] Only he may not multiply for himself horses . . .

[17] And he may not multiply for himself women/wives . . .

And silver and gold he may not multiply for himself greatly.

The law of the king in Deuteronomy 17 legislates three essential prohibitions. In the first two cases, the verbal clause occurs first, with the direct object ('horses' and 'women/wives') following. In the third instance, the direct object ('silver and gold') is fronted, with the verbal clause following. In addition, the first two prohibitions contain additional relevant material (indicated here by the ellipses), while the third statement stands by itself. Finally, the third one includes the adverbial מְאֹד *məʾod* 'greatly', a term that is lacking in the first two proscriptions.

10. Isaiah 2:7–8

7 וַתִּמָּלֵא אַרְצוֹ כֶּסֶף וְזָהָב

וְאֵין קֵצֶה לְאֹצְרֹתָיו

וַתִּמָּלֵא אַרְצוֹ סוּסִים

וְאֵין קֵצֶה לְמַרְכְּבֹתָיו:

8 וַתִּמָּלֵא אַרְצוֹ אֱלִילִים

לְמַעֲשֵׂה יָדָיו יִשְׁתַּחֲווּ

לַאֲשֶׁר עָשׂוּ אֶצְבְּעֹתָיו:

[7] And his land is filled with silver and gold,
and there is no end to his treasuries;
and his land is filled with horses,
and there is no end to his chariots.
[8] And his land is filled with false-gods,
to his handiwork they prostrate themselves,
to that which his fingers made.

The law of the king in Deuteronomy is referenced in this passage near the beginning of the book of Isaiah, as the prophet decries the arrogance of the people of Judah. In keeping with the device studied here, the text presents the first two statements in strictly parallel fashion: 'his land is filled with X, and there is no end to his Y'. The third declaration introduces stylistic change to mark closure: (a) the third item mentioned is 'idols', which is not specifically indicated in the source passage of Deut 17:16–17;[11] and (b) the expression וְאֵין קֵצֶה לְ- wə-ʾen qeṣɛ lə- 'and there is no end to . . .', what scholars call a verbless clause (using grammatical terminology), is replaced by a verbal sentence, with a subordinate clause following, namely, 'to his handiwork they prostrate themselves, to that which his fingers made'.

11. Jeremiah 50:35–38

חֶרֶב עַל־כַּשְׂדִּים נְאֻם־יְהוָה וְאֶל־יֹשְׁבֵי בָבֶל וְאֶל־שָׂרֶיהָ וְאֶל־חֲכָמֶיהָ: ³⁵

חֶרֶב אֶל־הַבַּדִּים וְנֹאָלוּ חֶרֶב אֶל־גִּבּוֹרֶיהָ וָחָתּוּ: ³⁶

חֶרֶב אֶל־סוּסָיו וְאֶל־רִכְבּוֹ וְאֶל־כָּל־הָעֶרֶב אֲשֶׁר בְּתוֹכָהּ וְהָיוּ לְנָשִׁים ³⁷
חֶרֶב אֶל־אוֹצְרֹתֶיהָ וּבֻזָּזוּ:

חֹרֶב אֶל־מֵימֶיהָ וְיָבֵשׁוּ כִּי אֶרֶץ פְּסִלִים הִיא וּבָאֵימִים יִתְהֹלָלוּ: ³⁸

³⁵ A sword against the Chaldeans, declares YHWH;
and against the inhabitants of Babylon,
and against her princes, and against her wise-men.
³⁶ A sword against the diviners, that they may be foolish,
A sword against her heroes, that they may be dismayed.
³⁷ A sword against his horses and against his chariotry,
and against all the mixed-crowd that is in her midst,
that they may become women;
A sword against her treasuries, that they may be plundered.
³⁸ A drought against her waters, that they may be dried-up,
for it is a land of idols, and for the dreads they go mad.

---

11. Note, however, that the reference to 'false-gods' here may allude to the 'women/wives' mentioned in Deut 17:17, especially in light of a passage such as 1 Kgs 11:1–8, which attributes Solomon's worship of foreign deities to the foreign women whom he married.

The prophet Jeremiah envisions a series of five swords to be unleashed against Babylon (referred to frequently as Chaldea during this period). Each line, accordingly, is introduced by the word חֶרֶב *ḥereb* 'sword'. In most clever fashion, the sixth and culminating line ever-so-slightly changes the crucial word to חֹרֶב *ḥoreb* 'drought'. In the original Hebrew text, with no vowel points, the words would have looked exactly the same, thus חרב ḤRB, though the reader would have known to intone the first five as *ḥereb* 'sword' and the last one as *ḥoreb* 'drought'—most fitting, of course, given the reference to 'her waters' in this final line.[12]

We now build upon the work of Mirsky, Par'an, and Frisch by presenting additional examples of the phenomenon, beginning with two wordings in Gen 1:31, mentioned already in Chapter 1 (see above, p. 25).

12. Genesis 1

| Gen 1:31 | יוֹם הַשִּׁשִּׁי | *yom haš-šišši* 'the sixth day' |
| Gen 1:31 | וְהִנֵּה־טוֹב מְאֹד | *wə-hinne tob mə'od* 'and behold, very good' |

(1) During the first five days of creation, the names of the days of the week are presented without the definite article, thus: יוֹם אֶחָד *yom 'eḥad* 'day one' (v. 5), יוֹם שֵׁנִי *yom šeni* 'a second day' (v. 8), יוֹם שְׁלִישִׁי *yom šəliši* 'a third day' (v. 13), יוֹם רְבִיעִי *yom rəbiʻi* 'a fourth day' (v. 19), and יוֹם חֲמִישִׁי *yom ḥamiši* 'a fifth day' (v. 23).[13] For the final day of creation, however, we read יוֹם הַשִּׁשִּׁי *yom haš-šišši* 'the sixth day', with the definite article.

---

12. To be totally accurate, though, notwithstanding the same *written* letter ח, the pronunciation of the first consonant would have been different in ancient Israel, with the noun 'sword' realized with /ḥ/, a pharyngeal fricative (cf. Ugaritic ḥrb 'sword'), and with the verb 'dry up' realized with /ḫ/, a velar fricative (cf. Ugaritic ḫ-r-b 'dry up'). As noted earlier in our introduction to alliteration (see Chapter 5, p. 81, n. 22), from the third century B.C.E. onward the two consonants merged to /ḥ/, but this was not the case originally, including in Jeremiah's time. For details, see Rendsburg, "Ancient Hebrew Phonology," 71–72; and Rendsburg, "Phonology: Biblical Hebrew," 102–3.

13. Standard Hebrew usage calls for the cardinal number 'one' in this instance, as opposed to the ordinal number 'first' (for another instance, see Gen 2:11–14, where the rivers of Eden are enumerated). Accordingly, the

(2) Throughout Genesis 1 the reader encounters the refrain כִּי־טוֹב *ki tob* 'that it was good' (vv. 4, 10, 12, 18, 21, 25). In its last iteration, however, the author writes וְהִנֵּה־טוֹב מְאֹד *wə-hinne tob mə'od* 'and behold, very good' (v. 31), with two differences: (a) the particle כִּי *ki* 'that' is changed to וְהִנֵּה *wə-hinne* 'and behold'; and (b) the word טוֹב *tob* 'good' receives the adverb מְאֹד *mə'od* 'very'.[14]

These changes, however slight, inform the reader that she has reached the end of the story, which in this case also describes the end of God's creative actions.

13. Genesis 41:26–27

שֶׁבַע פָּרֹת הַטֹּבֹת שֶׁבַע שָׁנִים֙ הֵנָּה ²⁶

וְשֶׁבַע הַֽשִּׁבֳּלִים֙ הַטֹּבֹת שֶׁבַע שָׁנִים הֵנָּה חֲלוֹם אֶחָד הֽוּא׃

וְשֶׁבַע הַ֠פָּרוֹת הָֽרַקּוֹת וְהָֽרָעֹת הָעֹלֹת אַחֲרֵיהֶן שֶׁבַע שָׁנִים֙ הֵנָּה ²⁷

וְשֶׁבַע הַֽשִּׁבֳּלִים֙ הָֽרֵקוֹת שְׁדֻפוֹת הַקָּדִים יִהְי֕וּ שֶׁבַע שְׁנֵי רָעָֽב׃

²⁶ The seven good cows, they are seven years,
And the seven good ears-of-grain, they are seven years
—it is one dream.
²⁷ And the seven thin and bad cows that come-up after them, they are seven years,
And the seven empty ears-of-grain, blasted by the east-wind, they will be seven years of famine.

These lines constitute the key portion of Joseph's interpretation of Pharaoh's parallel dreams.[15] Each of the dream components represents seven years. The first three are marked by the identical clause שֶׁבַע שָׁנִים

---

ordinals commence only with 'second'. My glosses include the indefinite article 'a', which is necessary in English, though note that there is no such part of speech in Hebrew.

14. Ancient Jewish exegesis made much of the addition of מְאֹד *mə'od* 'very' in Gen 1:31, reading all sorts of meaning into the word. To my mind, however, we can explain the usage as simply another instance of variation, though with the specific function of marking closure.

15. I am grateful to Everett Fox (oral communication), who directed my attention to this example.

הֵנָּה *šɛbaʿ šanim henna* 'they are seven years', without further comment. The fourth and culminating expression is יִהְי֛וּ שֶׁ֥בַע שְׁנֵ֖י רָעָ֑ב *yihyu šebaʿ šəne raʿab* 'they will be seven years of famine', with a future tense verb, a different way of expressing 'seven years', and the climactic word רָעָב *raʿab* 'famine'.

14. Numbers 1

Num 1:42   בְּנֵי נַפְתָּלִי   *bəne naptali*
                                         'the sons of Naphtali'

Numbers 1 constitutes a census of the twelve tribes of Israel. In order to commence the census, the tribe descended from the firstborn son of Jacob—namely, Reuben—is introduced with a special formula: וַיִּהְי֣וּ בְנֵי־רְאוּבֵן֩ בְּכֹ֨ר יִשְׂרָאֵ֜ל *wayyihyu bəne rəʾuben bəkor yiśraʾel* 'and the sons of Reuben, the firstborn of Israel, were' (v. 20), with both the epithet 'firstborn of Israel' and an actual verb, 'were'. The following tribes are each introduced with the simple phrase לִבְנֵ֣י שִׁמְעוֹן *li-bne šimʿon* 'of the sons of Simeon' (v. 22), לִבְנֵ֣י גָד *li-bne gad* 'of the sons of Gad' (v. 24), לִבְנֵ֣י יְהוּדָ֗ה *li-bne yəhuda* 'of the sons of Judah' (v. 26), etc. One would expect the last tribe in the enumeration to follow suit, but with characteristic flair the text diverges, so that the final tribe is introduced as בְּנֵי נַפְתָּלִי *bəne naptali* 'the sons of Naphtali' (v. 42). Textual critics typically emend the passage to include the preposition לְ- *li-* 'to, of', so that the Naphtali passage will accord with the ones referring to the ten preceding tribes (Simeon [v. 22] through Asher [v. 40]).[16] In doing so, they rely on the Samaritan Torah, which reads לבני נפתלי LBNY NPTLY 'of the sons of Naphtali' here, along with additional versional testimony, e.g., Vulgate *de filiis Nepthali* 'of the sons of Naphtali'. These other ancient versions, however, are simply harmonizing. In light of the many examples of variation to mark closure presented in this chapter, the Masoretic Text not only should be retained, but should also stand as a reminder of the creative abilities of the ancient Hebrew literati. Indeed, even in the most mundane of texts—a census list!—the literary imagination shines through.

---

16. See, for example, *BHS*, ad loc.

15. Numbers 2 — the tribal encampment around the Tabernacle (census figures)

⁹ כָּל־הַפְּקֻדִים לְמַחֲנֵה יְהוּדָה מְאַת אֶלֶף וּשְׁמֹנִים אֶלֶף וְשֵׁשֶׁת־אֲלָפִים
וְאַרְבַּע־מֵאוֹת לְצִבְאֹתָם רִאשֹׁנָה יִסָּעוּ:

----

¹⁶ כָּל־הַפְּקֻדִים לְמַחֲנֵה רְאוּבֵן מְאַת אֶלֶף וְאֶחָד וַחֲמִשִּׁים אֶלֶף
וְאַרְבַּע־מֵאוֹת וַחֲמִשִּׁים לְצִבְאֹתָם וּשְׁנִיִּם יִסָּעוּ:

----

²⁴ כָּל־הַפְּקֻדִים לְמַחֲנֵה אֶפְרַיִם מְאַת אֶלֶף וּשְׁמֹנַת־אֲלָפִים וּמֵאָה
לְצִבְאֹתָם וּשְׁלִשִׁים יִסָּעוּ:

----

³¹ כָּל־הַפְּקֻדִים לְמַחֲנֵה דָן מְאַת אֶלֶף וְשִׁבְעָה וַחֲמִשִּׁים אֶלֶף וְשֵׁשׁ
מֵאוֹת לָאַחֲרֹנָה יִסְעוּ לְדִגְלֵיהֶם:

⁹ All those counted of the camp of Judah (totaled) one hundred thousand and eighty thousand and six thousand and four hundred [186,400], according to their armies; they would proceed first.

----

¹⁶ All those counted of the camp of Reuben (totaled) one hundred thousand and fifty-one thousand and four hundred and fifty [151,450], according to their armies; and they would proceed second.

----

²⁴ All those counted of the camp of Ephraim (totaled) one hundred thousand and eight thousand and one hundred [108,100], according to their armies; and they would proceed third.

----

³¹ All those counted of the camp of Dan (totaled) one hundred thousand and fifty-seven thousand and six hundred [157,600]; they would proceed last, according to their flags.

Selected verses from Numbers 2 were studied above, in Chapter 12 (see section no. 12 therein), to illustrate the technique of repetition with variation. We return to that section of the Torah here, with specific attention to the verses presented above, in which changes in the final iteration of the census are used to mark closure.

This section of the book of Numbers describes the camp of the Israelites, divided into four sections, each with a tribal unit as its lead organizer, one on each flank of the Tabernacle. The verses above provide the number of adult males (capable of military service, apparently) in each section, as a summary statement for the more individualized census figures listed in this chapter. The first three verses follow the same pattern, while the fourth one (v. 31) departs in two distinct ways: (a) the word לְצִבְאֹתָם *lǝ-ṣib'otam* 'according to their armies' is omitted; and (b) the word לְדִגְלֵיהֶם *lǝ-diglehɛm* 'according to their flags' is added.

16. Numbers 28–29 — festival sacrifices

28:9 (Sabbath)   וּבְיוֹם֙ הַשַּׁבָּ֔ת
'and on the day of the Sabbath'

28:11 (New Moon)   וּבְרָאשֵׁי֙ חָדְשֵׁיכֶ֔ם
'and on your new moons'

28:16 (Pesaḥ, day 1)   וּבַחֹ֣דֶשׁ הָרִאשׁ֗וֹן בְּאַרְבָּעָ֥ה עָשָׂ֛ר י֖וֹם לַחֹ֑דֶשׁ
'and in the first month, on the fourteenth day of the month'

28:25 (Pesaḥ, day 7)   וּבַיּוֹם֙ הַשְּׁבִיעִ֔י
'and on the seventh day'

28:26 (Shavuʿot)   וּבְי֣וֹם הַבִּכּוּרִ֗ים
'and on the day of first-fruits'

29:1 [Rosh ha-Shana]   וּבַחֹ֨דֶשׁ הַשְּׁבִיעִ֜י בְּאֶחָ֣ד לַחֹ֗דֶשׁ
'and in the seventh month, on the first (day) of the month'

29:7 (Yom Kippur)   וּבֶעָשׂוֹר֩ לַחֹ֨דֶשׁ הַשְּׁבִיעִ֜י הַזֶּ֗ה
'and on the tenth (day) of this the seventh month'

29:12 (Sukkot, day 1)   וּבַחֲמִשָּׁה֩ עָשָׂ֨ר י֜וֹם לַחֹ֣דֶשׁ הַשְּׁבִיעִ֗י
'and on the fifteenth day of the seventh month'

29:17 (Sukkot, day 2)   וּבַיּ֣וֹם הַשֵּׁנִ֗י
'and on the second day'

29:20 (Sukkot, day 3)   וּבַיּוֹם הַשְּׁלִישִׁי
    'and on the third day'

29:23 (Sukkot, day 4)   וּבַיּוֹם הָרְבִיעִי
    'and on the fourth day'

29:26 (Sukkot, day 5)   וּבַיּוֹם הַחֲמִישִׁי
    'and on the fifth day'

29:29 (Sukkot, day 6)   וּבַיּוֹם הַשִּׁשִּׁי
    'and on the sixth day'

29:32 (Sukkot, day 7)   וּבַיּוֹם הַשְּׁבִיעִי
    'and on the seventh day'

29:35 (Sukkot, day 8 / ʿAṣeret)   בַּיּוֹם הַשְּׁמִינִי
    'on the eighth day'

Numbers 28–29 comprises the most detailed exposition of the daily and festival sacrifices found in the Torah. The long section commences with the daily sacrifices (Num 28:3–8) and then proceeds to the new moon and festival offerings. Each of the new subsections is introduced with -וּבְ *u-bə-* 'and on' (in two instances the translation 'and in' obtains), with the details following. The exception, as the above list demonstrates, is the last and final holiday in the annual calendar, to wit, the eighth-day festival that follows Sukkot (Shemini ʿAṣeret in Jewish parlance). As we have seen on other occasions, once more we note how two of the ancient versions harmonize this passage with the preceding ones. The Septuagint adds καὶ 'and' at the beginning of v. 35; while the Samaritan Torah reads וביום השמיני WBYWM HŠMYNY 'and on the eighth day'.

17. Judges 3:20–23

20 . . . וַיֹּאמֶר אֵהוּד דְּבַר־אֱלֹהִים לִי אֵלֶיךָ
    וַיָּקָם מֵעַל הַכִּסֵּא:
21 וַיִּשְׁלַח אֵהוּד אֶת־יַד שְׂמֹאלוֹ
    וַיִּקַּח אֶת־הַחֶרֶב מֵעַל יֶרֶךְ יְמִינוֹ
    וַיִּתְקָעֶהָ בְּבִטְנוֹ:

וַיָּבֹא גַם־הַנִּצָּב אַחַר הַלַּהַב 22

וַיִּסְגֹּר הַחֵלֶב בְּעַד הַלַּהַב כִּי לֹא שָׁלַף הַחֶרֶב מִבִּטְנוֹ

וַיֵּצֵא הַפַּרְשְׁדֹנָה:

וַיֵּצֵא אֵהוּד הַמִּסְדְּרוֹנָה 23

וַיִּסְגֹּר דַּלְתוֹת הָעֲלִיָּה בַּעֲדוֹ

וְנָעָל:

[20] And Ehud said, "I have a word of God for you"; and he [sc. Eglon] arose from the chair.

[21] And Ehud sent his left hand, and he took the sword from his right thigh, and he blasted it into his stomach.

[22] And also the hilt entered after the blade, and the fat closed around the blade, because he did not withdraw the sword from his stomach; and the feces exited.

[23] And Ehud exited via the colonnade, and he closed the doors of the upper-chamber about him, and he locked.

Hebrew narrative prose, as the present excerpt illustrates,[17] utilizes a special past-tense form, known to biblical scholars as the *wayyiqtol* form.[18] Ten such forms occur in Judg 3:20–23[19]—until we reach the final verb in this scene. Here we find, quite atypically, וְנָעָל *wə-naʿal* 'and he locked', formed by conjunctive -וְ *wə-* 'and' + *qatal* נָעָל *naʿal* 'he locked'.

Robert Longacre has noted this atypical usage, with the following explanation:

[Judg 3:20–23] constitutes a rather celebrated case where a *weqatal* form occurs at the end in place of the expected *wayyiqtol* form. The passage is a graphic and detailed description of what is undoubtedly depicted as a high point in the story. . . . The problem here is the occurrence of the *weqatal* form in [the final clause] after the long string of *wayyiqtol* forms.

17. For additional treatments of the Ehud account, see above, Chapter 10, nos. 6–7, and below, Chapter 19, no. 10.

18. See Jan Joosten, *The Verbal System of Biblical Hebrew* (Jerusalem Biblical Studies 10; Jerusalem: Simor, 2012), 164–80.

19. There is also one *qatal* form in a subordinate clause, 'because he did not withdraw the sword from his stomach', as expected.

Ingenious attempts have been made to explain it as a frequentative: perhaps there were a series of bolts to draw or bolts on several doors. But if we take this as a special marking, what is the rationale for its use here? Is it climactic or anticlimactic? . . . At any rate, we are at a great moment of a story and we can expect the narrator to indulge in a few tricks.[20]

While he did not state so explicitly, Longacre is correct: our narrator has played a trick, with a focus on the word וְנָעַל *wə-naʿal* 'and he locked', given its position as the closing act (sorry for the pun) in this action-packed scene.[21]

18. Judges 16 — Samson and Delilah

Judg 16:9

וַתֹּאמֶר אֵלָיו פְּלִשְׁתִּים עָלֶיךָ שִׁמְשׁוֹן

And she said to him, "The Philistines are upon you, Samson."

Judg 16:12

וַתֹּאמֶר אֵלָיו פְּלִשְׁתִּים עָלֶיךָ שִׁמְשׁוֹן

And she said to him, "The Philistines are upon you, Samson."

Judg 16:14

וַתֹּאמֶר אֵלָיו פְּלִשְׁתִּים עָלֶיךָ שִׁמְשׁוֹן

And she said to him, "The Philistines are upon you, Samson."

Judg 16:20

וַתֹּאמֶר   פְּלִשְׁתִּים עָלֶיךָ שִׁמְשׁוֹן

And she said, "The Philistines are upon you, Samson."

---

20. Longacre, "*Weqatal* forms in Biblical Hebrew Prose," 71–72.

21. All of this, of course, renders the proposal by some scholars (e.g., *BHS, ad loc.*) to emend the last verb to וַיִּנְעַל unnecessary.

These verses were treated in greater detail above, at Chapter 9, no. 12; here we focus on a specific element. Four times Delilah attempts to gain from her lover, Samson, the desired information regarding the source of his strength. Four times she toys with him and then warns him about the presence of the Philistines about him. The first three statements are introduced by וַתֹּאמֶר אֵלָיו *watto'mɛr 'elaw* 'and she said to him'. The fourth iteration involves only a slight change, hence simply וַתֹּאמֶר *watto'mɛr* 'and she said' (note the white space that I have left in the presentation above, to highlight this change)—thereby informing the reader that she has reached the denouement of the narrative.

19. 1 Samuel 8:11–17

וַיֹּאמֶר זֶה יִהְיֶה מִשְׁפַּט הַמֶּלֶךְ אֲשֶׁר יִמְלֹךְ עֲלֵיכֶם אֶת־בְּנֵיכֶם יִקָּח ¹¹
וְשָׂם לוֹ בְּמֶרְכַּבְתּוֹ וּבְפָרָשָׁיו וְרָצוּ לִפְנֵי מֶרְכַּבְתּוֹ:

וְלָשׂוּם לוֹ שָׂרֵי אֲלָפִים וְשָׂרֵי חֲמִשִּׁים וְלַחֲרֹשׁ חֲרִישׁוֹ וְלִקְצֹר קְצִירוֹ ¹²
וְלַעֲשׂוֹת כְּלֵי־מִלְחַמְתּוֹ וּכְלֵי רִכְבּוֹ:

וְאֶת־בְּנוֹתֵיכֶם יִקָּח לְרַקָּחוֹת וּלְטַבָּחוֹת וּלְאֹפוֹת: ¹³

וְאֶת־שְׂדוֹתֵיכֶם וְאֶת־כַּרְמֵיכֶם וְזֵיתֵיכֶם הַטּוֹבִים יִקָּח וְנָתַן לַעֲבָדָיו: ¹⁴

וְזַרְעֵיכֶם וְכַרְמֵיכֶם יַעְשֹׂר וְנָתַן לְסָרִיסָיו וְלַעֲבָדָיו: ¹⁵

וְאֶת־עַבְדֵיכֶם וְאֶת־שִׁפְחוֹתֵיכֶם וְאֶת־בַּחוּרֵיכֶם הַטּוֹבִים וְאֶת־ ¹⁶
חֲמוֹרֵיכֶם יִקָּח וְעָשָׂה לִמְלַאכְתּוֹ:

צֹאנְכֶם יַעְשֹׂר וְאַתֶּם תִּהְיוּ־לוֹ לַעֲבָדִים: ¹⁷

¹¹ And he [sc. Samuel] said, "This is the rule of the king who will rule over you: your sons he will take, and he will place them for himself in his chariotry and as his horsemen, and they will run before his chariot;

¹² and he will place (them) for himself (as) officers of the thousands and (as) officers of the hundreds; and to plow his plowing and to harvest his harvesting, and to make his implements of war and his implements of chariotry;

¹³ and your daughters he will take, as perfumers and as cooks, and as bakers;

¹⁴ and your fields and your vineyards, and your good olive-groves he will take, and he will give (them) to his servants;

¹⁵ and your seeds and your vineyards he will tithe, and he
will give (them) to his eunuchs and to his servants;
¹⁶ and your servants and your maidservants and your good
young-men and your donkeys he will take, and he will make
(them) for his labor;
¹⁷ your flocks he will tithe, and you will be unto him as
servants."

In this famous passage, the prophet Samuel cautions the people about
the future actions of the king whom they seek as their ruler. His initial
warning commences 'your sons he will take', with each subsequent
declaration beginning, not surprisingly, with the conjunction -וְ wə-
'and'. It is rather striking, accordingly, to find the last admonition
omitting this particle, hence simply צֹאנְכֶם יַעְשֹׂר ṣoʾnkɛm yaʿśor 'your
flocks he will tithe'. The experienced reader, of course, understands this
slight change as the author's method of indicating closure. Once more
the Septuagint follows an independent course by adding καὶ 'and' at
the beginning of v. 17 (see similarly above, no. 16)—but this evidence
should not serve as a license for scholars to emend the Masoretic Text.

20. Isaiah 40:12

מִי־מָדַד בְּשָׁעֳלוֹ מַיִם

וְשָׁמַיִם בַּזֶּרֶת תִּכֵּן

וְכָל בַּשָּׁלִשׁ עֲפַר הָאָרֶץ

וְשָׁקַל בַּפֶּלֶס הָרִים

וּגְבָעוֹת בְּמֹאזְנָיִם׃

Who has measured with the hollow of his hand the water,
And gauged the heavens with a span,
And contained with a third the dust of the earth,
And weighed with a scale the mountains,
And the hills with a balance?

We now return to some examples of poetic verses (as are most of the
passages identified by Mirsky), with a change indicated in the final
stich. The present example has five lines characterized by synonymous

parallelism.[22] Each of the first four cola includes a verb, a measuring tool, and the item measured; in the final colon, no verb is included, as a way to indicate closure. Obviously, 'verb gapping' is involved here (to use the technical term employed by scholars, referring to the absence of a verb), but one notes how the poet did not employ this technique until the final line.

21. Isaiah 44:5

זֶה יֹאמַר לַיהוָה אָנִי
וְזֶה יִקְרָא בְשֵׁם־יַעֲקֹב
וְזֶה יִכְתֹּב יָדוֹ לַיהוָה
וּבְשֵׁם יִשְׂרָאֵל יְכַנֶּה׃

This-one will say, "To Yʜwʜ am I,"
And this-one will call in the name of "Jacob";
And this-one will write (on) his hand "To Yʜwʜ,"
And in the name of "Israel" he shall be branded.

The first three lines follow the pattern of זֶה *zɛ* 'this-one' + verb + name (relating either to God or the people of Israel). This arrangement is altered in the final stich, with זֶה *zɛ* 'this-one' omitted and with the name preceding the verb.

22. Isaiah 58:13

If you honor it, (refraining)	וְכִבַּדְתּוֹ
From doing your ways,	מֵעֲשׂוֹת דְּרָכֶיךָ
From seeking your desire,	מִמְּצוֹא חֶפְצְךָ
And (from) speaking (your) business.	וְדַבֵּר דָּבָר׃

The prophet urges his listeners to honor the Sabbath by desisting from business activities. Note that the first two actions are introduced by the preposition -מ *m-* 'from', plus the nouns bear the pronoun suffix -ךָ *-ka* 'your'. In the third and final stich, however, these two grammatical

---

22. Once more, for my basic treatment of poetic parallelism, see below, Chapter 17, no. 2.

items are lacking (thus my use of parentheses around 'from' and 'your' in the translation above).[23]

23. Psalm 19:8–10

$$\text{8 תּוֹרַת יְהֹוָה תְּמִימָה מְשִׁיבַת נָפֶשׁ}$$
עֵדוּת יְהֹוָה נֶאֱמָנָה מַחְכִּימַת פֶּתִי׃
$$\text{9 פִּקּוּדֵי יְהֹוָה יְשָׁרִים מְשַׂמְּחֵי־לֵב}$$
מִצְוַת יְהֹוָה בָּרָה מְאִירַת עֵינָיִם׃
$$\text{10 יִרְאַת יְהֹוָה ׀ טְהוֹרָה עוֹמֶדֶת לָעַד}$$
מִשְׁפְּטֵי־יְהֹוָה אֱמֶת צָדְקוּ יַחְדָּו׃

8 The teaching of Yʜᴡʜ is perfect, it restores the life-essence;
The testimony of Yʜᴡʜ is truthful, it makes-wise the
    simpleton.
9 The decrees of Yʜᴡʜ are upright, they gladden the heart;
The commandment of Yʜᴡʜ is clear, it enlightens the eyes.
10 The fear of Yʜᴡʜ is pure, it abides forever;
The laws of Yʜᴡʜ are truth, they are-righteous together.

These three verses from a well-known psalm include six stichs praising God's ways, as embodied in his teaching / testimony / decrees / commandment / fear / laws—for our present purposes, we may consider these six terms as essentially synonymous. The first five stichs follow the same structure: the a-line in each is comprised of 'X of Yʜᴡʜ' followed by a predicate adjective; while the b-line in each contains a participle followed by an appropriate object.[24] The sixth stich, v. 10b, departs from the pattern. In the a-line, 'X of Yʜᴡʜ' is followed by a noun, אֱמֶת *'ɛmɛt* 'truth' (that is, not an adjective); while in the b-line a suffix-conjugation verb, צָדְקוּ *ṣadqu* 'they are-righteous', appears (that

---

23. Note the comment of Amos Ḥakham, *Isaiah 36–66* (Daʿat Miqraʾ; Jerusalem: Mosad ha-Rav Kook, 1984), 721: שִׁעוּרוֹ׃ וּמְדַבֵּר דָּבָר.
24. In the fifth line, v. 10a, the participle, עוֹמֶדֶת *'omɛdɛt* 'endures' (lit., 'stands'), is followed by the adverb לָעַד *la-ʿad* 'forever' (and hence not an object). This represents a slight change, though we also must recognize that this phrase is a standard idiom in Biblical Hebrew psalmody (see Pss 111:3, 111:10, 112:3, 112:9).

is, not a participle).[25] The reader of the poem is expected to notice the syntactic differences in the sixth stich, thereby realizing that she has reached the final 'X of Y<small>HWH</small>' statement.

24. Psalm 135:16–17

16 פֶּה־לָהֶם וְלֹא יְדַבֵּרוּ עֵינַיִם לָהֶם וְלֹא יִרְאוּ:

17 אָזְנַיִם לָהֶם וְלֹא יַאֲזִינוּ אַף אֵין־יֶשׁ־רוּחַ בְּפִיהֶם:

16 A mouth they have, but they do not speak;
Eyes they have, but they do not see.
17 Ears they have, but they do not listen;
However/nose, there is no breath in their mouth.

This passage is a shorter version of our paradigm example above (see no. 1), with the description of the idols limited to their facial body parts—mouth, eyes, ears, mouth (with wordplay on 'nose', see anon). In the first three stichs (vv. 16a, 16b, 17a), the sentence order is body part followed by verbal action (in the negative). A different syntax presents in the final stich: (a) the author utilizes a verbless clause; and (b) the body part, בְּפִיהֶם *bə-pihɛm* 'in their mouth', appears at the end of the verse. The attentive reader recognizes the difference and realizes that she has reached the end of the unit.

This passage allows us to see other literary devices at work. First, not wishing to engage in verbatim repetition throughout, the poet alters the expression from Ps 115:6, אָזְנַיִם לָהֶם וְלֹא יִשְׁמָעוּ *'oznayim lahɛm wə-lo' yišma'u* 'ears they have, but they do not hear', to אָזְנַיִם לָהֶם וְלֹא יַאֲזִינוּ *'oznayim lahɛm wə-lo' ya'azinu* 'ears they have, but they do not listen' in Ps 135:17, replacing 'hear' with its synonym 'listen' (a denominative verb based on the noun 'ear'). By this statement I do not mean to imply that the same poet is responsible for both Psalms 115 and 135. But at some point in the creation of the Psalter, I can imagine that an overarching scribe/author/editor exerted effort to ensure as little duplication as possible in the various phrases that appear within the canonical book.[26]

---

25. This change, unfortunately, cannot be captured in English translation—but it is clearly present in the Hebrew.

26. See further Chapter 15 on repeated phrases in both Psalms and Proverbs.

The second additional feature to be studied here is the delightful wordplay introduced by the use of אַף 'ap 'however/nose' at the head of v. 17b. If the reader had any sense of the longer list of the non-actions of the body parts of idols presented in Ps 115:5–7, then she would expect v. 17b to describe a non-action associated with the nose. After all, Ps 115:6 flows from v. 6a, concerning the ears (reproduced in the previous paragraph), to v. 6b, concerning the nose: אַף לָהֶם וְלֹא יְרִיחוּן 'ap lahɛm wə-lo' yərihun 'a nose they have, but they do not smell'. In the most clever of linguistic turns, the author of Psalm 135 also follows the 'ears' line with the word אַף 'ap—but at some point in the reading process the listener to v. 17b becomes aware that her expectation for this one-syllable word to mean 'nose' has not been realized, for instead the word is employed here with the connotation 'however'. Indeed, given the wording אַף אֵין־יֶשׁ־רוּחַ בְּפִיהֶם 'ap 'en yɛš ruah bə-pihɛm 'however/nose, there is no breath in their mouth', this awareness does not surface until the very last word of the verse. For until this point, the string of four words אַף אֵין־יֶשׁ־רוּחַ 'ap 'en yɛš ruah makes perfect sense,[27] with the assumption that the final word would be בּוֹ* *bo 'in it' presumably. In fact, I might argue that the exceedingly rare negator אֵין־יֶשׁ 'en yɛš 'there is no'[28] in this stich (for אֵין 'en alone would suffice) is used in order to extend the string of words as much as possible before the reader has her expectation dashed at the very end of the verse.

25. Psalm 119:176 — the last verse of the longest psalm

תָּעִיתִי כְּשֶׂה אֹבֵד בַּקֵּשׁ עַבְדֶּךָ כִּי מִצְוֹתֶיךָ לֹא שָׁכָחְתִּי׃

I have strayed like a lost sheep—seek your servant—
For your commandments I have not forgotten.

This example from biblical poetry is rather banal, and yet it illustrates the technique studied here nonetheless. Psalm 119 is the longest poem

---

27. Especially given the fact that in Ps 115:6 אַף 'ap 'nose' is collocated with the denominative verb ר-\ו-י-ח r-w/y-h 'breathe' and the fact that the two key nouns אַף 'ap 'nose' and רוּחַ ruah 'breath' appear together in Gen 7:22, Exod 15:8, 2 Sam 22:16 // Ps 18:16, Prov 14:29, 16:32, Job 4:9, 27:3, Lam 4:20.

28. The only other instance of this usage in the Bible is 1 Sam 21:9 אֵין יֶשׁ 'in yeš 'there is not' (actually 'is there not', since the construction occurs in a question), though with dialectal variation reflected in the /i/ vowel instead of expected /e/.

of the Bible, an alphabetic acrostic with eight lines for each of the twenty-two letters of the Hebrew alphabet. As a glance at any Bible will demonstrate, the first 175 verses of this psalm proceed in like fashion, line after line, stanza after stanza, with only two stichs to each verse. In the last verse, however, the author interposes a two-word phrase between the two stichs, as he turns to God with his plea בַּקֵּשׁ עַבְדֶּךָ *baqqeš ʿabdɛka* 'seek your servant'. The inclusion of this phrase hardly constitutes literary creativity at its finest, but its presence in the last line nevertheless serves as a signal to the reader (not that such is necessary, given the structure of the poem) that she has reached the final line of this exceedingly long composition.

26. Psalm 146:6–9

⁶ עֹשֶׂה ׀ שָׁמַיִם וָאָרֶץ אֶת־הַיָּם וְאֶת־כָּל־אֲשֶׁר־בָּם
הַשֹּׁמֵר אֱמֶת לְעוֹלָם:
⁷ עֹשֶׂה מִשְׁפָּט ׀ לָעֲשׁוּקִים
נֹתֵן לֶחֶם לָרְעֵבִים
יְהוָה מַתִּיר אֲסוּרִים:
⁸ יְהוָה ׀ פֹּקֵחַ עִוְרִים
יְהוָה זֹקֵף כְּפוּפִים
יְהוָה אֹהֵב צַדִּיקִים:
⁹ יְהוָה ׀ שֹׁמֵר אֶת־גֵּרִים
יָתוֹם וְאַלְמָנָה יְעוֹדֵד
וְדֶרֶךְ רְשָׁעִים יְעַוֵּת:

⁶ Who makes heaven and earth, the sea, and all that is in them,
Who guards truth forever.
⁷ Who makes judgment for the oppressed,
Who gives bread to the hungry,
Yнwн releases the imprisoned.
⁸ Yнwн opens-(the-eyes) of the blind,
Yнwн makes-upright the bent-over,
Yнwн loves the righteous.
⁹ Yнwн guards the resident-aliens,
The orphan and the widow he sustains,
And the path of the wicked he makes-tortuous.

This poetic selection ascribes a series of moral and ethical actions and qualities to God. In the first nine lines, the pattern is participial verb followed by object (in the first four cola, God is implied as subject, based on the mention of the deity in the preceding v. 5; in the next five stichs, the divine name יְהוָה 'Yhwh' appears explicitly). In the final two lines of this litany, the poet produces a different configuration, with object mentioned first (as indicated in my rendering above), followed by a *yiqtol* form of the verb (a point that cannot be reflected in the English).

27. Job 1:16–18 — the series of calamities

Job 1:16

עוֹד | זֶה מְדַבֵּר וְזֶה֙ בָּא וַיֹּאמַר֒

This one still was speaking, and this one came and said.

Job 1:17

עוֹד | זֶה מְדַבֵּר וְזֶה֙ בָּא וַיֹּאמַר֒

This one still was speaking, and this one came and said.

Job 1:18

עַד זֶה מְדַבֵּר וְזֶה בָּא וַיֹּאמַר

This one yet was speaking, and this one came and said.

We treated these passages earlier in Chapter 9, no. 23, as part of the many variations within the recurring phrases of Job 1–2. It remains to point out here that the variation in this particular case is introduced in the third and final iteration. Horrific as each one is, the reader is hereby notified that the calamity to be described by the current messenger is the last of the series.

28. Ruth 1:16–17

16 כִּי אֶל־אֲשֶׁר תֵּלְכִי אֵלֵךְ וּבַאֲשֶׁר תָּלִינִי֙ אָלִין עַמֵּךְ עַמִּי וֵאלֹהַיִךְ אֱלֹהָי׃
17 בַּאֲשֶׁר תָּמוּתִי֙ אָמוּת וְשָׁם אֶקָּבֵר

¹⁶ For wherever you go, I will go; and wherever you lodge, I
will lodge; your people, my people; your God, my God;
¹⁷ Wherever you die, I will die; and there I will be buried.

These words, which bridge Ruth 1:16–17 (they are properly v. 16b and
v. 17a), are part of a long (and famous) speech from Ruth to Naomi. The
basic point is: whatever and wherever are associated with Naomi, so shall
they be with Ruth as well. For the first five items, the key words—which
we may list as 'go', 'lodge', 'people', 'God', and 'die'—are repeated within
each clause, whether they are verbal (the first, second, and fifth) or simply
nominal (the third and fourth). The pattern is broken with the last item,
however: וְשָׁם אֶקָּבֵר *wǝ-šam 'ɛqqaber* 'and there I will be buried'. The
reader notes the lack of an a-phrase, which we may postulate as 'and
wherever you are buried', with only the b-phrase present. Obviously,
burial by itself marks closure, though to emphasize the point the author
employs the literary device of phraseological change to mark conclusion.

29. Qohelet 3:2–8 — 'time for x, time for y'

עֵת לָלֶדֶת וְעֵת לָמוּת עֵת לָטַעַת וְעֵת לַעֲקוֹר נָטוּעַ: ²

עֵת לַהֲרוֹג וְעֵת לִרְפּוֹא עֵת לִפְרוֹץ וְעֵת לִבְנוֹת: ³

עֵת לִבְכּוֹת וְעֵת לִשְׂחוֹק עֵת סְפוֹד וְעֵת רְקוֹד: ⁴

עֵת לְהַשְׁלִיךְ אֲבָנִים וְעֵת כְּנוֹס אֲבָנִים ⁵

עֵת לַחֲבוֹק וְעֵת לִרְחֹק מֵחַבֵּק:

עֵת לְבַקֵּשׁ וְעֵת לְאַבֵּד עֵת לִשְׁמוֹר וְעֵת לְהַשְׁלִיךְ: ⁶

עֵת לִקְרוֹעַ וְעֵת לִתְפּוֹר עֵת לַחֲשׁוֹת וְעֵת לְדַבֵּר: ⁷

עֵת לֶאֱהֹב וְעֵת לִשְׂנֹא עֵת מִלְחָמָה וְעֵת שָׁלוֹם: ⁸

² A time to give-birth, and a time to die;
A time to plant, and a time to uproot what is planted.
³ A time to kill, and a time to heal,
A time to break-down, and a time to build.
⁴ A time to cry, and a time to laugh,
A time to mourn, and a time to dance.
⁵ A time to cast stones, and a time to gather stones;
A time to hug, and a time to be-distant from hugging.

⁶ A time to seek, and a time to lose,
A time to guard, and a time to cast-away.
⁷ A time to tear, and a time to sew,
A time to be-quiet, and a time to speak.
⁸ A time to love, and a time to hate,
A time of war, and a time of peace.

This famous passage from Qohelet presents fourteen pairs of opposites. The first thirteen pairs are all verbs, in fact, all infinitive forms. The last pair, עֵת מִלְחָמָה וְעֵת שָׁלוֹם *ʿet milḥama wǝ-ʿet šalom* 'a time of war, and a time of peace', presents two nouns as opposites. The reader thereby realizes that she has reached the end of the litany.

As we have seen in the foregoing, Mirsky's seminal article merely touched the tip of the proverbial iceberg. Not only are there many more examples of the device of change to mark closure in the Bible, the ancient authors engaged in a variety of 'tricks' (to use Longacre's term, noted above) while employing this technique.

CHAPTER FOURTEEN

MARKING CLOSURE (WRIT LARGE)

In this chapter we introduce something new into the mix, building upon
Mirsky's original discovery. In the passages surveyed in the previous
chapter, the modification to mark closure occurs within a single verse
or a single set of verses or, at most, a single chapter, as per Mirsky's
analysis. But this technique could be extended to indicate closure of
larger swaths of material, be they sections of books, entire books, and
in one case the Torah as a whole.

1. Genesis — death notices

Gen 25:8 (Abraham)

וַיִּגְוַע וַיָּמָת אַבְרָהָם . . . וַיֵּאָסֶף אֶל־עַמָּיו:

And he expired, and Abraham died, . . . and he was gathered to his kin.

Gen 25:17 (Ishmael)

וַיִּגְוַע וַיָּמָת וַיֵּאָסֶף אֶל־עַמָּיו:

And he expired, and he died, and he was gathered to
his kin.

Gen 35:29 (Isaac)

וַיִּגְוַע יִצְחָק וַיָּמָת וַיֵּאָסֶף אֶל־עַמָּיו

And Isaac expired, and he died, and he was gathered to
his kin.

Gen 49:33 (Jacob)

וַיִּגְוַע וַיֵּאָסֶף אֶל־עַמָּיו:

And he expired, and he was gathered to his kin.

The four passages above comprise one of the repeating phrases in the book of Genesis, as the deaths of Abraham, Ishmael, Isaac, and Jacob are duly noted. The deaths of other individuals are noted, of course (Sarah in Gen 23:2, Rachel in Gen 35:19, Joseph in Gen 50:26, etc.), but only these four heroes (the three patriarchs, plus Ishmael) gain the full notice. Well, almost the full notice, for while the first three deaths are described via three separate actions—'expired', 'died', and 'was gathered to his kin'—in the fourth and final iteration one notes the use of only two of the verbs.[1] The reader, who has been attuned to expect all three verbs, has her eyebrow raised upon hearing only two verbs in Gen 49:33. She knows, accordingly, that the book of Genesis is reaching its end, and/or that the patriarchal narratives are soon to be a thing of the past.

2. Exodus 7–9 — 'and he did not listen to them, as Yhwh had spoken'

Exod 7:13

וַיֶּחֱזַק לֵב פַּרְעֹה וְלֹא שָׁמַע אֲלֵהֶם כַּאֲשֶׁר דִּבֶּר יְהוָה:

And the heart of Pharaoh was strong, and he did not listen to them, as Yhwh had spoken.

Exod 7:22

וַיֶּחֱזַק לֵב־פַּרְעֹה וְלֹא־שָׁמַע אֲלֵהֶם כַּאֲשֶׁר דִּבֶּר יְהוָה:

And the heart of Pharaoh was strong, and he did not listen to them, as Yhwh had spoken.

Exod 8:11

וְהַכְבֵּד אֶת־לִבּוֹ וְלֹא שָׁמַע אֲלֵהֶם כַּאֲשֶׁר דִּבֶּר יְהוָה:

And he made-heavy his heart, and he did not listen to them, as Yhwh had spoken.

---

1. The lack of the verbal root מ-ו-ת *m-w-t* 'die' in Gen 49:33 was not lost on the rabbis; R. Yoḥanan went so far as to state, "Our forefather Jacob never died" (Bavli Taʿanit 5b). See further Aaron Koller, "Diachronic Change and Synchronic Readings: Midrashim on Stative Verbs and Participles," *Journal of Semitic Studies* 57 (2012): 266.

Exod 8:15

וַיֶּחֱזַק לֵב־פַּרְעֹה וְלֹא־שָׁמַע אֲלֵהֶם כַּאֲשֶׁר דִּבֶּר יְהוָה:

And the heart of Pharaoh was strong, and he did not
listen to them, as Yʜwʜ had spoken.

Exod 9:12

וַיְחַזֵּק יְהוָה אֶת־לֵב פַּרְעֹה וְלֹא שָׁמַע אֲלֵהֶם כַּאֲשֶׁר דִּבֶּר יְהוָה
אֶל־מֹשֶׁה:

And Yʜwʜ strengthened the heart of Pharaoh, and he
did not listen to them, as Yʜwʜ had spoken to Moses.

In Chapter 3, we observed the repetition with variation that occurs
in the related phrases about the hardening of Pharaoh's heart and
his concomitant refusal to allow the Israelites to leave Egypt. Within
the many iterations, however, we also noticed one set of phrases that
repeats verbatim, to wit, וְלֹא שָׁמַע אֲלֵהֶם כַּאֲשֶׁר דִּבֶּר יְהוָה 'and he [sc.
Pharaoh] did not listen to them, as Yʜwʜ had spoken'. We observed
how this set of passages is an instance of 'form follows content':
Pharaoh remains obstinate, hence the language remains adamant,
as it were.

There are, however, two changes—one stylistic, one significant—
that appear in the last of the verses presented above. The stylistic
change is indicated by the addition of אֶל־מֹשֶׁה 'to Moses' in 9:12, at
the end of the sixth plague. The more significant marker is the change
from 'and the heart of Pharaoh was strong' (7:13, 7:22, 8:15)—or, in the
one instance, 'and he [sc. Pharaoh] made-heavy his heart' (8:11)—to the
fact that now God is responsible for Pharaoh's obstinacy: 'And Yʜwʜ
strengthened the heart of Pharaoh'.[2] Through the changes introduced in
9:12, the attentive reader can anticipate that the narrative has reached
a crucial point, and in fact such is the case, since henceforth Pharaoh's
position will change, as reflected in Exod 9:28, within the context of
the seventh plague.

---

2. I owe this keen observation to Jonathan Kline. See also Alter, *Five
Books of Moses*, 360.

3. Leviticus 16–22 — the resident-alien

Lev 16:29

וְהַגֵּר הַגָּר בְּתוֹכְכֶם:

and the resident-alien who resides in your midst

Lev 17:8

וּמִן־הַגֵּר אֲשֶׁר־יָגוּר בְּתוֹכָם

and from the resident-alien who will reside in their midst

Lev 17:10

וּמִן־הַגֵּר הַגָּר בְּתוֹכָם

and from the resident-alien who resides in their midst

Lev 17:12

וְהַגֵּר הַגָּר בְּתוֹכְכֶם

and the resident-alien who resides in your midst

Lev 17:13

וּמִן־הַגֵּר הַגָּר בְּתוֹכָם

and from the resident-alien who resides in their midst

Lev 18:26

וְהַגֵּר הַגָּר בְּתוֹכְכֶם:

and the resident-alien who resides in your midst

Lev 19:34

הַגֵּר | הַגָּר אִתְּכֶם

and the resident-alien who resides with you

Lev 20:2

וּמִן־הַגֵּר | הַגָּר בְּיִשְׂרָאֵל

and from the resident-alien who resides in Israel

Lev 22:18

וּמִן־הַגֵּר בְּיִשְׂרָאֵל

and from the resident-alien in Israel

The גֵּר *ger* 'resident-alien' (older translations typically use the word 'stranger') who resides among the people of Israel is the subject of a host of laws found throughout the three major law codes (Exodus 20–23, Leviticus, and Deuteronomy). The author of Leviticus favors a particular phrase when the resident-alien is mentioned in such contexts, typically הַגֵּר הַגָּר *hag-ger hag-gar* 'the resident-alien who resides', thus 8x in the list above, with one case of the verb changed from the participle to the future (Lev 17:8). Striking, therefore, is the last mention in Lev 22:18, וּמִן־הַגֵּר בְּיִשְׂרָאֵל *u-min hag-ger bə-yiśra'el* 'and from the resident-alien in Israel', which lacks a form of the verb ג-ו-ר *g-w-r* 'dwell, settle, reside'. Textual critics are wont to emend the reading, based on the inclusion of הגר HGR 'who resides' in the Samaritan Torah, along with reflections thereof in the Septuagint, the Peshitta, and the Vulgate.[3] The attentive reader, however, realizes that Lev 22:18 is the last such mention in the book, or at least in this section of Leviticus (since the resident-alien is mentioned in chs. 23–25, though in different contexts, with altogether different phraseologies). In short, the Masoretic Text should stand as it is, serving as a witness to the ancient author's/scribe's capacity to fashion an irregular version of a repeating formula as a signal of conclusion.

4. Leviticus 25:1 — 'at Mount Sinai'

וַיְדַבֵּר יְהוָה אֶל־מֹשֶׁה בְּהַר סִינַי לֵאמֹר:

waydabber YHWH *'el mošε bə-har sinay le'mor*

And YHWH spoke to Moses at Mount Sinai, saying:

On twenty-six occasions in the book of Leviticus (4:1, 5:14, 5:20, 6:1, 6:12, 6:17, 7:22, 7:28, 8:1, 12:1, 14:1, 17:1, 18:1, 19:1, 20:1, 21:16, 22:1, 22:17, 22:26, 23:1, 23:9, 23:23, 23:26, 23:33, 24:1, 24:13), speeches from the God of Israel to his prophet are introduced with the phrase וַיְדַבֵּר יְהוָה אֶל־מֹשֶׁה לֵאמֹר *waydabber* YHWH *'el mošε le'mor* 'and YHWH spoke to Moses saying' (each time with the same string of accent marks, as included here). Strikingly, the introduction to the last speech from YHWH to Moses (25:1) contains the additional phrase בְּהַר סִינַי *bə-har sinay* 'at

---

3. See, e.g., *BHS, ad loc.*

Mount Sinai'. The point is not lost on the reader: the last divine speech presented in the book of Leviticus is duly marked.[4]

5. Numbers — the daughters of Zelophehad

26:33

מַחְלָה וְנֹעָה חָגְלָה מִלְכָּה וְתִרְצָה:

Maḥla, and Noʿa, Ḥogla, Milka, and Tirṣa

27:1

מַחְלָה נֹעָה וְחָגְלָה וּמִלְכָּה וְתִרְצָה:

Maḥla, Noʿa, and Ḥogla, and Milka, and Tirṣa

36:11

מַחְלָה תִרְצָה וְחָגְלָה וּמִלְכָּה וְנֹעָה

Maḥla, Tirṣa, and Ḥogla, and Milka, and Noʿa

The purpose and placement of the appendix to the book of Numbers, as ch. 36, remains a bit of an enigma to biblical scholars. After all, the daughters of Zelophehad are mentioned in the census in ch. 26, and the issue of their inheritance is treated in relatively fine detail in ch. 27. Why, accordingly, does the book of Numbers return to the subject in ch. 36? Regardless of how one approaches this issue, our attention is drawn to the listing of the five daughters. While the first two iterations present the five names in the same order (though note the slight variations concerning the placement of the conjunction -וְ/-וּ wə-/u- 'and' within these lists), in the final rehearsal the order

---

4. See already John E. Hartley, *Leviticus* (Word Biblical Commentary 4; Dallas: Word, 1992), 433. There are other factors underlying the use of the expression 'at Mount Sinai', for which see Gary A. Rendsburg, "The Two Screens: On Mary Douglas's Proposal for a Literary Structure to the Book of Leviticus," *Jewish Studies Quarterly* 15 (2008): 175–89. Our present purpose, however, is to focus only on the change to mark closure. The knowledgeable reader will realize that an additional speech from God to Moses occurs in Leviticus 27, with the standard introductory formula in place in v. 1—but this chapter represents an appendix to the book, as is widely noted by scholars.

of the names is changed. The reader has arrived at the conclusion of the book (in fact, only two more verses appear), an attainment that is marked by the author/editor/compiler/redactor by means of this nimble maneuver. The Samaritan Torah, we hasten to add, harmonizes the three passages in verbatim fashion: מחלה ונעה חגלה מלכה ותרצה MḤLH WNʿH ḤGLH MLKH WTRṢH ʿMaḥla and Noʿa, Ḥogla, Milka, and Tirṣaʾ—though to our mind this exercise reveals a lack of creativity in literary production.

6. Deuteronomy 31:20 — 'flowing with milk and honey'

Exod 3:8, etc.

אֶרֶץ זָבַת חָלָב וּדְבַשׁ

ʾereṣ zabat ḥalab u-dbaš

a land flowing with milk and honey

Deut 31:20

הָאֲדָמָה . . . זָבַת חָלָב וּדְבַשׁ

ha-ʾadama . . . zabat ḥalab u-dbaš

the land . . . flowing with milk and honey

The expression in Exod 3:8 is one of the most recognizable in the Torah and indeed in the Bible as a whole. The words אֶרֶץ זָבַת חָלָב וּדְבַשׁ ʾereṣ zabat ḥalab u-dəbaš 'a land flowing with milk and honey' appear not only in Exod 3:8, but again, in verbatim fashion, in Exod 3:17, 13:5, 33:3, Lev 20:24, Deut 6:3, 11:9, 26:9, 26:15, 27:3. The same words also appear in the ironic speech of Dathan and Abiram in their challenge to Moses's leadership in Num 16:13–14. While the wording is slightly different in Num 13:27 and 14:8, the key words are nonetheless all still present, including the headword אֶרֶץ ʾereṣ 'land'. It is quite striking, therefore, to find the synonym אֲדָמָה ʾadama 'land' used in Deut 31:20—though this shift in lexical choice becomes explicable upon the reader's realization that this is the last time that she will encounter this description of the land of Canaan both in the book of Deuteronomy and in the Torah as a whole. Other changes are visible as well: (a) the word is preceded by the definite article, -הָ *ha-* 'the'; and (b) several intervening words occur (as indicated by the ellipsis).[5]

In the very least, we may assume that the variant phraseology in Deut 31:20 serves to prepare the reader for the conclusion of the book of Deuteronomy. Does it serve a larger purpose, indicating the conclusion of the Torah as a whole? After all, notwithstanding the disparate sources, at some point an individual or a team of learned bookmen must have produced the Torah in its final, present, canonical state. I raise the issue without providing a definitive answer, even if I for one tend toward a positive response to the question posed.

7. Judges — 'and the land was quiet for forty years'

Judg 3:11 (Othniel)

וַתִּשְׁקֹט הָאָרֶץ אַרְבָּעִים שָׁנָה וַיָּמָת עָתְנִיאֵל בֶּן־קְנַז:

And the land was quiet for forty years; and Othniel ben Qenaz died.

Judg 3:30 (Ehud)

וַתִּכָּנַע מוֹאָב בַּיּוֹם הַהוּא תַּחַת יַד יִשְׂרָאֵל וַתִּשְׁקֹט הָאָרֶץ שְׁמוֹנִים שָׁנָה:

And Moab was subdued on that day, under the hand of Israel; and the land was quiet for eighty years.

Judg 5:31 (Deborah)

כֵּן יֹאבְדוּ כָל־אוֹיְבֶיךָ יְהוָה וְאֹהֲבָיו כְּצֵאת הַשֶּׁמֶשׁ בִּגְבֻרָתוֹ וַתִּשְׁקֹט הָאָרֶץ אַרְבָּעִים שָׁנָה:

"So shall all your enemies be defeated, O YHWH, and may his devotees be like the sun rising in its strength"; and the land was quiet for forty years.

---

5. The standard phrase appears again in Josh 5:6; Jer 11:5; 32:22; and with slight variation in Ezek 20:6, 20:15. On further variation in the latter passages, see Chapter 15, no. 12.

Judg 8:28 (Gideon)

וַיִּכָּנַע מִדְיָן לִפְנֵי בְּנֵי יִשְׂרָאֵל וְלֹא יָסְפוּ לָשֵׂאת רֹאשָׁם וַתִּשְׁקֹט
הָאָרֶץ אַרְבָּעִים שָׁנָה בִּימֵי גִדְעוֹן:

And Midian was subdued before the children of Israel,
and they did not continue to raise their head; and the
land was quiet for forty years, in the days of Gideon.

Four times in the first half of the book of Judges, the author/editor/com-
piler/redactor (or shall we call him 'framer' in this instance?) incorporated
statements mentioning that the land was quiet for forty years (or, in one
case, eighty years). Each of these comments serves as the concluding
statement for the cycles of the first four major judges (Othniel, Ehud,
Deborah, Gideon),[6] revealing an editorial hand whose goal was a redactional framework. The four remarks are verbatim (save for the change of
'forty' to 'eighty' in one instance), though the fourth one departs from the
others by adding the phrase בִּימֵי גִדְעוֹן *bi-me gid'on* 'in the days of Gideon'.[7]

8. Judges — 'X ruled Israel for Y years'

Judg 10:2 (Tola)

וַיִּשְׁפֹּט אֶת־יִשְׂרָאֵל עֶשְׂרִים וְשָׁלֹשׁ שָׁנָה וַיָּמָת וַיִּקָּבֵר בְּשָׁמִיר:

And he judged Israel for twenty and three years; and he
died and was buried in Shamir.

Judg 10:3 (Yair)

וַיָּקָם אַחֲרָיו יָאִיר הַגִּלְעָדִי וַיִּשְׁפֹּט אֶת־יִשְׂרָאֵל עֶשְׂרִים וּשְׁתַּיִם
שָׁנָה:

And after him arose Yair the Gileadite; and he judged
Israel for twenty and two years.

---

6. The one-verse statement about Shamgar (Judg 3:31) obviously does
not constitute a cycle.

7. See the convenient chart in Robert H. O'Connell, *The Rhetoric of the Book
of Judges* (Supplements to Vetus Testamentum 63; Leiden: Brill, 1996), 50. Note
especially the placement of [בימי גדעון] within brackets. While O'Connell makes
no comment on this tactic, his layout highlights nicely the point made herein.

Judg 12:7 (Jephthah)

וַיִּשְׁפֹּט יִפְתָּח אֶת־יִשְׂרָאֵל שֵׁשׁ שָׁנִים וַיָּמָת יִפְתָּח הַגִּלְעָדִי וַיִּקָּבֵר
בְּעָרֵי גִלְעָד:

And Jephthah judged Israel for six years; and Jephthah the Gileadite died, and he was buried in the cities of Gilead.

Judg 12:9 (Ibzan)

וַיְהִי־לֹו שְׁלֹשִׁים בָּנִים וּשְׁלֹשִׁים בָּנֹות שִׁלַּח הַחוּצָה וּשְׁלֹשִׁים בָּנֹות
הֵבִיא לְבָנָיו מִן־הַחוּץ וַיִּשְׁפֹּט אֶת־יִשְׂרָאֵל שֶׁבַע שָׁנִים:

And he had thirty sons, and thirty daughters he sent-away (to marry) outside (the clan), and thirty daughters he brought to his sons from outside (the clan); and he judged Israel for seven years.

Judg 12:11 (Elon)

וַיִּשְׁפֹּט אַחֲרָיו אֶת־יִשְׂרָאֵל אֵילֹון הַזְּבוּלֹנִי וַיִּשְׁפֹּט אֶת־יִשְׂרָאֵל עֶשֶׂר
שָׁנִים:

And after him Elon the Zebulunite judged Israel; and he judged Israel for ten years.

Judg 12:14 (Abdon)

וַיְהִי־לֹו אַרְבָּעִים בָּנִים וּשְׁלֹשִׁים בְּנֵי בָנִים רֹכְבִים עַל־שִׁבְעִים עֲיָרִם
וַיִּשְׁפֹּט אֶת־יִשְׂרָאֵל שְׁמֹנֶה שָׁנִים:

And he had forty sons and thirty grandsons, riding on seventy asses; and he judged Israel for eight years.

Judg 15:20 (Samson)

וַיִּשְׁפֹּט אֶת־יִשְׂרָאֵל בִּימֵי פְלִשְׁתִּים עֶשְׂרִים שָׁנָה:

And he judged Israel, in the days of the Philistines, for twenty years.

Judg 16:31 (Samson)

וַיֵּרְדוּ אֶחָיו וְכָל־בֵּית אָבִיהוּ וַיִּשְׂאוּ אֹתוֹ וַיַּעֲלוּ | וַיִּקְבְּרוּ אוֹתוֹ בֵּין
צָרְעָה וּבֵין אֶשְׁתָּאֹל בְּקֶבֶר מָנוֹחַ אָבִיו וְהוּא שָׁפַט אֶת־יִשְׂרָאֵל
עֶשְׂרִים שָׁנָה:

And his brothers and all the house of his father came-
down; and they carried him, and brought (him) up and
buried him, between Ṣorʿa and Eshtaʾol, in the grave
of Manoah his father; and he had judged Israel for
twenty years.

In the second half of the book of Judges, which includes the seven
individual leaders enumerated above, the reader encounters the repeated phrases displayed here. The pattern is always the same: וַיִּשְׁפֹּט
אֶת־יִשְׂרָאֵל *wayyišpoṭ ʾet yisraʾel* 'and he judged Israel', using the typical
wayyiqtol verbal form used for prose storytelling, with the number of
years immediately following. (Note two minor variants: in 12:7, where
the name יִפְתָּח *yiptaḥ* 'Jephthah' appears immediately after the verb,
and in 12:11, where the adverbial אַחֲרָיו *ʾaḥaraw* 'after him' is included;
though these slight changes are not relevant to our present discussion.)

For the last judge, however, we note a variety of changes to mark
closure. Most obviously, and quite strangely, there are two such statements regarding Samson, in 15:20 (even though there is one more chapter about Samson to follow) and 16:31 (the final statement about this
character). In the first remark, one notes the phrase בִּימֵי פְלִשְׁתִּים *bi-me
pəlištim* 'in the days of the Philistines' interposed between 'Israel' and
the number of years (in my translation above, I have set this expression
off with commas, to make the point clear). More significantly, in the
second comment the verbal tense is changed, so that וְהוּא שָׁפַט *wə-huʾ
šapaṭ* 'and he had judged' appears in place of the expected *wayyiqtol*
(I have captured this change in my rendering via use of the English
pluperfect). The reader knows, through these departures from the anticipated pattern, that she has read of the last of the judges.[8]

---

8. O'Connell, *Rhetoric of the Book of Judges*, 49, noted the two formulae
in the Samson narrative, 15:20 and 16:31, about which he commented: "Of the
two occurrences in the Samson account . . . it is the former that conforms most

9. Judges — the burial of the hero

Judg 8:32 (Gideon)

וַיִּקָּבֵ֗ר בְּקֶ֙בֶר֙ יוֹאָ֣שׁ אָבִ֔יו בְּעָפְרָ֖ה אֲבִ֥י הָעֶזְרִֽי׃

And he was buried in the grave of Joash his father, in
Ophrah of the Abiezrites.

Judg 10:2 (Tola)

וַיִּקָּבֵ֖ר בְּשָׁמִֽיר׃

And he was buried in Shamir.

Judg 10:5 (Yair)

וַיִּקָּבֵ֖ר בְּקָמֽוֹן׃

And he was buried in Kamon.

Judg 12:7 (Jephthah)

וַיִּקָּבֵ֖ר בְּעָרֵ֥י גִלְעָֽד׃

And he was buried in the cities of Gilead.

Judg 12:10 (Ibzan)

וַיִּקָּבֵ֖ר בְּבֵ֥ית לָֽחֶם׃

And he was buried in Bethlehem.

Judg 12:12 (Elon)

וַיִּקָּבֵ֤ר בְּאַיָּלוֹן֙ בְּאֶ֣רֶץ זְבוּלֻֽן׃

And he was buried in Ayyalon in the land of Zebulun.

Judg 12:15 (Abdon)

וַיִּקָּבֵ֨ר בְּפִרְעָת֜וֹן בְּאֶ֣רֶץ אֶפְרַ֗יִם בְּהַ֖ר הָעֲמָלֵקִֽי׃

And he was buried in Pirathon in the land of Ephraim, in
the mount of the Amaleqites.

---

closely to the standard form of the motif. This suggests that the latter was either
primary, if the difference was unmotivated, or altered for rhetorical reasons."

Judg 16:31 (Samson)

וַיִּקְבְּרוּ אוֹתוֹ בֵּין צָרְעָה וּבֵין אֶשְׁתָּאֹל בְּקֶבֶר מָנוֹחַ אָבִיו

And they buried him between Zorah and Eshtaol, in the
grave of Manoah his father.

Burial notices appear in the book of Judges for eight of the individual
judges (from Gideon onward). Each of the first seven cases begins
with the verb in the passive, וַיִּקָּבֵר *wayyiqqaber* 'and he was buried'.
For the eighth and final judge, Samson, we find a different wording:
וַיִּקְבְּרוּ אוֹתוֹ *wayyiqbəru ʾoto* 'and they buried him' (the subject is 'his
brothers', mentioned earlier in the verse).[9] On the one hand, the author's motivation may have been to create an inclusio, since the same
phrase is used in Judg 2:9, with reference to Joshua, which in turn is a
rehearsal of the same phrase in Josh 24:30. On the other hand, within
the list of individual judges, as indicated by the above passages, only
the last of the burial notices uses this formula, as a way of marking
closure once more. And of course, we do not need to choose between
these two considerations, since they are not mutually exclusive.

The Samson cycle is different from the earlier cycles of the (major)
judges in so many ways. It includes a birth story about the hero, replete
with the barren woman motif (evocative of the ones in Genesis and the
one to follow regarding Samuel); it is the longest of the narratives; the
hero acts alone, as opposed to mustering and leading other Israelites to
battle; the hero has romantic interests; and so on. As if these features
were not enough, the author of the book of Judges incorporated other
elements to set off the Samson narrative from the earlier accounts,
including the items noted herein (nos. 8 and 9) that mark closure. The
days of the judges have come to an end, with the phraseology of the
Samson cycle serving as a literary-linguistic clue to the reader.

As we have seen in this chapter, in several key places within the
biblical canon, authors/editors/compilers/redactors elected to utilize
the stylistic device of marking closure, writ large, in order to inform
the reader that she has reached the conclusion of the text. This finding
should have implications for further research, specifically into how
biblical books came to be as the result of scribal and editorial activity.

---

9. This point may be seen in the convenient chart in O'Connell, *Rhetoric
of the Book of Judges*, 53.

CHAPTER FIFTEEN

REPETITION WITH VARIATION: POETIC AND PROPHETIC TEXTS

By poetic texts, I mean, of course, books such as Psalms, Proverbs, Job, Song of Songs, and Lamentations. By prophetic texts, I mean, of course, most of the material in Isaiah, Jeremiah, Ezekiel, and the Twelve, which is either clear poetry or on that difficult cusp between prose and poetry. The two genres of poetry and prophecy are brought together in this chapter, because collectively they stand in opposition to other genres such as narrative prose and legal-cultic texts. As with these latter categories (for which see Chapters 2, 3, 4, 9, and 12), the poetic and prophetic books also include manifold examples of repetition with variation.

Scott Noegel and I already devoted an entire chapter of our co-authored book on Song of Songs to this technique in that short poetic book.[1] There is no need to repeat all that material here, but a handful of select examples will be helpful to set the stage.

1. Song of Songs 2:5; 5:8

Song 2:5

כִּי־חוֹלַת אַהֲבָה אָנִי׃

for I am sick with love.

Song 5:8

שֶׁחוֹלַת אַהֲבָה אָנִי׃

that I am sick with love.

---

1. Noegel and Rendsburg, *Solomon's Vineyard*, 107–27. For earlier treatment, see Michael V. Fox, *The Song of Songs and the Ancient Egyptian Love Songs* (Madison: University of Wisconsin Press, 1985), 209–15; he referred to the parallel non-verbatim passages as 'repetends'.

The two lines are nearly identical, differentiated only by the coordinating particle used to introduce them, כִּי *ki* 'for, because' in the former, -שֶׁ *še-* 'that' in the latter.

2. Song of Songs 2:6; 8:3

Song 2:6

שְׂמֹאלוֹ תַּחַת לְרֹאשִׁי

His left-hand is beneath my head.

Song 8:3

שְׂמֹאלוֹ תַּחַת רֹאשִׁי

His left-hand is under my head.

These two lines also are almost identical, with the sole distinction being the form of the preposition. The form used in 2:6, תַּחַת לְ *taḥat lə-* 'beneath', is very rare in the Bible, appearing only one or two other times.[2] In light of the rarity of this preposition, one can imagine listeners to the Song of Songs noticing the linguistic oddity of תַּחַת לְ- *taḥat lə-* 'beneath' at 2:6, only to be treated to a smile when the reader/performer reaches 8:3 near the poem's end, with the standard usage, simple תַּחַת *taḥat* 'under', now in place.

3. Song of Songs 2:16; 6:3

Song 2:16

דּוֹדִי לִי וַאֲנִי לוֹ הָרֹעֶה בַּשּׁוֹשַׁנִּים:

My beloved is mine, and I am his,
Grazing among the lilies.

---

2. The only true parallel occurs in 2 Chr 4:3, in the expression תַּחַת לוֹ *taḥat lo* 'beneath it' (in place of the standard form תַּחְתָּיו *taḥtaw*), in addition to which note the more complex form אֶל תַּחַת לְ- *'el taḥat lə-* in Ezek 10:3. The form מִתַּחַת לְ- *mit-taḥat lə-*, attested 13x in the Bible (Gen 1:7, etc.), is a different preposition altogether, standard in its own right.

Song 6:3

אֲנִי לְדוֹדִי וְדוֹדִי לִי הָרֹעֶה בַּשּׁוֹשַׁנִּים:

I am my beloved's, and my beloved is mine,
Grazing among the lilies.

In this pair of verses, a number of points are noteworthy. Both passages
are spoken by the female lover, obviously, with their b-lines exactly
the same and with the variation present in the respective a-lines. Song
2:16 reads דּוֹדִי לִי וַאֲנִי לוֹ *dodi li wa-ʾani lo* 'my beloved is mine, and I
am his', while 6:3 reads אֲנִי לְדוֹדִי וְדוֹדִי לִי *ʾani lə-dodi wə-dodi li* 'I am
my beloved's, and my beloved is mine'. Note how (a) the order of the
words in the two phrases is reversed: in the former the female voice
leads with 'my beloved', while in the latter she leads with 'I'; and (b) the
former uses the pronoun form in the phrase וַאֲנִי לוֹ *wa-ʾani lo* 'and I am
his', while the latter utilizes the noun form in the wording אֲנִי לְדוֹדִי
ʾani lə-dodi 'I am my beloved's', thereby repeating the word דּוֹדִי *dodi*
'my beloved' in this line.

4. Song of Songs 1:15; 4:1

Song 1:15

הִנָּךְ יָפָה רַעְיָתִי הִנָּךְ יָפָה עֵינַיִךְ יוֹנִים:

Behold you are beautiful, my darling,
Behold you are beautiful, your eyes are doves.

Song 4:1

הִנָּךְ יָפָה רַעְיָתִי הִנָּךְ יָפָה עֵינַיִךְ יוֹנִים מִבַּעַד לְצַמָּתֵךְ

Behold you are beautiful, my darling,
Behold you are beautiful, your eyes are doves,
behind your braids.

The simple statement concerning the beauty of the female lover in 1:15,
along with the focus on the eyes, sets the stage for similar passages
throughout the poem. As such, the verset is but an entrée to things to
come, for as the poem develops the reader is treated to several full-
blown descriptions of the female lover's exquisiteness. The first of these

(known as the *waṣf* in biblical studies, based on the parallel strophes found in Arabic poetry) appears in Song 4:1–7. The poet takes the opportunity to enrich the text, expanding the earlier line and thereby introducing variation, via the addition of the expression מִבַּעַד לְצַמָּתֵךְ *mib-baʿad lə-ṣammatek* 'behind your braids'.

5. Song of Songs 4:1; 6:5

Song 4:1

שַׂעְרֵךְ כְּעֵדֶר הָעִזִּים שֶׁגָּלְשׁוּ מֵהַר גִּלְעָד:

Your hair is like a flock of goats
That flow down from Mount Gilead.

Song 6:5

שַׂעְרֵךְ כְּעֵדֶר הָעִזִּים שֶׁגָּלְשׁוּ מִן־הַגִּלְעָד:

Your hair is like a flock of goats
That flow down from the Gilead.

The description of the female lover in 4:1 continues with the move from eyes to hair. The same line reoccurs in 6:5, though naturally the poet introduces variation into the composition. In the first iteration, the prepositional phrase is מֵהַר גִּלְעָד *me-har gilʿad* 'from Mount Gilead', while in the second instance we read מִן־הַגִּלְעָד *min hag-gilʿad* 'from the Gilead'. In 4:1, the form of the preposition is prefixed -מֵ *me-*, the noun הַר *har* 'mountain' is included, and the toponym גִּלְעָד *gilʿad* 'Gilead' occurs without the definite article. In 6:5, by contrast, the preposition occurs as the independent form מִן *min*, the noun הַר *har* 'mountain' is absent, and the toponym הַגִּלְעָד *hag-gilʿad* 'the Gilead' occurs with the definite article. I have reflected the second and third of these differences in the translation above (one cannot vary the English to indicate the different forms of 'from').

These are all minor differences, but they serve as evidence of the extent to which the poet would go to vary the language of the composition. We also note that the expression הַר גִּלְעָד *har gilʿad* 'Mount Gilead' in 4:1 is the only attestation of this usage in the Bible; in all other cases, the definite article is present: הַר הַגִּלְעָד *har hag-gilʿad* (Gen

31:21, 31:23, 31:25, Deut 3:12, Judg 7:3). Poetry is less inclined to use the definite article, but nevertheless one wonders if the poet has not created the expression—notwithstanding its grammaticality (cf. אֶרֶץ גִּלְעָד ʾereṣ gilʿad 'land of Gilead' 3x in the Bible)—in order to distinguish the usage in 4:1 from that in 6:5 in one more minor way.

6. Song of Songs 2:9, 17; 8:14

Song 2:9

דּוֹמֶה דוֹדִי לִצְבִי אוֹ לְעֹפֶר הָאַיָּלִים

My beloved is-like a gazelle, or a fawn of the hinds.

Song 2:17

סֹב דְּמֵה־לְךָ דוֹדִי לִצְבִי אוֹ לְעֹפֶר הָאַיָּלִים עַל־הָרֵי בָתֶר:

Turn, liken yourself, my beloved, to a gazelle,
or to a fawn of the hinds,
Upon the mountains of cleavage.

Song 8:14

בְּרַח | דּוֹדִי וּדְמֵה־לְךָ לִצְבִי אוֹ לְעֹפֶר הָאַיָּלִים עַל הָרֵי בְשָׂמִים:

Flee, my beloved, and liken yourself to a gazelle,
or to a fawn of the hinds,
Upon the mountains of spices.

The first five examples in this chapter dealt with a comparison of two verses only, with the variations between them all relatively simple. We here present a set of three verses, with more complicated alterations. Three times in the Song of Songs the female lover compares (using the verb ד-מ-ה d-m-h 'liken, be similar') her lover to a gazelle or a fawn of the hinds. The plain statement appears in 2:9, with 2:17 and 8:14 expanding the thought in several ways.

In the latter two passages the verb ד-מ-ה d-m-h 'liken, be similar' occurs in the imperative, and in both cases it is preceded by another verb in the imperative. The differences are as follows: (a) In 2:17 the first verb is סֹב sob 'turn', while in 8:14 the first verb is בְּרַח bərah 'flee'. (b) In 2:17 the two verbs appear in asyndetic fashion (that is, with no conjunction between them), with the word דּוֹדִי *dodi* 'my beloved' following; while in 8:14 the two imperatives are separated by the insertion of the word דּוֹדִי *dodi* 'my beloved' between them. (c) The enigmatic phrase עַל־הָרֵי בָתֶר *ʿal hare bater* 'upon the mountains of cleavage' (one of many possible meanings) occurs in 2:17; whereas the wording in 8:14 is עַל הָרֵי בְשָׂמִים *ʿal hare bəśamim* 'upon the mountains of spices'.

As indicated above, these passages from Song of Songs constitute but a sampling. We move now to further examples of polyprosopon within poetic and prophetic texts.

7. Jeremiah 1:11, 13

Jer 1:11

וַיְהִי דְבַר־יְהוָה אֵלַי לֵאמֹר מָה־אַתָּה רֹאֶה יִרְמְיָהוּ וָאֹמַר מַקֵּל שָׁקֵד אֲנִי רֹאֶה:

And the word of YHWH was to me, saying, "What do you see, Jeremiah?" And I said, "A staff of almond I see."

Jer 1:13

וַיְהִי דְבַר־יְהוָה | אֵלַי שֵׁנִית לֵאמֹר מָה אַתָּה רֹאֶה וָאֹמַר סִיר נָפוּחַ אֲנִי רֹאֶה וּפָנָיו מִפְּנֵי צָפוֹנָה:

And the word of YHWH was to me a second-time, saying, "What do you see?" And I said, "A boiling pot I see, and its face is toward the north."

Twice in Jeremiah 1, Yahweh shows Jeremiah an item, with the fitting question, "What do you see?"—to which the prophet responds appropriately. The two passages present their content, as we have come to expect, in different fashion: (a) in v. 13, not surprisingly, the text introduces the word שֵׁנִית *šenit* 'a second-time'; (b) in the first instance, God includes the name of the prophet in his question, while the addressee is not mentioned specifically in the second version; and (c) v. 11 ends with the phrase אֲנִי רֹאֶה *ʾani roʾɛ* 'I see', while in v. 13 the prophet adds an additional description of the shown item after אֲנִי רֹאֶה *ʾani roʾɛ* 'I see'.[3]

---

3. On the alliteration in the second of these verses, see Chapter 16, no. 10.

8. Jeremiah 1:10; 18:7, 9; 31:38

Jer 1:10

רְאֵ֞ה הִפְקַדְתִּ֣יךָ ׀ הַיּ֣וֹם הַזֶּ֗ה עַל־הַגּוֹיִם֙ וְעַל־הַמַּמְלָכ֔וֹת לִנְת֥וֹשׁ
וְלִנְת֖וֹץ וּלְהַאֲבִ֣יד וְלַהֲר֑וֹס לִבְנ֖וֹת וְלִנְטֽוֹעַ׃

"See, I appoint you this day over the nations and over the
kingdoms, to uproot and to pull-down, and to defeat and
to destroy—to build and to plant."

Jer 18:7, 9

⁷ רֶ֣גַע אֲדַבֵּ֔ר עַל־גּ֖וֹי וְעַל־מַמְלָכָ֑ה לִנְת֥וֹשׁ וְלִנְת֖וֹץ וּלְהַאֲבִֽיד׃

⁷ "In an instant I speak concerning a nation and concerning a kingdom, to uproot and to pull-down, and to defeat."

⁹ וְרֶ֣גַע אֲדַבֵּ֔ר עַל־גּ֖וֹי וְעַל־מַמְלָכָ֑ה לִבְנ֖וֹת וְלִנְטֽוֹעַ׃

⁹ "In an instant I speak concerning a nation and concerning a kingdom, to build and to plant."

Jer 31:28

וְהָיָ֞ה כַּאֲשֶׁ֧ר שָׁקַ֣דְתִּי עֲלֵיהֶ֗ם לִנְת֧וֹשׁ וְלִנְת֛וֹץ וְלַהֲרֹ֖ס וּלְהַאֲבִ֣יד
וּלְהָרֵ֑עַ כֵּ֣ן אֶשְׁקֹ֧ד עֲלֵיהֶ֛ם לִבְנ֥וֹת וְלִנְט֖וֹעַ נְאֻם־יְהוָֽה׃

"And it will be, as I have watched over you, to uproot
and to pull-down, and to destroy, and to defeat and to
bring-disaster, so I will watch over you, to build and to
plant," declares Yʜᴡʜ.

These verses occur in different contexts within the book of Jeremiah,
and yet they are united by shared thought and similar vocabulary. The
general sense is that Jeremiah's role is to announce both destruction
and rebirth. For the nonce we focus our attention on the string of infinitive verbs used in the different verses. The opening call in 1:10 uses
four verbs to announce destruction: לִנְת֥וֹשׁ וְלִנְת֖וֹץ וּלְהַאֲבִ֣יד וְלַהֲר֑וֹס *lintoš
wə-lintoṣ u-lhaʾabid wə-laharos* 'to uproot and to pull-down, and to
defeat and to destroy', followed by the two verbs proclaiming rebirth:
לִבְנ֖וֹת וְלִנְטֽוֹעַ *libnot wə-lintoaʿ* 'to build and to plant'. The second version is split over two verses in ch. 18, with v. 7 opting for only three
synonymous verbs of destruction: לִנְת֥וֹשׁ וְלִנְת֖וֹץ וּלְהַאֲבִ֣יד *lintoš wə-lintoṣ*

u-lha'abid 'to uproot and to pull-down, and to defeat', and with v. 9 echoing the two verbs of rebirth: לִבְנֹת וְלִנְטֹעַ *libnot wə-lintoaʿ* 'to build and to plant'—though one notes the *defectiva* spelling of both forms, in contrast to the *plene* spellings in 1:10. In the third exemplar, five verbs of destruction now appear: לִנְתוֹשׁ וְלִנְתוֹץ וְלַהֲרֹס וּלְהַאֲבִיד וּלְהָרֵעַ *lintoš wə-lintoṣ wə-laharos u-lha'abid u-lharea*' 'to uproot and to pull-down, and to destroy, and to defeat and to bring-disaster'—in addition to which one notes the deft switch in order of the third and fourth verbs, with the standard phrase of rebirth following, as expected.

9. Jeremiah 1:19; 15:20

Jer 1:19

וְנִלְחֲמוּ אֵלֶיךָ וְלֹא־יוּכְלוּ לָךְ כִּי־אִתְּךָ אֲנִי נְאֻם־יְהוָה לְהַצִּילֶךָ:

And they will fight against you, but they will not be able (to defeat) you, for I am with you, declares YHWH, to rescue you.

Jer 15:20

וְנִלְחֲמוּ אֵלֶיךָ וְלֹא־יוּכְלוּ לָךְ כִּי־אִתְּךָ אֲנִי לְהוֹשִׁיעֲךָ וּלְהַצִּילֶךָ
נְאֻם־יְהוָה:

And they will fight against you, but they will not be able (to defeat) you, for I am with you, to save you and to rescue you, declares YHWH.

According to the approach we have used in this book, one will assume that the author/editor/redactor/compiler of the diverse oracles within the book of Jeremiah could expect his reader to retain in her mind the wording of a passage heard chapters earlier. So as not to repeat himself, accordingly, the creator of our text altered the wording in the second iteration, notwithstanding the fourteen chapters that separate the two passages. Two differences occur here: (a) in 1:19 the phrase נְאֻם־יְהוָה *nə'um YHWH* 'declares YHWH' is inserted within the divine word, while in 15:20 said expression appears at the end of the verse; and (b) the former verse uses only one verb, לְהַצִּילֶךָ *ləhaṣṣilɛka* 'to rescue you', while the latter verse presents two verbs, לְהוֹשִׁיעֲךָ וּלְהַצִּילֶךָ *ləhoši'aka u-lhaṣṣilɛka* 'to save you and to rescue you'.

10. Jeremiah 6:15; 8:12

Jer 6:15

הֹבִ֗ישׁוּ כִּ֤י תוֹעֵבָה֙ עָשׂ֔וּ גַּם־בּ֣וֹשׁ לֹֽא־יֵב֗וֹשׁוּ גַּם־הַכְלִים֙ לֹ֣א יָדָ֔עוּ
לָכֵ֞ן יִפְּל֣וּ בַנֹּפְלִ֗ים בְּעֵת־פְּקַדְתִּ֛ים יִכָּשְׁל֖וּ אָמַ֥ר יְהוָֽה׃

They acted-shamefully, indeed they committed abomination; yet they indeed are not ashamed, even to humiliate
they do not know, therefore they shall fall among those
who fall, at the time (when) I punish them they shall
stumble—says YHWH.

Jer 8:12

הֹבִ֗שׁוּ כִּ֤י תוֹעֵבָה֙ עָשׂ֔וּ גַּם־בּ֣וֹשׁ לֹֽא־יֵב֗וֹשׁוּ וְהִכָּלֵ֖ם לֹ֣א יָדָ֔עוּ
לָכֵ֞ן יִפְּל֣וּ בַנֹּפְלִ֗ים בְּעֵ֧ת פְּקֻדָּתָ֛ם יִכָּשְׁל֖וּ אָמַ֥ר יְהוָֽה׃

They acted-shamefully, indeed they committed abomination; yet they indeed are not ashamed, and to be humiliated they do not know, therefore they shall fall among
those who fall, at the time of their punishment they shall
stumble—says YHWH.

These passages are selected from two larger chunks of text, which
parallel each other (6:13–15 // 8:10–12), though with numerous minor
divergences.[4] In the verses presented here, two main differences occur:
(a) the first one uses גַּם הַכְלִים *gam haklim* 'even to humiliate', with an
emphasizing particle and the root כ-ל-ם *k-l-m* in the Hiphʿil; while the
second one reads וְהִכָּלֵם *wə-hikkalem* 'and to be humiliated', with the
simpler conjunction וְ- *wə-* 'and' and the root כ-ל-ם *k-l-m* in the Niphʿal;
and (b) 6:15 uses the expression בְּעֵת־פְּקַדְתִּים *be-ʿet pəqadtim* 'at the time
(when) I punish them' (an usual syntagma, with a finite verb serving

---

4. See the treatments by William L. Holladay, *Jeremiah 1: A Commentary
on the Book of the Prophet Jeremiah, Chapters 1–25* (Hermeneia; Philadelphia:
Fortress, 1986), 274–75 (though he would follow the Septuagint and omit 8:10–
12); and William McKane, *A Critical and Exegetical Commentary on Jeremiah*
(International Critical Commentary; Edinburgh: T&T Clark, 1986) 1:187–88.

as *nomen rectum* of a construct chain),[5] whereas 8:12 employs the more standard grammatical structure בְּעֵת פְּקֻדָּתָם *be-ʿet pəquddatam* 'at the time of their punishment'.

In addition, I note the different orthographies present, which allow the oral reader, holding the written text in his/her hand, an additional delight: הֹבִישׁוּ *hobišu* and יֵבוֹשׁוּ *yebošu* in the first instance (with *matres lectionis*), and הֹבִשׁוּ *hobišu* and יֵבֹשׁוּ *yebošu* in the second (without *matres lectionis*). Finally, also present is a scribal device that was introduced by the Masoretes but that presumably harks back to the ancient oral reading tradition. I refer to the presence of *maqqef* in בְּעֵת־פְּקַדְתִּים *be-ʿet pəqadtim* in 6:15 and the absence thereof in בְּעֵת פְּקֻדָּתָם *be-ʿet pəquddatam* in 8:12. This represents the finest distinction possible in the performance of a text (with concomitant accent on בְּעֵת *be-ʿet* in 8:12, in contrast to the lack of one on בְּעֵת־ *be-ʿet* in 6:15), and yet even this most minute divergence participates in the overall effect of polyprosopon. All of this at a distance of two chapters, with the assumption that someone listening to a sustained recitation of Jeremiah's oracles would recall the wording of 6:15 upon reaching 8:12.[6]

11. Ezekiel 8:12; 9:9

Ezek 8:12

כִּי אֹמְרִים אֵין יְהוָה רֹאֶה אֹתָנוּ עָזַב יְהוָה אֶת־הָאָרֶץ׃

For they say, "Yнwн does not see us, Yнwн has forsaken the land."

---

5. We encountered this syntagma at the very outset of our book; see above Chapter 1, pp. 15–16. For further study, see Daniel Grossberg, "Nominalization in Biblical Hebrew," *Hebrew Studies* 20–21 (1979–1980): 29–33.

6. For these reasons and more, I concur with McKane, *Jeremiah* 1:187–88, in his criticism of J. Gerald Janzen, *Studies in the Text of Jeremiah* (Cambridge: Harvard University Press, 1973), 95–96, who believes that the differences between 6:15 and 8:12 represent nothing more than orthographic variants. As McKane pointed out, "they were not regarded as orthographical variants by the Masoretes[,] whose pointing imposes morphological distinctions, and הַכְּלִים would be an unusual spelling of the Niphal infinitive construct in Biblical Hebrew as would פְּקַדְתָּם of a 1st person sing. verb + suffix." However, the Masora did not impose anything, but rather simply recorded in graphic notation the oral reading tradition, on which see above, Introduction, pp. 3–7.

Ezek 9:9

כִּי אָמְרוּ עָזַב יְהוָה אֶת־הָאָרֶץ וְאֵין יְהוָה רֹאֶה׃

For they said, "Y<small>HWH</small> has forsaken the land, and Y<small>HWH</small>
does not see."

These two passages present the viewpoint of the general populace (or
at least a significant portion thereof), which has lost its faith in God,
who to their mind has abandoned his people and the land of Israel.

While the individual words are essentially the same, verbatim repetition is avoided in a host of ways. (a) The first statement is introduced
with כִּי אֹמְרִים *ki ʾomrim* 'for they say', using the participle form of the
verb; the second statement is introduced with כִּי אָמְרוּ *ki ʾamru* 'for
they said', using the past-tense *qatal* form of the verb. (b) In the first
iteration, the quoted speech leads with God's not seeing, with his for-
saking the land following; in the second iteration, these two comments
are reversed. (c) In 8:12, the two parts of the declaration are asyndetic
(that is, no 'and' appears); in 9:9, the two parts are separated by the
conjunction ־וְ *wə-* 'and'. (d) Finally, in the first passage, an object is
present in the clause אֵין יְהוָה רֹאֶה אֹתָנוּ *ʾen yhwh roʾɛ ʾotanu* 'Y<small>HWH</small>
does not see us'; while in the second passage, no object is present, וְאֵין
יְהוָה רֹאֶה *wə-ʾen yhwh roʾɛ* 'and Y<small>HWH</small> does not see'. The result of
these minor changes is a stellar instance of repetition with variation.[7]

12. Ezekiel 20:6, 15

Ezek 20:6

אֶל־אֶרֶץ אֲשֶׁר־תַּרְתִּי לָהֶם זָבַת חָלָב וּדְבַשׁ

to (the) land that I explored for them, flowing with milk
and honey

---

7. Pancratius C. Beentjes, "Inverted Quotations in the Bible: A Neglected
Stylistic Pattern," *Biblica* 63 (1982): 506–23 (see esp. 508–9), may be correct
that this example is part of a larger stylistic pattern in the Bible, as indicated
in the title of his article. For earlier work in this direction, by Moshe Seidel
and Meir Weiss, see the references cited by Beentjes on p. 508 n. 4; indeed,
the device is typically referred to as 'Seidel's Law' within biblical studies
(for references, see ahead, p. 531, n. 7). Regardless, the two passages display
the kind of repetition with variation treated throughout the present volume.

Ezek 20:15

אֶל־הָאָרֶץ אֲשֶׁר־נָתַ֫תִּי זָבַת חָלָב֮ וּדְבַ֑שׁ

to the land that I gave (them), flowing with milk
and honey

Twice within the severe condemnation of Israel in ch. 20, the prophet
Ezekiel references the promised land of Canaan. Not wishing to repeat
himself verbatim, however, the author alters his words. In v. 6, we note
the use of the indefinite form אֶרֶץ *’ɛrɛṣ* 'land', the verbal root ת-ו-ר *t-w-r*
'seek', and the inclusion of the word לָהֶם *lahɛm* 'for them'. In v. 15, we note
the use of the definite form הָאָרֶץ *ha-’arɛṣ* 'the land', the verbal root נ-ת-ן
n-t-n 'give', and the omission of the expected word לָהֶם *lahɛm* 'to them'.[8]

13. Psalm 49:13, 21

Ps 49:13

וְאָדָ֣ם בִּ֭יקָר בַּל־יָלִ֑ין נִמְשַׁ֖ל כַּבְּהֵמ֣וֹת נִדְמֽוּ׃

And man in (his) honor does not abide;
he is like the beasts that perish.

Ps 49:21

אָדָ֣ם בִּ֭יקָר וְלֹ֣א יָבִ֑ין נִמְשַׁ֖ל כַּבְּהֵמ֣וֹת נִדְמֽוּ׃

Man in (his) honor, and he does not understand;
he is like the beasts that perish.

Refrains in ancient Hebrew poetry are not refrains in the generally
understood sense of that term, that is, verbatim repetition of a line at
regular (or at times irregular) intervals. Rather, as this example and
the next one demonstrate, the language is varied (and almost always
there is no regular distance between the lines). In these two lines from
Psalm 49, we note the following divergences:[9] (a) v. 13 begins with

---

8. For an earlier treatment of the key phrase 'flowing with milk and
honey', see above, Chapter 14, no. 6.

9. For brief mention of these verses, see John Goldingay, "Repetition and
Variation in the Psalms," *Jewish Quarterly Review* 68 (1977): 148. I owe this
reference to Knut Heim (Denver Seminary).

conjunctive -וְ *wə-* 'and', while v. 21 does not; (b) the former uses the
rarer negative particle בַּל *bal* 'not',[10] whereas the latter uses the more
standard negative particle לֹא *loʾ* 'not'; (c) the first iteration reads simply
בַּל *bal* 'not', while the second one reads וְלֹא *wə-loʾ* 'and not', with the
conjunction; and (d) v. 13 employs the verb ל-י-ן *l-y-n* 'lodge, abide',
while v. 21 opts for the verb ב-י-ן *b-y-n* 'understand'. This last alternation, the most major one among the four, actually generates different
meanings for the two lines, as is reflected in my English translations.

14. Psalm 107

Ps 107:6

וַיִּצְעֲקוּ אֶל־יְהוָה בַּצַּר לָהֶם מִמְּצוּקוֹתֵיהֶם יַצִּילֵם:

And they cried to Yhwh in their trouble,
from their straits he rescues them.

Ps 107:13

וַיִּזְעֲקוּ אֶל־יְהוָה בַּצַּר לָהֶם מִמְּצֻקוֹתֵיהֶם יוֹשִׁיעֵם:

And they cried to Yhwh in their trouble,
from their straits he saves them.

Ps 107:19

וַיִּזְעֲקוּ אֶל־יְהוָה בַּצַּר לָהֶם מִמְּצֻקוֹתֵיהֶם יוֹשִׁיעֵם:

And they cried to Yhwh in their trouble,
from their straits he saves them.

Ps 107:28

וַיִּצְעֲקוּ אֶל־יְהוָה בַּצַּר לָהֶם וּמִמְּצוּקֹתֵיהֶם יוֹצִיאֵם:

And they cried to Yhwh in their trouble,
and from their straits he extracts them.

---

10. The particle בַּל, typically an Israelian Hebrew feature, was available
to the author of this psalm due to its origin in northern Israel; see Gary A.
Rendsburg, *Linguistic Evidence for the Northern Origin of Selected Psalms*
(Society of Biblical Literature Monograph Series 43; Atlanta: Scholars Press,
1990), 24–25, 57.

Psalm 107 presents the relevant line 4x, twice (vv. 13, 19) verbatim, twice (vv. 6, 28) with variation. If we consider vv. 13 and 19 to be the base wording, we note the following deviations in vv. 6 and 28: (a) both use the root צ-ע-ק *ṣ-ʿ-q* 'call, cry out', rather than the root ז-ע-ק *z-ʿ-q*, which bears the same meaning (and thus my translations do not differ on this point); (b) v. 6 uses the Hiphʿil of the root נ-צ-ל *n-ṣ-l* 'rescue', while v. 28 uses the Hiphʿil of the root י-צ-א *y-ṣ-ʾ* 'take out, bring out, extract'—in contrast to the Hiphʿil of the root י-שׁ-ע *y-š-ʿ* 'save', which appears in vv. 13 and 19;[11] and (c) the final iteration prefixes the conjunction -ו *u-* 'and' to מִמְּצוּקֽוֹתֵיהֶם *mim-məṣuqotehɛm* 'from their straits' to create the unique form וּמִמְּצֽוּקֽוֹתֵיהֶם *u-mim-məṣuqotehɛm* 'and from their straits'. In addition, there are orthographic differences in מִמְּצֻקֽוֹתֵיהֶם *mim-məṣuqotehɛm* (thus vv. 13, 19), with the form in v. 6 employing *waw* (i.e., *šurɛq*) to represent long /u:/, and with the form in v. 28 doing likewise, though not employing *waw* (i.e., *ḥolɛm maleʾ*) to represent long /o:/. As a result, there is delight here both for the listener to the poem and for the oral reciter who held the written text in his hand.

15. Psalm 148:7–12

7 הַֽלְל֣וּ אֶת־יְהוָה מִן־הָאָ֑רֶץ
תַּ֝נִּינִ֗ים וְכָל־תְּהֹמֽוֹת׃

8 אֵ֣שׁ וּ֭בָרָד שֶׁ֣לֶג וְקִיט֑וֹר
ר֥וּחַ סְ֝עָרָ֗ה עֹשָׂ֥ה דְבָרֽוֹ׃

9 הֶהָרִ֥ים וְכָל־גְּבָע֑וֹת
עֵ֥ץ פְּ֝רִ֗י וְכָל־אֲרָזֽים׃

10 הַֽחַיָּ֥ה וְכָל־בְּהֵמָ֑ה
רֶ֝֗מֶשׂ וְצִפּ֥וֹר כָּנָֽף׃

11 מַלְכֵי־אֶ֭רֶץ וְכָל־לְאֻמִּ֑ים
שָׂ֝רִ֗ים וְכָל־שֹׁ֥פְטֵי אָֽרֶץ׃

12 בַּחוּרִ֥ים וְגַם־בְּתוּל֑וֹת
זְ֝קֵנִ֗ים עִם־נְעָרִֽים׃

---

11. My use of 'rescue' for נ-צ-ל *n-ṣ-l* (Hiphʿil) and 'save' for י-שׁ-ע *y-š-ʿ* (Hiphʿil) is simply for the sake of convenience. As far as I can determine, the meanings of the two verbs are essentially equivalent.

⁷ Praise YHWH from the earth,
Sea-creatures and all the depths.
⁸ Fire and hail, snow and smoke,
Wind (and) storm (that) does his word.
⁹ The mountains and all hills,
Fruit tree(s) and all cedars.
¹⁰ The beast and every domesticated-animal,
Creeping-thing and fowl of wing.
¹¹ Kings of (the) earth, and all peoples,
Princes and all (the) judges of (the) earth.
¹² Young-men and also young-women,
Elders with youths.

The variation in this stanza is not in wording per se, but in phraseology, to wit, the manner in which the poet generates different ways of saying 'X + Y'. In the translation above, I have inserted the word 'the' in parentheses, to allow for a smoother English reading, though in these instances the definite article is not present in the Hebrew original.

This section of Psalm 148 opens with the call to praise God (v. 7a). After this, eleven different phrases are used to connote the diverse elements of the world that are commanded to respond to the call. We may graph them as follows, with the nouns' number (singular or plural) indicated, the presence or absence of 'the', the use of the quantifier 'all' at times, the occasional employment of conjoined nouns X–Y (construct phrase), and so on:

7b: X(pl) + all Y(pl)

8a: W(sg) + X(sg), Y(sg) + Z(sg)

8b: X(sg)–Y(sg), *with verbal clause*

9a: the–X(pl) + all Y(pl)

9b: X(sg)–Y(sg) + all Z(pl)

10a: the–X(sg) + all Y(pl)

10b: X(sg) + Y(sg)–Z(sg)

11a: X(pl)–Y(sg) + all Z(pl)

11b: X(pl) + all Y(pl)–Z(sg)

12a: X(pl) + also Y(pl)

12b: X(pl) with Y(pl)

A less imaginative poet most likely would have repeated some of these patterns, but not the composer of Psalm 148.

16. Proverbs 1:8; 6:20

Prov 1:8

שְׁמַ֣ע בְּ֭נִי מוּסַ֣ר אָבִ֑יךָ וְאַל־תִּ֝טֹּ֗שׁ תּוֹרַ֥ת אִמֶּֽךָ׃

Listen, my son, (to) the instruction of your father,
And do not forsake the teaching of your mother.

Prov 6:20

נְצֹ֣ר בְּ֭נִי מִצְוַ֣ת אָבִ֑יךָ וְאַל־תִּ֝טֹּ֗שׁ תּוֹרַ֥ת אִמֶּֽךָ׃

Guard, my son, the command of your father,
And do not forsake the teaching of your mother.

No book of the Bible is more rife with non-verbatim doublets than the book of Proverbs; by one count there are approximately one hundred such instances.[12] In this chapter, naturally, we can present only a sampling—four cases, to be exact—all with rather simple variation; in other cases the modifications are more complex. In the first pair of passages presented above, the b-lines repeat verbatim (including even the accent marks), but the a-lines include two cases of variation: (a) the difference between the imperative verbs שְׁמַע *šamaʿ* 'hear, listen' in 1:8 and נְצֹר *nəṣor* 'guard' in 6:20; and (b) the alternation between the object מוּסַר *musar* 'instruction' in the former and מִצְוַת *miṣwat* 'command' in the latter.

---

12. Daniel C. Snell, *Twice-Told Proverbs and the Composition of the Book of Proverbs* (Winona Lake, IN: Eisenbrauns, 1993). For a thorough study of the differences between the variant wordings, see Knut M. Heim, *Poetic Imagination in Proverbs: Variant Repetitions and the Nature of Poetry* (Winona Lake, IN: Eisenbrauns, 2012). For a brief summary, see Rendsburg, "Literary and Linguistic Matters in the Book of Proverbs," 130–31.

17. Proverbs 2:16; 7:5

Prov 2:16

לְהַצִּ֣ילְךָ מֵאִשָּׁ֣ה זָרָ֑ה מִ֝נָּכְרִיָּ֗ה אֲמָרֶ֥יהָ הֶחֱלִֽיקָה׃

To rescue you from a strange woman,
From a foreign-woman (who) makes her words slick.

Prov 7:5

לִשְׁמָרְךָ֗ מֵאִשָּׁ֣ה זָרָ֑ה מִ֝נָּכְרִיָּ֗ה אֲמָרֶ֥יהָ הֶחֱלִֽיקָה׃

To guard you from a strange woman,
From a foreign-woman (who) makes her words slick.

Once more the b-lines in these two verses are precisely the same (again, including the accent marks); the variation occurs in the a-line, in fact, with the first word: לְהַצִּילְךָ *ləhaṣṣilka* 'to rescue you' in 2:16 and לִשְׁמָרְךָ *lišmorka* 'to guard you' in 7:5.

18. Proverbs 20:16; 27:13

Prov 20:16

לְקַח־בִּגְדוֹ כִּי־עָ֣רַב זָ֑ר וּבְעַ֖ד [נכרים] נָכְרִיָּ֣ה* חַבְלֵֽהוּ׃

Tak (*sic*) his garment, when he has stood-surety for a
　　　stranger,
And on behalf of a foreign-woman, hold him in pledge.

Prov 27:13

קַח־בִּגְדוֹ כִּי־עָ֣רַב זָ֑ר וּבְעַ֖ד　　　　　נָכְרִיָּ֣ה חַבְלֵֽהוּ׃

Take his garment, when he has stood-surety for a
　　　stranger,
And on behalf of a foreign-woman, hold him in pledge.

The only difference in the two passages is the form of the imperative 'take' at the beginning of each verse, with 20:16 using the irregular לְקַח *ləqaḥ* and 27:13 using the standard form, קַח *qaḥ*. (The first verse also has a Ketiv variant, indicated by the brackets, but the Qeri, indicated by the asterisk, conforms with the second verse, so we do not consider this a difference.) I have elected to render the first imperative form with atypical English 'tak' (on which see more anon, at the end of this chapter, no. 22), to highlight the alternation between the two verses in the English translations.

One notes that the first two pairs of proverbs presented above (nos. 16 and 17) appear within the same collection, the one that begins the book of Proverbs and comprises chs. 1–9; note the superscriptions at 1:1 ('the proverbs of Solomon son of David, king of Israel') and 10:1 ('the proverbs of Solomon'), demarcating originally discrete compilations within the canonical book. In the present instance, by contrast, the two verses occur in different sections of the book, 20:16 being found within the unit introduced by the superscription at 10:1 ('the proverbs of Solomon') and 27:13 within the unit introduced by the phrase at 25:1 ('these too are the proverbs of Solomon, which the men of Hezekiah king of Judah imported'). Which is to say, it was not only a single assembler of proverbial wisdom (say, the person responsible for chs. 1–9) who varied the individual maxims (once more see nos. 16 and 17 above), but the ultimate compiler of the entire canonical book of Proverbs followed suit by ensuring that repeated axioms across boundary divisions also did not repeat verbatim.[13]

19. Proverbs 21:9; 25:24

Prov 21:9

טוֹב לָשֶׁבֶת עַל־פִּנַּת־גָּג מֵאֵשֶׁת   מִדְיָנִים וּבֵית חָבֶר׃

Better to dwell on the corner of a roof,
Than with a woman of contention in a house of noise/
   storage.

Prov 25:24

טוֹב שֶׁבֶת עַל־פִּנַּת־גָּג מֵאֵשֶׁת [מדונים] מִדְיָנִים* וּבֵית חָבֶר׃

Better (to) dwell on the corner of a roof,
Than with a woman of contention in a house of noise/
   storage.

---

13. See the summary statement by Heim, *Poetic Imagination in Proverbs*, 535: "variant repetition in Proverbs is a conscious, ubiquitous editorial strategy." As the reader of the current monograph may imagine, I agree wholeheartedly.

Once more only a very simple modification occurs, with the first iteration including the preposition 'to' before the infinitive, hence לָשֶׁבֶת
lašebet 'to dwell', and with the second iteration not including this grammatical particle (which is perfectly acceptable in Hebrew), hence the
shorter form שֶׁבֶת šebet 'dwell'. (Again, we ignore the Ketiv that occurs
in 25:24, especially since the Qeri aligns perfectly with 21:9.) Moreover,
again we have two verses appearing in separate subdivisions of the
book of Proverbs, with 21:9 and 25:24 occurring within the same two
units discussed in the preceding example (see above, no. 18).

20. Job 28:12, 20

Job 28:12

> וְהַחָכְמָה מֵאַיִן תִּמָּצֵא וְאֵי זֶה מְקוֹם בִּינָה׃

"And wisdom, from where may it be found, and where is
the place of understanding?"

Job 28:20

> וְהַחָכְמָה מֵאַיִן תָּבוֹא וְאֵי זֶה מְקוֹם בִּינָה׃

"And wisdom, from where does it come, and where is the
place of understanding?"

These verses begin two strophes within the crucial chapter, Job 28,
the poem about wisdom.[14] Not wishing to repeat himself verbatim, the
composer of these lines varied his vocabulary with תִּמָּצֵא timmaṣeʾ 'be
found' in the first instance and תָּבוֹא taboʾ 'comes' in the second.

The book of Job is the most complex composition within the biblical
canon. I could cite many more examples of repetition with variation
within the complicated and at times convoluted poetry of the book,
but this one simple example from a relatively well-known chapter will
suffice by way of illustration.

---

14. For discussion, see Jan Fokkelman, "Job 28 and the Climax in Chapters
29–31: Crisis and Identity," in Hanna Liss and Manfred Oeming, eds., *Literary
Construction of Identity in the Ancient World* (Winona Lake, IN: Eisenbrauns,
2010), 301–22.

21. Lamentations 1:20; 2:11

Lam 1:20

מֵעַי חֳמַרְמָרוּ נֶהְפַּךְ לִבִּי בְּקִרְבִּי

My innards ferment, my heart is overturned in my midst.

Lam 2:11

חֳמַרְמְרוּ מֵעַי נִשְׁפַּךְ לָאָרֶץ כְּבֵדִי

My innards ferment, my liver is poured-out to the earth.

The two passages state essentially the same point, to wit, the poet's utter anguish upon the destruction of Jerusalem in 586 B.C.E. But the author has varied every possible element within the two iterations. First, although the English translation does not reveal the difference, the word order in 1:20 is subject-verb (SV), מֵעַי חֳמַרְמָרוּ *meʿay ḥomarmaru* 'my innards ferment',[15] while in 2:11 the order is reversed to verb-subject (VS), חֳמַרְמְרוּ מֵעַי *ḥomarmǝru meʿay* 'my innards ferment'.[16] Second, the latter part of the quoted passages occurs either as נֶהְפַּךְ לִבִּי בְּקִרְבִּי *nehpak libbi bǝ-qirbi* 'my heart is overturned in my midst' or as נִשְׁפַּךְ לָאָרֶץ *nišpak la-ʾareṣ kǝbedi* 'my liver is poured-out to the earth'. Note that both of these three-word phrases include a verb (in the Niphʿal stem, to be specific), a body part, and a prepositional phrase—though the poet has displayed his lexical and stylistic virtuosity: (a) none of the lexical items is duplicated; and (b) in the first case the body part appears before the prepositional phrase, while in the second instance the order of these two elements is reversed. Finally, it remains to point out that the words for 'heart' and 'liver' appear frequently as a parallel pair in Ugaritic poetry (*lb* and *kbd*, respectively, clear cognates to the

---

15. Hebrew מֵעַי *meʿay* 'my innards' is literally 'my intestines'; this internal organ was seen as the seat of emotion in the world of ancient Israel (and elsewhere). See further n. 17 below.

16. The reversal in word order suggests that 'Seidel's Law' (on which see above, p. 322, n. 7) is operative again. In addition, the use of the same words in specifically *two* separate verses in the book of Lamentations constitutes its own literary device, as identified and explicated by David Marcus, "Non-Recurring Doublets in the Book of Lamentations," *Hebrew Annual Review* 10 (1986): 177–95.

Hebrew forms),[17] so that the author of Lamentations is playing on a deep knowledge of ancient literature in his construction of the two verses.

22. Ezekiel 37:16

וְאַתָּה בֶן־אָדָם

קַח־לְךָ עֵץ אֶחָד וּכְתֹב עָלָיו לִיהוּדָה   וְלִבְנֵי יִשְׂרָאֵל חֲבֵרָיו

וּלְקַח עֵץ אֶחָד וּכְתוֹב עָלָיו לְיוֹסֵף עֵץ אֶפְרַיִם וְכָל־בֵּית יִשְׂרָאֵל חֲבֵרָיו:

"And you, son of man,

Take for you one wood, and write on it 'for Judah and for the
    children of Israel his comrades';

And tak (*sic*) one wood, and write on it 'for Joseph—the wood
    of Ephraim—and all the house of Israel his comrades'."

I have elected to place our final example in this chapter out of canonical order, because I consider it to be one of the most brilliant instances of polyprosopon in the entire Bible. In this well-known passage (reproduced here with the Qeri חֲבֵרָיו *ḥaberaw* 'his comrades' [2x]), God instructs the prophet Ezekiel to take two pieces of wood, to inscribe each of them (one for Judah and one for Israel), and then to bring them together to create a diptych (in v. 17)[18]—thereby symbolizing the promise for a reunited single kingdom of Israel (see v. 22). The set of double instructions to Ezekiel allows the reader to compare the language between v. 16a and v. 16b.

(a) The Judah portion begins with קַח־לְךָ *qaḥ ləka* 'take for you', using the standard imperative form, followed by the emphasizing dative form. The Israel section commences with the nonstandard imperative לְקַח *ləqaḥ* 'tak' (*sic*), without the emphasizing dative form, though with conjunctive -וּ *u-* 'and' (admittedly a near necessity here). This

---

17. For a listing of passages, see Gregorio del Olmo Lete and Joaquín Sanmartín, *A Dictionary of the Ugaritic Language in the Alphabetic Tradition*, trans. Wilfred G. E. Watson (Leiden: Brill, 2003), 1:424–25. Once more these body parts operate as seats of emotion (see n. 15 above).

18. See further Cyrus H. Gordon, "אחדים = *iltênêtu* 'pair'," in Yehoshua M. Grintz and Jacob Liver, eds., *Sefer Segal: Studies in the Bible Presented to Professor M. H. Segal* (Jerusalem: Kiryat Sepher, 1964), 5*–9*.

form, לְקַח *ləqaḥ*, with *lamed* retained, is a feature of Israelian Hebrew, as can be determined from its presence in 1 Kgs 17:11 (in the feminine) and Prov 20:16.[19] In the former, Elijah addresses the woman of Zarepath; while the latter appears in a book replete with Israelian Hebrew features.[20] In short, the author of Ezekiel 37 has taken advantage of the two available forms for the imperative 'take', one Judahite (in v. 16a), one Israelian (in v. 16b). Finally, note that I have attempted to replicate this distinction by using the regional dialectal English form 'tak' (not a misprint above) in my translation; this form occurs chiefly in Scotland, used, for example, by Walter Scott in his novel *Old Mortality* (1816).[21]

(b) Ezekiel is instructed to write on the first stick as follows: לִיהוּדָה וְלִבְנֵי יִשְׂרָאֵל חֲבֵרָיו *li-huda wə-li-bne yiśra'el ḥaberaw* 'for Judah and for the children of Israel his comrades'; the parallel line regarding the second stick reads: לְיוֹסֵף עֵץ אֶפְרַיִם וְכָל־בֵּית יִשְׂרָאֵל חֲבֵרָיו *lə-yosep 'eṣ 'eprayim wə-kol bet yiśra'el ḥaberaw* 'for Joseph—the wood of Ephraim—and all the house of Israel his comrades'. The variable language here consists of several components: (i) v. 16b incorporates an additional phrase, עֵץ אֶפְרַיִם *'eṣ 'eprayim* 'the wood of Ephraim', which is unparalleled in v. 16a (thus the white space above in the presentation of the full Hebrew text); (ii) v. 16a uses the expression בְּנֵי יִשְׂרָאֵל *bəne yiśra'el* 'children of Israel', while v. 16b opts for the phrase בֵּית יִשְׂרָאֵל *bet yiśra'el* 'house of Israel'; (iii) v. 16b includes the word כָּל־ *kol* 'all', which is lacking in v. 16a; (iv) by contrast, v. 16a includes an additional preposition, לְ- *li-* 'for' (in the phrase וְלִבְנֵי יִשְׂרָאֵל *wə-li-bne yiśra'el* 'and for the children of Israel'), which is wanting in v. 16b (in the phrase וְכָל־בֵּית יִשְׂרָאֵל *wə-kol bet yiśra'el* 'and all the house of Israel'). The total effect, incidentally, creates a Joseph line that is longer than its corresponding

---

19. Rendsburg, *Israelian Hebrew in the Book of Kings*, 46–47.

20. See H. L. Ginsberg, *The Israelian Heritage of Judaism* (New York: Jewish Theological Seminary, 1982), 34–36; Chen, "Israelian Hebrew in the Book of Proverbs"; and Rendsburg, "Literary and Linguistic Matters in the Book of Proverbs," 136–41. In the rehearsal of this maxim in Prov 27:13, note that the standard form קַח *qaḥ* 'take' occurs; on which see above, no. 18 in the present chapter. The one remaining example of the imperative of ל-ק-ח *l-q-ḥ* 'take' with the *lamed* retained is Exod 29:1, which the presumably Judahite author employed *alliterationis causa*; see above, Chapter 11, no. 1.

21. Cf. *OED*, s.v. 'take' *v.*

Judah line—an outcome that may be intentional, given the greater size of northern Israel in comparison to southern Judah.

Finally, once more we may observe an orthographic difference, with the first line reading וּכְתֹב WKTB *u-ktob* 'and write' (*defectiva*) and the second line reading וּכְתוֹב WKTWB *u-ktob* 'and write' (*plene*). The author of this passage clearly was a master of the literary device under discussion here, as he introduced a panoply of (mainly minor) variations within the ten and twelve words comprising lines vv. 16a and 16b, respectively.

Of all the passages that one could use to illustrate the technique of repetition with variation in the Bible, this one, if I may wax subjective for the moment, is my personal favorite. No other verse, to my mind, involves so many minor alterations, including dialectal variation, scribal variation, and more. Ezekiel 37:16 truly is a stunning gem of literary inventiveness.

CHAPTER SIXTEEN

ALLITERATION IN POETIC AND PROPHETIC TEXTS

On the basis of comparison with other world literature, one expects to find more examples of alliteration in poetic texts in the Bible than in the prose portions of the corpus.[1] Indeed, the abundance of such examples is so great, both within poetic books (such as Psalms and Proverbs) and within prophetic books written in poetic style (such as Amos and Isaiah), that this chapter can present only a representative sampling. Before presenting examples from these two corpora, we begin this chapter with four illustrations from the occasional poems embedded within the grand narrative prose account of Genesis through Kings.

1. Deuteronomy 32:15

וַיִּשְׁמַן יְשֻׁרוּן וַיִּבְעָט שָׁמַנְתָּ עָבִיתָ כָּשִׂיתָ

"And Jeshurun grew-fat, and he kicked;
You grew-fat, you became-thick, you became-coarse."

The rare verbs in this line of poetry alliterate with one another: וַיִּבְעָט *wayyibʿaṭ* 'and he kicked' and עָבִיתָ *ʿabita* 'you became-thick'. The first one derives from the root ב-ע-ט *b-ʿ-ṭ* 'kick', which occurs again only in 1 Sam 2:29. The second one derives from the root ע-ב-ה *ʿ-b-h* 'be thick', which occurs again only in 1 Kgs 12:10 // 2 Chr 10:10.

---

1. While I have not done a statistical survey (were such even possible) to either prove or disprove this postulate, even the casual reader would agree, I believe, that more alliteration is to be found in the poetic corpus than in the prose corpus. To be sure, alliteration is included in the standard work by Watson, *Classical Hebrew Poetry*, 225–29, while one rarely sees mention of alliteration in discussions of narrative prose.

In addition, two forms of the verbal root ש-מ-ן *š-m-n* 'grow fat' appear in this half-verse, namely, וַיִּשְׁמַן *wayyišman* 'and he grew-fat' and שָׁמַנְתָּ *šamanta* 'you grew-fat'—two of only five attestations of this verb in the Bible (for the others, see Isa 6:10, Jer 5:28, Neh 9:25). The two forms occur in conjunction with the rare designation יְשֻׁרוּן *yəšurun* 'Jeshurun', a poetic term for Israel (see elsewhere Deut 33:5, 33:26, Isa 44:2). The result is an alliterative string carried throughout the poetic line.

This leaves only one word on which to comment, namely, the final one, כָּשִׂיתָ *kaśita* 'you became-coarse', from the root כ-ש-ה *k-ś-h* 'be coarse'. This word is a *hapax legomenon* in the Bible, and even its exact meaning is not known: the gloss 'be coarse' is determined simply from the context. In light of the approach taken in this book, with many more examples to be presented in this chapter, one might expect that this word also was employed *alliterationis causa*. Alas, however, there is no like-sounding word in close proximity—thereby providing a moment of pause, as this instance reminds us that not every rare or unique word in the Bible is selected for the aural effect.

2. Deuteronomy 32:18

צוּר יְלָדְךָ תֶּשִׁי וַתִּשְׁכַּח אֵל מְחֹלְלֶךָ:

> The Rock who bore you—*tɛši*,
> And you forgot the God who birthpanged you.

No one, to the best of my knowledge, has solved the riddle of the third word in this verse, תֶּשִׁי—and hence I have elected to leave it untranslated, opting instead to use the transliteration *tɛši* in lieu of any conjecture.[2] Regardless of its meaning, there can be little doubt that the poet selected this vocable in anticipation of the next word, וַתִּשְׁכַּח *wattiškaḥ* 'and you forgot'. The /t/–/š/ sounds resonate in these consecutive words.

---

2. Most translations connect the word to the verbal root נ-ש-ה *n-š-h* 'forget', based on the theme announced in the second half of the verse. But I remain unconvinced of this approach, especially since the Masora transmitted the form as a noun.

3. Deuteronomy 33:14, 16

¹⁴ וּמִמֶּ֖גֶד תְּבוּאֹ֣ת שָׁ֑מֶשׁ וּמִמֶּ֖גֶד גֶּ֥רֶשׁ יְרָחִֽים׃

----

¹⁶ וּמִמֶּ֗גֶד אֶ֚רֶץ וּמְלֹאָ֔הּ וּרְצ֥וֹן שֹׁכְנִ֖י סְנֶ֑ה תָּב֙וֹאתָה֙ לְרֹ֣אשׁ יוֹסֵ֔ף
וּלְקָדְקֹ֖ד נְזִ֥יר אֶחָֽיו׃

¹⁴ And the bounty of the harvests of the sun,
And the bounty of the output of the moons.

----

¹⁶ And the bounty of the earth and its fullness,
And the favor of the One-who-dwells in the Bush,
May these come to the head of Joseph,
And to the pate of the elect of his brothers.

The unusual word that captures our attention is תָּבוֹאתָה *tabo'ta* (v. 16), rendered here as 'may these come'. The word derives from the exceedingly common verbal root ב-ו-א *b-w-ʾ* 'come', but the specific form constitutes a grammatical oddity—some would say impossibility—since it is marked as both the prefix-conjugation (with -תָּ *ta-* preceding the root) and the suffix-conjugation (with תָה- *-ta* following the root). Upon hearing such a form, the listener's literary antennae are aroused, at which point she realizes that she recently heard the like-sounding word תְּבוּאֹת *təbuʾot* 'harvests' (lit., 'in-comings') in v. 14. The verb in v. 16 and the noun in v. 14 derive from the same root (ב-ו-א *b-w-ʾ* 'come'), with both forms containing the consonant /t/ both before and after the root. As we have seen on earlier occasions, the biblical writer has employed a grammatical peculiarity to generate alliteration.[3]

4. 2 Samuel 23:7

וְאִ֚ישׁ יִגַּ֣ע בָּהֶ֔ם יִמָּלֵ֥א בַרְזֶ֖ל וְעֵ֣ץ חֲנִ֑ית וּבָאֵ֥שׁ שָׂר֖וֹף יִשָּׂרְפ֥וּ בַשָּֽׁבֶת׃

And the man who touches them, he is filled (with) iron and
    the shaft of a spear;
And in fire they are utterly consumed, in extreme-heat.

---

3. I hasten to add that the grammatical form remains unexplained, since to the best of my knowledge such forms do not occur elsewhere in Northwest Semitic (or in Semitic generally).

The meaning of the last word of this poetic line continued to elude scholars until the proper elucidation was proffered by Shlomo Naeh.[4] At first glance, the word שֶׁבֶת *šebet* (pausal שָׁבֶת *šabet*, as here in 2 Sam 23:7) is the infinitive construct of the verb י-שׁ-ב *y-š-b* 'sit'; hence the renderings 'in their place' (JPS), 'on the spot' (NJPS), etc. As Naeh noted, however, the noun שֶׁבֶת *šebet* occurs in Rabbinic Hebrew with the meaning 'hot wind, extreme heat' (Bereshit Rabba 29:2)—a connotation that fits the context of 2 Sam 23:7 perfectly (see my translation above).[5] The only point that remains to be recognized is the alliteration produced by using this rare word: וּבָאֵשׁ שָׂרוֹף יִשָּׂרְפוּ בַּשָּׁבֶת *u-ba-'eš śarop yiśśarpu baš-šabet*. Each of the items in this four-word series has either /š/ or /ś/ (close-sounding sibilants) and either /b/ or /p/ (corresponding voiced and voiceless labials). The result goes beyond alliteration: it is about as close to a tongue twister as one finds in the Bible.

5. Isaiah 24:16–17

¹⁶ בֹּגְדִים בָּגָדוּ וּבֶגֶד בּוֹגְדִים בָּגָדוּ:

¹⁷ פַּחַד וָפַחַת וָפָח עָלֶיךָ יוֹשֵׁב הָאָרֶץ:

¹⁶ The traitors have been treasonous,
And treason the traitors have been treasonous.
¹⁷ Terror and pit and trap, upon you, O inhabitant of the earth.

All who have read Isa 24:17 have noticed the threefold ring of the fate that awaits the cursed inhabitants of the earth: פַּחַד וָפַחַת וָפָח *paḥad wa-paḥat wa-paḥ* 'terror and pit and trap'. While I cannot be certain, I also suspect that the Jewish Publication Society's epoch-making translations (1917; 1970), from which my rendering is borrowed,[6] attempted

---

4. Shlomo Naeh, "A New Suggestion Regarding 2 Samuel xxiii 7," *Vetus Testamentum* 46 (1996): 260–65.

5. See also Gary A. Rendsburg, "Notes on Israelian Hebrew (I)," in Yitzhak Avishur and Robert Deutsch, eds., *Michael: Historical, Epigraphical and Biblical Studies in Honor of Prof. Michael Heltzer* (Tel Aviv: Archaeological Center Publications, 1999), 258.

6. To be more specific, the 1970 *Prophets* volume, which was incorporated into the complete 1985 *Tanakh* volume, reads: 'Terror, and pit, and trap' (with-

to capture the soundplay of the Hebrew with English alliteration.[7] Note the consonants /t/–/r/–/r/, /p/–/t/, /t/–/r/–/p/, respectively, in the three words.

What has been less noticed, however, is the preceding half-verse (v. 16b), with the fivefold repetition of the Hebrew root ב-ג-ד *b-g-d* 'commit treason, be treacherous, etc.', including in the noun form בֶּגֶד *beged* 'treason'. As Hugh Williamson pointed out, the soundplay carries over both verses, with the sounds of the root ב-ג-ד *b-g-d* in v. 16 (5x) anticipating the sounds of פַּחַד *paḥad* 'terror' and פַּחַת *paḥat* 'pit' at the beginning of v. 17.[8] Note the corresponding labials /b/ ~ /p/ at the start, velar /g/ or guttural /ḥ/ in the middle, and dental /d/ ~ /t/ concluding the aural effect. Finally, the reader may observe how I have attempted to capture also this part of the alliteration in my English rendering, with the /t/–/r/ sounds of 'traitors', 'treason', and 'treasonous' presaging the /t/–/r/ sounds of 'terror' and so on.

6. Isaiah 25:10

כִּי־תָנ֤וּחַ יַד־יְהוָה֙ בָּהָ֣ר הַזֶּ֔ה וְנָ֥דוֹשׁ מוֹאָ֖ב תַּחְתָּ֑יו כְּהִדּ֥וּשׁ מַתְבֵּ֖ן [במי]
בְּמ֥וֹ מַדְמֵנָֽה׃

For the hand of Yнwн shall rest on this mountain;
And Moab shall be threshed in its place,
As a straw-heap is threshed in a dung-pit.

Our attention is drawn to the last three words in the verse: מַתְבֵּן בְּמוֹ מַדְמֵנָה *matben bəmo madmena* 'a straw-heap in a dung-pit'.[9] The first word, מַתְבֵּן *matben* 'straw-heap' (at least such is the presumed meaning, related to תֶּבֶן *teben* 'straw'), occurs only here in the Bible. The second word, בְּמוֹ *bəmo* 'in', is the expanded form of the preposition

---

7. Other translations that I have consulted use 'fear' for 'terror' (KJV, NJB), 'snare' for 'trap' (KJV, RSV, NRSV, NIV), and so on.

8. H. G. M. Williamson, "Sound, Sense and Language in Isaiah 24–27," *Journal of Jewish Studies* 46 (1995): 1–9, esp. 3.

9. Once more, see ibid., 6–7.

-בְּ *bə-* 'in', used only in poetry within the Bible (10x: Ps 11:2; Job 5x; Isaiah 4x). The third word, מַדְמֵנָה *madmena* 'dung-pit', derived from the word דֹּמֶן *domɛn* 'dung', also occurs only here in the Bible. At the same time, the term alludes to a city in Moab, namely, Madmen, which is mentioned in Jer 48:2 (see Isa 10:31 for a like-named city in the territory of Benjamin).

In sum, the listener to this text hears similar sounds and structures in the two nouns, as follows: /m/ + dental (either /t/ or /d/) + labial (either /b/ or /m/) + /n/. To link the two nouns in the phrase, the author employed not the standard prepostion -בְּ *bə-* 'in', but rather the longer form בְּמוֹ *bəmo* 'in', to allow the double-labial combination /b/–/m/ to be heard.

7. Isaiah 27:1

בַּיּוֹם הַהוּא יִפְקֹד יְהוָה בְּחַרְבּוֹ הַקָּשָׁה וְהַגְּדוֹלָה וְהַחֲזָקָה עַל לִוְיָתָן
נָחָשׁ בָּרִחַ וְעַל לִוְיָתָן נָחָשׁ עֲקַלָּתוֹן וְהָרַג אֶת־הַתַּנִּין אֲשֶׁר בַּיָּם:

On that day, Yʜwʜ will visit with his hard and great and
strong sword upon Leviathan, (the) evil serpent, and upon
Leviathan, (the) crooked serpent; and he will kill the Tannin
that is in the sea.

This well-known verse—well known due to both its evocation of themes known from Ugaritic literature and its eschatological resonances within later Jewish sources—employs yet another rare Biblical Hebrew lexeme for the purpose of producing alliteration. The rare word is the adjective בָּרִחַ *bariaḥ* 'evil',[10] in line with the evil nature of Yam/Tannin/Leviathan in ancient Ugaritic mythological texts. While it is true that the cognate term *brḥ* 'evil' occurs in the closely related Ugaritic phrase *bṯn brḥ* 'evil serpent', and thus to some extent the word

---

10. Though many scholars continue to hold to the definition 'fleeing', incorrectly in my mind. The basic studies are Cyrus H. Gordon, "Leviathan: Symbol of Evil," in Alexander Altmann, ed., *Biblical Motifs: Origins and Transformations* (Cambridge: Harvard University Press, 1966), 1–9 (see p. 2 for the relevant Ugaritic and Hebrew texts, along with Gordon's translations); and Eduardo Zurro, "La raíz 'brḥ' II y el hápax *mibraḥ (Ez 17,21)," *Biblica* 61 (1980): 412–15.

בָּרִחַ *bariaḥ* 'evil' is totally expected in Isa 27:1, the alliteration with בְּחַרְבוֹ *bə-ḥarbo* 'with his sword' earlier in the verse remains central to the passage nonetheless.[11]

8. Isaiah 41:24

הֵן־אַתֶּם מֵאַיִן וּפָעָלְכֶם מֵאָפַע תּוֹעֵבָה יִבְחַר בָּכֶם׃

Behold, you are less than nothing,
And your work is of naught;
He who chooses you is an abomination.

The context of this passage is Second Isaiah's mock of the Babylonian gods, which are seen as delusions of their worshippers, in contrast to the one true God, Yahweh. The word that attracts our attention in this passage is the *hapax legomenon* אָפַע *'apaʿ* 'naught'.[12] Many scholars deny the existence of this vocable altogether, preferring instead to emend the word to אֶפֶס *'epes* 'non-existence', especially in light of verses such as Isa 34:12, 40:17, 41:12, Prov 26:20, etc., in which the two words אַיִן *'ayin* 'nothing' and אֶפֶס *'epes* 'non-existence' are collocated.[13] Since they are a standard word pair in Biblical Hebrew, they also must occur together—so the reasoning goes—in Isa 41:24; note אַיִן *'ayin* 'nothing' in the first stich, hence אֶפֶס *'epes* 'non-existence' must follow in the second stich.

Except that Lawrence Boadt astutely perceived the sound effect created by the use of אָפַע *'apaʿ* 'naught' in Isa 41:24, inserted as it is

---

11. As we learn from Ugaritic *ḥrb* 'sword' and *brḥ* 'evil', the *ḥet* in these two words represents the same phoneme, the pharyngeal fricative /ḥ/. The phrase נָחָשׁ בָּרִחַ *naḥaš bariaḥ* 'evil serpent' occurs one other time in the Bible, at Job 26:13 (with *plene* spelling: נָחָשׁ בָּרִיחַ), on which see below, Chapter 16, no. 22.

12. I cite the word in its pausal form, as it appears in the text. The reconstructed citation form of this word would be אָפַע *'epaʿ* 'naught'. The reader will note how I have used a rare English word, 'naught', to render a rare Hebrew word, with the synonym 'nothing' reserved for the more common Hebrew word אַיִן *'ayin* in the first stich.

13. See, e.g., BDB, 67.

between פָּעָלְכֶם *paʿolkɛm* 'your work' and תּוֹעֵבָה *toʿeba* 'abomination'.[14] The three words include the consonants /p/–/ʿ/, /p/–/ʿ/, and /ʿ/–/b/.[15] Emending the key word אָפַע *'apaʿ* 'naught' to the non-existent (ha!) אָפֶס *'ɛpɛs* 'non-existence' in this verse would denude the passage of its strong aural effect, which draws attention to the nothingness and abomination of the Babylonian gods derided by Second Isaiah here.

9. Isaiah 57:20

וְהָרְשָׁעִים כַּיָּם נִגְרָשׁ כִּי הַשְׁקֵט לֹא יוּכָל וַיִּגְרְשׁוּ מֵימָיו רֶפֶשׁ וָטִיט:

And the wicked are like the tossing sea;
For it cannot be quieted,
And its waters toss-up mire and mud.

In this verse, the prophet employs the *hapax legomenon* רֶפֶשׁ *rɛpɛš* 'mire' in order to complete a masterful string of like-sounding lexemes. The passage includes the more common words הָרְשָׁעִים *ha-rəšaʿim* 'the wicked', נִגְרָשׁ *nigraš* 'tossing', and וַיִּגְרְשׁוּ *wayyigrəšu* 'toss-up' (the latter two from the same verbal root ג-ר-שׁ *g-r-š* 'expel, dismiss, discharge, etc.'). All four words include the consonants *reš* and *šin* (/r/ and /š/), which when sounded together suggest the noise of the tossing sea.[16]

10. Jeremiah 1:13

וָאֹמַר סִיר נָפוּחַ אֲנִי רֹאֶה וּפָנָיו מִפְּנֵי צָפוֹנָה:

And I said, "A boiling pot I see, and its face is toward the north."

In the previous chapter (Chapter 15, no. 7), we discussed Jer 1:13 (especially the first part of the verse) as an instance of repetition with variation (when compared to v. 11). We now highlight the exquisite

---

14. Lawrence Boadt, "Intentional Alliteration in Second Isaiah," *Catholic Biblical Quarterly* 45 (1983): 353–63.

15. Note that /b/ is the voiced labial equivalent of the voiceless labial /p/.

16. Compare, perhaps, English 'rush', as in 'rush of water' (though also used for 'rush of people', etc.). *OED*, s.v. 'rush', *v.*², states, "etymology uncertain and disputed," the host of like-sounding Germanic cognates notwithstanding, and then observes, "probably ultimately of imitative origin."

alliteration in this verse. In the two previous verses a rather rudimentary instance of alliteration occurs (one even hesitates to use the term here): God showed Jeremiah מַקֵּל שָׁקֵד *maqqel šaqed* 'an almond branch' (v. 11), upon doing which he stated כִּי־שֹׁקֵד אֲנִי *ki šoqed 'ani* 'for I am watching' (v. 12). In the second instance, however, the author reveals himself to be quite adept at soundplay. God shows Jeremiah סִיר נָפוּחַ *sir napuaḥ* 'a boiling pot', but its description by Jeremiah, וּפָנָיו מִפְּנֵי צָפוֹנָה *u-panaw mippəne ṣapona* 'and its face is toward the north', treats the listener to exquisite alliteration. Note that the consonants /n/–/p/, which commence the adjective נָפוּחַ *napuaḥ*, occur in all three of the aforecited words that follow, albeit in reverse order, /p/–/n/.[17]

Just as the soundplay increases from basic to brilliant in the two scenes, so does the impact of the two messages. In the first one, the reader (as well as Jeremiah) learns that God is watching, though this should represent nothing new for the faithful worshipper of Yahweh. In the second one, however, the message is sterner, for the reader (and Jeremiah once more) learns, 'From the north evil shall break-open upon all the inhabitants of the land' (v. 14). As such, we may consider these verses as a prime example of 'build-up and climax', a literary device not surveyed systematically within the present book, but one that we have mentioned on several occasions.[18]

11. Jeremiah 2:2

הָלֹךְ וְקָרָאתָ בְאָזְנֵי יְרוּשָׁלַם לֵאמֹר
כֹּה אָמַר יְהוָה זָכַרְתִּי לָךְ חֶסֶד נְעוּרַיִךְ אַהֲבַת כְּלוּלֹתָיִךְ
לֶכְתֵּךְ אַחֲרַי בַּמִּדְבָּר בְּאֶרֶץ לֹא זְרוּעָה:

Go and proclaim in the ears of Jerusalem, saying:
Thus says Yʜwʜ: I remember you, the fealty of your youth,
    the love of your bridal;
Your going after me in the wilderness, in a land not sown.

---

17. For another instance of such soundplay in the book of Jeremiah, based on an object in the prophet's hand, see וּבַקֹּתִי *ubaqqoti* 'and I will frustrate' in 19:7 as a reflex of the key noun בַּקְבֻּק *baqbuq* 'bottle' in 19:1, 19:10.

18. See Chapter 9, p. 177, n. 27.

The context of Jeremiah's stirring words is the contrast between the past, as portrayed here, when the love between God and the people of Israel was as secure as the youthful wedding couple, and the present, as described in most of the book, in which God pleads with Israel to repent for its sins.

The listener apprehends that the word כְּלוּלֹתָיִךְ *kəlulotayik* 'your bridal' is unusual—indeed, it appears only here in the Bible. While some English translations render the word as 'your espousal' (see already KJV 'thine espousals'), and while others weave the word 'bride' into the rendering, as in 'your love as a bride' (thus RSV, NJPS), I have opted for 'your bridal'. My word choice recognizes the etymological connection of כְּלוּלֹת- *kəlulot-*, typically rendered 'espousal' or the like, to the common noun כַּלָּה *kalla* 'bride', and at the same time exploits its unfamiliar nature, hence my use of 'bridal'. The word is relegated to an adjective nowadays, but was used as a noun in centuries past, for example, by Shakespeare in *Othello* (1622), "Such obseruances as fits the Bridall" (Act III, Scene 4), and by Alfred Lord Tennyson in *Idylls of the King*, 'Enid' (1859), "I . . . will clothe her for her bridals like the sun."[19]

But to return now to the Hebrew itself, we may understand the prophet's selection of the *hapax legomenon* כְּלוּלֹתָיִךְ *kəlulotayik* 'your bridal' in light of the following word, לֶכְתֵּךְ *lektek* 'your going', from the common verb ה-ל-ך *h-l-k* 'go'.[20] Note how the consonants of the former, /k/–/l/–/l/–/t/–/k/, recur in the latter, which contains the string /l/–/k/–/t/–/k/. The result is a stunning instance of wordsmithing at its best.

12. Jeremiah 2:22

כִּי אִם־תְּכַבְּסִי בַּנֶּתֶר וְתַרְבִּי־לָךְ בֹּרִית נִכְתָּם עֲוֺנֵךְ לְפָנַי נְאֻם אֲדֹנָי יְהוִה:

Even if you cleanse with natron, and multiply for yourself
borax, your sin is stained before me, utters the Lord Yʜwʜ.

This verse presents two examples of alliteration, one readily apparent, the other less obvious. The former is the nexus between תַּרְבִּי *tarbi* 'you

---

19. *OED*, s.v. 'bridal'.

20. See also the first word of the verse, הֲלֹךְ *halok* 'go'. The form is the infinitive, though used here with the force of the imperative.

multiply' and בֹּרִית *borit* 'borax',[21] which are separated by only the one-syllable vocable לָךְ *lak* 'for yourself'. The two words, one a verb, one a noun, share the same three consonants in anagrammatic fashion. The inclusion of the long /i:/ vowel in both forms enhances the aural effect.[22]

The second example is, as indicated above, more concealed, but its presence once more demonstrates our literatus's mastery of the Hebrew language. The verb נִכְתָּם *niktam* 'stained', from the root כ-ת-ם *k-t-m*, appears only here in the Bible—though the noun derived therefrom, כֶּתֶם *kɛtɛm* 'stain', occurs more commonly in the Mishna.[23] As we have come to expect, rare words are selected purposefully by biblical authors in order to achieve alliteration. Such is the case here once more, as נִכְתָּם *niktam* 'stained' echoes the consonants heard earlier in the verse, at the bridge between אִם־תְּכַבְּסִי *'im təkabbəsi* 'if you cleanse'—in fact, in reverse order, as first the listener hears /m/–/t/–/k/ and then she hears /k/–/t/–/m/.

13. Jeremiah 46:14–15

14 הַגִּידוּ בְמִצְרַיִם וְהַשְׁמִיעוּ בְמִגְדּוֹל וְהַשְׁמִיעוּ בְנֹף וּבְתַחְפַּנְחֵס

אִמְרוּ הִתְיַצֵּב וְהָכֵן לָךְ כִּי־אָכְלָה חֶרֶב סְבִיבֶיךָ:

15 מַדּוּעַ נִסְחַף אַבִּירֶיךָ לֹא עָמַד כִּי יְהוָה הֲדָפוֹ:

14 Declare in Egypt, and announce in Migdol,
And announce in Memphis and in Tahpanhes;
Say: Position yourself and be-prepared,

---

21. I take advantage of the English word 'borax' here, since it sounds like the Hebrew word *borit* 'soap'. As an aside, note that the source of 'borax' is indeed Semitic, though from a different root, namely, Arabic *būraq* 'white, shiny'.

22. Interestingly, in the only other attestation of בֹּרִית *borit* 'borax' in the Bible, the word is once again employed *alliterationis causa*. See Mal 3:1–2, with the unique expression מַלְאַךְ הַבְּרִית *mal'ak hab-bərit* 'messenger of the covenant' in v. 1 and the noun בֹּרִית *borit* 'borax' in v. 2.

23. See Mishna Shabbat 9:5, with reference to the stain in a garment; and then 14x in Mishna Niddah and 15x in Tosefta Niddah, with reference to a woman's bloodstain. As a verb, the root *k-t-m* 'to be stained, to be soiled' occurs more commonly in Syriac. See also the form כתימין *kətimin* 'stained' in Targum Jonathan to Isa 1:18, as a more direct way of expressing the prophet's metaphorical reference to the people's sin as שָׁנִים *šanim* 'scarlet'.

For the sword shall devour round-about you.
¹⁵ Why are your steeds beaten-down?
They do not stand-firm
For Yʜwʜ thrusts them down.

The present example could have been included in Chapter 18 below, which is devoted to wordplay based on proper names, though I have elected to include it here, mainly because the chapter still to come focuses almost exclusively on passages within the great prose narrative that stretches from Genesis through Kings. The verses presented above, by contrast, occur in the book of Jeremiah, hence this example is better suited to our current treatment of alliteration within the poetic and prophetic books.

The key word in these verses is נִסְחַף *nisḥap* 'beaten-down' (v. 15), from the root ס-ח-ף *s-ḥ-p*, occurring elsewhere in the Bible only in Prov 28:3 (with reference to beating rain). The specific form of the verb here is the Niphʻal past tense, as indicated by the prefixed *nun*. The result is a precise echo, in anagrammatic fashion, of the four consonants heard at the end of the Egyptian city name תַחְפַּנְחֵס *taḥpanḥes* 'Tahpanhes' (later 'Daphnae'; modern Tell Defenneh in the eastern Delta). Also assisting in the alliterative effect are the two consonantal sounds in the shorter Egyptian city name נֹף *nop* 'Noph' (= 'Memphis'). We thus hear /n/–/p/ in the first toponym, /p/–/n/–/ḥ/–/s/ at the end of the second toponym, and then /n/–/s/–/ḥ/–/p/ in the crucial verb at the beginning of v. 15.

14. Zechariah 9:3

וַתִּבֶן צֹר מָצוֹר לָהּ וַתִּצְבָּר־כֶּסֶף כֶּעָפָר וְחָרוּץ כְּטִיט חוּצוֹת:

And Tyre has built a fortress for herself;
And she has amassed silver like dust,
And gold like the mud in the streets.

The city name צֹר *ṣor* 'Tyre' elicits a series of like-sounding words in this verse: מָצוֹר *maṣor* 'fortress', וַתִּצְבָּר *wattiṣbor* 'and she has amassed', and חָרוּץ *ḥaruṣ* 'gold'—all with both /ṣ/ and /r/ sounds. The last of these items, in turn, elicits another alliterative lexeme, חוּצוֹת *ḥuṣot* 'streets'—these two words share the consonants /ḥ/ and /ṣ/. The result is an entire catena of sounds resonating throughout the verse.[24]

15. Psalm 55:9

אָחִישָׁה מִפְלָט לִי מֵרוּחַ סֹעָה מִסָּעַר:

I would hasten me a refuge,
From the wind, sweeping from the storm.

I used this example to introduce the entire subject of alliteration, back in Chapter 5, but it bears repeating the information here as well. The adjective סֹעָה *soʿa* 'sweeping' represents the only attestation of the root ס-ע-ה *s-ʿ-h* in the Bible. It has been employed here *alliterationis causa*, as a match for the *samekh-ʿayin* combination in the following word, the more familiar noun סַעַר *saʿar* 'storm, tempest'. In addition, note how the first member of this three-word phrase adds to the aural effect, with מֵרוּחַ סֹעָה מִסָּעַר *me-ruaḥ soʿa mis-saʿar* producing not only /s/–/ʿ/ combinations but also /m/–/r/ sounds in two of the three words.

16. Psalm 120:5

אוֹיָה־לִי כִּי־גַרְתִּי מֶשֶׁךְ
שָׁכַנְתִּי עִם־אָהֳלֵי קֵדָר:

Woe to me, for I reside in Meshekh,
I dwell among the tents of Qedar.

Meshekh and Qedar are two geographical entities known from elsewhere in the Bible. The former is located far to the north, somewhere in Anatolia, to be equated with the Mushki of Assyrian records and the Moschoi of classical sources (for example, Strabo), with the current-day

---

24. The *ḥet* in the word חָרוּץ *ḥaruṣ* 'gold' represents /ḫ/ (cf. Ugaritic *ḫrṣ*, Akkadian *ḫurāṣu*); but to the best of my knowledge, there are no Semitic cognates to the word חוּץ *ḥuṣ* 'outside, street'. For an additional aspect to the use of the word חָרוּץ *ḥaruṣ* 'gold' in this verse, see below, Chapter 25, no. 8.

echo to be found in Moschia/Meskheti, a region of Georgia.[25] The latter is to be associated with the vast desert regions to the south, somewhere in Arabia, to be equated with the Qidri/Qadri of Assyrian records and the Cedrei of classical sources (for example, Pliny).[26]

This information allows us to understand the poet's geography, as he sees himself in exile, far removed from Jerusalem, at the northernmost and southernmost extremes of an ancient Israelite's terrestrial horizons.[27] But clearly there were other ethnic, political, or geographical entities to which the psalmist could have referred. For example, in Gen 10:2, 1 Chr 1:5, and all 5x in Ezekiel (see n. 25), Meshekh is mentioned alongside Tubal, known to us from classical sources (Herodotus et al.) as Tiberani, located along the shore of the Black Sea in modern-day Turkey; while in Gen 25:13, Isa 60:7, and 1 Chr 1:29, Qedar is paired with Nebaioth, a closely related desert tribe. So why does Ps 120:5 use 'Meshekh' and 'Qedar' and not 'Tubal' and 'Nebaioth'? The answer, as the reader of this book no doubt will divine for herself by this point, is the demands of alliteration.

The alliterative matches are the two verbs גַּרְתִּי *garti* 'I reside' and שָׁכַנְתִּי *šakanti* 'I dwell'. The attentive reader, however, will discern that the matches are not perfect, for מֶשֶׁךְ *mɛšɛk* 'Meshekh' of the a-line finds its mate with the latter verb, which is found in the b-line, while קֵדָר *qedar* 'Qedar' of the b-line finds its mate with the former verb, found in the a-line. For the former aural effect, note the correspondences between the three consonants of the first toponym, /m/–/š/–/k/, and the three root letters of the verb שׁ-כ-ן *š-k-n* 'dwell'; two are exact, while the consonants comprising the third pair are both nasal sounds. For the latter aural effect, note the correspondence between the three consonants of the second toponym, /q/–/d/–/r/, and the first three consonants in the verbal form גַּרְתִּי *garti* 'I reside', namely, /g/–/r/–/t/; the imperfect

---

25. For other mentions of Meshekh in the Bible, see Gen 10:2, Ezek 27:13, 32:26, 38:2, 38:3, 39:1, 1 Chr 1:5, 1:17.

26. For other mentions of Qedar in the Bible, see Gen 25:13, Isa 21:16, 21:17, 42:11, 60:7, Jer 2:10, 49:28, Ezek 27:21, Song 1:5, 1 Chr 1:29.

27. Note that in Jer 2:10, Qedar is paired with the islands of the Kittim, located in the Mediterranean, to once more evoke the extremes of geographical horizons, in this case, from the far west to the far southeast, apparently.

matches work fine, since /q/ and /g/ are both velars, while /d/ and /t/ are voiced and voiceless counterparts of the same dental sound.

The effect is clear, though the question remains: Why not match the geographical entity with its alliterative verbal form in the same stich? Why switch them up in this fashion? I would propose that the spread across two lines creates the effect of the geographical spread of the exile, real or imagined, in the poet's mind. The distance reaches from Meshekh to Qedar, and the alliterative words must reach similarly to find their mates.

There is one more item to mention, though, for another alliteration operates across the stichs. The verse begins with אוֹיָה לִי *'oya li* 'woe is me', whose sounds resonate in אָהֳלֵי *'ahole* 'tents of' in the second stich. In short, all the major elements (that is, save the particles כִּי *ki* 'for, because' and עִם *'im* 'with, among') in this poetic verse find their alliterative mates in the matching stich.

This seems to me to be the apposite place to quote the famous line of Vladimir Nabokov. Most readers know him as one of the most important modernist writers of the twentieth century, though in scientific circles he is equally famous for his contributions to lepidoptery, the study of moths and butterflies. When once asked what enthralls him in his two very dissimilar disciplines, Nabokov responded, "the beauty of science and the precision of poetry."[28] In light of the structure of Ps 120:5, elaborated above, and many other such passages treated in the present tome, one understands this remark all the more.

17. Psalms 120:7; 121:1, 3

אֲנִי־שָׁלוֹם וְכִי אֲדַבֵּר הֵמָּה לַמִּלְחָמָה: [7]

שִׁיר לַמַּעֲלוֹת אֶשָּׂא עֵינַי אֶל־הֶהָרִים מֵאַיִן יָבֹא עֶזְרִי: [1]

---

28. I must admit that I have not been able to locate these exact words attributed to Nabokov, but such was the lore at Cornell University, at which institution both Nabokov (1948–1959) and the present author taught (1986–2004). And while we naturally did not overlap, the long shadow of the former's distinguished career was still very much present during my years in Ithaca, NY. For similar expressions attributed to Nabokov, to wit, "the passion of science and the patience of poetry" and "the precision of poetry and the excitement of pure science," see Bruno Osimo, "Nabokov's Selftranslations: Interpretation Problems and Solutions in Lolita's Russian Version," *Sign Systems Studies* 27 (1999): 215–33.

----

³ אַל־יִתֵּן לַמּוֹט רַגְלֶךָ אַל־יָנוּם שֹׁמְרֶךָ:

⁷ I am (for) peace;
But when I speak, they are for war.
¹ A Song for Ascents.
I lift-up my eyes to the mountains,
From where will my help come?

----

³ He will not let your foot give-way,
Your guardian will not slumber.

While I have provided translations for these verses, their meanings are not the point. Rather, our attention is drawn to the superscription to Psalm 121, namely, שִׁיר לַמַּעֲלוֹת *šir lam-maʿalot* 'a song for ascents'. In all of the fourteen remaining psalms of this collection (Psalms 120–134), the superscription is always שִׁיר הַמַּעֲלוֹת *šir ham-maʿalot* 'a song of ascents' (120:1, 122:1, 123:1, etc., through 134:1). Why the peculiarity in Ps 121:1, with the preposition -לְ *l-* 'to, for'? On the one hand, the purpose may be simply to vary the monotony of the repeated verbatim superscription. However, as we saw in our chapters on repetition with variation, typically we encounter several variations on a theme, not simply one instance among fifteen. And if only one instance of varied language, why in the second slot? Why not further on in the litany of Ascents psalms?

The answer, it seems to me, lies in the preceding word, which in this case is the last word of Psalm 120, to wit, לַמִּלְחָמָה *lam-milḥama* 'for war' in Ps 120:7. We note at the head of these two words the same chain of sounds: *lamed* (/l/) with *pataḥ* vowel (/a/), followed by *mem* with *dageš*, that is to say, double /mm/. Which is to say, the reader goes from לַמִּלְחָמָה *lam-milḥama* 'for war' in Ps 120:7 to לַמַּעֲלוֹת *lam-maʿalot* 'for ascents' in Ps 121:1—and then two verses later the reader encounters לַמּוֹט *lam-moṭ* 'to give-way'. Strikingly, this exact concatenation of sounds, to wit, *lamm-*, will not be repeated anywhere else in the entire collection (be it an anthology of disconnected poems or an intentional assemblage from the pen of a single poet). They cluster right here, at the bridge between Psalms 120 and 121, thereby supplying the reason for the variant לַמַּעֲלוֹת lam-maʿalot 'for ascents' at precisely this spot, Ps 121:1.[29]

Finally, note that I happily follow the lead of the NJPS, which uses 'a song of ascents' for the fourteen poems introduced with the standard formulation, but 'a song for ascents' at Ps 121:1.

18. Psalm 137:2–3

עַל־עֲרָבִים בְּתוֹכָהּ תָּלִינוּ כִּנֹּרוֹתֵינוּ׃ [2]

כִּי שָׁם שְׁאֵלוּנוּ שׁוֹבֵינוּ דִּבְרֵי־שִׁיר וְתוֹלָלֵינוּ שִׂמְחָה [3]

שִׁירוּ לָנוּ מִשִּׁיר צִיּוֹן׃

[2] On the willows in her [sc. Babylon's] midst,
We hung our lyres.
[3] For there our captors asked us for words of song, and our
draggers (for) joy:
"Sing for us a song of Zion."

The word תוֹלָלֵינוּ tolalenu 'our draggers' (v. 3) is a *hapax legomenon*, whose exact meaning generally has eluded scholars. The proper solution was proffered by Alfred Guillaume, who called attention to the fact that the same root *t-l-l* means 'bind and drag away' in Arabic (4th form).[30] Additional support is forthcoming from Jibbali (a Semitic language spoken in Oman), where the verb *t-l-l* means 'drag a train behind one'.[31] But why, we may ask, did the author of this famous psalm select such a rare verb, especially when a more common synonym exists in the language, to wit, the root ס-ח-ב *s-ḥ-b* 'drag' (attested 5x in the Bible)? The answer, naturally, lies within the domain of alliteration,

---

29. I will admit to a slight fudge here, since the word אֲלַמְּדֵם *ʾalammədem* 'I will teach them' occurs in Ps 132:12. Note that this form also includes -*lamm*-, but the sounds appear in the inner portion of this word, not at the start, and the *lamed* here functions as part of the verbal root ל-מ-ד *l-m-d* 'teach', and not as its own morpheme, viz., the preposition 'to, for'.

30. Alfred Guillaume, "The Meaning of תולל in Psalm 137:3," *Journal of Biblical Literature* 75 (1956): 143–44.

31. T. M. Johnstone, *Jibbāli Lexicon* (Oxford: Oxford University Press, 1981), 270.

with תּוֹלָלֵינוּ *tolalenu* 'our draggers' echoing the sounds of the verb תְּלִינוּ *talinu* 'we hung' in the previous verse.[32]

19. Psalm 146:3–4

3 אַל־תִּבְטְחוּ בִנְדִיבִים בְּבֶן־אָדָם | שֶׁאֵין לוֹ תְשׁוּעָה:

4 תֵּצֵא רוּחוֹ יָשֻׁב לְאַדְמָתוֹ בַּיּוֹם הַהוּא אָבְדוּ עֶשְׁתֹּנֹתָיו:

³ Do not trust in nobles;
In a human being, for in him there is no salvation.
⁴ His breath departs, he returns to his humus,
On that day his devisings perish.

Hebrew has two words for 'salvation', used virtually interchangeably: יְשׁוּעָה *yəšuʿa* and תְּשׁוּעָה *təšuʿa* (attested 78 and 34 times, respectively). The latter is employed in Ps 146:3, in anticipation of the rare noun עֶשְׁתֹּנֹתָיו *ʿeštonotaw* 'his devisings' (v. 4). (See Job 12:5 for a byform of the noun, and Jonah 1:6 for the verbal root ע-שׁ-ת *ʿ-š-t* 'devise'.) Note the presence of the same three consonants in the two words, /t/–/š/–/ʿ/ ~ /ʿ/–/š/–/t/.

As to the presence of the word 'humus' in my translation, note my attempt to capture the relationship between Hebrew אָדָם *ʾadam* 'human' (v. 3) and אֲדָמָה *ʾadama* 'soil, earth, ground, humus' (v. 4). Fortunately for the translator, both Hebrew and Latin (and hence English) share the association between the two words, based on the widespread belief that humans are created from the soil/humus, as embodied most famously in Genesis 2.[33]

---

32. See Gary A. Rendsburg and Susan L. Rendsburg, "Physiological and Philological Notes to Psalm 137," *Jewish Quarterly Review* 83 (1993): 385–99, esp. 396–99.

33. See Saul Levin, "Homo : Humus and the Semitic Counterparts: The Oldest Culturally Significant Etymology?" in J. Peter Maher, Allan R. Bomhard, and E. F. K. Koerner, eds., *Papers from the Third International Conference on Historical Linguistics, Hamburg, August 22–26 1977* (Amsterdam: John Benjamins, 1982), 207–16.

20. Proverbs 23:2

וְשַׂמְתָּ שַׂכִּין בְּלֹעֶךָ אִם־בַּעַל נֶפֶשׁ אָתָּה:

And you shall put a knife in your gullet,
If you are a 'lord of appetite'.

One of the features of proverbial sayings in most of the world's languages is the use of soundplay (rhyme, assonance, alliteration, etc.).
Consider, for example, such English examples as 'forgive and forget',
'practice makes perfect', and 'a stitch in time saves nine' (it also saves
eight or ten stitches, but 'nine' produces the proper semi-rhyme with
'time'), or the much more complicated saying 'many a mickle makes
a muckle' (with 'mickle' bearing its Scots-English meaning 'little').

One will not be surprised, accordingly, to learn that two monographs written during the twentieth century focus on alliteration in the
book of Proverbs alone, with scores of examples provided by the two
authors, Gustav Boström and Thomas P. McCreesh.[34] Given the major
coverage of the topic available in the two studies, I content myself here
with but two examples.[35]

In the first illustration (see above), the noun לֹעַ *loaʿ* 'gullet' is yet
another *hapax legomenon* invoked for alliterative purpose—hence my
rendering 'gullet', instead of 'throat', which I would reserve for the
common Hebrew noun גָּרוֹן *garon*, attested 8x in the Bible. In this sole
attestation of לֹעַ *loaʿ* 'gullet' in the Bible, the word is introduced by the
prefix -בְּ *bə-* 'in', thereby producing the string of consonants /b/–/l/–/ʿ/.
Two words later comes the common Hebrew noun בַּעַל *baʿal* 'lord,
master', as the first component in the idiom בַּעַל נֶפֶשׁ *baʿal nɛpɛš* 'lord
of appetite', that is, someone with a healthy appetite—with the three
consonants /b/–/ʿ/–/l/ in anagrammatic fashion.

---

34. Gustav Boström, *Paronomasi i den äldre hebreiska maschallitteraturen*
(Lund: C. W. K. Gleerup, 1928); and Thomas P. McCreesh, *Biblical Sound and
Sense: Poetic Sound Patterns in Proverbs 10–29* (Journal for the Study of the Old
Testament Supplement Series 128; Sheffield: JSOT Press, 1991).

35. For further instances, see Rendsburg, "Literary and Linguistic Matters
in the Book of Proverbs," 113–17.

21. Proverbs 25:26

מַעְיָן נִרְפָּשׂ וּמָקוֹר מָשְׁחָת צַדִּיק מָט לִפְנֵי־רָשָׁע:

(Like) a muddied spring and a ruined water-source,
A righteous-man totters before a wicked-one.

The rare word in this proverb is נִרְפָּשׂ *nirpaś* 'muddied', a Niphʿal (passive) form from the root ר-פ-שׂ *r-p-ś* 'befoul, muddy'. The root generates only one other word in Biblical Hebrew, namely, מִרְפָּשׂ *mirpaś* 'that which has been muddied', found in Ezek 34:19.[36] The author of the proverb deftly placed נִרְפָּשׂ *nirpaś* 'muddied' near the beginning of the verse, with the alliterative phrase לִפְנֵי־רָשָׁע *lipne rašaʿ* 'before a wicked-one' as balance at the end of the verse. The four consonants at the center of this two-word phrase are /p/–/n/–/r/–/š/, a nearly identical match to /n/–/r/–/p/–/ś/ present in נִרְפָּשׂ *nirpaś* 'muddied'.

22. Job 26:13

בְּרוּחוֹ שָׁמַיִם שִׁפְרָה חֹלְלָה יָדוֹ נָחָשׁ בָּרִיחַ:

With his wind the heavens were calmed,
His hand pierced the evil serpent.

The expression נָחָשׁ בָּרִיחַ *naḥaš bariaḥ* 'evil serpent' was discussed above at Isa 27:1 (Chapter 16, no. 7). In its only other occurrence in the Bible, presented here, once more we observe the use of alliteration.[37]

---

36. Incidentally, in Ezek 34:19 the noun מִרְפָּשׂ *mirpaś* 'that which has been muddied' follows closely upon מִרְמַס *mirmas* 'that which has been trodden', creating both alliteration and assonance, indeed something akin to rhyme, given the same morphological structure of these two nouns.

37. I owe this example to Jonathan G. Kline, *Allusive Soundplay in the Hebrew Bible* (SBL Ancient Israel and Its Literature 28; Atlanta: SBL Press, 2016), 39–40. I take the opportunity to note that this recently published book is based on the author's doctoral thesis, "Transforming the Tradition: Soundplay as an Interpretive Device in Innerbiblical Allusions" (PhD dissertation, Harvard University, 2014), for it was my privilege both to teach Dr. Kline as an undergraduate student at Cornell University and then to serve on his doctoral committee at Harvard University. See further in the Acknowledgments to the present volume.

The verse opens with בְּרוּחוֹ *bə-ruḥo* 'with his wind', providing the same consonantal string /b/–/r/–/ḥ/ as occurs in the rare word בְּרִיחַ *bariaḥ* 'evil', which follows.[38] It goes without saying that the brilliant poetry of the book of Job is filled with examples of rare words, locutions, and the like, with wordplays and soundplays throughout.[39] We content ourselves here with but one example from among many.

23. Song 4:4

כְּמִגְדַּל דָּוִיד צַוָּארֵךְ בָּנוּי לְתַלְפִּיּוֹת
אֶלֶף הַמָּגֵן תָּלוּי עָלָיו כֹּל שִׁלְטֵי הַגִּבּוֹרִים:

As the tower of David is your neck, built to the heights;
A thousand shields hang upon it, all the weapons of the heroes.

As Scott Noegel and I demonstrated in our co-authored monograph devoted to the Song of Songs, there are literally dozens of instances of alliterative verse within the eight chapters of that exquisite poetic book. Since that territory has been well covered, I will limit myself herein to just a few stellar examples, beginning with the present instance.

The word תַלְפִּיּוֹת *talpiyyot* 'heights', yet another *hapax legomenon* within the biblical corpus, strikes the reader/listener as wholly exceptional. One might expect a noun derived from the more common roots relating to 'height, elevation, etc.', such as ג-ב-ה *g-b-h*, ר-ו-ם *r-w-m*, and ס-ל-ל *s-l-l*. Instead, we encounter the noun תַלְפִּיּוֹת *talpiyyot* 'heights', from whose morphology we may deduce the root ל-פ-ה *l-p-h* (ל-פ-י *l-p-y*). This very root, in the form of the verb *l-f-y*, occurs in Mehri and Jibbali (two South Arabian languages) with the meaning 'be able to climb easily (as, for example, a ladder or a mountain)'.[40] Which is

---

38. Once more, as we learn from Ugaritic *rḥ* 'wind' and *brḥ* 'evil', the *ḥet* in these two words represents the same phoneme, the pharyngeal fricative /ḥ/; hence the sound correspondence is exact and not an approximation.

39. See the many studies by Edward L. Greenstein, of which I cite here but one: "The Language of Job and Its Poetic Function," *Journal of Biblical Literature* 122 (2003): 651–66.

40. Johnstone, *Jibbāli Lexicon*, 160; and T. M. Johnstone, *Mehri Lexicon* (London: School of Oriental and African Studies, 1987), 251–52. For the verb in actual use, see Aaron D. Rubin, *Omani Mehri: A New Grammar with Texts* (Studies in Semitic Languages and Linguistics 93; Leiden: Brill, 2018), 694 (text

to say, a good Semitic cognate allows us to uncover the true meaning of the Hebrew noun תַּלְפִּיּוֹת *talpiyyot* 'heights', a word that generally confounded Hebraists throughout the centuries.

Why, however, did our poet reach deep into the Hebrew lexicon to pluck this rare noun? Once more the answer is attributable to the alliterative effect, with the key sounds of תַּלְפִּיּוֹת *talpiyyot* 'heights' echoed in two of the three following words: first אֶלֶף *'elep* 'thousand' and then תָּלוּי *taluy* 'hang'. Note how the first captures the /l/ and /p/ of the key noun, while the latter rehearses the /t/ and /l/ sounds.[41]

24. Song 5:3, 5

³ פָּשַׁטְתִּי אֶת־כֻּתָּנְתִּי אֵיכָכָה אֶלְבָּשֶׁנָּה
רָחַצְתִּי אֶת־רַגְלַי אֵיכָכָה אֲטַנְּפֵם:

----

⁵ קַמְתִּי אֲנִי לִפְתֹּחַ לְדוֹדִי וְיָדַי נָטְפוּ־מֹור
וְאֶצְבְּעֹתַי מֹור עֹבֵר עַל כַּפּוֹת הַמַּנְעוּל:

³ I have removed my tunic, how shall I put it on?
I have washed my feet, how shall I soil them?

----

⁵ I arose to open for my beloved; and my hands dripped myrrh,
And my fingers flowing myrrh, on the handles of the latch.

Yet another *hapax legomenon* appears in this selection, as the extraordinary poet who produced these lines elected to use the word אֲטַנְּפֵם *'aṭannəpem* 'how shall I soil them' (v. 3), from the root ט-נ-ף *ṭ-n-p* 'soil, begrime', within the context of the female lover's dream sequence (5:2–6). The attentive listener understands that she has encountered an unusual lexical item, but the reason for its presence in the stanza is

---

77, paragraph 1), with the form *əwfōh* 'climb'. For the shift of /l/ to /w/, under certain phonological conditions (as here), see 28–30.

41. For a more extended treatment, see Gary A. Rendsburg, "תַּלְפִּיּוֹת (Song 4:4)," *Journal of Northwest Semitic Languages* 20 (1994): 13–19.

revealed only two verses later, when the poet employs the anagrammatic root ף-ט-נ *n-ṭ-p* 'flow, drip' in the word נָטְפוּ *naṭpu* 'flowing' (v. 5).[42]

25. Lamentations 1:21

נֶאֱנָחָה אָנִי אֵין מְנַחֵם לִי

nɛʾɛnaḥa ʾani ʾen mənaḥem li

I groan, there is none to comfort me.

One does not have to be a master Hebraist to appreciate the striking
alliteration here,[43] even as the message of the verse is filled with anguish.
Note that the two key verbal roots, ח-נ-א *ʾ-n-ḥ* 'groan' and ם-ח-נ *n-ḥ-m*
'comfort', which are collocated only here in the Bible, share two root
letters, /n/ and /ḥ/.[44] To enhance the soundplay, the /ʾ/-/n/ combination
in נֶאֱנָחָה *nɛʾɛnaḥa* 'groan' is echoed in the two shorter words that follow: אָנִי *ʾani* 'I' and אֵין *ʾen* 'there is none'.

---

42. For more on this passage, see below, Chapter 17, no. 17.

43. For this passage, see also Kline, *Allusive Soundplay in the Hebrew
Bible*, 24 n. 71.

44. Even if the phonological match is not perfect, since the *ḥet* of ח-נ-א
ʾ-n-ḥ 'groan' reflects the velar fricative /ḫ/ (cf. Ugaritic *ʾnḫ* 'moan, groan, be
wretched'; Akkadian *anāḫu* 'toil, exert, moan'); while the *ḥet* of ם-ח-נ *n-ḥ-m*
'comfort' reflects the laryngeal fricative /ḥ/ (cf. the Ugaritic personal names
mnḥm and *ynḥm*).

CHAPTER SEVENTEEN

WORDPLAY

We have already identified three instances of wordplay in the Bible (see above, in Chapter 10, no. 10, regarding Judg 14:18; Chapter 10, no. 17, regarding 2 Sam 13:9; and Chapter 13, no. 24, regarding Ps 135:17), each time noting that the subject would be treated more fully in a chapter devoted to it. We now have reached that point, with this chapter presenting a representative sampling of passages in the Bible that evoke wordplay. By the term 'wordplay', I refer to polysemy, double meaning, *double entendre*, and the like—with a single word carrying two connotations simultaneously.

As has been the case on other occasions in this book, before presenting examples from ancient Hebrew texts it may be helpful to consider famous instances of wordplay in English compositions. Moreover, as I have done elsewhere herein, there is no better writer to consider than the master Shakespeare. Fine examples of wordplay in his plays include: (a) the twofold meaning of 'grave' in *Romeo and Juliet*, Act III, Scene 1, in Mercutio's dying words, 'ask for me to-morrow, and you shall find me a grave man' (in the senses of both 'serious' and 'buried'); and (b) the *double entendre* with 'conceive' during the exchange between the Earl of Kent and the Earl of Gloucester in *King Lear*, Act 1, Scene 1 (with the meanings 'comprehend' and 'produce a child').

To cite examples from an American author, I again turn to Henry David Thoreau's *Walden*: (a) "the boat, after passing from hand to hand, has gone down the stream of time" (with 'stream' used metaphorically, though continuing the imagery of the boat); (b) "It is well to have some water in your neighborhood. . . . One value even of the smallest well is . . ." (with both meanings of 'well' present); and (c) the interplay of 'perch' (the fish), 'perch' (a place from which to view), and 'perchance' (admittedly a favorite word of Thoreau's) in the chapter entitled "The Ponds."[1]

And with that as a brief introduction, we turn now to the use of wordplay in the Bible. This chapter presents a rather eclectic collection of examples; taken together they serve to illustrate the various types of wordplay that may be found in the biblical text.[2] More standard surveys of wordplay in the Bible may be found conveniently in the standard reference works.[3]

1. Job 7:6

יָמַי קַלּוּ מִנִּי־אָרֶג וַיִּכְלוּ בְּאֶפֶס תִּקְוָה:

My days pass faster than a weaver's-shuttle,
And come-to-an-end without hope / thread (*tiqwa*).

Our attention in this volume typically has been directed toward passages from the biblical prose corpus, which is (a) more familiar to most readers, and (b) easier to comprehend than the Bible's poetry. In the current chapter, by contrast, slightly more than half of our examples, including the first four, appear in the poetic corpus. And while no one to my knowledge has produced a quantitative study to demonstrate the point, my sense, gained through the experience of reading, is that wordplay is more common in poetry than in prose (think Shakespeare, for example). To make matters worse perhaps, I elect to begin this

---

1. I again cite from the Penguin Classics edition of Thoreau, *Walden and Civil Disobedience*, with the first two citations found on pp. 129 and 131, respectively, and with the third example to be seen most prominently on p. 234, especially with the phrase "from my distant perch" following shortly after the word 'piscine' earlier in the sentence.

2. This chapter represents a reworking of my earlier study: Gary A. Rendsburg, "Word Play in Biblical Hebrew: An Eclectic Collection," in Scott B. Noegel, ed., *Puns and Pundits: Word Play in the Bible and in Near Eastern Literature* (Bethesda, MD: CDL, 2000), 137–62.

3. For general surveys see Jack M. Sasson, "Wordplay in the OT," in Keith R. Crim, ed., *The Interpreter's Dictionary of the Bible, Supplementary Volume* (Nashville: Abingdon, 1976), 968–70; and Edward L. Greenstein, "Wordplay, Hebrew," in David Noel Freedman, ed., *The Anchor Bible Dictionary* (New York: Doubleday, 1992), 6:968–71.

chapter with not only any poetic verse, but one from the book of Job, clearly the most difficult composition in the corpus. Fortunately, the verse is an easy one to comprehend, and it illustrates the technique of wordplay simply and elegantly.

As he does through much of his long speeches in the book, Job bemoans his losses, often reaching a point of desperation. The verse reproduced here is a case in point, as Job sees his days fleeting without hope. The comparison is to the speed at which a weaver's shuttle moves, that is, in an exceedingly fast way in the hands of a gifted artisan. The two ideas converge in the final portion of the poetic verse, with the word תִּקְוָה *tiqwa*, whose typical meaning is 'hope' (Ruth 1:12, Ps 9:19, etc.), but which can also mean 'thread' (Josh 2:18, 2:21). In Job's mind, his *hope* is running out, just as the spool of *thread* on a loom expires in time. The result is literary artistry at its best.[4]

2. Song 2:12

הַנִּצָּנִים נִרְאוּ בָאָרֶץ עֵת הַזָּמִיר הִגִּיעַ וְקוֹל הַתּוֹר נִשְׁמַע בְּאַרְצֵנוּ:

The blossoms appear in the land,
The time of pruning / song (*zamir*) has arrived,
And the voice of the turtledove is heard in our land.

Since we began with poetry, let us continue with a few more poetic passages that exhibit wordplay. For years scholars debated the meaning of the word זָמִיר *zamir* in the middle of this verse—for while the word typically means 'song' (see 2 Sam 23:1, Isa 25:5, Ps 95:2, etc.), the same three root letters, ז-מ-ר *z-m-r*, mean 'prune' (Lev 25:3–4), in addition to which note the related noun מַזְמֵרוֹת *mazmerot* 'pruning-hooks' (Isa 2:4, Mic 4:3, etc.). As we shall see, both meanings fit the context of Song 2:12.

Before proceeding, however, we need to provide some basic information about ancient Hebrew poetry. The number one characteristic of

---

4. For more on this verse, see Scott B. Noegel, *Janus Parallelism in the Book of Job* (Journal for the Study of the Old Testament Supplement Series 223; Sheffield: Sheffield Academic Press, 1996), 50–52; and Edward L. Greenstein, "Some Metaphors in the Poetry of Job," in Maxine L. Grossman, ed., *Built by Wisdom, Established by Understanding: Essays on Biblical and Near Eastern Literature in Honor of Adele Berlin* (Bethesda: University Press of Maryland, 2013), 186–87.

ancient Hebrew (and Semitic in general) poetry is parallelism—that is, two lines (or stichs, to use the scholarly parlance) that in essence state and restate the same idea, though typically with the a-line providing the basic declaration and the b-line delivering emphasis of some sort. To use the shorthand description: A, what's more B.[5]

To illustrate this technique, we present but one out of literally hundreds, nay, thousands, of biblical verses that could serve as a paradigm example. Our example is the preceding verse in Song of Songs:

Song 2:11

כִּי־הִנֵּה [הסתו] הַסְּתָיו* עָבָר הַגֶּשֶׁם חָלַף הָלַךְ לוֹ:

For behold, the winter has passed,
The rains have ceased and departed.

The first line of this verse, what scholars call 2:11a, states the point in the most basic of terms, to wit, the winter has passed. The second line, that is, 2:11b, restates this notion, but it is more specific by mentioning the cessation of rain. Moreover, the a-line uses a basic Hebrew verb, ע-ב-ר ʿ-b-r 'pass' (used more than 500x in the Bible), while the b-line introduces a much rarer synonym, ח-ל-ף ḥ-l-p 'pass, pass on, cease' (attested 28x in the Bible). Through such devices, the parallelism evokes the "A, what's more B" process.

With this brief digression into the workings of parallelism, we return now to our analysis of Song 2:12. The problem here is obvious: this verse includes three stichs, not two. On the one hand, if the key word זָמִיר zamir in the b-line means 'song', then it nicely parallels 'the voice of the turtledove' in the c-line; but this would leave the reference to the blossoms in the a-line dangling without an appropriate parallel. On the other hand, if זָמִיר zamir means 'pruning', or better 'pruning-season',[6] this would create a nice correspondence between the a- and

---

5. See James Kugel, *The Idea of Biblical Poetry* (New Haven: Yale University Press, 1981), 1–58, including the chapter subtitle, "A is so, and *what's more*, B" (with the most succinct statement to be found on p. 8); and Robert Alter, *The Art of Biblical Poetry*, 2nd ed. (New York: Basic Books, 2011), 1–28, with the crisp locution on p. 11: "the assertion of *a fortiori*, 'how much more so'."

6. Note that the *qatīl* formation is used in Hebrew for words referring to agricultural work and seasons, such as קָצִיר *qaṣir* 'harvest', חָרִישׁ *ḥariš*

b-lines (blossoms / pruning), but then this would leave the c-line with its reference to song dangling without an appropriate semantic match.

The solution, of course, is to see *both* connotations inherent in זָמִיר *zamir*, as I have indicated in my translation of the b-line above 'the time of pruning / song has arrived'. There is more, though. Note how the meaning 'pruning' looks back to the a-line (with its key noun 'blossoms'), while the meaning 'song' looks ahead to the c-line (with its key phrase 'the voice of the turtledove')—so that the b-line generally and the key word זָמִיר *zamir* 'pruning / song' in particular generates the Janus effect. Hence we call this specific technique 'Janus parallelism', a term coined by my late teacher Cyrus H. Gordon, after the two-faced Roman god, who looks to both the past and the present (the month name 'January', at the turn of the new year, is based on his name).[7]

3. Genesis 15:1

אַל־תִּירָא אַבְרָם אָנֹכִי מָגֵן לָךְ שְׂכָרְךָ הַרְבֵּה מְאֹד:

Do not be afraid, Abram,
I am your shield / benefactor (*magen*),
Your reward shall be very great.

'plowing', אָבִיב *'abib* 'budding' (> 'spring'), אָסִיף *'asip* 'ingathering', and בָּצִיר *baṣir* 'vintage'. See also Chapter 10, p. 188, n. 3.

7. Cyrus H. Gordon, "New Directions," *Bulletin of the American Society of Papyrologists* 15 (1978): 59–60 (in the section entitled "Janus Parallelism"). And now a personal recollection: I was a graduate student in Professor Gordon's Song of Songs seminar in 1977 when we read this passage, as we worked our way through this exquisite book of love poetry, verse by verse. When we reached Song 2:12, and the students and teacher pondered which meaning fits better, 'song' or 'pruning', at that very moment, in that very place, Gordon suggested that both meanings are operative, in simultaneous fashion—as no doubt was originally intended by the poet in his word choice. It was either on that occasion or at the next class session when he suggested that we call this device 'Janus parallelism', at which point he composed the short note referenced above. I relate this story to my own students now, with the following quip: It was like being present in the laboratory at the very moment in 1953 when James Watson and Francis Crick discovered the molecular structure of deoxyribonucleic acid (DNA)—even if the microbiological discovery has had more far-reaching implications for humanity!

In the wake of Cyrus Gordon's discovery of Janus parallelism in Song 2:12 (see above, no. 2), I set about to identify other examples of this literary device in the Bible. After all, as my teacher used to say, if you see one sparrow in the woods, you can be fairly certain that there is another sparrow in the woods. My search yielded several examples, one of which I present here.

Once more we have a poetic line (embedded into the prose narrative of Genesis), a short speech by God to Abram that is divided into three stichs. The key word is מָגֵן *magen* in the second stich, which typically means 'shield' in Hebrew, a denotation that fits perfectly as a response to God's declaration in the first stich that Abram should not fear. But this leaves the third and final stich dangling by itself, with the phrase 'your reward shall be very great' unconnected. The solution to this problem arises when one realizes that the Hebrew verbal root מ-ג-ן *m-g-n* means 'grant, bestow'. In fact, this very verb is still present in the reader's memory, since it appears slightly earlier, in Gen 14:20. This verb, incidentally, is rare in the Bible, occurring elsewhere only in Hos 11:8 and Prov 4:9—so that its presence in Gen 14:20 is rather striking, serving to set the stage for the use of מ-ג-ן *m-g-n* as 'grant, bestow' in Gen 15:1 (among other reasons).

Given the two meanings inherent in this key word, the reader appreciates the Janus effect. With the meaning 'shield', the noun מָגֵן *magen* in the b-line looks back to the message delivered in the a-line; while with the meaning 'grant, bestow', the term looks ahead to the c-line with the promise of reward.

Admittedly, there is a slight problem here, since the Masoretic form of the word מָגֵן *magen* is not the expected form of 'benefactor' (per my translation above). Not that such a form is impossible, for it would equal what scholars call the stative form of the verb, but such forms are typically reserved to express states, such as זָקֵן *zaqen* 'old', מָלֵא *male'* 'full', רָעֵב *ra'eb* 'hungry', etc. The expected form here would be an active participle such as מֹגֵן* *mogen* or the *nomen agentis* form מַגָּן* *maggan*. The solution is to assume that the author intentionally wrote מגן MGN (with no vowels, of course), and that the oral reading tradition allowed both מָגֵן *magen* 'shield' and one of the other proposed forms, however the presenter of this text decided to declaim the word for his listeners. Regardless, the intentional use of a single word (at least in written form) with two meanings, both appropriate to the context, provides another illustration of wordplay generally and Janus parallelism specifically in the biblical text.[8]

4. Psalm 137:5–6

5 אִם־אֶשְׁכָּחֵךְ יְרוּשָׁלִָם תִּשְׁכַּח יְמִינִי:

6 תִּדְבַּק־לְשׁוֹנִי | לְחִכִּי אִם־לֹא אֶזְכְּרֵכִי

אִם־לֹא אַעֲלֶה אֶת־יְרוּשָׁלִַם עַל רֹאשׁ שִׂמְחָתִי:

5 If I forget (š-k-ḥ) you, O Jerusalem, may my right-hand be paralyzed (š-k-ḥ),

6 May my tongue cleave to my palate, if I do not remember you,
If I do not elevate Jerusalem over my chiefest joy.

We remain with poetry still, though we now consider other types of wordplay, not Janus parallelism per se. In this well-known verse (v. 5), the root שׁ-כ-ח š-k-ḥ occurs twice, with two different meanings. In the first case, it bears its common meaning, 'forget', while in the second instance, it bears a much rarer connotation, 'be paralyzed'. In fact, the latter constitutes the only attestation of this verb in the Bible, though it is better known in Arabic, as the root k-s-ḥ 'lame, crippled, paralyzed'.[9] The composer of Psalm 137 took advantage of the two meanings of the

---

8. In the rest of this chapter, I move to consider other types of wordplay. For more examples of Janus parallelism, see Noegel, *Janus Parallelism in the Book of Job*; Shalom M. Paul, "Polysensuous Polyvalency in Poetic Parallelisms," in Michael Fishbane and Emanuel Tov, eds., *"Shaʿarei Talmon": Studies in the Bible, Qumran, and the Ancient Near East Presented to Shemaryahu Talmon* (Winona Lake, IN: Eisenbrauns, 1992), 147–63; and Shalom M. Paul, "Polysemous Pivotal Punctuation: More Janus Double Entendres," in Michael V. Fox et al., eds., *Texts, Temples, and Traditions: A Tribute to Menahem Haran* (Winona Lake, IN: Eisenbrauns, 1996), 369–74.

9. As first suggested by Israel Eitan, "An Identification of *tiškaḥ yĕmīnī*, Ps 137:5," *Journal of Biblical Literature* 47 (1928): 193–95. See also James Barr, *Comparative Philology and the Text of the Old Testament* (Oxford: Clarendon Press, 1968), 336. The alert reader will realize that the order of the consonants in the cognate verbs Arabic k-s-ḥ and Hebrew שׁ-כ-ח š-k-ḥ do not match. One will assume, accordingly, a metathesis of consonants, perhaps due to attraction by the more common homonym שׁ-כ-ח š-k-ḥ 'forget'.

same Hebrew root ש-כ-ח *š-k-ḥ*, 'forget' and 'be paralyzed', and placed them in close proximity to each other, thereby producing an exquisite wordplay.

There is more, however. The paralysis of the right hand mentioned in v. 5 is coupled with the loss of speech in v. 6 'may my tongue cleave to my palate', suggesting a type of aphasia or apraxia. Taken together, these two symptoms (loss of right hand and loss of speech) suggest a cerebrovascular accident (stroke) in the left side of the brain, which both serves as the center of speech and controls the nerves and muscles on the right side of the body. In short, the psalmist, who lived in Babylonian exile (see v. 1 especially), declaims that should he forget Jerusalem, may he be stricken with a stroke.[10]

5. Genesis 39:6, 9

⁶ וַיַּעֲזֹב כָּל־אֲשֶׁר־לוֹ בְּיַד־יוֹסֵף וְלֹא־יָדַע אִתּוֹ מְאוּמָה כִּי אִם־הַלֶּחֶם
אֲשֶׁר־הוּא אוֹכֵל וַיְהִי יוֹסֵף יְפֵה־תֹאַר וִיפֵה מַרְאֶה׃

----

⁹ אֵינֶנּוּ גָדוֹל בַּבַּיִת הַזֶּה מִמֶּנִּי וְלֹא־חָשַׂךְ מִמֶּנִּי מְאוּמָה כִּי אִם־אוֹתָךְ
בַּאֲשֶׁר אַתְּ־אִשְׁתּוֹ וְאֵיךְ אֶעֱשֶׂה הָרָעָה הַגְּדֹלָה הַזֹּאת וְחָטָאתִי לֵאלֹהִים׃

⁶ And he left all that was his in the hand of Joseph, and he
did not know aught with him, except for the bread (*lɛhɛm*)
that he ate; and Joseph was handsome of form and handsome
of visage.

----

⁹ "There is no one greater in this house than I, and he has not
withheld from me aught, except for you, because you are his
wife; and how could I do this great evil and sin before God?"

We now segue back from our excursion into poetic material in order to return to an analysis of prose texts, which have provided and will continue to provide the fodder for the great majority of our discussions

---

10. For further details on both the science and the philology, see Rendsburg and Rendsburg, "Physiological and Philological Notes to Psalm 137," 385–92.

in this book. The two passages above, moreover, bring us to a specific type of wordplay, one imbued with sexual innuendo.[11]

In Gen 39:6, the narrator informs us that Potiphar entrusted his entire household to Joseph, כִּי אִם־הַלֶּחֶם אֲשֶׁר־הוּא אוֹכֵל *ki 'im hal-leḥem 'ašer hu' 'okel* 'except for the bread [i.e., food] that he ate'. This suggests a kind of dietary taboo, in which Egyptians would not allow foreigners to prepare their food, no matter how trustworthy an individual foreigner, in this case Joseph, may be. We gain a hint of this later in the narrative, in Gen 43:32, 'And they served him [sc. Joseph, now viceroy of Egypt] by himself, and them [sc. Joseph's brothers] by themselves, and the Egyptians who ate with him by themselves, for the Egyptians could not eat bread [i.e., food] with the Hebrews, for it is an abomination to Egypt'. And while we have no confirmation of such a taboo or practice from the ancient Egyptian records at our disposal, anthropologists can speak to many such habits among the various peoples of the world. In short, the passage in Gen 39:6 makes sense, given the broader picture, including the later reference in Gen 43:32 (whether it be an accurate reflection of matters in ancient times or simply something perceived or invented by the Israelite author).

In the following verses, Potiphar's wife makes sexual advances at Joseph, who resists the temptation and declares as above in v. 9. From Joseph's mouth, however, we learn that Potiphar has placed him in charge of the entire household כִּי אִם־אוֹתָךְ בַּאֲשֶׁר אַתְּ־אִשְׁתּוֹ *ki 'im 'otak ba-'ašer 'att 'išto* 'except for you, because you are his wife'. How can this be? In v. 6 the narrator refers to 'bread', while in v. 9 Joseph refers to Potiphar's wife. Which of these items is not in Joseph's charge?

Clearly, Joseph knows what he is talking about in v. 9, and his words make eminent sense. For while Potiphar entrusted Joseph with everything in the household, in his position as major-domo over the estate, obviously Potiphar would not allow Joseph to have control over his wife, given her position as lady of the house. How to dovetail the two statements?

The answer lies in the fact that לֶחֶם *leḥem* in v. 6 constitutes a *double entendre*: its basic meaning is 'bread, food', but as a metaphor

---

11. The best entrée to the subject remains Edward Ullendorff, "The Bawdy Bible," *Bulletin of the School of Oriental and African Studies* 42 (1979): 425–56.

it means 'wife, woman'. Similarly, the verb א-כ-ל *ʾ-k-l* means both 'eat' and 'engage in sexual intercourse'.[12] The latter may be demonstrated by a look at this verse from the book of Proverbs:

Prov 30:20

כֵּן | דֶּרֶךְ אִשָּׁה מְנָאָפֶת אָכְלָה וּמָחֲתָה פִיהָ וְאָמְרָה לֹא־פָעַלְתִּי אָוֶן:

Such is the way of an adulterous woman: she eats, she
wipes her mouth, and she says, "I have done no wrong."

Quite plainly, the sin of an adulterous woman is not any forbidden food that she might place in her mouth, but rather illicit sexual intercourse. This verse, accordingly, provides for us the prooftext that the verb א-כ-ל *ʾ-k-l* served as a euphemism for 'engage in sexual intercourse'. We also note, by the by, that Hebrew פֶּה *pɛ* 'mouth' was used euphemistically for 'vagina'.

Recognition of the euphemistic meaning of the Hebrew verb א-כ-ל *ʾ-k-l* is not new, for it was known to the rabbis of old already. For a source from the land of Israel, see Bereshit Rabba 86:6;[13] and for a source from Babylonia, see Bavli Ketubbot 65b. The latter text is instructive, as two sages debate whether the phrase in Mishna Ketubbot 5:9 והיא אוכלת עמו *wə-hiʾ ʾokɛlɛt ʿimmo* 'and she eats with him' refers to actual eating (thus R. Nahman) or to sexual intercourse (thus R. Assi). The latter sage, in fact, invoked Prov 30:20 to support his position.[14]

The second relevant lexeme in Gen 39:6 is לֶחֶם *lɛḥɛm* 'bread, food', but also 'wife, woman'. There is no explicit evidence for this

---

12. Compare (chiefly American) English 'eat' in its vulgar usage, as per *OED*, s.v. 'eat' *v.*, def. I.g: "*U.S. slang.* To practise fellatio or cunnilingus on (a person)," even if this usage is restricted to a specific non-penetrative type of sexual activity.

13. Juda Theodor and Chanoch Albeck, *Bereschit Rabba* (Jerusalem: Wahrmann, 1965), 2:1059, includes an extended discussion of rabbinic sources with this understanding of our passage. The Talmudic passages to be discussed below are cited by Albeck in the same work (3:142, in the section entitled "Einleitung und Registrar, Teil II").

14. The same issue is raised in Yerushalmi Ketubbot 5:9 (30b), with the very succinct comment לשון נקי *lašon naqi* 'euphemistic language' (thus the reading of the Leiden manuscript [Ms. Or. 4720 = Scal. 3]), and only minimal further discussion.

understanding elsewhere in the Bible, though the phrase in Prov 6:26 כִּי בְעַד־אִשָּׁה זוֹנָה עַד־כִּכַּר לָחֶם *ki bə'ad 'išša zona 'ad kikkar lahem* 'for through a harlot woman until a loaf of bread' (my translation is a bit too literal, but I prefer not to interpret for the moment) may allude to this usage as well. To be sure, this verse is invoked by the rabbinic source Midrash ha-Gadol in its commentary to Gen 39:6.[15]

The upshot of all of this is the following: when the narrator states in v. 6 that Potiphar put Joseph in charge of everything 'except for the bread that he ate', double meaning is present. The plain connotation works well, since socio-cultural-religious taboos presumably were at play regarding dietary habits; but the author also intended these words euphemistically as 'the wife/woman with whom he engages in sexual intercourse'. The clever listener to this text will realize the double meaning in v. 6; the slightly less astute listener will realize this once she reaches v. 9; while the least perceptive may not gain the sense at all, even after hearing v. 9. But that would be her loss.

6. Exodus 2:20

וַיֹּאמֶר אֶל־בְּנֹתָיו וְאַיּוֹ לָמָּה זֶּה עֲזַבְתֶּן אֶת־הָאִישׁ קִרְאֶן לוֹ וְיֹאכַל לָחֶם:

And he [sc. Reuel] said to his daughters, "And where is he? Why did you leave the man? Call him, so that he may eat bread (*lahem*)."

The example discussed above from Gen 39:6 is well known. Less well known is the fact that the same wordplay is present in Exod 2:20. Moses has rescued the seven daughters of Reuel from the rustlers who attempted to steal their sheep. The girls return home to their father, who then states as above, with the key phrase at the end, 'so that he may eat bread'. The very next verse describes not a meal, but Moses's decision to dwell with the man and to marry his daughter Zipporah. Thus once more the words א-כ-ל *'-k-l* 'eat' + לֶחֶם *lehem* 'bread' serve as a *double entendre*. In light of typical bedouin hospitality, we should understand these words literally, that is, Reuel is indeed inviting Moses

---

15. Mordecai Margaliot, ed., *Midraš ha-Gadol 'al Ḥamiša Ḥumše Torah: Sefer Berešit* (Jerusalem: Mosad ha-Rav Kook, 1947), 659.

to have a meal. But in light of the situation—a man living in the desert with seven daughters and a real hero happens by—and given what v. 21 narrates, the reader is to understand two meanings in Reuel's words. Certainly he was playing the hospitable host in offering Moses a meal, but clearly he had other things on his mind as well when uttering the words וְיֹאכַל לָחֶם *wə-yoʾkal laḥɛm* 'so that he may eat bread'. Once more this interpretation is to be found already in rabbinic sources, most prominently in Shemot Rabba 1:32.[16]

7. 2 Samuel 11:8

וַיֹּאמֶר דָּוִד לְאוּרִיָּה רֵד לְבֵיתְךָ וּרְחַץ רַגְלֶיךָ וַיֵּצֵא אוּרִיָּה מִבֵּית הַמֶּלֶךְ וַתֵּצֵא אַחֲרָיו מַשְׂאַת הַמֶּלֶךְ:

And David said to Uriah, "Go-down to your house, and wash your feet" (*u-rḥaṣ raglɛka*); and Uriah went-out from the house of the king, and a serving [of food] of the king went-out after him.

This verse includes another example of *double entendre*, with a plain surface meaning and a second sexual meaning. Uriah has just returned from the battlefront for the supposed purpose of reporting to the king. After their discussion (not recorded by the author!—one expects this information in the 'gap' between vv. 7 and 8), David commands Uriah, רֵד לְבֵיתְךָ וּרְחַץ רַגְלֶיךָ *red lə-betka u-rḥaṣ raglɛka* 'go-down to your house, and wash your feet'. After the long journey from Rabbah in Ammon to Jerusalem, a trek across the desert on both sides of the Jordan River, it would be very natural to instruct the traveler to wash his feet, as per typical Near Eastern practice. So the words are to be understood literally.

But at the same time, David's goal is to have Uriah sleep with his wife, Bathsheba. The word רֶגֶל/רַגְלַיִם *rɛgɛl/raglayim* 'foot'/'feet' means 'sexual organ(s)' elsewhere in the Bible: Isa 6:2, 7:20, Ruth 3:4, 3:7, 3:8,

---

16. I have checked numerous modern commentaries on Exodus, and none of them realizes the wordplay at work here. But I was happy to see that Victor P. Hamilton, *The Book of Genesis: Chapters 18–50* (Grand Rapids: Eerdmans, 1995), 461, referred to the wordplay in Exod 2:20 in his comments to Gen 39:6.

3:14 (in this set of examples the form is מַרְגְּלֹתָיו *margəlotaw* 'his feet'),
Song 5:3 (in this case once more with the verb ר-ח-ץ *r-ḥ-ṣ* 'wash').[17]
Accordingly, 'wash your feet' also means 'have intercourse', perhaps
with the intermediate nuance 'wet your genitals' (or some such phrase).
That Uriah undersood David correctly may be seen from his retort in
v. 11. When David asked Uriah why he had not gone to his house (end
of v. 10), Uriah responded (after the initial part of his explanation): וַאֲנִ֞י
אָב֧וֹא אֶל־בֵּיתִ֛י לֶאֱכֹ֥ל וְלִשְׁתּ֖וֹת וְלִשְׁכַּ֣ב עִם־אִשְׁתִּ֑י *wa-'ani 'abo' 'ɛl beti lɛ'ɛkol
wə-lištot wə-liškab 'im 'išti* 'and I should go to my house to eat, and to
drink, and to sleep with my wife?' (v. 11).

8. Proverbs 31:27

צוֹפִיָּ֗ה הֲלִיכ֥וֹת בֵּיתָ֑הּ וְלֶ֥חֶם עַצְל֗וּת לֹ֣א תֹאכֵֽל׃

She oversees (*ṣopiyya*) the ways of her house,
And the bread of laziness she does not eat.

At times the biblical writers engage in bilingual wordplay.[18] Al Wolters
noticed an excellent example of this device in Prov 31:27, involving Hebrew and Greek.[19] He noted that throughout the poem in Prov 31:10–31,
the third-person fem. sg. verb (in *qatal*, *yiqtol*, and *wayyiqtol* forms) is
used as the predicate of the woman as subject a staggering 23x. There
is one exception, though, in v. 27, where the feminine singular participle
is utilized. Moreover, the form utilized is not the normal form, which
in this case would be צוֹפָה *ṣopa* 'she oversees', but rather the unusual
form צוֹפִיָּה *ṣopiyya* 'she oversees'. This word choice allows the poet to
pun on the Greek word for wisdom, σοφία *sophia*. The result is that the
stich צוֹפִיָּה הֲלִיכוֹת בֵּיתָהּ may be read simultaneously in two different
ways, either 'she oversees the ways of her house' (with the first word

---

17. Not all scholars would agree that רֶגֶל/רַגְלַיִם *rɛgɛl/raglayim* 'foot'/'feet'
means 'sexual organ(s)' in these verses, but in my estimation the evidence is
clear. However, this is not the proper place to present all the evidence in order
to substantiate this claim. For more on Song 5:3, see below, Chapter 17, no. 17.

18. For wordplay across linguistic boundaries in classical literature, see
Ahl, *Metaformations*, 60–63.

19. Al Wolters, "*ṣôpiyyâ* (Prov 31:27) as Hymnic Participle and Play on
Sophia," *Journal of Biblical Literature* 104 (1985): 577–87.

as a Hebrew verb) or 'wisdom/*sophia* are the ways of her house' (with the first word understood as the Greek term).[20]

9. Exodus 10:10

וַיֹּאמֶר אֲלֵהֶם יְהִי כֵן יְהוָה עִמָּכֶם כַּאֲשֶׁר אֲשַׁלַּח אֶתְכֶם וְאֶת־טַפְּכֶם
רְאוּ כִּי רָעָה נֶגֶד פְּנֵיכֶם:

And he [sc. Pharaoh] said to them [sc. Moses and Aaron],
"May Yhwh indeed be with you, if I ever send-forth you and
your little-ones—see, for there is evil (*ra'a*) before you."

Another instance of bilingual wordplay may be found in Exod 10:10, in the words spoken above by Pharaoh. For the first time in the plagues narrative, there may be a hint that Pharaoh will allow the Israelites to leave, but he quickly adds רְאוּ כִּי רָעָה נֶגֶד פְּנֵיכֶם *rə'u ki ra'a nɛgɛd pənekɛm* 'see, for there is evil before you', which I have rendered here quite literally. The force of this expression seems to be, 'Look, you are up to no good', or something similar. In the mouth of Pharaoh, however, our attention is drawn to the word רָעָה *ra'a*, which in Hebrew means 'evil' but which in Egyptian is the name of the chief deity Ra, the sun-god. With this reading, the Pharaoh's words are to be understood along the lines of, 'Look, there is (only) Ra before you', which is to say, this Yahweh-god to whom you keep referring (and which Pharaoh has just mentioned by name) is inferior to 'my' god Ra. Should one object that the Hebrew word is comprised of two syllables, whereas the Egyptian divine name Ra is but one syllable, I should mention here that in ancient Egyptian the latter term was pronounced also as two syllables, and with the same two consonants as the Hebrew, /r/ (*reš*) and /ʿ/ (*ʿayin*), most likely as *ri'a*, and hence quite close to Hebrew *ra'a* 'evil'.

Proof (as it were) for reading 'Ra', the sun-god, here is forthcoming from the following three plagues. In the wake of Pharaoh's pronouncement in Exod 10:10 come the eighth plague of locusts, which

---

20. The underlying assumption is that native Hebrew speakers (at least more worldly and educated ones) would have recognized the Greek word here, even if they did not speak Greek, no less than today's native English speakers may recognize 'sophia' in an English context, even if they do not speak Greek.

blots out the sun (see 10:15), the ninth plague of darkness, which does likewise for three days (see 10:22), and the tenth plague of the death of the firstborn at midnight (see 12:29), when the sun is most distant from shining. Before the utterance in Exod 10:10, other deities were involved in the brunt of the plagues (Hapi, the Nile [plague 1]; Heqet, the frog-goddess of life [plague 2]; Apis and Hathor, the bull and cow deities, respectively [plague 5]; etc.), but not Ra. The story has withheld attacks on Ra until the very end of the plagues narrative, but they come in the wake of Pharaoh's unfortunate (for him) words in Exod 10:10.[21]

10. Jonah 3:7

וַיַּזְעֵק וַיֹּאמֶר בְּנִינְוֵה מִטַּעַם הַמֶּלֶךְ וּגְדֹלָיו לֵאמֹר הָאָדָם וְהַבְּהֵמָה
הַבָּקָר וְהַצֹּאן אַל־יִטְעֲמוּ מְאוּמָה אַל־יִרְעוּ וּמַיִם אַל־יִשְׁתּוּ׃

And he proclaimed, and he said in Nineveh, from the diktat (ta'am) of the king and his great-ones, saying: "Neither human nor beast, herd or flock, shall taste (ṭ-ʿ-m) anything; they shall not graze, and water they shall not drink."

The presence of the Assyrian king in the book of Jonah allows the author of this delightful little book to exploit a bilingual pun as well. But in this case it is not Akkadian and Hebrew per se (as one might expect) that is at play, but rather Aramaic and Hebrew (with a hint of Akkadian, as we shall see). For in Neo-Assyrian times Aramaic had gained the status of second language in Assyria alongside the native Akkadian. Our attention is drawn to the phrase מִטַּעַם הַמֶּלֶךְ וּגְדֹלָיו mit-ṭa'am ham-mɛlɛk u-gdolaw 'from the diktat of the king and his great-ones [i.e., nobles]', the contents of which is that neither humans nor animals should ט-ע-ם ṭ-ʿ-m 'taste' anything. The noun טַעַם ṭa'am 'taste' occurs elsewhere in the Bible (e.g., Exod 16:31, with relation to manna), but only here in Jonah 3:7 does it mean 'decree, command'. It bears this meaning in Aramaic, for which see Ezra 6:14 and 7:23,

---

21. In addition, note that an ancient Jewish midrashic tradition recorded in Shir ha-Shirim Rabba 15a–b understands רָעָה ra'a as an astral deity (see also Rashi on Exod 10:10). For further discussion, see Gary A. Rendsburg, "The Egyptian Sun-God Ra in the Pentateuch," *Henoch* 10 (1988): 3–15.

though more commonly the form is טְעֵם *ṭəʿem* (Dan 3:10, 3:29, etc.); the Akkadian cognate is *ṭēmu* 'decree, command'.

Our clever author, accordingly, has placed the noun טַעַם *ṭaʿam* 'decree, command' in the story at exactly the spot where the king of Nineveh, in whose city could be heard both Aramaic and Akkadian, issues a decree. The substance of the command, moreover, is not to taste anything, using the verbal root associated with this lexeme. I have rendered the key noun 'diktat' for two reasons: (a) to provide a sense of its foreignness, as a reflection of the non-native Hebrew usage; and (b) in order to produce, as best as possible, soundplay with the English word 'taste' later in the verse.

11. Exodus 16:15

וַיֹּאמְרוּ אִישׁ אֶל־אָחִיו מָן הוּא כִּי לֹא יָדְעוּ מַה־הוּא

And each-one said to the other, "What is it?" (*man huʾ*)—for they did not know what it is (*ma huʾ*).

An additional example of bilingual wordplay may occur in Exod 16:15. In the previous two verses, a dew-like substance covers the ground, though its exact quality and identification remains unknown to the Israelites. The people, accordingly, ask each other about the phenomenon, after which the author explains the inquisitive exchange. But the text uses two words for 'what': first מָן *man*, which appears nowhere else in the Bible with this sense; and then מַה *ma*, the standard form of the interrogative pronoun, occurring more than 500x in the canon. We anticipate the end of the narrative, which announces that מָן *man* becomes the name of this substance, that is, 'manna' (see v. 31). At this stage, however, the unique word serves only as a question word, 'what'.

For the wordplay to work, one must assume that *man* means 'what' in some other Semitic language(s). Such is indeed the case, even if the evidence is sparse, to wit, Ugaritic *mn*, Amarna *mannu*, *manna*, and Syriac *man*. The problem is that none of these usages places the reader in the context of the Sinai desert, which is where the manna story takes place. Of course, we have virtually no literary remains from that vast wasteland, so one is hard-pressed to know exactly what kind of Semitic language was used among the denizens of the Sinai in ancient times—never mind how said people expressed the interrogative 'what?' (a rather specific grammatical feature). Nonetheless, we will assume, in light of all the literary artistry present in the Bible, especially in foreign contexts (see Chapters 24 and 25), that the author of our text got it right, which is to say, somewhere in the Sinai desert the word *man* served for 'what', thereby allowing for the delightful (bilingual) wordplay inherent in Exod 16:15.[22]

12. 2 Samuel 11:1

וַיְהִי֩ לִתְשׁוּבַ֨ת הַשָּׁנָ֜ה לְעֵ֣ת | צֵ֣את הַמַּלְאֹכִ֗ים וַיִּשְׁלַ֣ח דָּוִ֡ד אֶת־יוֹאָ֣ב וְאֶת־עֲבָדָ֣יו עִמּוֹ֩ וְאֶת־כָּל־יִשְׂרָאֵל֒ וַיַּשְׁחִ֙תוּ֙ אֶת־בְּנֵ֣י עַמּ֔וֹן וַיָּצֻ֖רוּ עַל־רַבָּ֑ה וְדָוִ֖ד יוֹשֵׁ֥ב בִּירוּשָׁלָֽ͏ִם׃

And it was at the turn of the year, at the time of the going-out of kings (ʜᴍʟ'ᴋʏᴍ), and David sent Joab and his servants with him, and all Israel, and they assaulted the Ammonites, and they besieged Rabbah; but David sat in Jerusalem.

We now turn to another type of wordplay, of the visual variety. Throughout this book, we have referred to the manner in which the reader/performer/presenter of the literary composition held the text/scroll/document in his hand, while the gathered audience would listen and would absorb the spoken word. In instances of visual wordplay, only the reader realizes the frolic, for it is forthcoming solely from the written form of the text.[23]

In the passage cited above, the consonantal spelling of the word rendered 'the kings' is המלאכים ʜᴍʟ'ᴋʏᴍ (with the letter 'aleph inserted).[24] Any seasoned (or even neophyte) reader of Hebrew would read this word, certainly at first blush, as 'the messengers' (which always has the 'aleph), and yet the context demands 'the kings' here. For as we

---

22. This effect is expressly stated by Greenstein, "Wordplay, Hebrew," 971.

23. On "visual wordplay" in the cuneiform tradition, see Scott B. Noegel, "Wordplay in the Tale of the Poor Man of Nippur," *Acta Sumerologica* 18 (1996): 169–86, in particular 177–82.

24. A word of explanation: I have rendered the word as simply 'kings' in my translation, but the lemma includes the definite article, which serves to make definite the entire phrase 'at the time of the going-out of kings'.

know from ancient Near Eastern and indeed medieval history, the turn of the year, that is, the springtime, is when nations would commence battle again, since it was difficult to wage military campaigns during the rough winter months.[25] Moreover, notwithstanding this unique orthography, the ancient Jewish tradents transmitted the word with the pronunciation for 'the kings', emerging in the Masora as הַמְּלָאכִים *ham-məlakim*, exactly as it would be pronounced if the *'aleph* were not written.[26] Indeed, the reworking of this story in the book of Chronicles already points to this conclusion, since the reading in 1 Chr 20:1 is הַמְּלָכִים *ham-məlakim* 'the kings'. Furthermore, all the ancient versions (Septuagint, Targum Jonathan, Peshitta, Vulgate) understood the word as 'kings'. In short, there is absolute agreement that 'kings' is to be read in 2 Sam 11:1.[27]

But why, then, such a unique spelling at this point? As one reads the entire account of David and Bathsheba, one realizes how central messengers are to the narrative.[28] The word מלאכים ML'KYM *mal'akim*

---

25. The military endeavors of Charlemagne (r. 768–814) constitute a fine illustration from the world of medieval history. This monarch did not maintain a full-time regular army, but rather summoned his soldiers from their farms and towns each spring (eight thousand men seems to be a reasonable estimate) to conduct campaigns lasting three to six months.

26. Such is the reading of the Aleppo Codex, the most reliable medieval witness of the biblical text. Note the line above the *'aleph*, known as the *rafe* marker, which (in this case) instructs the reader to ignore the presence of the letter while reading aloud. The interested reader can access excellent photographs of the entire manuscript at http://aleppocodex.org/newsite /index.html, and then use the search and zoom features to see any verse very clearly (including the one under discussion here, 2 Sam 11:1). The St. Petersburg (Leningrad) Codex, quite oddly, provides a different pronunciation, הַמְּלָאכִים *ham-malkim*, though this too means 'kings' (and not 'messengers'). The reading of one additional (late) medieval manuscript, Oxford Bodleian MS. Kennicott 1, folio 175a, available at http://bav.bodleian.ox.ac.uk/digitized -items-hebrew-manuscripts (then scroll down for MS. Kennicott 1 in the long list of manuscripts), matches that of the Aleppo Codex exactly.

27. For full treatment, notwithstanding a contrary opinion, see Noam Mizrahi, "Kings or Messengers? The Text of 2 Samuel 11:1 in the Light of Hebrew Historical Phonology," *Zeitschrift für Althebräistik* 25–28 (2012–2015): 57–83.

28. I no longer recall whether my late graduate student Colin Smith suggested this to me or whether I realized this point independently of his

'messengers' appears in v. 4, when David sends messengers to fetch Bathsheba. But other messengers appear in the story as well, even if the word itself does not appear. I refer to v. 3, where David first inquires about Bathsheba's identity, and to v. 5, where Bathsheba informs David that she is pregnant. All of this was accomplished through messengers, a piece of information that the reader keeps in mind when she begins to wonder whether or not Uriah knows about the tryst between his wife and the king.[29]

But the most important messenger that appears in the story is the one who dominates the stage in vv. 19–25. Why do we learn so much detail about the manner in which the messenger reported the news of the battle and of Uriah's death to David? Why did the author not simply write something like 'And Joab sent word to David about the war and about Uriah's death'? My answer to this question is indebted to Meir Sternberg's treatment of the story, but he did not, in my opinion, develop the thought fully. Sternberg noticed, quite correctly, that the messenger did not carry out Joab's instructions as commanded (he changed the description of the battle to make the Israelites look better than they actually were, etc.), in the same manner that Joab did not carry out David's instructions as commanded (not only Uriah but other innocents were killed as well, though of course Joab could not orchestrate the battle in the way that David demanded).[30] By extending the chain of command further, the reader realizes that David did not follow God's commands, specifically the prohibitions against adultery and murder (found most succinctly in Exod 20:13–14 and Deut 5:17–18). The messenger, accordingly, plays a crucial role. He serves to point the reader to the lesson of the story. When the king abrogates God's command, generals no longer listen to the commander-in-chief, and privates (i.e., messengers) no longer listen to generals. All of this, I submit, is anticipated by the author in the enigmatic orthography המלאכים HML'KYM 'kings' in v. 1. The reader—in this case literally the

---

discovery. But he deserves credit regardless, for his discussion with me served as the catalyst for my further thoughts on the topic.

29. On the possibility, indeed the strong possibility, that Uriah knew that something had occurred, see Sternberg, *Poetics of Biblical Narrative*, 201–13.

30. Ibid., 213–19.

reader, that is, the individual actually reading with written document in hand—understands that 'kings' is intended, but questions why 'messengers' is spelled. As he proceeds through the story, our presenter keeps this piece of information in the back of his mind, and recalls it as 'messengers', especially the last and most important one, play a significant role in the narrative.[31]

As if all of the above were not enough, two additional points may be made here. First, note the collocation of the verb ש-ל-ח *š-l-ḥ* 'send' and our key noun המלאכים HML'KYM 'kings' (though looking like 'the messengers') in 2 Sam 11:1. These two words, 'send' and 'messengers', appear together approximately 70x in the Bible, so common is the expression—whether the messengers be human ones (e.g., Gen 32:4) or divine ones (e.g., Exod 23:20). The scribal tradition in 2 Sam 11:1, accordingly, plays with the reader's mind, which is so accustomed to seeing 'send' and 'messengers' together in a text—even if in this case 'kings' is to be understood.

Second, the word המלאכים HML'KYM 'kings' in v. 1 is not the only instance of an extra 'aleph introduced into the text in the story of David and Bathsheba. The scribe persisted in this practice, as can be seen in the words וַיֹּרְאוּ הַמּוֹרְאִים *wayyoru ham-morim* 'and the archers shot' (2 Sam 11:24), רָאשׁ *raš* 'poor' (2 Sam 12:1), and הָרָאשׁ *ha-raš* 'the poor' (2 Sam 12:4). Also relevant is the spelling וְלֹא־בָרָא *wə-loʾ baraʾ* 'and he did not eat' (2 Sam 12:17), for one expects the verb to end in *he*, not 'aleph; and in fact the scribe may have set the stage for all these 'aleph tricks toward the end of the previous account, with the word חֲלָאמָה *helama* 'to Helam' (2 Sam 10:17; cf. v. 16). Nowhere else in the Bible does one find such an assemblage of odd spellings involving the letter 'aleph, all present to retain the reader's focus on the most crucial of them, המלאכים HML'KYM 'kings' in 2 Sam 11:1.[32]

---

31. For a different understanding of the matter, see Robert P. Gordon, "Aleph Apologeticum," *Jewish Quarterly Review* 69 (1978): 112–16.

32. I am indebted to my former student Richard M. Wright (Livingston United Methodist Church [Livingston, LA]) for pointing out these additional atypical spellings.

13. Proverbs 31:21–22

²¹ לֹא־תִירָא לְבֵיתָהּ מִשָּׁלֶג כִּי כָל־בֵּיתָהּ לָבֻשׁ שָׁנִים:

²² מַרְבַדִּים עָשְׂתָה־לָּהּ שֵׁשׁ וְאַרְגָּמָן לְבוּשָׁהּ:

²¹ She does not fear for her house on account of snow,
Because her entire house is clothed in scarlet / doubly
    (*šanim*).
²² Coverings she has made for herself,
Linen and purple are her clothing.

The example presented by Wolters in Prov 31:27, discussed above (no. 8), is one of only several wordplays in the poem in Prov 31:10–31. Another is to be found in vv. 21–22, where the word שָׁנִים *šanim* (end of v. 21) operates as the pivot word in an asymmetrical Janus construction. The Masora transmitted the Janus word as שָׁנִים *šanim* 'scarlet', but as G. R. Driver pointed out, "scarlet is neither more nor less warm than other colours for clothing in snowy weather; further, the present form of *šānîm* is peculiar, if not impossible."[33] The Septuagint and the Vulgate suggest an alternative; both versions understood the word as 'double', no doubt reading the word as if it were pointed שְׁנַיִם *šənayim* 'two'. This, of course, makes much more sense, for with double layers of clothing the woman's household would be better protected from the cold of a snowy day. But the Masoretic reading of the word should not be discarded altogether (nor should the plural form be considered impossible).[34] Indeed, the term שָׁנִים *šanim* 'scarlet' foreshadows the mention of שֵׁשׁ וְאַרְגָּמָן *šeš wə-'argaman* 'linen and purple' (most likely a hendiadys here meaning 'purple linen'), the perfect parallel expression to שָׁנִים *šanim* 'scarlet' (see the well-known collocation of these three terms in the Tabernacle account [Exod 25:4, 28:5, etc.]).

In short, both readings of the consonantal form שנים šNYM are to be understood, with the word serving a Janus function: with the meaning

---

33. G. R. Driver, "On a Passage in the Baal Epic (IV AB iii 24) and Proverbs xxxi 21," *Bulletin of the American Schools of Oriental Research* 105 (1947): 11.

34. The plural form שָׁנִים *šanim* 'scarlet' occurs again in Isa 1:18. True, 1QIsaᵃ reads the singular שני šNY, but that is no reason to emend the Masoretic Text. For discussion, see E. Y. Kutscher, *Ha-Lašon ve-ha-Reqaʿ šel Megillat Yešaʿyahu ha-Šelema mi-Megillot Yam ha-Melaḥ* (Jerusalem: Magnes, 1959), 301.

'two, double' it looks back to the first part of the verse, responding to the need for double layers as protection against the snowy day; and with the meaning 'scarlet' it looks ahead to the next verse, with its focus on the aristocratic garments befitting the high-status woman described in Prov 31:10–31. Admittedly, our presenter would have encountered a problem, since he could pronounce the word in only one way, either as *šanim* 'scarlet' or *šǝnayim* 'two', though just possibly he uttered both forms of the word in a virtuosic performance.

14. Proverbs 31:19

יָדֶיהָ שִׁלְּחָה בַכִּישׁוֹר וְכַפֶּיהָ תָּמְכוּ פָלֶךְ׃

Her hands she sends-forth to the spindle / with skill (*kišor*),
And her palms grasp the whorl / (with) dexterity (*palɛk*).

A wordplay of another type—what we shall call double polysemy—occurs in the same poem at v. 19, as indicated above. A traditional translation of the verse reads as follows (reading with the word choices before the slash mark): 'Her hands she sends-forth to the spindle, and her palms grasp the whorl'.[35] But when one realizes that the root כ-שׁ-ר *k-š-r* is attested elsewhere in Hebrew (Qoh 2:21, etc., and more frequently in postbiblical Hebrew) with the meaning 'skill', and that the various talents of the woman are the main point of the poem, it becomes clear that the poet intended double meaning in the word כִּישׁוֹר *kišor*, hence both 'spindle' and 'skill'. For balance, one would expect the same or a similar double meaning to be inherent in the parallel term, פֶּלֶךְ *pɛlɛk*,[36] for such are the workings of Hebrew poetry. And while a parallel meaning is not attested elsewhere in Hebrew for the root פ-ל-ך *p-l-k*, the cognate root *f-l-k* bears the meaning 'clever' in Jibbali (a modern South Arabian language). Now at first glance it might seem far-fetched

---

35. In translating the two *termini technici* as 'spindle' and 'whorl', respectively, I accept the suggested definitions of Yael Yisraʾeli, "Melaʾkha: Malʾakhot ha-Bayit: Ṭevuyya," *ʾEnṣiqlopedya Miqraʾit* 4 (1962), cols. 998–1003. However, their actual meanings (the terms might be reversed, one could mean 'distaff', and so on) are not relevant to the current enterprise.

36. I use the standard form of the noun here, not as it occurs within the specific context of Prov 31:19.

to invoke a Jibbali cognate to substantiate a meaning in Biblical Hebrew. But it should be noted that quite a few words attested in ancient
Northwest Semitic have cognates only in modern South Semitic languages (South Arabian and Ethiopian).[37] In light of the two meanings
that both key words may bear (as attested in Hebrew for three of them,
and with the fourth one assumed for Hebrew, via a nod to Jibbali), I
suggest the translation appearing above for our passage, with apologies
for the slight encumbrance necessitated by the slash marks to bring out
the double polysemy.[38]

15. Proverbs 1:10, 15

Prov 1:10

בְּנִי אִם־יְפַתּוּךָ חַטָּאִים אַל־תֹּבֵא׃

My son, if the sinners entice you, do not consent (TB').

Prov 1:15

בְּנִי אַל־תֵּלֵךְ בְּדֶרֶךְ אִתָּם מְנַע רַגְלְךָ מִנְּתִיבָתָם׃

My son, do not go on the way with them (т.в.'.),
Restrain your foot from their path.

We now turn to yet another type of wordplay, one involving a cipher.
Prov 1:10 includes an unusual spelling and pointing in the final word,
תֹּבֵא tobe', from the root א-ב-ה '-b-h 'consent'; elsewhere in the Bible
the form appears as expected, as תֹּאבֶה to'be (Gen 24:5, 24:8, Deut 13:9,
1 Kgs 20:8). In fact, given the consonants תבא TB', an ancient Israelite
would naturally read the word as תבא tabo', but the Masora nonethe-

---

37. For examples and for a more detailed discussion of this verse, see
Gary A. Rendsburg, "Double Polysemy in Proverbs 31:19," in Asma Afsaruddin
and A. H. Mathias Zahniser, eds., *Humanism, Culture, and Language in the
Near East: Studies in Honor of Georg Krotkoff* (Winona Lake, IN: Eisenbrauns,
1997), 267–74.

38. Presumably the preposition -בְּ bə- 'in, with' in the first stich serves
as a double-duty preposition, thus yielding the second reading '(with) dexterity'. For additional examples of double polysemy, see Gary A. Rendsburg,
"Double Polysemy in Genesis 49:6 and Job 3:6," *Catholic Biblical Quarterly*
44 (1982): 48–51.

less transmitted the word as תֹּבֵא *tobe'* 'consent'. Why would the text include such an unusual form? Why not spell it the normal way?

The answer is that the three letters of this word, ת-ב-א T-B-', serve as a cipher for the phrase in v. 15. The connection is the first word in both verses, בְּנִי *bəni* 'my son', a common invocation in the book of Proverbs, to be sure, but within this section of the composition, the next one encountered by the reader/listener. So, the phrase אַל־תֹּבֵא *'al tobe'* means 'do not consent', but it also serves as the cipher for the phrase אַל־תֵּלֵךְ בְּדֶרֶךְ אִתָּם *'al telek bə-derek 'ittam* 'do not go on the way with them' (v. 15), the words of which (after the negative particle אַל *'al*) begin with the same three letters, ת-ב-א T-B-'.[39] This is an exceedingly clever maneuver, a wordplay of a totally different type, perhaps unique in the biblical corpus—but decoding the message is the self-stated purpose of the book of Proverbs, as revealed in Prov 1:6, לְהָבִין מָשָׁל וּמְלִיצָה דִּבְרֵי חֲכָמִים וְחִידֹתָם *ləhabin mašal u-mlişa dibre ḥakamim wə-ḥidotam* 'to understand proverb and saying, the words of the wise and their riddles'. From such an entrée to the book, the reader knows to expect various types of wordplay, including ciphers such as the present example, to be included in the collection. If we have continually returned to the book of Proverbs in this chapter, the reader will now more clearly understand why.

16. Proverbs 3:26

כִּי־יְהוָה יִהְיֶה בְכִסְלֶךָ וְשָׁמַר רַגְלְךָ מִלָּכֶד:

For Yhwh will be at your loin / your support (*kesel*),
And he will guard your leg from being-caught.

With a statement such as the one ending the previous section, it would be impertinent of me to leave the book of Proverbs, and thus we present

---

39. For this original insight, see Cyrus H. Gordon, "New Light on the Hebrew Language," *Hebrew Abstracts* 15 (1974): 29. For a more detailed treatment of the key word in v. 10, with a thorough review of the scholarly literature, see H. G. M. Williamson, "An Overlooked Suggestion at Proverbs 1.10," in David A. Baer and Robert P. Gordon, eds., *Leshon Limmudim: Essays on the Language and Literature of the Hebrew Bible in Honour of A. A. Macintosh* (London: Bloomsbury, 2014), 218–26.

here one more example from that remarkable collection of aphorisms, with so many of them displaying wordplay.[40]

The most common meaning of the Hebrew noun כֶּסֶל *kesel* is 'loin, thigh', as may be seen in the section of Leviticus dealing with the animal sacrifices (3:4, 3:10, 3:15, 4:9, 7:4), along with Ps 38:8 and Job 15:27; see also the Ugaritic cognate *ksl* 'back, behind' (not exactly the same body part, but close enough). In three instances, however, the word means 'support, confidence', namely, in Ps 78:7, Job 8:14, 31:24.

Strikingly, both connotations fit the context of Prov 3:26. The meaning 'loin, thigh' is appropriate given the use of רֶגֶל *regel* 'foot, leg' in the b-line; and yet 'support, confidence' makes perfect sense as well.[41] As with all wordplay, the reader need not decide which meaning is desired, for both senses of the word are to be understood in a single moment of reader comprehension: God will serve as your loins and as your support.

17. Song 5:2–6

2 אֲנִי יְשֵׁנָה וְלִבִּי עֵר קוֹל | דּוֹדִי דוֹפֵק פִּתְחִי־לִי אֲחֹתִי רַעְיָתִי יוֹנָתִי
תַמָּתִי שֶׁרֹאשִׁי נִמְלָא־טָל קְוֻּצּוֹתַי רְסִיסֵי לָיְלָה:

3 פָּשַׁטְתִּי אֶת־כֻּתׇּנְתִּי אֵיכָכָה אֶלְבָּשֶׁנָּה רָחַצְתִּי אֶת־רַגְלַי אֵיכָכָה
אֲטַנְּפֵם:

4 דּוֹדִי שָׁלַח יָדוֹ מִן־הַחֹר וּמֵעַי הָמוּ עָלָיו:

5 קַמְתִּי אֲנִי לִפְתֹּחַ לְדוֹדִי וְיָדַי נָטְפוּ־מוֹר וְאֶצְבְּעֹתַי מוֹר עֹבֵר עַל כַּפּוֹת
הַמַּנְעוּל:

6 פָּתַחְתִּי אֲנִי לְדוֹדִי וְדוֹדִי חָמַק עָבָר נַפְשִׁי יָצְאָה בְדַבְּרוֹ בִּקַּשְׁתִּיהוּ
וְלֹא מְצָאתִיהוּ קְרָאתִיו וְלֹא עָנָנִי:

2 I am asleep, but my heart is awake; hark, my beloved knocks, "Open for me, my sister, my darling, my dove, my perfect-one, for my head is full of dew, my locks (of) the droplets of the night."

---

40. For more examples, see Rendsburg, "Literary and Linguistic Matters in the Book of Proverbs," 117–20.

41. See Avigdor (Victor) Hurowitz, *Mišle* (Miqra' le-Yiśra'el; Jerusalem: Magnes, 2012), 1:188–89.

³ I have removed my tunic, how shall I put it on? I have
washed my feet, how shall I soil them?
⁴ My beloved sends his hand through the hole; my innards
are stirred for him.
⁵ I arose to open for my beloved; and my hands drip myrrh,
and my fingers, flowing myrrh, on the handles of the latch.
⁶ I opened for my beloved, but my beloved, turned, passed;
my life-essence went-out at his speaking, I sought him but I
did not find him, I called for him, but he did not answer me.

The reference to Song 5:3 in section no. 7 above (on David and Uriah)
raises the major question of how much sexual imagery may or may
not be present in the Song of Songs.[42] This is not the place for an extended exposition, but any treatment of wordplay or double meaning,
especially one that introduces the issue of sexual *double entendre*, must
return to this remarkable composition for at least some further discussion. As intimated above, scholars disagree as to how much of the book
should be read with sexual connotation; personally I am on the "more"
side rather than on the "less" side, especially in my reading of Song
5:2–6.[43] In this particular section, the poetry works on two levels: in
her dream world, the female protagonist at once prepares to open the
door to allow her beloved entrée into her chamber and engages (or at
least prepares to engage) in the sexual act as well.

The scene opens with קוֹל דּוֹדִי דוֹפֵק | *qol dodi dopeq* 'hark, my
beloved knocks' (v. 2), with 'knock' to be understood both literally,
that is, her lover approaches, and in a sexual sense (compare English
'knock', albeit with a somewhat vulgar tone, attested since 1598).[44] Next
we encounter the expression רָחַצְתִּי אֶת־רַגְלַי *raḥaṣti ʾet raglay* 'I have

---

42. We also studied alliteration in Song 5:3, 5:5, above in Chapter 16, no. 24.

43. For much of what follows, see also Marvin H. Pope, *Song of Songs*
(Anchor Bible 7C; Garden City, NY: Doubleday, 1977), 514–19. For scholars
more on the "less" side, see Jack M. Sasson's review of Pope, "On Pope's Song
of Songs (AB 7C)," *Maarav* 1 (1979): 177–96; and Fox, *The Song of Songs and the
Ancient Egyptian Love Songs*, 144–45. Pope responded to Sasson in "Response
to Sasson on the Sublime Song," *Maarav* 2 (1980): 207–14. For further discussion, see once more Ullendorff, "Bawdy Bible," 447–50.

44. *OED*, 'knock' *v.*, def. 2.e.

washed my feet' (v. 3), referred to above in our discussion of 2 Sam 11:8 (again, see no. 7). These words are to be understood literally (as per the gloss above), but also 'I have had intercourse', perhaps not literally in this case, but in the sense 'I have climaxed', presumably through female masturbation, in advance of her falling asleep (see the start of v. 2).[45] A similar *double entendre* occurs in the next verse: דּוֹדִי שָׁלַח יָדוֹ מִן־הַחֹר *dodi šalaḥ yado min ha-ḥor* 'my beloved sends his hand through the hole' (v. 4). In this case, יָד *yad* means literally 'hand', and חֹר *ḥor* means literally 'hole', with the image of the male lover attempting to enter the room by reaching his hand through the door hole to open the lock (recall דּוֹפֵק *dopeq* 'knock' in v. 2). But at the same time יָד *yad* means 'penis', in which case חֹר *ḥor* must mean 'vaginal opening'. For יָד *yad* = 'penis', the best biblical reference is Isa 57:8 אָהַבְתָּ מִשְׁכָּבָם יָד חָזִית *'ahabt miškabam yad ḥazit* 'you loved their bed, (their) "hand" [sc. penis] you have seen' (see below, p. 386, for another reference to this verse); in postbiblical literature see the two Qumran texts 1QS 7:13 and 11QT 46:13.[46] This sexual reading allows us to understand the female lover's reaction וּמֵעַי הָמוּ עָלָיו *u-meʿay hamu ʿalaw* 'my innards are stirred for him'.

The stanza continues with: קַמְתִּי אֲנִי לִפְתֹּחַ לְדוֹדִי וְיָדַי נָטְפוּ־מוֹר וְאֶצְבְּעֹתַי מוֹר עֹבֵר עַל כַּפּוֹת הַמַּנְעוּל *qamti 'ani liptoaḥ lə-dodi wə-yaday naṭpu mor wə-'eṣbəʿotay mor ʿober ʿal kappot ham-manʿul* 'I arose to open for my beloved; and my hands drip myrrh, and my fingers, flow-

---

45. Note that the phrase typically refers to a male 'washing his feet', as in 2 Sam 11:8, though in this case the phrase is uttered by the female, with reference to her own action. This would be one additional instance of the manner in which the female perspective dominates in the Song of Songs, with several reversals of usually male standpoints and orientations, for which see Noegel and Rendsburg, *Solomon's Vineyard*, 173.

46. See Mathias Delcor, "Two Special Meanings of the Word יד in Biblical Hebrew," *Journal of Semitic Studies* 12 (1967): 230–40, esp. 234–40, with reference to Ugaritic *yd* = 'penis' as well; and the more recent discussion by Shalom M. Paul, *Isaiah 40–66* (Eerdmans Critical Commentary; Grand Rapids: Eerdmans, 2012), 468–69. For recent discussion of the Qumran passages, see Elisha Qimron and James H. Charlesworth, "Rule of the Community," in James H. Charlesworth, ed., *The Dead Sea Scrolls: Hebrew, Aramaic, and Greek Texts with English Translations*, vol. 1, *Rule of the Community and Related Documents* (Tübingen: Mohr; Louisville: Westminster John Knox Press, 1994), 33 n. 185.

ing myrrh, on the handles of the latch' (v. 5), as the female lover both literally arises from her bed to open the door for her beloved and (perhaps, maybe) prepares to open herself for her beloved. The latter sense is certainly inherent in the climactic line: פָּתַחְתִּי אֲנִי לְדוֹדִי וְדוֹדִי חָמַק עָבָר *pataḥti ʾani lə-dodi wə-dodi ḥamaq ʿabar* 'I opened for my beloved, but my beloved, turned, passed [i.e., was gone]' (v. 6). At the very moment of the anticipated insertion—all still within her dream sequence—she opens for her beloved, but he is gone, poof, gone, as so often happens when one exits the dream world and returns to the world of reality.[47] The remainder of v. 6 conveys this transition, with 'my life-essence went-out at his speaking', still within the dream realm presumably; but with 'I sought him but I did not find him, I called for him, but he did not answer me' returning us to conscious awakeness, with the repetition of a trope that appeared earlier in Song 3:1–2.

18. Isaiah 23:16

קְחִי כִנּוֹר סֹבִּי עִיר זוֹנָה נִשְׁכָּחָה הֵיטִיבִי נַגֵּן הַרְבִּי־שִׁיר לְמַעַן תִּזָּכֵרִי:

> Take the lyre, go-about the city, harlot forgotten / sexually
>   active (*niškaḥa*),
> Play-music well, multiply song, so that you may be
>   remembered / fornicated (*tizzakeri*).

This passage affords another excellent illustration of sexual *double entendre* at play.[48] The verse occurs within Isaiah's oracle directed at Tyre, which the prophet predicts will be destroyed—after which it will become forgotten. Yet the poetic couplet is introduced by the expression at the end of the previous verse כְּשִׁירַת הַזּוֹנָה *kə-širat haz-zona* 'like the song of the harlot'—thereby inviting the listener to focus on the sexual innuendos.

The key phrases are זוֹנָה נִשְׁכָּחָה *zona niškaḥa* 'harlot forgotten' and לְמַעַן תִּזָּכֵרִי *lə-maʿan tizzakeri* 'so that you may be remembered'

---

47. We treated this passage above, in Chapter 8, no. 7, and we will return to it below, in Chapter 27, no. 8.

48. For what follows, see Zvi Rin and Shifra Rin, *ʿAlilot ha-ʾElim: Kol Širot ʾUgarit* (Philadelphia: Inbal, 1996), 379.

(thus their basic meanings), roughly parallel within the structure of the poetry. But an additional layer of meaning is forthcoming as well. Hence, the first expression connotes not only 'harlot forgotten' (from the verbal root *š-k-ḥ*), but also 'harlot sexually active' (from the root *ṯ-k-ḥ*, attested in Ugaritic).[49] And the second expression connotes not only 'so that you may be remembered' (from the root *z-k-r* with its standard meaning 'remember'), but also 'so that you may be fornicated' (from the homonymous root *z-k-r*, but with the sense 'fornicate'). The latter meaning of the root *z-k-r* is related to the common noun זָכָר *zakar* 'male'; though more pertinently it underlies two Hebrew nouns meaning 'male member': זִכְרוֹן *zikron* (bound form), which occurs in Isa 57:8 (a passage that we discussed above), and the second element of צַלְמֵי זָכָר *ṣalme zakar* 'phallic symbols' (lit., 'images of the male-member'), in Ezek 16:17. The result of all this is an exceedingly clever application of double polysemy by the poet/prophet responsible for Isa 23:16, within the address to Tyre.

19. Genesis 34:15

אַךְ־בְּזֹאת נֵאוֹת לָכֶם

"Only by this will we consent (*ne'ot*) to you."

The ingenuity of biblical writers in matters of wordplay is limitless. The present example is extremely subtle, for it entails the clue of a one-syllable noun embedded into a rare verb in the narrative text. The words cited above are spoken by Jacob's sons to Shechem and Hamor,

---

49. Cyrus H. Gordon, *Ugaritic Textbook* (Rome: Pontifical Biblical Institute, 1967), 501; and del Olmo Lete Sanmartín, *Dictionary of the Ugaritic Language*, 2:902–3. The relevant texts are *CAT* 1.11:1–2; 1.24:4. There have been attempts to locate this root elsewhere in Hebrew; for a survey see *HALOT* 2:1490–91. Isaiah 23:16 is not listed or discussed there, yet I find it to be the most convincing example. Most likely it is not a coincidence that the reflex of this root, best known from Ugaritic, appears in the prophet's address to Tyre, the major Phoenician city. Note that Ugaritic and Phoenician share many vocabulary items within the Canaanite umbrella. We would, accordingly, be dealing with an instance of addressee-switching, a literary device to be surveyed below in Chapter 25.

as the two parties negotiate an agreement that would include the intermarriage of Israelites and Shechemites. The members of the former party state that they are willing to enter into this arrangement, but only if the latter party agrees to be circumcised. But the verb choice used by Jacob's sons is an unusual one, to wit, the verb א-ו-ת ʾ-w-t 'consent'. Interestingly, this verb is then used, twice in fact, by the leaders of Shechem when they address their people: אַךְ־בְּזֹאת יֵאֹתוּ לָנוּ הָאֲנָשִׁים ʾak bə-zoʾt yeʾotu lanu ha-ʾanašim 'only by this will the men consent to us' (v. 22); and אַךְ נֵאוֹתָה לָהֶם ʾak neʾota lahem 'only let us consent to them' (v. 23).

The rarity of this verb may be seen from the fact that it occurs only one other time in the Bible (2 Kgs 12:9). The much more common verb for 'agree, consent' is the root א-ב-ה ʾ-b-h (discussed above, see no. 15, regarding Prov 1:10). This raises the question: Why did the author of Genesis 34 select the verb א-ו-ת ʾ-w-t 'consent' and in fact use it 3x? To my mind, the answer is: this unusual lexical choice allows the listeners to this text to hear the noun אוֹת ʾot 'sign', a word that is central to the context. For the Israelites, the rite of circumcision was the אוֹת ʾot 'sign' of the covenant, a point made explicit in Gen 17:11; and thus the author of Genesis 34 places this word, in the form of the prominent syllable within the verbal form נֵאוֹת neʾot 'we will consent' in v. 15, in the mouth of Jacob's sons as they address Shechem and Hamor. When the latter two individuals repeat the syllable, in the forms יֵאֹתוּ yeʾotu 'they will consent' in v. 22 and נֵאוֹתָה neʾota 'let us consent' in v. 23, no doubt unaware of the key word אוֹת ʾot 'sign' that they are invoking, we can imagine the Israelite audience of this story enjoying the subtle wordplay.[50]

---

50. On the centrality of circumcision to the story in Genesis 34, see Harvey E. Goldberg, "Cambridge in the Land of Canaan: Descent, Alliance, Circumcision, and Instruction in the Bible," *Journal of the Ancient Near Eastern Society* 24 (1996): 9–34, esp. 22–24. On p. 24, Goldberg observed that, "While the people of Shechem seem to offer all the signs of alliance, including the exchange of daughters, it is suggestive that, correlative to the feigned agreement, nowhere is the term *berit* used." The same is true of אוֹת ʾot 'sign', as just noted, except that the author managed to allude to this term by using the verb א-ו-ת ʾ-w-t 'consent' 3x in the story.

20. Exodus 15:19

וַיָּשֶׁב יְהוָה עֲלֵהֶם אֶת־מֵי הַיָּם וּבְנֵי יִשְׂרָאֵל הָלְכוּ בַיַּבָּשָׁה בְּתוֹךְ הַיָּם:

And YHWH returned upon them the waters of the sea, and
the Israelites walked on the dry-land in the midst of the sea.

In no. 12 above, we looked at a delightful visual wordplay within the biblical text. We end this chapter with another example of this technique, even if what follows cannot be substantiated for ancient Israel itself. In fact, almost undoubtedly this example of visual wordplay developed at a later time in Jewish history, but I find it so attractive that I take the opportunity to present it here nonetheless. The relevant text is Exodus 15, the majority of which includes the poem known as the Song of the Sea, aptly placed within the larger prose narrative.

The most ancient witness to this poem is 4QExod^c (4Q14), one of the biblical manuscripts among the Dead Sea Scrolls.[51] Notwithstanding this manuscript's fragmentary condition, it is clear that the poem was written out in it in block fashion and not in stanza fashion—which is to say, a mere glimpse of the lettering would not disclose to the reader whether the text before him was prose or poetry. Eventually, however, Jewish tradition mandated that the Song of the Sea should be written in stanza fashion (for lack of a better term), though to be sure several sub-traditions emerged on exactly how the poem should appear. One such variation employs a delightful visual play in v. 19, which actually is the first verse to return to the prose narrative, even though the scribal practice in this version continues to present the text as if it were part of the poem. In a representative Torah scroll, the visual wordplay in Exod 15:19 is presented like this (see Figure 1):

---

51. The text was published by Judith E. Sanderson, "4QExod^c," in Eugene Ulrich and Frank Moore Cross, eds., *Qumran Cave 4/VII* (Discoveries in the Judaean Desert 12; Oxford: Clarendon, 1994), 118 and Plate XIX. The only other Qumran text with our passage, 4QRP^c (4Q365), breaks off right at this point (and how often does that happen when one wishes to consult a Dead Sea Scrolls text!). See Emanuel Tov and Sidnie White, "Reworked Pentateuch," in Harold Attridge et al., *Qumran Cave 4/VIII* (Discoveries in the Judaean Desert 13; Oxford: Clarendon, 1994), 268 and Plate XXIII. The interested reader may consult the photographs at http://www.deadseascrolls.org.il /about-the-project/the-digital-library.

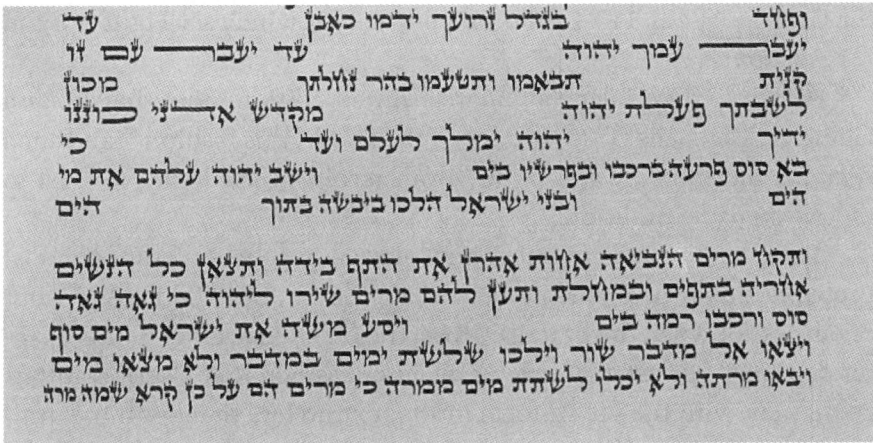

FIGURE 1: Exod 15:9 (and surrounding verses)
as presented in a contemporary Torah scroll.
[Torah scroll by scribe Rabbi Gustavo Surazski. Scroll
image courtesy of Temple Aliyah, Needham, MA.]

The penultimate line break of the poetic section occurs after the word
מֵי *me* 'waters of', thereby resulting in the final line looking like this:

הים	ובני ישראל הלכו ביבשה בתוך	הים
HYM	WBNY YŚR'L HLKW BYBŠH BTWK	HYM
the sea	and the Israelites walked on the dry-land in the midst of	the sea

Or, with Masoretic apparatus, the text looks like this:

הַיָּם:	וּבְנֵי יִשְׂרָאֵל הָלְכוּ בַיַּבָּשָׁה בְּתוֹךְ	הַיָּם
hay-yam	*u-bne yiśra'el halku bay-yabbaša bə-tok*	*hay-yam*
the sea	and the Israelites walked on the dry-land in the midst of	the sea

Note how the two occurrences of הים HYM *hay-yam* 'the sea' (the first
of which belongs to the preceding clause) are left and right justified,
with the remaining phrase 'and the Israelites walked on the dry-land
in the midst of' positioned in the middle of the line. The effect is to
give a visual image of the Israelites walking in the midst of the sea.

Among the medieval manuscripts that present the text in this
fashion, the reader is directed to Cambridge MS Add.652 (France, thirteenth century), folio 47v, line 10; and Oxford Bodleian MS. Kennicott 1

(La Coruña, Spain, 1476), folio 44b, line 6—for which see Figures 2 and 3, respectively.[52]

For an early modern standard printed edition, note that Johann Heinrich Michaelis (1720) produced the text in this fashion;[53] and such remains the standard format in Torah scrolls in use today, at least in the Ashkenazic tradition.[54]

To repeat: we cannot know how old this practice is,[55] though most probably this scribal custom developed only in the Middle Ages. But regardless of when the practice arose, the final illustration in this chapter demonstrates that later Jews also understood that a scribe/author could play with the visual form of the text no less than with the oral/aural nature of words.[56]

---

52. As noted above (n. 26), the wonders of the Internet now allow the reader to view these manuscripts for him- or herself. See, respectively, http://cudl.lib.cam.ac.uk/view/MS-ADD-00652/1, and http://bav.bodleian.ox.ac.uk/digitized-items-hebrew-manuscripts (as noted above, in n. 26, the reader then must scroll down to MS. Kennicott 1 in the long list of manuscripts). As an aside, note that the Kennicott Bible (as it is called generally) is the most lavishly illuminated Bible manuscript of the Middle Ages, produced only sixteen years before the expulsion of the Jews from Spain.

53. Johann Heinrich Michaelis, *Biblia Hebraica, ex aliquot manuscriptis* (Halae Magdeburgicae: Typis & Sumtibus Orpha notrophei, 1720), 58a, top line.

54. *Tiqqun Soferim la-Qore' ba-Torah* (Tel Aviv: Sinai, n.d.), 113. This text is based on an edition printed in Amsterdam in 1866. For an halakhic codification of this practice, see Shelomo Ganzfried, *Sefer Qeset ha-Sofer* (originally published in Ungvar, Hungary, 1835; 2nd ed., 1871; reprint: Brooklyn: Moriah, 1985), 272–73.

55. Our oldest post-Qumran exemplar does not produce the text of Exod 15:19 in this manner. I refer to the Ashkar-Gilson Hebrew manuscript no. 2, which is dated to ca. 700 C.E. and which fortunately includes Exodus 15, the Song of the Sea. Even though the text is not complete at this point in the extant portion of the manuscript, we are able to determine that a different layout for the relevant words was used. For general treatment and photograph, see Paul Sanders, "The Ashkar-Gilson Manuscript: Remnant of a Proto-Masoretic Model Scroll of the Torah," *Journal of Hebrew Scriptures*, vol. 14, article 7 (2014), available online at http://www.jhsonline.org/Articles/article_201.pdf. For a more popular version of the same article, see Paul Sanders, "Missing Link in Hebrew Bible Formation," *Biblical Archaeology Review* 41.6 (Nov.–Dec. 2015): 46–52, 74, 76.

56. For two stellar examples of visual wordplay in the ancient Egyptian story of The Shipwrecked Sailor, see Rendsburg, "Word Play in Biblical

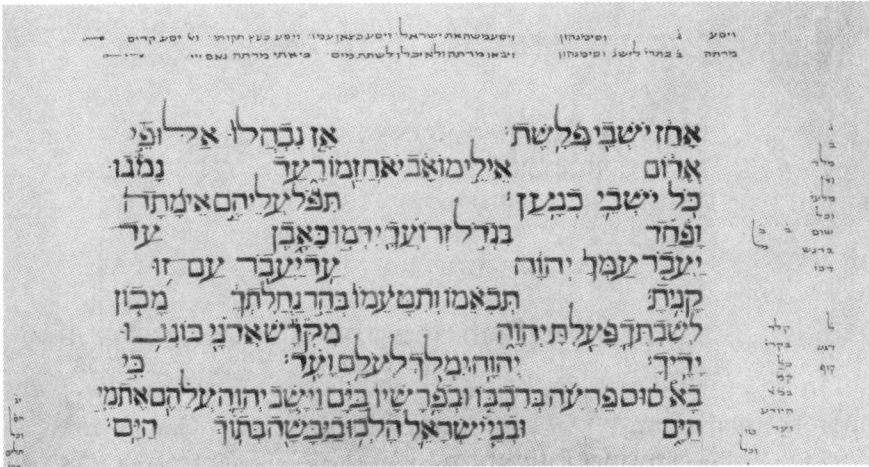

FIGURE 2: Cambridge MS Add.652 (France, thirteenth century), folio 47v. See line 10 (the bottom line in this cropped version of the page) for the layout of the relevant line. [Reproduced by kind permission of the Syndics of Cambridge University Library.]

FIGURE 3: Oxford Bodleian MS. Kennicott 1 (Spain, 1476), folio 44b. See line 6 (in this cropped version of the page) for the layout of the relevant line. [Used by kind permission of the Bodleian Library, University of Oxford.]

Hebrew: An Eclectic Collection," 160–61. For many other literary devices in this important composition, see Rendsburg, "Literary Devices in the Story of the Shipwrecked Sailor," 13–23.

CHAPTER EIGHTEEN

WORDPLAY ON NAMES

A special type of wordplay occurs in the Bible with proper names. I do not intend to discuss here the rather obvious ones—such as the plays upon the name of יַעֲקֹב *ya'aqob* 'Jacob', for which see Gen 25:26, with use of the noun עָקֵב *'eqɛb* 'heel' (Jacob grabs the heel of Esau), and Gen 27:36, where Esau employs the verbal root ע-ק-ב *'-q-b* 'supplant'—but rather the more subtle ones that appear in the biblical text. Almost all of the work in this arena has been accomplished by Moshe Garsiel, who has assiduously identified scores of examples throughout the Bible.[1] The present chapter is based almost entirely on his excellent research.[2]

Such wordplays may take several forms. We begin with the treatment of alliteration, by now well familiar to readers of this book. As one might expect, in light of the foregoing discussions of this device, at times the biblical authors selected unusual words and forms to echo the sounds present in the proper names (mainly personal names, but also place names, as we shall see).[3]

1. Genesis 4:4

וְהֶבֶל הֵבִיא גַם־הוּא מִבְּכֹרוֹת צֹאנוֹ וּמֵחֶלְבֵהֶן

And Abel brought, also he, from the firstborn of his flock, and from their suets.

---

1. The most important study is Moshe Garsiel, *Biblical Names: A Literary Study of Midrashic Derivations and Puns* (Ramat-Gan: Bar-Ilan University Press, 1971), with many additional articles on the subject by the same author in the decades since the book's publication.

2. Of the examples below, only nos. 5 and 6 are my original contributions.

3. I have called attention to an occasional example earlier, for example, the play between the root ה-ר-ס *h-r-s* 'destroy' and הַר סִינַי *har sinay* 'Mount Sinai'; see above, Chapter 6, no. 17.

Both the presence and the form of the last word in this sentence have caused scholars to raise an eyebrow. After all, the important point is that Abel brought animal sacrifices to God, parallel to Cain's offering of 'the fruit of the ground' (v. 3). While it is true that חֵלֶב *ḥelɛb* 'suet' is an essential component of the ritual of animal sacrifices (the word is attested 48x in Leviticus), its presence in Gen 4:4 is still a bit odd, especially since it appears at the end of the comment, almost as an afterthought. In addition, the form of the word is a bit odd, since grammatically חֶלְבֵהֶן *ḥɛlbehɛn* 'their suets' is plural, though it is written as if it were to be understood as singular (see Lev 8:16, 8:25).[4] This spelling, however, allows for the three letters ל-ב-ה L-B-H to appear together (that is, without the expected intervening *yod*), thus forming an anagram of the name ה-ב-ל H-B-L, that is, הֶבֶל *hɛbɛl* 'Abel'. The presenter would see the letters in his text, while the listener would hear the same sounds.[5]

Note further that while Cain's offering is described via use of the standard *wayyiqtol* form וַיָּבֵא *wayyabe'* 'and he brought' (v. 3), in the case of Abel the subject is fronted, thereby necessitating the use of a simple past-tense *qatal* verb, to wit, הֵבִיא *hebi'* '[he] brought'. This maneuver allows the consumer of this text to hear an additional /h/–/b/ combination, as in the beginning of the name הֶבֶל *hɛbɛl* 'Abel'. As we have seen time and again in our study, the ancient Israelite literati carefully planned every word in their compositions, all to enhance the pleasure of reading or hearing the text.[6]

---

4. See Emil Kautzsch, *Gesenius' Hebrew Grammar*, trans. A. E. Cowley (Oxford: Clarendon, 1910), 255, §91c: "[the form] perhaps intends the singular."

5. The Samaritan Torah supplies the *yod* in its reading ומחלביהן WMḤLBYHN, which means that the visual is lost a bit, though naturally the oral/aural effect remains.

6. For the alliteration here and for further insights into Genesis 4, see Karolien Vermeulen, "Mind the Gap: Ambiguity in the Story of Cain and Abel," *Journal of Biblical Literature* 133 (2014): 29–42, esp. 34.

2. Numbers 16:30

וְאִם־בְּרִיאָ֞ה יִבְרָ֣א יְהוָ֗ה וּפָצְתָ֨ה הָאֲדָמָ֤ה אֶת־פִּ֙יהָ֙ וּבָלְעָ֤ה אֹתָם֙ וְאֶת־
כָּל־אֲשֶׁ֣ר לָהֶ֔ם וְיָרְד֥וּ חַיִּ֖ים שְׁאֹ֑לָה וִֽידַעְתֶּ֔ם כִּ֧י נִֽאֲצ֛וּ הָאֲנָשִׁ֥ים הָאֵ֖לֶּה
אֶת־יְהוָֽה׃

> But if a creation YHWH creates, and the earth opens its
> mouth and swallows them and all that is theirs, and they
> descend alive to Sheol—then you will know that these men
> have spurned YHWH.

The unusual word here is בְּרִיאָה *bəriʾa* 'creation', the headword in the
sentence (after the short coordinating particle וְאִם *wə-ʾim* 'but if' (lit.,
'and if'). First, the root of this noun, ב-ר-א *b-r-ʾ* 'create', which is also
the root of the following verb, יִבְרָא *yibraʾ* 'creates', is rare in ancient Hebrew prose. Outside of the early chapters of Genesis, where it appears,
quite expectedly, 11x, the verb appears only in Exod 34:10, Deut 4:32,
and our verse, Num 16:30. Moreover, the noun בְּרִיאָה *bəriʾa* 'creation'
is a *hapax legomenon*; indeed, it is the only noun based on this verbal
root in the entire Bible. Furthermore, the form of this noun—what
scholars call a *qətīla* form, constituting a *nomen actionis*, hence, 'the act
of creating', even if rendered here 'creation'—is a rare morphological
category within Biblical Hebrew.[7]

All of this, accordingly, may cause a certain hesitation in the reading
process, as one can imagine both the presenter underscoring this word
and the listener pondering its purpose. The attentive reader, however,
will realize that בְּרִיאָה *bəriʾa* 'creation' occurs within the narrative of the
rebellion of Korah, Dathan, and Abiram, and hence alliterates with the
name of the last figure, אֲבִירָם *ʾabiram* 'Abiram' (5x in the chapter; most
recently, twice in v. 27). The soundplay is revealed even more when we
juxtapose the two-word phrase at the beginning of v. 30 with the name
of the rebel: וְאִם־בְּרִיאָה *wə-ʾim bəriʾa* 'but if a creation' ~ אֲבִירָם *ʾabiram*
'Abiram'. Note that in this instance, assonance combines with the alliteration, for the unusual noun form בְּרִיאָה *bəriʾa* 'creation' includes the long
/iː/ vowel, exactly as appears in the name אֲבִירָם *ʾabiram* 'Abiram' (even
if I do not indicate vowel length in my simplified transliteration system).

---

7. Nouns with this form are, however, a regular component of Mishnaic
Hebrew grammar.

3. Numbers 31:16

הֵן הֵנָּה הָיוּ לִבְנֵי יִשְׂרָאֵל בִּדְבַר בִּלְעָם לִמְסָר־מַעַל בַּיהוָה עַל־דְּבַר־
פְּעוֹר וַתְּהִי הַמַּגֵּפָה בַּעֲדַת יְהוָה:

Behold, these were to the children of Israel, at the word of
Balaam, to deliver a trespass against YHWH, on account of
Peʿor; and the plague was against the congregation of YHWH.

Earlier in the book of Numbers, the reader encountered the juxtaposition of two distinct narratives, the story of Balaam (chs. 22–24) and that
of the sinfulness of the Israelites at Baal Peʿor (ch. 25), though with no
apparent connection between the two.[8] Our author/editor/compiler/
redactor has reserved the explicit convergence of these two narratives
for a slightly later point in his larger composition, to wit, in Numbers
31. Soundplay to echo the convergence is employed in several ways.
First, the four-letter string of מַעַל בַּ *maʿal ba-* 'a trespass against' not
only alliterates with בִּלְעָם *bilʿam* 'Balaam', but serves as a graphic anagram: ב ל-ע-מ -מ-ע-ל ב ~ ב-ל-ע-מ B-L-ʿ-M (using regular *mem* here, since
final forms of the letters did not exist in the ancient Hebrew script).
Noteworthy here is the fact that while the noun מַעַל *maʿal* 'trespass,
treachery, faithlessness' is standard in Biblical Hebrew, only rarely is it
employed outside the legal texts of the Torah, that is, within narrative
prose. Its presence here, accordingly, represents yet another instance
of the author's mindful selection of a vocable *alliterationis causa*.

The second item here operates at the level of textual allusion: the
toponym פְּעוֹר *pəʿor* 'Peʿor' alludes to the name of Balaam's father,
בְּעוֹר *bəʿor* 'Beʿor' (Num 22:5, etc.), with /p/ and /b/ serving as voiceless
and voiced bilabial plosive counterparts (see below [no. 4] for another
example).

---

8. I say 'no apparent connection', though the experienced reader of biblical texts will realize that even the mere juxtaposition of narratives, including
seemingly unrelated ones, will frequently have a lesson to convey. This was
noted by the classical rabbis, who referred to this device as סמיכות פרשיות
semikut paršiyyot 'juxtaposition of sections'. See further Isaac Gottlieb, *Yeš
Seder la-Miqra'* [English title: *Order In the Bible: The Arrangement of the Torah
in Rabbinic and Medieval Jewish Commentary*] (Ramat-Gan: Bar-Ilan University Press, 2009).

4. Joshua 2:1–2

1 וַיִּשְׁלַ֣ח יְהוֹשֻֽׁעַ־בִּן־נ֠וּן מִֽן־הַשִּׁטִּ֞ים שְׁנַ֨יִם־אֲנָשִׁ֤ים מְרַגְּלִים֙ חֶ֣רֶשׁ לֵאמֹ֔ר לְכ֛וּ רְא֥וּ אֶת־הָאָ֖רֶץ וְאֶת־יְרִיח֑וֹ וַיֵּ֨לְכ֜וּ וַ֠יָּבֹאוּ בֵּית־אִשָּׁ֥ה זוֹנָ֛ה וּשְׁמָ֥הּ רָחָ֖ב וַיִּשְׁכְּבוּ־שָֽׁמָּה:

2 וַיֵּ֣אָמַ֔ר לְמֶ֥לֶךְ יְרִיח֖וֹ לֵאמֹ֑ר הִנֵּ֣ה אֲנָשִׁ֗ים בָּ֣אוּ הֵ֧נָּה הַלַּ֛יְלָה מִבְּנֵ֥י יִשְׂרָאֵ֖ל לַחְפֹּ֥ר אֶת־הָאָֽרֶץ:

¹ And Joshua bin Nun sent from the Shittim two men spies, silently, saying, "Go, see the land, and Jericho"; and they went, and they came to the house of a harlot woman, and her name was Rahab, and they lay-down there.
² And it was said to the king of Jericho, saying, "Behold, men have come here tonight, from the children of Israel, to dig the land."

Two unusual linguistic usages are present in these two verses, which introduce the character רָחָב *rahab* 'Rahab', resident in the city of יְרִיחוֹ *yəriho* 'Jericho' (2x). The first of these is the word חֶרֶשׁ *ḥereš* 'silently, secretly' in v. 1: while the verbal root ח-ר-שׁ *ḥ-r-š* 'be silent' and the noun/adjective חֵרֵשׁ *ḥereš* 'deaf' are well attested in Biblical Hebrew, only in Josh 2:1 do we encounter the adverb חֶרֶשׁ *ḥereš* 'silently, secretly'. Naturally, there is no other way to send out spies, so the word is superfluous (notice that the term does not occur in the Bible's other famous spy story, Numbers 13). Its presence in Josh 2:1 is to enhance the alliteration, with the /r/–/ḥ/ combination evoking the sounds of both 'Rahab' and 'Jericho'.

The second peculiarity is the verb לַחְפֹּר *laḥpor* 'to dig', which occurs both in v. 2 (see above) and in v. 3 (not reproduced here). As implied in my translation, the verbal root ח-פ-ר *ḥ-p-r* means literally 'dig', which by semantic extension means 'spy' in this story (compare English 'dig up dirt'). This usage occurs again only in Deut 1:22. The standard Hebrew verbs for 'spy' are ת-ו-ר *t-w-r* (12x in Numbers 13–14) and ר-ג-ל *r-g-l* (Pi'el) (Num 21:32, Deut 1:2, etc.), used in our story only in the participle form for the noun מְרַגְּלִים *məraggəlim* 'spies'.

The result of this combination of sounds is the following:

רָחָב	*raḥab* 'Rahab'
יְרִיחוֹ	*yəriḥo* 'Jericho' (2x)
חֶרֶשׁ	*ḥɛreš* 'silently, secretly'
לַחְפֹּר	*laḥpor* 'to dig' (2x)

Each of the words contains the combination /r/–/ḥ/ (or in reverse order, /ḥ/–/r/).[9] In addition, the verbal root ח-פ-ר *ḥ-p-r* produces even greater alliteration with רָחָב *raḥab* 'Rahab', when one realizes that the /p/ of the former is the voiceless bilabial stop corresponding to the /b/, or voiced bilabial stop, of the latter (as seen above [no. 3] in the case of 'Peʿor' ~ 'Beʿor').

At every turn, the author of these verses has introduced soundplay intended to be apprehended by the listeners to the story during an oral performance.

5. Judges 3:12

וַיֹּסִפוּ בְּנֵי יִשְׂרָאֵל לַעֲשׂוֹת הָרַע בְּעֵינֵי יְהוָה וַיְחַזֵּק יְהוָה אֶת־עֶגְלוֹן
מֶלֶךְ־מוֹאָב עַל־יִשְׂרָאֵל עַל כִּי־עָשׂוּ אֶת־הָרַע בְּעֵינֵי יְהוָה:

And the children of Israel continued to do evil in the eyes of
YHWH; and YHWH strengthened Eglon, king of Moab, over
Israel, for because they did evil in the eyes of YHWH.

This verse introduces the reader to the character of עֶגְלוֹן *ʿɛglon* 'Eglon', king of Moab, and the biblical author wastes no time in evoking the sounds of his name. Many scholars have noted the connection between this personal name and the word עֵגֶל *ʿɛgɛl* 'calf', with a potential connection to the king's portrayal (if such be intended by the author) as a fatted calf ready for the slaughter (see vv. 21–22, where Eglon is killed by Ehud). What has not been noticed, however, is the employment of

---

9. The sounds would not be exactly the same, since comparative Semitic evidence informs us that the relevant phoneme in the first and fourth items is /ḥ/ (cf. Ugaritic *rḥb* 'wide', the etymon of 'Rahab'; and Arabic *ḥafara* 'dig'), while in the second and third items it is /ḫ/ (cf. Ugaritic *yrḫ* 'moon', the etymon of 'Jericho', i.e., the city where the moon was worshiped in pre-Israelite times; Arabic *ḫarisa* 'be deaf').

the particle עַל כִּי *ʿal ki* 'for because', a rare grammatical usage, occurring elsewhere only in Deut 31:17, Jer 4:28, Mal 2:14, and Ps 139:14—so that Judg 3:12 represents the only attestation of this form in the narrative corpus.[10] Its presence here produces alliteration with עֶגְלוֹן *ʿeglon* 'Eglon'. The /ʿ/ and /l/ sounds are a perfect match,[11] while the /k/ of עַל כִּי *ʿal ki* is the voiceless equivalent of the voiced /g/ of עֶגְלוֹן *ʿeglon* (both are velar plosives, in linguistic parlance). One further notes the contrast between Judg 3:12 and other statements about the Israelites 'doing evil' before God in the book of Judges, for example, Judg 4:1, 6:1, 13:1. In these latter verses, the simple statement occurs, while in Judg 3:12 we get two mentions of the sinfulness, both the initial comment and then the explanatory remark subordinated via the connecting particle עַל כִּי *ʿal ki* 'for because'. All of this indicates that the author of our passage has plotted his prose quite consciously to produce the alliterative effect.

6. Judges 5:12

עוּרִי עוּרִי דְּבוֹרָה עוּרִי עוּרִי דַּבְּרִי־שִׁיר

"Awake, awake, O Deborah, awake, awake, speak (your) song."

This poetic line includes the only collocation in the entire Bible (prose or poetry) of the verb ד-ב-ר *d-b-r* (Piꜥel) 'speak' and the noun שִׁיר *šir* 'song'. Typically the verb שׁ-י-ר *š-y-r* 'sing' governs the noun שִׁיר *šir* 'song' or its feminine counterpart שִׁירָה *šira* 'song' (Exod 15:1, Pss 33:3, 96:1, 98:1, etc.). Alternatively, one may encounter other verbs for 'sing', such as ז-מ-ר *z-m-r* 'sing' and ר-נ-ן *r-n-n* 'sing aloud', often in parallelism with the basic verb שׁ-י-ר *š-y-r* 'sing' (especially the former, e.g., Judg 5:3, Ps 105:2; for the latter, see Ps 59:17). All of this highlights the singularity of the expression דַּבְּרִי שִׁיר *dabbəri šir* 'speak (your) song' in Judg 5:12. The reason for the use of the verb ד-ב-ר *d-b-r* (Piꜥel) 'speak' here, in the fem. sg. imperative form דַּבְּרִי *dabbəri*, is obvious: the sounds evoke the name of דְּבוֹרָה *dəbora* 'Deborah', the heroic figure of the

---

10. Deuteronomy 31:17 is within a prose book, but the context there is a speech by God to Moses, so not quite narrative per se.

11. In both instances, the letter *ʿayin* represents the laryngeal fricative /ʿ/, as determined through Ugaritic cognates.

poem. I would further note that all the lexemes in this stich contain the /r/ sound, thus allowing for a sustained alliteration: *ʿuri ʿuri dəbora ʿuri ʿuri dabbəri šir.*

7. Judges 11:34–36

³⁴ וַיָּבֹא יִפְתָּח הַמִּצְפָּה אֶל־בֵּיתוֹ וְהִנֵּה בִתּוֹ יֹצֵאת לִקְרָאתוֹ בְתֻפִּים וּבִמְחֹלוֹת וְרַק הִיא יְחִידָה אֵין־לוֹ מִמֶּנּוּ בֵּן אוֹ־בַת:

³⁵ וַיְהִי כִרְאוֹתוֹ אוֹתָהּ וַיִּקְרַע אֶת־בְּגָדָיו וַיֹּאמֶר אֲהָהּ בִּתִּי הַכְרֵעַ הִכְרַעְתִּנִי וְאַתְּ הָיִיתְ בְּעֹכְרָי וְאָנֹכִי פָּצִיתִי־פִי אֶל־יְהֹוָה וְלֹא אוּכַל לָשׁוּב:

³⁶ וַתֹּאמֶר אֵלָיו אָבִי פָּצִיתָה אֶת־פִּיךָ אֶל־יְהֹוָה עֲשֵׂה לִי כַּאֲשֶׁר יָצָא מִפִּיךָ אַחֲרֵי אֲשֶׁר עָשָׂה לְךָ יְהֹוָה נְקָמוֹת מֵאֹיְבֶיךָ מִבְּנֵי עַמּוֹן:

³⁴ And Jephthah came to Mizpah, to his house, and behold, his daughter is coming out to greet him, with timbrels and with dance; and indeed, she was the only-one, there was none to him other, son or daughter.
³⁵ And it was, when he saw her, and he tore his clothes, and he said, "Ah, my daughter, you indeed have brought me low, and you, you have become my trouble; and I, I opened my mouth to Yʜwʜ, and I cannot take (it) back."
³⁶ And she said to him, "My father, you opened your mouth to Yʜwʜ; do to me as has gone forth from your mouth, (especially) after Yʜwʜ did for you vengeances against your enemies, against the children of Ammon."

The background for these verses is Jephthah's vow, in which he promised to sacrifice unto Yahweh whoever or whatever (but presumably an animal) came out of his house to greet him upon his return home from victorious battle (see vv. 30–31). Alas, it was his daughter, his only child, who greeted him—and thus he was forced to fulfill his vow and (apparently) sacrifice her to God.[12]

---

12. I say 'apparently' because the text is never explicit about this, though to be sure such is strongly suggested (see v. 39). For the most thorough treatment of the subject, see David Marcus, *Jephthah and His Vow* (Lubbock: Texas Tech

The key verb in this passage is ה-צ-פ *p-ṣ-h* 'open', used in the expressions וְאָנֹכִי פָּצִיתִי־פִי *wa-ʾanoki paṣiti pi* 'and I, I opened my mouth' (v. 35; spoken by Jephthah) and אָבִי פָּצִיתָה אֶת־פִּיךָ *ʾabi paṣita ʾet pika* 'my father, you opened your mouth' (v. 36; spoken by his daughter). The verb alludes to the name יִפְתָּח *yiptaḥ* 'Jephthah', which derives from a synonymous verb פ-ת-ח *p-t-ḥ* 'open'. But more crucially for our present concern, ה-צ-פ *p-ṣ-h* 'open' alliterates with the toponym הַמִּצְפָּה *ham-miṣpa* 'Mizpah', lit., 'the lookout' (v. 34), where the action takes place, derived from the verbal root ה-פ-צ *ṣ-p-h* 'scout, watch, observe'.[13]

8. 1 Samuel 2:34, 36

34 וְזֶה־לְּךָ הָאוֹת אֲשֶׁר יָבֹא אֶל־שְׁנֵי בָנֶיךָ אֶל־חָפְנִי וּפִינְחָס בְּיוֹם אֶחָד יָמוּתוּ שְׁנֵיהֶם:

----

36 וְהָיָה כָּל־הַנּוֹתָר בְּבֵיתְךָ יָבוֹא לְהִשְׁתַּחֲוֺת לוֹ לַאֲגוֹרַת כֶּסֶף וְכִכַּר־לֶחֶם וְאָמַר סְפָחֵנִי נָא אֶל־אַחַת הַכְּהֻנּוֹת לֶאֱכֹל פַּת־לָחֶם:

34 And this will be for you the sign that is to come to your two sons, to Hophni and Pinḥas: on one day the two of them will die.

----

36 And it will be, all who are left in your house shall come and prostrate themselves to him, for a penny of silver and a loaf of bread, and he shall say, "Attach me, please, to one of the priestly-groups, in order to eat a piece of bread."

In these verses, God addresses the aging Eli with news of the impending fate of his two sons, Hophni and Pinḥas (traditional English 'Phineas'), the establishment of a new priestly line (v. 35, not reproduced here),

---

Press, 1986), esp. 13–32. For an earlier treatment of these verses in our study, see above, Chapter 10, no. 9. And for still more, see below, Chapter 19, no. 12.

13. Readers will be familiar with the name of the mountain that overlooks Jerusalem, and hence serves as a lookout, namely, הַר הַצּוֹפִים *har haṣ-ṣopim* 'the mount of the scouts', known in English as 'Mount Scopus', derived from the ancient Greek word *skopein* 'look, watch' (cf. English 'telescope', 'microscope', 'scope it out', etc.), per Josephus, *Antiquities of the Jews*, book 11, ch. 8, §5.

and the aftermath of the disaster, epitomized by the lack of basic food necessities. One word stands out in these verses as a linguistic oddity, namely סְפָחֵנִי *səpaḥeni* 'attach me' (v. 36). The root ס-פ-ח *s-p-ḥ* 'join, attach' is exceedingly rare in the Bible, occurring elsewhere only in 1 Sam 26:19, Isa 14:1, and Job 30:7 (the usage in Hab 2:15 appears to be a homonymous root, unrelated to the verb under discussion here). The author of our text has cleverly introduced it here, along with the first-person common sg. pronominal suffix נִי- *-ni* 'me', hence סְפָחֵנִי *səpaḥeni* 'attach me', in order to produce the alliteration with the names of the two sons: חָפְנִי וּפִינְחָס *ḥopni u-pinḥas* 'Hophni and Pinḥas'. The result is a stellar illustration of the technique under discussion: the employment of unusual forms and lexemes in order to augment the oral/aural character of the ancient text.

Throughout this book I have attempted to include analogous examples of the literary devices studied herein from more familiar literature, especially material composed in the English language. A stellar example of alliteration based on a personal name is forthcoming from Shakespeare's *Henry V*, namely, Fluellen's description of the Duke of Exeter as "as magnanimous as Agamemnon" (Act III, Scene 6). There are many other heroic and magnanimous figures from the ancient past, all or most of whom would have been well known to Shakespeare's audiences (in this case either through the Homeric corpus or through Aeschylus's tragedy),[14] but only Agamemnon fits the bill *alliterationis causa.*

There is more, however, for the biblical authors did not satisfy themselves with simple soundplays based on the characters' names in a story. At times they employed a more sophisticated technique, which Garsiel labels a "tacit" name derivation. In these cases, the text does not present alliteration, but rather demands that the reader and listeners apprehend a lexical nexus in order to mine the full meaning, and thereby enjoy the full pleasure, of the text.

---

14. Shakespeare would stage Agamemnon himself in *Troilus and Cressida* (1602), but that play was still a few years off for theatre-goers attending *Henry V* (1599).

9. Judges 4:15

וַיָּהָם יְהוָה אֶת־סִיסְרָא וְאֶת־כָּל־הָרֶכֶב וְאֶת־כָּל־הַמַּחֲנֶה לְפִי־חֶרֶב
לִפְנֵי בָרָק

And Yнwн confounded Sisera and all his chariotry and all
the camp, by the mouth of the sword, before Barak.

The verb וַיָּהָם *wayyahom*, from the uncommon verbal root ה-מ-ם *h-m-m*
'confound', brings the reader back to Exod 14:24, where it is used in
another military context with camp and chariotry present.[15] But it also
does something much more, in a far shrewder way. The verb ה-מ-ם
h-m-m 'amaze, confound' occurs in several poetic texts—2 Sam 22:15
// Ps 18:15, and Ps 144:6—with reference to בָּרָק *baraq* 'lightning', i.e.,
the same word as the personal name בָּרָק *baraq* 'Baraq' (anglicized as
'Barak'). In addition, 'lightning' is associated with 'the sword' in other
biblical passages—namely, Deut 32:41, Ezek 21:20, 21:33, Nah 3:3—in
the sense that the brandished sword evokes the glisten of lightning.
Hence, the phrase לְפִי־חֶרֶב לִפְנֵי בָרָק *lə-pi ḥereb lipne baraq* 'by the mouth
of the sword, before Baraq/lightning' in Judg 4:15 exploits this idiom.
The result is a pair of associations related to בָּרָק *baraq*, as both 'Baraq'
(personal name) and 'lightning' (common noun), which would not be
lost on the perceptive audience member listening to a performance of
this composition.

10. 2 Kings 9:37

[והית] וְהָיְתָה* נִבְלַת אִיזֶבֶל כְּדֹמֶן עַל־פְּנֵי הַשָּׂדֶה בְּחֵלֶק יִזְרְעֶאל

"And the carcass of Jezebel shall be as dung on the face of
the field, in the meadow of Jezreel."

---

15. In fact, this is but one of several features that links Exodus 14–15 and
Judges 4–5 (both with prose and poetic accounts of the same event)—so
much so that in Jewish tradition (according to the annual reading cycle) the
latter text, from the Prophets section of Tanakh, serves as the Haftarah for
the reading of the former text, from the Torah. To be more accurate, Ashke-
nazim read Judges 4–5, while Sephardim read only Judges 5, but the point
remains nonetheless.

The actual etymology of the name אִיזֶבֶל ʾizɛbɛl 'Jezebel' is available through the resources of Ugaritic language and literature, wherein one finds the expression ʾiy zbl bʿl ʾarṣ 'where is the Prince, Baʿal of the Earth?' (*CAT* 1.6:IV:16), a line stated about Baʿal, the most popularly worshipped deity in the Canaanite pantheon—and let us recall here the obvious, namely, Jezebel's identity as a Phoenician/Canaanite princess, who married Ahab, king of Israel. The Ugaritic passage quoted above provides the exact phrase that serves as Jezebel's name, letter-for-letter: ʾiy zbl 'where is the Prince' = אִיזֶבֶל ʾizɛbɛl.

The key noun here is zbl 'prince', derived from a root z-b-l 'be lofty, be exalted', which appears in Hebrew in the form זְבֻל zabul 'lofty abode', used for the Temple in concrete fashion (1 Kgs 8:13 // 2 Chr 6:2) and for the heavenly abode (Isa 63:15) and the domain of the sun and the moon (Hab 3:11) in poetic, metaphorical style.[16] Unfortunately, the Ugaritic (almost totally) consonantal writing system does not disclose the vowels of zbl, though presumably it was pronounced in some way approximate to the Hebrew vocalization זְבֻל zabul preserved by the much later Masoretes for this word, with positive connotation. Hebrew tradents, however, could not countenance the name of Jezebel, who put to death numerous prophets of Yahweh, in such lofty terms, and hence they 'changed' the second component in her name to זֶבֶל zɛbɛl. Now, this word does not occur in Biblical Hebrew, but it is a common noun in postbiblical Hebrew meaning 'dung, rubbish, garbage' (24x in the Mishna, e.g., Mishna Shabbat 4:1, 8:5, etc.).[17] Almost undoubtedly the word was known already in ancient Israel, even if it is not attested in our preserved texts in the Bible.

All of this serves as the necessary background information for understanding what the biblical author has accomplished in 2 Kgs 9:37, cited above. The prophecy attributed to Elijah states that Jezebel's carcass shall be כְּדֹמֶן ka-domɛn 'as dung', using a standard Biblical Hebrew word (Ps 83:11; Jeremiah [4x]) for this item. The alert reader

---

16. See also the Israelite tribal name זְבֻלוּן/זְבוּלֻן (two different spellings for the same word) zabulun 'Zebulun', along with the personal name זְבֻל zabul 'Zebul' (an officer of Abimelech [Judges 9]), both of which derive from the same base noun.

17. It may be related to the Ugaritic verb zbl meaning 'be sick' and the noun zbln 'illness'.

apprehends the allusion to the key component of the character's name, the synonymous noun זֶבֶל *zebel* 'dung, excrement, rubbish, garbage'. The effect is striking: in Garsiel's words, the verse constitutes "not merely a sarcastic pun, but a reflection of a deeper conviction that there is a link between the meaning inherent in the name and the doom of its owner."[18]

11. Zechariah 9:6

וְיָשַׁב מַמְזֵר בְּאַשְׁדּוֹד וְהִכְרַתִּי גְּאוֹן פְּלִשְׁתִּים:

And a bastard will dwell in Ashdod;
and I will cut-off the pride of the Philistines.

Among the prophetic oracles against the nations (on which see further in Chapter 25) are several proclamations directed at or against the Philistines. Amos (1:8), Jeremiah (47:4), Ezekiel (25:16), and Zechariah (9:6) all take advantage of the same wordplay, which we illustrate here with the last of these passages.

According to the biblical tradition, a tradition that has been corroborated by archaeological evidence unearthed in modern times, the Philistines migrated to the southern coastal plain of the land of Canaan from their original home in כַּפְתּוֹר *kaptor* 'Caphtor' (Deut 2:23, Amos 9:7, etc.). Modern scholars identify Caphtor with the Aegean in general or with Crete in particular. The latter name is attested in the Bible as כְּרֵתִים/ כְּרֵתִי *kəreti* (sg.)/*kəretim* (pl.) 'Cherethite(s)', that is, the Cretans, as an equivalent term for the Philistines (see especially Ezek 25:16 and Zeph 2:5, though also 2 Sam 8:18, 15:18, 20:7, 20:23, 1 Kgs 1:38, 1:44, 1 Chr 18:17).

Now, by sheer coincidence, the same three consonants in the Hebrew term כְּרֵתִים/כְּרֵתִי *kəreti* (sg.)/*kəretim* (pl.) 'Cherethite(s)/Cretan(s)', namely, כ-ר-ת *k-r-t*, constitute the verbal root 'cut-off, destroy, annihilate' (in the Hiph'il stem). The Hebrew prophets took full advantage of this happenstance, using this verb in the four aforementioned verses to refer to the prophesied defeat of the Philistines. Zechariah 9:6, the passage we utilize here by way of illustration, states וְהִכְרַתִּי גְּאוֹן פְּלִשְׁתִּים *wəhikratti gə'on pəlištim* 'and I will cut-off the pride of the Philistines'.

18. Garsiel, *Biblical Names*, 44.

12. Genesis 27:11

וַיֹּאמֶר יַעֲקֹב אֶל־רִבְקָה אִמּוֹ הֵן עֵשָׂו אָחִי אִישׁ שָׂעִר וְאָנֹכִי אִישׁ חָלָק:

And Jacob said to Rebekah his mother, "Behold, Esau my
brother is a hairy man, and I am a smooth man."

We conclude this chapter with one of the most brilliant wordplays in
the Bible, one that returns us to the book of Genesis. I label it 'brilliant' not only because of the manner in which the text builds upon the
characterizations of Jacob and Esau, but because in this instance, as we
shall see, not just *double* meaning is present, but indeed *triple* meaning.

The verse cited here appears within the well-known account of
Jacob's deception of his father, Isaac, and the subsequent procurement
of the blessing intended for his brother, Esau.[19] Rebekah, it will be
recalled, was the instigator of the plot, to which Jacob offered several
remonstrations, including the above remark. On the surface, the key
words שָׂעִר *śaʿir* 'hairy'[20] and חָלָק *ḥalaq* 'smooth' describe the presence
or absence of hair on the skin of the two brothers. At the same time,
though, the first one evokes the name of the mountain where the older
brother's descendants will live, for Edom is regularly associated with הַר
שֵׂעִיר *har śeʿir* 'Mount Seʿir' (Gen 36:8–9, etc.); while the southernmost
extreme of Israel is recorded in the book of Joshua as הָהָר הֶחָלָק *ha-har
he-ḥalaq* 'Mount Halaq'. In fact, the two toponyms are collocated in
the following expression:

Josh 12:7 (see similarly 11:17)

וְעַד־הָהָר הֶחָלָק הָעֹלֶה שֵׂעִירָה

wə-ʿad ha-har hɛ-ḥalaq ha-ʿolɛ śeʿira

and until Mount Halaq, which rises toward Seʿir

Presumably, Mount Halaq ('smooth') was a bald-faced mountain, while
Mount Seʿir was covered with trees ('hairy'), the contrast of which

---

19. For earlier treatment, in addition to Garsiel, *Biblical Names*, 66, see
Gevirtz, "Of Patriarchs and Puns," 48.

20. The expected spelling is שֵׂעִיר *śaʿir*, as occurs elsewhere in the Bible
when the noun means 'hairy-goat' (e.g., Lev 16:9).

elicited the names of the two mountains among the locals (compare, for example, Mount Baldy in southern California, among many similarly named peaks in the U.S. and Canada)—a point that the author of Genesis 27 exploited by placing the words cited above into the mouth of Jacob.

In the case of the Hebrew adjective חָלָק ḥalaq 'smooth' (and the verb derived therefrom), however, there is yet another connotation inherent, to wit, 'smooth-talking', with pejorative meaning (as obtains in English), for which see Prov 2:16, 7:5, 26:28, 28:23, 29:5.[21] Jacob, of course, is the smooth-talking one par excellence, ancient Israel's match for Odysseus.

In sum, then, the word שָׂעִר śaʿir 'hairy' refers to Esau's hairy skin, while also alluding to the name of הַר שֵׂעִיר har śeʿir 'Mount Seʿir' (hence double meaning is present); while the word חָלָק ḥalaq 'smooth' connotes three things at once: (a) Jacob's smooth skin, (b) the name of the mountain at Israel's southern terminus, and (c) the ability to engage in smooth talk. A master literatus has done it again—and one can imagine his audience celebrating the multiplicity of meaning.

The examples treated in this chapter represent only the tip of the iceberg; for the reader interested in a more in-depth treatment of this subject, I once more commend Moshe Garsiel's book and subsequent articles. Regardless, however, these dozen examples suffice to demonstrate the extent to which the ancient authors would utilize language in the service of literature. The first eight passages provide additional instances of alliteration, a feature examined in various chapters throughout the present book, though now within the more specific context of personal names. The last four passages treated move us into a new dimension, requiring much more of the listener than an ear trained to hear the same or similar sounds—for in these instances the audience member must be processing her internal vocabulary lists and literary interconnections in order to grasp the author's full intent.

In a contemporary setting, one can imagine authors playing on such names (both surnames and first names) as Sally Ride, first U.S.

---

21. We examined the first two of these verses in Chapter 15, no. 17, where I rendered the word הֶחֱלִיקָה heḥeliqa as 'she makes (her words) slick'.

female astronaut ("Ride, Sally, Ride"); the Canadian professional cyclist Ryder Hejsedal ("rides to victory"); the Olympic sprint champion Usain Bolt of Jamaica ("wins in lightning performance"); and Gal Fridman, Israel's first and only Olympic gold medalist, in the sport of windsurfing (*gal* means 'wave' in Hebrew).[22] As my simple examples indicate, newspaper headline writers are particularly fond of such wordings. For a parallel from a toponym, one can fancy the amusement that an ancient Israelite literary master would have allowed himself with the fact that John D. Rockefeller was born in Richford, New York (even though, in reality, the town is a very poor community, in the northern reaches of Appalachia).

One need not, however, simply imagine such plays upon proper names, for the present writer is able to tender three stellar examples of this device, in which the text demands specialized knowledge of a singular data point in order to allow the reader/listener to fully understand the lexical-historical connection.

The first comes from the realm of music, to wit, Edward Elgar's "Variations on an Original Theme" ("Enigma") Op. 36 (1899), with its initials and code-names for the fourteen individual variations, each with a particular person embedded therein. Of the fourteen, none bears more cryptic information than the ninth variation, "Nimrod," with reference to Elgar's friend and publisher, Augustus J. Jaeger of Novello & Co. (London). The person enjoying this composition would need to know that Jaeger means 'hunter' in German, and that Nimrod was a 'mighty hunter' according to the biblical tradition (Gen 10:9)— which means that a double leap is necessary to apprehend the title of the ninth variation.[23] Clearly, one simply can listen to and appreciate the music without such knowledge, and no doubt many attenders of a performance of this composition do so. The one with the specialized knowledge, however, does so with a smile. In like fashion, the reader of Zech 9:6 'and I will cut-off the pride of the Philistines' (see above)

---

22. Though in this instance, the athlete's father, Uri Fridman, intentionally named his son 'Gal', given his own commitment to nautical pursuits.

23. Nowadays such information typically is included in the program notes, though online sources also are helpful here: http://www.elgar.org/3enigma .htm and https://en.wikipedia.org/wiki/Enigma_Variations.

understands the message clearly; though the one who hears the echo of the noun כְּרֵתִים/כְּרֵתִי kəreti (sg.)/kəretim (pl.) 'Cherethite(s)/Cretan(s)' in the verbal form וְהִכְרַתִּי wəhikratti 'and I will cut-off' appreciates the writer's craft all the more.

My second example derives from the writing of J. R. R. Tolkien, whose central character Bilbo Baggins lives at Bag End, a rather curiously named locale in the Shire. The toponym actually carries two connotations. On the surface level, it was the name of the farmhouse home of Tolkien's aunt, Jane Neave, in Dormston, Worcestershire, which Tolkien would visit during his outings into the Cotswolds and beyond. But there is a more complicated understanding of the term as well: As professor of Anglo-Saxon (Old English) at the University of Oxford, Tolkien lamented the manner in which incursions from French had forever changed his beloved English language, from the Middle English period onward. As such, he resisted using French loanwords, especially whilst creating the world of Old England, as it were, in his mythopoeic works *The Hobbit* and *The Lord of the Rings*. Hence, translate Bag End into French and you get *cul-de-sac*, which describes the location of Bag End as a street with no outlet, but which term Tolkien could in no way employ in his writing.[24] To some extent, accordingly, the Bag End wordplay is a bit of a style-switching technique as well (on which see below, Chapter 24).

My third and final example comes from the British television series "Downton Abbey"—the current rage (as I write these words) of so many viewing enthusiasts—and has to do in particular with the name of Lord Grantham's dogs Isis (alas, now deceased) and Tio (introduced in season six, episode seven). The former is the name of the ancient Egyptian goddess of beauty, wisdom, and magic; while the latter is the name of the wife of Amenhotep II and mother of Thutmose IV.[25] What is the connection? The television programme is filmed at Highclere Castle in Hampshire, which in real life serves as home to the 8th Earl

---

24. See T. A. Shippey, *J. R. R. Tolkien: Author of the Century* (Boston: Houghton Mifflin, 2000), 10.

25. Since the ancient Egyptian writing system does not indicate the vowels, Tio is referred to in the scholarly literature by different forms: Tiaa/Tio/Tiya/Tiy.

of Carnarvon (b. 1956), great-grandson of the 5th Earl of Carnarvon (1866–1923), well known for his explorations and excavations in Egypt, often jointly with Howard Carter. Their most famous discovery, of course, was the tomb of King Tutankhamun, found in 1922. Indeed, Highclere Castle has a fine collection of Egyptian antiquities on exhibition in its lower level (even if the great finds from King Tut's tomb remain on display in the Egyptian Museum in Cairo). Now this is a lot of specialized information for the viewer to bear in mind, but such (to my mind at least) lies behind the decision of Julian Fellowes (b. 1949), creator and writer of "Downton Abbey," to name the family dogs Isis and Tio, as a minor nod and small homage to the real-life stately home and its aristocratic denizens. In fact, Lord Fellowes is a friend of the Carnarvon family and has stated publicly that in conceiving the television drama and its setting, he had Highclere Castle in mind.

Though there is more. Lord Fellowes's wife, Emma Joy Kitchener Fellowes (b. 1963), is the the great-grandniece of the 1st Earl Kitchener (1850–1916), who served the British Army with distinction in Egypt and the Sudan.[26] Moreover, Earl Kitchener and the 5th Earl of Carnarvon were personal friends who traveled in the same social circles, both in England and in Egypt. Indeed, Earl Kitchener stayed at Highclere Castle in June 1914, on the eve of World War I. Earl Kitchener also was close to Alfred de Rothschild (1842–1918), whose daughter Almina (1876–1969) married the 5th Earl of Carnarvon and thus became the 5th Countess of Carnavon. All of which indicates the multigenerational interconnections of the families that bridge the reality of Highclere Castle and its fictional alter ego Downton Abbey.[27]

---

26. Indeed, Kitchener's "Survey of Western Palestine," conducted with Claude R. Conder on behalf of the Palestine Exploration Fund during the years 1874–1877, remains to this day a valuable resource to all who research the historical geography and the archaeological sites of the land of Israel.

27. While I was well aware of the Egyptological connections outlined above, I am most grateful to Her Ladyship, the 8th Countess of Carnarvon, for receiving my wife Melissa and me at Highclere Castle in July 2017, for enlightening us about the relationship between the 1st Earl Kitchener and the 5th Earl of Carnarvon, and for directing me to the details recorded in her engaging book *Lady Almina and the Real Downton Abbey: The Lost Legacy of Highclere Castle* (London: Hodder, 2011), esp. 115 and 123.

Finally, it probably does not hurt that Julian Fellowes himself was born in Cairo, the city where his father was posted while serving in the British diplomatic corps. Somewhere in all of this lies the source of the names of Lord Grantham's dogs, Isis and Tio. In fact, when Lord Grantham names the newly arrived Tio in season six, episode seven, Lady Edith apparently takes the name to mean something else, for she states, "I thought we always had names from ancient Egypt"—at which point Lord Grantham explains her pharaonic connections.

In short, both in ancient Israel and in contemporary settings, artistic creators could expect their audiences to have considerable specialized knowledge that would allow them to gain the full pleasure of experiencing the text. Or at the very least, they had (and continue to have) a jolly good time with their own internal wordplays and allusive references.

CHAPTER NINETEEN

THE USE OF *wə-hinne* 'and behold'

One of the discoveries of modern biblical scholarship, especially in its literary bent, is the function of the particle וְהִנֵּה *wə-hinne* 'and behold'. Two scholars, working independently in the mid-1970s, brilliantly made the same insightful discovery. Francis Andersen, an Australian who then was teaching at the Church Divinity School of the Pacific (Berkeley),[1] and Jan Fokkelman, a Dutchman at the University of Leiden,[2] both noticed that וְהִנֵּה *wə-hinne* 'and behold' is employed to allow the reader to view the scene through the eyes of the character—what Andersen called 'participant perspective', the equivalent of the 'point-of-view shot' (POV shot) in film. Fokkelman's contribution was more limited, though just as insightful—more anon.[3]

The best way to describe the literary device is to illustrate the technique with a classic example:

---

1. Francis I. Andersen, *The Sentence in Biblical Hebrew* (The Hague: Mouton, 1974), 94–96.

2. J. P. Fokkelman, *Narrative Art in Genesis* (Assen: Van Gorcum, 1975), 50–51.

3. I also should mention Shimon Bar-Efrat here, who apparently made the same discovery as Andersen, albeit several years later. I do not have access to his 1979 Hebrew volume *Ha-ʿIṣṣuv ha-ʾOmanuti šel ha-Sippur ba-Miqraʾ* (Tel Aviv: Sifriyat Poʿalim, 1979), so I am unable to know for sure. Though in the English version, *Narrative Art in the Bible* (Sheffield: Almond Press, 1989), 35–36, Bar-Efrat writes in a very similar vein to Andersen. To be sure, the author would not have adopted Andersen's discovery without proper citation, since he cites earlier scholars at every opportunity. For further discussion, see also Berlin, *Poetics and Interpretation of Biblical Narrative*, 62–63 and 149 n. 37.

1. Genesis 22:13

וַיִּשָּׂא אַבְרָהָם אֶת־עֵינָיו וַיַּרְא וְהִנֵּה־אַיִל אַחַר נֶאֱחַז בַּסְּבַךְ בְּקַרְנָיו

And Abraham lifted-up his eyes, and he saw, *wə-hinne* [and behold], a ram behind (him),[4] caught in the thicket by its horns.

In the first five words of this verse (= nine in the English translations), we, the consumers of this text—by which I mean readers, hearers, viewers, et al.—see Abraham within our field of vision. Which is to say, we watch him lifting up his eyes and viewing the surrounding landscape. Were this scene to be filmed, Abraham would be 'on screen'. However, with the introduction of וְהִנֵּה *wə-hinne* 'and behold'—the sixth word in the text—the camera angle would change. At this moment in the text, we see what Abraham sees, through his eyes! With this change of perspective, we no longer see Abraham in our field of vision, but rather we, as consumers of the text, perceive only what Abraham beholds: a ram caught in the thicket by its horns. In a deft move, we become Abraham, as we are at one with him, for our field of vision is his and his field of vision becomes ours. How much more effective this device is, at this crucial point in the narrative, than the blander 'and Abraham saw a ram' would be. In short, we experience this key scene as Abraham experiences it—all through the employment of this little grammatical particle וְהִנֵּה *wə-hinne* 'and behold'.

Numerous other examples of this technique occur throughout biblical prose, a sampling of which are presented here.

2. Genesis 8:11

וַתָּבֹא אֵלָיו הַיּוֹנָה לְעֵת עֶרֶב וְהִנֵּה עֲלֵה־זַיִת טָרָף בְּפִיהָ וַיֵּדַע נֹחַ
כִּי־קַלּוּ הַמַּיִם מֵעַל הָאָרֶץ:

And the dove came to him at evening time, *wə-hinne* [and behold], an olive-leaf plucked in its mouth; and Noah knew that the waters had receded from upon the earth.

---

4. The presence of the word אַחַר *'aḥar* 'behind' in this passage, without anything following, remains a crux. Any attempt to solve the problem here—not that I have a ready solution—would take us too far afield. I content myself, accordingly, with the rendering 'behind (him)'.

Consider the scene: Noah already had sent forth the raven, but it had quickly returned (v. 7); and he had sent forth the dove, but it too had quickly returned (vv. 8–9). So, he waited a week and then sent forth the dove once more (v. 10). At the beginning of v. 11, we see the dove returning, but wait, 'וְהִנֵּה wə-*hinne* [and behold], an olive-leaf plucked in its mouth', a sight that we behold through the eyes of Noah. For a follow-up instance, where Noah learns that the earth is now dry, see two verses further, Gen 8:13.

3. Genesis 18:2

וַיִּשָּׂא עֵינָיו וַיַּרְא וְהִנֵּה שְׁלֹשָׁה אֲנָשִׁים נִצָּבִים עָלָיו

And he lifted-up his eyes, and he saw, wə-*hinne* [and behold], three men were stationed above him.

In yet another famous scene from the book of Genesis, Abraham is resting at the entrance of his tent on a hot day (v. 1), when suddenly he perceives three men stationed above him. To allow the reader to experience the arrival of the three visitors as Abraham himself experiences the action, the author employs the key word וְהִנֵּה wə-*hinne* 'and behold'.

4. Genesis 24:15

וַיְהִי־הוּא טֶרֶם כִּלָּה לְדַבֵּר וְהִנֵּה רִבְקָה יֹצֵאת אֲשֶׁר יֻלְּדָה לִבְתוּאֵל בֶּן־
מִלְכָּה אֵשֶׁת נָחוֹר אֲחִי אַבְרָהָם וְכַדָּהּ עַל־שִׁכְמָהּ:

And he barely had finished speaking, wə-*hinne* [and behold], Rebekah comes-out, who was borne to Bethuel son of Milcah, wife of Nahor, brother of Abraham, and her jug on her shoulder.

The longest narrative chapter in the Torah, Genesis 24, treats the reader to a series of verses employing the phrase וְהִנֵּה wə-*hinne* 'and behold'. The first of these occurs in v. 15. The servant has been praying to God in vv. 12–14, anticipating a young lass who might appear at the spring, who would lower her jug so that both the servant and his camels could drink, and who thus indeed would be Isaac's destined bride. And just as he concludes his words, wə-*hinne* 'and behold', Rebekah appears!

Note also the retelling of this scene in the voice of the servant, as he addresses Rebekah's household, in v. 45: וְהִנֵּה רִבְקָה יֹצֵאת וְכַדָּהּ עַל־שִׁכְמָהּ 'wə-hinne [and behold], Rebekah comes-out, and her jug on her shoulder', repeating verbatim what is told by the narrator in v. 15, minus the long insertion of the genealogical information necessary to identify Rebekah there.

5. Genesis 24:30

וַיְהִי | כִּרְאֹת אֶת־הַנֶּזֶם וְאֶת־הַצְּמִדִים עַל־יְדֵי אֲחֹתוֹ וּכְשָׁמְעוֹ אֶת־דִּבְרֵי רִבְקָה אֲחֹתוֹ לֵאמֹר כֹּה־דִבֶּר אֵלַי הָאִישׁ וַיָּבֹא אֶל־הָאִישׁ וְהִנֵּה עֹמֵד עַל־הַגְּמַלִּים עַל־הָעָיִן:

And it was, when he [sc. Laban] saw the nose-ring and the bracelets on the hands of his sister, and when he heard the words of Rebekah his sister, saying, "Thus the man spoke to me"; and he came to the man, wə-hinne [and behold], he is standing by the camels at the spring.

The subject of this verse is Laban, the brother of Rebekah, who sees the wealth represented by the jewelry adorning his sister and thus hurries to meet and greet the man who has bestowed these gifts. Laban's espying the man is not narrated with a bland, 'And he saw the man', but rather we, the readers, are treated to Laban's point of view: וְהִנֵּה עֹמֵד עַל־הַגְּמַלִּים עַל־הָעָיִן 'wə-hinne [and behold], he is standing by the camels at the spring'.

6. Genesis 24:63

וַיֵּצֵא יִצְחָק לָשׂוּחַ בַּשָּׂדֶה לִפְנוֹת עָרֶב וַיִּשָּׂא עֵינָיו וַיַּרְא וְהִנֵּה גְמַלִּים בָּאִים:

And Isaac went-out to urinate in the field,[5] at the turn of evening; and he lifted-up his eyes and he saw, wə-hinne [and behold], camels coming.

---

5. On לָשׂוּחַ lasuah 'to urinate' in this passage, see Gary A. Rendsburg, "Lasūah in Gen. xxiv 63," *Vetus Testamentum* 45 (1995): 558–60.

One final instance of וְהִנֵּה *wǝ-hinne* 'and behold' in this long chapter occurs in v. 63. Since most of the action has centered around the servant and his visit to Aram, where he meets Rebekah and her family, at story's end we are given a glimpse of Isaac, the groom-to-be. Isaac goes about his normal business (see n. 5), when—somewhat unexpectedly—he descries camels approaching from afar. We experience the scene through Isaac's eyes via the employment of וְהִנֵּה *wǝ-hinne* 'and behold' at the end of v. 63.

7. Genesis 26:8

וַיְהִ֗י כִּ֣י אָֽרְכוּ־ל֥וֹ שָׁם֙ הַיָּמִ֔ים וַיַּשְׁקֵ֗ף אֲבִימֶ֨לֶךְ֙ מֶ֣לֶךְ פְּלִשְׁתִּ֔ים בְּעַ֖ד
הַֽחַלּ֑וֹן וַיַּ֗רְא וְהִנֵּ֤ה יִצְחָק֙ מְצַחֵ֔ק אֵ֖ת רִבְקָ֥ה אִשְׁתּֽוֹ׃

And it was, when his days there lengthened, and Abimelech, king of the Philistines, espied through the window, and he saw, *wǝ-hinne* [and behold], Isaac playing with Rebekah his wife.

Since Isaac has passed Rebekah off as his sister—as did his father Abraham on two occasions with Sarah, including before the self-same (presumably) king Abimelech of Gerar—the reader is treated to Abimelech's point of view, when he espies the couple playing/cavorting/fondling/etc. The Hebrew verb here, ק-ח-צ *ṣ-ḥ-q* 'laugh, play'—which, by the way, also puns on Isaac's name, יִצְחָק *yiṣḥaq*—carries all of these meanings. Regardless of its specific denotation here, the actions of Isaac and Rebekah (or to be more precise, of Isaac toward Rebekah) led Abimelech to realize that the two were not siblings, as he had been steered to believe.

8. Exodus 3:2

וַיֵּ֠רָא מַלְאַ֨ךְ יְהֹוָ֥ה אֵלָ֛יו בְּלַבַּת־אֵ֖שׁ מִתּ֣וֹךְ הַסְּנֶ֑ה וַיַּ֗רְא וְהִנֵּ֤ה הַסְּנֶה֙ בֹּעֵ֣ר
בָּאֵ֔שׁ וְהַסְּנֶ֖ה אֵינֶ֥נּוּ אֻכָּֽל׃

And a manifestation of Yʜᴡʜ appeared unto him, in the flame of fire in the midst of the bush; and he saw, *wǝ-hinne* [and behold], the bush is burning, and the bush is not consumed.

In this famous scene, Moses encounters the God of Israel for the first time, indeed, in a most astonishing way, as the flame within the burning bush. To be sure, the reader wishes to experience the scene in the manner in which Moses experienced this singular manifestation of Yahweh—and the author of this passage does not disappoint.

9. Exodus 14:10

וּפַרְעֹה הִקְרִיב וַיִּשְׂאוּ בְנֵי־יִשְׂרָאֵל אֶת־עֵינֵיהֶם וְהִנֵּה מִצְרַיִם | נֹסֵעַ
אַחֲרֵיהֶם וַיִּירְאוּ מְאֹד וַיִּצְעֲקוּ בְנֵי־יִשְׂרָאֵל אֶל־יְהוָה:

And Pharaoh had approached; and the children of Israel
lifted-up their eyes, *wǝ-hinne* [and behold], Egypt traveling
after them, and they feared greatly, and the children of Israel
cried-out unto Yнwн.

The Israelites no doubt believed that they were free of the Egyptians, especially after Pharaoh had let the people go in Exodus 12, as a result of the tenth and culminating plague. Unbeknownst to the Israelites—though the reader is well aware by this point—the Egyptian army is in hot pursuit of the Israelites, and indeed draws near in the verse quoted above. As readers, we gain the perspective of the people of Israel as they witness the Egyptians approaching.

10. Judges 3:25 (2x)

וַיָּחִילוּ עַד־בּוֹשׁ וְהִנֵּה אֵינֶנּוּ פֹתֵחַ דַּלְתוֹת הָעֲלִיָּה וַיִּקְחוּ אֶת־הַמַּפְתֵּחַ
וַיִּפְתָּחוּ וְהִנֵּה אֲדֹנֵיהֶם נֹפֵל אַרְצָה מֵת:

And they [sc. Eglon's guards] waited, until embarrassed,
wǝ-hinne [and behold], he [sc. Eglon] is not opening the
doors of the upper-chamber, and they took the key, and
they opened, *wǝ-hinne* [and behold], their lord fallen to the
ground, dead.

One of the most entertaining stories in the Bible is the episode of King Eglon's death at the hands of Ehud, the Benjaminite hero, who attacked the king while he was seated on the 'throne' in his cool upper-chamber, that is, the toilet room.[6] The reader already knows that the deed has been done (see v. 22), and indeed Ehud has successfully fled already (see v. 23). In v. 24 we view the king's guards outside the chamber, waiting for the king to exit, though the wait continues in v. 25, quoted above. The passage includes two instances of *wə-hinne* 'and behold': (a) in the first of these we can imagine the eyes of the guards on the door and the lock, as time passes and nothing happens; while (b) in the second of these we sense their shock upon opening the door and finding their king on the ground, dead.

11. Judges 4:22 (2x)

וְהִנֵּה בָרָק רֹדֵף אֶת־סִיסְרָא וַתֵּצֵא יָעֵל לִקְרָאתוֹ וַתֹּאמֶר לוֹ לֵךְ וְאַרְאֶךָּ
אֶת־הָאִישׁ אֲשֶׁר־אַתָּה מְבַקֵּשׁ וַיָּבֹא אֵלֶיהָ וְהִנֵּה סִיסְרָא נֹפֵל מֵת
וְהַיָּתֵד בְּרַקָּתוֹ:

wə-hinne [and behold], Barak pursuing Sisera, and Yael went-out to greet him, and she said to him, "Come [lit., go], and I will show you the man whom you seek"; and he came unto her, *wə-hinne* [and behold], Sisera fallen, dead, and the tent-peg in his temple.

Once more we encounter a verse with two instances of *wə-hinne* 'and behold', though in this example the one experiencing the action is different in each case. (a) The previous verse (v. 21) narrates Yael's killing of Sisera, so that when the present verse (v. 22) commences with וְהִנֵּה *wə-hinne* 'and behold'—even though it is not preceded by an active verb, such as 'and she lifted-up her eyes' or 'and she saw'—the reader knows that the text provides us with Yael's perspective of the ensuing action. Said action is Barak approaching in pursuit of Sisera, which the reader experiences through Yael's viewpoint. (b) Even more crucial is the second וְהִנֵּה *wə-hinne* 'and behold' in the verse, which on this occasion provides the reader with Barak's point of view, as he perceives with astonishment the fallen and dead Sisera and then with greater focus the tent-peg driven through his temple.

---

6. For earlier analyses of this episode, see Chapter 10, nos. 6–7; and Chapter 13, no. 17.

12. Judges 11:34

וַיָּבֹא יִפְתָּח הַמִּצְפָּה אֶל־בֵּיתוֹ וְהִנֵּה בִתּוֹ יֹצֵאת לִקְרָאתוֹ בְתֻפִּים
וּבִמְחֹלוֹת וְרַק הִיא יְחִידָה אֵין־לוֹ מִמֶּנּוּ בֵּן אוֹ־בַת:

And Jephthah came to Mizpah, to his house, *wə-hinne* [and
behold], his daughter is coming out to greet him, with
timbrels and with dance; and indeed, she was the only-one,
there was none to him other, son or daughter.

In the previous chapter we looked at this verse, along with the following two verses, regarding the wordplay on the name of Mizpah, which
involves an allusion to the name of Jephthah (see Chapter 18, no. 7). In
this chapter, our attention is drawn to the use of וְהִנֵּה *wə-hinne* 'and
behold' in v. 34. As indicated in our earlier treatment, Jephthah returns
triumphant from battle, expecting to fulfill his vow to sacrifice whoever
or whatever greets him—with the presumption that said 'whoever' or
'whatever' will be a ram or some other animal.[7] As he arrives home,
though, he sees—alas!—his daughter coming out to greet him, with tim-
brel and with dance, in celebration of his victory. As we have come to
expect, the author passes on the option of a word such as וַיַּרְא *wayyar'*
'and he saw', and instead gets right to the point: וְהִנֵּה בִתּוֹ יֹצֵאת לִקְרָאתוֹ
wə-hinne bitto yoṣe't liqra'to 'and behold, his daughter is coming out
to greet him'. Alas, she now must serve the role of sacrificial victim,
in fulfillment of his vow (again, see above, Chapter 18, no. 7—though
see also n. 12 there).

These twelve examples suffice to demonstrate the point, though
in truth there are literally scores of such examples throughout Biblical
Hebrew prose narrative.

Among these scores we find a more specific usage of וְהִנֵּה *wə-hinne*
'and behold', namely, within the description of dreams. The key particle may occur within the narrator's relating of the dream, or it may
occur within the speech of the character as he recounts his dream to

---

7. The modern reader may wish to imagine a pet dog coming to greet
its master, but in the world of ancient Israel, it was just as possible to have a
pet sheep or similar domesticated animal (consider "Mary had a little lamb,"
which originates in nineteenth-century American lore).

others. For with dreams, quite obviously, *only* the dreamer perceives
the action—hence, during its telling or retelling, by definition we gain
the dreamer's perspective, and thus the text is suffused with instances
of וְהִנֵּה *wə-hinne* 'and behold'. While Andersen noted this point in his
seminal study, it was this specific usage of the וְהִנֵּה *wə-hinne* particle
that attracted Fokkelman's attention (see above).

We begin with instances in the voice of the narrator:

13. Genesis 28:12–13 (3x)

¹² וַיַּחֲלֹם וְהִנֵּה סֻלָּם מֻצָּב אַרְצָה וְרֹאשׁוֹ מַגִּיעַ הַשָּׁמָיְמָה וְהִנֵּה מַלְאֲכֵי
אֱלֹהִים עֹלִים וְיֹרְדִים בּוֹ:

¹³ וְהִנֵּה יְהֹוָה נִצָּב עָלָיו וַיֹּאמַר ...

¹² And he dreamed, *wə-hinne* [and behold], a staircase[8] stationed in the earth, and its head reaching unto the heavens,
wə-hinne [and behold], manifestations of God going-up and
going-down on it.
¹³ *wə-hinne* [and behold], Yʜᴡʜ positioned upon it, and he
said . . .

Three times in slightly more than one verse the reader experiences
Jacob's dream as the narrator relates what the dreamer sees: the staircase, the manifestations (or: angels, messengers), and finally God himself.

14. Genesis 41:1–4 (3x)

¹ וַיְהִי מִקֵּץ שְׁנָתַיִם יָמִים וּפַרְעֹה חֹלֵם וְהִנֵּה עֹמֵד עַל־הַיְאֹר:
² וְהִנֵּה מִן־הַיְאֹר עֹלֹת שֶׁבַע פָּרוֹת יְפוֹת מַרְאֶה וּבְרִיאֹת בָּשָׂר
וַתִּרְעֶינָה בָּאָחוּ:
³ וְהִנֵּה שֶׁבַע פָּרוֹת אֲחֵרוֹת עֹלוֹת אַחֲרֵיהֶן מִן־הַיְאֹר רָעוֹת מַרְאֶה
וְדַקּוֹת בָּשָׂר וַתַּעֲמֹדְנָה אֵצֶל הַפָּרוֹת עַל־שְׂפַת הַיְאֹר:

---

8. Hebrew סֻלָּם *sullam*, traditionally understood as 'ladder' (hence, 'Jacob's
ladder'), but more likely this *hapax legomenon* means 'staircase', especially
in the light of its Akkadian cognate, *simmiltu*. See Harold R. (Chaim) Cohen,
Biblical Hapax Legomena in the Light of Akkadian and Ugaritic (Society of Biblical Literature Dissertation Series 37; Missoula, MT: Scholars Press, 1978), 34.

^{4} וַתֹּאכַלְנָה הַפָּרוֹת רָעוֹת הַמַּרְאֶה וְדַקֹּת הַבָּשָׂר אֵת שֶׁבַע הַפָּרוֹת
יְפֹת הַמַּרְאֶה וְהַבְּרִיאֹת וַיִּיקַץ פַּרְעֹה:

^{1} And it was, at the end of two-years of days; and Pharaoh
dreamed, *wə-hinne* [and behold], he is standing by the Nile.
^{2} *wə-hinne* [and behold], from the Nile come-up seven cows,
beautiful of visage and healthy of flesh; and they grazed
among the reeds.
^{3} *wə-hinne* [and behold], seven other cows, coming-up after
them from the Nile, bad of visage and skinny of flesh; and
they stood next to the cows on the bank of the Nile.
^{4} And the cows, bad of visage and skinny of flesh, ate the seven
cows, beautiful of visage and healthy; and Pharaoh awoke.

Perhaps the most famous of all the dreams related in the Bible are
Pharaoh's dreams, which are described in vivid detail in Genesis 41.
The first dream includes three instances of וְהִנֵּה *wə-hinne* 'and behold',
as seen here, in vv. 1–3. Though one notes that the term is not used in
v. 4, in which the bad cows eat the good cows, at which point Pharaoh
awakes.

15. Genesis 41:5–7

^{5} וַיִּישָׁן וַיַּחֲלֹם שֵׁנִית וְהִנֵּה | שֶׁבַע שִׁבֳּלִים עֹלוֹת בְּקָנֶה אֶחָד בְּרִיאוֹת
וְטֹבוֹת:
^{6} וְהִנֵּה שֶׁבַע שִׁבֳּלִים דַּקּוֹת וּשְׁדוּפֹת קָדִים צֹמְחוֹת אַחֲרֵיהֶן:
^{7} וַתִּבְלַעְנָה הַשִּׁבֳּלִים הַדַּקּוֹת אֵת שֶׁבַע הַשִּׁבֳּלִים הַבְּרִיאוֹת וְהַמְּלֵאוֹת
וַיִּיקַץ פַּרְעֹה וְהִנֵּה חֲלוֹם:

^{5} And he slept, and he dreamed a second-time, *wə-hinne*
[and behold], seven ears-of-grain coming-up from one stalk,
healthy and good.
^{6} *wə-hinne* [and behold], seven ears-of-grain, skinny and
blasted by the east-wind, blossoming after them.
^{7} And the seven skinny ears-of-grain swallowed the seven
healthy and full ears-of-grain; and Pharaoh awoke, *wə-hinne*
[and behold], a dream.

The text continues with Pharaoh's second dream, with two instances of וְהִנֵּה wə-*hinne* 'and behold', in vv. 5–6. Once more the swallowing portion of the dream does not include this term, but then at the very end of the narrative, the reader experiences Pharaoh's realization that all was but a dream: וְהִנֵּה חֲלוֹם wə-*hinne ḥalom* 'and behold, a dream'.

As an aside, we note that while most readers consider the two accounts to be two dreams—which, of course, they are, since Pharaoh awoke after the 'first' one (v. 4)—for Pharaoh they are essentially a single dream, as indicated by the non-use of וְהִנֵּה חֲלוֹם wə-*hinne ḥalom* 'and behold, a dream' after the dream about the cows but the inclusion of this statement after the dream about the ears-of-grain.

This becomes apparent to the astute reader in the next verse, v. 8: וַיְסַפֵּר פַּרְעֹה לָהֶם אֶת־חֲלֹמוֹ וְאֵין־פּוֹתֵר אוֹתָם לְפַרְעֹה 'and Pharaoh recounted to them [sc. his wise-men and dream-interpreters] his dream, but there was none who could interpret them'. Which is to say, for Pharaoh the two visions were a single dream (note the use of חֲלֹמוֹ *ḥalomo* 'his dream', giving Pharaoh's perspective, even though this word is in the voice of the narrator), but the less-than-astute wise-men and dream-interpreters understood them as two dreams (note the use of אוֹתָם *'otam* 'them', providing the perspective of the men in the court). This all becomes even more explicit in v. 15, when Pharaoh says to Joseph, חֲלוֹם חָלַמְתִּי וּפֹתֵר אֵין אֹתוֹ 'a dream I have dreamed, but there is none who could interpret it'. This long paragraph has taken us on a long side-tour, but this point emanates from the singular use of וְהִנֵּה חֲלוֹם wə-*hinne ḥalom* 'and behold, a dream' (v. 7) only after Pharaoh awakens from the 'second' dream.

We now turn to examples expressed in the voice of the dreamer himself, as he recounts his dream to others.

16. Genesis 37:7 (3x)

וְהִנֵּה אֲנַחְנוּ מְאַלְּמִים אֲלֻמִּים בְּתוֹךְ הַשָּׂדֶה וְהִנֵּה קָמָה אֲלֻמָּתִי
וְגַם־נִצָּבָה וְהִנֵּה תְסֻבֶּינָה אֲלֻמֹּתֵיכֶם וַתִּשְׁתַּחֲוֶיןָ לַאֲלֻמָּתִי:

"*wə-hinne* [and behold], we are binding sheaves in the middle of the field, *wə-hinne* [and behold], my sheaf stood-up and indeed was positioned; *wə-hinne* [and behold], your sheaves surrounded (it), and they prostrated themselves to my sheaf."

In this passage, Joseph relates the first of his dreams to his brothers, with three occurrences of וְהִנֵּה wə-hinne 'and behold'. One can almost hear the words pouring out of his mouth, punctuated by our key phrase, as he progresses from one scene to the next in his recounting of what he has dreamed.

As a side note, we also observe the use of the verbal form תְסֻבֶּ֫ינָה təsubbena 'surrounded'. This is but one of a handful of prefix-conjugation forms used to express the past tense in all of biblical narrative prose, and the only instance of such a verbal form preceded by וְהִנֵּה wə-hinne 'and behold'.[9] I would explain this usage as another instance of confused syntax (see above, Chapter 8), with Joseph in his hurried and excited manner tripping over his words and unable to produce grammatically correct speech.

17. Genesis 37:9

וַיַּחֲלֹם עוֹד חֲלוֹם אַחֵר וַיְסַפֵּר אֹתוֹ לְאֶחָיו וַיֹּ֫אמֶר הִנֵּה חָלַ֫מְתִּי חֲלוֹם
עוֹד וְהִנֵּה הַשֶּׁ֫מֶשׁ וְהַיָּרֵחַ וְאַחַד עָשָׂר כּוֹכָבִים מִשְׁתַּחֲוִים לִי:

And he dreamed again, another dream, and he related it
to his brothers; and he said, "Behold,[10] I dreamed another
dream, wə-hinne [and behold], the sun and the moon and
eleven stars are prostrating themselves to me."

The significance of וְהִנֵּה wə-hinne 'and behold' here is self-evident, as Joseph now reports his second dream to his brothers.

18. Genesis 40:9

וַיְסַפֵּר שַׂר-הַמַּשְׁקִים אֶת-חֲלֹמוֹ לְיוֹסֵף וַיֹּ֫אמֶר לוֹ בַּחֲלוֹמִ֫י וְהִנֵּה-גֶ֫פֶן
לְפָנָי:

And the chief cupbearer recounted his dream to Joseph, and
he said to him, "In my dream, wə-hinne [and behold], a vine
before me."

---

9. See Joosten, *Verbal System of Biblical Hebrew*, 101, 279–80, 287.

10. Not וְהִנֵּה wə-hinne 'and behold', but rather simply הִנֵּה hinne 'behold', and thus less relevant to the main point under discussion here.

Once more the initial image within the dream is introduced by the key term surveyed in this chapter.

19. Genesis 40:16

וַיֹּאמֶר אֶל־יוֹסֵף אַף־אֲנִי בַּחֲלוֹמִי וְהִנֵּה שְׁלֹשָׁה סַלֵּי חֹרִי עַל־רֹאשִׁי:

And he said to Joseph, "Even I, in my dream, *wə-hinne* [and behold], three baskets of white-bread on my head."

Upon seeing that the chief cupbearer's dream was interpreted so brilliantly by Joseph, with the very positive outcome predicted, the chief baker steps forward to relate his dream to Joseph. As we have come to expect, he too commences with וְהִנֵּה *wə-hinne* 'and behold'. Though naturally, as the experienced reader of the book of Genesis is well aware, in the baker's case the result is not encouraging but devastating.

20.–21. Genesis 41:18–19, 22–23

As two additional examples of the presence of וְהִנֵּה *wə-hinne* 'and behold' in the dreamer's recounting of his dream, I direct the reader's attention to Gen 41:18–19 and 41:22–23, where Pharaoh relates his dreams to Joseph. Since we have reproduced the narrator's description of Pharaoh's two dreams above (nos. 14–15), I desist from presenting the passages containing their retellings here—even though there are key variations, as one would expect, given all that we have stated herein about non-verbatim repetition. Suffice it to say that all four statements in the cited verses commence with the key term וְהִנֵּה *wə-hinne* 'and behold'.

In sum, the use of וְהִנֵּה *wə-hinne* 'and behold' enlivens biblical narrative at every turn, as the reader/listener is able to experience the scene through the eyes of the main character—whether this be in 'real life action' or in dreams. Its discovery by groundbreaking scholars such as Andersen and Fokkelman during the 1970s constitutes one of the great findings of modern biblical scholarship.

CHAPTER TWENTY

SHORTER BEFORE LONGER—
AND DIVERGENCES THEREFROM

One of the linguistic universals identified by scholars is the propensity for languages to place shorter items before longer ones in a series.[1] Thus, for example, in English one finds two-item phrases such as 'bits and pieces', 'pins and needles', 'neat and tidy', 'nook and cranny', 'jot and tittle', 'bells and whistles', 'cease and desist', 'rough and tumble', 'first and foremost', 'straight and narrow', 'front and center', 'rest and relaxation', 'brick and mortar', 'part and parcel', 'fast and furious', 'quick and dirty', 'salt and pepper', 'ladies and gentlemen', 'checks and balances', 'trials and tribulations', 'done and dusted', 'pomp and circumstance', and 'kit and caboodle' (does anyone know what a caboodle is?). Note further such phrases as 'for all intents and purposes' (in British English: 'to all intents and purposes'), 'without let or hindrance' (a legal expression), 'without qualm or query' (virtually unknown in American English, and less heard nowadays even in British English), 'full faith and credit' (see Article IV, Section 1, of the United States Constitution), and 'Without fear and without favour' (the motto of the *Financial Times*). This pattern will explain the titles of famous works, such as *Troilus and Criseyde* by Geoffrey Chaucer, its adaptation by William Shakespeare as *Troilus and Cressida*, two other Shakespeare plays, namely, *Romeo and Juliet* and *Antony and Cleopatra*, the Jane Austen

---

1. For one such statement with reference to another literary corpus altogether, namely, Serbo-Croatian epic poems (*deseterac*), see John Miles Foley, *Traditional Oral Epic: The Odyssey, Beowulf, and the Serbo-Croatian Return Song* (Berkeley: University of California Press, 1991), 98. He there refers to the norm that establishes "the sequence of words according to their syllabic length and prescribes that longer words follow shorter ones, [with] the more extensive words characteristically appearing at the ends of cola and lines."

novels *Pride and Prejudice* and *Sense and Sensibility*,[2] the novel *Wives and Daughters* by Elizabeth Gaskell, and many more such examples. The names of businesses with two partners are likewise typically ordered from shorter to longer, as in: 'Lord and Taylor', 'Barnes and Noble', 'Marks and Spencer', 'Ede and Ravenscroft', 'Ben and Jerry's', 'Dun and Bradstreet', 'Bell and Howell', and so on.[3] One of my favorite examples is the television program 'Law and Order', obviously adapted from the basic English expression, but which shows the police work (that is, the 'order') during the first half of each episode and then the legal manuevers (that is, the 'law') during the second half—though by necessity the title must remain 'Law and Order', since no one would countenance 'Order and Law'.

The same holds for three-item expressions, such as 'hook, line, and sinker', 'lock, stock, and barrel', 'faith, hope, and charity', 'Tom, Dick, and Harry', and the marriage vow 'to love, honor, and cherish'. This pattern will explain the considered choices of wordsmiths, as in the following: 'friends, Romans, countrymen' (the beginning of Mark Antony's famous address in Shakespeare's *Julius Caesar*, Act III, Scene 2); 'life, liberty, and the pursuit of happiness' (near the start of the United States Declaration of Independence, as illustrations of 'unalienable rights'); and 'our Lives, our Fortunes and our sacred Honor' (the closing words thereto, pledged by the signatories whose names follow). Even when the relevant length of words is not readily apparent, authors will choose the same ordering, as in the closing words of Abraham Lincoln's "Gettysburg Address": 'and that government of the people, by the people, for the people, shall not perish from the earth'. Note the three prepositions, with 'of' consisting of vowel + consonant, 'by' consisting of consonant + diphthong, and 'for' consisting of consonant + vowel + consonant'—so that while all three are one-syllable words, they nonetheless expand from shortest to longest.

---

2. Note further the alliteration in both titles!

3. I do not deny that the expected order may be reversed at times, but in such cases there frequently is a gross imbalance between the two items, with a three-or-more-syllable word preceding a one-syllable word, as in 'Abraham and Straus' and 'Abercrombie and Fitch'. For a Hebrew parallel, note Ps 45:16 שְׂמָחֹת וָגִיל *śəmaḥot wa-gil* 'happiness and joy'. To return to English, in a phrase such as 'peanut butter and jelly', the core ingredient of the sandwich comes first, with the secondary component following.

This patterning will explain why in Hebrew two-item and three-item phrases are similarly placed in shorter-to-longer arrangement. Note the following two-noun phrases:[4]

(a) צֹאן וּבָקָר *ṣoʾn u-baqar* 'flocks and herds' (Gen 12:16, 13:5, 20:14, 21:27, 24:35, etc.).[5]

(b) כֶּסֶף וְזָהָב *kɛsɛp wə-zahab* 'silver and gold' (Deut 7:25, 8:13, 17:17, 29:16, etc.).[6]

(c) גֵּר וְתוֹשָׁב *ger wə-tošab* 'stranger and resident' = 'resident alien' (Gen 23:4, Lev 25:35, 25:47, etc.).

(d) חֹק וּמִשְׁפָּט *ḥoq u-mišpaṭ* 'statute and ordinance' (Exod 15:25, Josh 24:25).

---

4. For the standard treatment, see Shamma Friedman, "Kol ha-Qaṣar Qodem" [English title: The 'Law of Increasing Members' in Mishnaic Hebrew"], *Leshonenu* 35 (1971 / 5731): 117–29, 192–206. Notwithstanding the (English) title of this article, the author provides numerous examples of the 'shorter before longer' phenomenon in Biblical Hebrew as well, many of which are included in the present discussion. Friedman's findings, and the entire approach taken herein, has been challenged by Rosmari Lillas, "Hendiadys in the Hebrew Bible: An Investigation of the Applications of the Term" (PhD dissertation, University of Gothenburg, 2012), esp. 203–8. Part of the problem, however, is what constitutes 'hendiadys' (lit., 'one through two'). To be sure, Lillas has provided the scholarly community with a masterful collection of data (on pp. 371–607) that will serve anyone who wishes to investigate the matter further.

5. For a complete list and some further analysis, see Takamitsu Muraoka, "Biblical Hebrew Philological Notes (2)," *Jerusalem Studies in Arabic and Islam* 15 (1992) (= *Studies in Semitic Linguistics in Honour of Joshua Blau [I]*): 43–44.

6. The opposite order will be employed when the text wishes to emphasize the value of these two precious metals, especially when a third metal is added, for example, זָהָב וָכֶסֶף וּנְחֹשֶׁת *zahab wa-kɛsɛp u-nḥošɛt* 'gold and silver and bronze' (Exod 25:3, 35:5, etc.). For a thorough study, see Avi Hurvitz, "'Kiʾazmus Diʾakroni' ba-ʿIvrit ha-Miqraʾit," in Benjamin Uffenheimer, ed., *Ha-Miqraʾ ve-Toldot Yisraʾel: Meḥqarim ba-Miqraʾ u-ve-Sifrut Yeme Bayit Šeni le-Zikro šel Yaʿaqov Liver* (Tel Aviv: Tel Aviv University, 1972), 248–51. The author notes that while כֶּסֶף וְזָהָב *kɛsɛp wə-zahab* 'silver and gold' is the standard Biblical Hebrew order, during postexilic times the word order is changed, for reasons that are not altogether clear, to זָהָב וָכֶסֶף *zahab wa-kɛsɛp* 'gold and silver'.

(e) חֻקִּים וּמִשְׁפָּטִים *huqqim u-mišpaṭim* 'statutes and ordinances' (Deut 4:5, 4:8, 4:14, etc.).

(f) אוֹב וְיִדְּעֹנִי *'ob wə-yiddə'oni* 'ghost and wizard' (Deut 18:11, 2 Chr 33:6).

(g) אוֹתֹת וּמֹפְתִים *'otot u-moptim* 'signs and wonders' (Deut 6:22, with similar formulations elsewhere in Deuternomy; see also Jer 32:20, Ps 135:9, Neh 9:10).

(h) תְּכֵלֶת וְאַרְגָּמָן *təkelɛt wə-'argaman* 'blue and purple' (Jer 10:9, Ezek 27:7; see also below, in the next section).

(i) דַּל וְאֶבְיוֹן *dal wə-'ɛbyon* 'poor and downtrodden' (Pss 72:13, 82:4).

(j) צַר וְאוֹיֵב *ṣar wə-'oyeb* 'foe and enemy' (Lam 4:12, Esth 7:6).

(k) חֵן וָחֶסֶד *ḥen wa-ḥɛsɛd* 'grace and favor' (Esth 2:17).

(l) חֶסֶד וְרַחֲמִים *ḥɛsɛd wə-raḥamim* 'favor and compassion' (Zech 7:9).[7]

Similar patterns obtain with three-item phrases, most famously with the following:

(m) דָּגָן תִּירוֹשׁ וְיִצְהָר *dagan tiroš wə-yiṣhar* 'grain, wine, and oil'— thus Deut 28:51 and 2 Chr 31:5 in this specific format, but in the same order an additional 16x (!), to wit: Deut 7:13, 11:14, 12:17, 14:23, 18:4, Jer 31:12, Hos 2:10, 2:24, Joel 1:10, 2:19, Hag 1:11, Neh 5:11, 10:40, 13:5, 13:12, 2 Chr 32:28 (many of these with the definite article, pronominal suffix, etc.).[8]

---

7. Note that in the שִׂים שָׁלוֹם *śim šalom* 'Grant Peace' prayer (the last of the benedictions recitd in the 'Amidah prayer for Shaḥarit and Musaf), elements of these two-word phrases are combined into a three-word phrase, חֵן וָחֶסֶד וְרַחֲמִים *ḥen wa-ḥɛsɛd wə-raḥamim* 'grace and favor and compassion', with the expected order of shorter to longer retained.

8. Note, incidentally, that the three words are 'poetic' equivalents of the standard and more banal words לֶחֶם *lɛḥem* 'bread, grain', יַיִן *yayin* 'wine', and

(n) גֵּר יָתוֹם וְאַלְמָנָה *ger yatom wə-ʾalmana* 'stranger, orphan, and widow'—thus Deut 27:19, Jer 7:6, 22:3 in this specific format, but see also Deut 14:29, 16:11, 16:14, 24:19, 24:20, 24:21, 26:12, 26:13, with slightly different formulations, including the definite article, though retaining the same essential order.[9]

(o) תְּכֵלֶת וְאַרְגָּמָן וְתוֹלַעַת שָׁנִי *təkelɛt wə-ʾargaman wə-tolaʿat šani* 'blue and purple and crimson dye'—thus Exod 25:4 and 26:1, and 18x more with this specific wording within the Tabernacle account (Exodus 25–31, 35–40); see also Exod 28:5, 28:6, 35:25, 35:35, 39:1, 39:3 with slightly different formulations, though with the three items in the same order.

And for a truly long list of items, proceeding from shorter to longer, note the following:

Lev 7:37

זֹאת הַתּוֹרָה לָעֹלָה לַמִּנְחָה וְלַחַטָּאת וְלָאָשָׁם וְלַמִּלּוּאִים וּלְזֶבַח הַשְּׁלָמִים:

This is the law of the ʿola, of the minḥa, and of the ḥaṭṭaʾt, and of the ʾašam, and of the milluʾim, and of the zɛbaḥ haš-šəlamim.[10]

שֶׁמֶן *šɛmɛn* 'oil', respectively. I place 'poetic' in quotation marks here, because many of the passages are actually in prose, or at least in legal-cultic texts. Presumably, since the three terms are used in conjunction with God's blessing of the bounty of the land, the rarer terms are used instead of the more basic and prosaic equivalents in order to highlight God's beneficence.

9. I retain the conventional rendering 'orphan', even though יָתוֹם *yatom* most likely connotes 'fatherless', with the possibility, even probability, that the mother of the child still lives.

10. In order to demonstrate the point of shorter > longer, I have transliterated the Hebrew terms. Their usual English renderings are, respectively, 'burnt-offering', 'grain-offering', 'purification-offering', 'guilt-offering', 'ordination-offering', and 'sacrifice of well-being'. Note that חַטָּאת *ḥaṭṭaʾt* traditionally has been understood as 'sin-offering' (based on the connection to the verbal root ח-ט-א *ḥ-ṭ-ʾ* 'sin' and the noun חֵטְא *ḥeṭʾ* 'sin'), but modern scholarship has shown that the proper connotation in the cultic context is 'purgation, purification, decontamination'. See Baruch J. Schwartz, "Leviticus,"

Leviticus 6–7 comprises the second section in the book detailing the various sacrifices; the verse above comes at the end as a sort of caption or summary statement. Moreover, the individual sacrifices are presented in said order within chs. 6–7—with the exception of the מִלֻּאִים *millu'im* offering, which is nowhere mentioned in this section (more on this anon). The ordering commences with the shortest term, עֹלָה *'ola*, comprised of two syllables but only two consonants, since it ends with a vowel sound. The next three items also have two syllables, but each has three consonants and is thus slightly longer than the first term in the series. And the final member in the list is clearly the longest, the two-word phrase זֶבַח הַשְּׁלָמִים *zɛbaḥ haš-šəlamim* 'sacrifice of well-being'. Interposed, however, between the fourth and sixth members is the term מִלֻּאִים *millu'im* 'ordination-offering', even though, as noted above, this sacrifice is not discussed within Leviticus 6–7 (nor in the preceding section, Leviticus 1–5). Instead, this sacrifice, which is used for the investiture of the priests, is discussed in detail in Exod 29:19–34 (within the Tabernacle account), and then again in Lev 8:22–35 (when Aaron and his sons are actually inducted into their priestly office). Nonetheless, the author of Lev 7:37 saw fit to include the term מִלֻּאִים *millu'im* 'ordination-offering' in his list of sacrifices, in order to produce as complete a list as possible. Noteworthy for our present discussion is his placement of the word מִלֻּאִים *millu'im* 'ordination-offering' in precisely the spot where one would expect to find it, as the series progresses from shorter to longer.[11]

In light of the above, one will understand basic Hebrew collocations such as the following, selected at random from literally hundreds of instances:

(a) Exod 2:14 מִי שָׂמְךָ לְאִישׁ שַׂר וְשֹׁפֵט עָלֵינוּ *mi śamka lə-'iš śar wə-šopeṭ 'alenu* 'who placed you as a man, ruler and judge, over us?'—spoken by one of the Hebrew men to Moses, with the phrase שַׂר וְשֹׁפֵט *śar wə-šopeṭ* 'ruler and judge' eliciting the shorter before longer rule.

---

in Adele Berlin and Marc Zvi Brettler, eds., *The Jewish Study Bible*, 2nd ed. (New York: Oxford University Press, 2014), 202.

11. Friedman, "Kol ha-Qaṣar Qodem," 122.

(b) Exod 24:7 כֹּל אֲשֶׁר־דִּבֶּר יְהוָה נַעֲשֶׂה וְנִשְׁמָע *kol ʾašɛr dibber*
YHWH *naʿasɛ wə-nišmaʿ* 'All that YHWH has spoken, we will do
and we will obey'—One would expect, upon the people's hearing
God's commands, in particular the utterances in chs. 20–23
(the Decalogue and attendant laws), that they would proclaim,
'we will obey and we will do', since obedience to God's word
should logically precede observance of God's commands. Such
is implied, moreover, by God's proclamation at Exod 23:22, 'If
you indeed obey his voice,[12] and you do all that I have spoken',
with the logical progression from the act of obeying to the act
of doing. The reason behind the ordering of the two-verb phrase
נַעֲשֶׂה וְנִשְׁמָע *naʿasɛ wə-nišmaʿ* 'we will do and we will obey' in
the verse cited above is that the shorter word must precede the
longer one. Both verbs have two syllables,[13] though note how the
former has only three consonants (*nun–ʿayin–śin*), while the latter has four (*nun–šin–mem–ʿayin*).[14]

(c) Lev 23:37 עֹלָה וּמִנְחָה זֶבַח וּנְסָכִים *ʿola u-minḥa zɛbaḥ u-nsakim*
'burnt-offering and meal-offering, sacrifice and libations'—
comprised of two two-noun phrases, each with shorter before
longer.

(d) Deut 28:3 בָּרוּךְ אַתָּה בָּעִיר וּבָרוּךְ אַתָּה בַּשָּׂדֶה *baruk ʾatta ba-ʿir*
u-baruk ʾatta baś-śadɛ 'blessed shall you be in the city, blessed
shall you be in the field'.

---

12. The Hebrew text here indeed reads בְּקֹלוֹ *bə-qolo* 'his voice', instead
of the expected 'my voice'. As is my wont, I have rendered the text literally,
without attempting, as some modern translations do, to conceal a difficulty
in the original.

13. That is, in Iron Age Hebrew pronunciation, before the introduction of
the helping vowel /a/ after the ʿayin in the former verb within the Masoretic
system, which turned this form into a three-syllable vocable.

14. Jewish readers of this book may realize that this passage has been
used throughout the ages, especially in Jewish sermonics, to demonstrate the
virtual blind faith of the ancient Israelites—with reference to the people's
willingness to do whatever God commands, even before they hear (the literal
meaning of the verb ש-מ-ע *š-m-ʿ*, though translated 'obey' in this context)
the divine orders. The literary-linguistic explanation provided here renders
such eisegesis unnecessary.

(e) Deut 28:5 בָּרוּךְ טַנְאֲךָ וּמִשְׁאַרְתֶּךָ *baruk ṭanʾaka u-mišʾartɛka* 'blessed shall be your basket and your kneading-bowl'.

(f) Judg 18:19 וֶהְיֵה־לָנוּ לְאָב וּלְכֹהֵן *wɛ-hye lanu lǝ-ʾab u-l-kohen* 'and be for us as a father and as a priest'—spoken by the Danites to Micah, as they ask him to become their sacerdotal leader.

(g) Judg 18:19 לְשֵׁבֶט וּלְמִשְׁפָּחָה בְּיִשְׂרָאֵל *lǝ-šebɛṭ u-l-mišpaḥa bǝ-yiśraʾel* 'for a tribe and a clan in Israel'—within the continuation of the previous clause, as the Danites convince Micah that it is better to serve an entire tribe than a single household.

(h) Gen 12:1 לֶךְ־לְךָ מֵאַרְצְךָ וּמִמּוֹלַדְתְּךָ וּמִבֵּית אָבִיךָ *lɛk lǝka me-ʾarṣǝka u-mim-moladtǝka u-mib-bet ʾabika* 'go forth from your land, and from your birthplace, and from the house of your father'—God's famous words to Abram, instructing him to leave his homeland, beginning with the shorter word 'your land', then the longer word 'your birthplace', and finally the two-word phrase 'house of your father'.

Note further the order of the three statements of the priestly blessing in Num 6:24–26:

²⁴ יְבָרֶכְךָ יְהוָה וְיִשְׁמְרֶךָ:

²⁵ יָאֵר יְהוָה ׀ פָּנָיו אֵלֶיךָ וִיחֻנֶּךָּ:

²⁶ יִשָּׂא יְהוָה ׀ פָּנָיו אֵלֶיךָ וְיָשֵׂם לְךָ שָׁלוֹם:

²⁴ "May Yʜᴡʜ bless you, and may he guard you.
²⁵ May Yʜᴡʜ shine his face unto you, and may he be-gracious to you.
²⁶ May Yʜᴡʜ lift-up his face unto you, and may he grant you peace."

While the English rendering does not reflect the shorter-to-longer arrangement as clearly as one might hope, one need only count the words in the Hebrew text to realize that v. 24 is comprised of three words, v. 25 of five words, and v. 26 of seven words.[15]

---

15. See the treatment by Sharon R. Keller, "An Egyptian Analogue to the Priestly Blessing," in Meir Lubetski, Claire Gottlieb, and Sharon Keller, eds.,

The same pattern of shorter to longer obtains in poetry: that is, in parallel lines the norm is to place the shorter lexeme from the selected word pair in the a-line and the longer corresponding word in the b-line. Frequently, the former will be a more common, even prosaic word, while the latter will be a less common, at times strictly poetic word. Thus, for example, in the four instances in which ראֹשׁ *roʾš* 'head' and קָדְקֹד *qodqod* 'pate' are parallel, the former is always in the a-line and the latter is always in the b-line:[16]

(a) Gen 49:26

תִּהְיֶ֙יןָ֙ לְרֹ֣אשׁ יוֹסֵ֔ף וּלְקָדְקֹ֖ד נְזִ֥יר אֶחָֽיו׃

"May they [sc. the blessings] be on the head (*roʾš*) of Joseph,
And on the pate (*qodqod*) of the elect of his brothers."

(b) Deut 33:16

תָּב֙וֹאתָה֙ לְרֹ֣אשׁ יוֹסֵ֔ף וּלְקָדְקֹ֖ד נְזִ֥יר אֶחָֽיו׃

"May they [sc. the bounties] come to the head (*roʾš*) of Joseph,
And to the pate (*qodqod*) of the elect of his brothers."[17]

(c) Ps 7:17

יָשׁ֣וּב עֲמָל֣וֹ בְרֹאשׁ֑וֹ וְעַ֥ל קָ֝דְקֳד֗וֹ חֲמָס֥וֹ יֵרֵֽד׃

His mischief returns upon his head (*roʾš*),
And upon his pate (*qodqod*) his violence descends.

Boundaries of the Ancient Near Eastern World: A Tribute to Cyrus H. Gordon (Sheffield: Sheffield Academic Press, 1998), 338–45, esp. 342.

16. The same obtains in Ugaritic poetry; for extended discussion, see Stanley Gevirtz, *Patterns in the Early Poetry of Israel* (Chicago: University of Chicago Press, 1963), 7–8.

17. For an earlier discussion of the first word in this verset, see Chapter 16, no. 3. Note, incidentally, that the two verses, Gen 49:26 and Deut 33:16—the former the blessing of Jacob to Joseph, the latter the blessing of Moses to Joseph—reflect repetition with variation. I did not treat these verses in Chapter 15, since the two passages appear in poetic compositions separated by a vast amount of material (essentially, four books of the Torah). Whoever is responsible for the final product of the Torah seems to have ensured the variation, nonetheless. The sole alternation in the two lines is the verb תִּהְיֶיןָ *tihyɛn* 'may they be' in Gen 49:26 versus תָּבוֹאתָה *taboʾta* 'may they come' in Deut 33:16.

(d) Ps 68:22

אַךְ־אֱלֹהִים יִמְחַץ רֹאשׁ אֹיְבָיו קָדְקֹד שֵׂעָר מִתְהַלֵּךְ בַּאֲשָׁמָיו:

Indeed God will smite the head (*roʾš*) of his enemies,
The hairy pate (*qodqod*) of him who walks-about in his guilt.

For a second example of this phenomenon, note that when יַעֲקֹב *yaʿaqob* 'Jacob' and יִשְׂרָאֵל *yiśraʾel* 'Israel' are parallel, the former regularly stands before the latter,[18] as in the following passages: Gen 49:7, 49:24, Num 23:7, 23:10, 23:21, 23:23, 24:5, 24:17, Deut 33:10, Isa 14:1, 27:6, 29:23, 40:27, 41:14, 42:24, 43:1, 43:22, 43:28, 44:1, 44:5, 45:4, 46:3, 48:12, 49:5, 49:6, Jer 2:4, 10:16, 30:10, 46:27, Hos 12:13, Mic 2:12, 3:1, 3:8, 3:9, Nah 2:3, Pss 14:7, 22:24, 53:7, 78:5, 78:21, 78:71, 105:10, 135:4, 147:19. A few verses from this list are presented here:[19]

(a) Gen 49:7

אֲחַלְּקֵם בְּיַעֲקֹב וַאֲפִיצֵם בְּיִשְׂרָאֵל

"I will divide-them throughout Jacob,
And I will scatter them throughout Israel."

(b) Deut 33:10

יוֹרוּ מִשְׁפָּטֶיךָ לְיַעֲקֹב וְתוֹרָתְךָ לְיִשְׂרָאֵל

"They will teach your laws to Jacob,
And your Torah unto Israel."

(c) Hos 12:13

וַיִּבְרַח יַעֲקֹב שְׂדֵה אֲרָם וַיַּעֲבֹד יִשְׂרָאֵל בְּאִשָּׁה

And Jacob fled (to) the field of Aram,
And Israel worked for a woman.

---

18. Note that the name יַעֲקֹב *yaʿaqob* 'Jacob' would have contained two syllables in Iron Age Hebrew (expanded to three in Masoretic Hebrew, through the use of the *ḥaṭaf-pataḥ* vowel under the *ʿayin*), while the name יִשְׂרָאֵל *yiśraʾel* 'Israel' contains three syllables. Or, to look at this another way, the former is comprised of four consonants, while the latter has five (including *ʾaleph*, which serves as a true consonant in Hebrew).

19. For further discussion, see Gevirtz, *Patterns in the Early Poetry of Israel*, 52–55.

(d) Ps 14:7 (= Ps 53:7)

יָגֵל יַעֲקֹב יִשְׂמַח יִשְׂרָאֵל

Jacob shall rejoice,
Israel shall be happy.

And for a third set of examples, note that when the individual
elements in the two-noun phrases listed earlier in this chapter are disjoined and placed in parallel lines of poetry, the norm is, as expected,
to place the shorter word in the a-line and the longer one in the b-line.
Thus, for instance, to use the word pair דַּל וְאֶבְיוֹן dal wə-ʾɛbyon 'poor
and downtrodden':

(a) 1 Sam 2:8

מֵקִים מֵעָפָר דָּל מֵאַשְׁפֹּת יָרִים אֶבְיוֹן

He raises from the dust the poor (dal),
From the rubbish-piles he elevates the downtrodden
     (ʾɛbyon).[20]

(b) Amos 4:1

הָעֹשְׁקוֹת דַּלִּים הָרֹצְצוֹת אֶבְיוֹנִים

Who oppress the poor (dallim),
Who crush the downtrodden (ʾɛbyonim).[21]

(c) Prov 14:21

עֹשֵׁק־דָּל חֵרֵף עֹשֵׂהוּ וּמְכַבְּדוֹ חֹנֵן אֶבְיוֹן:

He who oppresses the poor (dal) insults his maker;
But he who honors him is gracious to the downtrodden
     (ʾɛbyon).

Notwithstanding all of the above data and illustrations, what we
truly are interested in in this chapter, as adumbrated in its title, is not
the norm, but rather the abnorm—which is to say, departures from the

---

20. This passage occurs with slight variation in Ps 113:7.
21. In this instance, the two key words appear in the plural form, but the
ordering remains as expected.

standard arrangement of shorter to longer. The following discussion provides examples of how the biblical authors altered the expected order in order to achieve their literary aims, typically alliteration, though in one instance (no. 5 below) the purpose is to mark closure.

1. Numbers 18:11–12

11 . . . כָּל־טָהֹ֤ור בְּבֵיתְךָ֙ יֹאכַ֣ל אֹתֹֽו׃

12 כֹּ֚ל חֵ֣לֶב יִצְהָ֔ר וְכָל־חֵ֛לֶב תִּירֹ֥ושׁ וְדָגָ֖ן רֵאשִׁיתָ֛ם אֲשֶׁר־יִתְּנ֥וּ לַֽיהוָ֖ה לְךָ֥

נְתַתִּֽים׃

11 . . . every pure-person in your house shall eat it.
12 Every best-portion of oil, and every best-portion of wine
and grain; their first-offerings that they give to Yнwн, to you
I give them.

As indicated above, the words דָּגָן *dagan* 'grain', תִּירֹושׁ *tiroš* 'wine', and יִצְהָר *yiṣhar* 'oil' are a regular triad in Biblical Hebrew. The only exception to this standard order occurs in the verse presented above, Num 18:12, where the reader will note that the first of the three agricultural items mentioned is יִצְהָר *yiṣhar* 'oil'. Why?

At this point in our survey of the literary workings of ancient Hebrew composition, it should come as no surprise to learn that the author placed יִצְהָר *yiṣhar* 'oil' in primary position *alliterationis causa*. The alliterative partner is the word טָהֹור *ṭahor* 'pure', or in this particular case, 'pure-person', that is, 'person in a state of ritual purity', which occurs toward the end of v. 11 (see above). Not only do the two words share the /h/–/r/ combination, but the initial consonants are both 'emphatic' consonants (to use the technical linguistic term), that is, they are pronounced in the mouth with a special distinctive quality (indicated by the dot beneath /ṣ/ and /ṭ/).[22]

---

22. Scholars have suggested a variety of options for the special distinctive quality of these consonants, including ejective, glottalized, velarized, pharyngealized, etc. Truth be told, there is no absolute way to know precisely how these consonants were realized in ancient Hebrew, though their glottalized nature is theorized by many students of ancient Hebrew phonology.

One still is left with the remaining two words in the triad, which appear later in v. 12 as תִּירוֹשׁ וְדָגָן *tiroš wə-dagan* 'wine and grain', that is, in reverse order. I would suggest that the author, once he moved יִצְהָר *yiṣhar* 'oil' to its primary position, simple elected to play with the order of all three words and hence created an atypical order with the two remaining words as well.

2. Numbers 22:40

וַיִּזְבַּח בָּלָק בָּקָר וָצֹאן

wayyizbaḥ balaq baqar wa-ṣoʾn

And Balak sacrificed herds and flocks.

One of the standard shorter-to-longer word pairs noted above is צֹאן וּבָקָר *ṣoʾn u-baqar* 'flocks and herds'—and yet here in Num 22:40 the reverse order occurs. The issue once more hinges on consideration of alliteration, for by placing the two items in reverse order the author is able to juxtapose the words בָּלָק *balaq* 'Balaq' (anglicized as 'Balak') and בָּקָר *baqar* 'herd', without צֹאן *ṣoʾn* 'flock' intervening. Assisting in the alliterative string is the first word, the verb וַיִּזְבַּח *wayyizbaḥ* 'and (he) sacrificed', with the labial /b/ and the guttural /ḥ/.

3. Deuteronomy 12:6, 17; 14:23; 15:19 — 'firstlings of herds and flocks'

Deut 12:6

וּבְכֹרֹת בְּקַרְכֶם וְצֹאנְכֶם:

u-bkorot bəqarkɛm wə-ṣoʾnkɛm

and the firstlings of your (pl.) herds and your (pl.) flocks

Deut 12:17

וּבְכֹרֹת בְּקָרְךָ וְצֹאנֶךָ

u-bkorot bəqarka wə-ṣoʾnɛka

and the firstlings of your (sg.) herds and your (sg.) flocks

Deut 14:23

וּבְכֹרֹת בְּקָרְךָ וְצֹאנֶךָ

u-bkorot bəqarka wə-ṣoʾnɛka

and the firstlings of your (sg.) herds and your (sg.) flocks

These three verses in Deuteronomy refer to the agricultural items (among both plants and animals) that the Israelites must dedicate to God. In our excerpts therefrom (with reference to the domesticated animals), the only difference in wording is the use of the second-person plural form כֶם- *-kɛm* 'your' in the first verse and the second-person singular form ךָ- *-ka* 'your' in the second and third verses; this is typical of Deuteronomic style, which frequently alternates between addressing the community as a whole with the former and then individuals with the latter.[23]

More pertinent to our present concern is the atypical ordering, which places בָּקָר *baqar* 'herd' before צֹאן *ṣoʾn* 'flock' in these passages. This arrangement once more enhances the alliterative effect, since the first word in these phrases is וּבְכֹרֹת *u-bkorot* 'and firstlings'.

Deut 15:19

כָּל־הַבְּכוֹר אֲשֶׁר יִוָּלֵד בִּבְקָרְךָ וּבְצֹאנְךָ הַזָּכָר תַּקְדִּישׁ לַיהוָה אֱלֹהֶיךָ

kol hab-bəkor ʾašɛr yiwwaled bi-bqarka u-b-ṣoʾnka
*haz-zakar taqdiš la-*YHWH* ʾelohɛka*

And every male firstling that is born to your herd and to your flock you shall dedicate to YHWH your God.

The word pair occurs one more time in Deuteronomy, once more with בְּכוֹר *bəkor* 'firstling' in the verse; and even though this time several words intervene, the author retains the atypical order by placing בָּקָר *baqar* 'herd' before צֹאן *ṣoʾn* 'flock'. The result is כָּל־הַבְּכוֹר אֲשֶׁר יִוָּלֵד בִּבְקָרְךָ וּבְצֹאנְךָ *kol hab-bəkor ʾašɛr yiwwaled bi-bqarka u-b-ṣoʾnka* 'and

---

23. See Moshe Weinfeld, *Deuteronomy 1–11* (Anchor Bible 5; New York: Doubleday, 1991), 15–16.

every male firstling that is born to your herd and to your flock', with
the words for 'firstling' and 'herd' still in relatively close proximity in
order to achieve the desired aural effect.

4. Nehemiah 10:37

וְאֶת־בְּכֹרֵי בְקָרֵינוּ וְצֹאנֵינוּ

wə-ɛt bəkore bəqarenu wə-ṣoʾnenu

"and the firstlings of our herds and our flocks"

We jump way out of canonical order to include this verse from the
book of Nehemiah, at the very end of the Bible. Once more the presence
of the word בְּכוֹר *bəkor* 'firstling' elicits the change in the usual word
order, with בָּקָר *baqar* 'herd' appearing before צֹאן *ṣoʾn* 'flock'. Interestingly, the Jews who speak the words quoted above (as part of their long
declaration, which comprises all of Nehemiah 10) understand them as
a direct citation from the Torah: כַּכָּתוּב בַּתּוֹרָה *kak-katub bat-tora* 'as it
is written in the Torah' (earlier in v. 37). And even though this precise
phrase does not occur anywhere within the Torah, clearly the author
of Nehemiah and the people who spoke these words had the aforecited
passages from the book of Deuteronomy in mind.

5. Numbers 23–24[24]

Num 23:7

לְכָה אָרָה־לִּי יַעֲקֹב וּלְכָה זֹעֲמָה יִשְׂרָאֵל

"Go, curse for me Jacob,
And go, execrate Israel."

Num 23:10

מִי מָנָה עֲפַר יַעֲקֹב וּמִסְפָּר אֶת־רֹבַע יִשְׂרָאֵל

"Who can count the dust of Jacob,
Indeed, number the dust-cloud of Israel?"

---

24. For this example, see already Moyer, "Literary and Linguistic Studies
in *Sefer Bilʿam*," 367.

Num 23:21

לֹא־הִבִּיט אָ֫וֶן בְּיַעֲקֹב וְלֹא־רָאָה עָמָל בְּיִשְׂרָאֵל

"He has not beheld misfortune in Jacob,
And he has not seen travail in Israel."

Num 23:23a

כִּי לֹא־נַחַשׁ בְּיַעֲקֹב וְלֹא־קֶסֶם בְּיִשְׂרָאֵל

"For there is no divination in Jacob,
And there is no magic in Israel."

Num 23:23b

כָּעֵת יֵאָמֵר לְיַעֲקֹב וּלְיִשְׂרָאֵל מַה־פָּעַל אֵל

"Now it shall be said of Jacob and of Israel,
'What has God done?' "

Num 24:5

מַה־טֹּבוּ אֹהָלֶיךָ יַעֲקֹב מִשְׁכְּנֹתֶיךָ יִשְׂרָאֵל

"How goodly are your tents, O Jacob,
Your dwelling-places, O Israel."

Num 24:17

דָּרַךְ כּוֹכָב מִיַּעֲקֹב וְקָם שֵׁבֶט מִיִּשְׂרָאֵל

"A star treads-forward from Jacob,
And a scepter shall rise from Israel."

Num 24:18–19

¹⁸ וְהָיָה אֱדוֹם יְרֵשָׁה וְהָיָה יְרֵשָׁה שֵׂעִיר אֹיְבָיו וְיִשְׂרָאֵל עֹשֶׂה חָיִל:
¹⁹ וְיֵרְדְּ מִיַּעֲקֹב וְהֶאֱבִיד שָׂרִיד מֵעִיר:

¹⁸ "And it will be, Edom shall be dispossessed,
And it will be, Seir shall be dispossessed (by) its enemies;
While Israel does valiantly.
¹⁹ And (a ruler) will rule from Jacob,
And he shall annihilate the remnant from ʿIr."

We return now to the Balaam material (see above, no. 2, for our first item from this section of the Torah). Seven times in his poetic oracles, Balaam follows standard Hebrew usage by placing 'Jacob' in the a-line and 'Israel' in the b-line—seen already above, where the relevant verses were included in the long list of biblical poetic passages with this order. The pattern is broken, however, with the eighth and final mention of Jacob/Israel in this pericope. In this case, accordingly, the author wished to alert the reader that she has reached Balaam's final pronouncement on the people of Israel, in line with our discussion of "Marking Closure" in Chapter 13. Numbers 24:18–19 is not easy to translate (my rendering above is but one of many possibilities), plus the poetic stichs are not perfectly parallel, but one thing remains clear: 'Israel' appears before 'Jacob' (spread over two verses) as a means of signaling the end of a long series of poetic oracles.

6. Psalm 114:1

בְּצֵאת יִשְׂרָאֵל מִמִּצְרָיִם

בֵּית יַעֲקֹב מֵעַם לֹעֵז:

> When Israel went-forth from Egypt,
> The house of Jacob from a people of foreign-tongue.

In this case, going against the grain, 'Israel' appears in the a-line, while 'Jacob' appears in the b-line. When poets construct their couplet in such fashion, the latter is typically expanded into a two-word phrase, as here: בֵּית יַעֲקֹב *bet yaʿaqob* 'house of Jacob'. For other examples, see:

(a) Deut 33:28 וַיִּשְׁכֹּן יִשְׂרָאֵל בֶּטַח בָּדָד עֵין יַעֲקֹב 'And Israel dwelt securely, the habitation of Jacob alone', in which 'Jacob' becomes עֵין יַעֲקֹב *ʿen yaʿaqob* 'habitation of Jacob', and hence this designation is now longer than 'Israel'.[25]

---

25. The noun עֵין *ʿen* 'habitation' is a byform of the more familiar מָעוֹן *maʿon* (masc.) / מְעֹנָה *məʿona* (fem.), both meaning 'habitation, residence'. For all my respect for his immense learning, I find the reading offered here to be more straightforward than that proffered by Richard C. Steiner, "דָּת and עֵין: Two Verbs Masquerading as Nouns in Moses' Blessing (Deuteronomy 33:2, 28)," *Journal of Biblical Literature* 115 (1996): 693–98, esp. 696–98. Note that

(b) Isa 10:20 לֹא־יוֹסִיף עוֹד שְׁאָר יִשְׂרָאֵל וּפְלֵיטַת בֵּית־יַעֲקֹב לְהִשָּׁעֵן עַל־מַכֵּהוּ 'No longer will the remnant of Israel and the vestige of the house of Jacob lean upon he-who-strikes him', once more with בֵּית־יַעֲקֹב *bet yaʿaqob* 'house of Jacob' in the b-line.

(c) Ps 81:5 כִּי חֹק לְיִשְׂרָאֵל הוּא מִשְׁפָּט לֵאלֹהֵי יַעֲקֹב 'For it is a law for Israel, and an ordinance of the God of Jacob', even if the expression לֵאלֹהֵי יַעֲקֹב *le-ʾlohe yaʿaqob* 'of the God of Jacob' introduces something new, that is, the divine, into the b-line.

To return to Ps 114:1, though, there is another factor at work, to wit, alliteration. In the first stich, בְּצֵאת יִשְׂרָאֵל מִמִּצְרָיִם *bə-ṣeʾt yiśraʾel mim-miṣrayim* 'when Israel went-forth from Egypt', a string of sibilants (ṣade–śin–ṣade) attracts the reader's ear; while even more strikingly the second stich is governed by the presence of ʿayin in the three final words of בֵּית יַעֲקֹב מֵעַם לֹעֵז *bet yaʿaqob me-ʿam loʿez* 'the house of Jacob from a people of foreign-tongue'.

7. Psalm 94:6

אַלְמָנָה וְגֵר יַהֲרֹגוּ
וִיתוֹמִים יְרַצֵּחוּ:

The widow and the stranger they kill,
and orphans they murder.

As we saw above, in Hebrew composition the three individuals requiring special protection from society at large regularly appear in the order גֵּר יָתוֹם וְאַלְמָנָה *ger yatom wə-ʾalmana* 'stranger, orphan, and widow'. In Ps 94:6, by contrast, we find the three words in scrambled order. Even if we were to account for this by the requirements of biblical poetic parallelism, which necessitates splitting up the three members of the expression in uneven fashion, we still are left with the peculiar arrangement. For while one may understand וִיתוֹמִים *wi-tomim* 'and orphans' (notably in the plural) in the b-line, the reader still would be

---

Steiner explains עֵז as a verb, in which case the placement of 'Jacob' in the b-line would require explanation.

puzzled by the order אַלְמָנָה וְגֵר ʾalmana wə-ger 'widow and stranger' in the a-line, with the longer before the shorter.

The solution to this problem was adduced by Patrick Miller, who correctly noticed that the reversal of the two nouns in the first stich allows גֵר ger 'stranger' to precede יַהֲרֹגוּ yaharogu 'they kill' directly.[26] This phrasing, accordingly, permits the /g/–/r/ of the noun גֵר ger 'stranger' to echo immediately within the verbal root ה-ר-ג h-r-g 'kill'. The aural effect is sudden and instantaneous, driving home the point of the wicked's actions, which not only are horrific by any standard, but which run counter to the Torah's call to defend the stranger, or-phan, and widow (see the long list of Deuteronomy passages registered above). Indeed, I also would propose that the jumbling of the lexical triad in Ps 94:6 is an instance of form following content. The actions are wrong, contrary to the Torah: hence the wording is wrong, shuf-fling the Torah's repeated formulation.[27]

---

26. Patrick Miller, "Studies in Hebrew Word Patterns," *Harvard Theological Review* 73 (1980): 79–89, esp. 81.

27. For a more thorough treatment of 'form follows content' in the Bible, see Chapter 27, with this example treated there as no. 10.

CHAPTER TWENTY-ONE

WHEN WAS ALL THIS WRITTEN?

So, when was all this written? By 'all this', I do not mean the entire Bible (which spans a millennium of literary activity, from the Song of the Sea [Exodus 15], composed ca. 1150 B.C.E., to the book of Daniel, written ca. 164 B.C.E.),[1] but rather the main texts with which we are engaged in this book. I refer here especially to the Torah, with a particular focus on the book of Genesis, but also to other biblical texts as well, such as the book of Samuel. As we have seen, these two narratives have provided numerous examples for our literary treatment of the Bible. More pertinent to the present chapter, however, is the manner in which the two compositions are inextricably linked together. In order to better comprehend the interconnectedness of the two works, however, we will need to provide a considerable amount of background information, mainly of a historical nature. I am, of course, keenly aware that the question 'When was all this written?' is less relevant to the major subject at hand, 'how the Bible is written', though there is a connection between the two issues, as we shall see. Regardless, given the intense interest in the dating of the Torah, and given my earlier considerations of that question,[2] I have opted to include this chapter within the current enterprise.

---

1. The date of the former continues to be debated, but I side with those scholars who contend that Exodus 15 is the oldest text in the Bible, a relic of archaic poetry embedded into the prose narrative of the Torah. At the other end of the continuum, note that while much of the book of Daniel is set in the court of Nebuchadnezzar, king of Babylon in the sixth century B.C.E., closer scrutiny reveals that the book achieved its final form during the Maccabean revolt in 164 B.C.E.

2. See my earlier studies: (1) *Redaction of Genesis*, 107–20; (2) "Biblical Literature as Politics: The Case of Genesis," in Adele Berlin, ed., *Religion and Politics in the Ancient Near East* (Bethesda: University Press of Maryland,

Let us begin by recalling Israel's history, in particular the events of the tenth century B.C.E., with special attention to the rapid developments of that epoch, especially in comparison with earlier Israelite history. For starters, there was a new polity in Israel, a monarchy, which traditionally had not been a feature of the society—indeed, since according to normative Israelite theology only God could be king, any human king was a compromise of that basic tenet.

Secondly, for the first time power was concentrated in a single place, namely, Jerusalem—in contrast to traditional Israelite society, which was formed by a loose confederation of twelve tribes that shared many beliefs and customs, especially the worship of one God, but that otherwise retained autonomy from each other. The establishment of a monarchy in Jerusalem in fact brought about a greatly diminished emphasis on the entire tribal system. Israel was in a new stage of social development altogether, shifting from a tribal, pastoral, and village lifestyle to a new urbanism.

These major transformations did not occur without opposition. The Bible records a resistance to the new monarchic system, first in the book of Judges (see, for example, Gideon's famous declaration in Judg 8:23), and then most forcefully in 1 Samuel 8, with the prophet Samuel's denunciation of human kingship. But the liberals of the day, if we may call them that, won out, and Israel moved to a monarchy, first in the person of Saul, a transitional figure, and then in complete fashion under David and Solomon, by which point human kingship was a *fait accompli*. When David died, there was a question as to who specifically would succeed him, but no one doubted that it would be one of his sons, so quickly had kingship taken hold in Israel. Similarly, when Solomon died, the northern tribes expressed their discontent with the Davidic dynasty, but there was no turning back at this point to an earlier system of governance. Thus, when the northern tribes refused

---

1996), 47–70; (3) "Reading David in Genesis: How We Know the Torah Was Written in the Tenth Century B.C.E.," *Bible Review* 17.1 (Feb. 2001): 20–33, 46; and (4) "The Genesis of the Bible," in *The Blanche and Irving Laurie Chair in Jewish History,* separatum published by the Allen and Joan Bildner Center for the Study of Jewish Life, Rutgers, The State University of New Jersey (2005), 11–30. The present chapter is based mainly on the last of these four previous treatments.

to follow Rehoboam, son of Solomon, grandson of David, their only choice was to set up a rival kingship, with a parallel royal dynasty established by Jeroboam from the tribe of Ephraim.

There was also a major new religious development during the tenth century B.C.E. Until this point, the Ark of the Covenant, the centerpiece of the Israelite cult, had been housed in the Tabernacle, a tent structure, in the village of Shiloh in the territory of Ephraim. David brought the Ark to Jerusalem amid great ceremony, and a generation later Solomon built the Temple to house the Ark. The Temple, a structure of stone, was something totally alien to Israelite religious life. Temples of stone were features of urban life—indeed, one might say, of Canaanite culture. The Israelites were traditionalists, with a tent-like Tabernacle, portable during their wandering period, then housed in a smallish village, but by no means to be replaced by the urban wonder. In fact, the Temple was so foreign to the Israelite lifestyle that Solomon needed to import Phoenician architects and builders to undertake the project (see 1 Kings 5).

The very notion of Jerusalem as the religious and administrative capital of the nation was altogether new and striking. After all, Jerusalem had not been an Israelite city until this point. The traditional capital was Shechem, where representatives of the twelve tribes would gather when necessary (Josh 24:1, 24:25, 1 Kgs 12:1; see also the references to Mount Gerizim and Mount Ebal in Deut 11:29, 27:12, Josh 8:33). Jerusalem, by contrast, had been an independent city-state of the Jebusites (either a local autochthonous people or a subgroup of the Canaanites), but that was exactly the point. Since it had not belonged to any of the twelve tribes, and since David sought to diminish the influence of the tribes, the choice of Jerusalem was intentional: it would serve him well as the capital of the new political entity. (Americans will compare the selection of Washington, DC, which belongs to no state. Parallel examples include Canberra and the surrounding Australian Capital Territory, which belongs to none of the six states comprising Australia; and Brasília and the surrounding Distrito Federal, which belongs to none of the twenty-six states comprising Brazil.)

David built an international empire, first by quashing the Philistine threat and gaining control of remaining Canaanite pockets within the ideal boundaries of Israel; then by conquering Moab and Ammon to

the east, Edom to the southeast, and Aram to the northeast; and all the
while securing good relations with the Phoenicians to the northwest
via treaty alliance. The result was an empire stretching from the Sinai
desert in the southwest to the Euphrates River in the far northeast.[3]

To return to religious issues, something even more shocking occurred during David's reign: the new king in Jerusalem allowed the
former Canaanite (or Jebusite) high priest of the city to remain in that
position, even though the deity now worshipped there was Yahweh.
Which is to say, the priest who served Yahweh in the Jerusalem Temple
had earlier worshipped a Canaanite deity, before David's conquest.
What is the evidence for this reconstruction of events? There are two
priests mentioned in the book of Samuel in connection with David's
reign: Abiathar and Zadok. The former appears very early in the narratives, as early as 1 Samuel 22, long before David comes to the throne.
The latter, on the other hand, appears out of nowhere, quite suddenly,
in 2 Sam 15:24–29.[4] In fact, this passage is quite telling. In the first of
these verses, Abiathar is the subject of the main verbal clause, with
Zadok and the accompanying Levites as the subject of a subordinate
clause (v. 24). Next, David addresses Zadok twice (vv. 25–26, 27–28),
with instructions on how to proceed. And finally we read וַיַּ֤שֶּׁב צָד֨וֹק
wayyašɛb ṣadoq wə-ʾɛbyatar וְאֶבְיָתָר֙ אֶת־אֲר֣וֹן הָאֱלֹהִ֔ים יְרוּשָׁלָ֖͏ם וַיֵּ֥שְׁבוּ שָֽׁם

---

3. I need to mention here that many scholars today doubt the historicity
of the material in 2 Samuel and 1 Kings concerning David and Solomon, the
building projects in Jerusalem, the extent of the empire, and so on. This is not
the forum in which to enter into an extended discussion on this matter, so I
will need to beg the reader's forbearance and ask one to join me in accepting
the biblical record as more or less historical. For an accessible treatment on
one aspect of the debate, see Jane Cahill, "Jerusalem in David and Solomon's
Time: It Really Was a Major City in the 10th Century B.C.E.," *Biblical Archaeology Review* 30.6 (Nov.–Dec. 2004): 20–31, 62–63.

4. Zadok appears already in 2 Sam 8:17, in a list of David's officials. But
this text must originate from relatively late in David's reign, since the second
priest listed there is Ahimelech son of Abiathar. Naturally, there is no way
to dovetail this passage with the apparent fact that Abiathar served as priest
until after David died (see 1 Kgs 2:27, 2:35). One solution is to assume a scribal
error in 2 Sam 8:17 and posit a reading 'Abiathar son of Ahimelech' (see 1 Sam
22:20). Regardless of how this issue is resolved, note the important fact that
Zadok appears first among the two priests listed in 2 Sam 8:17.

ʾet ʾaron ha-ʾɛlohim yərušalayim wayyešbu šam 'And Zadok and Abia-thar returned the Ark of God to Jerusalem; and they dwelt there', with Zadok in first position (v. 29).

So, who was this Zadok? A complete presentation of the data would require a major excursus at this point, so suffice it to state that I accept the conclusion of those scholars who posit that Zadok was the former king and high priest of Jebusite Jerusalem. In the Canaanite city-state system, these two roles were filled by one individual: one person served both as royal ruler of the city and as high priest in the temple of the city. Zadok, therefore, should be identified with אֲרַוְנָה *ʾarawna* 'Araunah' (see 2 Samuel 24), which in fact is not a proper name at all, but rather an old Hurrian word, *iwre-ne*, meaning 'the lord'. Note especially 2 Sam 24:23, where this individual is called אֲרַוְנָה הַמֶּלֶךְ *ʾarawna ham-mɛlɛk* 'Araunah the king'.[5] Accordingly, we can reconstruct the matter thus: David conquered Jerusalem, and he stripped Zadok/Araunah of his civil authority as king of the city, but he permitted him to retain his sacerdotal authority as high priest over the cult of the city.

How to get the people to go along with all these major changes of the tenth century? Monarchy—an international empire—the central-ity of Jerusalem—Zadok as priest. The answer is: write a national epic incorporating all of the earlier traditions back to Abraham, and embed into that narrative anticipations of the present. That is to say, there is a social, religious, and indeed political message in the book of Genesis (less so in the other four books of the Torah, though even there oc-casional points shine through). Or in other words: tell the story about the past, but reflect upon the present. This was the major accomplish-ment of the anonymous authors in Jerusalem who created the book of Genesis, to be dated, in my opinion, to the tenth century B.C.E.[6]

---

5. Most scholars, unable to accept the fact that Araunah was the king of Jerusalem, emend this verse or explain the usage in some other fashion. See, for example, P. Kyle McCarter, *II Samuel* (Anchor Bible 8A; New York: Doubleday, 1984), 508.

6. Some may object to this dating by claiming that writing and, by ex-tension, literacy were relatively rare in tenth-century B.C.E. Israel. But the picture continues to change with each archaeological season, for there is now a considerable number of inscriptions dated to the tenth and ninth centuries B.C.E. For recent discussion, see Shmuel Ahituv and Amihai Mazar, "The

Let us turn now to specific examples in defense of my hypothesis, beginning with three prominent illustrations. The first is God's promise to Abraham that kings shall stem from him and Sarah: Gen 17:6 וּמְלָכִים מִמְּךָ יֵצֵאוּ *u-mlakim mimməka yeṣeʾu* 'and kings will come-forth from you'; and Gen 17:16 מַלְכֵי עַמִּים מִמֶּנָּה יִהְיוּ *malke ʿammim mimmɛnna yihyu* 'kings of peoples will be from her'. The issue of monarchy, as indicated above, was a public concern during the late eleventh century and the first half of the tenth century (or perhaps a bit longer, if there was any lingering resistance), but at no other time. In the earlier period there still was a strong opposition to kingship; while after the time of David and Solomon monarchy was a reality from which there was no turning back.

Second, the boundaries of the land of Canaan promised to Abraham in Gen 15:18, אֶת־הָאָרֶץ הַזֹּאת מִנְּהַר מִצְרַיִם עַד־הַנָּהָר הַגָּדֹל נְהַר־פְּרָת *ʾet ha-ʾarɛṣ haz-zoʾt min-nəhar miṣrayim ʿad han-nahar hag-gadol nəhar pərat* 'this land, from the river of Egypt to the great river, the Euphrates River',[7] match the extent of the Davidic-Solomonic empire. At an earlier time an Israelite could only have laughed at such an idea—for Israel was a very minor player in the geopolitics of the twelfth and eleventh centuries B.C.E.—and after the death of Solomon the empire collapsed, never again to be realized.

The third item is the emphasis placed on Judah in the book of Genesis, especially the royal imagery in Jacob's deathbed words to his fourth son in Gen 49:10, לֹא־יָסוּר שֵׁבֶט מִיהוּדָה וּמְחֹקֵק מִבֵּין רַגְלָיו עַד כִּי־יָבֹא שִׁילֹו* [שילה] וְלֹו יִקְּהַת עַמִּים: *loʾ yasur šebɛṭ mi-yhuda u-mhoqeq mib-ben raglaw ʿad ki yaboʾ šilo wə-lo yiqqəhat ʿammim* 'and the staff shall not depart from Judah, nor the ruler from between his legs, until tribute

Inscriptions from Tel Rehov and their Contribution to the Study of Script and Writing during Iron Age IIA," in Esther Eshel and Yigal Levin, eds., "*See, I will bring a scroll recounting what befell me*" (Ps 40:8): Epigraphy and Daily Life from the Bible to the Talmud, Dedicated to the Memory of Professor Hanan Eshel (Journal of Ancient Judaism Supplements 12; Göttingen: Vandenhoeck & Ruprecht, 2014), 40–68 (with plates on 189–203), esp. 59, 63. Most importantly, see the programmatic essay by Matthieu Richelle, "Elusive Scrolls: Could Any Hebrew Literature Have Been Written Prior to the Eighth Century BCE?" *Vetus Testamentum* 66 (2016): 556–94.

7. Most likely the former river refers to the Wadi el-ʿArish in the Sinai.

comes to him, and his is the obedience of peoples'.[8] In addition, Judah is the most noble of the brothers in the Joseph story: it is his long speech in Gen 44:18–34 that brings Joseph to tears and prompts him to reveal himself to his brothers. Moreover, Judah is the only brother—other than Joseph—to receive an independent tale, notwithstanding the fact that said tale portrays him in a less-than-favorable light (more on this anon).

These three items converge to demonstrate that the book of Genesis, or at least its greatest part, derives from the tenth century B.C.E. The anonymous authors responsible for this masterpiece of literature told the story of Israel's patriarchs, but that story is at all times refracted through the prism of the present. God approves kingship, which is to reside with the tribe of Judah, and the boundaries of the realm were preordained in hoary antiquity. Or to put this in other terms, the story of the patriarchs is narrated, but the shadow of David and Solomon is evident throughout.

This technique is well known in world literature. The best example from American literature is Arthur Miller's "The Crucible," which narrates the past, specifically the Salem witch trials of late seventeenth-century Massachusetts, but reflects the present, with specific reference to the McCarthyism of the 1950s, of which Miller himself was a victim. Or to take an example from film, the movie $M^*A^*S^*H$, written by Ring Lardner Jr. and directed by Robert Altman in 1970, tells the story of American troops during the Korean War; but as all who see that film know, in essence it is about another land war in Asia, the one that was still raging in 1970, the one in Vietnam. The anti-war, pro-peace stance of the lead character, Benjamin Franklin "Hawkeye" Pierce, reflects the present, which is the late 1960s (when the movie was made) and early 1970s (when the movie was released)—but it is anachronistic for the early 1950s. These themes would continue, of course, in the television series $M^*A^*S^*H$, which dominated the small screen during the 1970s. From the world of opera we may cite "Nabucco" (1842), by Giuseppe Verdi, with its famous choral song "Va, pensiero." The opera narrates the enslavement of the Jews by Nebuchadnezzar in the sixth century B.C.E., but the storyline speaks to the "enslavement" of the northern

---

8. Understanding Ketiv שילה šYLH / Qeri שִׁילוֹ šilo (presumably the toponym Shiloh) as שַׁי לוֹ šay lo 'tribute to him', with many scholars.

Italians by the Habsburg Empire during the composer's time. Finally, let us recall that Shakespeare's histories tell the lives of earlier kings, but at the same time are informed by the English monarchy of his day; we will return to this point at the end of this chapter.

Having established the main point about Genesis and its connection to the Jerusalem court of King David and King Solomon, let us now look at additional details in the text that support our hypothesis. As noted above, David established his rule over the small kingdoms to the east and southeast, Ammon, Moab, and Edom. The author of Genesis reflects this development by relating the ancestors of these nations to the family of Abraham: the first two are descended from Abraham's nephew Lot (Gen 19:37–38),[9] while the third is descended from Abraham's grandson Esau (Gen 25:30). Furthermore, the twinning of Jacob and Esau, representing Israel and Edom, as opposed to the more distant relationship seen with Ammon and Moab as descended from Lot, reflects a difference in the manner in which the Transjordanian kingdoms were ruled by David. In the case of Ammon and Moab, it appears that David allowed their kings to remain on the throne, as vassals to Israel's suzerainty (explicit for Ammon, see 2 Sam 10:1; only implicit for Moab, perhaps see 1 Sam 22:3–4, even though this event occurs before David becomes king). In the case of Edom, however, the king of that realm was deposed, and David served as king over Edom (2 Sam 8:14). This also will explain why the author incorporated into his narrative the list of Edomite rulers in Genesis 36, for David and Solomon were seen as the royal successors to all the individuals mentioned there (see especially Gen 36:31). Finally, note that Isaac's blessing to Esau in Gen 27:40 foretells a time when Esau (read: Edom) will throw off the yoke of his brother (read: Israel), exactly as 1 Kgs 11:14–22 records in detail how Edom rebelled against Solomon toward the end of his reign.[10]

---

9. We looked at the larger setting of these verses earlier, in another context; see Chapter 9, no. 2.

10. It is unclear from 1 Kgs 11:14–22 whether or not the Edomites were successful in their rebellion against Solomon, but at some point they clearly must have become independent, either during Solomon's reign or soon after his death. The same would be true of Ammon and Moab (the latter is confirmed by the statement in the Mesha Stele that Omri had conquered Moab,

Jerusalem appears in the book of Genesis in several places. The most explicit reference is in Gen 14:18, where מַלְכִּי־צֶדֶק מֶלֶךְ שָׁלֵם *malki-ṣedɛq mɛlɛk šalem* 'Melchizedek, king of Salem' occurs (all agree that 'Salem' is a shortened form of 'Jerusalem'). Note, moreover, that this individual is referred to not only as the king of Salem but as כֹהֵן לְאֵל עֶלְיוֹן *kohen lə-ʾel ʿɛlyon* 'priest to El Elyon [i.e., 'God Most High]', reflecting the reality of the heads of Canaanite city-states, who served as both king and priest. Furthermore, the story includes the important detail that Abram tithes to this individual (v. 20). The message for someone in tenth-century B.C.E. Israel is clear: do not object to tithing to the new Canaanite king-priest who supervises the cult in Jerusalem, namely, Zadok, for it is something that father Abraham did in the distant past already. And note that the names of these two Jerusalemite figures include the same root, *ṣ-d-q* 'righteous', thereby further solidifying the connection.

A more subtle reference to Jerusalem occurs in Genesis 22, in the famous story of the Aqedah (lit., 'the binding', that is, the binding of Isaac), as the episode is known in Jewish tradition. Here we encounter the earliest reference in the Bible to the expression הַר יְהוָה *har YHWH* 'the mount of YHWH' (v. 14), which in every other attestation refers unambiguously to Mount Zion (the other instances are in Isaiah, Micah, and Psalm 24). Presumably this phrase already was in use in tenth-century Jerusalem, or we may even wish to suggest that the author of Genesis 22 coined the term right here before our eyes.[11] In addition, even more subtle is the use of two key words in v. 14 that begin with the letter combination *yod–reš*, viz., יִרְאֶה *yirʾɛ* 'will see' and יֵרָאֶה *yeraʾɛ* 'is seen', thereby evoking the sounds found at the beginning of the word יְרוּשָׁלַם *yərušalayim* 'Jerusalem'. Accordingly, the listener to this story would hear the very sounds of יְרוּשָׁלַם *yərušalayim* 'Jerusalem' at this

---

which means that the small kingdom must have been independent in the fifty or so years between Solomon and Omri), but note that only with Edom is there explicit mention of rebellion against Israelite rule: thus Edom in 1 Kgs 11:14–22, thus Esau in Gen 27:40.

11. In a different vein, note that both Abraham ibn Ezra in the twelfth century and his supercommentator Yosef ben Eliezer Tov Elem (Bonfils) in the fourteenth century recognized that the expression הַר יְהוָה *har YHWH* 'the mount of YHWH' would be anachronistic in the time of Moses, and thus they suggested that the phrase must have arisen at a later date.

crucial moment in the text. Later Jewish tradition, beginning with 2 Chr 3:1, would make this point explicit, that Mount Moriah is the spot on which the Temple was built; the author of Genesis 22 makes the same point, but much more subtly. Moreover, while Abraham builds altars in a variety of locations (see Gen 12:7, 12:8, 13:18), only here does he sacrifice. The point could not be clearer: the ram caught in the thicket would be but the first of countless rams sacrificed on that spot.

The third reference to Jerusalem in Genesis is the mention of Gihon in Gen 2:13 as one of the four rivers of Eden. This is the name of the large spring in Jerusalem, the city's largest water source by far, whose presence makes life in the locale possible. We must, of course, disregard the geographical impossibility of the confluence of the Tigris and Euphrates Rivers and the Gihon (regardless of how one identifies the Pishon, the fourth river mentioned), but that is beside the point. We are dealing here with the transfiguration of a myth, or of a mythic feature, that has the great life-giving water sources of the world flowing together, including the main water source of Jerusalem. The author of Genesis, faced with a people unaccustomed to ascribing any special quality to Jerusalem, embedded into his narrative these three key passages—the Melchizedek episode, the reference to expression הַר יְהוָה *har* YHWH 'the mount of YHWH' in the Aqedah, and the mention of the Gihon as one of the waters of Eden—in order to demonstrate the centrality of Jerusalem to the tradition, indeed to the divine order.

A dominant theme in Genesis, perceived by everyone who reads the book, is the motif of the younger son, which is present in all four generations of the patriarchal narratives. Generation one: Isaac supersedes Ishmael. Generation two: Jacob supersedes Esau. Generation three: Judah (the youngest of the original four sons of Leah) supersedes Reuben, Simeon, and Levi; and Joseph (the youngest of the twelve save one) supersedes his older brothers. Generation four: Perez supersedes Zerah, and Ephraim supersedes Manasseh. In addition, if we look at the first brothers in the history of mankind, God favors the younger, Abel, over the older, Cain; and if we look at the book immediately following Genesis, we note that Moses is three years younger than Aaron (Exod 7:7). What lies behind this repeated motif?

Three reasons may be put forward: literary, theological, and political. On the literary level, this motif represents the extraordinary in life, and the extraordinary is what drives literature. The ordinary does not make for good storytelling: it is the departure from the quotidian norm that generates drama and makes for interesting reading, and such is the case throughout the ages, no less in antiquity than in modern times. Primogeniture, which was the norm in the ancient world, would hardly require mention in belletristic writing. Ultimogeniture, on the other hand, was apparently a topos for which ancient readers had an insatiable appetite. I say this because the theme appears not only in the numerous instances in the Bible listed above, but in Ugaritic epic as well.[12]

But our biblical author did not have in mind only a literary purpose for including this theme. Rather, the topos served him well on the theological level too. In the mind of the writer, Israel as a nation was likened to a younger son, one without the natural gifts that descend on the firstborn nations of the world, well-established entities like Egypt, Assyria, and Babylonia, with great political, economic, and military power, much larger populations, and an unending supply of fresh water provided by the major rivers that flow through these lands (the Nile, Tigris, and Euphrates, respectively). Israel had none of this. It was a fledgling nation, a people only recently (or relatively so) settled in the land of Canaan, living in a land without the bounty of water found in these other countries, and thus at a natural disadvantage, and only presently coming into its own as a nation among the nations. In light of this dichotomy between Israel and the nations—and even when measured against neighbors closer to home, Israel (at least until David's time) paled in comparison with city-states such as Tyre and Hazor—the biblical author expanded the younger son motif into another plane altogether. God had chosen none of the firstborn nations of

---

12. Specifically in the Epic of Kirta, in which the eighth and youngest child of the title character (called Thitmanit, a name based on the numeral 'eight'; cf. Latin/English 'Octavia') rises to prominence over her seven older siblings. For the text and an English translation, see Edward L. Greenstein, "Kirta," in Simon B. Parker, ed., *Ugaritic Narrative Poetry* (Writings from the Ancient World 9; Atlanta: Society of Biblical Literature, 1997), 9–48. References to Thitmanit appear in *CAT* 1.15:III:12 (on p. 26) and *CAT* 1.16:I:29 (on p. 32). The key passage is *CAT* 1.15:III:16: *ṣġrthn abkrn* 'the youngest of them I designate-as-firstborn'.

the world to be his people, but rather he selected Israel, a lowly nation, a last-born nation, if you will, to be his covenant partner, elevating it to firstborn status, as the book of Exodus states explicitly: בְּנִי בְכֹרִי יִשְׂרָאֵל *bəni bəkori yiśra'el* 'Israel is my firstborn son' (Exod 4:22).[13]

But there is more to this. Could anyone in the tenth century B.C.E. read these stories in Genesis and not see the lives of King David and King Solomon before their eyes? Recall that David was the youngest son of Jesse (the seventh according to 1 Sam 16:10–11; the eighth according to 1 Chr 2:13–15), a point emphasized in the story of Samuel's mission to the house of Jesse to anoint the next king of Israel (1 Samuel 16). Even more relevant is the extended narrative of who would succeed David on the throne in 1 Kings 1–2, for here the point is expressed overtly. Adonijah was the oldest of David's remaining sons, and under normal circumstances the throne would have been his (see especially 1:6, 2:22). But as events unfolded, it was not Adonijah, but rather Solomon, one of David's youngest sons—if not the youngest—who succeeded his father on the throne.[14] Kingship was still new in Israel, but the average Israelite could expect that the firstborn son of the king would succeed him on the throne. Such did not occur, however, in the succession from David to Solomon. Lest someone criticize the king for his decision, the author reminds his readers that God has always favored the younger or youngest son: thus Isaac, Jacob, Joseph, Perez, Ephraim—thus Solomon.

Yet another theme that dominates the book of Genesis is the theme of fraternal strife. The conflict is mild in the case of Isaac and Ishmael, where truly it is more a case of their mothers, Sarah and Hagar, at odds with each other (Gen 16:4–9, 21:9–10). It increases in the next generation, in the persons of the twins Jacob and Esau (Gen 25:22–23, 27:40–41). Finally, the theme of fraternal strife blossoms fully in the

---

13. A second motif present in Genesis, that of the barren wife, also fits here. Other nations are blessed with natural fecundity. Israel, on the other hand, is likened to a barren woman; and only through God's direct intervention does she prosper.

14. According to the narrative in 2 Samuel, it would appear that Solomon is indeed the youngest of David's sons. The genealogy in 1 Chr 3:5–8 may suggest otherwise, since there are sons listed after Solomon; though we cannot be sure if they are younger than Solomon or simply are listed after Solomon since they were born to other wives, and not Bathsheba.

case of Joseph and his brothers (Genesis 37–50). Once more we can point to the present conditions of the tenth century B.C.E. as the background for a repeated motif in the book of Genesis. In David's family there are two major conflicts: the one between Amnon and Absalom (2 Samuel 13) and the aforementioned one between Adonijah and Solomon (1 Kings 1–2). In each of these cases, in fact, the conflict ends violently: Absalom kills Amnon (2 Sam 13:28–29), and Solomon kills Adonijah (through his agent Benaiah; see 1 Kgs 2:25). In light of these actions, our attention should be drawn to yet another instance of fraternal strife in Genesis, indeed, the one present in the world's first set of brothers. The familiar tale of Cain and Abel now comes into even greater focus for the reader. To echo a rhetorical question asked above in reference to another theme, would anyone in the tenth century B.C.E. have missed the connection between Cain's killing of Abel and the two fratricides among David's sons? And if the reader of the biblical material needed a still more specific reference, note that Cain killed Abel בַּשָּׂדֶה *baś-śadɛ* 'in the field' (Gen 4:8), exactly as occurs in the mouth of the wise woman of Tekoa in her allusive account of Absalom's slaying of Amnon (2 Sam 14:6).

Certain stories in the book of Samuel portray David in a less than favorable light, most famously the account of his adultery with Bathsheba. The author of Genesis, whose main goal was to valorize David (as we saw above in those verses that promote the monarchy in general and kingship resident in the tribe of Judah in particular), could not pass over the less positive aspects of David's career, especially if they were widely known in Jerusalem and beyond. Accordingly, he included one extended story about Judah, the most obvious reflex of David in Genesis, in which the former is similarly portrayed in a negative light. I refer, of course, to the story of Judah and Tamar in Genesis 38. Note the connections between Judah in Genesis and David in Samuel. Both are shepherds; both separate from their kinsmen by moving to Adullam (Gen 38:1, 1 Sam 22:1); the one has a friend named Hirah (Gen 38:1), the other a friend named Hiram (2 Sam 5:11, 1 Kgs 5:15). Judah's wife, whose actual name is not given, is described as בַּת . . . שׁוּעַ *bat . . . šua‘* 'the daughter of . . . Shua' (Gen 38:2), a close match to the name of David's wife בַּת־שֶׁבַע *bat-šɛba‘* 'Bathsheba'. There is an even closer nexus when one reads the book of Chronicles, for in this later version

the wife of Judah is now called by the proper name בַּת־שׁוּעַ *bat-šuaʿ*
'Bathshua' (1 Chr 2:3), and the wife of David is similarly called בַּת־שׁוּעַ
bat-šuaʿ 'Bathshua' (1 Chr 3:5). Judah and David both have a Tamar
in their lives: in the former case, a daughter-in-law; in the latter, a
daughter. And the ultimate connection between the two stories: in
both cases the protagonist commits a major sin involving sexual intercourse with a woman, and in both cases he is forced to admit his
guilt (Gen 38:26, 2 Sam 12:13). To repeat the kind of question we have
been asking throughout this chapter: Could anyone in tenth-century
Jerusalem have read the account of Judah and Tamar without seeing
the present-day David and Bathsheba in the text? We actually have
two interpretative options here: either the author of Genesis 38 sought
to lampoon David through the story of Judah and Tamar; or he was
writing an apologia, as if to state, do not worry too much about the
king's sexual peccadilloes, for such comes with the territory, or at least
is part of the family legacy.[15]

Another story that repeats in Genesis is the threefold attempt by
one of the patriarchs to pass his wife off as his sister. Abraham does
this twice (Gen 12:10–20, 20:1–18), and then Isaac does likewise (Gen
26:6–11). Much has been written about the wife-sister motif, but to my
mind the most important issue has been missed by most scholars. While
space does not allow for full documentation here, suffice it to note that
the books of Samuel and Chronicles provide adequate evidence to demonstrate that David and Abigail were not only husband and wife, but
also brother and sister.[16] Furthermore, implicit in the book of Samuel is
the fact that Amnon and Tamar, half-brother and half-sister, could have
married each other (2 Sam 13:13), the law in Lev 18:11 notwithstanding.
Abraham, one will recall, when pressed by Abimelech to explain why
he passed Sarah off as his sister, states that in fact he and Sarah are
half-brother and half-sister, with the same father though with different mothers (Gen 20:12). Many scholars read this passage as simply a
white lie from Abraham's mouth, but we should accept the basic fact

---

15. For a more detailed look at this material, see Gary A. Rendsburg,
"David and His Circle in Genesis xxxviii," *Vetus Testamentum* 36 (1986): 438–46.

16. See Jon D. Levenson and Baruch Halpern, "The Political Import of
David's Marriages," *Journal of Biblical Literature* 99 (1980): 507–18.

that these individuals were indeed half-siblings. Thus Abraham and Sarah, thus David and Abigail, thus Amnon and Tamar.

There are still other items that link the Genesis stories with events of the tenth century, though here I will briefly summarize only. Jacob's antagonist Laban and David's antagonist Nabal have much in common, not the least of which is their names, which are anagrams of each other (LBN and NBL, respectively). Rachel steals her father Laban's *teraphim*, deceives him, and sides with her husband, Jacob, in the clash between the two men (Gen 31:19, 31:34–35); in similar fashion, Michal uses the *teraphim* to fool her father, Saul, in order to protect her husband, David (1 Sam 19:11–17). Places significant to the career of David reverberate in Genesis: I already mentioned the case of Adullam, to which we may add more famous places, such as Hebron, David's first capital, and Bethlehem, David's birthplace. Another less well-known case is Mahanaim, the place in Transjordan to which David fled during Absalom's revolt (2 Sam 17:24, 17:27, 19:33), and where earlier Jacob had encamped during his return to the land of Canaan after twenty years away in Aram (Gen 32:3). Of the hundreds of toponyms in the land of Israel, I find it striking that relatively minor places such as Adullam and Mahanaim appear both in Genesis and in Samuel.

We must note that the matches between the characters in Genesis and those in Samuel are not always perfect. A prime example was noted above: Tamar in Genesis is the daughter-in-law of Judah, while Tamar in Samuel is the daughter of David. But we have to recognize the fact that the author of Genesis had to work within his tradition—a tradition that we must assume was known to his readers. I do not want to open the large question of how historical the patriarchal narratives may or may not be, but the fact is this: these stories work better if the characters are real people known to later Israelites, and not fictional literary creations. In like manner, Miller's play works better because the Salem witch trials were a real event in American history; if the playwright had invented this story out of whole cloth, the dramatic effect would have been greatly reduced. And the same holds, of course, for the Korean War in *M*A*S*H* and the history of the Plantagents in Shakespeare's *Richard II*.

I have focused this chapter on the book of Genesis, but in passing I should note that other books of the Torah also evoke material from the

early monarchy. In Num 24:7, for example, Balaam declares: וְיָרֹם מֵאֲגַג
מַלְכּוֹ וְתִנַּשֵּׂא מַלְכֻתוֹ *wə-yarom me-ʾagag malko wə-tinnaśśeʾ malkuto* 'its [sc.
Israel's] king shall rise above Agag, and his kingdom shall be established',
with reference to the king of Amalek defeated by Saul in 1 Samuel 15.

Or to take another example, the law of the king in Deut 17:16–17
limits the monarch in three ways: he is not to multiply wives, he is
not to hoard large amounts of silver and gold, and he is not to engage
in horse trade with Egypt. All three of these acts were committed by
Solomon, and indeed served, either directly or indirectly, to propel the
split of the kingdom into the two separate entities, Judah and Israel,
upon this king's death. To my mind, the law in Deuteronomy 17 limiting the king's powers must date to the late tenth century B.C.E., for it
constitutes a reaction to the excesses of Solomon. In like manner, the
Twenty-Second Amendment to the United States Constitution, limiting the president to two terms, was passed in the years immediately
following the presidency of Franklin Roosevelt, whose four terms were
seen as excessive. It hardly seems likely that Deuteronomy 17 would
date from centuries after Solomon, as most scholars opine.

Let us imagine now a scene in tenth-century Jerusalem in which a
group of ancient Israelite literati is gathered in some setting or other,
and there, on the spot, they invent ancient Hebrew literature.[17] Given
the chronological distance of ca. 3000 years, such a scene may be difficult to conjure; allow me, accordingly, to present two other depictions—
one imagined, one real—that may serve as analogies.

The former brings us to the year 1593 (C.E., that is, not B.C.E.). The
scene is a tavern in London. The following seven men are seated around
a table: the playwrights William Shakespeare, Christopher Marlowe,
and Ben Johnson; the poets John Donne and Edmund Spenser; and the
essayists Francis Bacon and Walter Raleigh. If the movie *Shakespeare
in Love* (1998) helps to imagine the scene, great. There, on the spot,
these seven men create modern English literature.

What led to this moment in time in 1593, when, in my little fantasy
world, these seven individuals launched the great enterprise known

---

17. For another imagined scenario, which takes a similar approach to the
one offered here, see the entertaining fictional account by Loren Fisher, *The
Jerusalem Academy* (Willits, CA: Fisher Publications, 2002).

as modern English literature? Let us review the events of the previous century. In 1476 William Caxton brought the first printing press to England, introduced from the continent, representing a new technology that allowed for the easier production of books, thereby stimulating a greater desire to read by the public at large. In the 1500s the Renaissance reached England, and with it the rediscovery of the classics of Greek and Roman literature, especially the former material. New literary forms were introduced from the continent, in particular the sonnet, borrowed from Italy, which Shakespeare and Donne mastered, and the essay, borrowed from France, which Bacon and Raleigh mastered.

In 1588 the English defeated the Spanish Armada, and with that event England became the dominant political and military force in Europe. It was an age of glory for England, characterized by patriotism, exploration, and foreign colonization. Fifteen years before our seven men are sitting in the London tavern, Francis Drake circumnavigated the globe, claiming lands on distant shores for England, including present-day northern California and Oregon. All of this created a new class of wealthy Englishmen, a rich merchant class, a new nobility even, an urban elite, not necessarily people of the landed-gentry type. With increased leisure time, these people desired entertainment, especially in the form of literature to read and plays to see.

Ruling over England at this time was Elizabeth I, whose long and successful reign fostered the arts. The queen herself, in fact, could read or speak six or seven languages, including classical Greek and Latin, and most probably Hebrew as well. The connection between political power and the flowering of the arts is a well-established one in world history. One need only consider Classical Greece, Imperial Rome, Medieval Spain, the seventeenth-century Dutch Republic, Napoleonic France, England's second go-round under Queen Victoria, and twentieth-century America: the height of these countries' political and military power corresponded to the height of their artistic creative endeavors.

A new religion was aswirl in England. Elizabeth's father, Henry VIII, had broken with the Church in Rome and had established the new Church of England. The Roman-Anglican wars continued to be fought after his death, but the new Church became firmly established under his daughter Elizabeth, whose anti-Catholic stance characterized her reign. Within a year of ascending the throne, she oversaw the Act of

Uniformity, which required the use of the Protestant *Book of Common Prayer*; she removed all the Catholics from her Privy Council; and she established herself as the Supreme Governor of the Church of England.

Against the backdrop of all this political, military, and religious activity stands an important event, which occurred in 1576: James Burbage built England's first theatre. This singular act meant that plays could evolve from informal street performances into serious theatrical productions. In this new setting, plays no longer were silly little things of no value; henceforth, they would be major productions of lasting import.

And thus was invented modern English literature during the reign of Elizabeth I—or in my imaginary world, by the seven men (note the good biblical number!) seated in a London tavern in 1593, during the heyday of Her Majesty's rule.

John Dryden, writing only a century later, would refer to these writers as "that great race of men who lived before the flood," employing, quite felicitously, a well-known biblical topos. Indeed, not a single English play written after 1633 would be produced on the London stage with any regularity for the next 250 years, so canonical had Marlowe, Shakespeare, and Johnson become (along with their slightly younger contemporaries, including John Webster, John Ford, and Thomas Middleton); the monopoly would not be broken until Oscar Wilde and George Bernard Shaw arrived on the scene in the late nineteenth century (moreover, both from Dublin, I hasten to add; neither was an Englishman).

More historical than my imagined London tavern scene is the reality of what transpired in Concord, Massachusetts, during the years 1834–1868. Living in the same village were Ralph Waldo Emerson, Henry David Thoreau, Nathaniel Hawthorne, William Ellery Channing, Bronson Alcott, and his more famous daughter Louisa May Alcott—the core individuals of the Transcendentalist movement and their literary fellow travelers.[18] Living nearby in other Massachusetts towns or

18. For a brief outline of the lives of these authors, see Alex W. Moore, *Concord Authors: Biographical Notes* (Concord, MA: Anaxagoras Publications, 1989). For a more developed study, see Susan Cheever, *American Bloomsbury: Louisa May Alcott, Ralph Waldo Emerson, Margaret Fuller, Nathaniel Hawthorne, and Henry David Thoreau: Their Lives, Their Loves, Their Work* (New York: Simon & Schuster, 2006). These authors were interconnected not only in life,

in Boston proper were Margaret Fuller (first editor of *The Dial* and sister-in-law of Channing), Elizabeth Peabody (student of Emerson and sister-in-law of Hawthorne), and Henry Wadsworth Longfellow (lifelong friend of Hawthorne, since their student days at Bowdoin College). The lives of these individuals reached other contemporary writers, at a geographical remove, including, most prominently, Herman Melville (who dedicated *Moby-Dick* to Hawthorne, especially after the two authors' mythic lunch and encounter in the Berkshire Mountains), Walt Whitman (whom both Thoreau and Bronson Alcott visited in Brooklyn, and whose *Leaves of Grass* was promoted by Emerson), Horace Greeley (who hired Fuller and promoted both Emerson and Thoreau), and Horace Mann (brother-in-law of Hawthorne).

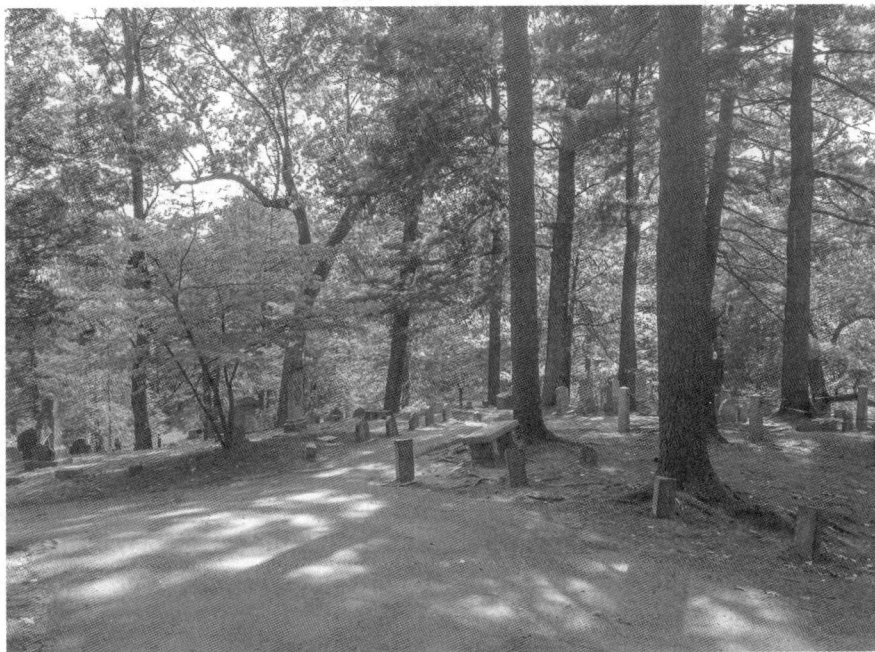

FIGURE 4: Authors Ridge section of Sleepy Hollow Cemetery, Concord, Massachusetts, with the Alcott, Thoreau, and Hawthrone family plots seen here, as photographed while standing in front of the Emerson family plot. Photograph by Melissa A. Rendsburg, August 2016.

but in death. The main group, comprised of Emerson, Thoreau, Hawthorne, and the Alcotts, are all buried within the small Authors Ridge section of Sleepy Hollow Cemetery in Concord. See Figure 4.

Without diminishing the work and influence of other writers, such as Washington Irving and Edgar Allan Poe, one may rightly claim that this remarkable group of writers created American literature during the middle of the nineteenth century. In fact, one may make an even greater claim: they created America! Consider, for example, Emerson's poem "Concord Hymn" (1837) and Longfellow's poem "Paul Revere's Ride" (1860), with their evocations of the events of April 1775 that marked the beginning of the Revolutionary War. And to bring this story full circle, one should recall that the Emerson family home, the Old Manse, stands next to the Old North Bridge crossing the Concord River, where "the shot heard round the world" was fired. Moreover, Emerson's grandfather, William Emerson Sr., witnessed the battle of Concord in April 1775 from the house itself.

Again we may ask: What led to this moment in time in the middle of the nineteenth century, which allowed for this circle of people to create the great enterprise known as American literature? In the generations prior, the United States was still a fledgling nation. The War of 1812, sometimes called "the Second War of Independence," had secured the status of the U.S. as an autonomous nation. The construction of long-range canals during the 1820s and the 1830s (such as the Erie Canal in New York, and the Delaware and Raritan Canal in New Jersey) allowed for travel and transportation toward new horizons. Even more significantly, the development of the railroads during the 1830s and 1840s allowed for the nation to see itself, well, as a nation, as the individual states became more and more interconnected. Western lands continued to be added to the United States, either as territories or as states admitted to the union. Manifest destiny (the term was coined in 1845) informed the spirit of America. With all of this, the United States came of age, and with it, its new national literature, as described above.

Let us now bring this picture back to tenth-century Jerusalem. Due to the anonymous nature of ancient Israelite literature (and ancient Near Eastern literature more generally), we cannot know the names of the individuals responsible for the creation of so much of the material that eventually was canonized as the Torah. But in some way, I like to imagine a circle of individuals (presumably all men, though even on this point one cannot be certain) akin to our Elizabethan friends in a London tavern in 1593, or to the Transcendentalists and their literary heirs in mid-nineteenth-century Concord and its environs, who collectively created the national literature at the heart of ancient Israel.

Let us now address the question: In what way, then, did these authors create ancient Hebrew literature? To answer this question, we must emphasize the point that most ancient stories were narrated in poetry, as opposed to prose. From Babylonia we may point to *Enuma Elish* ('When on High' = the Creation Epic) and the Gilgamesh Epic, both of which are written in poetry. In Canaan, both the myths of the gods, such as the Baʿal Myth, and the epics about human heroes, such as Aqhat and Kirta, were written in poetry. If we go further afield, we also may note that the earliest Greek literature—the epics of Homer and the mythological material of Hesiod—is poetic; only at a later stage do we encounter the prose material, whether historical (Herodotus, Thucydides, et al.) or philosophical (Plato, Aristotle, et al.).

Israel forged a new religious path, and that new path required a new medium to express its new religious ideas. The poetic tradition of the ancient Near East and the eastern Mediterranean was too heavily laden with the polytheistic mythologies of Israel's neighbors—as the cases of Enuma Elish, the Baʿal Myth, and Hesiod's *Works and Days* indicate clearly—and Israel's writers simply could not countenance utilizing that medium for expressing their revolutionary ideas about the divine. We segue, therefore, from the social and political issues that we have discussed above to the religious and theological issues that dominate the biblical text. Most obviously, we can point to the worship of only one God in ancient Israel, which was a radical departure from the veneration of a multiplicity of deities in the surrounding cultures. But this quantitative difference is only half the equation, for the qualitative difference is equally crucial. In Israel, Yahweh, the one God worshipped, was not a nature deity (associated with the sun, moon, rain, earth, sea, desert, river, etc.), but rather a deity who manifested himself in history, the history of mankind in general and the history of the people of Israel in particular. In the words of 1 Kgs 19:11–12, Yahweh is not to be found in the wind, or the earthquake, or the fire, but rather as קוֹל דְּמָמָה דַקָּה *qol dəmama daqqa* 'a still small voice' that speaks to mankind. One need only consider the manner in which the literature of Ugarit, our number one source for Canaanite mythology, describes Baʿal, ʿAnat, Mot, Yamm, and the other gods, all of whom are associated with nature and all of whose actions are narrated in poetry. Given this difference, Israel's writers rejected the poetic tradition and created an entirely new literary mode: narrative prose. The chart below presents the dichotomy for the two great bodies of literature at our disposal emanating from the land of Canaan:

Place:	Ugarit	Israel
Deity:	Ba'al et al.	Yahweh
Manifestation:	nature	history
Mode of storytelling:	poetry	prose

The evidence from the Bible suggests strongly that at one point Israel too narrated its stories in poetry, as part of its legacy as an ancient Near Eastern people. Snippets remain in the Bible: Exodus 15 (the Song of the Sea), Judges 5 (the Song of Deborah), two quotations from the Book of Yashar (Josh 10:12–13, 2 Sam 1:18–27), and a single passage from the Book of the Wars of YHWH (Num 21:14–15). But this is all that remains—just a few pages total, nothing more.[19] Otherwise, Israel's story is told in prose, and what eventually developed was the glorious narrative that stretches from Genesis 1 through 1 Kings 2, the core of which, if not the bulk of which, dates from the tenth century B.C.E., emanating from people close to the court of King David and King Solomon.

The question arises: Did Israel invent prose narration *de novo* or did it borrow this literary style from elsewhere? The answer lies in the latter option, and the source of that borrowing is the one country not mentioned up to this point: Egypt. Unlike the other peoples of the ancient Near East, the Egyptians told their stories not in poetry, but in prose. One rightly may ask: But were not the ancient Egyptians as polytheistic as the other neighboring peoples? Why should their prose

---

19. While Israel shifted from poetic storytelling to prose narrative, the poetic tradition remained very much alive in ancient Israel for other genres, such as hymns (Psalms), wisdom writing (Proverbs), love poetry (Song of Songs), dirges (Lamentations), and the like. It also would achieve new heights in the writings of the Prophets, a distinctly Israelite development with no parallels known from elsewhere in the ancient Near East.

storytelling style have been more acceptable to Israel than the poetry of the Canaanites or the Babylonians? The answer lies in the nature of the Egyptian prose stories: they typically are adventure tales, devoid of overriding theological messages. The best examples of such tales are Sinuhe, Wenamun, and The Shipwrecked Sailor, about which we will say more below.[20] Deities are rarely mentioned in these accounts, and when the divine is referred to, rarely do we read the name of a specific god, such as Ra or Horus or Isis; instead we usually encounter the term *nṯr*, the generic Egyptian term for 'god, deity'. These tales, I would argue, served as the model for the Hebrew prose literary tradition. Moreover, one finds signs of Egyptian cultural influence at the Jerusalem court during the reigns of King David and King Solomon, especially in the area of government administration (officialdom, bureaucracy, etc.).[21] Such influence reached Israel directly (for example, through the marriage of Solomon to the daughter of Pharaoh [1 Kgs 3:1]) and/or indirectly (for example, via the intermediation of Tyre). Within this picture we can situate the adaptation of Egyptian narrative prose by Israelite literati in tenth-century Jerusalem. As an analogy, one may point to new literary styles imported into England from Europe during the early modern period, including (as noted above) the essay and the sonnet.

Finally, we may reflect on a major literary motif that appears not only in the Bible and in these Egyptian tales, but in other ancient epics as well, most notably the *Odyssey* and Gilgamesh. I refer to the homecoming motif, or the *nostos* theme. Five major stories referred to above focus on the episodic journey of a hero who must leave his

---

20. For translations of these texts, see Miriam Lichtheim, *Ancient Egyptian Literature*, 3 vols. (Berkeley: University of California Press, 1973–1980) (Sinuhe and The Shipwrecked Sailor are in the first volume, while Wenamun is in the second); and Parkinson, *The Tale of Sinuhe and Other Ancient Egyptian Poems 1940–1640 BC* (Wenamun does not appear in this collection, since it postdates 1640 B.C.E.). Note that, per the title of his book, Parkinson considers the Egyptian tales to be poetry, but this is highly debatable. For bibliography on the issue, see Rendsburg, "Literary Devices in the Story of the Shipwrecked Sailor," 14 n. 4.

21. For general guidance, see John D. Currid, *Ancient Egypt and the Old Testament* (Grand Rapids, MI: Baker, 1997), 159–71.

native land, travel from locale to locale, and then return home successfully. The title characters in Gilgamesh, Sinuhe, Wenamun, and The
Shipwrecked Sailor, along with Odysseus in Homer's epic, all fit into
this pattern.[22] The Bible utilizes this motif as well, and includes one
such hero who also must leave home and who then returns after years
away. I refer to Jacob, and one even may wonder whether his twenty
years in Aram (Gen 31:38) is not coincidentally the same number of
years that Odysseus was away from Ithaca.[23]

But the Bible goes beyond all these narratives, with their focus on
a single hero figure, by adapting the homecoming motif to the major
story that dominates the Torah and the following book of Joshua. The
story is the same—the *nostos* theme still dominates—but in this case
the focus has been shifted from the travails of a particular individual
to that of an entire nation: עַם יִשְׂרָאֵל *'am yiśra'el* 'the people of Israel'.
This is the genius of the Israelite writers: their combining of a major
epic motif of antiquity with the collective history of the people of Israel.[24] The individual recedes in importance, and even though Moses
may dominate the narrative, the journey is that of the Israelites—in
fact, this will serve as an additional explanation as to why Moses cannot enter the Promised Land, for the journey is Israel's, not Moses's.
History plus epic, with an overlay of theology, all combined in a unique
way, expressed in prose, and unparalleled in ancient literature—that is
the creation of the brilliant Israelite literati of the tenth century B.C.E.

Throughout this book, I have used examples from English literature—
especially from the works of William Shakespeare—to illustrate various points. The end of this chapter provides yet another opportunity
to invoke the world of the bard. Shakespeare's histories deal with real
people—Richard II, Richard III, Henry V, and so on—but he takes liberties with the history in order to accomplish two things: (a) to create an
aesthetically pleasing play, and (b) to reflect the present, with a special
nod to the monarchy of his day. Shakespeare had a bit of a problem,

---

22. The end of Wenamun is missing, but no one doubts that the hero
successfully returned home, for the tale is narrated in the first person by the
title character.

23. See my earlier article, Gary A. Rendsburg, "Notes on Genesis xxxv,"
Vetus Testamentum 34 (1984): 361–66, esp. 361–64.

24. See Gordon and Rendsburg, *The Bible and the Ancient Near East*, 192.

however, for his monarch was a woman, Elizabeth I, but nothing could stand in the way of the great master—and indeed, Her Majesty understood well the messages of the plays performed in her presence at the royal residences in Greenwich, Whitehall, and Richmond.[25] To wit, Elizabeth is reported to have said to the Keeper of the Tower, "I am Richard II, know ye not that?"[26]

And thus I envision David turning to Benaiah, the captain of his personal bodyguard, after a reading of Genesis 38 in whatever version one may imagine it (if I may be permitted this little fantasy), and saying, אֲנִי יְהוּדָה הֲלֹא תֵדַע *'ani yəhuda ha-lo' teda'* 'I am Judah, know ye not that?'.

---

25. It is most unlikely that the queen would have attended performances at the Rose, the Curtain, or the Globe—the delightful portrayal of her presence in the theatre at the end of "Shakespeare in Love" notwithstanding.

26. For a recent treatment of this quotation, see Jason Scott-Warren, "Was Elizabeth I Richard II? The Authenticity of Lambarde's 'Conversation'," *The Review of English Studies* 64 (2013): 208–30.

CHAPTER TWENTY-TWO

A CHALLENGE TO THE DOCUMENTARY HYPOTHESIS

In the previous chapter, I attempted to demonstrate that the Torah stems essentially from the tenth century B.C.E., the time of David and Solomon. Anyone familiar with the Documentary Hypothesis (also known as the JEDP Theory, or more generally, as "source criticism"), which has dominated biblical scholarship during the last two centuries, will recognize at once that my approach to the problem is totally different. Actually, it is different on two levels. First, the Documentary Hypothesis proposes that the Torah is comprised of four major sources, which were all written independently and then combined by a redactor at a later stage to create the canonical text. Second, these sources are hypothesized to span centuries, from the tenth century through the fifth century, so that they supposedly existed as independent texts for a relatively long period of time before they were combined into a single final product. The four hypothesized sources (with their traditional dates indicated) are as follows:[1]

- Yahwist (J)—tenth century: a narrative that stretches from the creation of the world through the life of Moses.

- Elohist (E)—ninth century: a narrative that stretches from the life of Abraham through the life of Moses.

---

1. I say "traditional dates," because there has been a move by some scholars who recognize the Yahwist as an independent source to date the composition to the sixth century B.C.E. See, for example, John Van Seters, *Prologue to History: The Yahwist as Historian in Genesis* (Louisville: Westminster John Knox, 1992).

- Deuteronomist (D)—seventh century: a short narrative about the Wandering, followed by a very long presentation of law and cult, all placed in the mouth of Moses.

- Priestly (P)—sixth to fifth century: a major presentation of law and cult, with some narrative material as well, from the creation of the world through the life of Moses.

And then, according to those scholars who follow this approach, the four sources were combined by the Redactor (R) in the fifth century to create the Torah. This final editorial work often is linked to the activity of Ezra, who elevated the Torah to canonical status, as witnessed by the ceremony described in relatively fine detail in Nehemiah 8.

The origins of the Documentary Hypothesis lie in an attempt to explain all the doublets and contradictions that appear in the Torah. Paradigm examples include: the two creation accounts (Genesis 1–2); the number of animals that Noah takes on board the ark (Gen 6:19, 7:2); the lists of Esau's wives (Gen 26:34, 28:9, 36:2–3); the identity of the people who took Joseph down to Egypt, either Medanites (Gen 37:36) or Ishmaelites (Gen 39:1); the name of Moses's father-in-law as either Reuel (Exod 2:18) or Jethro (Exod 3:1, 4:18, 18:1, etc.); the name of the holy mountain as either Horeb (Exod 3:1, 17:6, 33:6, Deut 1:2, etc.) or Sinai (Exod 19:11, 24:16, 34:2, Lev 25:1, Num 3:1, etc.); the very different approaches to cultic worship presented in Leviticus and Deuteronomy; and so on.[2] All of these items, and many more, are explained in the Documentary Hypothesis by assigning the varying terms and contradictory information to different sources.

As I will attempt to demonstrate herein, however, a macroscopic view of the narratives reveals their essential literary unity. I do not wish to minimize the aforementioned issues, nor sweep them under the rug, for they clearly are present in the biblical text—but to my mind the majority of them remain rather inconsequential matters. By contrast, the macroscopic approach, which treats the narratives as

---

2. This is not the place to enter into a detailed study of the JEDP Theory, so this outline of the matter will need to suffice. For those seeking more details, the best and most accessible treatments of the subject remain the publications of Richard E. Friedman, especially his two books *Who Wrote the Bible?* and *The Bible with Sources Revealed*.

literary wholes, allows the reader to understand the biblical narrative in all of its glory and with all of its interconnectivity.

Having said that, however, I here must distinguish between the two major genres within the Torah: narrative, on the one hand, and legal-cultic material, on the other. There can be no doubt that the two great legal-cultic sections of the Pentateuch derive from separate schools. In this conclusion the Documentary Hypothesis is obviously correct, and in fact said finding remains one of the great accomplishments of modern biblical scholarship. The two relevant chunks of text are: (a) the Priestly material that spans Exodus 25 to Numbers 10 (and hence includes the entire book of Leviticus), along with selected chapters elsewhere; and (b) the bulk of the book of Deuteronomy.

In the former, for example, there is a great concern for ritual purity (see Leviticus 12–15, Numbers 19); no meat is to be consumed outside the sacrificial system (Lev 17:3–7); and there is a hierarchy distinguishing between priests (kohanim) and Levites (ləwiyyim) (Num 3:5–9). In the latter, by contrast, nary a word is said about ritual purity (the sole exception may be Deut 24:8);[3] meat may be consumed outside the sacrificial system (Deut 12:20–22); and there is no hierarchal distinction among the Levites, hence the term hak-kohanim ha-lwiyyim 'the Levitical priests' (Deut 17:9, etc.). But these contrasts only scratch the surface, because the entire tenor of the Priestly material and that of the Deuteronomic material are wholly different.[4]

But back to narrative: In opposition to the JEDP Theory's dividing the stories into small component parts, time and again the literary approach to biblical prose has demonstrated that these narratives operate as literary wholes (not 'holes'!). In what follows, I will present several such instances, proceeding in canonical order.

1. The Flood Story (Genesis 6–8)

Based on the aforementioned contradiction concerning the number of animals that Noah brought aboard the ark, along with other assumed

---

3. This passage was treated above, Chapter 11, no. 13.

4. For important studies, see Moshe Weinfeld, Deuteronomy and the Deuteronomic School (Oxford: Clarendon, 1972); and Israel Knohl, The Divine Symphony: The Bible's Many Voices (Philadelphia: Jewish Publication Society, 2003).

inconsistencies that have been espied in Genesis 6–8, including the back-and-forth use of the two divine names (יהוה 'Yнwн ' and אֱלֹהִים *'ɛlohim* 'God, Elohim'), scholars have divided the Flood Story into two sources, 'J' and 'P', as follows:

The Biblical Flood Story according to the Source Theory

	Yahwist (J)	Priestly (P)	Story Element
1.	6:5–8	6:9–13	morality factor
2.		6:14	materials
3.		6:15	dimensions
4.		6:16	decks
5.		6:17–22	covenant / population
6.	7:1–5		population
7.	7:7–10, 12, 16b, 17b, 22–23	7:6, 11, 13–16a, 17a, 18–21	flood
8.		7:24–8:5	mountaintop landing
9.	8:6–12		birds sent forth
10.		8:13–14	dry land
11.		8:15–19	all set free
12.	8:20–22		sacrifices

The problem for this approach arises when one brings the parallel flood account from the Gilgamesh Epic (Tablet XI) into the picture. As is well known, the Akkadian tale of Utnapishtim's surviving the great flood parallels the biblical account of Noah's exploits in exceedingly great detail, down to such items as the sending out of birds, the mountaintop landing, and so on. Moreover, the individual elements of the story are presented in the same order, even when some variation is possible. For example, at the end of the story, Noah and/or Utnapishtim could have offered sacrifices first and then sent everyone forth, but in both cases the survivor of the flood first sends everyone free and then offers sacrifices. An expansion of the above chart, now with the Gilgamesh Epic material in the fourth column, looks like this:[5]

The Biblical Flood Story according to the Source Theory and in Comparison to the Gilgamesh Epic Tablet XI

	Yahwist (J)	Priestly (P)	Story Element	Gilgamesh Epic XI
1.	6:5–8	6:9–13	morality factor	-
2.		6:14	materials	+
3.		6:15	dimensions	+
4.		6:16	decks	+
5.		6:17–22	covenant / population	-
6.	7:1–5		population	+
7.	7:7–10, 12, 16b, 17b, 22–23	7:6, 11, 13–16a, 17a, 18–21	flood	+
8.		7:24–8:5	mountain-top landing	+
9.	8:6–12		birds sent forth	+
10.		8:13–14	dry land	-
11.		8:15–19	all set free	+
12.	8:20–22		sacrifices	+

5. A plus-sign (+) indicates that the feature is present in both the biblical and Babylonian versions, while a minus-sign (-) indicates that the feature is present in the biblical account but not in the Babylonian one.

One notices in this scenario that the 'J' account does not include the materials/dimensions/decks trio, the mountaintop landing, and the setting free of the ark inhabitants, while the 'P' account does not include the elements of the birds being sent forth and the sacrifices.[6]

If the biblical story were the (haphazard?) compilation by the Redactor of two previously existing sources, one will wish to ask: Then how is it that the final product just happens to cohere perfectly with the flood narrative embedded into the Gilgamesh Epic, down to such details, precise order of elements, and so on? It is much better to assume that the flood story in Genesis 6–8 originates as a single coherent text. No doubt the biblical flood tradition was based on Mesopotamian precursors, most likely the one recorded in Gilgamesh Epic, Tablet XI, specifically. But it was transmitted in ancient Israel as a single unified account, not in two forms—one Yahwist, one Priestly—that somehow just magically happened to cohere with the Gilgamesh Epic version upon their being joined at a later stage by the Redactor.[7]

The attentive reader will have noted that three elements in the biblical account do not appear in the Gilgamesh Epic flood story (see above, n. 5). These features are (a) the morality factor, (b) the covenant, and (c) the emphasis on the dry land. Strikingly, these items, especially the first two, stand at the core of ancient Israelite religion. In the Gilgamesh Epic the decision to destroy humankind is more or less a capricious one, while in the Bible's version Yahweh is motivated to do so on account of the depravity on earth. The covenant concept is lacking in ancient Near Eastern religious traditions, but it stands at the core of biblical religion, as the concrete expression of the close relationship between Yahweh and his people Israel. And while the emphasis on the dry land

---

6. According to the JEDP Theory, the Priestly source does not countenance animal sacrifice until Aaron, the first high priest in the Tabernacle; hence, Noah's offering of the animals at story's end must be assigned to the Yahwist source (note also the use of יהוה 'Yᴀʜᴡʜ' to refer to the deity in Gen 8:20–21).

7. See Gordon J. Wenham, "The Coherence of the Flood Narrative," *Vetus Testamentum* 28 (1978): 336–48; and Gary A. Rendsburg, "The Biblical Flood Story in the Light of the Gilgameš Flood Account," in Joseph Azize and Noel Weeks, eds., *Gilgameš and the World of Assyria: Proceedings of the Conference Held at Mandelbaum House, The University of Sydney, 21–23 July 2004* (*Ancient Near Eastern Studies*, Supplement 21; Leuven: Peeters, 2007), 115–27.

may not be as significant as these first two items, here too one may explain its inclusion in the biblical account on theological grounds. I would claim that the biblical author wanted to underscore this point more so than his Mesopotamian predecessors, because it demonstrated for his readership in very explicit language that God was restoring the world to the condition that was needed for mankind to begin afresh. In the Gilgamesh Epic, this point naturally is implied, but it is striking how one goes very quickly from Utnapishtim's sending forth of the birds to his releasing everyone from the ship. The biblical author, by contrast, takes the time to describe the drying up of the earth explicitly. So to repeat, I admit that this point is not as theologically crucial as the morality and covenant issues, but its presence in the biblical story is telling nonetheless.

In sum, the author of the flood story in Genesis 6–8 adapted his account from the preexisting Mesopotamian flood tradition generally, most likely the Gilgamesh Epic version specifically. The two stories proceed in the same order, even when variable order was possible, with parallel element after parallel element. But the biblical writer remained a creative force nonetheless, for far from limiting himself to a simple retelling or adaptation of the Babylonian flood story, he introduced into his narrative three features that spoke to the core of ancient Israelite theology. Genesis 6–8 is a literary whole that is not to be subdivided into two parallel accounts ('J' and 'P'), which purportedly were woven together to create the existing narrative.

2. The Abraham Narrative (Genesis 12–22)

These eleven chapters have been divided by adherents of the Documentary Hypothesis into three sources, J, E, and P. There is far too much material in these eleven chapters to present herein, so I will limit myself to a detailed analysis of just one pair of episodes within the greater Abraham narrative.[8]

The first major episode in Abraham's (still called Abram at this juncture) life story is the call from God to leave his homeland and to

---

8. For the fuller analysis, see Rendsburg, *Redaction of Genesis*, 27–52 (= Chapter 2, "The Abraham Cycle").

journey to Canaan (Gen 12:1–9). The last major episode in his life story is the most famous and most challenging of them, the near-sacrifice of Isaac, in the Aqedah account (Gen 22:1–19). The former is assigned by the JEDP theorists to the Yahwist source, not least because the divine name used in Gen 12:1–9 is יהוה 'YHWH '; while the latter is assigned to the Elohist source, not least because the divine name used in Gen 22:1–19 is אֱלֹהִים ʾɛlohim 'God, Elohim'. And yet since the two episodes have so many lexical and thematic linkages between them,[9] a better approach is to consider them (along with the rest of the Abraham narrative) to be the work of a single author. I present these linkages in the following list:

1. 12:1–9 marks the first occasion in which God speaks to Abra(ha)m; 22:1–19 marks the last such occasion.

2. In both 12:1 and 22:2 God issues the command לֶךְ־לְךָ lɛk ləka 'go-you-forth', an expression that occurs nowhere else in the Bible.

3. In 12:1 the command is followed by a three-tiered phrase, מֵאַרְצְךָ וּמִמּוֹלַדְתְּךָ וּמִבֵּית אָבִיךָ me-ʾarṣəka u-mim-moladtəka u-mib-bet ʾabika 'from your land, and from your birthplace, and from the house of your father'.[10] In 22:2 the command is likewise preceded by a three-tiered phrase, אֶת־בִּנְךָ אֶת־יְחִידְךָ אֲשֶׁר־אָהַבְתָּ אֶת־יִצְחָק ʾɛt binka ʾɛt yəhidka ʾašer ʾahabta ʾɛt yiṣhaq 'your son, your only-one whom you love, Isaac'.[11] These descriptive epithets are accumulated in order to heighten the tension of the drama. Note further the threefold

9. Many of these have been noted by prior scholars, including: Benno Jacob, *Das erste Buch der Torah: Genesis* (Berlin: Schocken, 1934), 493; Umberto Cassuto, *From Noah to Abraham*, trans. Israel Abrahams (Jerusalem: Magnes, 1964), 296; Robert Davidson, *Genesis 12–50* (Cambridge: Cambridge University Press, 1979), 94; Fox, *Five Books of Moses*, 92; and most significantly, Nahum M. Sarna, *Understanding Genesis* (New York: Schocken, 1966), 160–61.
10. We studied this passage earlier in Chapter 20, p. 431, example (h).
11. In the Hebrew of 22:2, each of the three items is preceded by the particle אֶת ʾɛt, which is used to mark the definite object but is left untranslated. This grammatical usage thus parallels the threefold use of the preposition 'from' in 12:1.

use of 'your' (*-ka*) in 12:1 and the same technique with either 'your' (*-ka*) or 'you' (marked by *-ta* suffixed to the one
verb) in 22:2, all of which directs the reader's attention to
Abraham.

4. In both journeys, the specific destination is unknown to
Abra(ha)m, hence: 12:1 אֶל־הָאָרֶץ אֲשֶׁר אַרְאֶךָּ *'εl ha-'areṣ 'ašer
'ar'εkka* 'unto the land that I will show' // 22:2 עַל אַחַד הֶהָרִים
אֲשֶׁר אֹמַר אֵלֶיךָ *'al 'aḥad he-harim 'ašer 'omar 'elεka* 'on one
of the mountains that I will indicate (lit., "say") to you'.

5. In Gen 12:1–9 father and son leave each other; in Gen 22:1–19
father and son were prepared to see each other for the final
time. The former scene represents a break with the past; the
latter scene, had it been carried out to its fullest, would have
represented a break with the future.

6. In 12:6, Abra(ha)m's journey brings him to מוֹרֶה *morε*
'Moreh', while in 22:2 the destination is הַמֹּרִיָּה *ham-moriyya*
'(the land of) Moriah'.[12]

7. Both in 12:7 and in 22:9 Abra(ha)m builds an altar, with
both clauses commencing with וַיִּבֶן שָׁם *wayyibεn šam* 'and
he built there'.

8. The blessings given to Abra(ha)m in 12:2–3 and 22:17–18 are
strikingly similar, with many lexical overlaps.

9. In 12:4 we read וַיֵּלֶךְ אִתּוֹ לוֹט *wayyelεk 'itto loṭ* 'and Lot went
with him'; while in 22:6, 22:8 we read וַיֵּלְכוּ שְׁנֵיהֶם יַחְדָּו *wayy-
elku šənehεm yaḥdaw* 'and the two went together'. In both
scenes the protagonist is joined on his journey by a single
member of the next generation (either nephew Lot or son
Isaac).[13]

---

12. The Septuagint translators rendered both words the same, ὑψηλήν
hypsēlēn 'high', that is, 'elevated terrain'. Were these latter-day scholars attempting to show the relationship between the two stories even more closely?

13. This helps explain the focus on Lot in 12:4, especially since in reality
Abram was accompanied by his wife, Sarai, and others, as described in v. 5.

10. The verb וַיִּקַּח *wayyiqqaḥ* 'and he took' is predicated of
Abra(ha)m in both 12:5 and 22:3, with reference to the people
he took with him on the respective journeys.

11. The place name שְׁכֶם *šɛkɛm* 'Shechem' in 12:6 has an echo
in the verb וַיַּשְׁכֵּם *wayyaškem* 'and he arose-early' in 22:3.

12. 12:7 commences וַיֵּרָא יְהוָה אֶל־אַבְרָם *wayyera' YHWH 'ɛl 'abram*
'and Yʜᴡʜ appeared to Abram', and then later in the verse
occurs the expression לַיהוָה הַנִּרְאֶה אֵלָיו *la-YHWH han-nir'ɛ*
'elaw 'to Yʜᴡʜ who appeared unto him'. Resonances of
these phrases occur in 22:14, when Abraham names the place
יְהוָה | יִרְאֶה *YHWH yir'ɛ* 'Yʜᴡʜ sees', hence the expression
בְּהַר יְהוָה יֵרָאֶה *bə-har YHWH yera'ɛ* 'on the mount of Yʜᴡʜ
he appears'.¹⁴

13. In the first episode God speaks to Abram on two occasions,
to wit, in 12:1–3 and 12:7; in the second episode also, God
speaks to Abraham on two occasions, namely, in 22:12 and
22:16–18.

14. The first journey ends with Abram traveling to the Negev
(12:9), and the second journey ends with Abraham returning
to Beersheba (22:19), the most significant town in the Negev.

15. The first episode is preceded by the genealogical information
presented in 11:26–32, including reference to Nahor; while
the latter episode is followed by the genealogical information
in 22:20–24, with a focus on Nahor.

To my mind, these multiple lexical and thematic links are far too
many to be coincidental. The followers of the J–E separation of these
two chapters must assume that the Yahwist wrote 12:1–9 using such-
and-such words and ideas and that the Elohist wrote 22:1–19 using
such-and-such words and ideas, which—when placed in their respective positions in the final narrative by the Redactor—just happened
to echo each other in these manifold ways. A far better approach is

---

14. In Hebrew the same verbal root, ר־א־ה *r-'-h*, produces the meanings
'see' (Qal) and 'appear' (Niphʿal).

to presume a single author, or what I would call a single narrative voice (see further below), from the outset. A single long narrative about Abraham was authored by an ancient Israelite literary genius, with all of the interweavings indicated above consciously included in his text.

There is more, however, for I have saved until this point in my treatment one additional item that unites the two chapters. I have done so because of the emphasis placed earlier in this book on the use of alliteration to achieve literary effect. As we have seen repeatedly, alliterative words—which often are rare lexemes in the language—stand at close proximity to one another. In the present instance of Genesis 12 and Genesis 22, the two accounts are separated by ten chapters, and yet even here the author introduced an alliteration of the kind surveyed earlier (see Chapters 5–6, 10–11, 16). The key words are the rare verbs וַיַּעְתֵּק *wayyaʿteq* 'and he proceeded' in 12:8 and וַיַּעֲקֹד *wayyaʿqod* 'and he bound' in 22:9.[15] The former occurs only here in Gen 12:8 and (as a clear echo) in Gen 26:22. (The root ע-ת-ק *ʿ-t-q* does occur twelve other times in the Bible, with a range of meanings, among which are three additional instances of the Hiphʿil stem [Prov 25:1, Job 9:5, 32:15], though with different connotations than 'proceed'.) The latter verb, from the root ע-ק-ד *ʿ-q-d*, is a *hapax legomenon* in the Bible, used here instead of the common root ק-שׁ-ר *q-š-r* 'tie, bind' (see, e.g., Gen 38:28, Josh 2:18, 2:21, Job 39:10, etc.).[16] Note the precise equivalences of /ʿ/ and /q/ in both verbs, along with the corresponding voiced and voiceless dentals /d/ ~ /t/.[17] To my mind, the author of these two stories selected these rare lexemes deliberately, as one additional long-range nexus to solidify the association of the two pericopes. *Nota bene*: 'the author', in the previous sentence, and not two or more authors.

---

15. For my earlier discussion on this point, see Rendsburg, *Redaction of Genesis*, xix–xx (of the book's second edition only).

16. I cite here only passages that entail actual tying or binding, not metaphorical acts. See also Deut 6:8 and 11:18, as per rabbinic and apparently other (e.g., Qumran) Jewish interpretation.

17. The *ʿayin* in both verbs represents the same laryngeal fricative, as determined through the cognates, Ugaritic *ʿtq* 'pass' and Arabic *ʿaqada* 'tie, knot'.

3. Three items in the Jacob Story (Genesis 25–35)

In lieu of a similarly detailed analysis of matching units within the Jacob cycle,[18] I here prefer to focus our attention on several specific items within these chapters.[19]

First, in Gen 27:44, Rebekah instructs Jacob to flee to her brother Laban יָמִים אֲחָדִים *yamim 'aḥadim* '(for) a few days', until Esau's anger subsides. The next time we encounter this phrase is in Gen 29:20, where the seven years that Jacob labors to gain Rachel are in his eyes but כְּיָמִים אֲחָדִים *kə-yamim 'aḥadim* 'as a few days'.[20] As we read on, we realize that the 'few days' were in fact not just seven years, but another seven years, and then eventually another six years, for a total of twenty years (Gen 31:38, 31:41). All this as a reflection of Rebekah's original comment that Jacob should flee the household and live with Laban for a 'few days'. Clearly, the two occurrences of the phrase are interconnected, but the JEDP Theory will have none of this, for Gen 27:44 is assigned to 'J' and Gen 29:20 is ascribed to 'E'. The whole thing must be a coincidence, accordingly.

Second, and perhaps more striking: in Gen 29:26, after hearing Jacob's complaint that he labored for Rachel but was tricked into marrying Leah, his father-in-law, Laban, responds, לֹא־יֵעָשֶׂה כֵן בִּמְקוֹמֵנוּ לָתֵת הַצְּעִירָה לִפְנֵי הַבְּכִירָה *lo' ye'aśe ken bi-mqomenu latet haṣ-ṣə'ira lipne hab-bəkira* 'it is not done thus in our place to give the younger before the firstborn'.[21] These words no doubt are intended to take the reader back to the story in Genesis 27, in which Jacob (as the younger) placed himself before Esau (the firstborn). And yet once more the source critics would have us believe that these stories originated from different pens, since Gen 29:26 is assigned to 'E', while ch. 27 is ascribed to 'J'. Or, to repeat the above comment, once more this all must be a coincidence.

---

18. See Michael Fishbane, "Composition and Structure in the Jacob Cycle (Gen. 25:19–35:22)," *Journal of Jewish Studies* 26 (1975): 15–38; Michael Fishbane, *Text and Texture* (New York: Schocken, 1979), 40–62; and Rendsburg, *Redaction of Genesis*, 53–69.

19. For my earlier treatment of these passages, see Rendsburg, *Redaction of Genesis*, p. xxi (of the book's second edition only).

20. We will study this verse again in Chapter 29, during our detailed analysis of the Jacob and Rachel story.

21. Once more, see the more detailed treatment in Chapter 29.

These two items are more important, however, than the simple issue of single source versus multiple sources. For these interrelated passages speak to the very heart of biblical narrative. Jacob sinned by deceiving his father Isaac, and he deserves to be punished therefore. Now, while God can punish reprobates directly when he so desires (see, for instance, Gen 38:7, 38:10), how much more delightful the literary effect when a human character playfully exacts the revenge on the sinning individual. That is precisely what transpires here: (a) Laban takes advantage of Jacob at every turn so that the 'few days' turn into 7 + 7 + 6 = 20 years; and (b) when Jacob complains about the ruse performed upon him with the switch of Leah for Rachel, Laban informs the reader, via his words to Jacob, that the deceiver has in turn been deceived. It is almost as if W. S. Gilbert had the biblical story in mind with his lyrics, set to Arthur Sullivan's music, in "The Mikado" (Act II—in the mouth of the eponymous character): "My object all sublime / I shall achieve in time / To let the punishment fit the crime / The punishment fit the crime."

And yet the division of Genesis into its theoretical sources deprives the reader of all this. For by attributing these passages to different authors, source criticism not only rends the connection asunder but denudes Laban's words and actions of their powerful impact.

Let us go back for a moment, though, and recall that the actual mastermind behind the deception of Isaac was not Jacob, but rather Rebekah.[22] She too, accordingly, deserves punishment. Rebekah's comeuppance, however, is narrated in an even more subtle way. Once she sends her son Jacob away to live with her brother Laban in the land of Aram, we, the readers, never see her again. The camera, as it were, accompanies Jacob on his journey to Aram,[23] so that we leave Isaac, Rebekah, and Esau behind. When Jacob returns to the land of his birth, he is reunited with his brother, Esau (Gen 33:4), and with his father, Isaac (Gen 35:27)—but not a word about Rebekah. The reader is to surmise, accordingly, that sometime during the intervening twenty

---

22. For what follows, see my earlier study "Notes on Genesis xxxv," esp. 364–66.

23. For the linguistic evidence that serves the literary needs of this story, see below, Chapter 24, "Style-Switching."

years Rebekah died. Her punishment, then, is to be stricken from the record. To repeat what I said above, we never see her again. All of this is adumbrated by her own flippant words to Jacob, upon his objection to the plan to deceive Isaac, which might bring upon him a curse and not a blessing: עָלַי קִלְלָתְךָ בְּנִי ʿalay qiləlatka bəni 'may your curse be upon me, my son' (Gen 27:13). Words glibly spoken are sure to come to fruition, certainly so in the mindset of ancient Israel, which placed great emphasis on the power of the word.[24]

There is, I should add, one hint at all this in the book of Genesis, for in truth Rebekah is mentioned one additional time, in Gen 35:8: וַתָּמָת דְּבֹרָה מֵינֶקֶת רִבְקָה וַתִּקָּבֵר מִתַּחַת לְבֵית־אֵל תַּחַת הָאַלּוֹן וַיִּקְרָא שְׁמוֹ אַלּוֹן בָּכוּת wattamot dəbora meneqɛt ribqa wattiqqaber mit-taḥat lə-bet-ʾel taḥat ha-ʾallon wayyiqraʾ šəmo ʾallon bakut 'and Deborah, the nursemaid of Rebekah, died, and she was buried beneath Bethel, under the oak-tree, and they called the place Allon-bakut'. Here we receive mention of the death of Deborah, Rebekah's nursemaid. Scholars have been puzzled by the inclusion of this oblique comment, which is unconnected to what precedes or to what follows. The solution to the problem is as follows: Gen 35:8 allows the reader to hear the name 'Rebekah' one more time, with the expectation presumably that this will be her death notice—though she is fooled, as it were, upon learning that this is the notification of Deborah's demise. This in turn serves as a reminder that we never receive the expected death notice of Rebekah, the only one of the six leading ancestral heroes without a statement of death and burial.[25] All of this, I submit, is part of Rebekah's punishment for her primary role in the deception of Isaac: she is, indeed, totally written out of the record, even unto her death and burial.

---

24. See Isaac Rabinowitz, *A Witness Forever: Ancient Israel's Perception of Literature and the Resultant Hebrew Bible* (Occasional Publications of the Department of Near Eastern Studies and the Program of Jewish Studies, Cornell University, 1; Bethesda, MD: CDL, 1993).

25. See the following verses in Genesis, in canonical order: 23:1–2, 23:19–20 (Sarah); 25:8–10 (Abraham); 35:19 (Rachel); 35:28–29 (Isaac); 49:33, 50:13 (Jacob). True, Rebekah's burial is mentioned *post facto* by her son Jacob (49:31), but the point remains: Genesis does not include a death and burial notice of Rebekah within the narrative. Some of these passages were studied in another context above, in Chapter 14, no. 1.

Now back to source criticism: As we have seen above, ch. 27 is assigned to the Yahwist, and yet if the Documentary Hypothesis were correct, one would have to assume that not only 'J' but also his cohorts 'E' and 'P' conspired to exclude any further mention of Rebekah from the extended narrative that follows, through ch. 35. This is, to my mind, a bit too much to swallow. A better tack is to assume, once more, a literary whole incorporating the life story of Jacob, starting with his birth in Genesis 25, with a focus on his peregrinations to Aram and back, and concluding, in Genesis 35, with his reentry into the land of Canaan. His life will continue, of course, though in the next major section of Genesis, chs. 37–50, the (narrative) baton is passed to the next generation, represented most of all by Joseph.

4. The Plagues as Pairs

As others have noted previously,[26] the extended narrative of Exodus 7–12 presents the ten plagues as five pairs of two plagues each, with each member of the pair corresponding to its mate. This can be presented in chart form as follows:

Pair I	Pair II	Pair III	Pair IV	Pair V
1. Blood 2. Frogs	3. Lice 4. Insect Swarm	5. Pestilence 6. Boils	7. Hail 8. Locusts	9. Darkness 10. Firstborn

The first two plagues are connected to the Nile River; the third and fourth plagues are both insects;[27] the third pair comprises different diseases; each member of the fourth pair is a calamity that originates in the sky and devours crops; and finally, the last two plagues are connected by darkness, with number nine being darkness itself during the daytime, and the tenth plague occurring at midnight. In short, the long narrative that extends from ch. 7 through ch. 12 has a built-in unity, which is readily seen by this analysis and in the chart above.

---

26. See especially Cassuto, *Commentary on the Book of Exodus*, 93.

27. On the identity of the fourth plague, see Gary A. Rendsburg, "Beasts or Bugs? Solving the Problem of the Fourth Plague," *Bible Review* 19.2 (Apr. 2003): 18–23.

The Documentary Hypothesis, by contrast, divides the plagues narrative into different sources. Though I hasten to add that devotees of this approach do not agree on the assignment of the individual plagues. According to the classical view of S. R. Driver, the ten plagues are authored mainly by 'J' and 'P', with some 'E' material;[28] while the leading source critic today, Richard E. Friedman, opines that the plagues are chiefly 'E' and 'P', with some 'R' (that is, the Redactor).[29] And while this point by itself does not represent sufficient cause to upset the entire J–E–P applecart, it nevertheless raises an eyebrow: if the source critics themselves cannot agree in the main, then perhaps an entirely new approach is worthy of consideration.

In this particular case, let us examine how the source division would work with the design noted above. Driver's analysis yields the following:[30]

Pair I	Pair II	Pair III	Pair IV	Pair V
1. Blood (J)	3. Lice (P)	5. Pestilence (J)	7. Hail (J)	9. Darkness (E)
2. Frogs (J)	4. Insect Swarm (J)	6. Boils (P)	8. Locusts (J)	10. Firstborn (J)

Note that only the first and fourth pairs of plagues stem from the same voice, with the other pairs crossing the traditional source boundaries.

Friedman's analysis looks like this:

Pair I	Pair II	Pair III	Pair IV	Pair V
1. Blood (E)	3. Lice (P)	5. Pestilence (E)	7. Hail (E)	9. Darkness (E)
2. Frogs (E)	4. Insect Swarm (E)	6. Boils (P)	8. Locusts (E)	10. Firstborn (E)

In this scenario, three pairs of plagues (first, fourth, and fifth) derive from the same source, though the two other pairs divide. In addition, these

---

28. S. R. Driver, *An Introduction to the Literature of the Old Testament* (New York: Charles Scribner's Sons, 1913), 24–28. See also the convenient chart based on Driver's analysis in Moshe Greenberg and S. David Sperling, "Exodus, Book of," *Encyclopaedia Judaica*, 2nd ed. (Detroit: Macmillan, 2007), 6:619.

29. Friedman, *Bible with Sources Revealed*, 130–40, with extensive discussion in two notes on preceding pages, 125 n. ** and 126 n. *.

30. Both here and below, by the tenth plague, concerning the death of the firstborn, I intend both the prediction of the plague in 11:1–8 and the event itself in 12:29–30.

two charts allow one to see the point made above: Driver assigned most of the non-'P' material to 'J' (the exception is the plague of darkness, attributed to 'E'); while Friedman assigns all of the non-'P' material to 'E'.[31]

In either case, the source-critical analysis must assume that the Redactor took the individual pericopes and organized them (again, haphazardly?) in a way that, voilà, produced the final, canonical version, in which the plagues are organized as five pairs, with each member corresponding to its mate.

To my mind, a far simpler and less complicated approach is to discard the entire source-critical method and to assume an intentional ordering of the plagues in the manner described above.

5. The Plagues as Triads

A second pattern is visible in the plagues narrative, one that divides the first nine plagues into three sets of three each,[32] with the tenth plague standing outside this configuration as the climactic event. The defining feature in this design is whether or not Pharaoh is forewarned of each impending plague, and if he is forewarned, when, where, and how the warning is expressed. In the first member of each triad, Moses is to position himself before Pharaoh in the morning; in the second member of each triad, the warning is a general one, without a specific time and position indicated; and in the third member of each triad, no warning is given. Hence, we read as follows:

---

31. Note that a standard work on the subject, Antony F. Campbell and Mark A. O'Brien, *Sources of the Pentateuch* (Minneapolis: Fortress, 1993), presents the source division according to Martin Noth, which in turn is quite close to that of S. R. Driver, except for the fact that Driver countenanced 'E' material in the plagues narrative, which Noth denied. The reader can access Noth's system in one of two ways: (a) in chart form in Martin Noth, *A History of Pentateuchal Traditions*, trans. Bernhard W. Anderson (Chico, CA: Scholars Press, 1981), 268–69 (within the section entitled "Translator's Supplement: Analytical Outline of the Pentateuch," not included in the German original); and (b) in narrative form in Campbell and O'Brien, *Sources of the Pentateuch*, 38–39 (for 'P'), 136–42 (for 'J').

32. This arrangement was noted already by both Rashbam (1085–1158) and Abarbanel (1437–1508). See also Cassuto, *Commentary on the Book of Exodus*, 93; and Nahum M. Sarna, *Exploring Exodus* (New York: Schocken, 1986), 76–77.

Plague 1 [Exod 7:15]

לֵ֣ךְ אֶל־פַּרְעֹה֮ בַּבֹּ֒קֶר֒ הִנֵּה֙ יֹצֵ֣א הַמַּ֔יְמָה וְנִצַּבְתָּ֥ לִקְרָאת֖וֹ עַל־שְׂפַ֣ת
הַיְאֹ֑ר וְהַמַּטֶּ֛ה אֲשֶׁר־נֶהְפַּ֥ךְ לְנָחָ֖שׁ תִּקַּ֥ח בְּיָדֶֽךָ׃

"Go to Pharaoh in the <u>morning</u>—behold, he (will be) coming
out to the water—and you shall <u>position (yourself)</u> to greet
him at the edge of the Nile; and the staff that turned into a
snake you shall take in your hand."

Plague 2 [Exod 7:26]

וַיֹּ֤אמֶר יְהוָה֙ אֶל־מֹשֶׁ֔ה בֹּ֖א אֶל־פַּרְעֹ֑ה וְאָמַרְתָּ֣ אֵלָ֗יו כֹּ֚ה אָמַ֣ר יְהוָ֔ה
שַׁלַּ֥ח אֶת־עַמִּ֖י וְיַֽעַבְדֻֽנִי׃

And Yhwh said to Moses, "<u>Come to Pharaoh</u>, and you shall
say to him, 'Thus says Yhwh: Send-forth my people, so that
they may worship me'."

Plague 3 [no warning]

Plague 4 [Exod 8:16]

וַיֹּ֨אמֶר יְהוָ֜ה אֶל־מֹשֶׁ֗ה הַשְׁכֵּ֤ם בַּבֹּ֙קֶר֙ וְהִתְיַצֵּב֙ לִפְנֵ֣י פַרְעֹ֔ה הִנֵּ֖ה יוֹצֵ֣א
הַמָּ֑יְמָה וְאָמַרְתָּ֣ אֵלָ֗יו כֹּ֚ה אָמַ֣ר יְהוָ֔ה שַׁלַּ֥ח עַמִּ֖י וְיַֽעַבְדֻֽנִי׃

And Yhwh said to Moses, "Arise-early in the <u>morning</u> and
<u>position yourself</u> before Pharaoh—behold, he (will be) com-
ing out to the water—and you shall say to him, 'Thus says
Yhwh: Send-forth my people, so that they may worship me'."

Plague 5 [Exod 9:1]

וַיֹּ֤אמֶר יְהוָה֙ אֶל־מֹשֶׁ֔ה בֹּ֖א אֶל־פַּרְעֹ֑ה וְדִבַּרְתָּ֣ אֵלָ֗יו כֹּֽה־אָמַ֤ר יְהוָה֙
אֱלֹהֵ֣י הָֽעִבְרִ֔ים שַׁלַּ֥ח אֶת־עַמִּ֖י וְיַֽעַבְדֻֽנִי׃

And Yhwh said to Moses, "<u>Come to Pharaoh</u>, and you shall
speak to him, 'Thus says Yhwh the God of the Hebrews:
Send-forth my people, so that they may worship me'."

Plague 6 [no warning]

Plague 7 [Exod 9:13]

וַיֹּ֤אמֶר יְהוָה֙ אֶל־מֹשֶׁ֔ה הַשְׁכֵּ֣ם בַּבֹּ֗קֶר וְהִתְיַצֵּב֙ לִפְנֵ֣י פַרְעֹ֔ה וְאָמַרְתָּ֣ אֵלָ֔יו
כֹּֽה־אָמַ֤ר יְהוָה֙ אֱלֹהֵ֣י הָֽעִבְרִ֔ים שַׁלַּ֥ח אֶת־עַמִּ֖י וְיַֽעַבְדֻֽנִי׃

And Yʜᴡʜ said to Moses, "Arise-early in the <u>morning</u> and
<u>position yourself</u> before Pharaoh; and you shall say to him,
'Thus says Yʜᴡʜ the God of the Hebrews: Send-forth my
people, so that they may worship me'."

Plague 8 [Exod 10:1]

וַיֹּ֤אמֶר יְהוָה֙ אֶל־מֹשֶׁ֔ה בֹּ֖א אֶל־פַּרְעֹ֑ה כִּֽי־אֲנִ֞י הִכְבַּ֤דְתִּי אֶת־לִבּוֹ֙ וְאֶת־לֵ֣ב
עֲבָדָ֔יו לְמַ֗עַן שִׁתִ֛י אֹתֹתַ֥י אֵ֖לֶּה בְּקִרְבּֽוֹ׃

And Yʜᴡʜ said to Moses, "<u>Come to Pharaoh</u>, for I have
made-heavy his heart, and the heart of his servants, in order
that I may place these my signs in his midst."

Plague 9 [no warning]

Now, it is true that according to the classical source division,
plagues 1–2, 4–5, and 7–8 (that is, those with warnings) are assigned
to the same source ('J' by Driver, 'E' by Friedman), which means that
the pattern just noted could be dovetailed with the Documentary Hypothesis. But the design breaks down when we consider plagues 3,
6, and 9, that is, those without warnings. For according to the source
critics, while the third and sixth plagues are assigned to 'P' (so far, so
good), the ninth plague is allocated by Driver mainly to 'E', with some
'J' verses, and by Friedman to 'E' wholly. Once more, it is better to
posit a single, unified authorial voice than to reconstruct hypothetical
sources that in truth are only the constructs of scholars, unattested in
the actual record.

6. Alliteration in Exodus 32:12–15

At numerous times in this book (again, see Chapters 5–6, 10–11, 16), we have paid attention to the use of alliteration to enhance the literary text. For these soundplays to operate, one must assume that each is the conscious product of a single author, who has thoughtfully woven the alliterative lexemes into his literary creation. When such similar-sounding words occur within the same verse, the odds are that they are ascribed to the same source by adherents of the JEDP Theory. But when such alliterations span several verses, frequently the alliterative words wind up appearing in the hypothetical different sources. We have shown this above for the case of the two words at a distance from one another in Genesis 12 and 22, so here we provide another example, this time involving a cluster of words that appear in rapid succession and yet are ascribed to different sources according to the Documentary Hypothesis. Of the many examples that I could use to illustrate this point, I present here the passage of Exod 32:12–15, studied earlier.[33]

The following seven words occur within these six verses:

בְּרָעָה   *bə-raʿa* 'with evil' (v. 12)

הָרָעָה   *ha-raʿa* 'the evil' (v. 12)

אַרְבֶּה   *ʾarbɛ* 'I will multiply' (v. 13)

זַרְעֲכֶם   *zarʿakɛm* 'your seed' (v. 13)

הָרָעָה   *ha-raʿa* 'the evil' (v. 14)

עֶבְרֵיהֶם   *ʿɛbrehɛm* 'their (two) sides' (v. 15)

בְּרֵעֹה   *bə-reʿo* 'in its [sc. the people's] shouting' (v. 17)

As we noted in our first treatment of these words, the consonantal trio /b/ *bet* – /r/ *reš* – /ʿ/ *ʿayin* forms the basis for the alliteration, as seen in the first, sixth, and seventh of these words. Three others (the second, fourth, and fifth) include the /r/ *reš* and /ʿ/ *ʿayin* elements; while the remaining one (the third) includes the /r/ *reš* and /b/ *bet* sounds.

---

33. See Chapter 6, no. 18.

Included in this string of lexemes are two unusual items, עֶבְרֵיהֶם
ʿebrehɛm 'their (two) sides' (v. 15) and רֵעַ 'shouting' (v. 17)—again, see
above in Chapter 6, no. 18. More significantly for our present purposes,
however, is the unusual orthography of this last item, with the archaic
spelling ה- -H for the third masc. sg. pronominal suffix (normally one
expects -ו -w), thus permitting ברעה BRʿH 'with evil' (v. 12) and ברעה
BRʿH 'in its shouting' (v. 17) to look exactly alike.[34]

Now, what does all this have to do with the Documentary Hypothesis? According to the source critics, vv. 12–14 are ascribed to the 'J'
source, while vv. 15–17 are attributed to the 'E' source. And yet our alliterative string of words spans the two conjectured sources, including,
most tellingly, the twofold use of ברעה BRʿH in vv. 12 and 17, though
with different meanings. Those who would divide our text into separate
sources would have one believe that 'J' used the /b/ bet – /r/ reš – /ʿ/
ʿayin string and its congeners in vv. 12–14 (five such items), while the
'E' source did likewise in vv. 15–17 (two such items)—and that the latter source used the atypical spelling ברעה BRʿH in v. 17 only by coincidence, notwithstanding its matching mate, ברעה BRʿH, in v. 12. A far
better approach, here and in other such instances, is simply to assume
a single literary text that is not to be divided into microscopic parts.

* * * * *

The five texts presented above (with the plagues narrative analyzed
through two different lenses, for a total of six sections to this chapter)
are but a sampling of the narratives that could be examined in such
manner. A proponent of the JEDP Theory could respond with the notion
that the Redactor is the one responsible for all this apparent literary
unity: which is to say, he in fact was the one who took, for example,
the different 'J' and 'P' accounts of the flood and weaved them into a
unitary whole, consistent with the Mesopotamian flood tradition; or,
to use another example, he was the one who took the different 'J', 'E',
and 'P' versions of the plagues and organized them so that they work
as both pairs and triads in the final literary form. But if this were the

---

34. I intentionally omit the vowel signs here, in order to have the two
words appear as they would in a pre-Masoretic manuscript.

case, then why continue along this path? Why not simply surrender to the obvious and proclaim that a single narrative voice is responsible for these literary creations in their final form?

The main point is: we know absolutely nothing about the prehistory of the biblical text, for all we possess is the text in its final form. This stands in contrast to the developments of other literary creations in world history. To start with one of the oldest, we are able to trace the development of the Gilgamesh Epic from its earliest witnesses as independent poems, written in Sumerian and dated to the third millennium B.C.E., to the final, 'standard' version, written in Akkadian and dated to ca. 1100 B.C.E., with our best copies from Neo-Assyrian times, ca. 700 B.C.E.[35] More familiar to English readers is just about any play by William Shakespeare, for example, *King Lear* (1606): among the sources of the great bard's masterpiece was Raphael Holinshed's *Chronicles of England, Scotlande, and Irelande* (1587), which in turn used Geoffrey of Monmouth's *Historia Regum Brittanniae* (ca. 1135) as a source. With this information in hand, we are able to determine how Shakespeare changed the ending of the drama: in Geoffrey's account, Cordelia restores Lear to the throne and then succeeds her father as monarch; while in Shakespeare's more tragic version, as is well known, both lead characters die. This is precisely the kind of thing that we cannot determine about biblical texts: to repeat, all we have is the final form.[36]

Sometimes a single author is responsible for a text, but it changes over the course of time. A classic example is William Wordsworth's *The Prelude*, which was first published in 1799, then reworked for the 1805 edition (which, incidentally, was not found until 1926), and then finally the 1850 edition, published posthumously. Here too we are able to trace the work from its origins to its final form—but again, this is a process that we are unable to reconstruct for any biblical text. If the

---

35. The standard treatment remains Jeffrey H. Tigay, *The Evolution of the Gilgamesh Epic* (Philadelphia: University of Pennsylvania Press, 1982).

36. To be honest, we do have something similar in the Bible, to wit, the Chronicler's use of Samuel–Kings, with changes throughout (for example, the lack of a David-Bathsheba adulterous affair in the former, even though this event holds center stage in the latter). But this is the exception, for we have nothing comparable with earlier books such as Genesis, Exodus, etc., which have played a major role in the present work.

author of, say, Genesis or Exodus reworked his composition at any time during his lifetime, we have no evidence thereof.

At other times we have multiple contributors to a single text—which we may call 'composition by committee'—but even in recent examples thereof we still are unsure of who wrote what. Here my best illustration is the musical *Candide*, with an all-star cast of writers, including Lillian Hellman, who wrote the original libretto (1956), but with additions by Richard Wilbur, Dorothy Parker, Stephen Sondheim, Leonard Bernstein, et al., all of which culminated in the final revised version (1989). And while some of these individuals are yet alive (most famously, Sondheim), I am not sure if anyone has unraveled the entire final version to elucidate which of these lyricists is responsible for this line or that line, this song or that song. Could such a development underlie the book of Genesis? The answer is, naturally, yes—though the burden of proof for such a prehistory of the text would lie with the proponent of such a 'composition by committee' view.

In all of these instances, whether Gilgamesh or Shakespeare, Wordsworth or the modern American musical, the consumer of the text is best served simply by sitting back, listening, and enjoying—listening, that is, to what I call the single narrative voice. And thus my approach to the Torah is as follows: a single narrative voice is responsible for everything from Genesis 1 through Deuteronomy 34, with the legal-cultic material inserted at the proper places (the relatively short section in Exodus 21–23; the divine voice in the Exodus–Leviticus–Numbers material spoken at Sinai; and the Mosaic voice in the Deuteronomy material articulated in Moab). In such a way we are best able to explain the many interconnections in the text of the Torah, only a sampling of which are presented above. I certainly would not advocate an extreme position that might proclaim that Genesis 36, with its list of Edomite rulers, stems from the same pen as the exquisite novella that follows in Genesis 37–50, the Joseph story. Apart from some exceptions, such as this one, however, a single narrative voice constitutes, in my opinion, the best way to explain the creation of the Torah transmitted to us from ancient Israel.

CHAPTER TWENTY-THREE

ISRAELIAN HEBREW

There is no doubt that the Bible comes to us from Judah.[1] Kingship is promised to Judah in Gen 49:10; Judah has more adult men in the censuses in both Numbers 1 (vv. 26–27) and Numbers 26 (vv. 19–22) than any other tribe; Judah is the first tribe mentioned in the alignment of the people of Israel around the Tabernacle, and indeed it gains prime position as the dominant tribe on the prominent eastern flank (Num 2:3–9); there is far more information on the territorial allotment to Judah than for any other tribe in the book of Joshua (see ch. 15); God selects Judah as the first tribe to answer the call in Judg 1:2; the first of the judges presented is Othniel of Judah (Judg 3:7–11); and on it goes.

Taken together, these elements indicate that Judahite authors/ editors/scribes/compilers/redactors are responsible for the long narrative of Genesis through Samuel, based on their ideology that kingship should rest in the tribe of Judah generally and in the family of David in particular (2 Samuel 7). The picture continues in the book of Kings, where each monarch of the northern kingdom of Israel receives the notice, 'He did evil in the eyes of Yhwh, and he followed in the way of Jeroboam and in his sin, which he caused Israel to commit' (1 Kgs 15:34, with variations throughout)—a statement that makes sense only from the vantage point of Judah, with its aforementioned commitment to the Davidic-Solomonic monarchy. Classical prophecy begins in the north, in the persons of Amos and Hosea (mid- to latter eighth century), but otherwise all of our prophets, from Isaiah and Micah (latter eighth century) onward, are Judahites or exiles from Judah (as in the case of Ezekiel and Second Isaiah). Note further that when the people of the northern kingdom march off into Assyrian exile, the camera remains

---

1. For some of the basic argumentation, especially concerning the Torah and the book of Samuel, see above, Chapter 21.

behind in the land of Israel/Judah, as the reader waves goodbye, as it were, to the Samarians—in contrast to what occurs in 586 B.C.E., when the camera follows the Judahite people into Babylonian exile, through the short snippet concerning King Jehoiachin that closes the book of Kings (2 Kgs 25:27–30), and more importantly through the two prophets active in Babylonia (Ezekiel and Second Isaiah, as noted above).

Notwithstanding this remarkable Judahite focus, however, it is important to note that the Bible incorporates texts (of all genres) that originated in the north. I already mentioned the books of Amos and Hosea above, but we also may note portions of Judges with a geographical setting in the north (e.g., the story of Deborah and Barak in Judges 4–5 [one chapter in prose, one in poetry] and the stories of Gideon in Judges 6–8); the stories about Elijah and Elisha, which dominate 1 Kings 17 through 2 Kings 7; the annalistic material about the monarchs of the northern kingdom of Israel, commencing in 1 Kings 12 and continuing until 2 Kings 17 (with the Elijah and Elisha narratives incorporated therein); and poetic texts such as selected psalms, the book of Proverbs, and Song of Songs. Attention to language allows us to identify the northern provenance of these compositions.

Which is to say, a thorough linguistic analysis of the Bible has revealed that ancient Hebrew was characterized by regional dialects. In the main, these dialects align with the areas of the two kingdoms that coexisted for two centuries, ca. 930–721 B.C.E., though obviously these two dialects would have been present in their respective regions during the years beforehand and in the period thereafter. We call the southern dialect Judahite Hebrew, which corresponds to Standard Biblical Hebrew, since the vast majority of the Bible emanates from Judah in general and Jerusalem in particular (see above); while we call the northern dialect Israelian Hebrew,[2] characterized by many lexical and grammatical departures from the typical Hebrew found in the majority of the biblical books. As one would expect, these Israelian Hebrew

---

2. Note that 'Israelite' refers to pan-Israel during the biblical period, while 'Israeli' is the adjectival form correlating to modern Israel. In search of an appropriate adjective to refer to the northern kingdom of Israel in ancient times, Ginsberg, *Israelian Heritage of Judaism*, coined the term 'Israelian', which I and other scholars have adopted.

lexical and grammatical features frequently tally with usages found in Phoenician (spoken to the northwest of Israel), Ugaritic (spoken further north, albeit at a slightly earlier chronological period), and/or Aramaic (spoken to the northeast of Israel). In addition, many of these items appear more frequently in the much later attested Mishnaic Hebrew, which makes sense once one realizes that the Mishna was compiled by Rabbi Judah ha-Nasi in Zippori/Sepphoris, in the Galilee, ca. 200 C.E.

For the reader not conversant with dialect studies, let us digress from Hebrew to note a few contemporary examples here. While a German speaker from Berlin and a Dutch speaker from Amsterdam may be able to understand each other only with some considerable effort, speakers on the Germany-Netherlands border actually have no difficulty whatsoever, and in fact speak essentially the same language, with the 'German' in this region resembling Dutch to a great extent. Thus, for example, people on the German side of the border say *maken* for 'make,' (and not *machen*), *Appel* for 'apple' (and not *Apfel*), and *ik* for 'I' (and not *ich*)—all of which are standard Dutch. Similar isoglosses (to use the technical term) may be found along the French-Italian border; the Alpine villagers in this region communicate with each other without difficulty, though obviously a French speaker from Paris and an Italian speaker from Rome would not be able to understand one another.

To return to German, many regional dialects, even those not spoken in borderlands, use different words for even the most basic items. Among the most famous examples are the following: *Samstag* and *Sonnabend* for 'Saturday', *Kartoffel* and *Erdapfel* for 'potato', *Senf* and *Mostrich* for 'mustard', and *Karotten* and *Möhren* for 'carrots'. But German includes literally hundreds of such examples, as a glance at any standard dialect atlas of the German language will indicate, including numerous words limited to a very small area, e.g., *Diern* for 'girl' (instead of *Mädchen*), *Metzger* for 'butcher' (instead of *Fleischer*), *Onnern* for 'afternoon' (instead of *Nachmittag*), and so on. Some of these words will be unfamiliar to even native speakers of German.

There also are regional differences in grammatical usage, as the following two examples illustrate. Depending on one's place of origin, one will be inclined to say "Der Junge ist grösser als das Mädchen," "Der Junge ist grösser wie das Mädchen," or "Der Junge ist grösser als wie das Mädchen" (with both *als* and *wie* appearing side by side), and even "Der Junge ist grösser as das Mädchen" (using a very rare form *as*)—all of which mean 'the boy is bigger than the girl'. Similarly, for the telling of time, let's say 5:45, one will be inclined to use either "viertel vor sechs" or "dreiviertel sechs," depending on one's place of origin.

And lest one object by stating that Israel is a small place and cannot possibly have had regional dialects, let me note that small countries such as the Netherlands and Switzerland indeed have dozens of dialects (one per canton, in the latter country, according to some experts), and that Britain has far more dialects (indeed, one per county, some might say, as revealed through Kentish, Yorkshire dialect, Lancashire dialect, Northumbrian, Scots, etc.) than the United States, even though the former country is much, much smaller than the vast latter.

Of the literally hundreds, if not thousands, of dialect words in British English, two examples from Yorkshire English and one example from Scots English will suffice to illustrate the point. The word 'mistal' (cow shed) is first attested in the *Depositions of the Castle of York* (1673) in the following context: "Henry Cordingley, of Tonge, saith, that . . . he sawe the said Mary Sikes riding upon the backe of one of his cowes. And he endeavouring to strike att her stumbled and soe the said Mary flewe out of his mistall window." The word continues to be used three hundred years later in Yorkshire, as exemplified by its occurrence in the crime novel *Night Is a Time to Die* (1972), written by John Wainwright, a native of Leeds who served for twenty years as a police officer in the West Riding Constabulary, Yorkshire: "The cows were waiting in the mistal" (p. 7).[3] People from elsewhere may or may not recognize the word, but 'mistal' remains a hallmark of Yorkshire dialect even centuries after its earliest attestation.

The second example is a more familiar one, at least to anyone who has visited the city of York and who has paid attention to its street signs and so on, especially within the vicinity of the medieval walls that still grace the city and give York its defining character. I refer to the use of 'bar' for 'city gate', whose semantic extension and development is easily reconstructable. While the term is attested occasionally

---

3. Citations from *OED*, s.v. 'mistal'. For the complete text of the former citation, see also http://www.archive.org/stream/depositionsfromc00grea /depositionsfromc00grea_djvu.txt.

in other parts of England, its identification with York remains strong. In 1691, the naturalist John Ray included an entry on 'bar' in his book *A collection of English words not generally used . . . in two alphabetical catalogues, the one of such as are proper to the northern, the other to the southern counties; with catalogues of English birds and fishes: and an account of the preparing and refining such metals and minerals as are gotten in England,* as follows: "*Barr,* a Gate of a City, as Bootham Bar, Monkbar . . . in the City of York." In light of what I wrote above concerning 'mistal', the reader will not be surprised to learn that this usage is still present in York, and indeed the very places Monk Bar and Bootham Bar are still on the map to this day.[4]

For a third example, from a specific sub-dialect of Scots English, note that Aberdeen residents continue to use 'quean/quine' for 'lass, young woman', akin to the word's original meaning of simply 'woman'[5]—even though for the rest of the English-speaking world the term evolved into 'queen', with its royal connotation. And on and on one could go, with such wonderful illustrations from the native language of the current writer—though let us return now to our main subject.

Research into the language of the Bible has revealed the same situation in ancient Hebrew, with, as noted above, two main dialects, a northern one and a southern one—with the dialect of Benjamin serving as a border dialect, much like the situation along the current Germany-Netherlands boundary, described above. Israelian Hebrew, moreover, may have been further divided into sub-dialects, such as Samarian, Galilean, and Transjordanian, though typically the evidence does not allow us to finesse the picture to such a fine extent. Here we may mention the one famous instance where the Bible self-consciously reveals dialectal differences, the famous "shibboleth incident" in Judg 12:6. The Gileadites were able to identify the Ephraimites crossing the fords of the Jordan River because the former pronounced the word for 'river current' (see Ps 69:3, for example) as *ṯibbolɛt* [θibbolet], that is, with the /th/ sound as in English *thin, thing, think,* etc., since said phoneme was retained in Transjordanian Hebrew—but the Ephraimites were not able to replicate this pronunciation, since this sound did not occur in Cisjordanian Hebrew.

---

4. For further information, see *OED,* s.v. 'bar' *n.*[1], 13.a.

5. See further *OED,* s.v. 'quean'.

Upon being asked to recite the word, accordingly, the Ephraimites realized it as *sibbolɛt*, with [s] at the beginning. As an analogy, note the way
German speakers pronounce the aforecited English /th/ sound as [s], so
that 'thing' comes out sounding more like [sing].[6]

The present work is devoted to literary matters, so I do not wish
this chapter to digress too much into abstruse linguistic details—and
yet I consider this issue significant enough to devote a chapter to
the subject, with some simple illustrations. First, though, we need to
provide some method and some guidelines for the identification of
northern Hebrew features. If a rare word or feature occurs in the Bible
in identifiably northern texts, frequently in contrast to its counterpart
in Standard Biblical Hebrew, then one may consider the item to be an
Israelian Hebrew trait. This will especially be the case if the item has
a parallel in Phoenician, Ugaritic, and/or Aramaic, and/or if it is more
common in Mishnaic Hebrew than in Standard Biblical Hebrew. The
best way to proceed, then, is through a few basic examples.

The noun סֵפֶל *sepɛl* 'cup, bowl' appears in the Bible in only two
places, Judg 5:25 and 6:38. The former occurs in the Song of Deborah,
which lauds the victory over the Canaanites led by King Jabin of Hazor
(in the far north), while the latter occurs in the story of Gideon, who
was from the town of Ophrah in the territory of Manasseh (its exact
identification is unknown,[7] but based on clues in the narrative, one
assumes a location in the northern reaches of Manasseh, in or near
the Jezreel Valley). The word is known from Ugaritic, and it appears
22x in the Mishna and related Tannaitic texts.[8] These facts converge to
demonstrate that סֵפֶל *sepɛl* 'cup, bowl' was a lexeme at home only in
northern Israel. In southern Judah, the word was not used, as presumably כּוֹס *kos* 'cup' and other terms served.

---

6. I have treated the "shibboleth incident" in greater detail in several articles. See, for example, Gary A. Rendsburg, "More on Hebrew *šibbōlet*," *Journal
of Semitic Studies* 33 (1988): 255–58; and Gary A. Rendsburg, "Shibboleth," in
Geoffrey Khan, ed., *Encyclopedia of Hebrew Language and Linguistics* (Leiden:
Brill, 2013), 3:556–57.

7. Michael Avi-Yonah, "Ophrah," *Encyclopaedia Judaica*, 2nd ed. (Detroit:
Macmillan, 2007), 15:439.

8. By "related Tannaitic texts," I mean the Tosefta, Mekhilta, Sifra, Sifre
be-Midbar, and Sifre Devarim.

The word הֵיכָל *hekal* means both 'temple' and 'palace' (its ultimate etymology is Sumerian É.GAL, meaning 'great house', from which it passed into Akkadian as *ekallu* and thence into other ancient Semitic languages), but the distribution of these two meanings is informative for our reconstruction of ancient Hebrew dialects. In Judahite texts, the term means 'temple', with specific reference to the Temple in Jerusalem or the inner sanctum thereof; while in Israelian texts the term means 'palace', that is, the royal palace. Examples of the latter are to be found in 1 Kgs 21:1 (Ahab's palace), Hos 8:14, Amos 8:3 (the two northern prophets), Ps 45:9, 45:16 (in a poem that celebrates the wedding of a royal couple of Israel and Tyre), Prov 30:28 (royal palaces generally), and Joel 4:5 (with reference to Phoenicia).[9] This latter usage finds a cognate in Ugaritic, where *hkl* also refers to the palace of the king.

The noun חֵלֶק *heleq* usually means 'part, portion', but in Israelian texts the word means 'field', as may be seen in 2 Kgs 9:10, 9:36, 9:37 (with reference to a field in the Jezreel Valley) and in Hos 5:7 and Amos 7:4 (again, the two northern prophets). This Israelian Hebrew usage finds a cognate in Aramaic (חקל(א) *ḥaql(aʾ)* 'field', with metathesis caused by the presence of the /l/ sound in the word (a common phenomenon in world languages).[10]

We turn now to two grammatical illustrations. Once in the Bible, at 2 Kgs 15:10, the text uses the preposition קָבָל *qabol* 'before', in place of the exceedingly common לִפְנֵי *lipne* 'before', in the expression קָבָל־עָם *qabol ʿam* 'before the people'. This verse narrates the murder of the Israelian king Zechariah by the usurper Shallum; the use of קבל QBL as the regular preposition for 'before' in Aramaic solidifies the identification of this form as an Israelian Hebrew feature.

The second example is the use of the preposition מִן *min* 'from' before a following noun that either (a) lacks the definite article or (b) is a proper noun and yet the /n/ of the preposition does not assimilate.

---

9. On this usage, which is part of the style-switching technique of the biblical authors, see below, Chapter 24.

10. Note, for example, the following three words within the transition from Latin to Spanish: Latin *parabola* > Spanish *palabra* 'word'; Latin *miraculum* > Spanish *milagro* 'miracle'; Latin *periculum* > Spanish *peligro* 'danger, peril'—though in these three cases, the chance of metathesis is enhanced by the presence of both /l/ and /r/ in these lexemes.

Note the following: Judg 5:20 מִן־שָׁמַיִם *min šamayim* 'from heaven',
Judg 7:23 מִן־אָשֵׁר *min ʾašer* 'from Asher', Judg 7:23 מִן־כָּל־מְנַשֶּׁה *min kol
mənašše* 'from all of Manasseh', Judg 10:11 מִן־בְּנֵי עַמּוֹן *min bəne ʿammon*
'from the children of Ammon', Judg 10:11 מִן־פְּלִשְׁתִּים *min pəlištim* 'from
the Philistines', Judg 19:16 מִן־מַעֲשֵׂהוּ *min maʿaśehu* 'from his work',
2 Kgs 15:28 מִן־חַטֹּאות יָרָבְעָם *min ḥaṭṭoʾt yarobʿam* 'from the sins of Jeroboam', Ps 45:9 מִן־הֵיכְלֵי שֵׁן *min hekle šen* 'from palaces of ivory', Prov
27:8 מִן־קִנָּהּ *min qinnah* 'from its nest', etc. These examples all occur in
northern settings (Deborah, Gideon, an Israelian king, northern poems,
etc.), though one also notes the passage in Judg 19:16, in a story set in
Gibeah of Benjamin (recall our comment above about the dialect of
Benjamin as a border dialect, which means that at times it will unite
with Judahite Hebrew, while at other times with Israelian Hebrew).

Examples such as these could easily be multiplied, into the dozens
in fact, but the three lexical examples and the two grammatical illustrations presented here suffice to demonstrate the point.[11]

Now, what is remarkable about all this is that the ancient texts
were not altered, but rather were faithfully transmitted by the ancient
scribes and tradents—even during the process of the arrival of these
compositions from northern Israel into southern Judah (Jerusalem
in particular), where they found a home in what eventually would
emerge as Jewish canonical literature. One can only imagine what a
Judahite consumer of this material might have made of the expression
קָבָל־עָם *qabol ʿam* 'before the people' in 2 Kgs 15:10, and how tempting
it might have been for a scribe or tradent to change this to לִפְנֵי הָעָם
lipne ha-ʿam 'before the people', a phrase that occurs 11x in the Bible
(e.g., Exod 13:22, 17:5). Or how tempting it would have been to make
even slighter adjustments, such as changing Judg 7:23 מִן־כָּל *min kol*
'from all' to מִכָּל *mikkol* 'from all', a form that occurs 229x in the Bible.

But such did not occur: instead, the bookmen of Judah incorporated
the Israelian texts into their own literary canon, leaving the material
as they found it. A hint of this process is found in the Bible in Prov

---

11. For a more thorough treatment, see Rendsburg, "Comprehensive Guide
to Israelian Hebrew: Grammar and Lexicon," 5–35, with the references cited
therein. The one major work on this subject published since this article appeared is Noegel and Rendsburg, *Solomon's Vineyard*; see esp. ch. 1, 3–62.

גַּם־אֵלֶּה מִשְׁלֵי שְׁלֹמֹה אֲשֶׁר הֶעְתִּיקוּ אַנְשֵׁי | חִזְקִיָּה מֶלֶךְ־יְהוּדָה 25:1 'these also are the proverbs of Solomon, which the men of Hezekiah the king of Judah copied/imported/transferred'. Now most translations render the verb here as 'copy',[12] but in truth the word הֶעְתִּיקוּ *hεʿtiqu* is a Hiphʿil, or causative, form of the verbal root ע-ת-ק *ʿ-t-q*, which means 'pass' (that is, from one place to the next; e.g., Gen 12:8). This suggests that the form here should be rendered 'caused to pass', that is, 'imported' or 'transferred', in the sense that the proverbs that follow originated in the north and were brought into Jerusalem during the reign of Hezekiah.[13] The linguistic evidence bears this out, as illustrated by several examples included above from the latter chapters of Proverbs—though, to be sure, Israelian Hebrew is reflected in earlier sections of this biblical book as well.[14]

Note further that Hezekiah was the king of Judah at the time of the downfall of the northern kingdom of Israel, and in fact 2 Chronicles 30 records a tradition that he invited the northerners (that is, those who had not been exiled by the Assyrians but remained in the land) to come to Jerusalem to celebrate Passover. Moreover, archaeological evidence demonstrates that Jerusalem and its population greatly increased at this time, as many former denizens of northern Israel moved southward and settled in Judah.[15] In light of all this, it is easy to imagine how (large) sections of the book of Proverbs and other Israelian compositions—such as the stories concerning the northern judges (Deborah, Gideon, et al.) and prophets (Elijah and Elisha), the annalistic material concerning the northern kings, and the books of the northern prophets Amos and Hosea—found their way to Judah, where they were faithfully preserved. We can only marvel at the ancient scribes and tradents whose devotion served these texts so well

---

12. Which meaning this word bears in modern Hebrew.

13. Ginsberg, *Israelian Heritage of Judaism*, 37.

14. For details, see Chen, "Israelian Hebrew in the Book of Proverbs"; and Rendsburg, "Literary and Linguistic Matters in the Book of Proverbs," 112, 136–41.

15. For a summary of the evidence, see Gary A. Rendsburg and William M. Schniedewind, "The Siloam Tunnel Inscription: Historical and Linguistic Perspectives," *Israel Exploration Journal* 60 (2010): 188–203, esp. 189–91.

and through whose work we, millennia later, are able to establish the existence of regional dialects of ancient Hebrew.

So while this chapter has by necessity moved into the linguistic realm, even here—as the reader of this work now realizes—we learn something truly important about how the Bible was written, and how it was transmitted.[16]

---

16. For several more instances of Israelian Hebrew in the biblical text, used in the service of style-switching, see the end of the next chapter.

CHAPTER TWENTY-FOUR

STYLE-SWITCHING

I use the term 'style-switching' to refer to the intentional use of language to reflect either (a) the foreign setting of a particular story or (b) the foreignness of a particular character. The employment of 'literary dialect' (to use a more-or-less synonymous term) is yet another example of the brilliant use of language in the service of literature devised by the skillful authors of the biblical text.[1]

We begin with two stellar narratives that utilize the first type of style-switching referred to above, stories in Genesis that transport the reader from the main geographical context, that is, the land of Canaan, to the foreign land of Aram. In the former locale, various Canaanite dialects, Hebrew prime among them, were spoken. In the latter, Aramaic, a closely related but not mutually intelligible language, was used. Accordingly, in Genesis 24, when Abraham's servant visits the family homeland with the goal of obtaining a bride for Isaac, we must assume that the conversation took place in Aramaic. Similarly, in Genesis 29–31, when Jacob spends twenty years living with his uncle Laban in the land of Aram, we must assume that the characters (including Jacob and his two wives, Leah and Rachel) conversed in Aramaic. And yet the stories are narrated in Hebrew and the characters speak Hebrew.

To add the local color, however, the storywriter peppers his prose with Aramaic words, forms, and grammatical usages, in order to evoke the Aramean atmosphere. By so doing, both the camera (as it were)

---

1. For a parallel study to the present chapter, though with additional sections of the Bible not included here surveyed as well, see Gary A. Rendsburg, "Style-Switching in Biblical Hebrew," in Jeremy M. Hutton and Aaron D. Rubin, eds., *Epigraphy, Philology, and the Hebrew Bible: Methodological Perspectives on Philological and Comparative Study in of the Hebrew Bible in Honor of Jo Ann Hackett* (SBL Ancient Near East Monographs 12; Atlanta: SBL Press, 2015), 65–85.

and the language transport the reader to the land of Aram. Had the prose been written in Aramaic, the Israelite reader would not have been able to understand the proceedings—but by writing in Hebrew with an admixture of basic Aramaic, the storywriter is able to allow the consumer of this literature to enjoy the narrative to its fullest.

Parallels from our own modern experience may be helpful. In her delightful *Outlander* series, author Diana Gabaldon employs both Scots and Gaelic words to transport the reader from her current geographical (and chronological) setting to that of eighteenth-century Scotland. Hence, one encounters words such as 'bairn', 'ken', 'kirk', 'laird', 'parritch', and of course 'sassenach'.[2]

We encounter the same technique in cinema. When we (as Britons, Americans, etc.) watch a World War II movie, the entire dialogue is in English, but the Nazis speak a German-tinged English. Their German accent comes through at all times, and their English is sprinkled with words and phrases such as 'Achtung', 'mach schnell', 'jawohl, mein Kommandant', and the like. Had the Nazis spoken in German, subtitles would have been necessary—and of course this option is sometimes followed in cinema production. But in movie classics such as 'Casablanca', 'Stalag 17', and so on, the Germans speak English, though with their native tinge audible throughout.[3]

Though we also may cite a fine parallel from English literature of one thousand years ago, namely, the poem *The Battle of Maldon* (eleventh century C.E.; the battle occurred in 991 C.E.). When the Vikings speak, their speech is still Old English, but it is colored by many Scandinavicisms, that is, lexical and grammatical features associated with Old Norse. This technique allows the (anonymous) poet both to represent the foreignness of the Vikings and to add verisimilitude to his narrative.[4]

---

2. The first five words mean, respectively, 'child', 'know', 'church', 'lord', and 'porridge', while the final one is the term used by Scots for an English 'outlander' (sometimes with jest, sometimes with derision), thereby giving the series of novels its overall title.

3. Though in the latter film, the Nazis also speak German at times, without subtitles. Clearly the hand of producer, director, and co-screenwriter Billy Wilder is present here.

4. Fred C. Robinson, "Some Aspects of the 'Maldon' Poet's Artistry," *The Journal of English and Germanic Philology* 75 (1976): 25–40, esp. 25–28.

But back to our Genesis stories set in Aram. Actually, the narrator does something more than simply have the characters speak in Aramaic-tinged Hebrew. Just as frequently he narrates the story itself in typical third-person style, though with Aramaic-tinged Hebrew instead of standard diction. By so doing, the author transports his readership to the foreign land to an even greater extent.

We begin our survey with Genesis 24. While the contemporary reader, even the trained Hebraist, may not recognize the foreignness of these forms and words at first blush, I am quite certain that the ancient Israelite listening to this text would have identified the following features as atypical Hebrew, flavored with a hint of Aramaic. In an attempt to keep the material below accessible for the general reader, I present only the bare minimum of linguistic data. The reader interested in a full treatment is invited to consult my previous studies on the subject.[5]

(1) The stage is set already in the land of Canaan, with Abraham's instructions to his servant, during which he twice uses the expression אֱלֹהֵי הַשָּׁמַיִם *'ɛlohe haš-šamayim* 'God of heaven' (vv. 3, 7). This phrase occurs elsewhere in the Bible only in late texts: Jonah 1:9, Ezra 1:2, Neh 1:4, 1:5, 2:4, 2:20, 2 Chr 36:23, all under the influence of Aramaic אֱלָה שְׁמַיָּא *'ɛlah šəmayya'* 'God of heaven'. This epithet of God is attested in Aramaic texts in the Bible (Dan 2:18, 2:19, 2:37, 2:44, Ezra 5:12, 6:9, 6:10, 7:12, 7:21) and in such extrabiblical documents as the Elephantine papyri (e.g., Cowley 30:2 = *TAD* A 4.7:2).

(2) The phrase וְאַשְׁבִּיעֲךָ . . . אֲשֶׁר לֹא־תִקַּח אִשָּׁה לִבְנִי מִבְּנוֹת הַכְּנַעֲנִי *wə-'ašbi'aka . . . 'ašer lo' tiqqaḥ 'išša li-bni mib-bənot hak-kəna'ani* 'I adjure you . . . that you not take a woman for my son from among the daughters of the Canaanite' (v. 3) utilizes an unusual idiom for vowing. The verb שׁ-ב-ע *š-b-'* 'vow' (Qal, Niph'al), 'adjure' (Hiph'il) typically is followed by the particle אִם *'im*, which serves as the negator ('no, not')—see, for example, Gen 21:23, 1 Sam 19:6, 30:15 [2x], Song 2:7 [2x],

---

5. Rendsburg, "Some False Leads in the Identification of Late Biblical Hebrew Texts," 23–46; and Gary A. Rendsburg, "Aramaic-like Features in the Pentateuch," *Hebrew Studies* 47 (2006): 163–76. I refrain from providing additional footnotes with page numbers for each item registered below; suffice it to note that all of the usages discussed are treated in the cited articles.

3:5 [2x], 5:8, Neh 13:25 [2x], etc.—but this is not the case in Gen 24:3. Instead, Abraham's words to his servant employ the Aramaic-style idiom. In fact, the wording in Gen 24:3 is a calque (loan translation) of the Aramaic phrase.[6] In short, the ancient Israelite listener to this story would have stopped at this point and said something like, "Wait a minute, that's not how we speak Hebrew"—but that, of course, is precisely what the author intended.

(3) and (4) In v. 17 we read of the initial words spoken by the servant to the woman at the well (Rebekah, of course): הַגְמִיאִינִי נָא מְעַט־מַיִם מִכַּדֵּךְ hagmiʾini naʾ məʿaṭ mayim mik-kaddek 'cause-to-flow-forth for me please a bit of water from your jug'. Our attention is directed to two lexemes.

The first is the verb ג־מ־א g-m-ʾ (Hiphʿil) 'cause-to-flow-forth' (or more simply 'give-drink'). The root occurs elsewhere in the Bible only in Job 39:24 (albeit with a different nuance), in a book replete with Aramaisms—not because Job is a late composition necessarily, but rather because the setting of the book, in the Transjordanian desert fringe, prompts such usages.[7] The broader Aramaic picture provides some further usages of the root ג־מ־א g-m-ʾ. While it is true that one never finds the verb in regular or frequent use within Aramaic, the evidence is sufficient to allow the conclusion that an ancient Israelite would have recognized the Aramaic-ness of the verb.

The second item is the noun כַּד kad 'jug, pitcher, vessel', which occurs a remarkable 9x in Genesis 24 (vv. 14, 15, 16, 17, 18, 20, 43, 45, 46). This word is well attested in diverse Aramaic dialects, whereas it is restricted in the Bible to certain settings only, our story prime among them. The author's use of this distinctive word 9x in Genesis 24 is part of his effort to create the Aramean atmosphere.

(5) Several verses later we encounter the verb ע־ר־ה ʿ-r-h 'pour (liquids)' (v. 20), the only such case in the Bible. Once more we are

---

6. As witnessed by the manner in which the Targumim render the standard Hebrew imprecation formula.

7. See Stephen A. Kaufman, "The Classification of the North West Semitic Dialects of the Biblical Period and Some Implications Thereof," in *Proceedings of the Ninth World Congress of Jewish Studies*, vol. 5, *Panel Sessions*, part 1, *Hebrew and Aramaic Languages* (Jerusalem: World Union of Jewish Studies, 1988), 54–55.

dealing with a verb better attested in Aramaic, in which it means both 'pour (liquids)' and 'flow'.

(6) The reader is frozen for a moment by the phrase וְהָאִישׁ מִשְׁתָּאֵה לָהּ *wə-ha-ʾiš mišta'e lah* 'and the man is gazing at her', because of (a) the pause in the action, as the servant observes the woman's actions, and (b) the employment of the *hapax legomenon* שׁ-א-ה *š-'-h* (Hitpa'el) 'gaze, watch'. True, the corresponding Aramaic verb typically connotes 'stay, delay, hesitate', so the semantics are not identical; but once more we may observe (pun intended?) how an Aramaic-style lexeme is employed in Genesis 24 to enhance the literary effect.[8]

(7) In v. 38, while relating his story, the servant quotes Abraham as having instructed him as follows: אִם־לֹא אֶל־בֵּית־אָבִי תֵלֵךְ וְאֶל־מִשְׁפַּחְתִּי וְלָקַחְתָּ אִשָּׁה לִבְנִי 'but rather unto the house of my father you should go, and unto my family, and you shall take a wife for my son'. Our attention is drawn to the initial phrase, אִם־לֹא *ʾim lo'*, which in Hebrew normally means 'if not' (Gen 4:7, 18:21, etc.), but which in our passage means 'but rather'. This too represents the Aramaic usage, attested early on as אן לא *ʾin la'* and later אֶלָּא *ʾella'*, which actually passed into Hebrew in the postbiblical period and continues in use until the present day, with the force of 'but rather'.

(8) The final example from this episode is the noun מִגְדָּנֹת *mig-danot* 'choice gifts' (v. 53), which once more evokes an Aramaic usage. Elsewhere in the Bible this word is attested in Ezra 1:6, 2 Chr 21:3, 32:23—that is, in Late Biblical Hebrew, under the direct influence of Aramaic. Its presence in Genesis 24 is due to another reason, as we have outlined here, to flavor the narrative with Aramaic-like features, in order to create the proper ambiance.

The second narrative in the book of Genesis set in the land of Aram, namely, chs. 29–31, the account of Jacob in the household of Laban, provides ample additional specimens of this literary technique. Interestingly, the author does not introduce Aramaic-like features in ch. 29, perhaps because Jacob is still a recent arrival (notwithstanding the passage of seven years [see v. 20]). When we continue reading in chs. 30–31, by contrast, the text is once again heavily flavored with

---

8. The reader may recall that מִשְׁתָּאֵה *mišta'e* 'is gazing' was discussed earlier; see above, Chapter 5, no. 5.

atypical lexical and grammatical features—atypical in Hebrew, that is, but representative of Aramaic.

The linguistic features embedded in the story of Jacob in the land of Aram were first studied by Jonas Greenfield.[9] His pathbreaking research focused on three items, as follows:

(1) The verbs וַיַּצֵּל *wayyaṣṣel* 'and he [sc. God] removed' (31:9) and הִצִּיל *hiṣṣil* 'he [sc. God] removed' (31:16) are based on the root נ-צ-ל *n-ṣ-l* (Hiphʿil), which in Hebrew typically means 'save, rescue', but which in these two instances means 'remove, take away', a connotation it bears in Aramaic (in addition to 'save, rescue'). Note that the first verb is spoken by Jacob to his two wives, Rachel and Leah, while the second is spoken by the two wives themselves, whose native language in 'real life', of course, was Aramaic.

(2) At the end of Gen 31:23 we read וַיַּדְבֵּק אֹתוֹ בְּהַר הַגִּלְעָד *wayyadbeq ʾoto bə-har hag-gilʿad* 'and he [sc. Laban] overtook him in the Mount of Gilead'. In Hebrew the verbal root ד-ב-ק *d-b-q* means 'stick, adhere, cling' (both Qal and Hiphʿil). This is true of the Aramaic cognate as well, though in this language the verb gains the additional meaning 'overtake'. The author of our narrative took full advantage of this linguistic datum by introducing וַיַּדְבֵּק *wayyadbeq* 'and he overtook' at this key point in the story. For the reader unfamiliar with this usage, the author 'explains' it, as it were, two verses later with the phrase וַיַּשֵּׂג לָבָן אֶת־יַעֲקֹב *wayyaśśeg laban ʾet yaʿaqob* 'and Laban overtook Jacob', utilizing the standard Hebrew lexeme, the Hiphʿil of נ-שׂ-ג *n-ś-g* (see, for example, Gen 44:4, 44:6).

(3) In Gen 31:28, Laban says to Jacob, וְלֹא נְטַשְׁתַּנִי לְנַשֵּׁק לְבָנַי וְלִבְנֹתָי *wə-loʾ nətaštani lənaššeq lə-banay wə-li-bnotay* 'and you did not allow me to kiss my sons and my daughters'. Only here in the entire Bible does the verbal root נ-ט-שׁ *n-ṭ-š* mean 'allow, permit'; elsewhere it carries the meaning 'abandon, forsake'. The background for this unique usage was brilliantly deduced by Greenfield: in Aramaic a single verb, שׁ-ב-ק *š-b-q*, means both 'leave, abandon' and 'allow, permit', so that the clever Israelite author—placing much demand on his reader's knowledge and

9. Jonas C. Greenfield, "Aramaic Studies and the Bible," in John A. Emerton, ed., *Congress Volume: Vienna 1980* (Supplements to Vetus Testamentum 32; Leiden: Brill, 1981), 110–30, esp. 129–30.

equal cleverness—extended the semantics of the Hebrew verb נ-ט-שׁ
n-ṭ-š from its typical meaning, 'leave, abandon', to include 'allow, permit' as well.

Building on the strong foundation laid by Greenfield, I was able to identify numerous other elements of 'style-switching' within Genesis 30–31.[10] These include the following:

(4) The word גָּד *gad* 'fortune' (30:11), used in the naming of Gad, occurs only here in the Bible as a common noun.[11] In Aramaic, on the other hand, it is the common word for 'fate, fortune'.

(5) In 30:20, upon the birth of Zebulun, Leah states: זְבָדַנִי אֱלֹהִים |
אֹתִי זֵבֶד טוֹב *zəbadani ʾelohim ʾoti zebɛd ṭob* 'God has provided me with a good provision' (or perhaps, 'God has granted me a good dowry'). This passages includes the only two attestations of the root ז-ב-ד *z-b-d* 'provide, supply, give' (once as verb, once as noun) in the Bible. The root is part of the standard Aramaic lexis.

(6) The following expression in Gen 30:28 attracts our attention: נָקְבָה שְׂכָרְךָ עָלַי וְאֶתֵּנָה *noqba śəkarka ʿalay wə-ʾɛttena* 'designate your wage for me, and I will give it'. The verbal root נ-ק-ב *n-q-b* typically bears the core meaning 'bore, pierce', though in this instance by extension it comes to mean 'mark, specify, designate'.[12] This meaning is attested in the later Palmyrene and Nabatean dialects (also in later Amoraic Hebrew, presumably as a borrowing from Aramaic); while in Syriac the related noun form means 'weight', a connotation that also fits the passage in Gen 30:28, when one recalls that wages were paid in silver weighed out (before the invention of true money). The only other attestation in the Bible of נ-ק-ב *n-q-b* with the meaning 'mark, specify, designate' is in Isa 62:2, where it is a true Aramaism embedded in the words of Second Isaiah, who was living in Babylon during the

---

10. In addition to the aforecited article in *Hebrew Studies* (see above, p. 503, n. 5) see my earlier study: Gary A. Rendsburg, "Linguistic Variation and the 'Foreign' Factor in the Hebrew Bible," *Israel Oriental Studies* 15 (1996): 177–90, esp. 182–83. Note that item no. 6 below is identified here for the first time.

11. The term occurs elsewhere in Isa 65:11 as the name of a foreign deity, Gad/Fortune.

12. As a parallel, note the derivation of English/Latin 'designate', from 'sign', that is, 'incise, make a mark, etc.'.

sixth century B.C.E., during which time and in which place Aramaic was in standard use.

(7) The noun תְּיָשִׁים *təyašim* 'he-goats' in 30:35 is rare in Hebrew (in fact, it seems always to be used for style-switching effect),[13] though common in (at least Western) Aramaic dialects.

(8) The noun לוּז *luz* 'almond' (30:37) occurs only here in the Bible; it is the Aramaic word for this tree/nut, used here instead of standard Hebrew שָׁקֵד *šaqed* 'almond'.

(9) The noun רְהָטִים *rohaṭim* 'troughs' (30:38, 30:41) reflects Aramaic, in which the root ר-ה-ט *r-h-ṭ* 'run' corresponds to Hebrew ר-ו-ץ *r-w-ṣ* 'run'. Thus one reconstructs the semantic development of the word for 'trough' as derived from 'runner'.[14]

(10) The third-person fem. pl. form וַיֵּחַמְנָה *wayyeḥamna* 'and they [sc. the female members of the flock] were in heat' (30:38) reflects Aramaic morphology, with *y*- before the root and -*na* following. The standard Hebrew form would be וַתֵּחַמְנָה *watt eḥamna*, with *t*- and -*na* affixed to the root.

(11) In Gen 31:7, Jacob says to his two wives, וְהֶחֱלִף אֶת־מַשְׂכֻּרְתִּי עֲשֶׂרֶת מֹנִים *wə-heḥelip ʾet maśkurti ʿaśeret monim* 'and he changed my wage ten times', with reference to the unfair manner in which Laban treated him. In v. 31, Jacob addresses Laban with more or less the same expression: וַתַּחֲלֵף אֶת־מַשְׂכֻּרְתִּי עֲשֶׂרֶת מֹנִים *wattaḥalep ʾet maśkurti ʿaśeret monim* 'and you changed my wage ten times'. The wording in v. 7 contains no fewer than three Aramaic-like features, two lexical (both repeated in v. 31) and one grammatical. (a) The verb ח-ל-ף *ḥ-l-p* 'change, exchange' occurs elsewhere in the Bible (e.g., Gen 41:14, with reference to changing one's clothes), but with reference to monetary or fiscal change or exchange, the usage is rare.[15] It will come as no surprise, by this point, to learn that this usage has greater currency (pun intended?) in Aramaic (especially the Jewish Palestinian Aramaic dialect). (b) The noun מֹנִים *monim* 'times' is another nonstandard Hebrew term (limited

---

13. See Rendsburg, "Aramaic-like Features in the Pentateuch," 167, n. 11.

14. By way of comparison, note the English words 'runner' and 'runnel', meaning both 'small stream, rivulet' (that is, something natural) and 'a small channel in which water may flow' (that is, something manmade). See *OED*, s.v. 'runner' *n.¹*, def. 28; and *OED*, s.v. 'runnel' *n.¹*.

15. Elsewhere only Lev 27:10.

to our two verses) that is more common in Aramaic. (c) In v. 7, the verbal form וְהֶחֱלִף wə-heḥelip in Standard Biblical Hebrew would constitute a wəqatal form, pointing to the future; in the present instance, however, the tense is clearly past—hence, we designate this as a wə- + qatal form, to be translated 'and he changed', on par with Aramaic usage.

(12) The unique usage represented in לֹו הִגֵּיד עַל־בְּלִי ʿal bəli higgid lo 'by not telling him' (31:20) bespeaks Aramaic, which has an especially large number of compound particles based on עַל ʿal (e.g., עַל שֵׁם, עַל עָסִיק, עַל מְנָת, עַל גַּבֵּי, עַל אַפֵּי, etc.),[16] even if עַל בְּלִי ʿL BLY itself is not attested (to the best of my knowledge).

(13) The form גְּנֻבְתִי gənubti 'I was robbed' (31:39 [2x]) constitutes an inflected passive participle (note the suffix תִי- -ti, borrowed from the suffix-conjugation paradigm, yet attached to the participle here), a most unusual grammatical form. Such forms are known from later Jewish Palestinian Aramaic,[17] and one will assume that they were current in earlier Aramaic as well, including the dialect known to the author of Genesis 30–31.

(14) Our final example takes us one verse beyond the two chapters considered here, though there can be no doubt that its presence in Gen 32:1 is part of the same literary portrayal—especially since the action still concerns Laban and Jacob's family. The linguistic element is אֶתְהֶם ʾethem 'them', as opposed to standard Hebrew אֹתָם ʾotam 'them'.[18]

Now, if this were not enough to bring the reader/listener to the land of Aram, the author of this material included one final zinger as well, a pure Aramaic two-word expression, יְגַר שָׂהֲדוּתָא yəgar śahaduta⁾ 'mound of witness' (31:47), equaling Hebrew גַּלְעֵד galʿed 'mound of witness' (written as one word). The introduction of this pure Aramaic phrase serves as an explicit reminder that Laban and Jacob have been speaking Aramaic all along, and not Hebrew—just as Shakespeare's

---

16. Michael Sokoloff, *A Dictionary of Jewish Palestinian Aramaic* (Ramat-Gan: Bar-Ilan University Press, 1992), 406–8; and Michael Sokoloff, *A Dictionary of Jewish Babylonian Aramaic* (Ramat-Gan: Bar-Ilan University Press, 2002), 863.

17. See Gustaf Dalman, *Grammatik des jüdisch-palästinischen Aramäisch* (Leipzig: Hinrichs, 1905), 284.

18. For a related instance, see below, the section on the Balaam oracles, p. 514, item no. 12.

single phrase *Et tu, Brute?* (*Julius Caesar*, Act III, Scene 1) suffices to
remind the theatre-goer that Julius Caesar and his cohorts have been
speaking Latin all along, and not Elizabethan English.

We now turn to a third text in the Torah, though in this case something slightly different is at work. In the story of Balaam, the geographical setting remains in the land of Canaan (to be more specific, the land
of Moab, on the other side of the Jordan River, but still within the
Canaanite linguistic purview, since Moabite is a dialect of Canaanite
[along with Hebrew, Phoenician, etc.]), but the main character is an
Aramean prophet, brought from Pethor (= Pitru), in the heart of Aramean territory, by Balak king of Moab to curse the people of Israel.
Accordingly, Balaam's oracles, which comprise the key component of
his presence in the story, are heavily tinged with Aramaic-like features.

Again we may point to a parallel from the oeuvre of William Shakespeare, one found most conspicuously in *Henry V*. In this play, the
English military leader Captain Gower is joined by three others on the
campaign, Captain Fluellen of Wales, Captain Macmorris of Ireland,
and Captain Jamy of Scotland. Captain Gower speaks standard English,
no different than the patois of his king or other members of the royal
family. The dialects of the other three military men, by contrast, each
bears traits of the English used in the neighboring lands.

The most striking one, which would have been recognized by the
contemporary theatre-goer immediately, is the phrase 'look you', uttered by Fluellen 22x (!) during the performance, including a staggering
11x in Act III, Scene 2, with the remaining 11 scattered throughout the
remainder of the play. The phrase, by the way, still may be heard in
Welsh English at the present day. Furthermore, even the character's
surname rings with the audience, for in Welsh it clearly would have
been Llewellyn or Llywelyn. But since the English have great difficulty
in pronouncing the voiceless alveolar lateral fricative [ɬ] (yes, that is
what this sound is called in phonological studies, and that is its official International Phonetic Alphabet symbol), they typically replace
the sound with the combination [fl]—compare 'Floyd' for 'Lloyd'—as
reflected already in the Shakespearean adaptation 'Fluellen'.

The Irish officer, Captain Macmorris, also has distinctive aspects in
his English (e.g., 'Chrish' for 'Christ'), but most foreign of all are the
speeches of the Scot, Captain Jamy, which are virtually unintelligible

to one attending the play, a fact that no doubt reflects the reality of an Englishman's (in)ability to understand a Scotsman ca. 1600.[19] Consider, for example (*Henvy V*, Act III, Scene 2):

> By the mess, ere theise eyes of mine take themselves
> to slomber, ay'll de gud service, or ay'll lig i'
> the grund for it; ay, or go to death; and ay'll pay
> 't as valourously as I may, that sall I suerly do,
> that is the breff and the long. Marry, I wad full
> fain hear some question 'tween you tway.

This is so difficult to comprehend that further comment is hardly necessary.[20]

With this digression into English literature again serving as background for what follows, we may proceed to our analysis of Balaam's oracles embedded within Numbers 23–24. The following linguistic traits, all signifying Aramaic more than standard Hebrew, serve to signal the foreignness of the main character, as revealed through his own speech.[21]

(1) The reduplicated plural form of the common noun הַר *har* 'mountain' occurs in the phrase מֵהַרְרֵי־קֶדֶם *me-harare qɛdɛm* 'from the mountains of old' (23:7). The standard Hebrew construct form is הָרֵי *hare* 'mountains of' (32x).

(2) The noun צֻרִים *ṣurim* 'mountains' in 23:8, in the a-line of the couplet, replaces standard Hebrew הָרִים *harim* 'mountains', and is paired with גְּבָעוֹת *gəbaʿot* 'hills' in the b-line (the only such case in the Bible).

---

19. In some cases, not much has changed, one could say. See the playful description by Bill Bryson, *Notes from a Small Island* (London: Doubleday, 1993), 366–67, 369–70.

20. For elucidation and further information on the speech of all three non-English officers, see Dennis Freeborn, *From Old English to Standard English*, 3rd ed. (New York: Palgrave Macmillan, 2006), 322–23, with Text Commentary Book 16.2.

21. The first effort in this direction was the seminal article by Kaufman, "The Classification of the North West Semitic Dialects," 41–57, esp. 54–55. Another important study is Shelomo Morag, "Rovde Qadmut," *Tarbiz* 50 (1981): 1–24, many of whose interpretations are accepted in what follows.

The form צֻרִים ṣurim evokes Aramaic טוּרִים ṭurim 'mountains', and no doubt reflects an attempt to include that Aramaic word in the poetry.[22]

(3) The phrase וּבַגּוֹיִם לֹא יִתְחַשָּׁב u-bag-goyim lo' yithaššab 'and among the nations he [sc. Israel] is not reckoned' (23:9) includes an unusual usage. The Hitpaʿel verb יִתְחַשָּׁב yithaššab 'is not reckoned' does not bear its usual reflexive connotation (i.e., 'does not reckon himself'), but instead occurs with a passive meaning—exactly as occurs in the t-stem in Aramaic (in standard Hebrew one expects the Niphʿal for the passive).

(4) The noun רֹבַע robaʿ 'dust-cloud' in 23:10 occurs only here, but is explicable via its cognates in Christian Palestinian Aramaic and in Akkadian.

(5) The expression מוֹת יְשָׁרִים mot yašarim, lit. 'death of the upright' (23:10), was nicely elucidated by Menahem Kister as the opposite of the Aramaic expression מות לחה mwt lḥh 'evil death' in Nerab tomb inscription, no. 1, line 4—and indeed, this entire biblical verse shares much in common with Nerab tomb inscription, no. 2, lines 3–4.[23]

(6) In 23:18 Balaam addresses Balak with the words הַאֲזִינָה עָדַי ha'azina ʿaday. The phrase frequently is translated 'give-ear to me', but a problem arises since the verb א-ז-ן '-z-n (Hiphʿil) typically governs the preposition אֶל 'ɛl or לְ- lə-, both meaning 'to' (see especially Deut 1:45, Ps 77:2, Job 34:2).[24] We elect, accordingly, to interpret the expression differently, with עָדַי ʿaday meaning 'my warnings', closely related to the noun עֵדִי ʿdy 'covenant, testimony', which occurs repeatedly in the Aramaic Sefire treaty texts.

---

22. The form צֻרִים ṣurim uses the Old Aramaic orthography still, in which the emphatic interdental /ẓ/ is represented by צ ṣ (before the shift to ט ṭ occurred). In fact, this orthography occurs still in the Adon letter, line 8, where 'he guarded' appears as נצר nṣr (not the expected נטר nṭr).

23. Menahem Kister, "Some Blessing and Curse Formulae in the Bible, Northwest Semitic Inscriptions, Post-Biblical Literature and Late Antiquity," in M. F. J. Baasten and W. Th. van Peursen, eds., Hamlet on a Hill: Semitic and Greek Studies Presented to T. Muraoka on the Occasion of His Sixty-Fifth Birthday (Orientalia Lovaniensia Analecta 118; Leuven: Peeters, 2003), 325.

24. The only other collocation of the verb א-ז-ן '-z-n (Hiphʿil) and the preposition עַד 'ad is in Job 32:11, אָזִין עַד־תְּבוּנֹתֵיכֶם 'azin 'ad təbunotekɛm 'I listen to your wise-sayings'. Note, however, that in this instance the preposition is followed by a reference to the speech heard, not a reference to the one speaking.

(7) The noun נַחַשׁ *naḥaš* 'divination' occurs in 23:23; a bit further on, in 24:1, within the prose narrative, one encounters the plural form נְחָשִׁים *nəḥašim* 'divinations'. These are the only two attestations of this noun in the Bible, though it is well distributed across Aramaic dialects with the meaning 'augury, divination'.

(8) The fossilized form נְאֻם *nə'um* 'said, spoken, uttered'[25] is used with reference to human speech (to introduce words delivered by Balaam) in 24:3–4 (3x) and 24:15–16 (3x). This rare usage in the Bible (almost always the form introduces divine speech, especially within the prophetic books) occurs elsewhere only in northern settings in the Bible, that is, in the area of Israel geographically closest to Aram. While the word is not attested in Aramaic per se, most likely Hebrew נְאֻם *nə'um* is related to Eblaite *en-ma*,[26] which once more takes us to the general region of Aram, even if the floruit of Ebla was at the end of the Early Bronze Age, a millennium and then some before Aramaic first emerges in the written record.

(9) Twice in the poetry we encounter the verb ח-ז-ה *ḥ-z-h* 'see', which is standard in Aramaic, though not in Hebrew. Note, for example, that the Targumim regularly use this verb to render the standard Hebrew verb ר-א-ה *r-ʿ-h* 'see'. The two passages are the parallel expressions אֲשֶׁר מַחֲזֵה שַׁדַּי יֶחֱזֶה *'ašɛr maḥaze šadday yɛḥɛzɛ* 'who views the vision of Shadday' (24:4) and מַחֲזֵה שַׁדַּי יֶחֱזֶה *maḥaze šadday yɛḥɛzɛ* '(who) views the vision of Shadday' (24:16).[27]

(10) The verbal form נְטָיוּ *niṭṭayu* 'inclining' (or perhaps 'standing tall')[28] in 24:6 retains the third root letter *yod*, as in Aramaic. We have just noted two possible meanings for this verb, though a third one also

---

25. The term 'fossilized' means that the verb is not productive, it never occurs in any other form, it is not conjugated, and so on—so that all 377 occurrences of the word are in the same form.

26. See Cyrus H. Gordon, "Vocalized Consonants: The Key to *um-ma/ en-ma*/נאם," in Mark E. Cohen, Daniel C. Snell, and David B. Weisberg, eds., *The Tablet and the Scroll: Near Eastern Studies in Honor of William W. Hallo* (Bethesda, MD: CDL, 1993), 109–10; and Gary A. Rendsburg, "Hebrew Philological Notes (I)," *Hebrew Studies* 40 (1999): 29–30.

27. As such, the two passages constitute an example of repetition with variation, as studied above in Chapter 4, no. 11.

28. See Menahem Moreshet, "ki-nḥalim niṭṭayu," *Bet Miqra'* 48 (1971–1972 / 5732): 51–56; and Morag, "Rovde Qadmut," 15–16, esp. n. 54.

may be present, namely 'be damp', known from Syriac, especially given the overall intent of this verse, with the recurrent water imagery: כִּנְחָ־ לִים נִטָּיוּ כְּגַנֹּת עֲלֵי נָהָר כַּאֲהָלִים֙ נָטַע יְהֹוָה כַּאֲרָזִים עֲלֵי־מָיִם *ki-nḥalim niṭṭayu kə-gannot ʿale nahar ka-ʾahalim naṭaʿ* YHWH *ka-ʾarazim ʿale mayim* 'like palm-trees inclining, like gardens along the river, like aloes planted by YHWH, like cedars along the water'.

(11) The noun מַלְכֻת *malkut* 'kingdom' in 24:7 constitutes the classic Aramaic form of this noun, used here in place of the standard Hebrew form, מַמְלָכָה *mamlaka* 'kingdom'. The former term, in its fuller spelling מַלְכוּת *malkut*, entered Hebrew as a genuine loanword from Aramaic with the passage of time, so that it comes to dominate in books such as Ezra–Nehemiah (8x), Chronicles (28x), Esther (26x), and Daniel (16x), all written during the postexilic period. The attestation in Num 24:7, however, is to be explained otherwise, as part of the style-switching effect achieved by the author, who places this vocable in the mouth of Balaam.

(12) The word עַצְמֹתֵיהֶם *ʿaṣmotehɛm* 'their bones' in 24:8 includes the pronominal suffix הֶם ָ - *-ehɛm* 'their' added to a plural noun ending in וֹת- *-ot*. Standard Biblical Hebrew prefers the form ם ָ - *-am* after this ending, while Late Biblical Hebrew prefers the form הֶם ָי - *-ehɛm*, as a result of Aramaic influence.[29] In the case of the Balaam narrative, however, we are firmly within Standard Biblical Hebrew, save for the Aramaic-like features branding Balaam's speech. And while not every instance of הֶם ָי - *-ehɛm* 'their' in preexilic texts is an example of style-switching, in the present instance, in the mouth of Balaam, this is most likely the proper explanation.[30]

(13) The full phrase in which the preceding form occurs is the following: וְעַצְמֹתֵיהֶם יְגָרֵם *wə-ʿaṣmotehɛm yəgarem* 'and their bones he devours' (24:8). The linguistic oddity here is the verbal root ג-ר-ם *g-r-m* 'devour bones', a denominative verb based on the Aramaic noun גֶּרֶם *gəram* 'bone'.

---

29. For general discussion, see Avi Hurvitz, *A Linguistic Study of the Relationship between the Priestly Source and the Book of Ezekiel* (Cahiers de la Revue Biblique 20; Paris: Gabalda, 1982), 24–27. For the most recent treatment, see Moshe Bar-Asher, "Lešon Qumran ben ha-Miqraʾ li-Lšon Ḥazal ('Iyyun ba-Seʿif be-Morfologya)," *Meghillot* 2 (2004): 137–49.

30. For a related feature, see above, regarding the story of Jacob and Laban, item no. 14.

In short, the Balaam oracles are filled with Aramaic-like usages, which together serve the purpose of the style-switching employed by the ancient Israelite author.

Style-switching also may occur within inner-Hebrew contexts—in which case the definition presented in the first paragraph of this chapter may require slight tweaking, since the characters are still Israelites and thus not quite foreigners. Again, analogies from English literature (mainly British, but also American) may be helpful.

The earliest (or at least earliest surviving) attempt by an English author to represent the regional dialect of a character or characters from another part of the country occurs in *The Canterbury Tales*, by Geoffrey Chaucer, specifically in "The Reeve's Tale." For while the great poet hailed from London, and while his collective oeuvre reflects southern English, in "The Reeve's Tale" something unique occurs. The storyteller, who hails from Norfolk, narrates his tale with tinges of his East Anglian dialect; and even more significantly, he conveys the speech of John and Aleyn, the two clerks (that is, students) who hail from Northumbria, in the dialect of that region in the far northeastern corner of England. Thus, for example, one finds *hame* for *home*, along with other instances of /a/ for /o/, reflecting retention of the Old English long /a:/ vowel; *swilk* for *swich* (that is, Middle English for 'such') and *whilk* for *whilch* (that is, Middle English for 'which'), with the distinctive Scandinavian /k/ for English /ch/; and other instances of Scandinavian influence, remnants of the Viking settlement in northeastern England.[31]

Jumping ahead in time, nineteenth-century authors, it seems, were particularly fond of casting their prose in the local dialect—in Britain one thinks of Charles Dickens and Elizabeth Gaskell; in America

---

31. The classic article on the subject is by (none other than) J. R. R. Tolkien, "Chaucer as a Philologist: The Reeve's Tale," *Transactions of the Philological Society* (1934): 1–70. For some recent challenges and corrections to Tolkien's approach, based on advances in Chaucerian manuscript studies and in Middle English dialectological research, see S. C. P. Horobin, "J. R. R. Tolkien as a Philologist: A Reconsideration of the Northernisms in Chaucer's *Reeve's Tale*," *English Studies* 82 (2001): 97–105; and Philip Knox, "The 'Dialect' of Chaucer's Reeve," *The Chaucer Review* 49 (2014): 102–24. To my mind, though, and I believe that both authors would agree, Tolkien's basic statement, especially regarding the speech of the two clerks, remains valid.

writers such as Mark Twain and George Washington Harris stand
out. One single word from the works of Mrs. Gaskell, representative
of Lancashire English, will suffice to illustrate: 'liefer', in the sense of
'gladly', as in: "I'd liefer sweep th' streets" (*North and South*) and "I
would liefer live without fire" (*Mary Barton*).[32] Such examples, of course,
could be multiplied, for Mrs. Gaskell, for the aforecited authors, and
for countless more not mentioned here—but these illustrations from
English literature (both medieval and Victorian) hopefully will help the
reader new to the subject of 'style-switching' or 'literary dialect' with
the point under consideration in Biblical Hebrew prose.

And with that digression into English literature, we may return to
our main subject. The best illustration of inner-Hebrew dialect representation occurs in 2 Samuel 14, in which the presumably Judahite
author of the David story incorporates Israelian Hebrew elements into
the speech of the wise woman of Tekoa (to be associated with Tekoa
of the Galilee, not Tekoa near Bethlehem). Israelian Hebrew traits
include the following.[33]

(1) In telling her tale, the woman of Tekoa employs the locution
הָאֶחָד אֶת־הָאֶחָד *ha-ʾeḥad ʾet ha-ʾeḥad* 'the one [struck] the one' (2 Sam
14:6) to express the correlative or reciprocal, whereas Standard Biblical Hebrew uses the collocation אִישׁ אֶת־רֵעֵהוּ *ʾiš ʾet reʿehu* 'the one
the other' (lit., 'each man his friend'; e.g., Exod 21:18), or the similar
expression אִישׁ אֶת־אָחִיו *ʾiš ʾet ʾaḥiw* 'the one the other' (lit., 'each man
his brother'; e.g., Exod 32:27).[34] The expression employed by the woman
of Tekoa finds parallels in Aramaic חדא עם חדא *ḥada ʿim ḥada* 'one
with one' (e.g., Targum Onqelos and Targum Pseudo-Jonathan to Exod
26:3 [2x], with similar constructions in Targum Neofiti and Samaritan
Targum) and in the Aramaic-tinged Hebrew in Job 41:8, אֶחָד בְּאֶחָד
ʾeḥad be-ʾeḥad 'one [touches] one'.

---

32. For guidance, see Wendy A. Craik, *Elizabeth Gaskell and the English
Provincial Novel* (London: Methuen, 1975). For some instances in American
literature, see Michael Ellis, "Literary Dialect as Linguistic Evidence: Subject-
Verb Concord in Nineteenth-Century Southern Literature," *American Speech*
69 (1994): 128–44.

33. For more on Israelian Hebrew, see the preceding chapter.

34. Joüon and Muraoka, *Grammar of Biblical Hebrew*, 546–47.

(2) Later in the narrative, during her response to David's question about whether Joab has played a role in her performance, the woman of Tekoa uses the particle of existence אֵשׁ *'iš* 'there is, there are' (2 Sam 14:19), attested elsewhere only in Israelian Hebrew texts (Mic 6:10, Prov 18:24—the latter with *plene* spelling אִישׁ *'iš*), in contrast to Standard Biblical Hebrew יֵשׁ *yeš*.[35]

(3) Immediately following are the forms לְהֵמִין וּלְהַשְׂמִיל *ləhemin u-lhaśmil* 'to go-right and to go-left' (2 Sam 14:19). Both of these forms are irregular—the former not to a great extent, though note the *defectiva* spelling, without the first root letter *yod* indicated; the latter more so, since the expected *'aleph* is elided. And while we cannot state unequivocally that these forms reflect the speaker's northern regional dialect,[36] or even her colloquial speech, there is a good chance that they do, or at the very least, that they add to the literary portrayal of the wise woman of Tekoa.[37]

The texts surveyed herein (Genesis 24, Genesis 30–31, Numbers 23–24, 2 Samuel 14) illustrate well yet another facet of the use of language in the service of literature. The ancient Israelite bookmen knew their language well, as they were able to differentiate 'standard' and 'native' Hebrew usages from 'dialectal' and 'Aramaic-like' words and phrases. Moreover, they no doubt could depend on at least some segment of their audience (indeed, perhaps a significant portion thereof) possessing the linguistic competence both to appreciate their efforts and to delight in the results.

---

35. Gary A. Rendsburg, "Millat ha-Qiyyum אֵשׁ," *Meḥqarim be-Lašon* 9 (2003): 251–55.

36. Note that these two verbs are particularly susceptible to nonstandard forms. The standard (or at least expected) forms appear in Gen 13:9, but there is something atypical about one or the other verb in all other instances: Isa 30:21, Ezek 21:21, 1 Chr 12:2.

37. Naama Zahavi-Ely, "'Turn Right or Left': Literary Use of Dialect in 2 Samuel 14:19?" *Hebrew Studies* 53 (2012): 43–53.

CHAPTER TWENTY-FIVE

ADDRESSEE-SWITCHING

The term addressee-switching refers to the manner in which the prophets pepper their oracles to the foreign nations with linguistic traits indicative of the speech variety of the nation being addressed. Such prophetic speeches appear in Amos (ch. 1), Isaiah (chs. 13–23), Zephaniah (ch. 2), Jeremiah (chs. 46–51), Obadiah (most of ch. 1, the sole chapter in this shortest of biblical books), and Ezekiel (chs. 25–32).[1] The literary effect is as follows: although the people who actually heard these speeches were the Israelites themselves, the addition of such foreign linguistic elements no doubt added a veneer of reality and authenticity to the prophetic pronouncements. As such, addressee-switching is closely related to the technique of style-switching that was surveyed in the previous chapter.

The first to identify this device appears to have been Chaim Rabin:

> It is a feature of First Isaiah's style that, when speaking of or addressing a foreign nation, he creates "atmosphere" by using some word or words in that nation's language. Of course such phrases must not be expected to be correct expressions in the foreign language in all respects. Over-correctness in such "stage" use of a foreign language would defeat its purpose. The point is to give the listener some feature which strongly suggests the other language, but which is sufficiently familiar to be understood.[2]

---

1. This list of the prophets places them in chronological order.

2. Chaim Rabin, "An Arabic Phrase in Isaiah," in *Studi sull'Oriente e la Bibbia: Offerti al P. Giovanni Rinaldi nel 60° compleanno da ellievi, colleghi, amici* (Genoa: Studio e Vita, 1967), 303–9, esp. 304–5. See also Kaufman, "The Classification of the North West Semitic Dialects of the Biblical Period and Some Implications Thereof," 41–57, esp. 55.

Rabin's parade example was Isaiah's oracle to Dumah in ch. 21, as follows:

1. Isaiah 21:11–12

מַשָּׂא דּוּמָה אֵלַי קֹרֵא מִשֵּׂעִיר שֹׁמֵר מַה־מִלַּיְלָה שֹׁמֵר מַה־מִלֵּיל: ¹¹

אָמַר שֹׁמֵר אָתָה בֹקֶר וְגַם־לָיְלָה אִם־תִּבְעָיוּן בְּעָיוּ שֻׁבוּ אֵתָיוּ: ¹²

¹¹ Oracle of Dumah: Unto me someone calls from Seir, "Watchman, what of the night? Watchman, what of the night?"
¹² The watchman says, "Morning comes, and also the night; if you inquire, inquire, return, come again."

This passage is one of the most enigmatic in the entire Bible, so much so that we will not even venture any insights into its overall meaning and intent. Instead, we will focus on the lexical and grammatical peculiarities in these two short verses. The addressee is Dumah, identified with the archaeological site of Dumat al-Jandal in northwest Arabia (= modern al-Jawf). Hence, one finds in this passage the following features that evoke the linguistic milieu of that region:[3] (a) the verbal roots ב-ע-י *b-ʿ-y* (= ב-ע-ה *b-ʿ-h*) 'seek, inquire' and א-ת-י *ʾ-t-y* (= א-ת-ה *ʾ-t-h*) 'come';[4] and (b) the retention of the root letter *yod* in three verbal forms derived from these roots, to wit, תִּבְעָיוּן *tibʿayun* 'inquire', בְּעָיוּ *bəʿayu* 'inquire', and אֵתָיוּ *ʾetayu* 'come'. To be more precise, all of these words occur within the phrase uttered by the watchman, presumably someone from Dumah. Thus, on the one hand, this first example may

---

3. The language used in ancient northwest Arabia, including at Dumah, is called Ancient North Arabian, an umbrella term for various dialects (Ṣafaitic, etc.), but Aramaic inscriptions have been found in the area as well. The features noted here are found in both languages.

4. In the Bible, the verb ב-ע-ה *b-ʿ-h* 'seek, inquire' is always used for dialect effect. In addition to the two occurrences in Isa 21:12 studied here, see also Obad 1:6, addressed to Edom, or at least concerning Edom. (The cases of the same verbal root in Isa 30:13 and 64:1 are derived from a homonym meaning 'swell, bulge'.) Similarly, the verb א-ת-ה *ʾ-t-h* 'come' is either poetic or regional-dialectal or occurs in style-switching and addressee-switching contexts.

fall more into the realm of style-switching than addressee-switching, though, on the other hand, it occurs within a prophetic oracle to a foreign people, so it may be considered a case of the latter as well. Regardless of this technical issue, Rabin certainly pointed the way, for his discovery allowed other scholars to identify more examples of foreign elements in the oracles to the nations. Such examples include the following.[5]

2. Isaiah 17:12

הוֹי הֲמוֹן עַמִּים רַבִּים כַּהֲמוֹת יַמִּים יֶהֱמָיוּן וּשְׁאוֹן לְאֻמִּים כִּשְׁאוֹן מַיִם כַּבִּירִים יִשָּׁאוּן:

Ah, the roar of many peoples, like the roar of the seas they roar; and the rage of nations, like the rage of mighty waters they rage.

In this verse, addressed by Isaiah to the people of Aram (see the mention of 'Damascus' in v. 1), two Aramaic features occur, one grammatical and one lexical: (a) יֶהֱמָיוּן *yehɛmayun* 'they roar', once more with the consonant *yod* retained; and (b) כַּבִּירִים *kabbirim* 'great, mighty', which is common in Aramaic but is limited in Biblical Hebrew to style-switching and addressee-switching settings only.[6]

3. Isaiah 23:13

זֶה הָעָם

zɛ ha-ʿam

this people

---

5. See already my earlier treatments: Gary A. Rendsburg, "The Strata of Biblical Hebrew," *Journal of Northwest Semitic Languages* 17 (1991): 96–97; and Rendsburg, "Linguistic Variation and the 'Foreign' Factor in the Hebrew Bible," 184–87.

6. Gary A. Rendsburg, "*Kabbîr* in Biblical Hebrew: Evidence for Style-Switching and Addressee-Switching in the Hebrew Bible," *Journal of the American Oriental Society* 112 (1992): 649–51.

This phrase occurs within the prophecy to Phoenicia (see 'Tyre' in vv. 1, 5, 8, and 'Sidon' in vv. 2, 4, 12), even if v. 13 also introduces Chaldea, an Aramean group, into the mix.[7] The standard Hebrew way to express 'this people' is הָעָם הַזֶּה *ha-ʿam haz-zɛ* (Exod 3:21, 18:18, 18:23, etc., for a total of 78x). The atypical syntax employed in Isa 23:13 evokes an alternative grammatical pattern, attested in both Phoenician and Aramaic.[8]

4. Jeremiah 48:36

עַל־כֵּן יִתְרַת עָשָׂה אָבָדוּ׃

Therefore the abundance he has made has perished.

Our attention is drawn to the noun יִתְרַת *yitrat* 'gain, riches, abundance' within Jeremiah's speech to Moab. This is the only attestation of this form of the noun in the Bible: here it occurs as feminine, while elsewhere the form is masculine: יֶתֶר *yetɛr* 'gain, riches, abundance' (Gen 49:3 [2x], Ps 17:14, Job 22:20). The key issue, however, lies elsewhere, for the feminine singular noun יִתְרַת *yitrat* retains the *-at* ending, precisely as occurs in Moabite. The effect would have been fully realized by the ancient Israelite consumers of Jeremiah's pronouncement—a singular Moabite grammatical feature to remind the audience that the addressee here is the people of Moab.

5. Jeremiah 50:15

אֲשִׁיוֹתֶיהָ

ʾošyotɛha (Qeri) [Ketiv: אשויתיה]

her towers

---

7. While the reference is somewhat obscure, most likely Chaldea here refers not to the later Neo-Babylonian Empire (see, for example, 2 Kings 25 [7x]), but rather to the original homeland of the Chaldeans in the northern reaches of the Fertile Crescent. For the evidence, see Cyrus H. Gordon, "Abraham and the Merchants of Ura," *Journal of Near Eastern Studies* 17 (1958): 28–31, esp. 30.

8. For a detailed studied of this syntagma, see Gary A. Rendsburg, "Šimuš Bilti Ragil šel Kinnuy ha-Remez ba-Miqraʾ: ʿEdut Nosefet le-ʿIvrit Ṣefonit bi-Tqufat ha-Miqraʾ," *Shnaton* 12 (2000): 83–88.

This noun constitutes a *hapax legomenon* in the Bible, used here in the prophetic address to Babylon specifically to evoke the Akkadian word *asītu* 'tower'. There are some (minor?) linguistic matters that need to be resolved, such as the /a/ vowel in the Akkadian word versus the /o/ vowel in the Hebrew equivalent, and perhaps more seriously, the /s/ sibilant in the Akkadian versus the /š/ sibilant in the Hebrew—but both the correspondence between the two and the purposeful employment of this lexeme within the speech concerning Babylon are assured.[9]

6. Ezekiel 26:11

וּמַצְּבוֹת עֻזֵּךְ לָאָרֶץ תֵּרֵד

u-maṣṣəbot ʿuzzek la-ʾareṣ tered

Your pillar of strength to the ground will fall.

This passage appears within Ezekiel's proclamation directed at Tyre (see vv. 2–3); hence the author utilizes the Phoenician feminine singular nominal ending -*ot* for the noun מַצְּבוֹת *maṣṣəbot* 'pillar' (the standard Hebrew form would be מַצֵּבָה *maṣṣeba* 'pillar'). While the noun in Ezek 26:11 at first glance may look plural, one notes that the verb at the end of the phrase is the third fem. sg. form, demonstrating that the subject of the clause, מַצְּבוֹת *maṣṣəbot* 'pillar', must be singular. Once more, one assumes an Israelite audience apprehending the significance of this Phoenicianism within the oracle directed at Tyre.

7. Amos 1:5

וְתוֹמֵךְ שֵׁבֶט

wə-tomek šebeṭ

and he who holds the scepter

The book of Amos commences with a series of short oracles directed at the foreign nations, with the aforecited phrase appearing within the

---

9. For the correspondence between the Akkadian and the Hebrew, see Cohen, *Biblical Hapax Legomena in the Light of Akkadian and Ugaritic*, 46–47.

Aram section (vv. 3–5). The two-word expression serves as an epithet for the ruler of Aram—though this particular example of addressee-switching is a bit more subtle than the others surveyed in this chapter.[10] For neither of the two words evokes Aramaic per se, but rather the Hebrew phrase is the interdialectal equivalent of the Aramaic phrase יאחז חטר Yᵉ'ḤZ ḤṬR 'he who holds the scepter', attested in the Panamuwa inscription (line 20).[11]

8. Zechariah 9:3

וַתִּבֶן צֹר מָצוֹר לָהּ וַתִּצְבָּר־כֶּסֶף כֶּעָפָר וְחָרוּץ כְּטִיט חוּצוֹת׃

> And Tyre has built a fortress for herself;
> And she has amassed silver like dust,
> And gold like the mud in the streets.

This verse was discussed earlier in the book, in Chapter 16, no. 14, as part of our treatment of alliteration in poetic and prophetic texts. We return to this passage now, which occurs within Zechariah's short blast at Tyre and Sidon (vv. 2b–4), in order to emphasize the use of the word חָרוּץ ḥaruṣ 'gold', which occurs here instead of the standard Hebrew term, זָהָב zahab 'gold'. As noted in the earlier treatment, this lexical choice enhances the alliteration in the verse. But its function in the verse is twofold, for it also serves to elicit addressee-switching. The word חרץ ḤRṢ 'gold' is the only term attested for this precious metal in Phoenician; while from an earlier epoch the cognate form ḥrṣ is attested in Ugaritic.[12] In short, the prophetic author selected the term חָרוּץ ḥaruṣ 'gold' deftly, for it served his literary artistry doubly.

---

10. See the earlier discussion by Shalom M. Paul, *Amos* (Hermeneia; Minneapolis: Fortress, 1991), 52–53 and n. 94. Within the treatment of Amos 1:5, he also adduced Zech 9:3, our next example.

11. To be more accurate, the Panamuwa inscription is written in Samalian, a dialect of Old Aramaic used in the area of Zincirli, located in modern-day southern Turkey. We assume that the expression would have been familiar throughout the Aramaic-speaking milieu, including in Damascus itself.

12. Incidentally, through trans-Mediterranean trade, the word was borrowed into Greek as χρυσός *chrysos* 'gold'. In time, this form entered English as the first element in the word 'chrysanthemum', lit., 'gold flower'.

9. Jeremiah 49:11

וְאַלְמְנֹתֶיךָ עָלַי תִּבְטָחוּ

wə-ʾalmənotɛka ʿalay tibṭaḥu

And let your widows trust in me.

This verse occurs within Jeremiah's oracle directed at Edom (vv. 7–22). Our knowledge of the Edomite dialect (part of the Canaanite umbrella) is so scant that any inference regarding a feature relevant to the addressee-switching effect must remain somewhat hypothetical. The passage quoted above, nevertheless, is a most promising one. The verb in this phrase, תִּבְטָחוּ *tibṭaḥu* 'trust', represents the only third fem. pl. *tiqtəlū* form (to use its technical designation) in the Bible. I would venture to suggest that this form reflects Edomite morphology, though to repeat, we know precious little about this subject and can make no definitive statement.[13]

---

13. For additional forays with the goal of identifying Edomite dialectal traits represented in the Bible, see Gary A. Rendsburg, "What We Can Learn about Other Northwest Semitic Dialects from Reading the Bible," in Athalya Brenner-Idan, ed., *Discourse, Dialogue, and Debate in the Bible: Essays in Honour of Frank H. Polak* (Hebrew Bible Monographs 63; Amsterdam Studies in Bible and Religion 7; Sheffield: Sheffield Phoenix, 2014), 172–73.

CHAPTER TWENTY-SIX

TELLING AND RETELLING: VARIATION WITHIN DIRECT SPEECH

I unabashedly borrow the title of this chapter from the excellent book by George Savran, *Telling and Retelling: Quotation in Biblical Narrative*.[1] In his monograph, Savran studies different versions of quoted speech: for example, (i) when character A relates a story in one way to character B, and then in another way to character C, changing the wording to suit his/her needs; and (ii) when character A states something that is then repeated, typically in different fashion, by character B. Savran counts more than one hundred examples of this phenomenon in the grand narrative of Genesis through Kings.

In light of the use of 'repetition with variation' in general prose narrative (as surveyed repeatedly in the current volume), the reader will not be surprised to learn that in the vast majority of the hundred-plus cases in which direct speech is recorded and then repeated, the reiterated version deviates from the original statement. Indeed, Savran counts only ten instances in Genesis through Kings (Gen 20:5, 26:9, 38:22, 44:25, Exod 32:8, 1 Sam 21:12, 29:5, 1 Kgs 18:11, 18:14, 22:18) in which verbatim repetition occurs, though "each of these discourses is very short (from two to seven words), increasing the statistical probability of literal repetition."[2] One of these passages was studied above, namely, Gen 38:22 לֹא־הָיְתָה בָזֶה קְדֵשָׁה *loʾ hayta ba-ze qədeša* 'There has not been a *qedesha* in this [sc. 'here']', in connection with the alliteration evoked therein (see Chapter 5, no. 10).

There is no need for me to rehearse all or even many of the fine examples presented by Savran in his book. But a few illustrative examples

---

1. George W. Savran, *Telling and Retelling: Quotation in Biblical Narrative* (Bloomington: Indiana University Press, 1988).
    2. Ibid., 29.

are essential to my project, especially as they relate to the topic of repetition with variation, a crucial component of the present study.

1. Genesis 39:14, 17

Gen 39:14

רְאוּ הֵבִיא לָנוּ אִישׁ עִבְרִי לְצַחֶק בָּנוּ בָּא אֵלַיֹ לִשְׁכַּב עִמִּי

"See, he brought to us a Hebrew man, to sport with us;
he came to me, to lie with me."

Gen 39:17

בָּא־אֵלַיֹ הָעֶבֶד הָעִבְרִי אֲשֶׁר־הֵבֵאתָ לָנוּ לְצַחֶק בִּי׃

"He came to me, the Hebrew slave, whom you brought to
us, to sport with me."

We begin with a very simple example of the first pattern noted above.[3] Both quotations are in the mouth of Potiphar's wife, as she crafts her story, first while speaking to the household staff, and then while speaking to her husband. We note some similarities in the two speeches, most importantly, (a) the presence of the phrase בָּא אֵלַי *ba' 'elay* 'he came to me'; and (b) the use of the Hiphʿil form of the verb ב-ו-א *b-w-'* 'come', hence 'bring', namely, הֵבִיא לָנוּ *hebi' lanu* 'he brought to us', הֵבֵאתָ לָנוּ *hebe'ta lanu* 'you brought to us'.

Our focus, however, remains with the differences. First, in v. 14, Potiphar's wife leads with the mention of Joseph, whom her husband brought to the household (since the staff would be more interested in this matter) and then proceeds to the sexual encounter; whereas in v. 17, she leads with the latter (since this will increase the ire of her husband) and then proceeds to blame him, so it seems, with the phrase, 'whom you brought to us'.

Second, in v. 14, Joseph is designated an אִישׁ עִבְרִי *'iš 'ibri* 'a Hebrew man', while in v. 17 she refers to him as הָעֶבֶד הָעִבְרִי *ha-'ɛbɛd ha-'ibri* 'the

---

3. See the detailed study in Sternberg, *Poetics of Biblical Narrative*, 425–27. For a more recent treatment, see Simcha Kogut, "Keṣad huṭreda 'ešet Poṭifar u-maduaʿ *wǝ-hab-bor req* (Berešit 37:24) lo' haya req? Pešaṭ u-Draš be-he'ara lǝšonit," in Lea Mazor, ed., *Sippur Yosef ba-Miqra' u-ve-Re'i ha-Dorot* (= *Bet Miqra'* 55 [2009–2010 / 5770]), 77–83, esp. 77–79.

Hebrew slave'. If she had referred to Joseph as a slave when speaking to the household staff, among whom were slaves and servants, their response might have been to show allegiance to Joseph, with whom they would share a common social-legal status. By referring to him as 'a Hebrew man', by contrast, she plays the ethnic card, us (that is, we Egyptians, who need to stand together) versus him (that is, the foreigner Hebrew). None of this is necessary, though, when she speaks to her husband; quite the contrary, by referring to Joseph as 'the Hebrew slave', she nimbly reminds Potiphar of his status as master to said slave.

Third, in the first iteration, Potiphar's wife states that Joseph's role was לְצַחֶק בָּנוּ *ləṣaḥɛq banu* 'to sport with us', with an emphasis on the 'us', as again she attempts to garner the support of the household staff, who would see themselves as part and parcel of the 'us' and thus would sympathize with her. In the second iteration, once more this ploy is unnecessary, for now she must set Joseph not against the the staff but against her husband, and hence she uses the phrase לְצַחֶק בִּי *ləṣaḥɛq bi* 'to sport with me'.

There are still other points of comparison that could be made here (as well as with the other components of her larger twin speeches, which comprise vv. 14–15 and vv. 17–18, respectively), but these three items illustrate the technique in fine fashion.

2. Genesis 27:3–4, 7

Gen 27:3–4

‎3 וְעַתָּה שָׂא־נָא כֵלֶיךָ תֶּלְיְךָ וְקַשְׁתֶּךָ וְצֵא הַשָּׂדֶה וְצוּדָה לִּי [צידה] צָיִד*:
‎4 וַעֲשֵׂה־לִי מַטְעַמִּים כַּאֲשֶׁר אָהַבְתִּי וְהָבִיאָה לִּי וְאֹכֵלָה בַּעֲבוּר תְּבָרֶכְךָ נַפְשִׁי בְּטֶרֶם אָמוּת:

³ "And now, take please your items, your quiver and your bow, and go-out to the field, and hunt for me game.
⁴ And make for me delicacies, as I love, and bring (them) to me, so that I may eat; in order that my inner-being may bless you, afore I die."[4]

---

4. I have used the archaic English preposition 'afore' here, to reflect the rarer Hebrew term בְּטֶרֶם *ba-ṭɛrɛm*, reserving 'before' for the much commoner Hebrew term לִפְנֵי *lipne*. See the discussion below for the contrast. For an

Gen 27:7

הָבִיאָה לִּי צַיִד וַעֲשֵׂה־לִי מַטְעַמִּים וְאֹכֵלָה וַאֲבָרֶכְכָה לִפְנֵי יְהוָה
לִפְנֵי מוֹתִי:

"Bring to me game, and make for me delicacies, so that
I may eat; so that I may bless you, before Yʜwʜ, before
my death."

We now move to an example of type (ii) above, where the words spoken
by one character are represented in a different manner by a second
character.[5] The first citation, vv. 3–4, reproduces the words spoken by
Isaac to Esau; while the second citation, v. 7, presents Rebekah's report
of said words to Jacob. The differences are striking.

We first notice the length of Isaac's instructions, twenty-four words,
versus the brevity of Rebekah's take, twelve words. Isaac is deliberate
in speaking to Esau; for Rebekah, by contrast, time is of the essence and
hence every word matters, if the ruse is to work. Upon closer inspection,
we note that she essentially omits all of what Isaac stated in the first sentence, repeating only the key word צַיִד ṣayid 'game'. Among the words
she omits are כֵלֶיךָ תֶּלְיְךָ וְקַשְׁתֶּךָ kelɛka tɛlyəka wə-qaštɛka 'your items,
your quiver and your bow'. The second of these nouns appears only
here in the Bible: one may consider it a technical term used by archers,
whether they be hunters or warriors. Rebekah may not even know what
the word means. Each endeavor has its own technical vocabulary, so
when non-specialists speak about the endeavor they are inclined to use
less technical language. A modern analogy might be ice hockey, which
has such technical terms as 'forechecking', 'backchecking', 'delayed
offside', 'stretch pass', 'change on the fly', 'odd-man rush', 'long change',
'blocker save', 'toe drag', and so on—words understood by true devotees
but less known to casual observers. By analogy, all Rebekah knows is
that Isaac instructed Esau to bring him game (whatever the specific
meaning of the exact words), and that is what she repeats to Jacob.

---

example of 'afore' in English literature, note John Bunyan, *Pilgrim's Progress*
(1684), Second Part, ii.63: "That they were hanged afore we came hither" (see
OED, s.v. 'afore', adv., prep., and conj.).

5. For earlier treatments, see Sternberg, *Poetics of Biblical Narrative*, 391;
and Savran, *Telling and Retelling*, 41–42.

Also unnecessary, of course, is the phrase כַּאֲשֶׁר אָהַבְתִּי *ka-ʾašɛr ʾahabti* 'as I love', which she omits as well. Yet another difference is the order of the two verbs: Isaac used the order וְהָבִיאָה . . . וַעֲשֵׂה־לִי *wa-ʿase li . . . wə-habiʾa li* 'and make for me . . . and bring to me'; whereas Rebekah states, הָבִיאָה לִי . . . וַעֲשֵׂה־לִי *habiʾa li . . . wa-ʿase li* 'bring to me . . . and make for me'. Whether the change in word order is significant or not is unclear, but it is present for the reader to ponder nonetheless.

Finally, Isaac ends his statement to Esau with בַּעֲבוּר תְּבָרֶכְךָ נַפְשִׁי בְּטֶרֶם אָמוּת *baʿabur təbarekəka napši bə-ṭɛrɛm ʾamut* 'in order that my inner-being may bless you, afore I die'. Interestingly, Rebekah alters this when she speaks to Jacob, using instead the phrase וַאֲבָרֶכְכָה לִפְנֵי יְהוָה לִפְנֵי מוֹתִי *wa-ʾabarekəka lipne yhwh lipne moti* 'so that I may bless you, before Yнwн, before my death'. Apart from the minor grammatical changes, the reader is led to ask: Does Rebekah's introduction of the divine name here reflect the author's belief that the spirituality of women surpasses that of men?

In short, a host of changes are introduced by Rebekah in her report of Isaac's original words (spoken to Esau) to Jacob. What is truly striking, though, is the following. When Jacob actually appears before Isaac, with the pretense of being Esau, he invites his father to eat and then states בַּעֲבוּר תְּבָרֲכַנִּי נַפְשֶׁךָ *baʿabur təbarakanni napšɛka* 'in order that your inner-being may bless me' (v. 19)—using the very words (save for the changes in person) that Isaac actually spoke to Esau (see v. 4), even though Jacob was not present, did not hear the words spoken, and gained knowledge of them only through Rebekah's reportage, which used different vocables! The attentive reader realizes the change back to the original speech and wishes to know: How did Jacob know which words to use? Was he simply so familiar with his father's speech patterns to know that Isaac would not invoke the divine name Yнwн in such contexts? Or, following a different tack, was Jacob also eavesdropping when Isaac spoke to Esau in vv. 3–4, even though the narrator informs us that only Rebekah overheard the conversation? In typical Hebrew storytelling fashion, we are given no clues that would allow us to answer these questions. We simply must recognize the change and ponder. We are, however, given an extra treat when Esau himself arrives on the scene, invites his father to eat, and then employs the selfsame

expression (word-for-word, letter-for-letter, accent-for-accent): בַּעֲבוּר
תְּבָרֲכַנִּי נַפְשֶׁךָ *baʿabur təbarakanni napšɛka* 'in order that your inner-being may bless me' (v. 31). Obviously Esau would know exactly what to say—but how did Jacob know to do so?

3. Genesis 24:3–6, 37–40

The most complicated example of the device studied here occurs in Genesis 24, with iteration upon iteration of both repeated direct speech and repeated narration. As per the topic of this chapter, we will focus on examples of the former.[6]

At the beginning of the tale, Abraham and his servant hold the following conversation:

> 3 וְאַשְׁבִּיעֲךָ בַּיהוָה אֱלֹהֵי הַשָּׁמַיִם וֵאלֹהֵי הָאָרֶץ אֲשֶׁר לֹא־תִקַּח אִשָּׁה
> לִבְנִי מִבְּנוֹת הַכְּנַעֲנִי אֲשֶׁר אָנֹכִי יוֹשֵׁב בְּקִרְבּוֹ:
> 4 כִּי אֶל־אַרְצִי וְאֶל־מוֹלַדְתִּי תֵּלֵךְ וְלָקַחְתָּ אִשָּׁה לִבְנִי לְיִצְחָק:
> 5 וַיֹּאמֶר אֵלָיו הָעֶבֶד אוּלַי לֹא־תֹאבֶה הָאִשָּׁה לָלֶכֶת אַחֲרַי אֶל־הָאָרֶץ
> הַזֹּאת הֶהָשֵׁב אָשִׁיב אֶת־בִּנְךָ אֶל־הָאָרֶץ אֲשֶׁר־יָצָאתָ מִשָּׁם:
> 6 וַיֹּאמֶר אֵלָיו אַבְרָהָם הִשָּׁמֶר לְךָ פֶּן־תָּשִׁיב אֶת־בְּנִי שָׁמָּה:

3 "And I adjure you by Yhwh the God of Heaven and the God of Earth, not to take a wife for my son from the daughters of the Canaanite, in whose midst I dwell.
4 Rather, unto my land and unto my birthplace you shall go; and you shall take a wife for my son, for Isaac."
5 And the servant said to him, "Perhaps the woman will not consent to go after me to this land; shall I indeed return your son to the land from which you came-forth?"
6 And Abraham said to him, "Guard yourself, lest you return my son there."

---

6. The role of Genesis 24 as fodder for our discussion may be seen from the numerous citations to this chapter in the Index of Biblical Passages to Savran, *Telling and Retelling*, 156, with a full column of references to pages within the book.

Now, when the servant relates this dialogue to his hosts, that is, Rebekah's family in Aram, he speaks as follows:

37 וַיַּשְׁבִּעֵנִי אֲדֹנִי לֵאמֹר לֹא־תִקַּח אִשָּׁה לִבְנִי מִבְּנוֹת הַכְּנַעֲנִי אֲשֶׁר אָנֹכִי יֹשֵׁב בְּאַרְצוֹ:

38 אִם־לֹא אֶל־בֵּית־אָבִי תֵּלֵךְ וְאֶל־מִשְׁפַּחְתִּי וְלָקַחְתָּ אִשָּׁה לִבְנִי:

39 וָאֹמַר אֶל־אֲדֹנִי אֻלַי לֹא־תֵלֵךְ הָאִשָּׁה אַחֲרָי:

40 וַיֹּאמֶר אֵלָי יְהֹוָה אֲשֶׁר־הִתְהַלַּכְתִּי לְפָנָיו יִשְׁלַח מַלְאָכוֹ אִתָּךְ וְהִצְלִיחַ דַּרְכֶּךָ וְלָקַחְתָּ אִשָּׁה לִבְנִי מִמִּשְׁפַּחְתִּי וּמִבֵּית אָבִי:

[37] "And my lord adjured me, saying: 'Do not take a wife for my son from the daughters of the Canaanite, in whose land I dwell.
[38] Rather, unto the house of my father you shall go, and unto my family, and you shall take a wife for my son.'
[39] And I said to my lord, 'Perhaps the woman will not go after me'.
[40] And he said to me, 'YHWH, in whose presence I have walked, he will send his messenger with you, and he will make-successful your way, and you shall take a wife for my son, from my family and from the house of my father'."

The attentive listener to the original conversation and then the servant's retelling observes several crucial differences (in addition to some minor ones). First, whereas Abraham used the the words אַרְצִי *'arṣi* 'my land' and מוֹלַדְתִּי *moladti* 'my birthplace' (v. 4)—essentially geographical terms, of the sort that one needs to state on a landing or immigration card—the servant replaces these with the much more family-oriented expressions בֵּית־אָבִי *bet 'abi* 'house of my father' and מִשְׁפַּחְתִּי *mišpaḥti* 'my family' (v. 38). And if this were not enough, he actually repeats the same two words—in reverse order, as befits biblical style[7]—in v. 40.

---

7. As noted above in Chapter 15, this device is known to biblical scholars as Seidel's Law, named for Moshe Seidel. See his "Maqbilot ben Sefer Yešaʿyahu le-Sefer Tehillim," *Sinai* 38 (1955–1956): 149–72, 229–40, 272–80, 335–55, with particular attention to p. 150. This essay was reprinted in Moshe Seidel, *Ḥiqre Miqra'* (Jerusalem: Mosad ha-Rav Kook, 1978), 1–99. For an English discussion,

Secondly, in the original conversation, when the servant raised the possibility that the woman might not wish to go with him, he continued with the question, 'Shall I indeed return your son to the land from which you came-forth?' (v. 5)—which in turn elicited Abraham's rather stern comment, "Guard yourself, lest you return my son there" (v. 6). In the servant's reformulation, however, he alters this exchange. In his retelling of the initial conversation between Abraham and himself, the servant never raises the possibility of Isaac's journeying to Aram, thereby eliminating any need to relate Abraham's stern words. Had he reported this portion of the conversation, no doubt his words would not be well received in Aram—"how dare he speak so negatively about our land," one can imagine his interlocutors thinking. Moreover, in the servant's version, divine intervention all but guarantees a successful mission (v. 40)!

4. Genesis 24:22–25, 47

Gen 24:22–25

22 וַיְהִי כַּאֲשֶׁר כִּלּוּ הַגְּמַלִּים לִשְׁתּוֹת וַיִּקַּח הָאִישׁ נֶזֶם זָהָב בֶּקַע
מִשְׁקָלוֹ וּשְׁנֵי צְמִידִים עַל־יָדֶיהָ עֲשָׂרָה זָהָב מִשְׁקָלָם:

23 וַיֹּאמֶר בַּת־מִי אַתְּ הַגִּידִי נָא לִי הֲיֵשׁ בֵּית־אָבִיךְ מָקוֹם לָנוּ לָלִין:

24 וַתֹּאמֶר אֵלָיו בַּת־בְּתוּאֵל אָנֹכִי בֶּן־מִלְכָּה אֲשֶׁר יָלְדָה לְנָחוֹר:

25 וַתֹּאמֶר אֵלָיו גַּם־תֶּבֶן גַּם־מִסְפּוֹא רַב עִמָּנוּ גַּם־מָקוֹם לָלוּן:

22 And it was, when the camels finished drinking, and the man took a nose-ring of gold, one half-shekel its weight, and two bracelets on her hands, ten (shekels) of gold their weight.

23 And he said, "Whose daughter are you? Tell me, please. Is there in the house of your father a place for us to lodge?"

24 And she said to him, "The daughter of Bethuel am I, son of Milcah, whom she bore to Nahor."

25 And she said to him, "There is also straw, also much fodder with us, also a place to lodge."

---

see Shemaryahu Talmon, "The Textual Study of the Bible—A New Outlook," in Frank M. Cross and Shemaryahu Talmon, eds., *Qumran and the History of the Biblical Text* (Cambridge: Harvard University Press, 1975), 321–400, esp. 362–63.

Gen 24:47

וָאֶשְׁאַ֣ל אֹתָ֗הּ וָאֹמַר֙ בַּת־מִ֣י אַ֔תְּ וַתֹּ֗אמֶר בַּת־בְּתוּאֵל֙ בֶּן־נָח֔וֹר אֲשֶׁ֥ר
יָֽלְדָה־לּ֖וֹ מִלְכָּ֑ה וָאָשִׂ֤ם הַנֶּ֙זֶם֙ עַל־אַפָּ֔הּ וְהַצְּמִידִ֖ים עַל־יָדֶֽיהָ׃

"And I asked her, and I said, 'Whose daughter are you?',
and she said, 'The daughter of Bethuel son of Nahor,
whom Milcah bore to him'; and I put the nose-ring on
her nose and the bracelets on her hands.'"

In the original scene, as reported by the narrator, we learn that Abraham's servant—so astonished by the young woman's exertion and hospitality in providing drink both to him and to his ten camels[8]—adorned her with gifts of jewelry and only then asked who she was. When he recounts the scene to Rebekah's household, however, he realizes that his audience may think that his action was a bit hasty: perhaps he would bestow gifts on any woman who provided drink and hospitality—and not just the specifically intended Rebekah. Accordingly, in his version, he changes the order of the events, so that first he inquired about her identity, learned that she was Rebekah daughter of Bethuel, son of Nahor and Milcah—and hence a cousin of Isaac—and only then presented her with the nose-ring and bracelets.

In addition, in the original scene, Abraham's servant had the temerity to ask, even before learning the identity of his interlocutor, "Tell me, please. Is there in the house of your father a place for us to lodge?" (v. 23). To which the young woman responded, "There is also straw, also much fodder with us, also a place to lodge" (v. 25). This portion of their exchange is omitted when the servant describes the scene before the members of the household. After all, they may find his question rather impudent, and they also may not be very cheerful about Rebekah's offering hospitality of 'room and board' to the man and his camels. In short, better simply not to mention this part of the dialogue.

---

8. Let us recall that camels may drink up to twenty-five liters (= 6.5 U.S. gallons) of water in a single take, within three minutes. Rebekah, accordingly, would have needed to draw 250 liters (= 65 gallons) of water from the well! In light of this calculation, one can comprehend the servant's amazement and astonishment (see v. 21 especially) at her assiduousness. See our earlier analysis of this scene in Chapter 5, no. 5.

5. Judges 13:3–5, 7

Judg 13:3–5

3 וַיֵּרָ֥א מַלְאַךְ־יְהוָ֖ה אֶל־הָאִשָּׁ֑ה וַיֹּ֣אמֶר אֵלֶ֗יהָ הִנֵּה־נָ֤א אַתְּ־עֲקָרָה֙ וְלֹ֣א יָלַ֔דְתְּ וְהָרִ֖ית וְיָלַ֥דְתְּ בֵּֽן׃

4 וְעַתָּה֙ הִשָּׁ֣מְרִי נָ֔א וְאַל־תִּשְׁתִּ֖י יַ֣יִן וְשֵׁכָ֑ר וְאַל־תֹּאכְלִ֖י כָּל־טָמֵֽא׃

5 כִּי֩ הִנָּ֨ךְ הָרָ֜ה וְיֹלַ֣דְתְּ בֵּ֗ן וּמוֹרָה֙ לֹא־יַעֲלֶ֣ה עַל־רֹאשׁ֔וֹ כִּֽי־נְזִ֧יר אֱלֹהִ֛ים יִהְיֶ֥ה הַנַּ֖עַר מִן־הַבָּ֑טֶן וְה֗וּא יָחֵ֛ל לְהוֹשִׁ֥יעַ אֶת־יִשְׂרָאֵ֖ל מִיַּ֥ד פְּלִשְׁתִּֽים׃

³ And the messenger of Yʜwʜ appeared unto the woman; and he said to her, "Behold, please, you are barren, and you have not borne, but you will conceive, and you will bear a son.
⁴ And now, guard-yourself, please, and do not drink wine or strong-drink, and do not eat anything impure.
⁵ For behold, you are to conceive, and you are to bear a son, and a razor shall not go-up on his head, for the lad will be a *nazir* of God from the womb;⁹ and he, he will begin to save Israel from the hand of the Philistines."

Judg 13:7

וַיֹּ֣אמֶר לִ֗י הִנָּ֥ךְ הָרָ֖ה וְיֹלַ֣דְתְּ בֵּ֑ן וְעַתָּ֞ה אַל־תִּשְׁתִּ֣י ׀ יַ֣יִן וְשֵׁכָ֗ר וְאַל־תֹּֽאכְלִי֙ כָּל־טֻמְאָ֔ה כִּֽי־נְזִ֤יר אֱלֹהִים֙ יִהְיֶ֣ה הַנַּ֔עַר מִן־הַבֶּ֖טֶן עַד־י֥וֹם מוֹתֽוֹ׃

And he said to me, "Behold, you are to conceive, and you are to bear a son; and now, do not drink wine or strong-drink, and do not eat any impurity, for the lad will be a *nazir* of God from the womb, until the day of his death."

---

9. Literally, 'stomach' (see also v. 7), but obviously 'womb' in this context, as often in Biblical Hebrew. In fact, the principal meaning of 'womb' in English is 'the abdomen or abdominal cavity of a person or animal' (*OED*, s.v. 'womb' *n.*).

In Judges 13, a messenger of Yahweh appears to the unnamed wife of Manoah, with the primary message of her forthcoming conception and birth of a savior. As frequently happens when an original discourse is retold, Manoah's wife greatly condenses the message in her conversation with her husband.[10] Note the two and one-half verses of original speech (vv. 3b–5) versus the single verse of repeated speech (v. 7). Even within her shortened version, some phrases are repeated verbatim, most significantly, כִּי־נְזִיר אֱלֹהִים יִהְיֶה הַנַּעַר מִן־הַבָּטֶן / מִן־הַבָּטֶן *ki nəzir 'ɛlohim yihyɛ han-na'ar min hab-baṭen / min hab-bɛṭen* 'for the lad will be a *nazir* of God from the womb' (v. 5 = v. 7).[11]

But then there are the variations, including one stylistic one, to wit, כָּל־טָמֵא *kol ṭame'* 'anything impure' (v. 4) > כָּל־טֻמְאָה *kol ṭum'a* 'any impurity' (v. 7), and one substantive one, namely, וְהוּא יָחֵל לְהוֹשִׁיעַ אֶת־יִשְׂרָאֵל מִיַּד פְּלִשְׁתִּים *wə-hu' yaḥel ləhošia' 'et yiśra'el miy-yad pəlištim* 'and he, he will begin to save Israel from the hand of the Philistines' (v. 5) > עַד־יוֹם מוֹתוֹ *'ad yom moto* 'until the day of his death' (v. 7). How did the wife of Manoah know that her son's (Samson's) saving the Israelites from the hand of the Philistines would be coterminous with his death? The reader, to be sure, does not know this information yet, and in fact she will not apprehend this point until ch. 16 (see v. 30 especially). Only then will the reader realize how prescient the wife of Manoah was, as the reader recalls (upon reaching the end of the Samson narrative) this anonymous character's substitution of the messenger's longer phrase 'and he will begin to save Israel from the hand of the Philistines' in 13:5 with her curt 'until the day of his death' in 13:7.[12] The two expressions look so different from one another in ch. 13; but they become one and the same in ch. 16. Such is the wonder of biblical narrative.

---

10. For an earlier treatment, see Savran, *Telling and Retelling*, 31–32.

11. The very minor change from הַבָּטֶן *hab-baṭen* 'the womb' to הַבֶּטֶן *hab-bɛṭen* 'the womb' in v. 7 is not a change at all, in fact, for the variants are based on phonological considerations within the Masoretic system. In ancient Israel, the two forms would have been identical.

12. On the role of anonymous characters in the Bible, with special attention to the wife of Manoah, see Adele Reinhartz, *Why Ask My Name? Anonymity and Identity in Biblical Narrative* (New York: Oxford University Press, 1998), 95–101.

6. 1 Kings 21:2–3, 6, 15

1 Kgs 21:2–3

² וַיְדַבֵּ֣ר אַחְאָ֣ב אֶל־נָב֣וֹת ׀ לֵאמֹ֣ר ׀ תְּנָה־לִּ֣י אֶֽת־כַּרְמְךָ֗ וִֽיהִי־לִ֣י
לְגַן־יָרָ֗ק כִּ֣י ה֤וּא קָרוֹב֙ אֵ֣צֶל בֵּיתִ֔י וְאֶתְּנָ֤ה לְךָ֙ תַּחְתָּ֔יו כֶּ֖רֶם ט֣וֹב
מִמֶּ֑נּוּ אִ֚ם ט֣וֹב בְּעֵינֶ֔יךָ אֶתְּנָה־לְךָ֥ כֶ֖סֶף מְחִ֥יר זֶֽה׃
³ וַיֹּ֥אמֶר נָב֖וֹת אֶל־אַחְאָ֑ב חָלִ֧ילָה לִּ֛י מֵֽיהוָ֖ה מִתִּתִּ֛י אֶת־נַחֲלַ֥ת
אֲבֹתַ֖י לָֽךְ׃

² And Ahab spoke to Naboth, saying, "Give me your vineyard, so that it will be for me as a vegetable garden, for it is near to my house, and let me give to you in its place a better vineyard; (or) if it is good in your eyes, let me give you silver (as) this price."
³ And Naboth said to Ahab, "Profanity to me from Yнwн, my giving the inheritance of my fathers to you."

1 Kgs 21:6

וַיְדַבֵּ֣ר אֵלֶ֗יהָ כִּֽי־אֲדַבֵּ֣ר אֶל־נָב֣וֹת הַיִּזְרְעֵאלִ֜י וָאֹ֧מַר ל֣וֹ תְּנָה־לִּ֣י אֶת־
כַּרְמְךָ֣ בְּכֶ֗סֶף א֤וֹ אִם־חָפֵ֣ץ אַתָּ֔ה אֶתְּנָה־לְךָ֥ כֶ֖רֶם תַּחְתָּ֑יו וַיֹּ֕אמֶר
לֹֽא־אֶתֵּ֥ן לְךָ֖ אֶת־כַּרְמִֽי׃

And he spoke to her, "For I spoke to Naboth the Jezreelite, and I said to him, 'Give me your vineyard for silver, or if it please you, let me give you a vineyard in its stead'; and he said, 'I will not give you my vineyard'."

1 Kgs 21:15

וַתֹּ֤אמֶר אִיזֶ֙בֶל֙ אֶל־אַחְאָ֔ב ק֣וּם רֵ֗שׁ אֶת־כֶּ֤רֶם ׀ נָב֣וֹת הַיִּזְרְעֵאלִ֗י
אֲשֶׁ֤ר מֵאֵן֙ לָתֶת־לְךָ֣ בְכֶ֔סֶף כִּ֣י אֵ֥ין נָב֛וֹת חַ֖י כִּי־מֵֽת׃

And Jezebel said to Ahab, "Arise, possess the vineyard of Naboth the Jezreelite, who refused to give (it) to you for silver, for Naboth is not alive, but dead."

This narrative episode unfolds with Ahab, king of the northern kingdom of Israel, asking his neighbor Naboth for his vineyard, in exchange

either for a better vineyard or for silver payment. The request is polite
and non-demanding (v. 2), and certainly does not fall within the category of eminent domain (U.S.) or compulsory purchase (U.K.)—even
though such was feared by the prophet Samuel in his denunciation of
kingship (1 Sam 8:14). Naboth's response, in turn, is perfectly understandable, as he does not wish for the land that belongs to his family
legacy to pass to another, even the king of Israel (v. 3).[13]

When Ahab reports this conversation to his wife, Jezebel, in v. 6,
both portions of the dialogue are truncated. The most striking differences in the first half of the dialogue are: (a) Ahab does not mention
his desire to turn Naboth's vineyard into a vegetable garden; (b) Ahab
fronts the silver and mentions the exchange of another vineyard secondarily, though in the original conversation he led with the vineyard
and mentioned the option of silver payment secondarily; and (c) the idea
of כֶּרֶם טוֹב מִמֶּנּוּ *kɛrɛm ṭob mimmɛnnu* 'a better vineyard' is modified
to simply כֶּרֶם *kɛrɛm* 'a vineyard'. Regarding the first two differences,
Ahab must presume that his wife, as a *femme royale* with a life limited
to the palace (recall that Jezebel was both a daughter of the king of
Tyre and the wife of the king of Israel), does not understand land use
and land exchange but that she would understand capital purchase.
Regarding the third difference, Ahab presumably does not wish his
wife to know that he offered 'a better vineyard', as opposed to simply
'a [non-descript] vineyard'.

The retelling of the second part of the dialogue reveals an even
more striking omission. In the actual conversation, Naboth provided
a very good reason for his unwillingness to transfer his property to
Ahab: חָלִילָה לִּי מֵיהוָֹה מִתִּתִּי אֶת־נַחֲלַת אֲבֹתַי לָךְ *halila li me-YHWH mit-
titti ʾet naḥalat ʾabotay lak* 'Profanity to me from YHWH, my giving
the inheritance of my fathers to you' (with apologies for the over-
literalness of this rendering). When Ahab reports the conversation
to Jezebel, he represents Naboth's words thus: לֹא־אֶתֵּן לְךָ אֶת־כַּרְמִי *loʾ
ʾetten ləka ʾet karmi* 'I will not give you my vineyard'. After all, what
would a Baʿal-and-Asherah-worshipping Phoenician woman, who has

---

13. For earlier treatments, see Sternberg, *Poetics of Biblical Narrative*,
431–32; and Savran, *Telling and Retelling*, 102–3.

spent her time killing the prophets of Yahweh (see 1 Kgs 18:4, 18:13), understand of such matters!

Finally, while not directly related to the topic of 'telling and retelling', we note Jezebel's words to Ahab, as she informs her husband of Naboth's death (which she orchestrated [see vv. 8–14]), in particular her statement אֶת־כֶּרֶם ׀ נָבוֹת הַיִּזְרְעֵאלִי אֲשֶׁר מֵאֵן לָתֶת־לְךָ בְכֶסֶף *'et kɛrɛm nabot hay-yizrəʿeʾli ʾašɛr meʾen latɛt ləka bə-kɛsɛp* 'the vineyard of Naboth the Jezreelite, who refused to give (it) to you for silver'. Through this expression, we gain further insight into the way words operate. While the reader knows that Naboth had an excellent reason not to transfer the vineyard that had been in his family for generations, Jezebel knows none of this. In her mind, his non-action was simple snub, hence her use of the verb מ-א-ן *m-ʾ-n* 'refuse'. Furthermore, she makes no reference whatsoever to the land exchange, but rather mentions only the proposed option of silver payment. None of this, of course, is explicated by the author; rather, the members of the audience are invited to be active participants in the reading process, to discern all this on their own.

CHAPTER TWENTY-SEVEN

FORM FOLLOWS CONTENT

At several points in this book we have observed the technique of form follows content (to use the literary term) or form follows function (to use the architectural term). In this chapter we review those instances and provide additional examples.[1]

1. Genesis 1 — the first creation account

As we saw in Chapter 1, the Bible's first creation account, found in Genesis 1, proceeds in orderly fashion, with each day enumerated separately, with refrains present, with repeated terms and phrases, and with the first three days of creation matching the second three days. The result is a well-designed literary structure, serving as the blueprint to creation. God brought order out of chaos, which is indicated in a variety of ways (e.g., the creation of 'light' in a world preexistent with 'darkness')—and the text of Genesis 1 reflects this process throughout.

2. Genesis 39:2–5 — in Potiphar's house

² וַיְהִי יְהוָה אֶת־יוֹסֵף וַיְהִי אִישׁ מַצְלִיחַ וַיְהִי בְּבֵית אֲדֹנָיו הַמִּצְרִי׃

³ וַיַּרְא אֲדֹנָיו כִּי יְהוָה אִתּוֹ וְכֹל אֲשֶׁר־הוּא עֹשֶׂה יְהוָה מַצְלִיחַ בְּיָדוֹ׃

⁴ וַיִּמְצָא יוֹסֵף חֵן בְּעֵינָיו וַיְשָׁרֶת אֹתוֹ וַיַּפְקִדֵהוּ עַל־בֵּיתוֹ וְכָל־יֶשׁ־לוֹ נָתַן בְּיָדוֹ׃

⁵ וַיְהִי מֵאָז הִפְקִיד אֹתוֹ בְּבֵיתוֹ וְעַל כָּל־אֲשֶׁר יֶשׁ־לוֹ וַיְבָרֶךְ יְהוָה אֶת־בֵּית הַמִּצְרִי בִּגְלַל יוֹסֵף וַיְהִי בִּרְכַּת יְהוָה בְּכָל־אֲשֶׁר יֶשׁ־לוֹ בַּבַּיִת וּבַשָּׂדֶה׃

---

1. As indicated, some of the passages treated in this chapter have been treated in earlier chapters. By necessity, accordingly, some of my prose will echo what I have written above.

² And YHWH was with Joseph, and he was a successful man, and he was in the house of his lord, the Egyptian.

³ And his lord saw that YHWH was with him; and all that he would do, YHWH would make-successful in his hand.

⁴ And Joseph found favor in his eyes, and he served him; and he appointed him over his household, and all that was his, he gave into his hand.

⁵ And it was, from when he appointed him in his household, and over all that was his, and YHWH blessed the house of the Egyptian on account of Joseph; and it was, the blessing of YHWH was on all that was his, in the house and in the field.

This passage repeats over and again the success that was had in the house of Potiphar due to Joseph's diligence and expertise. Potiphar's house is blessed with bounty on account of Joseph, and the effusive language reflects the abundance. The same information could have been conveyed in a single verse, but the effect would be much diminished. Note especially the repetition of key words: מַצְלִיחַ *maṣliaḥ* 'successful' (2x); בֵית-/בַּיִת *bet-/bayit* 'house(hold)' (5x); בְּיָדוֹ *bə-yado* 'in his hand' (2x); the verbal root פ-ק-ד *p-q-d* 'appoint' (2x); the variant phrases וְעַל כָּל־אֲשֶׁר יֶשׁ־לוֹ *wa-kol yeš lo* 'and all that was his' (v. 4), וְכָל־יֶשׁ־לוֹ *wa-ʿal kol ʾašer yeš lo* 'and over all that was his' (v. 5a), and בְּכָל־אֲשֶׁר יֶשׁ־לוֹ *bə-kol ʾašer yeš lo* 'on all that was his' (v. 5b); the root ב-ר-ך *b-r-k* 'bless', once as verb, וַיְבָרֶךְ *waybarɛk* 'and [YHWH] blessed' (v. 5a), once as noun, בִּרְכַּת *birkat* 'blessing (of)'; and of course, יהוה 'YHWH ' (5x).

3. Exodus 7–9 — Pharaoh's stubborn heart

Exod 7:13

וַיֶּחֱזַק לֵב פַּרְעֹה וְלֹא שָׁמַע אֲלֵהֶם כַּאֲשֶׁר דִּבֶּר יְהוָה:

And the heart of Pharaoh was strong, and he did not listen to them, as YHWH had spoken.

Exod 7:22

וַיֶּחֱזַק לֵב־פַּרְעֹה וְלֹא־שָׁמַע אֲלֵהֶם כַּאֲשֶׁר דִּבֶּר יְהוָה:

And the heart of Pharaoh was strong, and he did not listen to them, as YHWH had spoken.

Exod 8:11

וְהַכְבֵּד֙ אֶת־לִבּ֔וֹ וְלֹ֥א שָׁמַ֖ע אֲלֵהֶ֑ם כַּאֲשֶׁ֖ר דִּבֶּ֥ר יְהוָֽה׃

And he made-heavy his heart, and he did not listen to them, as Yhwh had spoken.

Exod 8:15

וַיֶּחֱזַ֤ק לֵב־פַּרְעֹה֙ וְלֹֽא־שָׁמַ֣ע אֲלֵהֶ֔ם כַּאֲשֶׁ֖ר דִּבֶּ֥ר יְהוָֽה׃

And the heart of Pharaoh was strong, and he did not listen to them, as Yhwh had spoken.

Exod 9:12

וַיְחַזֵּ֤ק יְהוָה֙ אֶת־לֵ֣ב פַּרְעֹ֔ה וְלֹ֥א שָׁמַ֖ע אֲלֵהֶ֑ם כַּאֲשֶׁ֛ר דִּבֶּ֥ר יְהוָ֖ה אֶל־מֹשֶֽׁה׃

And Yhwh strengthened the heart of Pharaoh, and he did not listen to them, as Yhwh had spoken to Moses.

Several chapters of this book have been devoted to 'repetition with variation', an omnipresent technique in Biblical Hebrew prose and poetry. On occasion, we have seen departures therefrom, as in the set of passages above, with five instances of וְלֹ֥א שָׁמַ֖ע אֲלֵהֶ֑ם כַּאֲשֶׁ֖ר דִּבֶּ֥ר יְהוָֽה 'and he did not listen to them, as Yhwh had spoken'. In fact, three of these five verses are wholly verbatim: וַיֶּחֱזַק לֵב פַּרְעֹה וְלֹא שָׁמַע אֲלֵהֶם כַּאֲשֶׁר דִּבֶּר יְהוָה (7:13, 7:22, 8:15)—save for the most minor of changes (presence or absence of *maqqef*, as noted in Chapter 3, no. 2). As discussed in Chapter 3, the consistency of the language is an example of 'form follows content': Pharaoh is unwavering in his opposition to the Israelites' leaving Egypt, hence the language is unwavering as well.

4. 1 Samuel 9:12–13 — the prattling girls before Saul

12 . . . יֵ֣שׁ הִנֵּ֤ה לְפָנֶ֙יךָ֙ מַהֵ֔ר ׀ עַתָּ֣ה כִּ֣י הַיּ֗וֹם בָּ֤א לָעִיר֙ כִּ֣י זֶ֧בַח הַיּ֛וֹם לָעָ֖ם בַּבָּמָֽה׃

13 כְּבֹאֲכֶ֣ם הָעִ֗יר כֵּ֣ן תִּמְצְא֣וּן אֹת֡וֹ בְּטֶרֶם֩ יַעֲלֶ֨ה הַבָּמָ֜תָה לֶאֱכֹ֗ל כִּ֠י לֹֽא־יֹאכַ֤ל הָעָם֙ עַד־בֹּא֔וֹ כִּֽי־הוּא֙ יְבָרֵ֣ךְ הַזֶּ֔בַח אַחֲרֵי־כֵ֖ן יֹאכְל֣וּ הַקְּרֻאִ֑ים וְעַתָּ֣ה עֲל֔וּ כִּֽי־אֹת֥וֹ כְהַיּ֖וֹם תִּמְצְא֥וּן אֹתֽוֹ׃

[12] "Yes, here before you; hurry now, because today he is coming to the city, because the sacrifice is today for the people at
the high-place.
[13] When you come to the city, thus you will find him, before
he goes up to the high-place to eat, because the people cannot eat until he comes, because he must bless the sacrifice;
afterward the invited-ones can eat. So now go up, because
him, this very day you will find him.'"

Chapter 8 was devoted to the intentional use of confused language in
the Bible as a means to portray the confusion, excitement, or bewilderment of the moment. There is no need to rehearse all that material
here, though clearly this device fits into the more general category of
'form follows content' studied in this chapter. I elect, accordingly, to
include two examples already treated in Chapter 8 (the present one,
and the next one, concerning Judg 18:17), in order to remind us of those
illustrative passages.

As discussed earlier (Chapter 8, no. 1), the words above comprise
the village maidens' response to the simple question posed by Saul
and his attendant, הֲיֵשׁ בָּזֶה הָרֹאֶה 'Is the seer here?' (v. 11). The literal
translation above allows the reader to comprehend the true intent of
the passage: by the use of such language, the text succeeds in depicting the girls' excitement over seeing the tall, handsome Saul, as they
prattle all at once, creating a cacophony of voices.

5. Judges 18:17 — the looting of Micah's house

In Judg 18:17, the action of the men who disturb and loot Micah's house is described with the phrase בָּאוּ שָׁמָּה לָקְחוּ 'they came
there, they took' (followed by the list of the four items taken). As
noted in Chapter 8, no. 7, several scholars have disapproved of this
phrase. George Foot Moore remarked that "the asyndeton is without
parallel in simple narrative,"[2] while Arnold Ehrlich used the rather
strong term "unhebräisch."[3] But certainly this view is a misunderstanding of what the author attempted to convey here. The lack of

---

2. Moore, *Judges*, 397.
3. Ehrlich, *Randglossen zur Hebräischen Bibel*, 3:146.

the conjunction is an indication of the suddenness by which the men swooped into the house and took the desired items. The text is not 'un-Hebraic', but rather, once more, form follows content: the speeded syntax (if I may use that term) reflects the speed with which the event occurred.

6. 1 Kings 19:10, 14 — steady Elijah

1 Kgs 19:10

קַנֹּא קִנֵּאתִי לַיהוָה | אֱלֹהֵי צְבָאוֹת כִּי־עָזְבוּ בְרִיתְךָ בְּנֵי יִשְׂרָאֵל
אֶת־מִזְבְּחֹתֶיךָ הָרָסוּ וְאֶת־נְבִיאֶיךָ הָרְגוּ בֶחָרֶב וָאִוָּתֵר אֲנִי לְבַדִּי
וַיְבַקְשׁוּ אֶת־נַפְשִׁי לְקַחְתָּהּ:

"I am indeed zealous for YHWH the God of Hosts, for the children of Israel have forsaken your covenant, your altars they have destroyed, and your prophets they have killed by the sword; and I remain, I alone, and they seek my life-force, to take it."

1 Kgs 19:14

קַנֹּא קִנֵּאתִי לַיהוָה | אֱלֹהֵי צְבָאוֹת כִּי־עָזְבוּ בְרִיתְךָ בְּנֵי יִשְׂרָאֵל
אֶת־מִזְבְּחֹתֶיךָ הָרָסוּ וְאֶת־נְבִיאֶיךָ הָרְגוּ בֶחָרֶב וָאִוָּתֵר אֲנִי לְבַדִּי
וַיְבַקְשׁוּ אֶת־נַפְשִׁי לְקַחְתָּהּ:

"I am indeed zealous for YHWH the God of Hosts, for the children of Israel have forsaken your covenant, your altars they have destroyed, and your prophets they have killed by the sword; and I remain, I alone, and they seek my life-force, to take it."

In Chapter 9, no. 21, we saw the workings of repetition with variation within the narrative of Elijah at Mount Horeb in 1 Kings 19. At that time, I observed the converse in Elijah's long answer (now reproduced above) to God's short question, מַה־לְּךָ פֹה אֵלִיָּהוּ *ma ləka po ʾeliyyahu* "Why are you here, Elijah?" (vv. 9, 13). The prophet's response appears verbatim in vv. 10, 14 (letter for letter, vowel for vowel, *ṭaʿam* for *ṭaʿam*), over the course of twenty-four words![4] Presumably, the fact that God's concise question was repeated word for word paves the way for his prophet's response to be stated verbatim. To my mind, however, there is something more significant at play here: given all the other variable phraseology present in 1 Kings 19 (and throughout the Bible), the lack of such variation in Elijah's retort provides the reader/listener with insight into the prophet's character. While the Israelites act not in accordance with God's will—כִּי־עָזְבוּ בְרִיתְךָ ki ʿazbu bəritka 'for they have forsaken your covenant'—Elijah his prophet is one who does not stray, either by action or in his words.

7. Psalm 73:19 — sudden destruction

אֵיךְ הָיוּ לְשַׁמָּה כְרָגַע סָפוּ תַמּוּ מִן־בַּלָּהוֹת:

How they are ruined, so suddenly; at an end, completely, by terrors.

Poetry allows for laxer syntax than prose, though even within poetry the use of asyndeton is quite atypical. As a parallel usage to the example in Judg 18:17 (see above, no. 5), we observe the two-word phrase סָפוּ תַמּוּ sapu tammu, lit., 'they ended, they completed', which follows immediately upon the word כְרָגַע ke-ragaʿ 'so suddenly'. In the translation provided above, I have rendered the two Hebrew verbs very loosely, as adverbials, 'at an end, completely', in an attempt to mimic the effect of a swift and complete ruin. Standard translations capture the hendiadys thus, for example: 'swept away utterly' (RSV), 'wholly swept away' (NJPS)—with one verb and one adverbial, and by deriving the verb from ס-פ-ה s-p-h 'sweep away' (and not from ס-ו-ף s-w-p 'end', as per the Masoretic accents). Regardless, the suddenness of the event is indicated by the Hebrew syntactic construction, with the two verbs juxtaposed, with not even a connective conjunction between them.

---

4. True, I could have presented Elijah's response only once, but the effect of the two verses is realized better upon their full and hence duplicated presentation above.

8. Song 5:6 — the lover's dream

פָּתַחְתִּי אֲנִי לְדוֹדִי וְדוֹדִי חָמַק עָבָר

"I opened for my beloved, but my beloved turned, passed."

Yet another asyndetic phrase is found in Song 5:6, where the verset וְדוֹדִי חָמַק עָבָר *wə-dodi ḥamaq ʿabar* 'but my beloved, turned, passed' (i.e., 'was gone') indicates the instantaneous disappearance of the male lover from the female lover's fantasy.[5] In her remarkably evocative dream, which commences in v. 2 and ends abruptly in v. 6, the female lover has been imagining her beau approaching and entering—both her room and her body, through the splendid employment of a magnificent series of *double entendres*—and then poof, he is gone, as she awakes to the reality of the night. As stated above, his sudden evaporation from her world is expressed by the syntagma חָמַק עָבָר *ḥamaq ʿabar* 'turned, passed', two verbs juxtaposed in rapid succession.

9. Psalm 22:17 — the sudden pounce

כִּי סְבָבוּנִי כְּלָבִים עֲדַת מְרֵעִים הִקִּיפוּנִי כָּאֲרִי יָדַי וְרַגְלָי׃

Yea, dogs surround me, a company of evildoers encircles me;
like a lion—my hands, my feet.

An even greater suddenness can be evoked by the lack of a verb altogether, as occurs in Ps 22:17. The absence of a verb in the second stich indicates the swiftness with which the attack comes. The reader experiences the anguish of the psalmist, who is surrounded by enemies, and then suddenly, the pounce—with the immediate cry about hands and feet under attack. The speed with which a lion (or better, lioness) pounces on its prey is indicated by the speed with which the verse reaches its climactic end, passing over the unnecessary verb in order to highlight the pain of the psalmist as if his very limbs are rent asunder.[6]

---

5. We treated this passage earlier in both Chapter 8, no. 7, and Chapter 17, no. 17.

6. See my earlier treatment: Gary A. Rendsburg, "Hebrew Philological Notes (III)," *Hebrew Studies* 43 (2002): 25–26.

10. Psalm 94:6 — something awry

אַלְמָנָה וְגֵר יַהֲרֹגוּ

וִיתוֹמִים יְרַצֵּחוּ׃

> The widow and the stranger they kill,
> And the orphans they murder.

As we saw above in Chapter 20, both in Hebrew composition and in language universally, the ordering of related words normally proceeds from shorter to longer. Thus, the three individuals requiring special protection from society at large regularly appear in the Bible in the order גֵּר יָתוֹם וְאַלְמָנָה *ger yatom wə-ʾalmana* 'stranger, orphan, and widow' (9x in Deuteronomy, 2x in Jeremiah). In Ps 94:6, by contrast, we find the three words in scrambled order. Even if we were to account for this by the requirements of biblical poetic parallelism, which necessitates splitting up the three members of the expression in uneven fashion, we still are left with the peculiar arrangement. For while one may understand the presence of וִיתוֹמִים *wi-tomim* 'and orphans' (notably in the plural) in the b-line, the reader still would be left puzzled by the order אַלְמָנָה וְגֵר *ʾalmana wə-ger* 'widow and stranger' in the a-line, with the longer before the shorter.

In our earlier treatment (Chapter 20, no. 7), we referred to the aural effect of the reordering, as observed by Patrick Miller, who correctly noticed that the reversal of the two nouns in the first stich allows גֵר *ger* 'stranger' to precede יַהֲרֹגוּ *yaharogu* 'they kill' directly, with the /g/–/r/ ~ /r/–/g/ combination present in the two words. I also indicated, however, that more is at stake. Not only are the actions of the wicked in this verse horrific by any standard, they also run counter to the Torah's call to defend the stranger, orphan, and widow (see especially the list of Deuteronomy passages registered above). Hence, I also would propose that the jumbling of the lexical triad in Ps 94:6 is an instance of form following content. The actions are wrong, contrary to the Torah: hence the wording is wrong, as the poet shuffles the elements of the Torah's regular formulation.

11. The book of Numbers — wandering in the desert

With one exception, each of the books of the Torah appears to be well organized. The book of Genesis has four major cycles (Primeval History, Abraham Cycle, Jacob Cycle, Joseph Story—along with some linking material).[7] The narrative portion of the book of Exodus proceeds in linear fashion from slavery to plagues to exodus to journey to Mount Sinai, etc.; then follows a section of law; and finally, there is the long segment describing the construction of the Tabernacle. The book of Leviticus occurs wholly at Mount Sinai; its contents cohere around the laws and cult of ancient Israel, especially from a priestly perspective; and it too reflects a unique literary design.[8] The book of Deuteronomy is comprised of a series of Moses's farewell discourses to the people of Israel, delivered from the Moab plateau; and within the central portion of the book, the individual laws are organized according to an established pattern.[9]

The one book of the Torah for which scholars have been unable to discern any obvious pattern is the book of Numbers.[10] In the words of Jacob Milgrom, "A striking feature of Numbers is that law (L) and narrative (N) alternate regularly, as follows: 1:1–10:10 (L); 10:11–14:45 (N); 15 (L); 16–17 (N); 18–19 (L); 20–25 (N); 26:1–27:11 (L); 27:12–23 (N); 28–30 (L); 31:1–33:49 (N); 33:50–56; 34–36 (L)."[11] Or, to look at the book in a different manner, again in Milgrom's words,

---

7. See Rendsburg, *Redaction of Genesis.*

8. See Mary Douglas, *Leviticus as Literature* (Oxford: Oxford University Press, 1999); and my study based thereon, Rendsburg, "The Two Screens: On Mary Douglas's Proposal for a Literary Structure to the Book of Leviticus."

9. Kaufman, "Structure of the Deuteronomic Law."

10. Though some have tried, to be sure. See, for example, Mary Douglas, *In the Wilderness: The Doctrine of Defilement in the Book of Numbers* (Journal for the Study of the Old Testament Supplement Series 158; Sheffield: JSOT Press, 1993). While I am thoroughly convinced by Douglas's analysis of the book of Leviticus (see above, n. 8), I find her attempt to find structure in Numbers less compelling. For the most recent survey of opinions, along with a new approach, see Josef Forsling, *Composite Artistry in the Book of Numbers: A Study in Biblical Narrative Conventions* (Studia Theologica Holmiensia 22; Åbo, Finland: Åbo Akademis förlag / Åbo Akademi University Press, 2013); available online at: https://www.doria.fi/bitstream/handle/10024/93413/forsling_josef.pdf.

11. Jacob Milgrom, *Numbers* (JPS Torah Commentary; Philadelphia: Jewish Publication Society, 1990), p. xv.

The generic variety that characterizes Numbers surpasses that of any other book in the Bible. Note these examples: narrative (4:1–3), poetry (21:17–18), prophecy (24:3–9), victory song (21:27–30, pre-Israelite), prayer (12:13), blessing (6:24–26), lampoon (22:22–35), diplomatic letter (21:14–19), civil law (27:1–11), cultic law (15:17–21), oracular decision (15:32–36), census list (26:1–51), temple archive (7:10–88), itinerary (33:1–49).[12]

Occasionally, there are associative links between the two main genres, law and narrative, as in the case of Num 15:39, which reads וְלֹא־תָת֫וּרוּ אַחֲרֵ֣י לְבַבְכֶם֮ וְאַחֲרֵ֣י עֵינֵיכֶ֔ם *wə-loʾ taturu ʾaḥare ləbabkɛm wə-ʾaḥare ʿenekɛm* 'and you shall not follow after your heart and after your eyes', with the verb ת-ו-ר *t-w-r* 'follow after' (in a relatively unique usage here) echoing its repeated presence, with the meaning 'spy, explore', in the narrative of Numbers 13–14 (12x).

By and large, however, the problem remains, for the book of Numbers is—as revealed by Milgrom's two comments cited above—the most meandering of the books of the Torah (even of the Bible as a whole).[13] But that is precisely the point: for the desert journey was a meandering one—in fact, one so confused that even with all the details provided in the wilderness itineraries of the book of Numbers, scholars still have a difficult time reconstructing the specific route. Such is life in the unsettled desert, with a journey here, then there, with a stop here, then there, with the need to turn this way, then that way. Hence, the book of Numbers lacks the obvious structure of the other books of the Torah (and of other books of the Bible), in a remarkable instance of form following content.

---

12. Ibid., p. xiii.

13. With apologies for the use of the word 'meander' here, since the book of Numbers is known in Hebrew as בְּמִדְבַּר *bə-midbar* 'in the wilderness' (after the first key word in Num 1:1, though how fitting for its contents), while the English verb derives from the name of the Meander River in Anatolia (modern Büyük Menderes, in Turkish), characterized by its many twists and turns and bends and windings.

12. The book of Job — tortured language

All scholars have noticed the exceedingly difficult language that dominates the book of Job. Raymond Scheindlin has gone further, however, with the following insightful remark: "the author of Job may have decided that a difficult texture was the right one for his emotionally wrenching theme—a tortured language to describe life's torment."[14] One could not agree more.[15]

---

14. Raymond P. Scheindlin, *The Book of Job* (New York: Norton, 1999), 31.

15. For detailed studies on the language of Job, see especially Greenstein, "The Language of Job and Its Poetic Function," 651–66; and Edward L. Greenstein, "The Invention of Language in the Poetry of Job," in James K. Aitken, Jeremy M. S. Clines, and Christl M. Maier, eds., *Interested Readers: Essays on the Hebrew Bible in Honor of David J. A. Clines* (Atlanta: Society of Biblical Literature, 2013), 332–46.

CHAPTER TWENTY-EIGHT

SOME FINAL ODDITIES

Throughout this book, I have paid attention to linguistic oddities in the Bible, including the presence of rare words, unusual grammatical constructions, and more. Typically I have grouped these in a specific way (under alliteration, style-switching, and so on). In this penultimate chapter, I present a selection of still other textual peculiarities, though they defy categorization and in fact frequently are *sui generis*, even within the extensive biblical corpus.

1. Genesis 20:2

וַיֹּאמֶר אַבְרָהָם אֶל־שָׂרָה אִשְׁתּוֹ אֲחֹתִי הִוא וַיִּשְׁלַח אֲבִימֶלֶךְ מֶלֶךְ גְּרָר וַיִּקַּח אֶת־שָׂרָה:

And Abraham said to Sarah his wife, "She is my sister";
and Abimelech king of Gerar sent (a messenger), and he
took Sarah.

The scene is the arrival of Abraham (and with him Sarah) at the city of Gerar (see v. 1), as part of the patriarch's travels and sojournings in different parts of the land of Canaan. Scholars long have puzzled how Abraham could have said *to* Sarah, "she is my sister"; after all, he must have said this *about* his wife. Hence one finds renderings such as the following: RSV, Robert Alter, "And Abraham said of Sarah his wife"; NJPS, NIV, Tikva Frymer-Kensky, "Abraham said of Sarah his wife"; Everett Fox, "Avraham said of Sara his wife"; Buber-Rosenzweig, "Abraham sprach von Sfara seinem Weibe," and so on.[1] But these modern

---

1. Alter, *Five Books of Moses*, 98; Frymer-Kensky, *Reading the Women of the Bible*, 95; Fox, *Five Books of Moses*, 85; and Martin Buber and Franz Rosenzweig, *Die Schrift* (Gerlingen: Verlag Lambert Schneider, 1976), 1:53.

translations are not the first to solve the apparent problem in this way, for the oldest Jewish translations do likewise. Hence, the Septuagint renders the key word as περί *peri* 'about, concerning', while all three Targumim of the Torah (Onqelos, Neofiti, and Pseudo-Jonathan) use the preposition עַל *ʿal* 'about'.

All of these scholars and translators are/were guided both by common sense (though see below) and by the fact that in Hebrew the prepositions אֶל *ʾel* 'to, for' and עַל *ʿal* 'on, over, about, concerning' are sometimes interchanged. But the confusion between these two words occurs most prominently (in fact, almost exclusively) in the Israelian Hebrew corpus, as I have demonstrated elsewhere.[2] Since there are no indications of northern Israelite material in the Abraham narrative, however, we should look elsewhere for a solution.

Let us return to the parallel account that appears earlier in the Abra(ha)m narrative, in Gen 12:10–20. In this story, as Abram and Sarai enter Egypt to escape the famine in the land of Canaan, the husband requests of his wife, אִמְרִי־נָא אֲחֹתִי אָתְּ *ʾimri naʾ ʾaḥoti ʾat* 'say, please, you are my sister' (v. 13). Later in the episode, after Pharaoh has taken Sarai into his palace, an act that results in the ensuing plagues, he calls for Abram and then berates him with that statement לָמָה אָמַרְתָּ אֲחֹתִי הִוא *lama ʾamarta ʾaḥoti hiʾ* 'why did you say, "she is my sister"?' (v. 19). From the latter we learn that Abram used the very phrase אֲחֹתִי הִוא *ʾaḥoti hiʾ* 'she is my sister' while present in Egypt, a declaration that led to the subsequent events.

With this as background, we return to the verse introduced above, Gen 20:2, which I prefer to interpret as follows. As the couple are entering Gerar, Abraham says *to* Sarah אֲחֹתִי הִוא *ʾaḥoti hiʾ* 'she is my sister', which he had used earlier while in Egypt. The two-word phrase constitutes code-language, which the two understand fully, along the following lines: 'Let's resort to the ruse we used last time, when I went about Egypt saying אֲחֹתִי הִוא *ʾaḥoti hiʾ* "she is my sister"; let's try that again here in Gerar.' (Never mind that the first effort to pass Sarah off as his sister got them into a heap of trouble.) And for added effect, I imagine Abraham sticking his elbow into Sarah's rib at this point, or whatever the ancient Israelite non-verbal communication equivalent

---

2. Rendsburg, *Israelian Hebrew in the Book of Kings*, 32–36.

might have been, to drive home the point. Understood this way, there is no need for translational gymnastics: the text means what is says, 'And Abraham said to Sarah his wife, "She is my sister." '

2. Genesis 38:25

וַתֹּאמֶר הַכֶּר־נָא לְמִי הַחֹתֶמֶת וְהַפְּתִילִים וְהַמַּטֶּה הָאֵלֶּה:

watto'mɛr hakkɛr na' lə-mi ha-ḥotɛmɛt wə-hap-pətilim wə-ham-maṭṭɛ ha-'ellɛ

And she said, "Recognize please, to whom (belong) these: the seale [*sic*], and the cords, and the staff?"

This verse appears near the denouement of the Judah and Tamar story, with Tamar addressing Judah as quoted above. The linguistic oddity here is the word חֹתֶמֶת *ḥotɛmɛt* 'seale' (see anon for this spelling). Throughout the history of the Hebrew language—indeed, throughout the history of other ancient Near Eastern languages as well, including Egyptian, Phoenician, Ammonite, Aramaic-Syriac, Arabic, etc.—the noun is universally masculine: in Hebrew, for example, חוֹתָם *ḥotam* 'seal' (16x).[3] In fact, the word occurs in this standard masculine form earlier in this very story, when Tamar (disguised as a prostitute) requested the seal and the other objects in the first place (see v. 18). Only in Gen 38:25 in all of Hebrew and its cognate languages does the word appear as feminine: חֹתֶמֶת *ḥotɛmɛt* 'seale'. To mark this difference, I have taken advantage of the early modern English spelling 'seale', as attested in, for example, Shakespeare, *The Merchant of Venice*, Act IV, Scene 1, and *A Midsummer Night's Dream*, Act III, Scene 2.[4]

---

3. To be more honest, there is one single exception, in ancient Egyptian, where the feminine form *ḥtmt* is attested in the tomb inscription of Nebwenenef in Thebes, dated to the 19th Dynasty, though most likely the meaning is 'ring' rather than 'seal'. For details, see Adolf Erman, *Wörterbuch der ägyptischen Sprache* (Berlin: Akademie-Verlag, 1982), 3:350; and Adolf Erman, *Wörterbuch der ägyptischen Sprache: Die Belegstellen* (Berlin: Akademie-Verlag, 1982), 3:72.

4. See *OED*, s.v. 'seal' *n.*².

But why use this odd feminine form? And is it a real form that was in use in ancient Hebrew, even if attested only here in the Bible? The answer to these questions and the key to our analysis comes from the fuller context of v. 25 and the first two words of v. 26. The text reads as follows (most of it appears above):

25 וַתֹּאמֶר הַכֶּר־נָא לְמִי הַחֹתֶמֶת וְהַפְּתִילִים וְהַמַּטֶּה הָאֵלֶּה: 26 וַיַּכֵּר יְהוּדָה

25 *watto'mɛr hakkɛr na' lǝ-mi ha-ḥotɛmɛt wǝ-hap-pǝtilim wǝ-ham-maṭṭɛ ha-'ellɛ* 26 *wayyakkɛr yǝhuda*

25 And she said, "Recognize please, to whom (belong) these: the seale, and the cords, and the staff?" 26 And Judah recognized.

As numerous scholars have observed, this passage links the story of Judah and Tamar to the story of Joseph in the preceding chapter.[5] The pertinent wording there is (Gen 37:32–33):

32 וַיֹּאמְרוּ זֹאת מָצָאנוּ הַכֶּר־נָא הַכְּתֹנֶת בִּנְךָ הִוא אִם־לֹא: 33 וַיַּכִּירָהּ

32 *wayyomru zo't maṣa'nu hakkɛr na' hak-kǝtonɛt binka hi' 'im lo'* 33 *wayyakkirah*

32 And they said, "This we found, recognize please, is this the tunic of your son, or not?" 33 And he recognized it.

Because the key noun in the Joseph story is the feminine form הַכְּתֹנֶת *hak-kǝtonɛt* 'the tunic', the author placed into Tamar's mouth the feminine form הַחֹתֶמֶת *ha-ḥotɛmɛt* 'the seale'. The two are of similar morphological structure and they sound alike. Everyone who reads Gen 38:25 is taken back to Gen 37:32, and the author has solidified the link with the unique form חֹתֶמֶת *ḥotɛmɛt* 'seale'. Almost without a doubt, the author of our story created the word for the specific literary purpose

---

5. See Rendsburg, *Redaction of Genesis*, 93, n. 32. The earliest individual to recognize this point was Rabbi Yoḥanan in Bereshit Rabba 85:2. For a recent, more detailed treatment, see Alter, *Art of Biblical Narrative*, 2–3, 10–11.

just described—something between a neologism and a portmanteau word, what some scholars term a 'stunt word'.

Finally, it is important to note that the reading tradition of the Torah seems to have noted the connection as well. The string of accent marks is the same for both phrases, to wit (reading from right to left), ׀ ו ײ ֖ , as follows:

Gen 37:32

הַכְּתֹנֶת בִּנְךָ הִוא אִם־לֹא

hak-kətonɛt binka hi' 'im lo'

is this the tunic of your son, or not?

Gen 38:25

הַחֹתֶמֶת וְהַפְּתִילִים וְהַמַּטֶּה הָאֵלֶּה

ha-ḥotɛmɛt wə-hap-pətilim wə-ham-maṭṭɛ ha-'ellɛ

these: the seale, and the cords, and the staff?

In both cases we encounter the series *darga, tevir, tifḥa,* and *silluq.*[6]

3. Genesis 35:22; 49:4

Gen 35:22

וַיְהִי בִּשְׁכֹּן יִשְׂרָאֵל בָּאָרֶץ הַהִוא וַיֵּלֶךְ רְאוּבֵן וַיִּשְׁכַּב אֶת־בִּלְהָה
פִּילֶגֶשׁ אָבִיו וַיִּשְׁמַע יִשְׂרָאֵל [פ] וַיִּהְיוּ בְנֵי־יַעֲקֹב שְׁנֵים עָשָׂר׃

And it was, when Israel dwelt in that land, and Reuben went, and he lay with Bilhah, the concubine of his father; and Israel heard. [P] And the sons of Jacob were twelve.

---

6. Admittedly, this is a common string in the Bible, but no other instance of this sequence occurs between the two interrelated verses of Gen 37:32 and Gen 38:25, so that the reader is thereby guided to make the connection. The verses with the same series of accent marks closest to the two cited passages are Gen 37:15 (preceding) and Gen 40:23 (following). I have utilized the information provided in James D. Price, *Concordance of the Hebrew Accents in the Hebrew Bible* (Lewiston, NY: Mellen, 1996), 1:148, in order to isolate these examples.

Gen 49:4

פַּחַז כַּמַּיִם אַל־תּוֹתַר כִּי עָלִיתָ כִּי מִשְׁכְּבֵי אָבִיךָ אָז חִלַּלְתָּ אָז יְצוּעִי עָלָה׃

"Wily as water, do not surpass, for you went-up on the
bed of your father; then you profaned—on my couch he
went-up."

The first of these passages offers something relatively uncommon in
the Bible, what in Hebrew is called פסקה באמצע פסוק *pisqa bə-ʾemṣaʿ
pasuq* 'a break in the middle of a verse', indicated in the actual manuscripts with a sizable chunk of white space in the text.[7] In the presentation of Gen 35:22 above, I have indicated this break with the
bolded Hebrew letter [פ] *pe* within brackets, denoted in the English
rendering with the equivalent letter [P].[8] The effect on the reader is
as follows: Reuben sleeps with Bilhah, Jacob learns about the affair,
but he takes no action. Instead, there is stark silence, represented by
the blank space in the text—until the passage continues in remarkably bland fashion with the listing of Jacob's twelve sons (vv. 23–26),

---

7. There are several dozen such instances in the Bible, depending on the
manuscript. According to one scholar's attempt to quantify the number of
examples, there are thirty sure instances; see Moshe Zvi Segal, "Le-Ḥeqer
ha-<Pisqaʾ be-ʾEmṣaʿ Pasuq>," *Tarbiz* 29 (1960): 203–6. Of these, only three
occur in the Torah (Gen 35:22, Num 27:1, Deut 2:8), with one each in Joshua,
Judges, Kings, and Ezekiel, and then a whopping twenty-three cases in Samuel.
For discussion, see Shemaryahu Talmon, "*Pisqah beʾEmṣaʿ Pasuq* and 11QPsª,"
Textus 5 (1966): 11–21 [reprinted in Shemaryahu Talmon, *Text and Canon of
the Hebrew Bible: Collected Studies* (Winona Lake, IN: Eisenbrauns, 2010),
369–82]; and more recently and more succinctly, Tov, *Textual Criticism of
the Hebrew Bible*, 50–51.

8. The [פ]/[P] siglum stands for the Hebrew word פתוחה *pətuḥa*, lit.,
'opened', a technical term devised by the Masoretes for a type of paragraph
break indicated by white space within the text. Almost always, such paragraph
breaks occur at the end of a verse in a fitting spot, or at the end of a narrative or section of narrative. The oddity here is the placement of this scribal
marker within the middle of a verse! There are other Masoretic peculiarities
here, e.g., (a) the use of two *ʾatnaḥ* markers in the lead-up to the white space;
and (b) the use of both *ʾatnaḥ* and *silluq* 'end of verse' markers on the word
יִשְׂרָאֵל *yiśraʾel* 'Israel'—even though technically the end of the verse has not
been reached.

introduced with the clause וַיִּהְיוּ בְנֵי־יַעֲקֹב שְׁנֵים עָשָׂר *wayyihyu bəne ya'aqob šənem 'aśar* 'And the sons of Jacob were twelve' (v. 22b). The performer of this text would read the mini-account of Reuben's action, then pause for several seconds, with our imagined audience waiting with bated breath[9] for the continuation—until the presenter carried on (and perhaps thereby disappointed his audience) with the insipid listing of Jacob's twelve sons.

Fourteen chapters later in the canonical organization of the book of Genesis, in 49:4—by which point the listeners to our text may long have forgotten the entire episode (entire, ha!—it is narrated in nine words)—the text returns to Reuben's dalliance with Bilhah. The context is Jacob's deathbed blessings to his twelve sons, though to be sure the first three sons, Reuben prime among them, receive critique rather than blessing. The most direct line, within the poetry placed into Jacob's mouth, is: כִּי עָלִיתָ מִשְׁכְּבֵי אָבִיךָ *ki 'alita miškəbe 'abika* 'for you went-up on the bed of your father', which serves to bring the reader's mind back to the tersely told episode in Gen 35:22. The astute listener to this verse will be braced for this declaration from the opening word of Gen 49:4, פַּחַז *paḥaz*, a rare lexeme, translated here as 'wily, beguiling, deceitful', but having sexual overtones as well, as may be seen by a nod to its Modern South Arabian cognate, the verb *f-ḫ-ḏ*, with the very specific meaning 'to arrange the thighs of a woman for sexual intercourse'[10]—even if the entire expression is not patient of easy explication: פַּחַז כַּמַּיִם אַל־תּוֹתַר *paḥaz kam-mayim 'al totar* 'wily as water, do not surpass'.

But the most interesting literary effect of Gen 49:4 comes at the end: יְצוּעִי עָלָה *yəṣu'i 'ala* 'on my couch he went-up'. All of a sudden, Jacob, who has been addressing Reuben until now, indeed since v. 3, refers to him in the third person: 'on my couch he went-up'. The effect here is the following: Jacob interrupts his speaking to Reuben in order to turn to the audience, breaking the 'fourth wall', as this procedure is called

9. I take the opportunity to note that the first attestation of the expression 'bated breath' is found in Shakespeare, *The Merchant of Venice*, Act I, Scene 3 (spoken by Shylock)—and also to point out the alliteration inherent in this phrase.

10. See Aaron D. Rubin, "Genesis 49:4 in Light of Arabic and Modern South Arabian," *Vetus Testamentum* 59 (2009): 499–502.

in theatrical performance. Examples range from tragedy to comedy, from Shakespeare (in *Richard III* most prominently) to Groucho Marx (in *Animal Crackers*), but here we have the biblical author employing this technique three thousand years ago.[11]

At the very point when the audience has forgotten about Reuben's actions, those gathered to listen to the reader's performance are reminded of what transpired, not by the author per se, but by Jacob himself, who indeed heard and kept his silence back in Gen 35:22 (hence the 'break in the middle of the verse'), only to reveal his knowledge in the most forthright fashion, directly to the audience—as if to say, "You see, you thought I had forgotten about the matter entirely, just as you have, but no, I have kept it within me all these years, only to produce it now, for the greatest impact, removing Reuben from my line of succession." And not only for the greatest impact, but also for the greatest literary effect.

Excursus: One would like to know, of course, how old is the tradition of including a *petuḥa* paragraph break in the middle of Gen 35:22. The older of the two great medieval codices, the Aleppo Codex (Tiberias, ca. 930 c.e.), lacks all of Genesis and indeed most of the Torah, so there is no way of determining this manuscript's scribal practice on our verse. However, since Maimonides (1140–1205) held this manuscript in the greatest esteem, and since Maimonides affirmed the presence of a *petuḥa* break in the middle of Gen 35:22, one will presume that the Aleppo Codex attested to such.

The second great medieval codex, that of St. Petersburg (Leningrad) (Tiberias, 1009 c.e.), is completely extant, with the *petuḥa* break in place, as one would expect. See Figure 5 (on the next page), where there is a small amount of white space at the end of the line after the phrase וַיִּשְׁמַע יִשְׂרָאֵל *wayyišmaʿ yiśraʾel* 'and Israel heard', and then a full line of white space following.

---

11. Most biblical scholars, devoid of literary sensitivity (apparently), simply emend the text, so that Jacob continues in the second person.

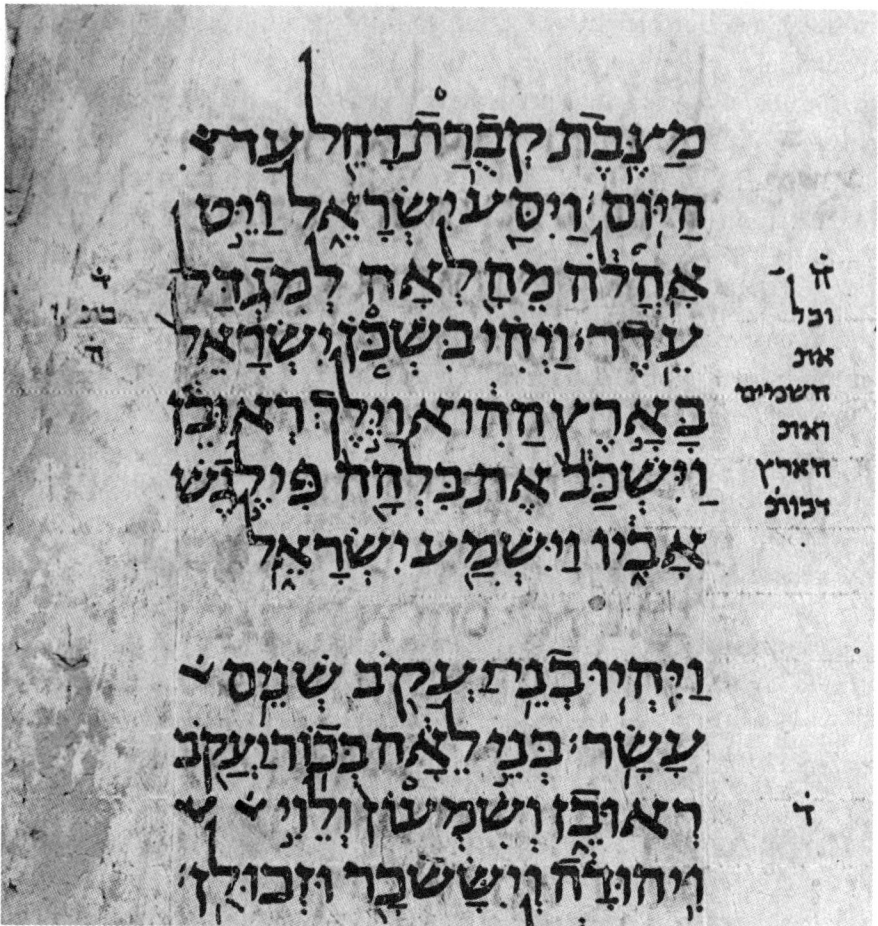

FIGURE 5: Gen 35:22 as presented in the St. Petersburg (Leningrad) Codex, folio 21v, column 3. [Photograph by Bruce and Kenneth Zuckerman, West Semitic Research, in collaboration with the Ancient Biblical Manuscript Center. Courtesy Russian National Library (Saltykov-Shchedrin).]

One could continue to cite other instances of medieval manuscripts, including unpointed Torah scrolls with the white space in place, though it will suffice here to refer to Bayerische Staatsbibliothek, Cod.hebr. 487 (Germany, ca. 1400 C.E.), since it has been the subject of a thorough investigation by Josef Oesch.[12] See Figure 6 for the layout of Gen 35:22 in this Torah scroll.

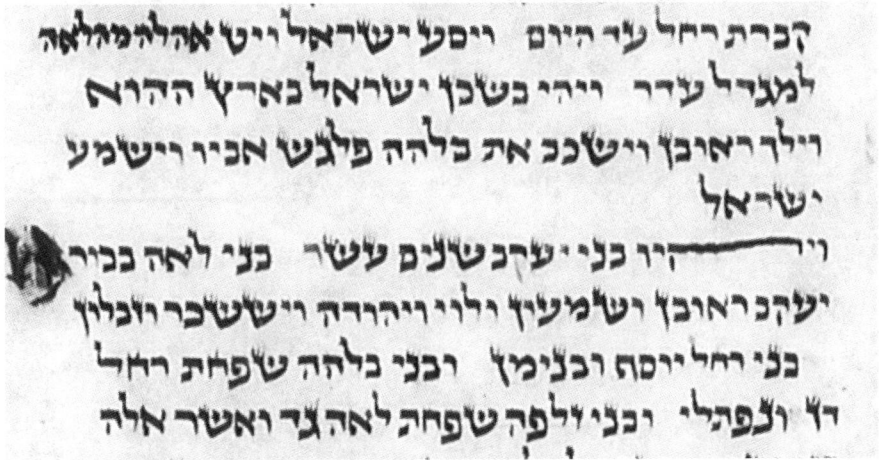

FIGURE 6: Gen 35:22 as presented in Bayerische Staatsbibliothek, Cod.hebr. 487, fol. 36r. [Used with kind permission of the Bayerische Staatsbibliothek (Munich).]

All well and good for medieval documents, but what about further back in the history of Jewish biblical manuscripts? This question leads us, of course, to the Dead Sea Scrolls. Fortunately, Gen 35:22 is attested in one document, namely, 4Q1 = 4QGen-Exod[a], frg. 5—though naturally the specific information we seek is unattested in the fragment, since it breaks off just at the point where the manuscript would reveal the presence or absence of a paragraph break. And how often does this happen in Dead Sea Scrolls research! Figure 7 (on the next page) presents the text.

---

12. Josef M. Oesch, "Skizze einer formalen Gliederungshermeneutik der Sifre Tora," in Marjo C. A. Korpel and Josef M. Oesch, eds., *Unit Delimitation in Biblical Hebrew and Northwest Semitic Literature* (Pericope 4; Assen: Van Gorcum, 2003), 162–203 (see esp. the chart on 198–200).

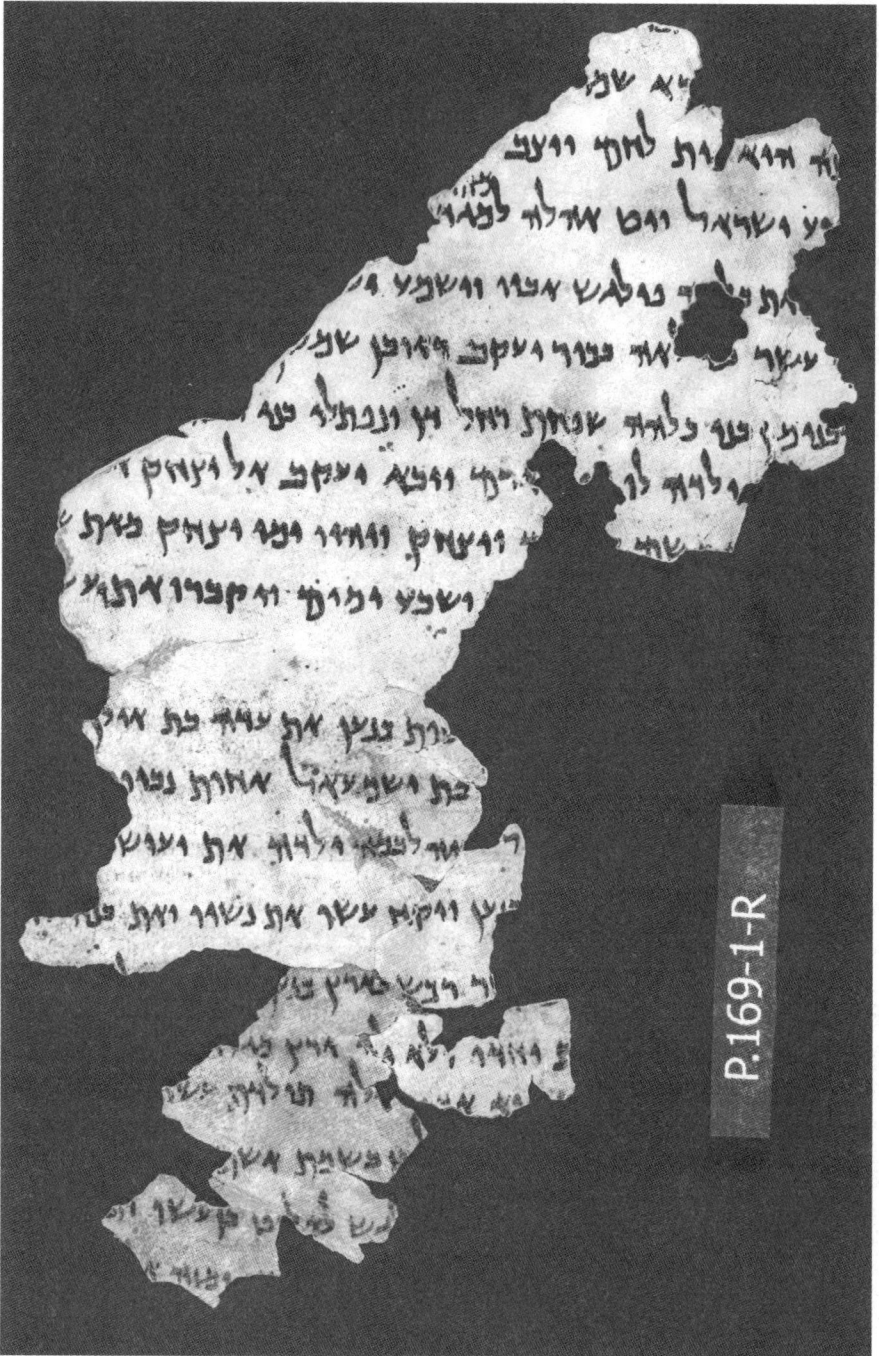

FIGURE 7: 4Q1 = 4QGen-Exodᵃ, frg. 5.
[Used with kind permission of the Israel Antiquities Authority (Jerusalem).]

The fourth line of writing reads as follows:

אֵת בל[ה]הֹ פילגש אביו וישמע יש[ראל]

]'T BL[H]H PYLGŠ 'BYW WYŠMʿ YŚ[RʾL

]Bil[h]ah the concubine of his father, and Is[rael] heard

Now, the editor of this text, James Davila, observed as follows regarding the line in which Gen 35:22a occurs: "The last 12–15 letter-spaces may be reconstructed as blank, or could contain the G [= LXX] addition."[13] Which is to say, if one reconstructs the missing parts of the fragmentary document (see Figure 7 above), one would notice that the line that includes Gen 35:22a is much shorter than all the other lines, by about twelve to fifteen letter-spaces. So something must have been there, either white space or some extra words. The addition to which Davila refers is an extra phrase that occurs in the Septuagint, namely, 'and it seemed evil in his sight', with a presumed Hebrew *Vorlage* וירע בעיניו WYRʿ BʿYNYW.[14]

Is there any way to judge which is the more likely option? To my mind, the white space is more probable, for the following reason. If one works through all of 4QGen-Exod[a], one notices that this document aligns much more frequently with the Masoretic Text than it does with the Septuagint.[15] And while this is not a foolproof argument, to my mind this evidence tilts the conclusion in the direction of the white-space option.[16]

---

13. James R. Davila, "4QGen-Exod[a]," in Eugene Ulrich and Frank Moore Cross, eds., *Qumran Cave 4/VII* (Discoveries in the Judaean Desert XII; Oxford: Clarendon, 1994), 10. See also his comment on p. 12.

14. I adopt the translation of the Greek from Robert J. V. Hiebert, "Genesis," in Albert Pietersma and Benjamin G. Wright, eds., *A New English Translation of the Septuagint* (New York: Oxford University Press, 2007), 30.

15. Notwithstanding an occasional counterexample, most famously, the use of 'seventy-five' and not 'seventy' in Exod 1:5, on which see Davila, "4QGen-Exod[a]," 18–19.

16. In addition, note that the presumed two-word Hebrew phrase וירע בעיניו WYRʿ BʿYNYW 'and it seemed evil in his eyes' comprises only eleven letter-spaces, four of which are *waw* and *yod*, which take up less space than the other letters of the alphabet. As such, the line still would be shorter than the other lines in the manuscript.

Most likely, then, our oldest witness to Gen 35:22 included the paragraph break in the middle of the verse. This visual sign serves to instruct the presenter of this text to pause after the words וישמע ישראל wyšmʿ yśrʾl 'and Israel heard'—thereby providing the dramatic hiatus described above before he continued with the remainder of the verse.

4. Leviticus 8:15, 19, 23

Lev 8:15

וַיִּשְׁחָ֓ט וַיִּקַּ֨ח מֹשֶׁ֤ה אֶת־הַדָּם֙ וַיִּתֵּ֜ן עַל־קַרְנ֨וֹת הַמִּזְבֵּ֤חַ סָבִיב֙ בְּאֶצְבָּע֔וֹ

And he slaughtered; and Moses took the blood, and he put (it) on the horns of the altar around, with his finger.

Lev 8:19

וַיִּשְׁחָ֑ט וַיִּזְרֹ֨ק מֹשֶׁ֧ה אֶת־הַדָּ֛ם עַל־הַמִּזְבֵּ֖חַ סָבִֽיב׃

And he slaughtered; and Moses dashed the blood on the altar around.

Lev 8:23

וַיִּשְׁחָ֓ט ׀ וַיִּקַּ֨ח מֹשֶׁה֙ מִדָּמ֔וֹ וַיִּתֵּ֛ן עַל־תְּנ֥וּךְ אֹֽזֶן־אַהֲרֹ֖ן הַיְמָנִ֑ית וְעַל־בֹּ֤הֶן יָדוֹ֙ הַיְמָנִ֔ית וְעַל־בֹּ֖הֶן רַגְל֥וֹ הַיְמָנִֽית׃

And he slaughtered; and Moses took of its blood, and he put (it) on the right earlobe of Aaron, and on his right thumb, and on his right big toe.

These three verses display the following grammatical curiosity. The verb וַיִּשְׁחָט wayyišḥaṭ 'and he slaughtered' stands by itself at the beginning of the verse, each time with its own disjunctive accent (indicated by semicolon in the translation), reviaʿ, ʾatnaḥ, and šalšelet, respectively. Two points may be noted. First, almost never does a verse begin with a word marked by a disjunctive accent, especially one that indicates a higher-level disjuncture (which is certainly true of the ʾatnaḥ and šalšelet, even if less so with the reviaʿ).[17] Secondly, when two verbs are

---

17. See Israel Yeivin, *Introduction to the Tiberian Masorah*, trans. E. J. Revell (Missoula, MT: Society of Biblical Literature, 1980), 169.

predicated of a single subject, the typical word order is: verb₁ + subject + verb₂; in the three verses from Leviticus 8 cited above, however, the word order is: verb₁ + verb₂ + subject. Examples of the standard syntax are as follows (four from prose texts, one from a prophetic text):

Gen 14:13

וַיָּבֹא הַפָּלִיט וַיַּגֵּד לְאַבְרָם הָעִבְרִי

And the escapee came, and he told Abram the Hebrew.

Gen 22:13

וַיֵּלֶךְ אַבְרָהָם וַיִּקַּח אֶת־הָאַיִל

And Abraham went, and he took the ram.

Gen 26:13

וַיִּגְדַּל הָאִישׁ וַיֵּלֶךְ הָלוֹךְ וְגָדֵל

And the man [sc. Isaac] grew, and he went going and growing.

2 Sam 5:17

וַיִּשְׁמַע דָּוִד וַיֵּרֶד אֶל־הַמְצוּדָה:

And David heard, and he went down to the citadel.

Mal 3:16

וַיַּקְשֵׁב יְהוָה וַיִּשְׁמָע

And Yʜwʜ heeded, and he heard.

In light of this standard usage, why, then, does Leviticus 8 present the atypical wording 3x? The issue lies in the following conundrum. This chapter of the Torah describes the investiture of Aaron and his sons as priests who henceforth will administer the cult, including the slaughtering and sacrificing of animals. But how can they slaughter the respective animals (one bull and two rams, in this ceremony) if they are not yet priests? And yet Moses cannot perform this act either, for while he is from the tribe of Levi, he is not a priest. The solution, accordingly, is to *imply* that Moses was the slaughterer, but not to state so explicitly. Though another interpretation also is possible, namely, that the subject of וַיִּשְׁחָט *wayyišḥaṭ* 'and he slaughtered' is an impersonal 'he', hence to be rendered 'and one slaughtered'. Either way, the result is an ingenious sentence structure, with the phrase 'and he/one slaughtered' at the outset, a disjuncture marking this clause off from the rest of the verse, and then the remainder of the action with Moses as clear subject of the ensuing verb(s).[18] One can only marvel at the inventive mind of the ancient author who devised this linguistic solution to the religious challenge at hand.

5. Deuteronomy 16:6

כִּי אִם־אֶל־הַמָּקֹום אֲשֶׁר־יִבְחַר יְהוָה אֱלֹהֶיךָ לְשַׁכֵּן שְׁמֹו שָׁם תִּזְבַּח
אֶת־הַפֶּסַח בָּעָרֶב

But rather unto the place that YHWH your God shall choose
to cause his name to dwell, there shall you sacrifice the
passover-offering at evening.

In truth, there is nothing odd about this verse at all, since it reads perfectly smoothly and makes perfect sense.[19] The oddity, however, is

---

18. This interpretation, I must add, obviates the solution (less ingenious, to my mind) proferred by many scholars and translators, including one of the most sensitive readers of biblical literature—which is to render the verb in the passive. Note, for example, NRSV, NJPS, and Alter, *Five Books of Moses*, 573–74, with the rendering 'and it was slaughtered' (in addition to which the phrase is affixed to the end of the preceding verse). For the impersonal understanding of the verb, note the translation 'man metzte' by Buber and Rosenzweig, *Die Schrift* 1:292, standing as a clause unto itself in the text's colometry. See also Fox, *Five Books of Moses*, 540–41. who retains the active form with 'and he slew (it)', though he too affixes the phrase to the end of the preceding verse.

19. I should note here that the force of Deut 16:6 (see also vv. 2 and 7, with repetition for emphasis) is to counter the command given in Exod 12:3–8, by which each family is to observe its own passover-offering ceremony in individual households. One of the major themes of the book of Deuteronomy is the centralization of worship at a single sanctuary site, so that even the passover-offering must take place at the central shrine. On the specific point, see Tigay, *Deuteronomy*, 155. On the general concept, see in the same volume, Excursus 14, "The Restriction of Sacrifice to a Single Sanctuary," 459–64.

the pause between the words שְׁמוֹ *šəmo* 'his name' and שָׁם *šam* 'there', as indicated by the comma in the above translation. Upon seeing the juxtaposition of these two small words (which, as an aside, actually look alike and share the same consonants [šmw ~ šm]), the informed reader of the book of Deuteronomy expects the two to flow together. Note the following seven passages elsewhere in the book where such occurs, including two instances in ch. 16:[20]

Deut 12:5

כִּי אִם־אֶל־הַמָּקוֹם אֲשֶׁר־יִבְחַר יְהוָה אֱלֹהֵיכֶם מִכָּל־שִׁבְטֵיכֶם
לָשׂוּם אֶת־שְׁמוֹ שָׁם

> But rather unto the place that Yʜwʜ your God
> shall choose from among all your tribes to place *his*
> *name there*;

Deut 12:11

וְהָיָה הַמָּקוֹם אֲשֶׁר־יִבְחַר יְהוָה אֱלֹהֵיכֶם בּוֹ לְשַׁכֵּן שְׁמוֹ שָׁם

> And it will be the place that Yʜwʜ your God shall
> choose to cause *his name* to dwell *there*,

Deut 12:21

כִּי־יִרְחַק מִמְּךָ הַמָּקוֹם אֲשֶׁר יִבְחַר יְהוָה אֱלֹהֶיךָ לָשׂוּם שְׁמוֹ שָׁם

> If the place that Yʜwʜ your God shall choose to place *his*
> *name there* is too far for you;

---

20. In the translations that follow, note (a) the use of italics for our key phrase; (b) the use at the beginning of the translation of either an uppercase letter, which indicates the start of the verse, or a lowercase letter, which indicates that the quoted text begins in the middle of the verse; and (c) the employment at the end of the translation of either a period (full stop), which indicates that the quoted text ends the verse, or another punctuation mark (comma or semicolon), which signals that the quoted text ends in the middle of the verse, with the specific mark chosen based on the degree of disjuncture. Regarding (a) above, in several instances English usage has required the insertion of the infinitive 'to dwell' between *his name* and *there*, though in the Hebrew original the two key words nonetheless appear side by side: שְׁמוֹ שָׁם *šəmo šam* 'his name there'.

Deut 14:24

כִּי־יִרְחַק מִמְּךָ֙ הַמָּק֔וֹם אֲשֶׁ֤ר יִבְחַר֙ יְהוָ֣ה אֱלֹהֶ֔יךָ לָשׂ֥וּם שְׁמ֖וֹ שָׁ֑ם

if the place that Yhwh your God shall choose to place *his name there* is too far for you;

Deut 16:2

בַּמָּקוֹם֙ אֲשֶׁר־יִבְחַ֣ר יְהוָ֔ה לְשַׁכֵּ֥ן שְׁמ֖וֹ שָֽׁם׃

at the place that Yhwh shall choose to cause *his name* to dwell *there*.

Deut 16:11

בַּמָּק֔וֹם אֲשֶׁ֤ר יִבְחַר֙ יְהוָ֣ה אֱלֹהֶ֔יךָ לְשַׁכֵּ֥ן שְׁמ֖וֹ שָֽׁם׃

at the place that Yhwh your God shall choose to cause *his name* to dwell *there*.

Deut 26:2

וְהָלַכְתָּ֙ אֶל־הַמָּק֔וֹם אֲשֶׁ֤ר יִבְחַר֙ יְהוָ֣ה אֱלֹהֶ֔יךָ לְשַׁכֵּ֥ן שְׁמ֖וֹ שָֽׁם׃

And you shall go to the place that Yhwh your God shall choose to cause *his name* to dwell *there*.

In the light of this series of passages, both the reader of and the listener to Deuteronomy have every reason to expect the word שָׁם *šam* 'there' to occur in a single breath after שְׁמוֹ *šǝmo* 'his name'. Not so fast, though, says our clever author, for in this case, in Deut 16:6, he has disjoined the two words, with שְׁמוֹ *šǝmo* 'his name' ending one clause, and with שָׁם *šam* 'there' beginning the next one. Clever indeed, very clever.

6. Judges 4:20

וַיֹּ֣אמֶר אֵלֶ֗יהָ עֲמֹ֛ד פֶּ֥תַח הָאֹ֖הֶל וְהָיָ֡ה אִם־אִישׁ֩ יָב֨וֹא וּשְׁאֵלֵ֜ךְ וְאָמַ֗ר
הֲיֵֽשׁ־פֹּ֥ה אִ֖ישׁ וְאָמַ֥רְתְּ אָֽיִן׃

And he [sc. Sisera] said to her [sc. Yael], "Stand at the entrance of the tent; and it will be, if a man comes and asks you, and says, 'Is there a man here?', then you shall say, 'None'."

The setting of this verse is as follows: Sisera, the Canaanite general, has fled from Barak's army and has taken refuge in the tent of Yael, whom he assumes to be an ally (see v. 17). The oddity is the following: Sisera addresses Yael using the masc. sg. imperative form עֲמֹד *ʿamod* (more properly *ʿămōd*, in standard Biblical Hebrew transliteration) 'stand!', when naturally one would expect to find the feminine form עִמְדִי *ʿimdi* 'stand!' (not attested in the Bible, but reconstructible from the verbal paradigm). Most scholars are content to emend the text here,[21] but D. F. Murray astutely discovered the literary device at play here.[22] Sisera is a general who spends his life ordering soldiers about, barking commands at them in the masculine singular form—especially, one might assume, the command 'stand!', as in 'stand here!', 'stand there!', 'stand guard!', and so on. It is as if he sees Yael as yet another subordinate to be ordered about, and/or is so masculine in his work that he does not even know the feminine form![23] All of which, of course, serves in stark contrast to Yael's infantilizing him, if not emasculating him, in the surrounding verses (vv. 19, 21). In short, the Masoretic Text should stand. And if any statement should serve as the final comment in this book, let it be that: *stet*.

---

21. Either by reading the infinitive absolute עֲמֹד *ʿamod* (more properly *ʿămōd*, in standard Biblical Hebrew transliteration), which can serve as the imperative in Biblical Hebrew grammar, hence, also 'stand!'; or by restoring the *yod*, to produce the aforecited fem. sg. imperative form עִמְדִי *ʿimdi*.

22. D. F. Murray, "Narrative Structure and Technique in the Deborah-Barak Story, Judges iv 4–22," in John A. Emerton, ed., *Studies in the Historical Books of the Old Testament* (Supplements to Vetus Testamentum 30; Leiden: Brill, 1979), 183 n. 49: "Sisera now passes from addressing Jael with polite request to commanding her as though she were one of his troops (hence the *masculine* imperative)."

23. Though to be fair, Sisera does use a feminine imperative form when, addressing Yael in v. 19, he says, הַשְׁקִינִי־נָא מְעַט־מַיִם *hašqini naʾ məʿaṭ mayim* 'give-drink to me please, a little water'.

CHAPTER TWENTY-NINE

GENESIS 29: PUTTING IT ALL TOGETHER

Well, not quite the final comment, for we have one more chapter. In this the final chapter of the book, I present an analysis of a single narrative prose chapter, in order to demonstrate how all (or at least much) of what we have discussed above coalesces to create a unified story. In theory, I could select virtually any chapter of biblical narrative prose as my specimen, though I have elected Genesis 29, if for no other reason than the tale of Jacob and Rachel at the well remains one of my favorite episodes in the Bible.[1] In addition, ending the book in this manner, with an analysis of a single narrative in the book of Genesis, serves as a nice bookend to the first chapter, which was devoted to Genesis 1, the first creation account. And this too, incidentally, is a literary device in the Bible, known to scholars as 'inclusio' or 'envelope structure'.[2] We proceed in a verse-by-verse fashion.[3]

Verse 1

וַיִּשָּׂא יַעֲקֹב רַגְלָיו וַיֵּלֶךְ אַרְצָה בְנֵי־קֶדֶם:

And Jacob lifted-up his feet, and he went to the land of the Bene Qedem.

---

1. Yes, even so-called objective scholars can have their favorites!

2. See, for example, Gary A. Rendsburg, "The Inclusio in Leviticus xi," *Vetus Testamentum* 43 (1993): 418–21.

3. I end the verse-by-verse analysis with 29:30, even though the chapter continues with five more verses. While there is no paragraph division here in the main Tiberian Masoretic tradition, the older system of Sedarim marks a Seder (section) break both before 29:1 and after 29:30, indicating that ancient Jewish readers understood these thirty verses as comprising a story unto itself. The St. Petersburg (Leningrad) Codex and related manuscripts mark these Seder breaks with a large *samekh* (ס) in the margin.

This short verse very quickly transitions the reader from the family home in the land of Canaan to the land of the Bene Qedem, that is, 'the Easterners'. This geographical term seems to cover a wide swath of land, though as we learn from the ensuing material, it clearly embraces the area of Aram, including the city of Harran (in modern-day southern Turkey).

Verse 2

וַיַּרְא וְהִנֵּה בְאֵר בַּשָּׂדֶה וְהִנֵּה־שָׁם שְׁלֹשָׁה עֶדְרֵי־צֹאן רֹבְצִים עָלֶיהָ כִּי מִן־הַבְּאֵר הַהִוא יַשְׁקוּ הָעֲדָרִים וְהָאֶבֶן גְּדֹלָה עַל־פִּי הַבְּאֵר:

And he saw, and behold, a well in the field, and behold, there were three flock-herds lazing at it, for from that well they would water the herds; and the stone was large on the mouth of the well.

Twice in this verse we encounter the particle וְהִנֵּה *wǝ-hinne* 'and behold' (see above, Chapter 19). This usage serves to change the point of view from that of the author/narrator along with his readers/audience to that of Jacob. Which is to say, in v. 1 we have Jacob in our field of vision, as we watch him proceed from the land of Canaan to the land of the Bene Qedem. Here in v. 2, however, we gain Jacob's perspective: we see what he sees, which in this case is first the well and then the flocks lazing by it.

The verse continues with additional information, to wit, 'for from that well they would water the herds; and the stone was large on the mouth of the well'. Now this is information that the storyteller conveys to us, but this is not information that Jacob knows, or at least not yet. As such, we have here an additional literary device, not commented upon thus far in our very long book, but which I present here: a situation whereby the reader knows something that the character does not (yet) know.[4]

---

4. This is similar to, but not quite identical with, 'dramatic irony', defined by the *OED* as follows: "the incongruity created when the (tragic) significance of a character's speech or actions is revealed to the audience but unknown to the character concerned; the literary device so used, orig. in Greek tragedy." Since there is no overriding significance to the information about the well and the flock here, I would not use the term 'dramatic irony' in this instance at Gen 29:2.

The most significant example of this in the Bible is Gen 22:1, where the author informs his readers וְהָאֱלֹהִים נִסָּה אֶת־אַבְרָהָם *wə-ha-ʾelohim nissa ʾet ʾabraham* 'and God tried Abraham'. Hence the reader knows that Abraham is (only) being put to the test, with reference to the command to sacrifice Isaac. This passage, accordingly, informs the reader (a) that the events that are to follow are about Abraham (and that is where the literary focus remains);[5] and (b) that we need not worry about Isaac (who operates in the narrative more as an agent than as a fully developed character).[6] But Abraham does not know any of this; for him, everything that unfolds is real.

Now back to Jacob. As we have just seen, Gen 29:2 collocates two distinct literary devices: (a) the use of וְהִנֵּה *wə-hinne* 'and behold'; and (b) the device whereby the reader knows information ahead of the character. In fact, each of these is employed twice in the verse: as we saw above, there are two instances of וְהִנֵּה *wə-hinne* 'and behold'; and there are two parts to the information conveyed to the reader, one about the well itself, and one about the stone covering the well. To be honest, I see no specific reason why any of this should have any intrinsic value here at v. 2; rather, the collocation of the two devices serves simply to sensitize the reader to their joint usage. Which is to say, the reader should pay attention to the next time these two devices are arranged side by side—for at that point in the narrative there will be something of great inherent value.

Verse 3

וְנֶאֶסְפוּ־שָׁמָּה כָל־הָעֲדָרִים וְגָלֲלוּ אֶת־הָאֶבֶן מֵעַל פִּי הַבְּאֵר וְהִשְׁקוּ
אֶת־הַצֹּאן וְהֵשִׁיבוּ אֶת־הָאֶבֶן עַל־פִּי הַבְּאֵר לִמְקֹמָהּ׃

And all the herds would be gathered there, and they would roll the stone from upon the mouth of the well, and they would water the flock; and they would return the stone upon the mouth of the well to its place.

---

5. So much so, in fact, that Sarah is totally absent from the narrative (!), since her presence would only obfuscate the scene.
6. On 'agent', see Berlin, *Poetics and Interpretation of Biblical Narrative*, 23, 27, 32, 56, 85–86.

This verse continues the second half of the preceding verse. The reader learns additional information about the daily practice of the shepherds, including the gathering of the flocks by the well, the watering of the flocks at this well, and the manner of removing and then replacing the stone above the well. But none of this is known to Jacob yet.

Verse 4

וַיֹּ֤אמֶר לָהֶם֙ יַעֲקֹ֔ב אַחַ֖י מֵאַ֣יִן אַתֶּ֑ם וַיֹּ֣אמְר֔וּ מֵחָרָ֖ן אֲנָֽחְנוּ׃

And Jacob said to them, "My brothers, from where are you?"
And they said, "From Harran are we."

The first three verses comprise the exposition. The only past-tense verbs that have occurred thus far are the two verbs of motion in v. 1, which narrates Jacob's journey to this new place, and the verb of sight in v. 2, which narrates Jacob's espying the well and the flock. The rest of v. 2 and all of v. 3, to repeat, is information outside the main storyline.

We return to real action, however, with v. 4, though as is typical in biblical narrative prose, much of the action is reported to the reader via direct discourse.[7] Jacob asks the men of the place where they are from, and they respond with the name of their city, Harran.

Verse 5

וַיֹּ֣אמֶר לָהֶ֗ם הַיְדַעְתֶּ֛ם אֶת־לָבָ֖ן בֶּן־נָח֑וֹר וַיֹּאמְר֖וּ יָדָֽעְנוּ׃

And he said to them, "Do you know Laban son of Nahor?"
And they said, "We know."

Once Jacob learns that the men are from Harran, he asks them whether or not they know Laban son of Nahor, who hails from the city (though actually Nahor is Laban's grandfather; see Gen 22:23 in conjunction with Gen 24:29). In fact, they do, comes the response. Note, as an aside, that Biblical Hebrew has no word for 'yes'. If the answer to a yes/no question was 'no', then an ancient Hebrew speaker simply said לֹא *loʾ* 'no'. But if the answer to a yes/no question was 'yes', then the ancient

---

7. See Alter, *Art of Biblical Narrative*, 79–110.

Hebrew speaker needed to repeat the predicate (or some other key element in the question) in some adjusted fashion. Thus, for example, here Jacob asks הַיְדַעְתֶּם אֶת־לָבָן בֶּן־נָחוֹר *ha-yda'tεm 'εt laban bεn naḥor* 'do you know Laban son of Nahor', and the men respond יָדָעְנוּ *yada'nu* 'we know'.[8]

Verse 6

וַיֹּאמֶר לָהֶם הֲשָׁלוֹם לוֹ וַיֹּאמְרוּ שָׁלוֹם וְהִנֵּה רָחֵל בִּתּוֹ בָּאָה עִם־הַצֹּאן׃

And he said to them, "Is it well with him?" And they said, "Well, and here is Rachel his daughter coming with the flock."

To continue the aside, the beginning of this verse provides an additional example of a 'yes' response to a yes/no question. Jacob inquires, הֲשָׁלוֹם לוֹ *ha-šalom lo* 'is it well with him?' (lit., 'is there peace unto him?'), and the men respond, שָׁלוֹם *šalom* 'well' (lit., 'peace').

What follows constitutes one of the most delightful wordplays in the Bible: וְהִנֵּה רָחֵל בִּתּוֹ בָּאָה עִם־הַצֹּאן *wə-hinne raḥel bitto ba'a 'im haṣ-ṣo'n* 'and here is Rachel his daughter coming with the flock'. First, though, note that the use of וְהִנֵּה *wə-hinne* 'and here' is slightly different than the usage studied in Chapter 19 and above, for in this case the particle appears in direct speech, and thus I have rendered it differently, to wit, 'and here'. The aforementioned wordplay is multilayered: (a) the proper name רָחֵל *raḥel* 'Rachel' means 'ewe' in Hebrew;[9] (b) this new character, introduced here in v. 6, is tending to הַצֹּאן *haṣ-ṣo'n* 'the flock';

---

8. See Edward L. Greenstein, "The Syntax of Saying 'Yes' in Biblical Hebrew," *Journal of the Ancient Near Eastern Society* 19 (1989): 51–59. Our passage is cited on p. 54. On the question of the *qatal* form (which typically connotes past tense) of the verb יָדָעְנוּ *yada'nu* 'we know', note the Egyptian parallel *rḫ-n-i* 'I know' (and similarly for other persons [you, he, she, we, they, etc.]), with past-tense marker, even though the knowledge is clearly present knowledge. See James P. Allen, *Middle Egyptian: An Introduction to the Language and Culture of Hieroglyphs*, 2nd ed. (Cambridge: Cambridge University Press, 2010), 236, §18.10.

9. Note that many Hebrew personal names derive from common nouns denoting animals, e.g., צִפֹּרָה *ṣippora* 'Zipporah' = 'bird', יָעֵל *ya'el* 'Yael' = 'ibex', דְּבוֹרָה *dəbora* 'Deborah' = 'bee', זְאֵב *zə'eb* 'Zeeb' = 'wolf', שָׁפָן *šapan* 'Shaphan' = 'hyrax', etc.

and (c) the verb in the clause, בָּאָה *ba'a* 'is coming', evokes the sound that sheep make![10] While the text, quite naturally, is to be rendered, 'and here is Rachel his daughter coming with the flock', the reader also will catch a hint of 'and here is Rachel his daughter baa-ing [sc. 'bleating'] with the flock'. Why not introduce a bit of humor into the text! Just brilliant!

Verse 7

וַיֹּאמֶר הֵן עוֹד הַיּוֹם גָּדוֹל לֹא־עֵת הֵאָסֵף הַמִּקְנֶה הַשְׁקוּ הַצֹּאן וּלְכוּ רְעוּ׃

And he said, "Here the day is still great, it is not time to gather the livestock; water the flock, and go and shepherd."

Jacob's attention will turn to Rachel in a moment, but for now he is interested in the daily rhythms of the shepherds. Perhaps in a bit of a bossy manner, he instructs the shepherds to give drink to the animals.

Verse 8

וַיֹּאמְרוֹ לֹא נוּכַל עַד אֲשֶׁר יֵאָסְפוּ כָּל־הָעֲדָרִים וְגָלֲלוּ אֶת־הָאֶבֶן מֵעַל פִּי הַבְּאֵר וְהִשְׁקִינוּ הַצֹּאן׃

And they said, "We are not able until all the herds are gathered, and they roll the stone from upon the mouth of the well, so that we may water the flock."

The shepherds respond with a description of their technique, which is to wait until all the herds are gathered, and only then to remove the stone from the mouth of the well. This is information that the reader

---

10. The parallel in Greek appears in Cratinus, *Dionysalexander* (an Attic comedy, ca. 450 B.C.E., known only from fragments discovered among the Oxyrhynchus papyri), where the bleating of sheep is reproduced as βῆ βῆ. See the discussion in E. B. Petrounias, "The Pronunciation of Ancient Greek: Evidence and Hypothesis," in A.-F. Christidis, ed., *A History of Ancient Greek: From the Beginnings to Late Antiquity* (Cambridge: Cambridge University Press, 2007), 552–53.

learned back in v. 2; we now observe how Jacob learns the same information, though at a later point in the narrative. As intimated above, we will see later in the story the significance of this delay in Jacob's learning what the reader already knows.

While not specifically stated by the men, apparently the various groups of shepherds all cooperate with one another, and they wait until everyone has arrived at the well before they remove the stone. That way, presumably, the well would be uncovered for a shorter period of time, which would prevent dust and dirt from falling into the water and would prevent the water from evaporating in the noonday sun.

Verse 9

עוֹדֶ֣נּוּ מְדַבֵּ֣ר עִמָּ֑ם וְרָחֵ֣ל ׀ בָּ֗אָה עִם־הַצֹּאן֙ אֲשֶׁ֣ר לְאָבִ֔יהָ כִּ֥י רֹעָ֖ה הִֽוא׃

He was still speaking with them, and Rachel came with the flock that was her father's, for she was a shepherdess.

That discussion is abandoned now, for while Jacob and the men still were speaking, Rachel approached with her flock, or rather her father's flock. The wordplay that appeared earlier, in v. 6, is repeated here; note the phrase וְרָחֵ֣ל ׀ בָּ֗אָה עִם־הַצֹּאן֙ wə-raḥel baʾa ʿim haṣ-ṣoʾn 'and Rachel came with the flock', once more evoking 'and Rachel baa-ed [i.e., 'bleated'] with the flock'. A very slight difference occurs between the two verbs: in v. 6, the form is the participle בָּאָה baʾá (accented on the second syllable), signaling present tense, while in v. 9 the form is the suffix-conjugation בָּאָה báʾa (accented on the first syllable), signaling past tense. The ever-so-slight rewordings allow the author to demonstrate his verbal virtuosity.

Of greater significance here is the use of the type-scene: 3x in the Bible we read of the Israelite bachelor in a foreign land, where he encounters his destined bride at the well.[11] The Jacob-Rachel episode,

---

11. See Alter, *Art of Biblical Narrative*, 55–78. Alter identified other less-recognized examples of this type-scene, specifically, the aborted type-scene with Saul and the maidens in 1 Samuel 9 and the inverted type-scene with Ruth and Boaz in Ruth 2. Alter's chapter is nothing less than a brilliant tour de force.

set in Aram, is the basic version of the type-scene, narrated with just the right amount of detail, one might say. The Moses-Zipporah episode (Exod 2:15–21), set in Midian, is slightly dissimilar, since there are multiple young women at the well, plus the story is narrated in very schematic fashion—with, for example, no indication as to why Zipporah among the seven daughters of Reuel is the one whom Moses marries. The Isaac-Rebekah episode (Genesis 24) has the greatest variation, both because it is not Isaac but rather his surrogate, Abraham's servant, who journeys to the foreign land (also Aram) and because it constitutes by far the longest telling (sixty-seven verses).

An ancient Israelite reader did not have to read beyond the first verse or two in such type-scenes. All she needed to do was to realize that all the elements were present: Israelite bachelor in a foreign land at a well, with an eligible young woman present. Clearly marriage will ensue.[12]

Verse 10

וַיְהִ֡י כַּאֲשֶׁר֩ רָאָ֨ה יַעֲקֹ֜ב אֶת־רָחֵ֗ל בַּת־לָבָן֙ אֲחִ֣י אִמּ֔וֹ וְאֶת־צֹ֥אן לָבָ֖ן אֲחִ֣י אִמּ֑וֹ וַיִּגַּ֣שׁ יַעֲקֹ֗ב וַיָּ֤גֶל אֶת־הָאֶ֙בֶן֙ מֵעַל֙ פִּ֣י הַבְּאֵ֔ר וַיַּ֕שְׁקְ אֶת־צֹ֥אן לָבָ֖ן אֲחִ֥י אִמּֽוֹ:

And it was, when Jacob saw Rachel the daughter of Laban
the brother of his mother, and the flock of Laban the brother
of his mother; and Jacob approached, and he rolled the stone
from upon the mouth of the well, and he watered the flock of
Laban the brother of his mother.

The phrase that stands out in this verse is clearly אֲחִי אִמּוֹ *'aḥi 'immo* 'the brother of his mother', used 3x, whenever Laban is mentioned. The reader already knows that Laban is the brother of Jacob's mother, Rebekah (see Gen 24:49, 25:20, 27:43, 28:2, etc.), so there is no real need for

---

12. If it helps, compare the type-scene of the American Western. All one needs to see is the 'bad guy' dressed in black, with a close shot of the big black boots, and another close shot of the saloon door swinging open, with scared locals seated at the bar. Every viewer of such a scene knows that all of this will eventuate in a good old-fashioned shoot-out on Main Street.

this appositional identifier in Gen 29:10, certainly not 3x. The purpose for its repeated use must lie elsewhere, therefore.

Up until this point, Jacob has mentioned Laban by name and he has heard Rachel's name as well, but by and large he has been engaged with the shepherds of the town gathered with their flocks at the well. For the first time, he turns his attention elsewhere, to Rachel and her flock. The identifier אֲחִי אִמּוֹ ʾaḥi ʾimmo 'the brother of his mother', accordingly, provides the reader with Jacob's perspective. At times, the perspective of a character will be marked, as with the use of the particle וְהִנֵּה wə-hinne 'and behold' (again, see Chapter 19, and above regarding vv. 1–2). At other times, the perspective is unmarked, but a phrase incorporated into the text allows the reader to understand that the view is nonetheless that of one of the characters.[13] This is especially the case with a naming tag, as we have here in Gen 29:10.

The best example of this technique occurs in Genesis 21, where Ishmael is never mentioned by name; instead, a series of tags or epithets provides the viewpoint of each of the four main characters in the chapter.[14] For Sarah, he is בֶּן־הָגָר הַמִּצְרִית אֲשֶׁר־יָלְדָה לְאַבְרָהָם ben hagar ham-miṣrit ʾašer yalda lə-ʾabraham 'the son of Hagar the Egyptian whom she bore to Abraham' (v. 9), evoking distance and even disdain; for Abraham he is בְּנוֹ bəno 'his son' (v. 11), demonstrating his close connection to his own son; for God he is הַנַּעַר han-naʿar 'the lad' (vv. 12, 17 [2x], 18), using the most neutral, dispassionate term available; and for Hagar he is הַיֶּלֶד hay-yɛlɛd 'the child' (vv. 14, 15, 16), since to a mother her son remains her child forever. Now some of these terms are used in speech (vv. 12, 16, 17 [second occurrence], 18), but the ma-

---

13. On the naming technique, see Berlin, *Poetics and Interpretation of Biblical Narrative*, 59–61, 87–91.

14. As first observed by Nehama Leibowitz, *Torah Insights*, trans. Alan Smith (Jerusalem: Eliner Library, Joint Authority for Jewish Zionist Education, Department for Torah and Culture in the Diaspora, 1995), 173. I have not been able to track down the first mention of this insight in the numerous publications by the author, though no doubt it occurred long before the 1995 publication date of the cited volume, a book that appeared very late in Leibowitz's long and distinguished career. See also Meir Weiss, *Miqraʾot kə-Kavvanatam: Leqeṭ Maʾamarim* [English title: *Scriptures in Their Own Light: Collected Essays*] (Jerusalem: Bialik, 1987), 304–5. I am grateful to my friend and colleague Walter Herzberg (Jewish Theological Seminary) for these references.

jority occur within the third-person narration, offering the reader the internal perspective of the character 'on stage' at each particular moment in the story.

Again, back to Jacob: when the reader encounters the phrase אֲחִי אִמּוֹ *'aḥi 'immo* 'the brother of his mother' 3x in quick succession, she is aware that the text offers here the internal perspective of Jacob. After all, the purpose of his journey was to arrive at the home of the brother of his mother; and here he now stands before daughter and flock of said relative. There is more, however, for the relationship between a young man and his maternal uncle is a very close one in many cultures. This phenomenon has been studied by anthropologists such as Claude Lévi-Strauss,[15] while linguists have observed that Latin *auunculus* 'maternal uncle' is the dimunitive form of *auus* 'grandfather'.[16] Literary echoes of the relationship occur with Aḥiqar and Nadin of ancient Near Eastern lore (even if the latter turned into a treacherous betrayer), both with Hygelac and Beowulf and with Arthur and Gawain of northwestern European lore, and (in the extreme) with Luqmān and Luqaym of Arabic lore.

It is for this reason that Rebekah instructs Jacob to flee their home and take refuge with *her* brother Laban; after all, it would have been easier for Jacob to flee home and take refuge with his paternal uncle Ishmael, who lived much closer. (Incidentally, note that Esau establishes a relationship with Ishmael when he marries one of the latter's daughters, for which see Gen 28:9.) But the maternal uncle is the one who will serve as his nephew's protector, as both anthropological fieldwork and literary trope demonstrate.

We will get to the relationship between Jacob and Laban below, but for now, our focus remains on the first interaction between Jacob and Rachel. No time to wait for all the shepherds to gather and to remove

---

15. Claude Lévi-Strauss, *Structural Anthropology* (New York: Basic Books, 1976), 2:83–98, incorporating material from Margaret Mead on the Mundugomor and Mary Douglas on the Lele.

16. Thomas V. Gamkrelidze and Vjačeslav V. Ivanov, *Indo-European and the Indo-Europeans: A Reconstruction and Historical Analysis of a Proto-language and a Proto-culture* (Trends in Linguistics: Studies and Monographs 80; Berlin: Mouton de Gruyter, 1994), 1:674–76. Note that Latin *auunculus* is the source of both English 'uncle' and the more learned word 'avuncular'.

the stone from the well: Jacob does this himself and gallantly waters Rachel's flock.

Mention of the stone here brings us to another literary device employed by the author of the extended Jacob narrative. I refer to the use of אֶבֶן *ʾɛbɛn* 'stone' as *Leitwort*, or 'leading word', a literary device first recognized by Martin Buber in his research into the workings of biblical literature.[17] The key word appears in these stories in ch. 28 (vv. 11, 18, 22), where Jacob places a stone under his head in order to sleep and then uses the stone to establish a cultic place for God (Bethel); here in ch. 29 (vv. 2–3, 8, 10), as we have seen, as the stone that covers the mouth of the well; in ch. 31 (vv. 45–46), where a pile of stones serves to mark the agreement between Jacob and Laban; and in ch. 35 (v. 14), where once more Jacob uses a stone to establish a cultic place for God (again, Bethel). All of this bespeaks a single hand as the creative force behind the extended Jacob narrative, in line with what we argued above in Chapter 22 concerning the inherent unity of biblical compositions.[18]

Verse 11

וַיִּשַּׁק יַעֲקֹב לְרָחֵל וַיִּשָּׂא אֶת־קֹלוֹ וַיֵּבְךְּ:

And Jacob kissed Rachel; and he lifted-up his voice and he cried.

Another delightful wordplay occurs here. The words for 'watered' in v. 10 and 'kissed' in v. 11 are spelled exactly the same, וישק *wyšq*, keeping in mind that the original text included nothing but the consonantal skeleton (see the Introduction). The first is pronounced וַיַּשְׁקְ *wayyašq*, while the second is pronounced וַיִּשַּׁק *wayyiššaq*. Note that Jacob is the

---

17. Martin Buber, "*Leitwort* Style in Pentateuch Narrative," in Martin Buber and Franz Rosenzweig, *Scripture and Translation*, trans. and ed. Lawrence Rosenwald and Everett Fox (Bloomington: Indiana University Press, 1994), 114–28. For the original publication, see Martin Buber and Franz Rosenzweig, *Die Schrift und ihre Verdeutschung* (Berlin: Schocken, 1936), 262–75.

18. For another example of *Leitwort*, serving to unite a series of scenes in the life of an individual character, see Rendsburg, "The Literary Approach to the Bible and Finding a Good Translation," 182–84 (regarding the word בַּת *bat* 'daughter' in Exodus 1–2). See also above, Chapter 6, no. 2.

subject of both verbs, with the flock serving as one object and Rachel as the other. The effect is even more playful when one recalls that the name Rachel means 'ewe'! The performer of this text needs to be careful here, lest he confuse matters and have Jacob kiss the flock and water Rachel!

The attentive reader will realize something else here, for this is the only place in all of biblical narrative where a bachelor male kisses a bachelorette female.[19] Elsewhere this action occurs between parents and children, between siblings, and with other close relationships, as follows—Gen 27:26–27: Jacob (posing as Esau) to Isaac; Gen 29:13: Laban to Jacob; Gen 32:1: Laban to his daughters and grandchildren; Gen 33:4: Esau to Jacob; Gen 45:15: Joseph to his brothers; Gen 48:10: Jacob to Joseph's children; Gen 50:1: Joseph to Jacob; Exod 4:27: Aaron to Moses; Exod 18:7: Moses to Jethro; Ruth 1:9: Naomi to Ruth and Orpah; Ruth 1:14: Orpah to Naomi; 1 Sam 10:1: Samuel to Saul; 2 Sam 14:33: David to Absalom; and so on.[20] In light of all these examples, Jacob's kiss to Rachel would be arresting to the reader's ears. Moreover, while Jacob already has learned her identity, Rachel does not yet know his—so that the kiss would be seen as exceedingly forward. All of this also explains, to my mind, why v. 11 is the shortest verse (at seven words comprised of twenty-five letters) of the chapter; the author wants the reader to hear these words alone, unencumbered by other action occurring within the recitation: pause before v. 11—seven short words, with the central action of the kiss—pause after v. 11.

I would suggest that the kiss here represents a type of literary foreshadowing. For typically love is not mentioned as a factor in the narratives of the lives of biblical couples (for example, none is expressed in the cases of Abraham and Sarah, Joseph and Asenath, Moses and Zipporah, Ruth and Boaz, or David and Abigail); or the root א-ה-ב *ʾ-h-b* 'love' is used only once, almost in passing fashion (Gen 24:67: Isaac for Rebekah; Judg 16:4: Samson for Delilah; 1 Sam 1:5: Elkanah for Hannah;

---

19. Samuel H. Dresner, *Rachel* (Minneapolis: Fortress, 1994), 32.

20. True, the verb נ-שׁ-ק *n-š-q* 'kiss' appears twice in Song of Songs (1:2, 8:1), but the setting is totally different within the exquisite love poetry of that unique biblical book. In the first verse, the female lover opens the entire poem with her desire for her beau's kisses and romantic love, but they are apart, so no real kisses are exchanged. In the second instance, note her desire to have a sibling relationship with her lover, so that kisses could be exchanged freely.

1 Sam 18:20: Michal for David).[21] By contrast, as we shall see below, romantic love is very much present in the story of Jacob and Rachel.

Verse 12

וַיַּגֵּד יַעֲקֹב לְרָחֵל כִּי אֲחִי אָבִיהָ הוּא וְכִי בֶן־רִבְקָה הוּא וַתָּרָץ וַתַּגֵּד
לְאָבִיהָ:

And Jacob told Rachel that he was a brother of her father,
and that he was the son of Rebekah; and she ran and she told
her father.

Only now, after kissing her, does Jacob reveal his identity to Rachel, an action that prompts her to run and inform her father. The reader perceives Jacob's use of the word אָח 'aḥ 'brother', used loosely here as 'male relative', for in actuality he was Laban's nephew, of course. The employment of this word creates an even closer bond between the two characters.

Verse 13

וַיְהִי כִשְׁמֹעַ לָבָן אֶת־שֵׁמַע | יַעֲקֹב בֶּן־אֲחֹתוֹ וַיָּרָץ לִקְרָאתוֹ וַיְחַבֶּק־לוֹ
וַיְנַשֶּׁק־לוֹ וַיְבִיאֵהוּ אֶל־בֵּיתוֹ וַיְסַפֵּר לְלָבָן אֵת כָּל־הַדְּבָרִים הָאֵלֶּה:

And when Laban heard the hearing-news about Jacob the
son of his sister, he ran to greet him, and he hugged him, and
he kissed him, and he brought him to his house; and he told
to Laban all these things.

At last, Jacob and Laban meet, with hugs and kisses and greetings and warmth abounding.

Verse 14

וַיֹּאמֶר לוֹ לָבָן אַךְ עַצְמִי וּבְשָׂרִי אָתָּה וַיֵּשֶׁב עִמּוֹ חֹדֶשׁ יָמִים:

And Laban said to him, "Indeed my bone and my flesh are
you"; and he sat with him a month of days.

---

21. Note additional uses of the verb א-ה-ב ʾ-h-b 'love' to express love between parent and child; see Gen 22:2: Abraham to Isaac; Gen 25:28: Isaac to Esau, Rebekah to Jacob; Gen 37:3: Jacob to Joseph; etc.

The relationship between maternal uncle and nephew is articulated even more solidly here, through the expression placed in the mouth of Laban, אַדְ עַצְמִי וּבְשָׂרִי אָתָּה ʾak ʿaṣmi u-bśari ʾatta 'indeed my bone and my flesh are you'. This brings concreteness to the theoretical framework of the maternal uncle–nephew relationship described above.

Verse 15

וַיֹּאמֶר לָבָן לְיַעֲקֹב הֲכִי־אָחִי אַתָּה וַעֲבַדְתַּנִי חִנָּם הַגִּידָה לִּי
מַה־מַּשְׂכֻּרְתֶּךָ:

And Laban said to Jacob, "Just because you are my brother, should you work for me for free? Tell me, what (should be) your wage?"

We infer that at some point during the month that has passed, Jacob began to work in the household of Laban as shepherd. (Alone? With his own flock? Alongside Rachel? With her flock?—We don't know.) But it would be unfair to have Jacob work gratis, and thus Laban asks him the question recorded here in v. 15. Note that Laban uses the selfsame word אָח ʾaḥ 'brother' (see above, v. 12), so that the bond between the two is now closer still and also bidirectional.

Verse 16

וּלְלָבָן שְׁתֵּי בָנוֹת שֵׁם הַגְּדֹלָה לֵאָה וְשֵׁם הַקְּטַנָּה רָחֵל:

And Laban had two daughters, the name of the older was Leah, and the name of the younger was Rachel.

Verse 17

וְעֵינֵי לֵאָה רַכּוֹת וְרָחֵל הָיְתָה יְפַת־תֹּאַר וִיפַת מַרְאֶה:

And the eyes of Leah were soft; and Rachel was beautiful of form and a beautiful sight.

I treat these two verses together, for they interrupt the dialogue be-tween Laban and Jacob (the former's question appears in v. 15; the latter's response appears in v. 18). Together they provide the reader with additional information regarding Laban's household, information about which she previously was ignorant. Until this point there was no mention of Leah as Rachel's older sister (v. 16); and we also had no idea of the physical properties of Rachel (or Leah, of course) (v. 17). The presence of Leah in the household simply was not relevant, and thus she was not mentioned until now—but, as we shall see, her status in the family becomes very relevant in the verses ahead.

Incidentally, the exact nuance of רַכּוֹת *rakkot*, lit., 'soft', the word used to describe Leah's eyes, is unknown. Does the word denote that she had beautiful eyes—implying, perhaps, that otherwise she was not attractive? Or does the term signify that something was wrong with her eyes—implying, perhaps, that otherwise she was quite attractive? Again, we do not know.

Verse 18

וַיֶּאֱהַב יַעֲקֹב אֶת־רָחֵל וַיֹּאמֶר אֶעֱבָדְךָ שֶׁבַע שָׁנִים בְּרָחֵל בִּתְּךָ הַקְּטַנָּה:

And Jacob loved Rachel; and he said, "I will work for you seven years, for Rachel, your younger daughter."

Here we find the key mention that Jacob loved Rachel, with the implication that he wished to marry her. But since he arrived in Aram penniless, without any means by which to obtain a bride, Jacob needed to labor seven years as an equivalent to paying the bride-price.[22]

Verse 19

וַיֹּאמֶר לָבָן טוֹב תִּתִּי אֹתָהּ לָךְ מִתִּתִּי אֹתָהּ לְאִישׁ אַחֵר שְׁבָה עִמָּדִי:

And Laban said, "Better that I give her to you than I give her to another man; stay with me."

---

22. In the ancient world, both marriage partners needed to bring something of value into the mix. English possesses the word 'dowry' to refer to the wife's (or her family's) contribution; we use the word 'bride-price', for lack of a better term, to refer to the husband's contribution. The Hebrew word is מֹהַר *mohar* 'bride-price', though it is not used here (see Gen 34:12, Exod 22:16, 1 Sam 18:25).

Laban agrees to the offer, both the bride-price and the marriage.

Verse 20

וַיַּעֲבֹד יַעֲקֹב בְּרָחֵל שֶׁבַע שָׁנִים וַיִּהְיוּ בְעֵינָיו כְּיָמִים אֲחָדִים בְּאַהֲבָתוֹ
אֹתָהּ:

And Jacob worked for Rachel seven years; and they were in
his eyes as a few days, such was his love for her.

As indicated above (see on v. 11), the love that Jacob feels for Rachel
is unparalleled in any other biblical story. The words here are among
the most romantic words ever penned by an ancient author (save for
love poetry, such as Song of Songs): '[the seven years] were in his eyes
as a few days, such was his love for her'. But there is much more to
this phrase.

First, as discussed earlier (see Chapter 22), the last time the reader
encountered the key two-word phrase יָמִים אֲחָדִים *yamim 'aḥadim* '(for)
a few days' was in Gen 27:44, when Rebekah instructed Jacob to flee
to her brother Laban until Esau's anger subsided. The use of the same
phrase here, כְּיָמִים אֲחָדִים *kə-yamim 'aḥadim* 'as a few days', brings the
reader back to that point in the narrative. Needless to say, this tempers
the romantic quality of the locution, but it also shows the interconnectedness of all the events that transpire in Jacob's life. As we read
on, we realize that the 'few days' were in fact not just the seven years
mentioned here (29:20), but another seven years (see below, v. 30),
and then eventually another six years, for a total of twenty years (Gen
31:38, 31:41). All this as a reflection of Rebekah's original comment that
Jacob should flee the household and live with Laban '(for) a few days'.
Moreover, and to repeat what we stated in Chapter 22, the approach
taken here contradicts the approach taken by the JEDP Theory, which
ascribes Gen 27:44 to 'J' and assigns Gen 29:20 to 'E'. The whole thing
must be a coincidence, accordingly—though we know better.

Secondly, and to bring something new into the picture, we observe
the difference between 'story time' and 'narrational time'.[23] As chapter

---

23. Others prefer the term 'discourse time', but to my mind 'discourse'
connotes direct speech; hence, I prefer 'narrational time'.

29 unfolds, vv. 2–13 narrate the events of a single day, from the moment that Jacob arrives at the well through his meeting Laban. To extend the story time a bit further, one also notes that vv. 2–19 narrate the events of a single month, from the moment that Jacob arrives until the agreement is reached concerning Jacob's working for seven years in order to obtain Rachel. And then all of a sudden, the author narrates the seven years in a single verse (v. 20) with breathtaking speed! If eighteen verses (vv. 2–19) are used to narrate the events of one month, then seven years would take 1512 verses (= 18 verses/month x 12 months x 7 years). Or, more to the extreme, if twelve verses (vv. 2–13) are used to narrate the events of one day, then seven years would take a staggering 30,660 verses (= 12 verses/day x 365 days/year x 7 years)—about one and one-third times the length of the entire Bible! Clearly, no one would expect the author to devote so much narrational time to the events of the intervening seven years, but the calculations help to demonstrate the point nonetheless. To be sure, something of interest must have happened during the seven years—but pausing to mention any of it would denude the text of its impact. For the goal of the text here is to allow the reader to experience the seven years as Jacob did, כְּיָמִים אֲחָדִים kə-yamim ʾaḥadim 'as a few days'; hence, she must experience that time period in the most minimal number of words possible. As such, the narrational time employed in v. 20 is another stellar instance of 'form follows content' (see above, Chapter 27): the seven years speed by both for Jacob and for the reader.

In short, when the writer of the story wishes to slow down the action, as he does on day one in Aram, he is able to do so. When he wants to fast-forward the action, as he does for the seven years that passed, he is able to accomplish this as well. He controls the pace, fast or slow. Narrational time, accordingly, is one more tool exploited by the ancient Israelite author, among the many tools he carried in his literary toolbox.

Verse 21

וַיֹּאמֶר יַעֲקֹב אֶל־לָבָן הָבָה אֶת־אִשְׁתִּי כִּי מָלְאוּ יָמָי וְאָבוֹאָה אֵלֶיהָ:

And Jacob said to Laban, "Bring my wife, because my days are fulfilled, so that I may come unto her."

With the seven years (quickly) passed, Jacob requests that Laban present Rachel to him officially as wife.

Verse 22

וַיֶּאֱסֹף לָבָן אֶת־כָּל־אַנְשֵׁי הַמָּקוֹם וַיַּעַשׂ מִשְׁתֶּה:

And Laban gathered all the men of the place, and he made a drinking-feast.

As is/was the traditional custom in the Near East (and elsewhere), the wedding festivities are accompanied by a feast, to which all the people of the place are invited.

Verse 23

וַיְהִי בָעֶרֶב וַיִּקַּח אֶת־לֵאָה בִתּוֹ וַיָּבֵא אֹתָהּ אֵלָיו וַיָּבֹא אֵלֶיהָ:

And it was in the evening, and he took Leah his daughter,
and he brought her to him; and he came unto her.

The famous ruse occurs in this verse. While the name לֵאָה *le'a* 'Leah' must perforce appear in this passage, after the mention of her name the text refers to the actors with pronouns only: וַיָּבֵא אֹתָהּ אֵלָיו וַיָּבֹא אֵלֶיהָ *wayyabe' 'otah 'elaw wayyabo' 'elɛha* 'and he brought her to him; and he came unto her'. The deception will work only through the anonymity, and the accumulation of pronouns here allows the reader to sense the scene better. We have, therefore, another instance of 'form follows content'.

One further observes how the two key verbs are written with the same four letters, ויבא *wyb'*, though obviously distinguished in vocalization and in meaning: וַיָּבֵא *wayyabe'* 'and he brought' and וַיָּבֹא *wayyabo'* 'and he came'.[24] This technique provides for further muddle, at least on a visual level for the presenter holding the written text.

---

24. In Hebrew, the verbs 'bring' and 'come' are built from the same verbal root, ב-ו-א *b-w-'*; the latter appears in the simple Qal pattern, while the former appears in the causative Hiph'il, that is, 'cause to come' > 'bring'.

Another example of the naming technique also occurs in this verse, for Leah is denoted not only by her name, but also by the phrase לֵאָה בִתּוֹ *leʾa bitto* 'Leah his daughter'. This provides for us the internal perspective of Laban: Leah is *his* daughter, and as paterfamilias, he has the right to do whatever he wishes in such role, including taking *his* daughter Leah (and not Rachel) to present to Jacob on his wedding night.

Verse 24

וַיִּתֵּן לָבָן לָהּ אֶת־זִלְפָּה שִׁפְחָתוֹ לְלֵאָה בִתּוֹ שִׁפְחָה׃

And Laban gave to her Zilpah his handmaid, for Leah his daughter (as) a handmaid.

The traditional wedding includes the exchange of gifts. The prime one in this case is the presentation of Zilpah as handmaid to Leah.

Verse 25

וַיְהִי בַבֹּקֶר וְהִנֵּה־הִוא לֵאָה וַיֹּאמֶר אֶל־לָבָן מַה־זֹּאת עָשִׂיתָ לִּי הֲלֹא
בְרָחֵל עָבַדְתִּי עִמָּךְ וְלָמָּה רִמִּיתָנִי׃

And it was in the morning, and behold, she is Leah; and he said to Laban, "What is this that you have done to me? Did I not work with you for Rachel? And why did you deceive me?"

The reader, who was apprised of the ruse two verses earlier, cannot wait to learn what Jacob's reaction will be once he discovers the truth, that he has married Leah and not Rachel. The author obliges her here in v. 25. In standard biblical style, we view the scene through Jacob's eyes; with the arrival of morning, we read וְהִנֵּה־הִוא לֵאָה *wə-hinne hiʾ leʾa* 'and behold, she is Leah'.

Above we discussed the manner in which the author of our chapter introduces two devices at the outset: (a) the use of וְהִנֵּה *wə-hinne* 'and behold'; and (b) the situation whereby the reader knows something that the character does not (yet) know. As we observed at that point, there is no inherent reason for the use of these two devices in v. 2, other than to sensitize the reader to their employment in the narrative, in anticipation of the crucial time when the two techniques would coincide again. That time is now.

In v. 23, the reader learned something that Jacob did not know: Leah, not Rachel, was given to him on his wedding night; while here in v. 25, the reader hears the phrase וְהִנֵּה *wə-hinne* 'and behold'. The conjoining of these two techniques (notwithstanding the interposition of v. 24, on which see below) alerts the reader to the very crucial scene unfolding here.

Verse 26

וַיֹּאמֶר לָבָן לֹא־יֵעָשֶׂה כֵן בִּמְקוֹמֵנוּ לָתֵת הַצְּעִירָה לִפְנֵי הַבְּכִירָה:

And Laban said, "It is not done thus in our place, to give the younger before the firstborn."

We also discussed this verse earlier (see Chapter 22), as another instance of how the Documentary Hypothesis fails the reader of biblical narrative. Upon Jacob's complaint that he labored for Rachel but was tricked into marrying Leah, his father-in-law, Laban, responds, לֹא־ יֵעָשֶׂה כֵן בִּמְקוֹמֵנוּ לָתֵת הַצְּעִירָה לִפְנֵי הַבְּכִירָה *loʾ yeʿaśe ken bi-mqomenu latet haṣ-ṣəʿira lipne hab-bəkira* 'it is not done thus in our place, to give the younger before the firstborn'. These words clearly are intended to take the reader back to the story in Genesis 27, in which Jacob (as the younger) placed himself before Esau (the firstborn). And yet once more the source critics would have us believe that the two passages originate from different pens, since Gen 29:26 is assigned to 'E', while ch. 27 is ascribed to 'J'. Or, to repeat the above comment, once more this all must be a coincidence.

A specific lexical linkage between the two stories is the root ר-מ-ה *r-m-h* 'deceive', which occurs one verse earlier (v. 25), in Jacob's words to Laban וְלָמָּה רִמִּיתָנִי *wə-lamma rimmitani* 'and why did you deceive me', as well as two chapters earlier, in the noun form, when Isaac speaks to Esau regarding Jacob's actions, saying, בָּא אָחִיךָ בְּמִרְמָה *baʾ ʾaḥika bə-mirma* 'your brother came with guile' (or 'deception', to reflect the lexical link more closely).

As also discussed earlier (again, see Chapter 22), the punishment that Jacob receives here for deceiving his father stands at the very core of the Bible's message.[25] And while God could have exacted this punishment on Jacob, as he does with other reprobates (see Gen 38:7, 38:10), how much more delightful the literary effect when a human character (in this case Laban) playfully exacts the revenge on the sinning individual. Indeed, as the reader may have noticed, God does not appear at all in the entire episode of Jacob's arrival at Harran and his early years in the household of Laban.

But wait a second: How did Laban know what had transpired back in the land of Canaan? By declaring 'it is not done thus in our place, to give the younger before the firstborn', Laban implies that he knows what happened, how Jacob the younger had placed himself before Esau the firstborn. To repeat the question: How did Laban know this?

The answer is provided by our storyteller in an *en passant* comment back in v. 13: וַיְסַפֵּר לְלָבָן אֵת כָּל־הַדְּבָרִים הָאֵלֶּה *waysapper lə-laban ʾet kol had-dəbarim ha-ʾellɛ* 'and he told to Laban all these things'. All what things? No doubt the story of his having cheated his brother Esau out of the blessing, which in turn precipitated his need to leave the household of his parents, Isaac and Rebekah. Otherwise, why would Jacob have made the trip to visit his uncle Laban? Nephew shows up at the doorstep (or perhaps, tent flap): he must have provided some background story to explain his long journey from Canaan to Aram.

Note how the author of our tale made very little of the comment at the end of v. 13, just as I passed over these words in my analysis of v. 13 above. This passage was of little concern to us then, though its significance becomes apparent now. In classical biblical storytelling style, however, the reader needs to figure this out for herself. She needs to be an active participant in the literary experience; she cannot be a passive listener, expecting to be spoon-fed all the necessary information, or else she will miss too much.

---

25. See, most familarly and most prominently, Exod 20:12 כַּבֵּד אֶת־אָבִיךָ וְאֶת־אִמֶּךָ 'Honor your father and your mother' (and its parallel in Deut 5:16).

Verse 27

מַלֵּא שְׁבֻעַ זֹאת וְנִתְּנָה לְךָ גַּם־אֶת־זֹאת בַּעֲבֹדָה אֲשֶׁר תַּעֲבֹד עִמָּדִי
עוֹד שֶׁבַע־שָׁנִים אֲחֵרוֹת:

"Fulfill the week of this-one; and also this-one will be given
to you, for the work that you will work with me, another
seven years more."

Laban imposes another seven years on Jacob. But to show that he is not
a total "bad guy," in this case, Laban will allow Jacob to marry Rachel
(via a promissory note, as it were) before working off the seven years
of debt. First, however, he must complete the traditional week-long
wedding festivities.

One observes how the daughters do not gain their names in Laban's
declaration, but rather each is referred to simply as זֹאת *zo't* 'this-one'.
The effect is to show that the two young women are more like pawns
on a chessboard, devoid of their names and character, as if they can be
moved about at will by the controlling Laban.

Verse 28

וַיַּעַשׂ יַעֲקֹב כֵּן וַיְמַלֵּא שְׁבֻעַ זֹאת וַיִּתֶּן־לוֹ אֶת־רָחֵל בִּתּוֹ לוֹ לְאִשָּׁה:

And Jacob did thus, and he fulfilled the week of this-one; and
he gave him Rachel his daughter as a wife for him.

Attention to the naming technique reveals that the narrator has adopted
Laban's use of זֹאת *zo't* 'this-one' to refer to Leah, but has reverted to
רָחֵל *raḥel* 'Rachel' in the second part of the verse. This clever maneuver
adumbrates for the reader what she already must know: Rachel, not
Leah, is the beloved wife, and she will remain so as the story develops
further.

Verse 29

וַיִּתֵּן לָבָן לְרָחֵל בִּתּוֹ אֶת־בִּלְהָה שִׁפְחָתוֹ לָהּ לְשִׁפְחָה:

And Laban gave to Rachel his daughter Bilhah his handmaid,
for her as a handmaid.

As we saw in the first wedding celebration (see above, v. 24), also here: Laban presents the gift of a handmaid to his daughter on the occasion. Though naturally the author does not narrate the two events in the same parallel language; rather, as we have come to expect (see above, Chapter 9), he varies his wording, as follows:

Gen 29:24

וַיִּתֵּן לָבָן לָהּ אֶת־זִלְפָּה שִׁפְחָתוֹ לְלֵאָה בִתּוֹ שִׁפְחָה:

And Laban gave to her Zilpah his handmaid, for Leah his daughter (as) a handmaid.

Gen 29:29

וַיִּתֵּן לָבָן לְרָחֵל בִּתּוֹ אֶת־בִּלְהָה שִׁפְחָתוֹ לָהּ לְשִׁפְחָה:

And Laban gave to Rachel his daughter Bilhah his hand-maid, for her as a handmaid.

In v. 24, the indirect object at the beginning of the sentence is expressed via a pronoun; while in v. 29 it is expressed via the personal name with epithet: hence, לָהּ *lah* 'to her' versus לְרָחֵל בִּתּוֹ *lə-raḥel bitto* 'to Rachel his daughter'. The readings are balanced in the second part of the verse, for in v. 24 one reads לְלֵאָה בִתּוֹ *lə-leʾa bitto* 'for Leah his daughter'; while in v. 29 only the pronoun לָהּ *lah* 'for her' is used. One final variation occurs in the last word of each sentence, with v. 24 reading שִׁפְחָה *šipḥa* '(as) a handmaid' and v. 29 reading לְשִׁפְחָה *lə-šipḥa* 'as a handmaid'. Note how my rendering places 'as' in parentheses in the first instance, to capture this distinction in English translation.

Verse 30

וַיָּבֹא גַּם אֶל־רָחֵל וַיֶּאֱהַב גַּם־אֶת־רָחֵל מִלֵּאָה וַיַּעֲבֹד עִמּוֹ עוֹד שֶׁבַע־שָׁנִים אֲחֵרוֹת:

And he came also unto Rachel, and also he loved Rachel more than Leah; and he worked with him another seven years more.

Jacob now consummates the marriage with Rachel. Our attention is drawn to a comparison between the way the two sex acts are narrated, the earlier one with Leah in v. 23 and the current one with Rachel here in v. 30. In the first instance the text reads וַיָּבֹא אֵלֶיהָ *wayyabo᾽ ᾽elɛha* 'and he came unto her'; while in the second case the text states וַיָּבֹא גַם אֶל־רָחֵל *wayyabo᾽ gam ᾽el raḥel* 'and he came also unto Rachel'. It is not the word גַם *gam* 'also' that attracts our attention so much, but rather the difference between אֵלֶיהָ *᾽elɛha* 'unto her' in v. 23 and אֶל־רָחֵל *᾽el raḥel* 'unto Rachel' in v. 30. Obviously the anonymity implied by the former was necessary (see above, on v. 23, for discussion of the accumulation of pronouns there), whereas here in v. 30 everything is now above board and thus Rachel can be mentioned explicitly.

A second feature of this verse is the alliteration produced by מִלֵּאָה *mil-le᾽a* 'more than Leah' and the two verbs derived from the root מ־ל־א *m-l-᾽* 'fill, fulfill', to wit, מַלֵּא *malle᾽* 'fulfill' (v. 27) and וַיְמַלֵּא *waymalle᾽* 'and he fulfilled' (v. 28). As we have seen throughout this book, the ancient authors peppered their prose and poetry with like-sounding words, so it is not unexpected to find at least one alliteration within the thirty verses comprising this account.

But the most significant literary effect forthcoming from this portion of the narrative is the ordering of events, especially when one compares the wedding scene with Leah and the wedding scene with Rachel. I withheld comment on the matter above, when I analyzed vv. 23–24, though I take the opportunity now to note the order of events there: (a) presentation of bride to groom (v. 23a); (b) consummation of the marriage through sexual intercourse (v. 23b); and (c) gift of the handmaid (v. 24). Are we to imagine that, *after* Jacob and his bride (ha! Leah!) engaged in the sex act, Laban entered with the gift of Zilpah to his daughter? Clearly not, for readers would realize that the exchange of gifts occurs during the wedding feast (v. 22).[26]

In the second marriage, the proper order occurs: (a) presentation of bride to groom (v. 28); (b) gift of the handmaid (v. 29); and (c) consummation of the marriage through sexual intercourse (v. 30). We know, of

---

26. If the latter-day parallel from the wedding scene at the end of Act I of "Fiddler on the Roof" (or its parallel in the film version) helps, that is fine.

course, that this order must have obtained in the first instance as well, but the author consciously chose to tell the events in nonchronological order—yet another technique of the biblical authors.[27]

The question is why? I hinted at the answer above: The reader, who was apprised of the ruse *two verses earlier*, cannot wait to learn what Jacob's reaction will be once he discovers the truth, that he has married Leah and not Rachel. But to extend the drama, to lengthen that wait—by this point the reader is on the edge of her seat—the writer of the story interposes the gift of Zilpah to Leah (v. 24) between the sexual intercourse (end of v. 23) and Jacob's awareness the next morning of what transpired the night before (v. 25).

The average reader may not have realized the chronological displacement while listening to the narration of the Jacob-Leah scene, while the alert reader very well may have taken note of the issue. Either way, one hopes that upon reaching the narration of the Jacob-Rachel wedding scene, both kinds of readers would have recalled the former order of events. And if not, well fine, the author had his way nonetheless.

---

27. See the fine study by David A. Glatt, *Chronological Displacement in Biblical and Related Literatures* (Society of Biblical Literature Dissertation Series 139; Atlanta: Scholars Press, 1993).

BIBLIOGRAPHY

Ackerman, James S. "The Literary Context of the Moses Birth Story (Exodus 1–2)," in Kenneth R. R. Gros Louis, James S. Ackerman, and Thayer S. Warshaw, eds., *Literary Interpretations of Biblical Narratives*, 74–119. Nashville: Abingdon, 1974.

Agamben, Giorgio. "Pascoli and the Thought of the Voice" (originally published in Italian in 1982), in *The End of the Poem*, 62–75. Translated by Daniel Heller-Roazen. Stanford: Stanford University Press, 1999.

Ahituv, Shmuel. *Echoes from the Past: Hebrew and Cognate Inscriptions from the Biblical Period.* Jerusalem: Carta, 2008.

Ahituv, Shmuel, and Amihai Mazar. "The Inscriptions from Tel Rehov and Their Contribution to the Study of Script and Writing during Iron Age IIA," in Esther Eshel and Yigal Levin, eds., *"See, I will bring a scroll recounting what befell me" (Ps 40:8): Epigraphy and Daily Life from the Bible to the Talmud, Dedicated to the Memory of Professor Hanan Eshel*, 40–68 (with plates on 189–203). Journal of Ancient Judaism Supplements 12. Göttingen: Vandenhoeck & Ruprecht, 2014.

Ahl, Frederick. *Metaformations: Soundplay and Wordplay in Ovid and Other Classical Poets.* Ithaca, NY: Cornell University Press, 1985.

Alcott, W. A. "On Reading, and Reading Books." *The Common School Journal* (edited by Horace Mann) 3.2 (Jan. 15, 1841): 17–20.

Allen, James P. *Middle Egyptian: An Introduction to the Language and Culture of Hieroglyphs.* 2nd ed. Cambridge: Cambridge University Press, 2010.

Alter, Robert. *Ancient Israel.* New York: Norton, 2013.

———. *The Art of Biblical Narrative.* 2nd ed. New York: Basic Books, 2011.

———. *The Art of Biblical Poetry.* 2nd ed. New York: Basic Books, 2011.

———. *The Book of Psalms.* New York: Norton, 2007.

———. *The Five Books of Moses*. New York: Norton, 2004.

———. *The Wisdom Books*. New York: Norton, 2010.

Andersen, Francis I. *The Sentence in Biblical Hebrew*. The Hague: Mouton, 1974.

Andrzejewski, B. W., and I. M. Lewis. *Somali Poetry: An Introduction*. Oxford: Clarendon, 1964.

Assis, Elie. "Ha-Mivneh ha-Sifruti šel Sippur Kibbuš ha-ʾAreṣ be-Sefer Yehošuaʿ (Peraqim 1–11) u-Mašmaʿuto." PhD dissertation, Bar-Ilan University, 1999.

Avi-Yonah, Michael. "Ophrah." *Encyclopaedia Judaica*, 2nd ed., 15:439. Detroit: Macmillan, 2007.

Baines, John. "Interpreting the Story of the Shipwrecked Sailor." *The Journal of Egyptian Archaeology* 76 (1990): 55–72.

Bar-Asher, Moshe. "Lešon Qumran ben ha-Miqraʾ li-Lšon Ḥazal (ʿIyyun ba-Seʿif be-Morfologya)." *Meghillot* 2 (2004): 137–49.

Bar-Efrat, Shimon. *Ha-ʾIṣṣuv ha-ʾOmanuti šel ha-Sippur ba-Miqraʾ*. Tel Aviv: Sifriyat Poʿalim, 1979.

———. *Narrative Art in the Bible*. Sheffield: Almond Press, 1989.

Barr, James. *Comparative Philology and the Text of the Old Testament*. Oxford: Clarendon, 1968.

———. *The Variable Spellings of the Hebrew Bible*. Oxford: Oxford University Press, 1989.

Barré, Michael L. "The Meaning of PRŠDN in Judges iii 22." *Vetus Testamentum* 41 (1991): 1–11.

Beattie, D. R. G. "A Midrashic Gloss in Ruth 2:7." *Zeitschrift für die alttestamentliche Wissenschaft* 89 (1977): 122–24.

Beentjes, Pancratius C. "Inverted Quotations in the Bible: A Neglected Stylistic Pattern." *Biblica* 63 (1982): 506–23.

Ben-Ḥayyim, Zeʾev. "ʾezɛr kə-nɛgdo: haṣṣaʿa." *Leshonenu* 61 (1998 / 5758): 45–50.

Berlin, Adele. *The Dynamics of Biblical Parallelism*. Bloomington: Indiana University Press, 1985. 2nd ed., Grand Rapids: Eerdmans, 2008.

———. *Poetics and Interpretation of Biblical Narrative*. Sheffield: Almond Press, 1983. Repr., Winona Lake: Eisenbrauns, 1994.

Blackman, A. M. *Middle-Egyptian Stories*. Bibliotheca Aegyptiaca 2. Brussels: Édition de la Fondation Égyptologique Reine Élisabeth, 1932.

Blau, Joshua. "Benoni Paʿul be-Horaʾa ʾAqtivit." *Leshonenu* 18 (1951 / 5713): 67–81.

Boadt, Lawrence. "Intentional Alliteration in Second Isaiah." *Catholic Biblical Quarterly* 45 (1983): 353–63.

Boling, Robert G. *Judges*. Anchor Bible 6A. Garden City, NY: Doubleday, 1975.

Boström, Gustav. *Paronomasi i den äldre hebreiska maschallitteraturen.* Lund: C. W. K. Gleerup, 1928.

Brenner, Athalya. "Lešono šel Sefer Yona ke-Maddad li-Qviʿat Zeman Ḥibburo." *Bet Miqraʾ* 24 (1978–1979 / 5739): 396–405.

Brettler, Marc Z. *How to Read the Bible*. Philadelphia: Jewish Publication Society, 2005.

———. *How to Read the Jewish Bible*. New York: Oxford University Press, 2007.

Brown, John Pairman. *Israel and Hellas*. Beihefte zur Zeitschrift für die Alttestamentliche Wissenschaft 231. Berlin: de Gruyter, 1995.

Bryson, Bill. *Notes from a Small Island*. London: Doubleday, 1993.

Buber, Martin. "Die Erzählung von Sauls Königswahl." *Vetus Testamentum* 6 (1956): 113–73.

———. "*Leitwort* Style in Pentateuch Narrative," in Martin Buber and Franz Rosenzweig, *Scripture and Translation*, 114–28. Translated and edited by Lawrence Rosenwald and Everett Fox. Bloomington: Indiana University Press, 1994.

Buber, Martin, and Franz Rosenzweig. *Die Schrift.* 4 vols. Gerlingen: Verlag Lambert Schneider, 1976.

———. *Die Schrift und ihre Verdeutschung*. Berlin: Schocken, 1936.

Buttin, François. *Du costume militaire au moyen âge et pendant la renaissance*. Memorias de la Real Academia de Buenas Letras de Barcelona 12. Barcelona: Real Academia de Buenas Letras, 1971.

Cahill, Jane. "Jerusalem in David and Solomon's Time: It Really Was a Major City in the 10th Century B.C.E." *Biblical Archaeology Review* 30.6 (Nov.–Dec. 2004): 20–31, 62–63.

Campbell, Antony F., and Mark A. O'Brien. *Sources of the Pentateuch*. Minneapolis: Fortress, 1993.

Campbell, Edward F. *Ruth*. Anchor Bible 7. Garden City, NY: Doubleday, 1975.

Carnarvon, 8th Countess of. *Lady Almina and the Real Downton Abbey: The Lost Legacy of Highclere Castle.* London: Hodder, 2011.

Casson, Lionel. *Ships and Seamanship in the Ancient World.* Princeton: Princeton University Press, 1971.

Cassuto, Umberto. *A Commentary on the Book of Exodus.* Translated by Israel Abrahams. Jerusalem: Magnes, 1967.

———. *From Noah to Abraham.* Translated by Israel Abrahams. Jerusalem: Magnes, 1964.

Chadwick, Nora K., and Victor Zhirmunsky. *Oral Epics of Central Asia.* Cambridge: Cambridge University Press, 1969.

Cheever, Susan. *American Bloomsbury: Louisa May Alcott, Ralph Waldo Emerson, Margaret Fuller, Nathaniel Hawthorne, and Henry David Thoreau: Their Lives, Their Loves, Their Work.* New York: Simon & Schuster, 2006.

Chen, Yiyi. "Israelian Hebrew in the Book of Proverbs." PhD dissertation, Cornell University, 2000.

Cohen, Harold R. (Chaim). *Biblical Hapax Legomena in the Light of Akkadian and Ugaritic.* Society of Biblical Literature Dissertation Series 37. Missoula, MT: Scholars Press, 1978.

Cole, R. Alan. *Exodus.* London: Tyndale House, 1973.

Craik, Wendy A. *Elizabeth Gaskell and the English Provincial Novel.* London: Methuen, 1975.

Crystal, David. *The Story of English in 100 Words.* New York: St. Martin's Press, 2011.

Currid, John D. *Ancient Egypt and the Old Testament.* Grand Rapids: Baker, 1997.

Dalman, Gustaf. *Grammatik des jüdisch-palästinischen Aramäisch.* Leipzig: Hinrichs, 1905.

Davidson, Robert. *Genesis 12–50.* Cambridge: Cambridge University Press, 1979.

Davila, James R. "4QGen-Exodᵃ," in Eugene Ulrich and Frank Moore Cross, eds., *Qumran Cave 4/VII*, 7–30. Discoveries in the Judaean Desert 12. Oxford: Clarendon, 1994.

Day, John. *From Creation to Babel: Studies in Genesis 1–11.* Library of Hebrew Bible / Old Testament Studies 592. London: Bloomsbury Academic, 2013.

Delcor, Mathias. "Two Special Meanings of the Word יד in Biblical Hebrew." *Journal of Semitic Studies* 12 (1967): 230–40.

Depuydt, Leo. "On the Notion of Movement in Egypto-Coptic and Biblical Hebrew," in Sarah Israelit-Groll, ed., *Pharaonic Egypt: The Bible and Christianity.* Jerusalem: Magnes, 1985.

Diamond, James S. *Scribal Secrets: Extraordinary Texts in the Torah and Their Implications.* Edited by Robert Goldenberg and Gary A. Rendsburg. Eugene, OR: Pickwick, 2019.

Dillon, H. A. "On a MS. Collection of Ordinances of Chivalry of the Fifteenth Century, Belonging to Lord Hastings." *Archaeologia, or Miscellaneous Tracts Relating to Antiquity Published by the Society of Antiquaries of London* 57 (1900): 29–70.

Douglas, Mary. *In the Wilderness: The Doctrine of Defilement in the Book of Numbers.* Journal for the Study of the Old Testament Supplement Series 158. Sheffield: JSOT Press, 1993.

———. *Leviticus as Literature.* Oxford: Oxford University Press, 1999.

Dresner, Samuel H. *Rachel.* Minneapolis: Fortress, 1994.

Driver, G. R. "Hebrew Poetic Diction," in *Congress Volume: Copenhagen 1953,* 26–39. Supplements to Vetus Testamentum 1. Leiden: Brill, 1953.

———. "On a Passage in the Baal Epic (IV AB iii 24) and Proverbs xxxi 21." *Bulletin of the American Schools of Oriental Research* 105 (1947): 11.

Driver, S. R. *An Introduction to the Literature of the Old Testament.* New York: Charles Scribner's Sons, 1913.

———. *Notes on the Hebrew Text of the Books of Samuel.* Oxford: Clarendon, 1890.

Ehrlich, Arnold B. *Randglossen zur Hebräischen Bibel.* 7 vols. Leipzig: Hinrichs, 1908–1914.

Eitan, Israel. "An Identification of *tiškaḥ yĕmīnī,* Ps 137:5." *Journal of Biblical Literature* 47 (1928): 193–95.

Ellis, Michael. "Literary Dialect as Linguistic Evidence: Subject-Verb Concord in Nineteenth-Century Southern Literature." *American Speech* 69 (1994): 128–44.

Erman, Adolf. *The Ancient Egyptians: A Sourcebook of their Writings.* Translated by A. M. Blackman. German original, 1923; first English edition, 1927. New York: Harper & Row, 1966.

———. *Wörterbuch der ägyptischen Sprache.* 7 vols. Berlin: Akademie-Verlag, 1982. Original publication: Leipzig: Hinrichs, 1926–1953.

———. *Wörterbuch der ägyptischen Sprache: Die Belegstellen.* 4 vols. Berlin: Akademie-Verlag, 1982. Original publication: Leipzig: Hinrichs, 1926–1953.

Faulkner, Raymond O. *The Ancient Egyptian Pyramid Texts.* Oxford: Clarendon, 1969.

Ffoulkes, Charles. *The Armourer and His Craft from the XIth to the XVIth Century.* Boston: Small, Maynard, 1912.

Fishbane, Michael. "Composition and Structure in the Jacob Cycle (Gen. 25:19–35:22)." *Journal of Jewish Studies* 26 (1975): 15–38.

———. *Text and Texture.* New York: Schocken, 1979.

Fisher, Loren. *The Jerusalem Academy.* Willits, CA: Fisher Publications, 2002.

Fokkelman, Jan P. "Job 28 and the Climax in Chapters 29–31: Crisis and Identity," in Hanna Liss and Manfred Oeming, eds., *Literary Construction of Identity in the Ancient World,* 301–22. Winona Lake, IN: Eisenbrauns, 2010.

———. *Narrative Art and Poetry in the Books of Samuel,* vol. 2, *The Crossing Fates.* Assen: Van Gorcum, 1986.

———. *Narrative Art and Poetry in the Books of Samuel,* vol. 4, *Vow and Desire.* Assen: Van Gorcum, 1993.

———. *Narrative Art in Genesis.* Assen: Van Gorcum, 1975.

Foley, John Miles. *Traditional Oral Epic: The Odyssey, Beowulf, and the Serbo-Croatian Return Song.* Berkeley: University of California Press, 1991.

Forsling, Josef. *Composite Artistry in the Book of Numbers: A Study in Biblical Narrative Conventions.* Studia Theologica Holmiensia 22. Åbo, Finland: Åbo Akademis förlag / Åbo Akademi University Press, 2013.

Fox, Everett. *The Early Prophets.* New York: Schocken, 2014.

———. *The Five Books of Moses.* New York: Schocken, 1995.

Fox, Michael V. *The Song of Songs and the Ancient Egyptian Love Songs.* Madison: University of Wisconsin Press, 1985.

Freeborn, Dennis. *From Old English to Standard English.* 3rd ed. New York: Palgrave Macmillan, 2006.

Freedman, David Noel. "Deliberate Deviation from an Established Pattern of Repetition in Hebrew Poetry as a Rhetorical Device," in *Proceedings of the Ninth World Congress of Jewish Studies, Division A: The Period of the Bible*, 45–52. Jerusalem: World Congress of Jewish Studies, 1986. [Reprinted in: John R. Huddlestun, ed., *Divine Commitment and Human Obligation: Selected Writings of David Noel Freedman*, 2:205–12. Grand Rapids: Eerdmans, 1997.]

Fretz, Mark J. "Weapons and Implements of Warfare," in David Noel Freedman, ed., *The Anchor Bible Dictionary*, 6:893–95. New York: Doubleday, 1992.

Friedman, Richard E. *The Bible with Sources Revealed.* San Francisco: Harper, 2003.

———. *A Commentary on the Torah.* San Francisco: Harper, 2001.

———. *Who Wrote the Bible?* Englewood Cliffs, NJ: Prentice-Hall, 1987.

Friedman, Shamma. "Kol ha-Qaṣar Qodem" (English title: "The 'Law of Increasing Members' in Mishnaic Hebrew"). *Leshonenu* 35 (1971 / 5731): 117–29, 192–206.

Frisch, Amos. "Hedim be-Sifre Nevi'im le-'Issure 'Ḥoq ha-Melek' še-be-Sefer Devarim," in Shmuel Vargon et al., eds., *Menaḥot Yedidut we-Hoqra le-Menaḥem Kohen* [= *'Iyyune Miqra' u-Paršanut* 7 (5765)], 263–81. Ramat-Gan: Bar-Ilan University Press, 2005.

Frymer-Kensky, Tikva. *Reading the Women of the Bible.* New York: Schocken, 2002.

Gábor, Ignaz. *Der hebräische Urrhythmus.* Beihefte zur Zeitschrift für die Alttestamentliche Wissenschaft 25. Giessen: Töpelmann, 1929.

Gamkrelidze, Thomas V., and Vjačeslav V. Ivanov. *Indo-European and the Indo-Europeans: A Reconstruction and Historical Analysis of a Proto-language and a Proto-culture.* 2 vols. Trends in Linguistics: Studies and Monographs 80. Berlin: Mouton de Gruyter, 1994.

Ganzfried, Shelomo. *Sefer Qeset ha-Sofer.* Originally published in Ungvar, Hungary, 1835; 2nd ed., 1871. Reprint: Brooklyn: Moriah, 1985.

Garsiel, Moshe. *Biblical Names: A Literary Study of Midrashic Derivations and Puns.* Ramat-Gan: Bar-Ilan University Press, 1971.

———. *The First Book of Samuel: A Literary Study of Comparative Structures, Analogies and Parallels.* Ramat-Gan: Revivim, 1983.

———. "The Story of David, Nabal and Abigail (1 Samuel 25): A Literary Study of Wordplay on Names, Analogies and Socially Structured

Opposites," in Daniel Bodi, ed., *Abigail, Wife of David, and Other Ancient Oriental Women*, 66–78. Sheffield: Sheffield Phoenix, 2013.

Gevirtz, Stanley. "Of Patriarchs and Puns: Joseph at the Fountain, Jacob at the Ford." *Hebrew Union College Annual* 46 (1975): 33–54.

———. *Patterns in the Early Poetry of Israel*. Chicago: University of Chicago Press, 1963.

Ginsberg, H. L. *The Israelian Heritage of Judaism*. New York: Jewish Theological Seminary, 1982.

Glatt, David A. *Chronological Displacement in Biblical and Related Literatures*. Society of Biblical Literature Dissertation Series 139. Atlanta: Scholars Press, 1993.

Goedicke, Hans. *Die Geschichte des Schiffbrüchigen*. Wiesbaden: Harrassowitz, 1974.

Goldberg, Harvey E. "Cambridge in the Land of Canaan: Descent, Alliance, Circumcision, and Instruction in the Bible." *Journal of the Ancient Near Eastern Society* 24 (1996): 9–34.

Goldingay, John. "Repetition and Variation in the Psalms." *Jewish Quarterly Review* 68 (1977): 146–57.

Gordon, Cyrus H. "Abraham and the Merchants of Ura." *Journal of Near Eastern Studies* 17 (1958): 28–31.

———. "אחדים = *iltênêtu* 'pair'," in Yehoshua M. Grintz and Jacob Liver, eds., *Sefer Segal: Studies in the Bible Presented to Professor M. H. Segal*, 5*–9*. Jerusalem: Kiryat Sepher, 1964.

———. "Build-up and Climax," in Y. Avishur and J. Blau, eds., *Studies in the Bible and Ancient Near East Presented to Samuel E. Loewenstamm*, 29–34. Jerusalem: E. Rubinstein, 1978.

———. "Leviathan: Symbol of Evil," in Alexander Altmann, ed., *Biblical Motifs: Origins and Transformations*, 1–9. Cambridge: Harvard University Press, 1966.

———. "New Directions." *Bulletin of the American Society of Papyrologists* 15 (1978): 59–60.

———. "New Light on the Hebrew Language." *Hebrew Abstracts* 15 (1974): 29–31.

———. *Ugaritic Textbook*. Rome: Pontifical Biblical Institute, 1967.

———. "Vocalized Consonants: The Key to *um-ma/en-ma*/נאם," in Mark E. Cohen, Daniel C. Snell, and David B. Weisberg, eds., *The Tablet and the Scroll: Near Eastern Studies in Honor of William W. Hallo*, 109–10. Bethesda, MD: CDL, 1993.

Gordon, Cyrus H., and Gary A. Rendsburg. *The Bible and the Ancient Near East.* New York: Norton, 1997.

Gordon, Robert P. "Aleph Apologeticum." *Jewish Quarterly Review* 69 (1978): 112–16.

Gottlieb, Isaac. *Yeš Seder la-Miqra*ʾ (English title: *Order In the Bible: The Arrangement of the Torah in Rabbinic and Medieval Jewish Commentary*). Ramat-Gan: Bar-Ilan University Press, 2009.

Greenberg, Moshe. *Ezekiel 1–20.* Anchor Bible 22. Garden City, NY: Doubleday, 1983.

———. *Ezekiel 21–37.* Anchor Bible 22A. New York: Doubleday, 1997.

Greenberg, Moshe, and S. David Sperling. "Exodus, Book of." *Encyclopaedia Judaica*, 2nd ed., 6:612–23. Detroit: Macmillan, 2007.

Greenfield, Jonas C. "Aramaic Studies and the Bible," in John A. Emerton, ed., *Congress Volume: Vienna 1980*, 110–30. Supplements to Vetus Testamentum 32. Leiden: Brill, 1981.

Greenspahn, Frederick E. *Hapax Legomena in Biblical Hebrew.* Society of Biblical Literature Dissertation Series 74. Chico, CA: Scholars Press, 1984.

Greenstein, Edward L. "An Equivocal Reading of the Sale of Joseph," in Kenneth R. R. Gros Louis, ed., *Literary Interpretations of Biblical Narratives*, Volume II, 114–25. Nashville: Abingdon, 1982.

———. "The Invention of Language in the Poetry of Job," in James K. Aitken, Jeremy M. S. Clines, and Christl M. Maier, eds., *Interested Readers: Essays on the Hebrew Bible in Honor of David J. A. Clines*, 332–46. Atlanta: Society of Biblical Literature, 2013.

———. "Jethro's Wit: An Interpretation of Wordplay in Exodus 18," in Stephen L. Cook and S. C. Winter, eds., *On the Way to Nineveh: Studies in Honor of George M. Landes*, 155–71. Atlanta: Scholars Press, 1999.

———. "Kirta," in Simon B. Parker, ed., *Ugaritic Narrative Poetry*, 9–48. Writings from the Ancient World 9. Atlanta: Society of Biblical Literature, 1997.

———. "The Language of Job and Its Poetic Function." *Journal of Biblical Literature* 122 (2003): 651–66.

———. "Some Metaphors in the Poetry of Job," in Maxine L. Grossman, ed., *Built by Wisdom, Established by Understanding: Essays on Biblical and Near Eastern Literature in Honor of Adele Berlin*, 179–95. Bethesda: University Press of Maryland, 2013.

———. "The Syntax of Saying 'Yes' in Biblical Hebrew." *Journal of the Ancient Near Eastern Society* 19 (1989): 51–59.

———. "Wordplay, Hebrew," in David Noel Freedman, ed., *The Anchor Bible Dictionary*, 6:968–71. New York: Doubleday, 1992.

Grintz, Yehoshua M. *Mivḥar ha-Sifrut ha-Miṣrit ha-ʿAtiqa*. Tel Aviv: Devir, 1958.

Grossberg, Daniel. "Nominalization in Biblical Hebrew." *Hebrew Studies* 20–21 (1979–1980): 29–33.

Guillaume, Alfred. "The Meaning of תולל in Psalm 137:3." *Journal of Biblical Literature* 75 (1956): 143–44.

Gunn, David M. *The Fate of King Saul*. Journal for the Study of the Old Testament Supplement Series 14. Sheffield: JSOT Press, 1980.

Ḥakham, Amos. *Isaiah 36–66*. Daʿat Miqraʾ. Jerusalem: Mosad ha-Rav Kook, 1984.

Hamilton, Victor P. *The Book of Genesis: Chapters 18–50*. Grand Rapids: Eerdmans, 1995.

Hartley, John E. *Leviticus*. Word Biblical Commentary 4. Dallas: Word, 1992.

Heim, Knut M. *Poetic Imagination in Proverbs: Variant Repetitions and the Nature of Poetry*. Winona Lake, IN: Eisenbrauns, 2012.

Heschel, Abraham Joshua. *The Sabbath*. New York: Farrar, Straus & Young, 1951.

Hiebert, Robert J. V. "Genesis," in Albert Pietersma and Benjamin G. Wright, eds., *A New English Translation of the Septuagint*, 1–42. New York: Oxford University Press, 2007.

Hodge, Carleton T. "Ritual and Writing: An Inquiry into the Origin of the Egyptian Script," in M. Dale Kinkade, Kenneth L. Hale, and Oswald Werner, eds., *Linguistics and Anthropology: In Honor of C. F. Voegelin*, 331–50. Lisse: Peter de Ridder Press, 1975. [Reprinted in: Scott B. Noegel and Alan S. Kaye, eds., *Afroasiatic Linguistics, Semitics, and Egyptology: Selected Writings of Carleton T. Hodge*, 199–220. Bethesda, MD: CDL, 2004.]

Holladay, William L. *Jeremiah 1: A Commentary on the Book of the Prophet Jeremiah, Chapters 1–25.* Hermeneia. Philadelphia: Fortress, 1986.

Holmstedt, Robert D. "The Story of Ancient Hebrew *ʾăšer.*" *Ancient Near Eastern Studies* 43 (2006): 7–26.

Horobin, S. C. P. "J. R. R. Tolkien as a Philologist: A Reconsideration of the Northernisms in Chaucer's *Reeve's Tale.*" *English Studies* 82 (2001): 97–105.

Hurowitz, Avigdor (Victor). "Healing and Hissing Snakes: Listening to Numbers 21:4–9." *Scriptura* 87 (2004): 278–87.

———. *Mišle.* 2 vols. Miqraʾ le-Yiśraʾel. Jerusalem: Magnes, 2012.

Hurvitz, Avi. "The Date of the Prose-Tale of Job Linguistically Reconsidered." *Harvard Theological Review* 67 (1974): 17–34.

———. "'Kiʾazmus Diʾakroni' ba-ʿIvrit ha-Miqraʾit," in Benjamin Uffenheimer, ed., *Ha-Miqraʾ ve-Toldot Yisraʾel: Meḥqarim ba-Miqraʾ u-ve-Sifrut Yeme Bayit Šeni le-Zikro šel Yaʿaqov Liver,* 248–51. Tel Aviv: Tel Aviv University, 1972.

———. *A Linguistic Study of the Relationship between the Priestly Source and the Book of Ezekiel.* Cahiers de la Revue Biblique 20. Paris: Gabalda, 1982.

———. "Ruth 2:7—'A Midrashic Gloss'?" *Zeitschrift für die alttestamentliche Wissenschaft* 95 (1983): 121–23.

Jacob, Benno. *Das erste Buch der Torah: Genesis.* Berlin: Schocken, 1934.

Janzen, J. Gerald. *Studies in the Text of Jeremiah.* Cambridge: Harvard University Press, 1973.

Johnson, Samuel. *A Dictionary of the English Language.* London: W. Strahan, 1755.

Johnstone, T. M. *Jibbāli Lexicon.* Oxford: Oxford University Press, 1981.

———. *Mehri Lexicon.* London: School of Oriental and African Studies, 1987.

Joosten, Jan. *The Verbal System of Biblical Hebrew.* Jerusalem Biblical Studies 10. Jerusalem: Simor, 2012.

Joüon, Paul, and Takamitsu Muraoka. *A Grammar of Biblical Hebrew.* 2 vols. Subsidia Biblica 14. Rome: Pontifical Biblical Institute, 1991.

Kaufman, Stephen A. "The Classification of the North West Semitic Dialects of the Biblical Period and Some Implications Thereof," in

Proceedings of the Ninth World Congress of Jewish Studies, vol. 5, *Panel Sessions*, part 1, *Hebrew and Aramaic Languages*, 41–57. Jerusalem: World Union of Jewish Studies, 1988.

———. "The Structure of the Deuteronomic Law." *Maarav* 1 (1978–1979): 105–58.

Kautzsch, Emil. *Gesenius' Hebrew Grammar*. Translated by A. E. Cowley. Oxford: Clarendon, 1910.

Kazin, Alfred. *The Portable Blake*. New York: Viking, 1968.

Keller, Sharon R. "An Egyptian Analogue to the Priestly Blessing," in Meir Lubetski, Claire Gottlieb, and Sharon Keller, eds., *Boundaries of the Ancient Near Eastern World: A Tribute to Cyrus H. Gordon*, 338–45. Sheffield: Sheffield Academic Press, 1998.

Kikawada, Isaac. "Literary Convention of the Primeval History." *Annual of the Japanese Biblical Institute* 1 (1975): 3–22.

Kim, Yoo-ki. *The Function of the Tautological Infinitive in Classical Biblical Hebrew*. Harvard Semitic Studies 60. Winona Lake, IN: Eisenbrauns, 2009.

Kister, Menahem. "Some Blessing and Curse Formulae in the Bible, Northwest Semitic Inscriptions, Post-Biblical Literature and Late Antiquity," in M. F. J. Baasten and W. Th. van Peursen, eds., *Hamlet on a Hill: Semitic and Greek Studies Presented to T. Muraoka on the Occasion of His Sixty-Fifth Birthday*, 313–32. Orientalia Lovaniensia Analecta 118. Leuven: Peeters, 2003.

Kline, Jonathan G. *Allusive Soundplay in the Hebrew Bible*. SBL Ancient Israel and Its Literature 28. Atlanta: SBL Press, 2016.

———. "Transforming the Tradition: Soundplay as an Interpretive Device in Innerbiblical Allusions." PhD dissertation, Harvard University, 2014.

Knohl, Israel. *The Divine Symphony: The Bible's Many Voices*. Philadelphia: Jewish Publication Society, 2003.

Knox, Philip. "The 'Dialect' of Chaucer's Reeve." *The Chaucer Review* 49 (2014): 102–24.

Kogut, Simcha. *Ha-Miqra' ben Ṭeʿamim le-Paršanut*. Jerusalem: Bialik, 1996.

———. "Keṣad huṭreda 'ešet Poṭifar u-maduaʿ *wə-hab-bor req* (Berešit 37:24) lo' haya req? Pešaṭ u-Draš be-he'ara lešonit," in Lea Mazor, ed., *Sippur Yosef ba-Miqra' u-ve-Re'i ha-Dorot = Bet Miqra'* 55 (2009–2010 / 5770): 77–83.

Koller, Aaron. "Diachronic Change and Synchronic Readings: Midrashim on Stative Verbs and Participles." *Journal of Semitic Studies* 57 (2012): 265–94.

Kugel, James. *How to Read the Bible: A Guide to Scripture, Then and Now.* New York: Free Press, 2007.

———. *The Idea of Biblical Poetry.* New Haven: Yale University Press, 1981.

Kutscher, E. Y. *A History of the Hebrew Language.* Leiden: Brill; Jerusalem, Magnes, 1982.

———. *Ha-Lašon we-ha-Reqaʿ šel Megillat Yešaʿyahu ha-Šelema mi-Megillot Yam ha-Melaḥ.* Jerusalem: Magnes, 1959.

Landes, George M. "Linguistic Criteria and the Date of the Book of Jonah," in *Eretz-Israel* 16 (Harry Orlinsky Volume), 147–70. Jerusalem: ha-Ḥevra le-Ḥaqirat Ereṣ-Yisra'el ve-ʿAtiqoteha, 1982.

Lattimore, Richard. *The Iliad of Homer.* Chicago: University of Chicago Press, 1951.

Leibowitz, Nehama. *Torah Insights.* Translated by Alan Smith. Jerusalem: Eliner Library, Joint Authority for Jewish Zionist Education, Department for Torah and Culture in the Diaspora, 1995.

Leithart, Peter. "Nabal and His Wine." *Journal of Biblical Literature* 120 (2001): 525–27.

Levenson, Jon D., and Baruch Halpern. "The Political Import of David's Marriages." *Journal of Biblical Literature* 99 (1980): 507–18.

Levin, Saul. "Homo : Humus and the Semitic Counterparts: The Oldest Culturally Significant Etymology?" in J. Peter Maher, Allan R. Bomhard, and E. F. K. Koerner, eds., *Papers from the Third International Conference on Historical Linguistics, Hamburg, August 22–26 1977*, 207–16. Amsterdam: John Benjamins, 1982.

———. "The 'Qeri' as the Primary Text of the Hebrew Bible." *General Linguistics* 35 (1997): 181–223.

———. *Semitic and Indo-European: The Principal Etymologies.* Amsterdam: John Benjamins, 1995.

———. *Semitic and Indo-European II: Comparative Morphology, Syntax and Phonetics.* Amsterdam: John Benjamins, 2002.

Levine, Nachman. "Ten Hungers/Six Barleys: Structure and Redemption in the Targum to Ruth." *Journal for the Study of Judaism* 30 (1999): 312–24.

Lévi-Strauss, Claude. *Structural Anthropology.* New York: Basic Books, 1976.

Lichtheim, Miriam. *Ancient Egyptian Literature.* 3 vols. Berkeley: University of California Press, 1973–1980.

Lillas, Rosmari. "*Hendiadys* in the Hebrew Bible: An Investigation of the Applications of the Term." PhD dissertation, University of Gothenburg, 2012.

Lipiński, Edward. *Semitic Languages: Outline of a Comparative Grammar.* Leuven: Peeters, 1997.

Longacre, Robert E. *Joseph: A Story of Divine Providence.* Winona Lake, IN: Eisenbrauns, 1989.

———. "*Weqatal* Forms in Biblical Hebrew Prose: A Discourse-modular Approach," in Robert D. Bergen, ed., *Biblical Hebrew and Discourse Linguistics,* 50–98. Dallas: Summer Institute of Linguistics, 1994.

Lord, Albert B. *The Singer of Tales.* Harvard Studies in Comparative Literature 24. Cambridge: Harvard University Press, 1960.

Lys, Daniel. "Résidence ou repos? Notule sur Ruth ii 7." *Vetus Testamentum* 21 (1971): 497–501.

Manguel, Alberto. *A History of Reading.* New York: Viking, 1996.

Marcus, David. "How Many Daughters Did Lot Have?" in Shamir Yona, ed., *Or le-Mayer: Studies in Bible, Semitic Languages, Rabbinic Literature, and Ancient Civilizations Presented to Mayer Gruber on the Occasion of His Sixty-Fifth Birthday,* 109*–20*. Beersheva: Ben-Gurion University of the Negev Press, 2010.

———. *Jephthah and His Vow.* Lubbock: Texas Tech Press, 1986.

———. "Non-Recurring Doublets in the Book of Lamentations." *Hebrew Annual Review* 10 (1986): 177–95.

Margalit, Baruch. "Alliteration in Ugaritic Poetry: Its Role in Composition and Analysis," *Ugarit-Forschungen* 11 (1979): 537–57.

———. "Alliteration in Ugaritic Poetry: Its Role in Composition and Analysis (Part II)." *Journal of Northwest Semitic Languages* 8 (1980): 57–80.

Margaliot, Mordecai, ed. *Midraš ha-Gadol ʿal Ḥamiša Ḥumše Torah: Sefer Berešit.* Jerusalem: Mosad ha-Rav Kook, 1947.

Mayes, A. D. H. *Deuteronomy.* Grand Rapids: Eerdmans, 1981.

McCarter, P. Kyle. *I Samuel.* Anchor Bible 8. Garden City, NY: Doubleday, 1980.

————. *II Samuel.* Anchor Bible 8A. New York: Doubleday, 1984.

McCarthy, Carmel. *Deuteronomy.* Biblia Hebraica Quinta 5. Stuttgart: Deutsche Bibelgeschellschaft, 2007.

McCreesh, Thomas P. *Biblical Sound and Sense: Poetic Sound Patterns in Proverbs 10–29.* Journal for the Study of the Old Testament Supplement Series 128. Sheffield: JSOT Press, 1991.

McKane, William. *A Critical and Exegetical Commentary on Jeremiah.* International Critical Commentary. Edinburgh: T&T Clark, 1986.

Meier, Samuel E. *Speaking of Speaking: Marking Direct Discourse in the Hebrew Bible.* Supplements to Vetus Testamentum 46. Leiden: Brill, 1992.

Merwe, C. H. J. van der. "Discourse Linguistics and Biblical Hebrew Grammar," in Robert D. Bergen, ed., *Biblical Hebrew and Discourse Linguistics,* 13–49. Dallas: Summer Institute of Linguistics, 1994.

Meyers, Carol L. "Having Their Space and Eating There Too: Bread Production and Female Power in Ancient Israelite Households." *Nashim: A Journal of Jewish Women's Studies* 5 (2002): 14–44.

Michaelis, Johann Heinrich. *Biblia Hebraica, ex aliquot manuscriptis.* Halae Magdeburgicae: Typis & Sumtibus Orpha notrophei, 1720.

Milgrom, Jacob. *Numbers.* JPS Torah Commentary. Philadelphia: Jewish Publication Society, 1990.

————. *Leviticus 1–16.* Anchor Bible 3. New York: Doubleday, 1991.

Miller, Geoffrey D. "Intertextuality in Old Testament Research." *Currents in Biblical Research* 9 (2010), 283–309.

Miller, Patrick. "Studies in Hebrew Word Patterns." *Harvard Theological Review* 73 (1980): 79–89.

Mirsky, Aharon. "Stylistic Device for Conclusion in Hebrew." *Semitics* 5 (1977): 5–23.

Mishor, Mordechay. "On the Language and Text of Exodus 18," in Steven E. Fassberg and Avi Hurvitz, eds., *Biblical Hebrew in Its Northwest Semitic Environment: Typological and Historical Perspectives,* 225–29. Jerusalem: Magnes; Winona Lake, IN: Eisenbrauns, 2006.

Mizrahi, Noam. "Kings or Messengers? The Text of 2 Samuel 11:1 in the Light of Hebrew Historical Phonology." *Zeitschrift für Althebräistik* 25–28 (2012–2015): 57–83.

Moore, Alex W. *Concord Authors: Biographical Notes.* Concord, MA: Anaxagoras Publications, 1989.

Moore, George Foot. *A Critical and Exegetical Commentary on Judges.* International Critical Commentary. Edinburgh: T&T Clark, 1895.

Moore, Michael S. "Two Textual Anomalies in Ruth." *Catholic Biblical Quarterly* 59 (1997): 238–43.

Morag, Shelomo. "Rovde Qadmut." *Tarbiz* 50 (1981): 1–24.

Moreshet, Menahem. "ki-nhalim nittayu," *Bet Miqraʾ* 48 (1971–1972 / 5732): 51–56.

Moyer, Clinton J. "Literary and Linguistic Studies in Sefer Bilʿam (Numbers 22–24)." PhD dissertation, Cornell University, 2009.

———. "Who Is the Prophet, and Who the Ass? Role-Reversing Interludes and the Unity of the Balaam Narrative (Numbers 22–24)." *Journal for the Study of the Old Testament* 37 (2012): 167–83.

Muraoka, Takamitsu. "Biblical Hebrew Philological Notes (2)." *Jerusalem Studies in Arabic and Islam* 15 (1992) (= *Studies in Semitic Linguistics in Honour of Joshua Blau [I]*): 43–54.

Murray, D. F. "Narrative Structure and Technique in the Deborah-Barak Story, Judges iv 4–22," in John A. Emerton, ed., *Studies in the Historical Books of the Old Testament*, 155–89. Supplements to Vetus Testamentum 30. Leiden: Brill, 1979.

Naeh, Shlomo. "A New Suggestion Regarding 2 Samuel xxiii 7." *Vetus Testamentum* 46 (1996): 260–65.

Naveh, Joseph. "A Hebrew Letter from the Seventh Century B.C." *Israel Exploration Journal* 10 (1960): 129–39.

Niehoff, Maren. "Do Biblical Characters Talk to Themselves? Narrative Modes of Representing Inner Speech in Early Biblical Fiction." *Journal of Biblical Literature* 111 (1992): 577–95.

Noegel, Scott B. *Janus Parallelism in the Book of Job.* Journal for the Study of the Old Testament Supplement Series 223. Sheffield: Sheffield Academic, 1996.

———. "The Significance of the Seventh Plague." *Biblica* 76 (1995): 532–39.

———. "Wordplay in the Tale of the Poor Man of Nippur." *Acta Sumerologica* 18 (1996): 169–86.

Noegel, Scott B., and Gary A. Rendsburg. *Solomon's Vineyard: Literary and Linguistic Studies in the Song of Songs.* SBL Ancient Israel and Its Literature 1. Atlanta: Society of Biblical Literature, 2009.

Noth, Martin. *A History of Pentateuchal Traditions.* Translated by Bernhard W. Anderson. Chico, CA: Scholars Press, 1981.

O'Connell, Robert H. *The Rhetoric of the Book of Judges.* Supplements to Vetus Testamentum 63. Leiden: Brill, 1996.

Oesch, Josef M. "Skizze einder formalen Gliederungshermeneutik der Sifre Tora," in Marjo C. A. Korpel and Josef M. Oesch, eds., *Unit Delimitation in Biblical Hebrew and Northwest Semitic Literature,* 162–203. Pericope 4. Assen: Van Gorcum, 2003.

Ogden, G. S. "Notes on the Use of הויה in Exodus ix 3." *Vetus Testamentum* 17 (1967): 483–84.

del Olmo Lete, Gregorio, and Joaquín Sanmartín. *A Dictionary of the Ugaritic Language in the Alphabetic Tradition.* Translated by Wilfred G. E. Watson. 2 vols. Leiden: Brill, 2003.

Osimo, Bruno. "Nabokov's Selftranslations: Interpretation Problems and Solutions in Lolita's Russian Version." *Sign Systems Studies* 27 (1999): 215–33.

Par'an, Meir. *Darkhe ha-Signon ha-Kohani ba-Torah.* Jerusalem: Magnes, 1989.

Parkinson, Richard B. *The Tale of Sinuhe and Other Ancient Egyptian Poems 1940–1640 BC.* Oxford: Clarendon, 1997.

Paul, Shalom M. *Amos.* Hermeneia. Minneapolis: Fortress, 1991.

———. "Exodus 1:21: 'To Found a Family': A Biblical and Akkadian Idiom," in Robert J. Ratner et al., eds., *Let Your Colleagues Praise You: Studies in Memory of Stanley Gevirtz,* Part II = *Maarav* 8 (1992): 139–42.

———. *Isaiah 40–66.* Eerdmans Critical Commentary. Grand Rapids: Eerdmans, 2012).

———. "Polysemous Pivotal Punctuation: More Janus Double Entendres," in Michael V. Fox et al., eds., *Texts, Temples, and Traditions: A Tribute to Menahem Haran,* 369–74. Winona Lake, IN: Eisenbrauns, 1996.

———. "Polysensuous Polyvalency in Poetic Parallelisms," in Michael Fishbane and Emanuel Tov, eds., *"Shaʿarei Talmon": Studies in the Bible, Qumran, and the Ancient Near East Presented to Shemaryahu Talmon,* 147–63. Winona Lake, IN: Eisenbrauns, 1992.

Person, Raymond F. "The Ancient Israelite Scribe as Performer." *Journal of Biblical Literature* 117 (1998): 601–9.

Petrounias, E. B. "The Pronunciation of Ancient Greek: Evidence and Hypothesis," in A.-F. Christidis, ed., *A History of Ancient Greek: From the Beginnings to Late Antiquity,* 545–55. Cambridge: Cambridge University Press, 2007.

Pope, Marvin H. *Song of Songs.* Anchor Bible 7C. Garden City, NY: Doubleday, 1977.

———. "Response to Sasson on the Sublime Song." *Maarav* 2 (1980): 207–14.

Price, James D. *Concordance of the Hebrew Accents in the Hebrew Bible.* 5 vols. Lewiston, NY: Mellen, 1996.

Propp, William H. C. *Exodus 1–18.* Anchor Bible 2. New York: Doubleday, 1999.

Qimron, Elisha, and James H. Charlesworth. "Rule of the Community," in James H. Charlesworth, ed., *The Dead Sea Scrolls: Hebrew, Aramaic, and Greek Texts with English Translations*, vol. 1, *Rule of the Community and Related Documents,* 1–52. Tübingen: Mohr; Louisville: Westminster John Knox, 1994.

Rabin, Chaim. "An Arabic Phrase in Isaiah," in *Studi sull'Oriente e la Bibbia: Offerti al P. Giovanni Rinaldi nel 60° compleanno da ellievi, colleghi, amici,* 303–9. Genoa: Studio e Vita, 1967.

Rabinowitz, Isaac. *A Witness Forever: Ancient Israel's Perception of Literature and the Resultant Hebrew Bible.* Occasional Publications of the Department of Near Eastern Studies and the Program of Jewish Studies, Cornell University, 1. Bethesda, MD: CDL, 1993.

Rahlfs, Alfred. "Zur Setzung der Lesemütter im Alten Testament," in *Nachrichten von der Königlichen Gesellschaft der Wissenschaften zu Göttingen: Philologisch-historische Klasse,* 315–47. Berlin: Weidmannsche Buchhandlung, 1916.

Rankin, O. S. "Alliteration in Hebrew Poetry." *Journal of Theological Studies* 31 (1930): 285–91.

Ratner, Robert J. "Morphological Variation in Biblical Hebrew Rhetoric," in Robert J. Ratner et al., eds., *Let Your Colleagues Praise You: Studies in Memory of Stanley Gevirtz,* Part II = *Maarav* 8 (1992): 143–59.

Reinhartz, Adele. *Why Ask My Name? Anonymity and Identity in Biblical Narrative.* New York: Oxford University Press, 1998.

Rendsburg, Gary A. "Alliteration in the Book of Genesis," in Elizabeth R. Hayes and Karolien Vermeulen, eds., *Doubling and Duplicating in the Book of Genesis: Literary and Stylistic Approaches to the Text,* 79–95. Winona Lake, IN: Eisenbrauns, 2016.

———. "Alliteration in the Exodus Narrative," in Chaim Cohen et al., eds., *Birkat Shalom: Studies in the Bible, Ancient Near Eastern Lit-*

erature, and Postbiblical Judaism Presented to Shalom M. Paul on the Occasion of His Seventieth Birthday*, 83–100. Winona Lake, IN: Eisenbrauns, 2008.

———. "Ancient Hebrew Phonology," in Alan S. Kaye ed., *The Phonologies of Asia and Africa*, 65–83. Winona Lake, IN: Eisenbrauns, 1997.

———. "Aramaic-like Features in the Pentateuch." *Hebrew Studies* 47 (2006): 163–76.

———. "Beasts or Bugs? Solving the Problem of the Fourth Plague." *Bible Review* 19.2 (Apr. 2003): 18–23.

———. "The Biblical Flood Story in the Light of the Gilgameš Flood Account," in Joseph Azize and Noel Weeks, eds., *Gilgameš and the World of Assyria: Proceedings of the Conference held at Mandelbaum House, The University of Sydney, 21–23 July 2004*, 115–27. Ancient Near Eastern Studies, Supplement 21. Leuven: Peeters, 2007.

———. "Biblical Literature as Politics: The Case of Genesis," in Adele Berlin, ed., *Religion and Politics in the Ancient Near East*, 47–70. Bethesda: University Press of Maryland, 1996.

———. "A Comprehensive Guide to Israelian Hebrew: Grammar and Lexicon." *Orient* 38 (2003): 5–35.

———. "Confused Language as a Deliberate Literary Device in Biblical Hebrew Narrative." *Journal of Hebrew Scriptures*, vol. 2, article 6 (1998–1999), available online at: http://www.jhsonline.org/Articles /article_12.pdf. [Reprinted in: Ehud Ben Zvi, ed., *Perspectives on Hebrew Scriptures I*, 197–213. Perspectives on Hebrew Scriptures and Its Contexts 1. Piscataway, NJ: Gorgias, 2006.]

———. "David and His Circle in Genesis xxxviii." *Vetus Testamentum* 36 (1986): 438–46.

———. "Double Polysemy in Genesis 49:6 and Job 3:6." *Catholic Biblical Quarterly* 44 (1982): 48–51.

———. "Double Polysemy in Proverbs 31:19," in Asma Afsaruddin and A. H. Mathias Zahniser, eds., *Humanism, Culture, and Language in the Near East: Studies in Honor of Georg Krotkoff*, 267–74. Winona Lake, IN: Eisenbrauns, 1997.

———. "The Egyptian Sun-God Ra in the Pentateuch." *Henoch* 10 (1988): 3–15.

———. "The Genesis of the Bible," in *The Blanche and Irving Laurie Chair in Jewish History*, separatum published by the Allen and

Joan Bildner Center for the Study of Jewish Life, Rutgers, The State University of New Jersey (2005): 11–30.

———. "The Guilty Party in 1 Kings iii 16–28." *Vetus Testamentum* 48 (1998): 534–41.

———. "Hebrew Philological Notes (I)." *Hebrew Studies* 40 (1999): 27–32.

———. "Hebrew Philological Notes (III)." *Hebrew Studies* 43 (2002): 25–26.

———. "The Inclusio in Leviticus xi." *Vetus Testamentum* 43 (1993): 418–21.

———. *Israelian Hebrew in the Book of Kings.* Occasional Publications of the Department of Near Eastern Studies and the Program of Jewish Studies, Cornell University, 5. Bethesda, MD: CDL, 2002.

———. "*Kabbîr* in Biblical Hebrew: Evidence for Style-Switching and Addressee-Switching in the Hebrew Bible." *Journal of the American Oriental Society* 112 (1992): 649–51.

———. "Lašon Mebulbelet ke-Takhsis Sifruti ba-Sippur ha-Miqra'i," in Shmuel Vargon et al., eds., *Menaḥot, Yedidut, ve-Hoqra le-Moshe Garsiel*, 27–43 = *'Iyyune Miqra u-Paršanut* 9 (5769). Ramat-Gan: Bar-Ilan University Press, 2009.

———. "*Lasûaḥ* in Gen. xxiv 63." *Vetus Testamentum* 45 (1995): 558–60.

———. "Late Biblical Hebrew in the Book of Haggai," in Rebecca Hasselbach and Naʿama Pat-El, eds., *Language and Nature: Papers Presented to John Huehnergard on the Occasion of His 60th Birthday*, 329–44. Studies in Ancient Oriental Civilization 67. Chicago: The Oriental Institute of the University of Chicago, 2012.

———. *Linguistic Evidence for the Northern Origin of Selected Psalms.* Society of Biblical Literature Monograph Series 43. Atlanta: Scholars Press, 1990.

———. "Linguistic Variation and the 'Foreign' Factor in the Hebrew Bible." *Israel Oriental Studies* 15 (1996): 177–90.

———. "Literary and Linguistic Matters in the Book of Proverbs," in John Jarick, ed., *Perspectives on Israelite Wisdom: Proceedings of the Oxford Old Testament Seminar*, 111–47. The Library of Hebrew Bible / Old Testament Studies 618. London: Bloomsbury T&T Clark, 2016.

———. "The Literary Approach to the Bible and Finding a Good Translation," in Frederick W. Knobloch, ed., *Biblical Translation in Context*, 179–94. Bethesda: University Press of Maryland, 2002.

———. "Literary Devices in the Story of the Shipwrecked Sailor." *Journal of the American Oriental Society* 120 (2000): 13–23.

———. "The Literary Unity of the Exodus Narrative," in James K. Hoffmeier, Alan Millard, and Gary A. Rendsburg, eds., *"Did I Not Bring Israel Out of Egypt?": Biblical, Archaeological, and Egyptological Perspectives on the Exodus Narratives*, 113–32. Bulletin for Biblical Research Supplement 13. Winona Lake, IN: Eisenbrauns, 2016.

———. "Marking Closure." *Vetus Testamentum* 66 (2016): 280–303.

———. "Millat ha-Qiyyum אשׁ." *Meḥqarim be-Lašon* 9 (2003): 251–55.

———. "More on Hebrew *šibbōlet*." *Journal of Semitic Studies* 33 (1988): 255–58.

———. "Moses as Equal to Pharaoh," in Gary M. Beckman and Theodore J. Lewis, eds., *Text, Artifact, and Image: Revealing Ancient Israelite Religion*, 201–19. Brown Judaic Studies 346. Providence: Brown Judaic Studies, 2006.

———. "Notes on Genesis xxxv." *Vetus Testamentum* 34 (1984): 361–66.

———. "Notes on Israelian Hebrew (I)," in Yitzhak Avishur and Robert Deutsch, eds., *Michael: Historical, Epigraphical and Biblical Studies in Honor of Prof. Michael Heltzer*, 255–58. Tel Aviv: Archaeological Center Publications, 1999.

———. "Phonology: Biblical Hebrew," in Geoffrey Khan, ed., *Encyclopedia of Hebrew Language and Linguistics*, 3:100–109. 4 vols. Leiden: Brill, 2013.

———. "Reading David in Genesis: How We Know the Torah Was Written in the Tenth Century B.C.E." *Bible Review* 17.1 (Feb. 2001): 20–33, 46.

———. *The Redaction of Genesis*. Winona Lake, IN: Eisenbrauns, 1986. Repr., with a new foreword, 2014.

———. "Repetition with Variation in Legal-Cultic Texts of the Torah," in Shamir Yona et al., eds., *Marbeh Ḥokmah: Studies in the Bible and the Ancient Near East in Loving Memory of Victor Avigdor Hurowitz*, 435–63. Winona Lake, IN: Eisenbrauns, 2015.

———. "Shibboleth," in Geoffrey Khan, ed., *Encyclopedia of Hebrew Language and Linguistics*, 3:556–57. Leiden: Brill, 2013.

———. "Šimuš Bilti Ragil šel Kinnuy ha-Remez ba-Miqraʾ: ʿEdut Nosefet le-ʿIvrit Ṣefonit bi-Tqufat ha-Miqraʾ." *Shnaton* 12 (2000): 83–88.

———. "Some False Leads in the Identification of Late Biblical Hebrew Texts: The Cases of Genesis 24 and 1 Samuel 2:27–36." *Journal of Biblical Literature* 121 (2002): 23–46.

———. "The Strata of Biblical Hebrew." *Journal of Northwest Semitic Languages* 17 (1991): 81–99.

———. "Style-Switching in Biblical Hebrew," in Jeremy M. Hutton and Aaron D. Rubin, eds., *Epigraphy, Philology, and the Hebrew Bible: Methodological Perspectives on Philological and Comparative Study in of the Hebrew Bible in Honor of Jo Ann Hackett*, 65–85. SBL Ancient Near East Monographs 12. Atlanta: SBL Press, 2015.

———. "תַּלְפִּיּוֹת (Song 4:4)." *Journal of Northwest Semitic Languages* 20 (1994): 13–19.

———. "The Two Screens: On Mary Douglas's Proposal for a Literary Structure to the Book of Leviticus." *Jewish Studies Quarterly* 15 (2008): 175–89.

———. "Unlikely Heroes: Women as Israel." *Bible Review* 19.1 (Feb. 2003): 16–23, 52–53.

———. "Variation in Biblical Hebrew Prose and Poetry," in Maxine Grossman, ed., *Built by Wisdom, Established by Understanding: Essays in Honor of Adele Berlin*, 197–226. Bethesda: University Press of Maryland, 2013.

———. "What We Can Learn about Other Northwest Semitic Dialects from Reading the Bible," in Athalya Brenner-Idan, ed., *Discourse, Dialogue, and Debate in the Bible: Essays in Honour of Frank H. Polak*, 160–78. Hebrew Bible Monographs 63; Amsterdam Studies in Bible and Religion 7. Sheffield: Sheffield Phoenix Press, 2014.

———. "Word Play in Biblical Hebrew: An Eclectic Collection," in Scott B. Noegel, ed., *Puns and Pundits: Word Play in the Bible and in Near Eastern Literature*, 137–62. Bethesda, MD: CDL Press, 2000.

Rendsburg, Gary A., and Susan L. Rendsburg. "Physiological and Philological Notes to Psalm 137." *Jewish Quarterly Review* 83 (1993): 385–99.

Rendsburg, Gary A., and William M. Schniedewind. "The Siloam Tunnel Inscription: Historical and Linguistic Perspectives." *Israel Exploration Journal* 60 (2010): 188–203.

Revell, E. J. *The Designation of the Individual: Expressive Usage in Biblical Narrative*. Kampen: Kok Pharos, 1996.

———. "The Two Forms of First Person Singular Pronoun in Biblical Hebrew: Redundancy or Expressive Contrast?" *Journal of Semitic Studies* 40 (1995): 199–217.

Richelle, Matthieu. "Elusive Scrolls: Could Any Hebrew Literature Have Been Written Prior to the Eighth Century BCE?" *Vetus Testamentum* 66 (2016): 556–94.

Rin, Zvi, and Shifra Rin. ʿAlilot ha-ʾElim: Kol Širot ʾUgarit. Philadelphia: Inbal, 1996.

Robinson, Bernard P. "The Theophany and Meal of Exodus 24." *Scandinavian Journal of the Old Testament* 25 (2011): 155–73.

Robinson, Fred C. "Some Aspects of the 'Maldon' Poet's Artistry." *The Journal of English and Germanic Philology* 75 (1976): 25–40.

Rofé, Alexander. "Sidduram šel ha-ḥuqqim be-Sefer Devarim," in Shemuʾel Reʾem, Haim Beinart, and Samuel E. Loewenstamm, eds., *Studies in the Bible: M. D. Cassuto Centennial Volume*, 217–35. Jerusalem: Magnes, 1987.

Roper, Jonathan. "Alliteration Lost, Kept and Gained: Translation as Indicator of Language-Specific Prosaics," in Anneli Baran, Liisi Laineste, and Piret Voolaid, eds., *Scala Naturae: Festschrift in Honour of Arvo Krikmann for His 75th Birthday*, 419–34. Tartu: ELM Scholarly Press, 2014.

Rosenberg, Joel. "1 and 2 Samuel," in Robert Alter and Frank Kermode, eds., *The Literary Guide to the Bible*, 122–45. Cambridge: Harvard University Press [Belknap], 1987.

Roshwalb, Esther H. "Build-up and Climax in Jeremiah's Visions and Laments," in Meir Lubetski, Claire Gottlieb, and Sharon Keller, eds., *Boundaries of the Ancient Near Eastern World: A Tribute to Cyrus H. Gordon*, 111–35. Journal for the Study of the Old Testament Supplement Series 273. Sheffield: Sheffield Academic, 1998.

Rubin, Aaron D. "Genesis 49:4 in Light of Arabic and Modern South Arabian." *Vetus Testamentum* 59 (2009): 499–502.

———. *Omani Mehri: A New Grammar with Texts.* Studies in Semitic Languages and Linguistics 93. Leiden: Brill, 2018.

Sanders, Paul. "The Ashkar-Gilson Manuscript: Remnant of a Proto-Masoretic Model Scroll of the Torah." *Journal of Hebrew Scriptures*, vol. 14, article 7 (2014): 1–25, available online at: http://www.jhsonline.org/Articles/article_201.pdf.

———. "Missing Link in Hebrew Bible Formation." *Biblical Archaeology Review* 41.6 (Nov.–Dec. 2015): 46–52, 74, 76.

Sanderson, Judith E. "4QExod^c," in Eugene Ulrich and Frank Moore Cross, eds., *Qumran Cave 4/VII*, 97–125. Discoveries in the Judaean Desert 12. Oxford: Clarendon, 1994.

Sarna, Nahum M. *Exploring Exodus*. New York: Schocken, 1986.

———. *Understanding Genesis*. New York: Schocken, 1966.

Sasson, Jack M. *Jonah*. Anchor Bible 24B. New York: Doubleday, 1990.

———. "On Jonah's Two Missions." *Henoch* 6 (1984): 23–30.

———. "On Pope's Song of Songs (AB 7C)." *Maarav* 1 (1979): 177–96.

———. *Ruth: A New Translation, with a Philological Commentary and a Formalist-Folkloristic Interpretation*. 2nd ed. Sheffield: JSOT Press, 1989.

———. "The 'Tower of Babel' as a Clue to the Redactional Structuring of the Primeval History (Genesis 1:1–11:9)," in Gary A. Rendsburg et al., eds., *The Bible World: Essays in Honor of Cyrus H. Gordon*, 211–19. New York: Ktav, 1980. [Reprinted in: Richard S. Hess and David T. Tsumura, eds., *I Studied Inscriptions from before the Flood: Ancient Near Eastern, Literary, and Linguistic Approaches to Genesis 1–11*, 448–57. Winona Lake, IN: Eisenbrauns, 1994.]

———. "Wordplay in the OT," in Keith R. Crim, ed., *The Interpreter's Dictionary of the Bible, Supplementary Volume*, 968–70. Nashville: Abingdon, 1976.

Satlow, Michael L. *How the Bible Became Holy*. New Haven: Yale University Press, 2014.

Savran, George W. *Telling and Retelling: Quotation in Biblical Narrative*. Bloomington: Indiana University Press, 1988.

Scheindlin, Raymond P. *The Book of Job*. New York: Norton, 1999.

Schniedewind, William M. *How the Bible Became a Book: The Textualization of Ancient Israel*. New York: Cambridge University Press, 2004.

Schwartz, Baruch J. "Leviticus," in Adele Berlin and Marc Zvi Brettler, eds., *The Jewish Study Bible*, 2nd ed., 193–266. New York: Oxford University Press, 2014.

Scott-Warren, Jason. "Was Elizabeth I Richard II? The Authenticity of Lambarde's 'Conversation'." *The Review of English Studies* 64 (2013): 208–30.

Segal, Moshe Zvi. "Le-Ḥeqer ha-<Pisqa> be-ʾEmṣaʿ Pasuq>." *Tarbiz* 29 (1960): 203–6.

Seidel, Moshe. "Maqbilot ben Sefer Yešaʿyahu le-Sefer Tehillim." *Sinai* 38 (1955–1956): 149–72, 229–40, 272–80, 335–55. [Reprinted in: Moshe Seidel, *Ḥiqre Miqra*ʾ, 1–99. Jerusalem: Mosad ha-Rav Kook, 1978.]

Seow, Choon-Leong. *Ecclesiastes.* Anchor Bible 18C. New York: Doubleday, 1997.

Shippey, T. A. *J. R. R. Tolkien: Author of the Century.* Boston: Houghton Mifflin, 2000.

Simpson, William Kelly. *The Literature of Ancient Egypt.* New Haven: Yale University Press, 1972.

Smith, Henry Preserved. *A Critical and Exegetical Commentary on the Books of Samuel.* International Critical Commentary. Edinburgh: T&T Clark, 1899.

Snell, Daniel C. *Twice-Told Proverbs and the Composition of the Book of Proverbs.* Winona Lake, IN: Eisenbrauns, 1993.

Sokoloff, Michael. *A Dictionary of Jewish Babylonian Aramaic.* Ramat-Gan: Bar-Ilan University Press, 2002.

———. *A Dictionary of Jewish Palestinian Aramaic.* Ramat-Gan: Bar-Ilan University Press, 1992.

Sommer, Benjamin D. *A Prophet Reads Scripture: Allusion in Isaiah 40–66.* Contraversions: Jews and Other Differences. Stanford: Stanford University Press, 1998.

Sperber, Alexander. *The Bible in Aramaic.* Leiden: Brill, 2004. Reprint of the original 1959–1968 four-volume set.

Steiner, Richard C. "דָּת and עֵין: Two Verbs Masquerading as Nouns in Moses' Blessing (Deuteronomy 33:2, 28)." *Journal of Biblical Literature* 115 (1996): 693–98.

Sternberg, Meir. *The Poetics of Biblical Narrative: Ideological Literature and the Drama of Reading.* Bloomington: Indiana University Press, 1985.

Stone, George Cameron. *A Glossary of the Construction, Decoration and Use of Arms and Armor.* New York: Jack Brussel, 1961.

Tadmor, Hayim. "Autobiographical Apology in the Royal Assyrian Literature," in Hayim Tadmor and Moshe Weinfeld, eds., *History, Historiography and Interpretation: Studies in Biblical and Cuneiform Literatures,* 36–57. Jerusalem: Magnes, 1983.

Talmon, Shemaryahu. "Pisqah be'Emṣaʿ Pasuq and 11QPsᵃ." *Textus* 5 (1966): 11–21. [Reprinted in: Shemaryahu Talmon, *Text and Canon of the Hebrew Bible: Collected Studies*, 369–82. Winona Lake, IN: Eisenbrauns, 2010.]

———. "The Textual Study of the Bible—A New Outlook," in Frank M. Cross and Shemaryahu Talmon, eds., *Qumran and the History of the Biblical Text*, 321–400. Cambridge: Harvard University Press, 1975.

Theodor, Julius, and Chanoch Albeck. *Bereschit Rabba.* Jerusalem: Wahrmann, 1965.

Thoreau, Henry David. *Walden and Civil Disobedience.* With an Introduction by Michael Meyer. Penguin Classics. New York: Penguin, 1983.

Tigay, Jeffrey H. *Deuteronomy.* JPS Torah Commentary. Philadelphia: Jewish Publication Society, 1996.

———. *The Evolution of the Gilgamesh Epic.* Philadelphia: University of Pennsylvania Press, 1982.

Tolkien, J. R. R. "Chaucer as a Philologist: The Reeve's Tale." *Transactions of the Philological Society* (1934): 1–70.

Tov, Emanuel. *Textual Criticism of the Hebrew Bible.* 3rd ed. Minneapolis: Fortress, 2012.

Tov, Emanuel, and Sidnie White. "Reworked Pentateuch," in Harold Attridge et al., *Qumran Cave 4/VIII*, 187–352. Discoveries in the Judaean Desert 13. Oxford: Clarendon, 1994.

Twain, Mark. *A Connecticut Yankee in King Arthur's Court.* New York: Oxford University Press, 1996. First published in 1889.

Ullendorff, Edward, "The Bawdy Bible." *Bulletin of the School of Oriental and African Studies* 42 (1979): 425–56.

———. "The Construction of Noah's Ark." *Vetus Testamentum* 4 (1954): 95–96. [Reprinted in: Edward Ullendorff, *Is Biblical Hebrew a Language?*, 48–49. Wiesbaden: Harrassowitz, 1977.]

Van Seters, John. *Prologue to History: The Yahwist as Historian in Genesis.* Louisville: Westminster John Knox, 1992.

Veldhuis, Nick C. "The Fly, the Worm, and the Chain: Old Babylonian Chain Incantations." *Orientalia Lovaniensia Periodica* 24 (1993): 41–64.

Vermeulen, Karolien. "Mind the Gap: Ambiguity in the Story of Cain and Abel." *Journal of Biblical Literature* 133 (2014): 29–42.

———. "Two of a Kind: Twin Language in the Hebrew Bible." *Journal for the Study of the Old Testament* 37 (2012): 135–50.

Waldman, Nahum M. "Some Aspects of Biblical Punning." *Shofar* 14 (1996): 38–52.

Watson, Wilfred G. E. *Classical Hebrew Poetry: A Guide to Its Techniques.* London: T&T Clark, 2005.

Weinfeld, Moshe. *Deuteronomy 1–11.* Anchor Bible 5. New York: Doubleday, 1991.

———. *Deuteronomy and the Deuteronomic School.* Oxford: Clarendon, 1972.

Weiss, Meir. *Miqraʾot kə-Kavvanatam: Leqeṭ Maʾamarim* (English title: *Scriptures in Their Own Light: Collected Essays*). Jerusalem: Bialik, 1987.

Wenham, Gordon J. "The Coherence of the Flood Narrative." *Vetus Testamentum* 28 (1978): 336–48.

Williamson, H. G. M. "An Overlooked Suggestion at Proverbs 1.10," in David A. Baer and Robert P. Gordon, eds., *Leshon Limmudim: Essays on the Language and Literature of the Hebrew Bible in Honour of A. A. Macintosh*, 218–26. London: Bloomsbury, 2014.

———. "Sound, Sense and Language in Isaiah 24–27." *Journal of Jewish Studies* 46 (1995): 1–9.

Wolters, Al. "*ṣôpiyyâ* (Prov 31:27) as Hymnic Participle and Play on Sophia." *Journal of Biblical Literature* 104 (1985): 577–87.

Yeivin, Israel. *Introduction to the Tiberian Masorah.* Translated by E. J. Revell. Missoula, MT: Society of Biblical Literature, 1980.

Yisraʾeli, Yael. "Melaʾkha: Malʾakhot ha-Bayit: Ṭevuyya," *ʾEnṣiqlopedya Miqraʾit* 4 (1962), cols. 998–1003.

Young, Ian. "Is the Prose Tale of Job in Late Biblical Hebrew?" *Vetus Testamentum* 59 (2009): 606–29.

Zahavi-Ely, Naama. "'Turn Right or Left': Literary Use of Dialect in 2 Samuel 14:19?" *Hebrew Studies* 53 (2012): 43–53.

Zakovitch, Yair. "Humor and Theology or the Successful Failure of Israelite Intelligence: A Literary-Folkloric Approach to Joshua 2," in Susan Niditch, ed., *Text and Tradition: The Hebrew Bible and Folklore*, 75–98. Atlanta: Society of Biblical Literature, 1990.

Zevit, Ziony. *The Anterior Construction in Classical Hebrew.* Society of Biblical Literature Monograph Series 50. Atlanta: Scholars Press, 1998.

Zewi, Tamar. "On רָאָה כִּי and רָאָה וְהִנֵּה in Biblical Hebrew," in Gregor Geiger, ed., *En pāsē grammatikē kai sophiā: Saggi di linguistica ebraica in onore di Alviero Niccacci, ofm,* 405–14. Jerusalem: Franciscan Printing Press / Edizioni Terra Sancta, 2011.

Zimmerman, Frank. *Before the Masora.* Lanham, MD: University Press of America, 2001.

Zurro, Eduardo. "La raíz 'brḥ' II y el hápax *mibraḥ (Ez 17,21)." *Biblica* 61 (1980): 412–15.

INDEX OF MODERN AUTHORS

INDEX OF BIBLICAL PASSAGES

INDEX OF OTHER SOURCES